WATER AND WATER POLICY
IN WORLD FOOD SUPPLIES

WATER AND WATER POLICY IN WORLD FOOD SUPPLIES

Proceedings of the Conference
May 26–30, 1985
Texas A&M University
College Station, Texas

Editor

WAYNE R. JORDAN

TEXAS A&M UNIVERSITY PRESS
COLLEGE STATION

Manufactured in the United States of America
First Edition

Library of Congress Cataloging-in-Publication Data

Water and water policy in world food supplies.

   1. Water-supply, Agricultural—Government policy—
Congresses. 2. Irrigation—Government policy—
Congresses. 3. Water resources development—Government
policy—Congresses. 4. Water quality management—
Government policy—Congresses. I. Jordan, Wayne R.,
1940–
HD1690.5.W38   1987   333.91'3   86-23065
ISBN 0-89096-278-2

CONTENTS

FOREWORD

An international conference, "Water and Water Policy in World Food Supplies," convened May 26 through May 30, 1985, on the Texas A&M University campus in College Station, Texas.

These are the proceedings from that conference.

Under the leadership of Texas A&M University president Dr. Frank E. Vandiver, this conference was organized as part of an effort to explore a broader, global role for the university. Major research universities are not only national but international resources. Dr. Vandiver's thought was that such universities, strategically located throughout the world, might be linked by a network of cooperative programs, sharing expertise and helping one another and the people they serve.

The framework of the conference was based on the relationship of water and water policy to food production throughout the world. At the time of the conference, drought and massive problems of food distribution were taking their toll, particularly in Africa. The challenges of famine and pestilence were persistent.

Other issues important to the provision of the optimal amounts of food were generally not included in the scope of this conference because some—such as population control and the storage, transportation, and distribution of food—have received repeated and wide consideration in other international conferences.

An additional element of the agenda of the conference included discussions of how institutions, national and international agencies, and governments can be coordinated to provide efficient, streamlined solutions to the problems of food supply.

In order to explore important aspects of institutional bridging, experts in the areas of water and agriculture were invited from all over the world to discuss as a single topic the problems associated with food and water. Participants came from governmental agencies, both international and national; from university faculties and research organizations from the United States and abroad, and from the private sector.

Plenary speakers dealt with broad topics such as national and international development; irrigation and drainage problems; new technologies for using water more efficiently, and institutions that develop programs and policies.

Six concurrent sessions dealt with technical aspects of the following subjects: water supply; water salinity; water demand, water policy, and economic development; integrated ecosystems management; energy and water; and technology.

The papers from both the plenary and concurrent sessions are included in these proceedings.

The second stage of the conference was an action-oriented postconference working session that convened at The Woodlands, Texas, on June 1. A small group of delegates and conferees gathered to develop general recommendations of the conference, based on responses from all conference participants. Using the "nominal group" technique, representatives at the postconference session sought to reconcile and prioritize major issues that emerged from two earlier rounds of deliberations by groups from the six technical areas listed above. The thirty-three recommendations considered during the postconference meeting are listed in Part XII of these proceedings.

The edited recommendations from the postconference meeting were:

1. *Policies for sustainable agriculture.* National policies for sustainable agriculture that are consistent with the prioritized use of water resources need to be developed to meet the needs of people. Needs in the areas of food production and economic growth must be balanced against environmental concerns.

2. *Education and training.* Practical and relevant education and training need to be provided to managers of water systems and rural development specialists, to other professionals, and to water users.

3. *Existing systems.* To increase productivity and efficiency, existing irrigation systems and management of those systems must be improved.

4. *Implementing the systems approach.* Production systems that integrate planting, tillage, harvesting, water management, pest control, crop selection, and responses to the environment must be developed. Flexible agricultural ecosystems that can enable people (particularly small and poor farmers), crops, and livestock to withstand the effects of extended droughts are also needed. The site-specific nature of many water and food issues must be recognized.

5. *Incentives.* Incentives for adoption of appropriate water use and food production measures must be established to ensure efficient use of the resource.

6. *Research and development.* Within target communities, integrated ecosystems management must be improved through multidisciplinary research and extension using local institutions and personnel, with priority on farmer inputs. Appropriate agricultural technology and management systems must be developed for higher and more stable yields in dryland and rainfed agriculture. Alternative energy sources should be selected and developed, with particular emphasis on small systems (less than 3 HP).

7. *Preservation and improved use efficiency.* Natural resources should be preserved. This should include water and soil, as well as germ plasm of plants, animals, and microorganisms (preferably in ecosystem preserves). The use of these resources should be optimized by keeping with sound agricultural, ecological, and social principles.

8. *Drainage and salinity control.* Waterlogging, salinization, and degradation of the production capacity of soils

must be alleviated or prevented through efficient drainage practices and other management measures.

9. *Local people.* Local people—water users—should be involved in water and energy development and management. It is critical to involve local consumers, producers, and managers of water supplies or new technology throughout the planning and implementation phases of projects designed to increase food production.

10. *Private sector.* The private sector should be involved in agricultural and agribusiness development and recognized as possessing the capabilities to accomplish development. Partnerships of government and private firms should be encouraged.

Dr. Vandiver provided the inspiration and leadership for the conference. The United States Agency for International Development, the United Nations Development Programme, the Mitchell Energy Corporation, the Whirlpool Corporation, the Conrad Hilton Foundation, the Inter-American Development Bank, Tenneco, Inc., Deere and Company, Pan American Airlines, and Jon L. Hagler provided financial and materiel support for the conference.

Organizers of the conference included Dr. H. O. Kunkel, chairman; Dr. Jack Cross, conference director; Dr. Bill Stout, chairman of the Program Committee; Dr. Orlando Olcese, chairman of the Advisory Committee; Dr. Wayne Jordan, chairman of the Editorial Committee; and Dr. John Hoyle, director of the nominal group technique process.

Our special thanks go out to these and many others for their unique and productive contributions.

H. O. Kunkel, Dean, College of Agriculture
Bill A. Stout, Professor, Department of
   Agricultural Engineering
Wayne R. Jordan, Director, Texas Water
   Resources Institute

THE CHARGE TO THE CONFERENCE

"May you live in interesting times!" So runs an ancient Oriental curse, and we surely live in times interesting, perilous, exciting, and challenging. No challenge looms more ominous, nor more constant, than a world shortage of water. Governments, agencies, associations, individuals, all either know of this threat or have suffered its consequences—which is why it is vital to the world that you are here today.

There are experts among you from governments, industry, private groups of concerned citizens, and the academic community—men and women versed in the areas of food production and water supply. And you have, I think, at this moment, an opportunity to help mankind in a manner which has probably never occurred before.

This is a unique occasion because you will be discussing at one meeting problems that have been treated separately. There have been numerous conferences on food production and ones dealing with water supply problems, but to my knowledge, this is the first time that a conference has linked these two areas which concern so much of the globe.

You have been most carefully selected to attend this conference. You come to Texas A&M University from all over the planet, for the problems to be addressed here are common to virtually every nation on earth. The most highly developed countries are not immune to decreasing water supplies. As our populations grow, feeding our citizens becomes an increasing burden. None of us have the luxury of putting off the problems of drought and famine.

In the past, nations have resorted to warfare when food ran scarce. Food and water have been used as political weapons. But here today, men and women of goodwill have the opportunity to work for the betterment of all mankind, regardless of ideological or political persuasion.

It is my hope that from this conference will come new approaches, new ways to cope with these problems. Perhaps, international organizations will find new ways to influence world policies. Perhaps, governments will discover new approaches to enhance standards of living in their own countries and their neighbors'. The English poet John Donne said "No man is an island." I think it is safe to extend that to say that no nation stands alone in the face of famine, pestilence, and death.

I charge you today to put aside all differences and labor together to break down the walls that exist, to link university research with public and private endeavors, so that mankind may push back the limitations of our time and bring comfort to the future.

Frank E. Vandiver
President
Texas A&M University

OPENING REMARKS

It is our pleasure to call to order this opening session of the first international conference on food and water to be held at Texas A&M University.

The convening of this conference is the dream of many of us, but of none so much as Dr. Frank E. Vandiver, president of Texas A&M University. For it was Professor Vandiver who thought that a university or a network of universities might take on a venture that governments and their agencies, international unions of scientific societies, or pan-world organizations may not be able to mount because of a variety of reasons. This conference is an experiment to that end.

The issue facing this proposition, in the absence of other initiatives toward a purpose, is to bring together men and women from places throughout the world to talk and think together on problems that are common to many peoples. Called together here are scientists, technologists, planners, and those concerned with national policies to ponder and talk of problems that have national or regional definitions, but which are based on universal principles. Perhaps a university has opportunities that consortia, international unions, scholarly societies, or multinational industrial organizations do not have. Some of the answers to these issues will be found during this week.

Of course, Texas A&M University has not put this conference together on its own. A wide range of institutions, notably the cosponsor, the U.S. Agency for International Development; the World Bank; the Foreign Agricultural Organization of the United Nations; the United Nations Development Programme; the Inter-American Development Bank; the Mitchell Energy Corporation; Deere and Company; Whirlpool Corporation; Tenneco, Inc.; and foundations. Individuals such as George Mitchell, Jon L. Hagler, Robert W. Heard, Orlando Olcese, Nyle Brady, and the many participants have rallied to the effort.

The principal limiting factors in increasing food production are land area and water. Because technology and policies can so greatly determine the presence and efficiency of water use and because concerns about water are an area of common interest to Texans, the theme of "Water and Water Policy in World Food Supplies" was selected for this conference.

The issues relating to water begin with climate. Freshwater is the ultimate renewable resource for agriculture. Its renewability comes about by cyclic events that lead to rain and snowfalls over the continents. But weather is inherently variable. Drought and floods occur. Famines can be triggered. And unlike other vital resources, water is required in such massive quantities that it is not a commodity of international commerce.

Great engineering feats can work beautiful changes. A dam can make a desert bloom. The same dam can increase the salinity of the soil, increase the number of cases of bilharziasis, cause the migration of thousands of people, and foul its waters with collected silt and pathogens of plants and animals.

Water is a complex issue, one at the heart of conflicts. It is at once a precious and a wasted resource. It is at once a commodity that feeds mankind and that is used in vast quantities for industry, commerce, and maintaining quality of life.

This conference has a diversity of participants, we believe quite unlike any other past conference. Here are scientists and technicians. Here are those who can influence policy. Here, too, are those who came to listen and those who came to say what they believe to be most important.

We are happy that you are here. We welcome you to Texas A&M University.

H. O. Kunkel
Dean, College of Agriculture
Texas A&M University

WELCOMING REMARKS

The needs of the nation and the world for increased food and fiber fluctuate around a general set of problems of increasing importance. Sometimes the problem is water; at other times, overproduction, low income for farmers, or local shortages and high prices for consumers. And still at other times, the problems are political, cultural, or sociological. In this setting, the university establishment faces a number of challenges. How do we train people, how do we perform research, and how do we transmit knowledge to meet the challenge of the world demand for food?

In our country, we have had a group of institutions that have dealt very effectively with America's agricultural problems. They are the land-grant institutions. Thus, it is fitting that our same land-grant institutions begin to utilize their tremendous capacities and expertise to focus on world problems such as shortages of food and water.

From our land-grant universities has come research that produces drought-resistant plants, controls injurious insects, manages meager water supplies, and controls drought. There has also been a vision that recognizes global issues. But we must do more. Texas A&M University, in its proud heritage and land-grant tradition, is responding to this challenge. We understand and appreciate the interdependence of our fragile world ecosystem. We accept the responsibility that our long-term success and viability is linked to our ability to provide the solutions to problems that are not only national but international in scope.

It is with this commitment to be involved, to become a part of the solution, that we bring together such renowned individuals as yourselves, to think, to innovate, to motivate, and to provide a vision of and a plan for what concrete steps we can take that will help us all to solve food and water problems.

It is thus, with extreme pleasure, that on behalf of the Board of Regents of the Texas A&M University System, our four academic institutions, and our eight services and agencies, that I welcome you to a conference with international relevance. We offer you our support, our hospitality, and our commitment. Feel free to call upon us for any help. Welcome, and have a great conference.

Arthur G. Hansen
Chancellor
Texas A&M University System

PART I. SPECIAL PRESENTATIONS

1. STATEMENT FROM THE UNITED NATIONS

Michel Doo Kingué, Under-Secretary-General, UNITAR, United Nations, New York, New York

Mr. Chairman, Ladies and Gentlemen:

It is for me a great honor and a privilege to address this important gathering on behalf of the Secretary-General of the United Nations, His Excellency Mr. Javier Pérez de Cuéllar, who was unable to be here today due to traveling commitments related to the performance of his demanding duties. He asked me to convey to you his very deep and sincere regrets as well as his best wishes for a successful conference.

As you all know, the need to ensure adequate food supplies for the world's rapidly growing population; famine, starvation, and malnutrition that unfortunately afflict many developing countries; and the challenge of ensuring and managing our essential water supplies are all matters of great concern to the United Nations and particularly its current Secretary-General. This is to say that Mr. Javier Pérez de Cuéllar and his senior staff have a keen interest in this important meeting and look forward to the adoption and implementation of its conclusions by all member states.

Although I am not an expert on the subject of this conference, which is "Water and Water Policy in World Food Supplies," I am delighted to be with you for a while as I am a son of Africa, a continent that has been facing for the last fifteen years a series of recurrent droughts that are devastating an increasing number of its countries. As a result, I have a personal and vested interest in your discussions. Furthermore, being the executive head of a United Nations agency the purpose of which is, inter alia, to enhance the effectiveness of the United Nations in the promotion of economic and social development all over the world, I am also deeply interested in the solutions that you will be able to recommend and which my agency is willing to consider and promote among the decisionmakers in Third World countries.

Perhaps as never before, and most likely because of the tragic situation prevailing in Africa today, the world's attention is now focused on the problems of ensuring food supplies for the world's growing population and on the vital role of water and water policy in meeting this challenge. The drought situation in Africa has underscored the crucial importance of water in maintaining human life. It has become eminently apparent that an increased emphasis has to be placed on the availability and management of water resources. I am told that soon after your conference, the International Water Resources Association will also be holding its congress in Brussels, Belgium, where the main theme will be "Water Resources for Rural Areas and their Population." One month later, from July 15 to 26 in Nairobi, Kenya, the World Conference to Review and Appraise the Achievements of the United Nations Decade for Women will meet and discuss several items, one of which is entitled "Food, Water, and Agriculture." We welcome all these discussions, which we feel are both important and timely.

Actually, it was in recognition of the vital importance of water to mankind that the United Nations organized the International Water Conference in Mar del Plata, Argentina, in 1977 and the International Conference on Desertification in that same year in Nairobi, Kenya. These two meetings had been preceded by a number of other United Nations conferences dealing notably and respectively with the environment, population, food, and human settlements. They were also followed by the International Conference on New and Renewable Sources of Energy in 1981 and more recently the International Conference on Population held in Mexico in 1984. Our work within the United Nations leads to the conclusion that these global problems are interconnected and that they cannot be entirely resolved independently.

It was also in recognition of the crucial role of water resources in human life that the General Assembly of the United Nations declared the years of the 1980s the International Drinking Water Supply and Sanitation Decade. That Decade is an international education and action campaign involving 100 governments in developing countries, donor governments in developed countries, 12 organizations of the United Nations system, and dozens of nongovernmental organizations. Since the launching of that Decade in 1980, bilateral aid agencies have increased their support to the drinking water and sanitation programs from 1 percent to between 4 and 15 percent of their total aid budgets.

Even in the brief period since the events I just mentioned took place, it has become increasingly apparent that it is a matter of life-saving urgency that immediate attention be given to ways in which our fixed global stock of water can be developed and used wisely for the decades ahead. Experts tell us that unsafe water and inadequate sanitation are responsible for 80 percent of all human illness and disease, as well as heavy losses in productivity. They also add that the major causes of death in the Third World are malnutrition and diseases resulting from polluted water. It is thus clear that to fight malnutrition in developing countries we should increase food production in those countries. Similarly, we should help their populations to get access to unpolluted water to fight contagious diseases. By the end of this century, the population of developing countries will have grown from around 3 billion now to approximately 5 billion. It is obvious that an essential need will be for water to provide food, manufactured goods, and energy to support this growth.

At the same time, in this Third World Development Decade declared by the General Assembly as the Third Development Decade, a most urgent problem is the need to develop strategies to stimulate food production in the Third World and to improve community water supplies. It is simply not acceptable that hundreds of millions in the Third World lack an adequate diet; that, in some low-income countries, as many as 40 percent of pre-school age children exhibit clinical signs of malnutrition. In the words of the Brandt Commission, "The idea of a community of nations has little meaning if that situation is allowed to continue, if hunger is regarded as a marginal problem that humanity can live with."

The meeting of basic human needs for food, drinking water, and sanitation undoubtedly calls into question such issues as the role of the agricultural sector in socioeconomic development, the allocation of resources to rural areas, the distribution of the benefits of growth, and the priorities to be accorded to crucial social services. And, while the pressing problems that are now attracting our attention are immediate, it is essential that they be approached within the context of both emergency needs and mid- and long-term development programs.

As we have witnessed most tragically in recent years, beyond the problem of securing access to adequate supplies of water to serve the development process and to meet priority social needs loom the devastating problems of drought and floods. Each year, more than 4 million hectares of crops are destroyed by floods in Southeast Asia alone. In Africa, we see the catastrophic effects of drought. These are situations that call for the formulation of effective strategies for flood and drought control.

Another area that cries for attention is the alarming pollution of our rivers, lakes, and groundwater. If we are to pass on an environmentally acceptable habitat to future generations, we must step up action in this regard at the national, regional, and international levels.

A complicating factor in water resource management, with political implications, arises from the fact that many of the great rivers and lakes of the world are common to two or more countries. Cooperation between riparian countries will become increasingly critical as the pressures increase for alternative uses of limited water supplies. Yet, it is heartening to know that many cooperative ventures have already started in this area. I personally witnessed the development of such cooperation in Africa when I was for eleven and a half years the assistant administrator of the United Nations Development Programme responsible for the African branch of that program.

While all of these considerations concerning the long-term and development aspects of water resource management require attention, it is on the drought-affected countries of Africa and the terrible situation of famine, starvation, and death that has arisen in consequence of the drought and declining food production in that region that the world's attention is focused at present.

As you know, the Secretary-General of the United Nations has been deeply concerned with the situation prevailing in the drought-affected African countries. As early as December 1983 he called the attention of the world community to the development of that tragic situation. Later on, he visited a number of those countries to gain a firsthand knowledge of the situation. He subsequently established in New York, with a network of field offices in the countries concerned, an Office for Emergency Operations in Africa which, inter alia, monitors the emergency situation on a continuous basis and coordinates the flow of assistance to the affected countries.

Twenty-one African countries[1] have been seared by drought this year, causing a massive 14 percent drop in their combined cereal production. The significance of this deterioration can only be fully appreciated if we realize that this output is now running at 21 percent below the average for the past five years.

Naturally, the effects of the poor harvests have been felt throughout the national economies of those countries. Not only are food stocks depleted, but the foreign reserves of many of the affected countries are also exhausted. As a result, the capacity of these countries to purchase the 12.2 million tons of cereals they need is problematical.

Reports from the most affected areas indicate that deaths from starvation continue relentlessly and that the destruction of pastures has been so severe that whole communities and the culture of some desert nomads could well be on the way to extinction. Emaciated refugees continue to pour across national borders, driven by the desperate search for food.

The actual number of victims to the African drought is not known; too many whose strength failed them before they reached the feeding camps lie in unmarked graves. But, of the living, 30 million persons, roughly the equivalent of twice the population of Australia, remain directly threatened by starvation and malnutrition.

The amount of damage suffered is not quantifiable either. The figures which emerge on production losses and swollen import bills reveal only a fraction of the damage sustained. They do not reveal the extent of disintegration in social institutions or the unraveling of the social and political fabric of whole nations. In any case, how can we quantify human suffering or put a price on human life? How do we place an accounting figure on the physical impairment suffered by millions of young people as a result of malnutrition which will condemn them to marginal lives? All of these aspects escape national accounting.

The international community, governments and individuals alike, have been responsive to the needs of the drought-affected African countries. Out of 7 million tons of food aid needed this year, 6.3 million tons have been pledged. A major cause of concern, however, is that only about 40 percent of the 6.3 million tons pledged has actually been received in the affected countries. To be effective, food aid has to reach the people for whom it is destined, and right now, unfortunately, logistical constraints are impeding

[1] For reference: Western Africa: Burkina Faso, Cape Verde, Chad, Mali, Mauritania, Niger, Senegal.

East Africa: Burundi, Ethiopia, Kenya, Rwanda, Somalia, Sudan, Tanzania.

Southern Africa: Angola, Botswana, Lesotho, Mozambique, Zambia, Zimbabwe.

North Africa: Morocco.

the distribution of food, particularly in some landlocked Sahelian countries. According to the United Nations Food and Agriculture Organization (FAO), only concerted action right now can avert a major disaster in the six most affected countries, namely Chad, Ethiopia, Mali, Mozambique, Niger, and Sudan. For the Sahelian countries and Sudan, it is essential to deliver as much aid as possible before the rains in June make distant settlements inaccessible by road.

It should also be stressed that despite its essential role, food aid can at best only ensure survival. If Africa is to be freed from the grip of famine, the productive capacities of its shattered agriculture must be rebuilt. This will entail the application of new and appropriate technologies of food and energy production, the vigorous implementation of appropriate national and regional policies and strategies, and the application of new technologies and management techniques to the continent's water resources. Experience already gained during the implementation of the International Drinking Water Supply and Sanitation Decade shows that the development of new low-cost appropriate technologies not only makes safe drinking water and sanitation facilities more affordable for poorer communities in developing countries but also helps financially strapped governments to realize considerable savings in the implementation of their Decade strategies. For example, Indonesia planned to invest $1.6 billion by 1990 to bring drinking water supplies to 75 percent of urban and 60 percent of rural people, and sanitation to 60 percent of the urban and 50 percent of the rural inhabitants. Now, by using low-cost technologies the cost of these expanded services can come down to about $1 billion—a savings of almost 40 percent.

Your conference is therefore right in putting emphasis on the need to develop and use the most appropriate technologies, which does not necessarily mean nonsophisticated technologies. It is also well known that effectiveness can be enhanced through improved management. As a result, better management techniques can play an important role in the use of water and implementation of water policies in food supplies. Your discussions on that issue are thus fully justified.

Substantial water resources are potentially available in Sub-Saharan Africa. In normal circumstances, the Niger River basin, including the Bénoué River basin, discharges 175 billion cubic meters per year into the Atlantic Ocean. At Niamey, in the subarid part of the basin, the Niger basin still conveys 32 billion cubic meters per year downstream, enough to meet the potential requirements of over 1 million hectares of irrigated agriculture. Lake Chad in normal years receives some 43 billion cubic meters per year from its two main tributaries—the Logone and Chari. The Senegal River at Bakel discharges, when there is no drought, an average of 24 billion cubic meters per year. These important water resources should not remain unutilized. Of course, individual water projects—whether simple or multipurpose—should form part of integrated development plans establishing a broad relationship between the availability of water and its possible uses in various ways: for irrigation, electric power production, navigation, and industrial and domesic consumption.

The United Nations Development Programme has been involved in supporting the efforts of a dozen and a half African countries in planning the integrated development and management of their river and lake basins, particularly the Senegal River Basin, the Gambia River Basin, the Niger River Basin, the Lake Chad Basin, and the Kagera River Basin. The relevant integrated basin development plans have been concerned with ways and means to make water serve different purposes and meet both common and specific objectives of the partner countries. For example, in the program for the development of the Senegal River Basin, which involves Mali, Mauritania, and Senegal, the construction of a major dam at Manantali to regulate the downstream flow is designed to help ease common constraints such as poor transportation infrastructure, vulnerability to drought, and high energy costs. At the same time, the program addresses the pressing needs of each country—agriculture and livestock development in the case of Mauritania, diversification of the groundnut-based agriculture in Senegal, and access to the sea in the case of landlocked Mali.

There is no doubt that the drought, or in other words, the unavailability of water, is only one of the complex variables that have contributed to the decline in per capita food production in Africa over the past decade. In 1980, each African had around 12 percent less homegrown food than twenty years earlier; and today, per capita African food production is 10 to 12 percent lower than five years ago. In a number of cases governments have allocated low priority and insufficient resources to agriculture; pricing policies have not always provided farmers with adequate incentives; research into improved crop varieties and growing methods has been insufficient; foreign aid has too often supported large-scale schemes and export-oriented commodities rather than food production. The external situation has also played a damaging role in the situation being faced by African countries as they have severely suffered from the world recession of the 1980s—to mention just one of the external factors. By mid-1982, real prices of primary commodities other than oil were lower than at any time in the last thirty years and 21 percent lower than in 1975, a recession year during which prices of primary commodities had fallen by 18 percent. According to the World Bank, between 1980 and 1982 alone price of non-oil primary commodities declined by 27 percent in current dollar terms. The resulting shortage of foreign exchange earned by African countries whose economies rely on the export of primary commodities has limited the availability of imported agricultural inputs. In the poorest countries budgets are so tight that governments have difficulties even paying the salaries of extension workers. Clearly, the reversal of the trend in agricultural production in Africa will call for a massive, concerted effort addressing the problem in its many facets.

I wish to conclude these remarks by stressing the paramount importance of ensuring adequate food for each human being. At the national level, mass hunger can lead to chaos, destroying social and political institutions. Security in Third World countries cannot only be ensured through military protective measures. It also has strong economic and social requirements. At the international level, the idea of a community of nations has little meaning so long as malnutrition and starvation remain at their present levels. As Secretary-General Javier Pérez de Cuéllar put it in his 1984 report on the work of the organization, "In our world of growing economic interdependence, impoverished people faced perpetually with a variety of overwhelming economic and social crises constitute not only a challenge to international conscience, but a threat to international stability as well." The elimination of hunger is therefore one of the most pressing tasks today before the world community.

In considering the present critical situation as well as ensuring global food supplies in the long run, the United Nations system has been engaged in an exercise of deep reflection and reassessment. A wealth of new policy initiatives have been put forward for the consideration of member states by the United Nations Food and Agriculture Organization and the World Food Council. Other pertinent suggestions like the ones your conference may make are also most welcomed.

There is no doubt that if we are to meet successfully the challenge of ensuring adequate food supplies to the world's population, radical new approaches will be required in water technology and management techniques. That is why the United Nations is so interested in your conference, an important endeavor which we consider a significant contribution to the achievement of our common goal.

2. FOOD AND WATER: THE WIDER INTERRELATIONSHIPS AND THE LATIN AMERICAN CONTEXT

Kirk P. Rodgers, Department of Regional Development, Organization of American States

Ladies and Gentlemen:

I bring you greetings from João Baena Soares, Secretary-General of the Organization of American States (OAS). Ambassador Baena Soares has asked me to extend to Texas A&M University and to the cosponsors of this meeting his heartiest congratulations. The convening of the First International Conference on Food and Water is a pioneering venture. It links two interdependent development issues and brings together policymakers, development practitioners, researchers, and teachers from around the world. We have come to learn from each other. The Organization of American States is proud to be associated with this important international endeavor.

My distinguished colleague, Michel Doo Kingué of the United Nations, will be speaking to you this evening from an international perspective. I would like now to speak to you from a hemispheric viewpoint. The Organization of American States joins together the countries of Latin America, the Caribbean, and the United States in a common search for peace through development. We strive to facilitate north-south dialogue and transfer of technology within the Americas. Our basic goal is to promote harmonious development within and between the countries of our region, and to help countries in their efforts to obtain more equitable distribution of the benefits of development among their peoples. Our tools are technical assistance, training, and facilitation of dialogue.

Ladies and gentlemen, this conference is about interrelationships. In the next few minutes, I want to speak to you about two sets of interrelations: one between concepts and the other between people.

Conceptually, I think it is important at this state in our conference to underscore the fact that while policies affecting water and food interact with each other, they are part of much broader relationships in development. It is important to keep clearly in mind that water and food policies must consider the economic, social, geographic, and environmental contexts in which development is taking place.

Let us look first at the environmental and geographic contexts. Water and land combine to produce food in particular pieces of space. These specific geographic contexts are called river basins. In the Americas, we must be concerned with the interactions that take place within our great river systems: the Amazon, the Plata, and the Orinoco, which are shared by many countries. Planning the development of land and water resources is a complex task. The approach must be an integrated one, both within individual countries and between them. Disregard of the downstream effects of land and water development can be just as damaging as failure to integrate water and food policies. If "downstream" is in a neighboring country, the failures may provoke political confrontations.

The hallmark of the approach of my organization to land and water resource development is geographic, and the context is environmental. We assist countries in development of river basins and of regions. We begin with an overview of the physical environment and proceed from there to help countries formulate specific investment projects. Recently, we produced a publication which reviewed twenty years of experience in technical cooperation in integrated regional development planning and the formulation of more than $4 billion in investment projects. It was a humbling experience. Mistakes and failed plans stood out clearly with the perspective of time, but so did the occasional highly successful projects that flowed from the plans. If there was one key lesson to be drawn from all that experience, it is that when we were effective integrators of data, institutions and people, and when we kept the geographic and environmental contexts clearly in mind, we succeeded. When we did not, we failed.

Let us turn now to the economic and social contexts of development in the Americas that often determine the outcome of our food and water policies. I think I hardly need to emphasize by now the fact that water and food issues cannot be seen in isolation from government socioeconomic development policies or international economic conditions that constrain these policies. Let me give you some concrete examples about current international economic conditions that are proving very frustrating to Latin American government policies on food security. Some Asian and African countries may be facing these same problems.

1. As Dr. Husain of the World Bank said in his keynote address on the first day of this conference, many developing countries are now being required to adopt stringent policies of "economic adjustment" to deal with their foreign-debt problems. These policies, as necessary as they may be for restoring those countries to financial health, are tending to favor production for export over production for domestic consumption—including food. If scarce investment dollars must go elsewhere, it doesn't matter how intelligent our water policies or food production strategies were.

2. Subsidized agricultural products from developed countries are sometimes sold in international markets at so called "dumping prices," which directly decreases the in-

centive for food production in the developing countries. Food prices and the availability of credit for food production are clearly just as decisive in their effects as proper water policies.

The lesson here is once again a matter of interrelationship. Just as land and water development can usefully be seen in a context of river-basin development, food production must be seen in the context of international market conditions and socioeconomic development policies. In the Americas, some of these interrelationships are sensitive indeed.

And now finally, let us turn to the other basic question of interrelationship—people and institutions. I want to address this broad issue in the context of transfer of technology in the areas of land and water development in the Americas. The example I will use should have wider relevance.

In the Western Hemisphere, we live in a region with long traditions of linkage. In Latin America and the Caribbean there are deep cultural ties that bind nations together. Between north and south, there are long traditions of interaction and dialogue. In the area of transfer of technology, we have for decades taken advantage of these linkages. During the Alliance for Progress, launched by President Kennedy in the 1960s, there was a greatly accelerated pace of interaction. Massive efforts in training and scientific interchange between the United States and Latin America were begun. A whole generation of Latin American professionals was affected. Some of them are here with us tonight, for nowhere was this interaction more strongly felt than in the fields associated with land and water resource development.

For the OAS, the 1960s was the period when the Inter-American Center for Integrated Development of Land and Water Resources (CIDIAT) was created jointly with the government of Venezuela. In the early years, Utah State University played a key role in helping OAS and Venezuela launch this important training institution. This year, CIDIAT celebrates its twentieth anniversary. It has achieved enormous successes. By 1984, it had graduated 10,317 students of which 4,015 are non-Venezuelans. Between 1973 and 1984, it granted a large number of master of science degrees in fields such as land and water resource development, hydrology, irrigation, and drainage.

It is practically impossible today to enter any major Latin American agency in water resource development without encountering a CIDIAT graduate or a former participant in one of its seminars or national courses. But quantity doesn't tell the whole story; qualitatively, this is a center in which Venezuela and Latin America as a whole can be very proud. Latin America can, in fact, be proud about the overall progress made in the past twenty years in its training of professionals in the field of land and water resource development and the upgrading of the quality of its institutions in these fields.

But now I come to a less happy part of this story. I have been stressing interrelationships between people and institutions. As I said, in the 1960s and 1970s, the technological interactions between North and South America were very broad-based and very intensive. Today they are less so. There are many reasons for this. Latin America has come of age in the scientific and technical fields of which we speak. It has a strong cadre of land and water professionals compared with many other parts of the world. But we have also seen that it still has many problems, and the powerful north-south linkages that existed in the sixties and seventies have withered somewhat. Many connections still exist between U.S. universities and research centers and Latin American institutions, but they are financially constrained today. The U.S. Agency for International Development is now active in only four of the ten South American countries. Its efforts are concentrated in Central America and the Caribbean. In several Latin American countries Europe has replaced the United States as the major source of bilateral funding of technical assistance. The Organization of American States, while its programs in the field of land and water development have remained relatively stable, has fewer resources in real-dollar terms. The United Nations Development Programme (UNDP) in particular, has drastically reduced its funds for Latin America in order to strengthen its services to Africa and Asia.

Severe shortages of funds for fellowships, seminars, and travel grants have constrained north-south interactions. The conference we are attending this week is a happy exception to this tendency.

This problem, while serious, is not without solutions. Latin America and the Caribbean after twenty years of intensive efforts have important concentrations of high-quality professional talent. The challenge is to mobilize this talent to enable these developing countries to help each other and to reopen the technical dialogue between Latin America and the United States. The private sector and U.S. universities have an important role to play in meeting this challenge.

Somehow, we all have to do a better job of tapping the talent that has been developed in the Americas. There is a huge investment here, and some of it is not fully utilized. We have to strengthen the linkages between Latin American and U.S. universities and research centers. We have to facilitate the process of horizontal cooperation that will enable Argentinians to teach Bolivians and Venezuelans teach Ecuadorians and vice versa. Horizontal cooperation at a broader international level would also be valuable.

Let us hope that this conference will stimulate us in the search for such interrelationships. From the perspective of the Americas, let us hope that this event will catalyze a re-strengthening of north-south cooperation and scientific interchange. We all stand to benefit.

PART II. PLENARY PRESENTATIONS

3. WORLD DEVELOPMENT, 1985–2000

S. Shahid Husain, Operations Policy Staff, The World Bank, Washington, D.C.

It is a privilege for me to participate in this important conference on Water and Water Policy in World Food Supplies. The themes of this meeting are major concerns to the World Bank, and we are pleased that we have been invited to participate.

Both the place and date of this conference have special significance. Texas is a state where water and food are major issues in the regional economy, and decisions made here have international impact. It is also fitting that this conference is convening in 1985, the midpoint in the International Drinking Water Supply and Sanitation Decade; it is a time for reflection on the progress that has been made and for charting a course of action toward the objective of extending water supply and sanitation to unserved millions in the developing world. The year 1985 has also demonstrated the contrast between our aspirations and the realities facing people in Africa, where the international community and African governments are seeking to avoid further tragedy from drought and famine. The theme of this conference is thus timely and closely related to priorities for development assistance.

A heavy obligation rests on all who participate in this conference—and the professional communities from which we come—to address these urgent issues. The management of natural resources through sound policy and effective institutions is an essential part of development at a global, regional, and national level. There is no country that can claim to have mastered its water resource problems, despite the extraordinary significance of this issue for present—and future—generations.

In my remarks, I would like to address some of the critical issues in policy and management in the water sector. The World Bank is the lead multilateral agency financing investment projects and programs in the developing countries. With 148 member governments, we are engaged in investment, development of technology, institutional development, and advising policymakers on ways to increase food supplies and develop water resources. We seek to provide policy advice to our member governments within the broader framework of their macroeconomic strategy and development objectives.

Let me begin by placing these issues within the global economic environment. In 1985, the developing countries find themselves in a difficult conjuncture of circumstances. After nearly two decades of unprecedented economic growth, a combination of global economic factors, domestic policy, and management has led to a period of adjustment for both the developed and developing countries. Slow growth, high interest rates, and increased unemployment in Europe and North America have all served to turn national attention to domestic concerns, and away from the needs of developing countries. There has been a perceptible decline in government commitment to open trading systems and capital flows to developing countries. Thus the developing countries have found themselves facing both trade barriers and reduced prices for raw materials and other goods they export. The reductions in income have been particularly serious as they face high costs of servicing debts entered into in more optimistic times. There are some parallels between the developing countries and American farmers: Both borrowed against optimistic prospects for the future and later found themselves in changed global and national situations. And both need help if they are to overcome their current dilemmas.

Difficult economic conditions have also been made more difficult by the declining commitment to internationalism by the developed countries. Despite pressing, indeed emergency, conditions in some regions, many developed countries have turned inward, reducing their contributions to official development assistance. Only recent special efforts have increased assistance to Africa. However, global aid flows, which can encourage governments in the adjustment process and cushion the poor from the pains of adjustment, have been relatively static. The developing countries, therefore, must face these dilemmas and their attendant political costs without much of a prospect of improvement in this environment. We at the World Bank are actively trying to provide financial assistance and advice to the developing countries, for both short-term adjustment and longer-term development strategy. Despite the World Bank's lending some $14.7 billion in 1985, our resources remain small in the face of the needs of the developing countries. An essential ingredient in this adjustment process is the political courage of national leaders. It is worth noting that despite occasional incidents of political violence, there has been remarkable political stability in developing countries during difficult economic times.

My conclusion from this brief review of the global situation is that the developing countries must improve their development policies more than ever, including those for water and food, both at the macroeconomic and sectoral levels. The costs of inefficiency are too great at this point for the developing countries to bear. Furthermore, sound policy must be backed with effective institutions and management, particularly with regard to resource allocation and finance. Many countries are making serious efforts to improve their policies. As committed members of the development community we must support them.

Let me now turn more specifically to the issues of food and water. First, I shall seek to define the issue of food security as we in the World Bank understand it, based on almost four decades of experience with agricultural policy and projects. I shall then relate long-term food prospects to the issue of a sustainable natural resource base and the management of competing uses of water. As you know well from experience in Texas, many of the problems in water resource management are common to developed and developing countries. They are also complex, controversial, and not easily resolvable.

Food security is an issue of great importance to all countries. It involves both the availability of food and the ability to obtain it. Despite enormous production of food in some regions, particularly North America, there are still some 750 million people in the world today who regularly lack food in amounts sufficient to permit them to be fully productive. This is an unacceptable waste for the planet as a whole. Since most of these people live in developing countries—in Africa and Asia—it is remarkable that countries in these areas have made as much progress as they have.

While increases in global food production have been very large over the past decades—India, for example, is now self-sufficient in grains—there is nevertheless the fact that food production is not always in the locations where it is needed the most. Even within a single country—again, take India—there are producing regions and consuming regions. The problem is how to ensure adequate trade and distribution systems.

In some countries—particularly in eastern Africa—there is a need to increase local production so that food is available throughout the year. This will require new approaches in agricultural technology. We cannot be satisfied with the gains of the Green Revolution. We are still relatively ignorant about effective approaches to African agriculture. There is also a need for research and careful evaluation of the many food-distribution systems on that continent. Even so, we must recognize that there is an upper limit to the potential for food production in many semiarid and arid areas because of insufficient and unreliable rainfall. This problem is exacerbated over large parts of Africa and northeastern Brazil by the absence of major rivers and limited potential for irrigation development.

In addition, questions of food security demonstrate the interdependence of the developed and developing countries. One of the major factors affecting food security is price variation. Changes in food prices strain the already limited purchasing power of vast numbers of people in developing countries. Decisions in major food production centers, such as the United States and the Soviet Union, have direct effects overseas. This was dramatically illustrated in the 1970s by short harvests in the Soviet Union and stocks policy in the United States. Food availability was much welcomed in the developing countries during this period. And I would like to say that generous U.S. food support to Africa again this year is to be very much applauded.

Price instability in today's world also comes from monetary disturbances in the international economy. They may have little to do with what has transpired in agriculture, but it has very great implications for agriculture. It is a reason why many low-income countries may want to be a bit more self-sufficient in food than they otherwise would be.

This view naturally leads to a concern about the inputs required for food production, not least the need for water. As I suggested at the beginning of my remarks, no country is adequately managing its natural resource base. Both the developed and developing countries have difficulty determining an appropriate balance between the present and the future for the use, development, consumption, and protection of natural resources. There has been considerable concern in Washington about the problems of the Ogallala Aquifer. Poor management of local resources can have regional and national implications. I believe that the case of Ogallala suggests important lessons for the developing countries. These include the following:

1. There is a need for a broad policy framework and regulations for groundwater use over the entire area of an aquifer.

2. Ogallala demonstrates the importance of limiting water use to sustainable yields over time.

3. And third, with limited rainfall, unbalanced use of water resources can result in unsustainable approaches to agriculture production.

I might add that while the United States may be able to afford some inefficiency in the use of its water resources, many developing countries cannot. The populations and the natural resource base in Ethiopia and Sudan are already at risk. The long-term prospects of both will worsen if sound policy is not put into place. Desertification cannot be explained by climate alone; clearly, man bears heavy responsibility for this process. On these issues, therefore, we must develop a framework for planning and decision making that acknowledges the many different claims for water, including irrigation, municipal supply, and industrial uses.

What are the components of such a framework? I submit that from a global perspective, we do not face a water crisis per se. On the supply side, most of the projections of water use made in the 1960s suggested such a crisis would come. However, these projections have been revised in the 1970s and 1980s to suggest that some efforts at demand management have been successful and that, on a global basis, we do not face an absolute shortage of water in the near future.

This is not to say that some regions are not facing a crisis with regard to water. The point is to address these issues at the national and regional levels, where action can be taken. What is at issue is the efficiency of water use in the developed and developing countries, and particularly in those countries with relatively scarce water resources. There is a need for well-defined water resource policies that (1) start with an inventory of what is available, (2) determine the quantity and quality of water required for each competing use, (3) manage the demand for water by investment planning, pricing, and regulation to ensure sustainable yields over the long run, (4) designate appropriate technologies for each use, and (5) ensure that water is used efficiently within those technologies. The instruments for these elements of policy are technological, economic, financial, and institutional. Serious demand management requires policies that are understood by users and the publc at large. It also requires effective institutions, which are sadly lacking in many developing countries.

The application of these policy instruments can vary from general environmental guidelines to strict regulations requiring conservation. Regardless of the context, the policy framework for managing water resources must be intersectoral: Agriculturalists must be communicating with industrialists and public utilities and vice versa. Governments must provide a framework in which disputes can be resolved.

An important component of demand management is pricing. Consumers must receive signals about the true cost of the water they consume. Public subsidies to water are not justified in most cases. Moreover, the failure to recover the costs of investment, operations, and maintenance is a major obstacle to the extension of water-supply systems in developing countries and has meant that the majority are condemned to inadequate water supplies for the forseeable future.

This issue was highlighted in the recent Mid-Decade report submitted in April to the committee on Natural Resources of the United Nations, to be forwarded to the General Assembly. This report, which the World Bank helped prepare, reflects a consensus of the international agencies working on drinking-water supply in developing countries. Unless local resources are mobilized for investment in water supply, there is little hope that the unserved millions of households will receive water. We are all too conscious of the fact that external resources are minimal in the face of the very large demand of water. Bank support for the Water Decade, therefore, is very much linked to our encouragement to governments to adopt replicable technical solutions that are affordable to beneficiaries and which are in large part financed by local resources.

The same points can be made in relation to irrigation. Heavy capital investments in irrigation must be considered within a broad framework of increasing yields over time. Reasonable economic rates of return must be matched by adequate financial returns as well. While irrigation has made very large contributions to increased agricultural production in much of Asia, North Africa, and the Middle East, new investments must be carefully analyzed in terms of additional costs and long-term benefits. It is possible to overinvest as well as underinvest in irrigation. The issue here is careful investment planning and good technical design.

Regardless of the use of water, it is important also to evaluate the costs of the depletion of natural resources. In many parts of the world, irreparable damage is occurring to forests, soils, water courses, and groundwater. Measuring the effects of depletion or pollution on the demand for one use underestimates the significance of lost resources. We must appreciate the intersectoral impacts within geographic regions. This suggests that a project-by-project approach to water resources management is not correct. Rather, we must develop a comprehensive, long-term view of the impact of public and private activities within river basins and ecologically bounded regions. We are currently working to develop such an approach to our own economic analysis, which in

the future may be used in projects involving natural resources. The impacts of individual, badly conceived projects are far-reaching, affecting soils, agricultural yields, and ultimately the incomes, health, and welfare of many rural and urban residents in developing countries. In the World Bank we have coordinated and been extensively involved in the comprehensive, long-term water planning for several of the world's major river basins, such as the Indus basin in the 1960s and 1970s and more recently the Narbada River basin in India—a multibillion dollar program that will continue to be implemented over the next fifty years. A recent World Bank–assisted water supply project in southern India—in the state of Tamil Nadu—illustrates the intersectoral aspects of this problem. The project would provide drinking water supply to some seventy-five towns outside the metropolitan area of Madras. The costs of using conventional water sources for these supplies are close to the limit of affordability of low-income households. If the investments are to be self-sustaining and replicable, these costs must be recovered from the beneficiaries. Tamil Nadu state, with some 60 million people, cannot afford to subsidize consumers. Moreover, at the same time, the sources for water for Madras itself are inadequate. To complicate the issue further, the preferred technical solution for metropolitan Madras involves bringing water from a neighboring state—a proposition whose political costs I suspect would be well appreciated here in Texas. World Bank staff, working with officials in Tamil Nadu, realized that this problem required a much broader view than provided by a single water-supply project. In fact, the major user of water—irrigated agriculture—is quite inefficient, with unlined canals and high rates of evaporation. This has led the government of Tamil Nadu, with the World Bank's financial and the United Nations' technical support, to initiate a statewide water resources management study.

This study will, among other things, identify options for pricing water for various uses and make recommendations for investments in resource management and irrigation that will have direct implications for the cost of water for drinking supply and industrial purposes. It will also provide a framework for irrigation investments in the future.

To sum up, we believe that management in the water sector means working on both supply and demand. It requires precise technical understanding and economic judgment about the uses of water if efficiency is to be improved. More important, however, effective management in this sector demands a broad, comprehensive view of the various uses of water and of the impacts of using water for one purpose on its availability for others. People do not live in project areas. They work and live in geographic regions, whether urban or rural, with particular environmental characteristics. Our use of natural resources for human well-being must reflect an appreciation of interdependence.

I would like to conclude by reflecting on the role of the international community in the resolution of these problems. The questions of food, water, and water resources have been addressed in global conferences under the auspices of the United Nations. Global, regional, and national concerns have been expressed; I believe that beyond raising official consciousness on these issues, a framework is now needed for action at the international and national levels. This framework must combine policy improvements, institutional development, resource mobilization, and coordination of external assistance.

First, governments must make efforts to articulate sensible policies in the management of their water resources. They must appreciate the financial and economic implications of their decisions. They must mobilize national and local financial resources for priority investments, including the rehabilitation, operation, and maintenance of existing facilities. Local capital can be selectively complemented by external assistance, but only on an exceptional basis. The bulk of investment in the management of water resources must come from the developing countries themselves.

Our responsibility is to see that the advice these countries receive is sensible and that external assistance is well used. Countries which are prepared to adopt sensible policies and strategies for the use of natural resources deserve external support; those countries which refuse to acknowledge the tradeoffs between short-term use and longer-term sustainable approaches should rethink their policies.

What is the World Bank doing in this regard? Over the past five years, World Bank lending for agriculture and irrigation development has amounted to about $3.5 billion annually, or one-quarter of our total lending. This is complemented by some $1 billion financing annually for drinking-water supply and sanitation investments within urban and rural development projects, as well as in free-standing water supply and sanitation programs. World Bank lending amounts to about half the annual totals of external assistance within the International Drinking Water Supply and Sanitation Decade. These funds assist national investments by the developing countries themselves, thus almost doubling the level of investment in these activities.

Money is only one part of the assistance being provided by the World Bank. We have evaluated many investments in the development of water resources and concluded that more attention should be devoted to appropriate low-cost technologies. The developing countries cannot afford to adopt the costly approaches that have been used with mixed success in the developed world. Together with UNDP, the World Bank is the executing agency for a program of research and development in low-cost technologies for drinking-water supply and sanitation, including such basic technologies as hand pumps and on-site sanitation. Most cities in developing countries will be unable to afford water-borne sewage; less costly means must be developed.

We are pleased that this joint World Bank–UNDP program has received extensive international attention and been well received in the developing countries themselves, such as India, China, Brazil, and many in Africa. Demonstration projects and technical assistance are in place in more than forty countries.

We are also working closely with other donors and agencies to coordinate aid. For many reasons, including the scarcity of development assistance, the need to improve aid effectiveness at the national level, and most of all, to help the developing nations formulate and implement sensible approaches to the management of natural resources, we are in close communication with other sources of external advice. For example, on May 13 and 14, 1985, the World Bank met with the members of Organization for Economic Cooperation and Development (OECD) to discuss how to improve aid coordination in the water sector, raising many of the same issues I have suggested here. I am pleased to report that many of the donors strongly support the thrust of these policies, and we are now moving to make our activities mutually supportive at the national level.

A recent meeting held in Sri Lanka, at the initiative of the government of Sri Lanka, brought together the sixteen official external donors working on water supply in Sri Lanka to ensure that we followed common objectives with the government. It is hoped that these types of coordination improve the quality and impact of external assistance. I should add, however, that official coordination is no replacement for active cooperation among professionals working in the sector. There is a need to share technical information, research, and operational experience so that a consensus emerges concerning appropriate technological solutions, financial policies, and organizational approaches. An important part of this process is the training of professionals in the developing countries.

In this connection, we have been asked to host an International Network of Training Centers for Water Supply and Sanitation, which will seek to strengthen training in this sector by providing materials and staff to existing training institutions in the developing countries. This network was created by the donors in 1984 and will be supported by bilateral and multilateral coordination as part of our effort to strengthen institutions responsible for water supply and sanitation.

Finally, let me reiterate that we do not underestimate the difficulties in developing effective policies and approaches to managing natural resources. To do so will require technical skill, political courage, and commitment. To do less, however, is to put the populations of the developing countries at risk. This is unacceptable. Let me end with a quotation from Seneca: "It is not because things are difficult that we do not dare to act. Rather, because we do not dare to act, things are difficult."

4. FOOD AND WATER AS IF POOR PEOPLE MATTERED: A PROFESSIONAL REVOLUTION

Robert Chambers, Institute of Development Studies, University of Sussex, Brighton, United Kingdom

ABSTRACT

Hunger is an extreme sign of deprivation. Failures to eliminate hunger, and past errors of belief, are reason for humility and re-appraisal. Hunger in the modern world is a problem not of production but of poverty, not of the total food available but of who produces it and who can command it. Normal professionalism is also part of the problem. To alleviate deprivation and hunger, professionals need to learn from and with those who are last—the poor—and to put their priorities first, including livelihoods and personal food security.

Irrigation's benefits to the land-poor—the landless and those with little land—are easily underestimated. They can include higher production, employment on more days, higher daily wages, less need to migrate, and reduced risks. From canal irrigation, benefits to the land-poor can be realized through redistribution of canal water, sliding scales of water entitlements, increases in cropping intensities, more predictability and less hassle in water supply, and equitable land distribution. From groundwater, benefits to the land-poor can be sought with pumps of ½ to 3 HP, rights and access to water, public policy with power tariffs, spacing wells and tubewells, and trees as poor people's solar pumps. Last-first approaches can also be applied to drinking water, water for pastoralism, common-property land, watershed development, energy, and agricultural research. Normal professionalism points away from these opportunities; to realize them and enable the poor to overcome hunger and deprivation demands a new professionalism which puts the last first.

THE CASE FOR PROFESSIONAL HUMILITY

In his Nairobi speech in September, 1973, Robert McNamara expressed a major shift that had been taking place in development thinking. He focused on the poverty of people in the developing world, and especially on what he termed absolute poverty, a condition of life marked by disease, illiteracy, malnutrition, and squalor, and so degrading as to insult human dignity. He asked: "And are not we who tolerate such poverty, when it is within our power to reduce the number afflicted by it, failing to fulfill the fundamental obligations accepted by civilized men since the beginning of time?" (McNamara, 1973, 6–7). His question is with us still, and if his language today sounds dated in its male bias, that serves to emphasize that it was twelve years ago when he asked it and brought antipoverty policies firmly to the fore.

The record of those 12 years is sobering and humbling. There have been successes. Life expectancy and literacy rates in most countries of the Third World have risen. Irrigated areas have extended. Bangladesh in 1984 averted a famine when faced with conditions similar to those which had caused terrible suffering ten years earlier. And the list could be extended. But the shameful fact remains that there are some 750 million people still trapped in absolute poverty.

At the World Food Conference in 1974 Henry Kissinger proclaimed the objective that within a decade no child would go to bed hungry, no family would fear for its next day's bread, and no human being's future and capacity would be stunted by malnutrition. But a decade later we have one of the worst. C. P. Snow's speculation twenty years ago was closer—that by 1984 we might be watching the world dying from starvation on our television screens. Such are the wonders of modern technology and the failures of human will that we do indeed now see children dying of hunger in our living rooms and yet still fail to enable the deprived to avoid such outrageous suffering.

Many dimensions of deprivation are discomforting. We often do not wish to look squarely at the truth, at the dependence of wealth on poverty and exploitation at unequal exchange between rich nations and poor, at transfer payments by transnational corporations, at obligations of low-income nations to repay debts in strong dollars, and so on. There is also an easy temptation to treat deprivation as if it were only "hunger." Thus in a recent speech (Clausen, 1985) the president of the World Bank defined absolute poverty as meaning that "people are too poor to obtain a calorie-adequate diet." Such hunger is the bottom line, an extreme deprivation, and points to those most in need. But overcoming deprivation entails much more, including access to basic services, and to basic goods such as matches, salt, soap, clothes, nails, thread, batteries, and so on which are no longer available in many parts of rural Sub-Saharan Africa (Chambers, 1985a). Food and water are among the least threatening and most easily accepted aspects of deprivation for elites to examine. But as we shall see, when poor people are put first, comfortable and conventional professionalism is challenged even by food and water.

The case for professional humility rests not only on failures of action but also on past errors of belief. At the level of general theory, trickle-down can now be seen as a naive wish fulfillment. At the technical level, too, there have been astonishing errors and ignorance. For many years, post-harvest losses at the village level were believed to be of the order of 30 percent, and special institutions, university courses, and research programs were set up to tackle this enormous waste. Yet as meticulous research began to be done at the village level, it emerged that farmers were not so foolish or incompetent, and that losses were lower, typically in the range of 5 to 8 percent (Greeley, 1982; Greeley [ed.],

1982; Lipton, 1982). Another technical field still in disarray is human nutrition, with continuing uncertainty about the human nutritional requirements. Perhaps the grossest error has been the view, gratifying to professionals and elites generally, that the poor are ignorant, lazy, and conservative. Some of the most important lessons of the past decade have been that it is less the poor who are ignorant, lazy, and conservative than professionals—that we are part of the problem.

Concerning food, the biggest error has been to see hunger as a problem of total production. For a long time it seemed commonsensical that world hunger resulted from a shortage of food and that producing more food would banish world hunger. This view cannot be sustained. World food supplies have been rising faster than population. Huge grain surpluses are stored in the rich world. The problem is that low-income countries cannot afford to buy them. Even more, poor people within those countries do not command or cannot afford to buy the food they need. Hunger is not a problem of total production; it is a problem of poverty of nations and especially of people.

A striking illustration of this truth for people is to be found in Amartya Sen's book *Poverty and Famines* (1981). He analyzes four major famines to show that starvation resulted from a loss of food entitlements—the ability to command food, whether through producing, earning, purchasing, or receiving it. The Great Bengal famine of 1943–44 in which perhaps 3 million people died, came after a fairly normal period in terms of food availability. Officials were right in saying that there was no serious shortage of food. People died because of sudden loss of earnings, high inflation, hoarding, and official bungling which meant that they could not command food although it was available.

Deprivation and hunger will not be overcome by increasing production in the rich world; that may even perversely inhibit production in low-income countries and make things worse. Deprivation and hunger will be overcome by enabling the deprived to grow the food themselves, or to earn it, or to command it in other ways. Increasingly, this has been recognized and emphasized by scientists. M. S. Swaminathan (n.d., 45) in an article entitled "Our Greatest Challenge: Feeding a Hungry World" has advocated "Social security to provide the needed purchasing power to the urban and rural poor through greater opportunities for gainful employment" as a component of a national food security system. Norman Borlaug (n.d., 135) has written that "the chief impediment to equitable food distribution is poverty—lack of purchasing power. . . ." But the danger remains that the main perceived professional frontiers of biotechnology, gene splicing, and the like will, as they work themselves through in history, serve the rich and not the poor, increasing production in the wrong places and for the wrong people, even if this is not what enlightened scientists intend.

The challenge, as the president of the World Bank put it in 1985, is "to generate growth among low-income countries and *low-income people within countries*" (Clausen, 1985, 7; author's italics). To do this, scientists and engineers have daunting power because their decisions have such vast, if distant, ramifications. In one of his songs Tom Lehrer had a well-known rocket scientist saying: "When the rockets go up, who cares where they come down. / That's not my department, says Werner von Braun."

Where the "rockets" come down is everyone's department. Technologies developed in laboratories, workshops, and on research stations can have massive impacts, for better or worse, on the distant rural poor, and those whose choices and actions develop them have causal and moral responsibility for these impacts.

NORMAL PROFESSIONALISM

Part of the problem is normal professionalism. We are trained and trapped in cores of knowledge, and our location, conditioning, preferences, and career incentives point us inward and upward toward greater "sophistication" instead of outward and downward toward the peripheries of knowledge, and especially the knowledge of the rural poor. "First" thinking, as it can be termed (Chambers, 1985), is powerfully pointed toward whatever is capital-intensive, mechanical, chemical, and quantifiable and away from whatever is labor-intensive, powered by animals or people, organic and difficult to quantify—away, that is, from the resources and techniques of the rural poor. Industrial, commercial, and large-farmer interests add their pull in directions scientists and engineers are already inclined to go.

Nor are these all "first" biases. Most normal professionalism deals with resources, not people. The point of entry, debate, and analysis is usually technical. Choices in research and development are influenced by the latest technology, skills, techniques, tools, and instruments, and by the priorities of peers and funding agencies, often commercial. Disciplines and professions specialize and tend to dig down into ruts, and to respond to challenges with reflexes that fit their specializations. Normal professionals, more than they realize, are trapped, blinkered, and biased in their view of reality. Above all, they see the world from the core, where they are, and not from the periphery where the deprived and hungry are.

Four bad effects follow:

1. Technologies generated in "first" conditions do not fit the needs and resources of those who are last. The cry is repeated for the transfer of technology, but a transfer-of-technology mentality is part of the problem. It is gratifying to believe that we have the knowledge, and they do not, and that they must be educated (in farming practices, in water management, and so on). But the ignorance is all too often that of the professionals. The transfer-of-technology paradigm (Chambers and Ghildyal, 1985) generates technologies that do not fit the conditions of the resource-poor, who then do not adopt them, not because they are ignorant but because they are rational.

2. The poor are a residual. Resources come before people, but then among people, the less poor come first, and the poorer last. So we have Chapter One—General Background, Chapter Two—Soils, Chapter Three—Hydrology, and then the token postscripts of Chapter Twelve—Sociological Constraints, and Chapter Thirteen—Impact on Women.

3. Disciplines and professions leave gaps. A tempting

view is that if all known and relevant disciplines are applied to a problem, every important aspect will be covered. With normal professionalism, that view is false. Canal irrigation provides an illustration. Sociologists, with few exceptions, have studied the village level and what happens among farmers below the outlet (the official water handover point between irrigation staff and groups of farmers). Engineers have concentrated on design, construction, and maintenance—the physical hardware dimensions of canal irrigation. Normal professionals, both sociologists and engineers, have in consequence neglected the operation of the main irrigation system, the allocation, scheduling, and distribution of water on the canals down to the outlets, and communications and controls. In textbooks used in professional training of canal-irrigation system managers, these crucial subjects are scarcely even mentioned.

4. Normal professionalism lacks the imagination to see that apparently technical decisions are normative. What scientists decide to do affects who gains and who loses in society. There are no neutral decisions. But to see the implications of decisions requires imagination to think through causal chains to those who may be affected, especially the poorer of the peripheries.

Normal professionalism is thus not just imperfect. It operates blindly, from the top down, from the center outward, with able and intelligent people seeing little more than their own parts of the system, cogs in the machine, not recognizing where they are going or the effects of their actions and inaction. Whether they harm or help the peripheral poor is then largely coincidental.

THE REVOLUTION: PUTTING POOR CLIENTS FIRST

A clue to the change needed can be found in Peters and Waterman's (1982) study of lessons from America's best-run companies. They quote (p. 156) Lew Young, editor-in-chief of *Business Week:*

> Probably the most important management fundamental that is being ignored today is staying close to the customer to satisfy his needs and anticipate his wants. In too many companies, the customer has become a bloody nuisance whose unpredictable behavior damages carefully made strategic plans, whose activities mess up computer operations, and who stubbornly insists that purchased products should work.

The authors find that the excellent companies are driven more by their direct orientation to their customers than by technology and in summary say that what their research uncovered on the customer attribute was that "the excellent companies *really are* close to their customers. That's it. Other companies talk about it; the excellent companies do it" (ibid, 156–57; their emphases).

For companies, there are practical, commercial reasons for putting clients first. Being close to them pays. With the rural poor the problem is different. They cannot exercise demand. They are precisely those who are most powerless, most scattered, most unable to articulate their needs, most unable to make demands on the system. They are, moreover, easily despised and rejected as ignorant and not knowing what is best for them. Neither commercial forces nor inclination draw normal professionals to learning from them and identifying their priorities. To serve them is largely a personal and moral question. Robert McNamara recognized that "The fundamental case for development assistance is the moral one. The whole of human history has recognized the principle—at least in the abstract—that the rich and the powerful have a moral obligation to assist the poor and the weak" (1973, 8). The problem is to make this abstract principle concrete. At issue is a moral choice, of a personal, professional revolution to put poor clients first.

This revolution leads to a new professionalism. It entails "flips" or reversals, taking hold of the other end of the stick, seeing things the other way around—from the point of view of poor clients, their priorities, their resources, their skills, and their knowledge. The effect is like taking a globe of the world and turning it upside down, or standing on one's head. Everything looks different. Criteria and agenda are new.

Three practical implications stand out. First, a key to the revolution is a sustained effort to learn from and with poorer clients. Research, especially over the past ten years, has shown the richness and validity of much indigenous technical knowledge (IDS, 1979; Brokensha et al. [eds.], 1980; Chambers, 1983, 75–102; Richards, 1985). Modern scientific knowledge is so linked with power and prestige that to learn from the poor requires a major role reversal from teaching and transferring technology to sitting down to listen and learn.

The second implication is to put the priorities of the poorer first. The temptation is to know what is best for others. For me to say now what the priorities of poorer people are, or may often be, is itself arrogant, and there is no substitute for asking them, again and again; but interim guesses are that their deprivations are multiple, not just poverty, but also physical weakness, isolation, vulnerability, and powerlessness; and that their priorities include livelihoods in the sense of adequate and secure stocks and flows of food and income, and reserves against contingencies. For this, access to and command over productive resources that give a degree of independence often seem to be the desired goal, together with assets for security against disasters and sudden large needs.

The third implication is for decisions by professionals on where to work, what to work on, what to seek funds for, or what to put in the syllabus. Many professionals have made reversals and decided to work on what matters to those who are last: root crops for famine reserves, pest and disease resistance to avoid purchase of chemicals, irrigation management to benefit smaller farmers and tailenders, agroforestry for improved traditional agriculture, and so on. But the great majority of professionals have not. The touchstone is for all to ask of their work: Who will gain? Who will lose? And how could the poorer lose less and gain more?

If putting the last first in this way appears the starry-eyed evangelism of a jet-lagged English academic, let us test it against practical potentials, taking first canal irrigation and second, groundwater and other small sources of water for irrigation.

IRRIGATION AS IF POOR PEOPLE MATTERED

Irrigation is usually seen as a means to production. Let us instead look at it as a means to enable the poorer to gain more secure and adequate livelihoods. For them, the importance of irrigation is not the volume of production that results, but the amount and stability of the food and income they can obtain. Silliman and Lenton (1985) in their study *Irrigation and the Land-Poor,* define the land-poor to include those who own no land, those who operate no land, and those whose major source of income is agricultural wage employment; note that this extended definition includes many small and marginal farmers. The authors find that although their subject has been neglected in research, there is considerable evidence of strongly positive employment and income effects from irrigation, much stronger than with high-yielding varieties. The benefits can take many forms: higher incomes for land-poor farmers; higher wages for laborers because of higher demand and the higher incomes of farmers, which enable them to pay their laborers more; work on more days of the year, and especially work during a second or third season when previously there was none; reduced need to migrate seasonally to seek work elsewhere, avoiding the disruptions and insecurities involved and giving a better chance to educate children; and migration to irrigated areas with direct benefits to the migrants and indirect benefits to laborers who stay behind because of deceased competition for work. Other potential benefits can be conjectured, for example, reduced vulnerability to indebtedness and impoverishment, and reduced dependence on patrons because incomes are higher and better spread throughout the year.

Such points can be confirmed by going directly to "last" people, such as laborers on the tail ends of canal irrigation systems. Women laborers on the tail end of the Kaudulla Project in Sri Lanka benefited from more work when additional supplies came to their project through the Mahaweli Scheme. In a Tamil Nadu village in India, Harijan women, asked how they felt about electric lighting installed in their huts by a government program, did not praise the light but complained that unreliable power supplies to their employers' irrigation pumps restricted their work and incomes as laborers.

The priorities of the land-poor with irrigation are likely, in short, to be for adequate, stable, predictable, and timely water supplies, both to generate employment and to enable those with some land to command and use the water.

From this perspective, let us now examine first, canal irrigation, and second, groundwater.

Canal Irrigation

Many large and medium irrigation systems in South and Southeast Asia operate far below their potential for generating employment and incomes for the poor. The deprived on canal irrigation are often laborers, marginal and small farmers, and tail enders. Providing better water supplies for tail end farmers helps both them and laborers on their land. Five priorities can be suggested.

Redistributing water from heads to tails. Each irrigation system is unique, but on many, permissive issues in headreaches create conditions of waterlogging that depress yields while tail ends are deprived of adequate, timely, and predictable supplies. The potential here is for redistribution of water so that all gain from more appropriate, adequate, timely, and predictable water supplies. At headreaches this might sometimes mean a shift to more employment-intensive, higher value, non-paddy crops, and at the tails, more employment because of a better water supply.

Raising intensities. Combinations of reservoir management, water-saving responses to rainfall, reduction or improvement of irrigation at night, improved communications, and decision making with farmers can be used to save water and increase intensities from one to two, or from two to three crops a year (Chambers, 1984). Increased intensities can also be expected to reduce out-migration, increase in-migration, and raise the incomes of the land-poor.

Progressive entitlements to water. As on the West Banas Project in Rajasthan, water entitlements can be determined on a progressive basis, with per-hectare entitlements decreasing with farm size. Besides increasing the productivity of water, this is likely to increase the livelihood-intensity of its use. Such rights are least difficult to establish before the start of a project.

Predictability and low hassle. For small and marginal farmers predictability and low hassle in gaining access to water are highly valued. On the Mahi-Kadana Project in Gujarat in India, researchers (Jayaraman et al, 1983) have reported farmers paying between seven and nine times as much for groundwater as for canal water; the groundwater is relatively reliable, but the canal water has to be obtained through a complex and unreliable bureaucratic process. A complex of questions concerning information, power, control, rights, and trust (Wade, 1985) is involved here, with the presumption that high predictability and low hassle in the supply of land-irrigation water will encourage farmers to irrigate more and generate more employment.

Land acquisition and allocation. Countries differ in policy as to whether new canal systems are built to supply water to farmers on their existing land, or whether the land is acquired and redistributed. Acquisition and redistribution are common in Africa, for example, as on the Mwea Irrigation Settlement in Kenya, and in the Dry Zone of Sri Lanka, but rare in India, one case being the Rajasthan Canal. The potential for the settlement of landless families on land secured by enforcing land ceilings, or from land acquisition or purchase by government when irrigation is provided, would seem very large in India and elsewhere.

Groundwater

Groundwater which is not fully exploited can be seen as a last frontier (IDS, 1980b), raising the question of who will get it, and who will benefit and who lose out from its development. In India the unexploited potential is still vast; estimates of the renewable recharge of groundwater roughly doubled between 1969 and 1983 (Sinha, 1983), and by 1984 the current official estimate was that 33 percent (probably a substantial underestimate) was still unexploited. Much unused groundwater potential in the lower Gangetic basin, in both India and Bangladesh, are coexisting with the greatest concentration in numbers, density, and desperation of poor people in the world. The normal pattern of groundwater development is spotty. Scattered larger farmers buy pumps and irrigate, and public tubewells are installed. Spots or islands of irrigation then appear, leaving between them unirrigated areas with many of the poorer farmers. Sometimes the cone of depression (the conical depression in the water table caused by pumping) lowers water in neighbors' wells so that they find irrigation harder, costlier, or impossible. Many other inequities have been documented with both public and private wells and tubewells.

Some of the poorer gain work and wages from this pattern of development, but they stand to gain much more from more targeted approaches. Of these, four can be outlined.

Small-scale pumps. In India and Bangladesh, and perhaps elsewhere, there is a curious gap in the pumps available on the market. At the lower end there is human and animal lift, but then little or nothing less than 3 or 5 HP pumps. This gap coincides with the needs of tens of millions of small farmers whose land lies above accessible groundwater and for whom a 3 or 5 HP pump may be too large, unless they sell water to neighbors. Many possibilities can be examined: solar (McGowan, 1985), pumps powered by batteries that are taken home at night and charged (Joshi, 1984), and decentralized electric systems based on producer gas (Joshi et al., 1983). There would appear to be a commercial opportunity here, requiring imaginative research and development close to the clients.

Rights to water. Rights to water are often proportional to land and limited to those with land. Recent innovations have shown that more equitable approaches can work. Three (see also Silliman and Lenton, 1985) deserve mention.

First, the Gram Gourav Pratisthan near Pune in India is a voluntary agency which has helped form groups of farm families for lift irrigation where water is scarcer than land. Water rights are allocated according to numbers of members of the family. This is subject to the payment of a contribution per head and the family having the necessary land. The allocation is half an acre per person subscribed at the time of starting (Morehouse, 1981; GGP, 1983). Thirty-four groups were operating in March, 1985, and other voluntary agencies were taking up the approach.

Second, Proshika in Bangladesh, as well as other organizations, had by 1984 enabled more than a hundred groups of landless peasants to acquire low-lift pumps for extracting water from common water sources for sale to farmers. Other organizations were doing likewise in Bangladesh, and groups often sell both water and their labor on a sharecropping basis. Though landless, they are thus enabled to gain from the underexploited common resource of water (Ahmed, 1983; Wood, 1984). Other organizations were doing likewise in Bangladesh, and there was interest in this approach in India as well.

The third example concerns not groundwater but small dams. Sukhomajri and Nada are villages near Chandigarh in northern India where the water in very small dams built for erosion control has been allocated equally to all families (hearths) in the village. This includes the landless, who can

sell their water or use it in sharecropping arrangements (SPWD, 1984). This may be replicated on the Adhikola Project in Nepal, as well as elsewhere in India.

All three approaches are small-scale but spreading. All allocate water more equitably than the more common system of water to the strongest. All have a higher livelihood-intensity of scarce water use than would otherwise be achieved.

Managing the groundwater market. Although they are amenable to policy interventions, markets for groundwater have been neglected. They present two types of opportunity.

1. Saturation. Where groundwater recharge is very good, as in much of the Gangetic basin, one approach to benefit the land-poor is to install pumping overcapacity. This creates a water-buyer's market. In parts of Gonda District in Uttar Pradesh, land is fragmented, and the same farmers may be sellers of water on some plots and buyers on others. Tubes are cheap and more numerous than the diesel pumps that are hired and moved around. In such conditions, small, poor farmers are in a strong position. They can purchase a secure and adequate supply of water for irrigation from their neighbors even though they may not own capital equipment or even tubes (Chambers and Joshi, 1983). "Saturation" in such areas appears a feasible policy. It could be introduced through camps of administrative, banking, and technical staff who could install overcapacity village by village and so generate a water-buyer's market for small farmers, and also a seller's market for laborers because of increased demand for labor.

2. Pricing, spacing, and public tubewell policy. In a recent study (Shah, 1985), Tushaar Shah of the Institute of Rural Management at Anand noted and investigated anomalies in the groundwater market in India, a subject that had largely escaped notice. He contrasts high rates of 15 to 35 rupees per hour in Gujarat with much lower rates of 4 to 8 rupees per hour in Punjab and Uttar Pradesh. The contrast is attributed to three factors. First, Punjab and Uttar Pradesh have a flat rate charge per horsepower per annum whereas in Gujarat the charge is based on units of power consumed. In consequence, the marginal cost of water to the seller is relatively high in Gujarat, while negligible in Punjab and Uttar Pradesh. Second, tubewell spacing policy in Gujarat gives a farmer with a tubewell a monopoly over some 203 hectares within which buyers of water lack alternate sources that might keep prices down. Third, public tubewells in Gujarat are so scattered and few that they do not compete effectively with private tubewells to keep the price of water down. High prices for water in Gujarat discriminate against small and poor farmers. Shah concludes that quite straightforward changes in government policies for power pricing, spacing, and public tubewells could transform groundwater markets in Gujarat into powerful instruments for small farmer development.

Trees as poor people's solar pumps. Trees with irrigation are a gap subject that has fallen between the slots of disciplines and professions. Foresters are concerned with trees in forests, not on farms; irrigation is usually thought of in terms of crops. Where water tables are high, however, trees can be poor people's solar pumps. They require planting, protecting, and cropping or cutting, but they do not require farmers to obtain credit and hardware for pumping. Thus they could sidestep much exploitive hassle. In the Gangetic basin and similar areas, trees could be a buffer against indebtedness for many poor people. To meet contingencies, they can cut and sell the trees. In Egypt, fodder trees might provide an alternative or supplement to berseem as an animal fodder. If the trees were more productive than berseem, they might release land for food and other crops. In any case, trees are a cheap and renewable means for the poor to tap groundwater.

OTHER RESOURCES AS IF POOR PEOPLE MATTERED

Similar approaches, starting with the priorities and needs of the poor, can be applied to other resources and developments. The same questions of who has access, who gains and who loses, and how the poorer can lose less and gain more, can be asked with each of the following: (1) drinking water, including ease and equity of access, quality, and maintainability; (2) water for livestock, including questions of location, density, technology, ownership and control of water supplies (Stanford, 1983, 1985); (3) appropriation of land through appropriation of water. On the fringes of the Sahel, as also in Botswana, the right to install a water supply gives de facto control over land, usually by the better-off members of society. The appropriation of these two common resources, water and land, is seen as development. One can reflect, though, on the jingle written at the time of the enclosure of common lands in England:

They clap in gaol the man or woman
Who steals the goose from off the common;
But let the bigger knave go loose
Who steals the common from the goose.

Those who appropriate water and land are denying to others what was before a common resource; (4) water falling in watersheds, where contour plowing, tie-ridging, grassing waterways, agroforestry, and other measures may enable disadvantaged rainfed farmers to retain more water; (5) energy, which has been regarded as a problem for the rich rather than an opportunity for the poor. Livelihood-intensive use of producer gas locomotion (Foley and Barnard, 1983) in remote wooded or bushed areas could both save foreign exchange, where oil is imported, and generate incomes for the poor who could bring wood to the roadside to sell as fuel to passing vehicles; and (6) agricultural research methodology, where a case has been argued (Chambers and Ghildyal, 1985) that a new paradigm is needed for research to serve resource-poor farmers.

In each of these cases, as with canal irrigation and groundwater for irrigation, starting with the poorest people and putting their priorities first present criteria and agenda that lead to new ideas of what should be done.

CONCLUSION

In alleviating deprivation and world hunger, normal professionalism is not only not enough, it can point in the wrong directions. While there is a world food surplus, any scientist who devotes his or her life successfully to increasing food production in the rich world may have a net effect of making things worse for the poor since low world food prices encourage imports by low-income countries and inhibit domestic production and income generation. Normal professionalism also starts with problems that are physical and scientific and with resources rather than people, let alone those who are deprived. The distant poor are the final residual in any analysis of implications, if indeed they are reached at all. Professions concerned with water have special problems. The inherent difficulties of water as a substance to manage and measure make them narrow their focus more than others. In consequence, and more than others, water-related professionals may overlook social implications of technical decisions and activities. Yet because water can do so much to reduce deprivation, their actions matter much, for better or for worse, for the deprived and hungry.

The argument for a professional revolution is both moral and practical. It is the deprived who are hungry, and their hunger will be overcome to the extent that they become less poor. Professional reversals to put people before resources, and the poorest first of all, generate new agendas for water policy and research. Priority for livelihoods for the deprived demands a flip of perception, and then presents the excitement and intellectual challenge of a new paradigm to elaborate and explore. Above all, it holds out better hope of reducing deprivation and hunger in the world. The question is whether enough professionals will have the vision and courage for the quiet personal revolutions that are needed.

REFERENCES

Ahmed, I. 1983. Irrigation projects for the landless in rural Bangladesh. *ADAB News,* January–February.

Borlaug, Norman E. 1983. Feeding the world during the next doubling of the world population. In G. Bixler and L. W. Shemilt (eds.) Chemistry and world food supplies: the new frontiers, Chemrawn II, perspectives and recommendations. Los Banos, Laguna, Philippines: International Rice Research Institute.

Brokensha, David W., D. M. Warren, and Oswald Werner (eds.). 1980. Indigenous systems of knowledge and development. Lanham, Md.: University Press of America, Inc.

Chambers, Robert. 1983. Rural development: Putting the last first. Harlow, England: Longman.

Chambers, Robert. 1984. Improving canal irrigation management: No need to wait. Paper No. 15, November. New Delhi: Ford Foundation.

Chambers, Robert. 1985a. The crisis of Africa's rural poor: Perceptions and priorities. IDS Paper No. 201, February. Brighton, England: Institute of Development Studies, University of Sussex.

Chambers, Robert. 1985b. Putting "last" thinking first: A professional revolution. pp. 78–94. In *Third World Affairs* 1985. London: Third World Foundation.

Chambers, Robert, and B. P. Ghildyal. 1985. Agricultural research for resource-poor farmers: The farmer-first-and-last model. IDS Paper No. 203. April. Brighton, England: Institute of Development Studies, University of Sussex.

Chambers, Robert, and Deep Joshi. 1983. Notes, reflections, and proposals on groundwater following a visit to Gonda District, Eastern U.P. Memorandum, March 9. New Delhi: Ford Foundation.

Clausen, A. W. 1985. Poverty in the developing countries, 1985. Address delivered January 11, 1985, at the Martin Luther King, Jr. Center for Nonviolent Social Change, Inc., Atlanta, Georgia, The Hunger Project Paper No. 3, March, 1985. San Francisco: The Hunger Project.

Foley, Gerald, and Geoffrey Barnard. 1983. Biomass gasification in developing countries. Technical Report No. 1. January. London: Earthscan.

GGP 1983. Pani Panchayat (Dividing line between poverty and prosperity), Gram Gourav Pratisthan, Shetkarinagar-Khalad, Taluka-Purandhar, District Pune, Maharashtra, India. November.

Greeley, Martin. 1982. Pinpointing post-harvest food losses. *Ceres* 15, 1, no. 85, (January–February): 30–37.

Greeley, Martin (ed.). 1982. Feeding the hungry: A role for post-harvest technology? IDS Bulletin 13, 3, June. Brighton, England: Institute of Development Studies, University of Sussex.

IDS. 1979. Rural development: Whose knowledge counts? IDS Bulletin 10, 2, January. Brighton, England: Institute of Development Studies, University of Sussex.

IDS. 1980. Who gets a last rural resource? The potential and challenge of lift irrigation. IDS Discussion Paper No. 156. Brighton, England: Institute of Development Studies, University of Sussex.

Jayaraman, T. K., M. K. Lowdermilk, L. J. Nelson, W. Clyma, J. M. Reddy, and M. I. Haider. 1983. Diagnostic analysis of farm irrigation systems in the Mahi-Kadana irrigation project, Gujarat, India. Water Management Synthesis Report No. 18, November. Fort Collins, Colo.: University Services Center, Colorado State University.

Joshi, Deep, David Seckler, and B. C. Jain. 1983. Social forestry, wood gasifiers, and lift irrigation: synergistic relations between technology and natural resources in rural India. Paper No. 3, June. New Delhi: Ford Foundation.

Joshi, Deep. 1984. Batteries, pumps, and small farmers. Memorandum, March 2. New Delhi: Ford Foundation.

Lipton, Michael. 1982. Post-harvest technology and the reduction of hunger. Pp. 4–11. *In* Martin Greeley (ed.) Feeding the hungry: A role for post-harvest technology? IDS Bulletin 13, 3, June.

McGowan, Richard. 1985. Current developments of photovoltaic irrigation in the developing world. Burlington, Vt.: Associates in Rural Development.

McNamara, Robert S. 1973. Address to the Board of Governors, Nairobi, Kenya, September 24, 1973. Washington, D.C.: International Bank for Reconstruction and Development.

Morehouse, Ward. 1981. Defying gravity: Technology and social justice. September. Geneva: United Nations Development Forum.

Peters, Thomas J., and Robert H. Waterman, Jr. 1982. In search of excellence: lessons from America's best-run companies. New York: Harper and Row.

Richards, Paulv. 1985. Indigenous agricultural revolution: Ecology and food production in West Africa. London: Hutchinson House.

Sandford, Stephen. 1983. Organisation and management of water supplies in tropical Africa. ILCA Research Report No. 8. December. Addis Ababa: International Livestock Centre for Africa.

———. 1985. The management of water development for livestock in dry zones of Africa. Addis Ababa: International Livestock Centre for Africa.

Sen, Amartya. 1981. Poverty and famines: An essay on entitlement and deprivation. Oxford: Clarendon Press.

Shah, Tushaar. 1985. Transforming groundwater markets into powerful instruments for small farm development: Lessons from the Punjab, Uttar Pradesh, and Gujarat. Mimeograph, January. Anand, Gujarat, India: Institute of rural management.

Silliman, Joel, and Roberto Lenton. 1985. Irrigation and the land-poor. New York: Ford Foundation.

Sinha, B. P. C. 1983. A critical review of the groundwater resource evaluation methodologies and estimates in India. Pp. K-13–25. *In* Central Ground Water Board, Ministry of Irrigation, Seminar on assessment, development and management of groundwater resources, Keynote Addresses and Special Papers. New Delhi, April 29–30. 1983.

SPWD [Society for Promotion of Wastelands Development]. 1984. Hill resource development and community management: lessons learnt on micro-watershed management from cases of Sukhomajri and Dasholi Gram Swarajya Mandal. August. New Delhi: Society for Promotion of Wastelands Development.

Swaminathan, M. S. 1982. Our greatest challenge: feeding a hungry world. *In* G. Bixler and L. W. Shemilt (eds.) Chemistry and world food supplies: the new frontiers. Chemrawn II, Perspectives and recommendations. Los Banos, Laguna, Philippines: International Rice Research Institute.

Wade, Robert. 1985. Managing water managers: deterring expropriation, or, equity as a control mechanism. Washington, D.C.: World Bank.

Wood, Geoffrey D. 1984. Provision of Irrigation Services by the Landless—An Approach to Agrarian Reform in Bangladesh. *Agricultural Administration* 17:55–80.

5. WATER AS A CONSTRAINT TO WORLD FOOD SUPPLIES

Manzur Ahmad, Pakistan Agricultural Research Council, Islamabad, Pakistan

ABSTRACT

Water is the most important input to agriculture, yet it is not an unlimited resource. As irrigation represents the best hope of quickly expanding world food supplies, a detailed discussion of Pakistan's case is considered to be the most relevant to the theme of this paper, Pakistan being a typical arid country primarily dependent on irrigation for its agriculture. With the construction of additional storage facilities, development of the groundwater potential and improved water management, the amount of water now available for raising crops can ultimately be raised to 278 percent. In addition, the benefits of available water itself can be optimized by better choice of crop varieties, cropping patterns, use of modern agricultural inputs, and adoption of appropriate agronomical practices, which should continuously be updated through research. Pakistan can thus make a substantial contribution to future world food supplies, but this requires mobilizing the huge investment needed for harnessing and utilizing its water potential and tackling socioeconomic problems as the development proceeds.

Water is the source of all life. The Holy Koran says "And We created from water everything living." No doubt, therefore, that it is the most important input in agriculture. It is essential for the very existence of plants and indispensable to their growth, being the main constituent of the protoplasm and making up 85 to 95 percent of the fresh weight of most of their green tissues. It has several functions to perform: It not only carries the nutrients from the soil to the plant but also is involved in essential physiological processes such as photosynthesis and various metabolism reactions. It is also vital for the maintenance of plant turgor which, *inter alia,* maintains the form and mechanical strength of the plant organs.

Water is the *sine qua non* of agriculture and food production, but it is not an ulimited resource. No authentic study is yet available as to whether water can support world food needs in the very distant future. In its monumental report entitled "Agriculture Towards 2000," the Food and Agriculture Organization examined the probable situation at the approaching turn of the century. In this study, FAO has come to the conclusion that irrigated areas can expand by 40 percent in twenty years over the 1980 level and can contribute about half the additional production required under an optimistic scenario. That conclusion is based on the premise that the developing countries will be able to achieve the overall economic growth of 7 percent envisioned in the new United Nations development strategy and double their food output in two decades from 1980 without water becoming a constraint for these countries, as a whole. Of course massive investment will have to be mobilized for this purpose. It has been estimated in this report that for irrigation facilities alone in the ninety developing countries studied, the gross investment required would be approximately $12.7 billion per annum in 1990 and $14.7 billion per annum in the year 2000 (both in terms of 1975 dollars).

Irrigation for agricultural production is a complex activity, In fact, it has six dimensions: three dimensions of space regarding point of delivery, the other three being quantity, quality, and time of supply. The last three dimensions are determined by soils, climate, crop varieties, and cropping patterns. On top of these dimensions is the multidisciplinary character of irrigation, embracing as it does the interaction of engineering, biological, and social sciences. Water cannot be considered to have become a real constraint to meeting the world food supplies as long as there is the scope for manipulation of the various underlying factors for further increasing the agricultural production.

In dealing with the subject of this paper, the case history of Pakistan has been kept in view because the conditions here are typical of many arid countries. The conclusions that can be drawn from a discussion of Pakistan's water problems, prospects, policies, plans, and programs will be valid for very large regions of the world and, therefore, highly relevant to the theme of this paper. The dependence of Pakistan's agriculture primarily on irrigation is yet another reason why the example of Pakistan is so appropriate to the theme; the relative contribution of irrigated areas to agricultural production around the world is much larger than the percentage of such areas in proportion to the total cultivated area. Moreover, irrigation holds the promise of being a major instrument of meeting food deficits in future, especially in the developing world.

Pakistan has a land area of 80 million ha, of which nearly one-fourth, i.e., 20 million ha, have been under cultivation and another 11.0 million ha have been classified as culturable waste. It has been a traditional exporter of rice and cotton and reached self-sufficiency in wheat for its 95 million people in 1983, when it produced 12.4 million tons. However, it has been importing edible oil to the extent of four-fifths of its requirements, the maximum import being 742,000 tons in 1983–84. More than two-thirds of the cultivated area is dependent on irrigation, the rest is by and large rainfed. Irrigation is responsible for more than 90 percent of the agricultural production. The annual cropping intensity has been about 110 to 115 percent, i.e., double cropping has been practiced in only a limited area.

Under the Indus Water Treaty, signed by India and Pakistan in September, 1960, to resolve the Indus Waters dispute, the three western rivers of the Indus System, namely, the Indus, the Jhelum, and the Chenab, have been allocated to Pakistan

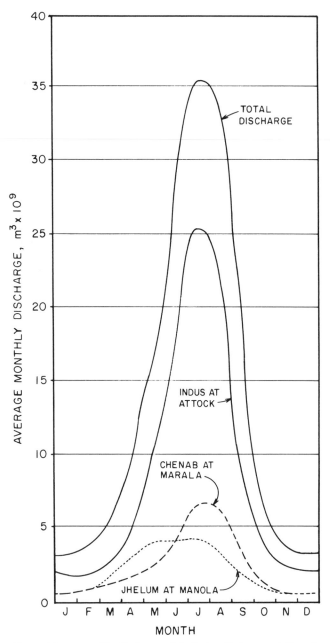

Fig. 1. Mean monthly discharge of the Indus, Jhelum, and Chenab rivers at the points indicated.

and the three eastern rivers to India. A transition period of ten years was allowed so that Pakistan could transfer use of irrigation water from the three eastern rivers to the new western rivers. The annual flow in the eastern rivers is distributed very unevenly over the seasons. About 84 percent of it occurs during summer, from April through September. Half of the remaining flow occurs in the months of March and October, and thus only 4 percent is available from November through February. The individual and combined hydrographs of the three western rivers giving mean monthly flow have been drawn in Fig. 1, which demonstrates the wide seasonal fluctuations in the river flows. The annual

flows are also marked by equally large fluctuations from year to year. They touched a peak of 223.48 billion cubic meters (BCM) in 1959–60 and dropped to a low of 115.2 BCM during 1974–75.

Until the 1950s, irrigation in Pakistan was entirely supply oriented, although there has subsequently been a gradual but only partial shift of orientation to resource development. In these conditions, the demand had been dictated by the availability of river water, the flow of which was under hardly any control. Nevertheless, effort was made to use the river hydrograph as much as possible through a system of interconnecting rivers and a blend of perennial, nonperennial, and inundation canals. The perennial canals are intended to run throughout the year, although with reduced discharge in winter as crop requirements are less in this period anyway. The nonperennial canals are meant to run only during summer from April 1 to October 15. The inundation canals operate for still shorter periods of very high river flows as there is no control structure such as a weir or a barrage on the feeding rivers.

The inundation canals and non-perennial canals were constructed for irrigation only in those areas where the underground water at shallow levels was sweet and could be taken out by Persian wheels for subsistence agriculture and for drinking in winter, when the canals are closed. As inundation canals drew most of their supply during the flood periods of summer, the quality and yields of the crops grown with this supply suffered. Almost all the inundation canals have now been brought under weir control. The water allowances for areas served by these canals have been kept high to preserve their right to the flow water, but obviously, the intensity of cropping has been low.

Agriculture is the mainstay of Pakistan's economy. It constitutes 30 percent of the gross national product of the country and provides employment to about 55 percent of its active labor force as well as raw materials for its major industries, and it is the biggest source of foreign exchange. With its population growing at the rate of 3 percent and expected to increase 50 percent to 150 million by the year 2000, Pakistan has to produce more food and other agricultural commodities not only for itself but also for export. Fortunately, there is a tremendous potential for developing the water resources of Pakistan to meet the rapidly growing demand for this vital agricultural input.

The total availability of water for irrigation can be increased by building storage areas and tapping the groundwater potential and through better water management, which aims at reducing the transit or conveyance losses and promoting improved agronomical practices on the farm. Each of these factors will now be discussed.

Of the annual average flow of 168 BCM of the three western rivers of the Indus System, allocated to Pakistan under the Indus Waters Treaty, only about 121.2 BCM is being diverted through canals. The canal diversions have steadily increased to this level from 99.41 BCM in 1960–61 as a result of the construction of major storage facilities at Tarbela and Mangla holding 13.56 and 7.06 BCM, respectively, and a small one at Chashma Barrage of 0.6 BCM. This improvement in supply should not be judged merely by the increase in the quantum of water as it also ensures better timing of supply because the water releases from storage areas can now be regulated to correspond more closely to the fluctuations in actual water requirements of the crops.

Even in a mean year, about 46.8 BCM of river water is still going to waste at sea. Some of it can be trapped by building additional storage facilities, for which there are a number of potential sites, especially on the Indus. One such project, namely the Kalabagh Dam on the Indus, with a reservoir capacity of 11.28 BCM, is already under active consideration of the government, with the additional possibility of generating 2,400 MW of electric power. It would not be economical to bottle up the entire surplus flow of the Indus even in a mean year because the storage facility required for this purpose would not fill up in many years. Only a partial regulation of the mean flow would, therefore, be feasible. Studies have shown that 144 BCM can be considered the upper limit for diversion through the canals by additional storages as compared with the present level of 121.2 BCM.

Groundwater is yet another source which can make a substantial contribution to water supply in Pakistan. The entire Indus plain is underlain with water to a depth of 100 m and more. This vast reservoir, one of the biggest in the world, can theoretically be tapped by "mining," which was being suggested earlier in the history of Pakistan by several experts. The idea of "mining" was given up, however, in view of the increasing use of expensive energy it would involve and more particularly because it was justifiably believed that the high salinity of water in the deeper portions would be brought up even to the shallower levels and thus adversely affect the usability of the groundwater potential as a whole. It has therefore been decided to depress the water table to no more than 3 to 4.5 m and to restrict pumping only to the annual recharge. This will have the additional advantage of subirrigation. Studies have shown that groundwater kept at this level, particularly at 3 m below the ground surface, can reduce the irrigation requirement by as much as 30 percent.

However, the entire annual recharge to the groundwater will not take place in sweet water zones from which it can be recovered more or less for direct use in irrigation. The recharge in the saline water zones can, however, be captured only through skimming wells, which will be shallow so as to draw water only from the sweet upper layers. Various estimates have been made from time to time of the usable groundwater potential. These range from 48 to 72 BCM of which at present 44.7 BCM is already being tapped both by tubewells in the public sector and of the farmers themselves. For the purpose of this paper, it has been assumed that only 52.8 BCM of water can ultimately be recovered for irrigation through pumpage, in view of the fact that the recharge itself will diminish and when the delivery losses are curtailed with better water management as discussed later on in this paper. Adoption of this figure implies a certain degree of liberalism in the interpretation of what is "usable" groundwater. The groundwater will, in general, have a higher content of dissolved salts and a certain amount of alkalinity, and some of it can be used only after mixing with canal water. Opinions differ about the acceptable level of salinity, expressed in terms of electric conductivity (EC), and of alkalinity, expressed in terms of sodium absorption ratio (SAR) and residual sodium content (RSC). But the higher these values are, the more careful and the better degree of management the use of such waters would require. As a result of field experiments conducted in Pakistan, it has been established that water with EC up to 1500, SAR of less than 10, and RSC of less than 2.5 can be used without much difficulty.

As has been stated earlier, a large quantity of floodwater will continue to flow into the sea unused for several years as it will not be economical to build storage facilities to tap the floods even in a mean year, not to mention the years with still heavier floods. A promising approach to long-term increased utilization of groundwater and conservation of floodwaters will be, therefore, to induce heavy recharge in the river flood plain by evacuating a large volume of the aquifer during the low flow season. Preliminary studies undertaken in connection with the Revised Action Program for Irrigated Agriculture (WAPDA, 1982) using analog models indicate that a total yield of 19.2 BCM from the riverine reservoir is practicable; one-fourth of this would be captured from the previous unused flood flows and the remaining would result from additional canal losses and reduced river flows.

A substantial addition can be made to the total water availability for irrigation by minimizing the losses that take place in the conveyance system, viz., canals, distributaries, and in watercourses as well in the farmers' fields themselves. A number of experiments have been carried out over several decades to determine these losses. The latest estimates put them at 25 percent in canals and distributaries, which are mostly unlined earthen channels; at 46 percent in watercourses, and at 26 percent in the farmers' fields. The high water losses in the watercourses are the result of neglect by the farmers who are responsible for their upkeep and the manner in which cuts are made in them by farmers drawing their share of the water during their weekly turns. The field losses are due to the poor application efficiency resulting from unleveled fields and unscientific irrigation practices followed by the farmers, leading to frequent instances of over- or under-irrigation. In preparing an annual water budget for the future, it has been assumed that the losses can be curtailed in the canals and distributaries to 10 percent (after rehabilitation and through better maintenance). In the watercourses losses could be cut to 15 percent through realignment, bank strengthening, concrete lining in pervious tracts, construction of concrete turnouts, culverts, and buffalo wallow ponds. In the fields losses could be cut also to 15 percent through precision land leveling and educating farmers by means of improved extension services.

Taking into account the possible increase in surface supplies, the potential contribution of groundwater, and the district potential for reduction of transit and field-application losses, a water budget has been prepared for Pakistan showing the goals in comparison with the existing situation, as shown in Table 1. It will be seen that there is a potential of increasing water supply for crops from the 1982–83 level of

Table 1. Present water availability and water resources potential (billion cubic meters).

Present (1982–83)

Source	Canal Head	Watercourse Head	Field	Crop Use
Surface water	124	93 (75%)	50 (54%)	37 (74%)
Groundwater	—	45	24 (54%)	18 (74%)
Total	124	138	74 (54%)	55 (74%)

Potential

Source	Canal Head	Watercourse Head	Field	Crop Use
Surface water	148	126 (85%)	113 (90%)	96 (85%)
Groundwater	—	54	49 (90%)	42 (85%)
Riverine reservoir	—	20	18 (90%)	15 (85%)
Total	148	200	180 (90%)	153 (85%)

55 BCM to 153 BCM ultimately, and this represents an expansion of 278 percent.

The water budget mentioned earlier shows only the quantitative picture, and as stated earlier, quantity of water is only one of several aspects of irrigation. The improvement in the timing of supplies made possible by properly scheduling storage releases and tubewell pumping will have an accelerating impact on raising agricultural production. Still another factor that cannot be brought out by a quantitative water budget is the fact that conjunctive use of surface and groundwater supplies offers a much more powerful lever for agricultural production than is indicated by the arithmetical sum of the availabilities from these two sources.

Management of water supply is not the only factor that determines food and agricultural production. It may also be possible to make adjustments in the irrigation water demand itself in order to avoid a mismatch with supply at any particular time because of canal capacity limitation or water availability. As the water demand is a function of the cropping patterns and crop varieties, any adjustment in it can be effected by changing these two elements singly or in combination. Greater emphasis in the cropping pattern to lower delta crops, which require less water, and on the use of varieties that are comparatively more drought resistant can bring about a significant reduction in the demand. Examples in Pakistan are cotton and maize, which are lower delta crops, as opposed to rice and oilseed crops in place of wheat as drought-resistant alternatives.

An optimum choice of crop varieties and cropping patterns may still leave some water deficits. Care has to be taken to reduce the impact of such a deficit on the crop yields by shifting the time of the deficit so that it coincides with the noncritical periods of the crop growth. Identification of the critical periods of the various crops, therefore, becomes a vital factor in scheduling canal supplies. For example, in the case of wheat, the most critical stage is the tillering stage, which is reached about eighteen to twenty-one days after the seed has been sown. This stage requires one-fifth of the total water applied to the wheat crop but if water is denied at this stage, the yield may go down by more than 50 percent. In the case of cotton, the early vegetative stage is the most critical one. On the other hand, anthesis in wheat and flowering in cotton fall into the noncritical category of their growth stages.

The development of water resources requires huge outlays of capital. It is therefore absolutely essential that optimum use is made of water by the application of the complementary agricultural inputs, viz. improved seed, fertilizer, and plant pesticides in addition to adoption of scientific cultural practices, such as land preparation and seed and fertilizer placement. Unless these other inputs are simultaneously provided, large production increases with irrigation alone will not take place. The impact of fertilizer, for example, with different irrigation dosages is evident from Fig. 2, which has been drawn from actual surveys undertaken by WAPDA Master Planning & Review Division in connection with the Revised Action Program for Irrigated Agriculture (WAPDA, 1982). Control of weeds is also necessary as these are known to take as much as a 30 percent toll of crops. Soil sodicity can also vitiate the benefits of irrigation despite the application of other agricultural inputs, unless the soils have been properly treated with gypsum, as a cheap soil-amendment agent. Congestion of drainage too can have an adverse effect on production as the proper aeration of the plant roots will then be impossible. Amelioration of such congestion is therefore an essential prerequisite.

The need for promoting the use of complementary inputs

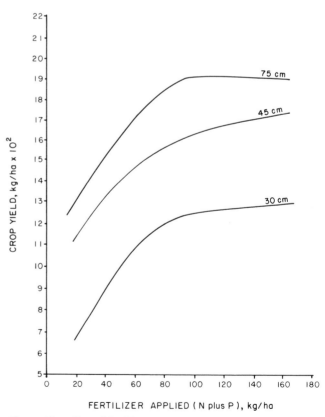

Fig. 2. The effect of fertilizer on crop yield response to irrigation.

Table 2. Yield of major crops.

	Weighted Mean	Median of Upper Range	Potential
	A	B	$\dfrac{B}{A} \times 100\%$
	100 kg/ha		
Wheat	13.8	46.0	333
Seed cotton	6.8	16.6	257
Rice	18.4	50.6	275
Maize	13.8	41.4	300
Sugarcane	294.5	782.0	266

and scientific cultivation practices also becomes apparent from the actual yields obtained by progressive farmers in Pakistan. The weighted average and the median upper range of yields differ by more than 250 percent, in the case of wheat by 333 percent, as shown in Table 2, taken from the Revised Action Program for Irrigation Agriculture (WAPDA, 1982). This tremendous yield gap, i.e., the differential between the average yield across the irrigated areas and the yield of the progressive farmers, is not entirely due to the differences in water supply but is primarily attributable to the efficient use of complementary agricultural inputs and improved management practices.

Optimization of the benefits of irrigation water in terms of increased agricultural production also requires a constant research effort. Some of the areas of research are:

1. Identification and development of drought-resistant varieties
2. Identification of the critical stages of crop growth for various crops when any moisture stress can be harmful
3. Identification and development of salt-tolerant varieties
4. Influence of water table and water and soil salinities on irrigation requirements
5. Role of water in relation to other agricultural inputs in increasing yields
6. Continuous improvement in water management techniques, from the technical as well as economic points of view.

Pakistan is aware of the key significance of this research on irrigated agriculture. With this objective in view, it has established extensive facilities within the framework of a development project at Mona (WAPDA, 1981), where research is being carried out under farmers' field conditions on an area of more than 70,000 ha and with their fullest cooperation. The results of the research have inspired several new policy initiatives by government, particularly in regard to improved water management on the farm.

The vast irrigation potential cannot be mobilized through engineering and biological measures alone. In developing countries the social aspects are no less important because the landholdings are usually very small. In Pakistan, a watercourse with a capacity of 28 liters per second ($L \cdot S^{-1}$) may be irrigating an area of about 220 ha or so, but it serves as many as fifty farmers, who have to work together to modernize their agricultural production. A beginning has been made in Pakistan by enacting a law for the formation of Water Users Associations, one for each watercourse, to ensure better water management downstream of the outlet from the canal. Some outstanding results have been achieved in generating cooperation among the farmers on the renovation, maintenance, and upkeep of their watercourses, but this cooperation has yet to be extended to the adoption of better cultivation practices, crop rotations, and cropping patterns. While the "turn" system in vogue for sharing of water by the farmers may be the most equitable, as the share of each is determined not on the basis of his influence but on the size of the land he possesses, it is certainly not the most efficient as there is no built-in mechanism for avoiding waste and misuse. Reconciliation of equity with efficiency cannot be achieved until the constraints involved are fully investigated and the possible solutions have been tried in field conditions. It is therefore with the keenest interest that Pakistan is looking forward to becoming the main cooperating center of the International Irrigation Management Institute, being established with headquarters in Sri Lanka, with the objective, inter alia, of sponsoring action-oriented research on all aspects of irrigation management, viz., biological, engineering, sociological, and economic, especially on their relative interaction.

Two other factors come into the picture. First, there should be adequate incentives to farmers for improving water management. This might be pricing policies with respect to irrigation water as well as farmers' crops. It is assumed that the farmers are continuously given the required technology that has been tested for its economic feasibility. Second, existence of any interprovincial, interstate, or interregional water disputes within a country may also seriously impair the prospects of optimizing the benefits from water as a limited natural resource.

The Pakistan case has demonstrated that with the available water resources, it can make a substantial contribution to world food supplies in the future, provided it can mobilize the huge capital investment required for harnessing them ($5 billion for the Kalabagh Dam alone) and tackle socioeconomic problems as the development proceeds.

REFERENCES

Agriculture Towards 2000. Food and Agriculture Organization, Rome.

Revised Action Program for Irrigated Agriculture. 1982. WAPDA, Lahore, Pakistan, April.

Evaluation of Research at Mona Reclamation Experimental Project. 1981. WAPDA, Lahore, Pakistan.

6. IRRIGATION AND DRAINAGE IN THE WORLD

W. Robert Rangeley, International Commission on Irrigation, London, England

ABSTRACT

Irrigation has expanded dramatically in this century, from about 40 million ha in 1900 to 270 million today, to the extent that it covers 18 percent of the cultivated land and provides one-third of the world's food. The current rate of expansion is about 4 million ha a year. However, technological advances have not kept pace with expansion, and many recently constructed projects are already becoming outmoded. In recent years there has been a growing awareness that expansion of irrigation is not sufficient in itself to meet future needs, and furthermore, is it always the least-cost solution? Today, there is a major thrust to increase production from the existing irrigated land, particularly in large parts of Asia where crop yields are about one-third those achieved elsewhere. This thrust involves programs to rehabilitate and modernize the old irrigation projects and to arrest the current decline in management standards.

The major drainage projects of the world were first built in the developed countries in Europe and North America. In recent years the emphasis has moved to the developing countries, where the old irrigation systems are suffering from waterlogging, and to central Asia where there is an urgent need to improve the productivity of what are now low-yielding lands.

Both the Green Revolution of the 1960s and abrupt increases in oil prices in 1972 and 1979 have had adverse effects on the production from the marginal lands of the world and have favored the high-yielding land that has good soils, irrigation, and drainage. This point is illustrated by the better rates of growth in agricultural output in those Asian countries with extensive irrigation compared with the rainlands of Africa.

Finally, this chapter stresses the need to improve irrigation-management standards. It is proposed that over the next decade there be a special endeavor to focus on the issues of management on a worldwide scale, involving the establishment of a network of national and international irrigation management training centers.

IRRIGATED AREAS OF THE WORLD

Irrigation has expanded dramatically in this century, from about 40 million ha in 1900 to 270 million today, to the extent that it covers 18 percent of the cultivated land and provides one-third of the world's food.

Table 1 shows growth in irrigation development by continents since the middle of the century.

The global rate of expansion has been particularly impressive since 1950. In the twenty years from 1950 to 1970 the gross irrigated area of the world was doubled. It is interesting to note that in any single decade since 1950, the expansion has approximately equaled the total development achieved during the first half of the century.

The worldwide rate of irrigation development in the 1960s averaged almost 6 million ha a year. By the 1970s it had declined to about 5 million ha a year. Within the whole, the most rapid growth has occurred in India where in the 1960s the gross area expanded from about 28 million to 37 million ha, and today it is about 55 million ha. In the 1980s the worldwide rate of growth had declined slightly because of economic recession, the adverse terms of trade for agriculture, and new emphasis on rehabilitation and modernization. Reliable figures are not available, but the current rate of growth has probably fallen to about 4 million ha a year.

CONTRIBUTION OF IRRIGATION TO FOOD PRODUCTION

The irrigated areas of the world are currently estimated to cover about 18 percent of the total cultivated area and contribute about one-third of world food production. The contribution of irrigation to food production in certain selected countries with a major irrigated component of total cultivated area is shown in Table 2.

DRAINED AREAS IN THE WORLD

In drainage development, statistics are too limited to attempt a serious tabulation, but using the information from member countries of the International Commission on Irrigation Development (ICID), the continental distribution is as given in Table 3.

OBJECTIVES AND CRITERIA THAT HAVE INFLUENCED IRRIGATION AND DRAINAGE DEVELOPMENT

The Early Aim—Famine Relief in Asia

In the early nineteenth century, irrigation projects were constructed in Asia and the Middle East as insurance against famines. When major irrigation works were first proposed in 1840 for the deltas of southern India, it was recorded that in the Cauvery Delta, "in one of the worst years of drought enough water had been allowed to flow into the sea which if used would have irrigated 10 times as much grain as would have supplied the whole population of the region." It was this kind of reasoning that prompted the construction of the great irrigation works of the Cauvery, Krishna, and Godavari deltas. By the end of the century this region of India had more than 1 million ha of irrigated land, and severe famines had almost become things of the past.

In the northern parts of the Indian subcontinent, work was started in the second half of the nineteenth century on the great irrigation systems of the Ganges and Indus plains. The Indus system today provides 80 percent of the agriculture output of Pakistan and covers about 14 million ha.

Table 1. Gross irrigated areas by continent (million ha).

	1950	1960	1970	Present Estimate
Europe (incl. part Soviet Union)	8	12	20	29
Asia (incl. part Soviet Union)	66	100	132	184
Africa	4	5	9	13
North American	12	17	29	34
South America	3	5	6	9
Australia and Pacific	1	1	2	2
	94	140	198	271

Table 2. The contribution of irrigation to food production.

Country	Irrigated Area/ Cultivated Area (percent)	Irrigated Food Production/Total Food Production (percent)
India	30	55
Pakistan	65	80
China	50	70
Indonesia	40	50
Chile	35	55
Peru	35	55
Mexico	30	N/A

Table 3. Gross drained and flood-protected areas (million ha).

Region	Area
Europe	29
Asia	50
Africa	1
North America	52
South America	10
Australia and Pacific	2

General Objectives

The general objectives of irrigation development have been either to achieve self-sufficiency in food and fiber or to maximize economic efficiency in the use of land and water. The former objective essentially belongs to the developing countries and the latter to the developed countries. Within these broad generalizations there are exceptions where projects are developed for export produce, and perhaps the most striking examples of this objective are found in the Sudan and Egypt. Although these export-oriented schemes have suffered setbacks in recent years as the terms of trade in agriculture have declined, there are signs of better stability and of some successful attempts to adjust to the new economic conditions.

The Issue of Cost

Irrigation is a high-cost form of agricultural development, and big projects have long lead times from project inception to full development. It is therefore not surprising that investment in irrigation gives rise to much debate among agricultural planners. There is an understandable desire to seek lower-cost solutions that will achieve similar objectives in terms of agricultural growth. In particular, planners, influenced by the high cost of capital, look for projects with shorter payback periods. Although the injection of "quick return" inputs such as fertilizers, seed, and low-cost infrastructure has brought an excellent response in recent years, there are many signs of a leveling-off in the absence of greater investment in irrigation and drainage.

Costs vary widely throughout the world depending on the type of system, water source costs, size of project, and availability resources for construction. The lowest costs of new major irrigation systems are found in Asia and particularly in India, where surface systems cost from \$2,000 to \$4,000 per hectare. In other countries where projects are large enough to provide economy of scale, costs are around \$5,000 per hectare.

In regions where projects are small and where there has been no long tradition of irrigation, costs are often \$10,000 per hectare and more. The higher range of costs is typical of most of Sub-Saharan Africa. Here, irrigable land is found only in small scattered entities, which results in not only a high average cost of development but also a higher cost of infrastructure for transportation, marketing, and supplies that must be improved as part of the project costs.

Drainage costs vary widely but are generally between \$1,000 and \$2,000 per hectare. Thus, for both irrigation and drainage a global average cost is some \$5,000 to \$6,000 per hectare.

Opportunity Cost of Capital

The high opportunity cost attached to capital has in recent years tended to influence irrigation strategies in several ways. For most projects there are options and trade-offs between high initial capital investment coupled with low running costs on the one hand and low capital costs with high running costs on the other hand. Clearly a high discount rate leads to a preference for projects with high running costs and low capital costs. To give a general example, pump schemes have been shown to be more attractive than gravity diversion dam schemes, especially in the period up to the mid-1970s when energy costs were low. Furthermore, high discount rates favored other energy-intensive modes of increasing crop production such as greater use of fertilizers and mechanization.

Despite such demonstrations of economic disadvantages for capital-intensive projects, experience in developing countries has shown that the large gravity flow projects have proved more resilient to economic changes than projects with high running costs. Furthermore, the traditional gravity flow projects have proved less vulnerable to the general decline in management standards that has occurred in many developing countries.

The Constraint of Poor Drainage

Whereas the growth in drained areas has in the past been in Europe and North America, the pattern has shifted to other regions, including the Soviet Union, China, Pakistan, Bangladesh, and the Middle East. In some regions such as Bangladesh, eastern India, southern Pakistan, and Cambodia, poor drainage and flooding represent the main constraint on agricultural production. Despite this constraint, the poor economic returns on investment have hitherto seriously restricted drainage projects.

Influence of the Green Revolution and the Oil Crisis on Irrigation Development

It is interesting to reflect on some of the factors that have influenced the pattern of growth in irrigation and drainage over the last fifty years. From the middle of this century new technologies that had remained latent during World War II were rapidly applied to agriculture throughout the world. At the same time large new investments were made in irrigation, particularly in those countries with an established tradition in irrigated crop production, India, Sudan, Egypt, and Pakistan, for example. The results of the new technologies and new investments are demonstrated in the growth rate in agricultural production. For example, grain production rose by about 3 percent a year in the period from 1950 to 1973. Of the new technologies, the most dramatic in its effect was the introduction of new crop varieties in the late 1960s—the so called "Green Revolution."

The new crop varieties were bred to respond better to farm inputs than the traditional varieties, and it was therefore not surprising to find that the main increases in yields were in areas with good water control from irrigation or drainage. In Pakistan, wheat yields rose by some 40 percent in a space of three years, and rice yields doubled in a decade. In the drained areas of the Mekong Delta the new rice varieties proved highly responsive. By contrast, in areas of uncertain rainfall such as Africa, or of poor irrigation such as in many parts of Southeast Asia, the response was disappointing. The Green Revolution therefore underlined the value of good systematic irrigation and drainage. India in particular recognized the enhanced value of irrigation and pursued a rate of expansion in irrigation of between 1 million and 1.5 million ha a year and has successfully improved grain production per capita despite a large demographic growth.

The second event that affected agricultural production and the value of irrigation and drainage was the oil crisis of 1973 with its second wave in 1979. Over this period oil prices rose about sevenfold in real terms. The 1973 increase contributed to a rapid decline in the growth rate of grain production from about 3 percent to 2 percent in the period from 1973 to 1977, and in recent years it has fallen toward 1 percent. In 1977, the underlying reason was that high oil prices meant high input costs, so areas with marginal yields fell out of production. Regions with poor climates and soils are the most affected as we see from the present situation in Africa.

High input prices favor irrigation and drainage simply because high yields justify the inputs. Thus, both the Green Revolution and the oil crisis have widened the gap in the returns obtainable from irrigated and well-drained land compared with those from marginal land or from good land with uncertain water control. These factors make a very strong case for the further development of irrigation and drainage and in particular for the rehabilitation and modernization of the existing irrigation systems.

PRESENT PROBLEMS AND SOLUTIONS

Limitations in Water Resources

In many countries where irrigated land represents a high proportion of the total cultivated land, the available water resources are approaching the economic if not the physical limits of exploitation. This applies to, for example, India, Sri Lanka, Egypt, the Sudan, and the southwestern United States. There are small island countries like Mauritius and arid zone countries like Somalia and Botswana that need irrigation but have a very poor distribution of water resources in relation to the irrigable land.

Possible options in regions of water shortage are to: (1) construct more storage reservoirs, (2) undertake major interbasin transfers of water, (3) better integrated use of ground and surface waters, and last but most important, (4) economize in present water use by raising water management standards and irrigation efficiencies.

In some regions the correct solution is to undertake most if not all of these measures as part of a long-term investment program, taking into account that some of them are longer term than others. This is indeed the policy being followed in countries such as India and Mauritius, to cite a large and small example.

Storage Reservoirs

The measure with least difficulty of implementation is to build storage reservoirs, but costs per unit of water delivered are often high. Given the necessary financing, the administrative and social constraints are rarely severe.

It is usually easier to implement a storage-dam project than to construct and bring into service the associated irrigation system. There are many unfortunate examples in the world where dams have been built without the means of realizing the total project benefits. Too often it is forgotten that in terms of finance alone the funding of a dam for a new irrigation project is only the beginning and involves perhaps no more than 15 or 20 percent of the total project investment costs.

One effect of the rise in oil prices has been to improve the economic value of multipurpose power/irrigation dams. Whereas before 1973 the energy component of an irrigation project was often small, being perhaps about one-third of total benefits or less, with irrigation two-thirds, for the same project today these proportions would be reversed. In some cases it is possible to obtain an acceptable rate of return from hydroelectric projects costing as much as $3,500 per kilowatt, and for some multipurpose projects this justifies a dam without allocation of any costs to irrigation or other purposes.

Table 4. Interbasin transfer schemes.

Location	Scheme	Capacity $(m^3 \cdot s^{-1})$	Length (km)
Iraq	Tigris to Tharthar depression	11,000	64
Iraq	Tharthar to Euphrates	1,100	37
Pakistan	Marala to River Ravi	610	100
India	Himalayas to Rajasthan	524	178
India	Ghagra River to Ganga Plains	481	250
Australia	Snowy Mountains to River Murray and River Murrumbidgee	260	211
California	San Joaquin River to Lake Perris	116	700
Soviet Union	Siberia to Aral Sea (planned)	2,400	2,273

Interbasin Transfers

River-basin transfer gives rise to legal problems between countries, regions, or even districts. Several projects have already been constructed, and these are listed in Table 4. There are many other projects in various stages of planning or development in the Soviet Union, Peru, United States, and South Africa, Iran, and Bangladesh.

It is expected that basin transfer projects will become a more common feature of water resource exploitation in the next century.

Groundwater and Its Integration with Surface Supplies

Groundwater exploitation has always made a major contribution to irrigation, but its effective integration with surface water supplies has eluded most authorities. Fig. 1 gives an example of a ground and surface water balance that could be developed in the Indus basin of Pakistan. It is, however, only achievable if the surface water storage reservoirs (Tarbela and Mangla) are used in conjunction with the groundwater aquifers. In effect, this means adopting a system of seasonal groundwater pumping to maximize abstractions when surface waters are scarce and to maximize canal deliveries during the flood season. Although such a mode of operation may sound simple, it is very difficult to apply in practice, particularly on an old established irrigation system where cultivators are inclined to treat historical canal flows as a right regardless of newly developed groundwater sources.

Superimposed on the legal and administrative constraints are the problems of operating public tubewell fields. Recent experience has shown that management standards in the surface irrigation projects have declined to seriously low levels, and it is therefore not surprising that the more complex management of the conjunctive use of ground and surface waters should have an even lower degree of success.

Improving Irrigation Efficiency

The improvement of irrigation efficiency is the most vital requirement of our time. Not only is improved efficiency a prerequisite to further expansion of irrigated areas in many regions of water shortage, but it is also a necessary ingredient for any program of improved crop production.

A survey by Wageningen University and ICID has shown that in surface systems, application efficiencies vary from

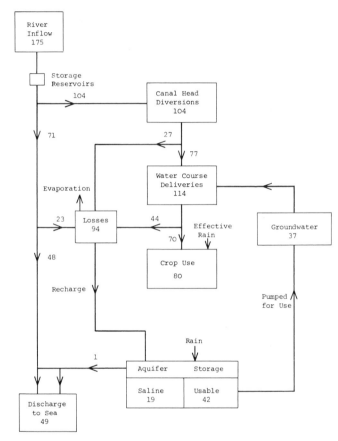

Fig. 1. Indicative ground- and surface water balance in Indus basin (10^9 m^3 per year).

35 to 75 percent and conveyance efficiencies from 30 to 90 percent. The overall efficiencies fall mostly between 10 and 50 percent. Many large surface systems in Asia have efficiencies about the middle of those ranges or about 30 percent compared with about 37 percent in some developed countries. By contrast the more advanced drip systems achieve 85 percent and sprinkler systems in developed countries have overall efficiencies of about 60 percent. However, such advanced systems are mainly applicable to industrialized countries or where crops of high-value are grown.

It is clear that the first step to raise irrigation efficiencies is to improve water management and farm management, and the former tends to be a prerequisite for the latter. For expediency we need to improve management without having the benefits of system improvement and modernization. These physical changes to existing systems involve long-term programs extending well into the next century.

For new systems there is a need to prepare designs and layouts that permit good standards of management taking into account such things as scheme size, canal command size, and rotational unit size as mentioned above. Furthermore, there is a need to link water management much closer to the work of the farmer or his progress toward more efficient application efficiencies will be seriously hindered.

Looking further ahead, new irrigation technology will play an important part in the achievement of better irrigation efficiency. It is to be noted that in countries with advanced technologies, the water use per hectare is about half that of the less advanced. Advanced technology includes the use of sprinklers, microsprinklers, and drip irrigation. Recently, more attention has been given to subsurface drip systems that inject water into the root zones with great efficiency. These modern technologies are rapidly penetrating the developed countries where water is usually charged by volume. They are unlikely to penetrate the developing world until a more realistic tariff structure is adopted for water.

In the absence of water tariff structures that provide farmers with incentives to increase irrigation efficiency, it is imperative that authorities for the irrigation project should dictate the water scheduling if not exercise complete physical control over it. The Sudan is a special example of centralized control among developing countries, and the irrigation efficiencies attained are well above average.

Outmoded Irrigation Systems

Earlier in this paper it was stated that technological progress had not kept pace with irrigation expansion, resulting in the existence of large areas of land that call for modernization. Added to this situation are the effects of a lack of maintenance and good management, with the result that many systems require both rehabilitation and modernization.

Several points of failure to meet modern requirements can be identified. First, most systems, and even those constructed in the last forty years, are based on cropping intensities that were too low to meet present needs. Second, there are inadequate control structures to permit good water management. Third, canals have excessive seepage losses. Fourth, there has been a failure to allow for the exploitation of groundwater resources as an integral part of the total water-supply system. Fifth, there was a failure to face up to the creation of waterlogging and salinity. Apart from those general observations, in the particular case of Sub-Saharan Africa some projects have been built that are too small to be viable from the points of view of management structure, supply of inputs, and marketing.

Modernization must be approached with great care. The risks of creating systems that are beyond the capability of the available management resources are quite real. Indeed,

there is a school of thought that believes the concepts of more vigorous water management to be fallacious and that they would lead to more sources of error, malfunction, and greater pressures in the operators than at present. Against that, it is doubtful whether the cost of modernization can be justified without associated improvements in water control.

Management

Of the 271 million ha of irrigated land in the world 75 percent are in developing countries. Many of these countries suffer shortages to varying degrees in human resources with trained management capability. Even where there is an adequate supply of technical resources, management resources may be lacking in many sectors.

The need for better management in irrigation and drainage is becoming widely recognized. The newly created International Irrigation Management Institute (IIMI) set up last year and based in Sri Lanka is about to embark on its initial programs of study. This institute is research oriented. It sets out to analyze management problems and formulate solutions.

There is an urgent need for training in management technology as a whole and irrigation management in particular. It is hoped that training centers can be set up both internationally and nationally to enhance the competence of managers at all levels. Some countries such as Morocco have already demonstrated the enormous returns that can be obtained from investment in better management.

Institutional and Sociological Problems

Many experts favor a structure for water management whereby the farmers play a leading role through the medium of water user associations. Such a structure is successful in most of the older irrigation systems of the developing world and in developed countries. However, it is often slow to take root in many other situations, particularly for those countries that are embarking on systematic irrigation for the first time. Often the failures that arise are caused by attempts to adopt unproven technology. The response of farmers is often difficult to predict, and there is a tendency to cling to traditions and practices even when these are based on rainfed crop husbandry. Responses must be tested and evaluated and irrigation methodologies proved at prototype scale before the farmers can assume active participation in water management.

Waterlogging, Salinity, and Salt Balance

In this century there has been a tendency to proceed with irrigation development and leave the drainage measures to be undertaken as and when the need arises. This has proved a sound economic approach save where the drainage works have been unduly delayed. Unfortunately, there are now large irrigated areas that suffer from the twin menaces of waterlogging and salinity. In some river basins—the Indus, Tigris, Euphrates, and Murray (Australia), for example—it is not simply a matter of drainage but also one of salt balance. The saline effluent has to be disposed of either outside the main river channel through outfall drains as in the Lower

Indus, within the basin in evaporation ponds as in Australia or Iraq, or by temporary retention for release at high flood.

Flood Control

In countries such as Bangladesh, Peru, Cambodia, and Vietnam flood control is essential to any real progress in achieving more intensive agriculture. Although the farmers have learned to exploit the floods for crop production, crop yields are very low and the hazards of the flood discourage the use of modern agricultural inputs. The investments required to achieve flood control on a substantive scale are enormous, involving as they do storage reservoirs, river channel improvement, embankments and polders, and either pumped drainage or costly outfall channels. Flood damage is unfortunately a feature of some of the more densely populated parts of the world, and so urgent measures are required. For example, Bangladesh, with a population of 100 million, has about 9 million ha of cultivated land of which more than half is subject to inundation to varying degrees.

THE WAY AHEAD

In 1979 the International Food Policy Research Institute (IFPRI) made a projection of potential food deficits in thirty-six selected developing market economy countries (DMEs). The deficits were calculated by comparing consumption with the production that would occur if the 1960–75 growth rate of about 2.4 percent per annum is extended to 1990. The study concluded that with allowance for income growth, a total deficit would arise in the thirty-six countries of about 60 million to 70 million tons if an accelerated investment program was not adopted for agriculture as a whole and for irrigation in particular. In general it was predicted that half this deficit could be made up from rainfed crops and half from irrigation.

The total gross irrigated area of the thirty-six countries was 75 million ha in 1975, having expanded by 19 million ha over the period from 1960 to 1975, or 2 percent per annum. A simple continuation of that growth rate would add 27 million ha by 1990, whereas to meet the IFPRI projections it would be necessary to add about 40 million ha in the same period in addition to a program of rehabilitation and modernization of existing systems. Two-thirds of the way through the time period, it can be said that it is unlikely that the rate of expansion in irrigation in those thirty-six countries will achieve even the lower of these two levels, and furthermore, poor progress has been made with rehabilitation. This means that in some countries nutritional standards will remain depressed and in others, food imports will need to be increased to maintain minimum standards.

The IFPRI projections identify the main food deficit areas as Bangladesh, India, Nigeria, Egypt, and the Sahel region of Africa. Of these areas, India is achieving a better growth rate than IFPRI projected, but others are doing worse, particularly in Africa. Part of the reason for the substantial growth in India is the high level of investment that has been maintained in irrigation and drainage. Cereal production has increased from about 35 million to 140 million tons a

Table 5. Food production index per capita in 1981 in Sub-Saharan Africa (1970 = 100).

Senegal	93
Mauritania	73
Mali	83
Upper Volta (Burkina Faso)	95
Niger	88
Chad	95
Ethiopia	82
Somalia	60

year in the period from 1950 to 1983, and more than 50 percent of this increase is attributable to irrigation.

If India is to sustain its present growth rate in agriculture, this will mean a continuation of the growth rate in irrigation of at least 1.5 million ha a year. In these conditions India should be self-sufficient in cereals at least up to the year 2000, by which time the gross irrigated area will have reached 90 million ha covering 80 percent of the total potentially irrigable land.

In Bangladesh the situation is less favorable than in India because very little progress has been made toward the provision of a sound agricultural infrastructure that is so necessary if full use is to be made of modern farm inputs. The weakness of the situation is reflected in the low food production index per capita, which fell 6 percent in the period 1970 to 1982, and in the growth rate in agricultural output, which fell from 2.7 to 2.3 percent between decades.

To turn to Sub-Saharan Africa, which is much in the news, the situation is now worse than predicted by IFPRI when they did their study seven years ago. In the eleven years from 1970 to 1981 the food production indexes have fallen in most of the countries in this region, as illustrated in Table 5.

Since 1982 there has been a further decrease in the production indexes that have been abnormally affected by drought. Cereal imports are rapidly approaching 3 million tons per annum, and deficits arising in the mid 1980s are comparable with those IFPRI predicted for 1990.

In the Sub-Saharan African countries listed in Table 5 there is a substantial potential for irrigation development, but it is unlikely that progress will be rapid enough to make a major contribution to total food production before the end of this century unless an accelerated program of investment is adopted. Even then, the social and institutional constraints will prove severe in regions that have no tradition in modern crop husbandry, let alone in irrigation.

None of the eight countries listed in Table 5 contains as much irrigable land as does the Sudan; nevertheless, the total irrigable area offers a large potential, being in aggregate between 2 million and 3 million ha depending on classification criteria. The cost of irrigation development will, however, be high because of the scattered pattern of the irrigable land, the seasonal nature of the river flows, and the need to provide infrastructure. It is interesting to reflect that systematic irrigation of even 1 million ha in these countries could provide a high degree of security against famine such as the delta projects did for southern India in the last century.

To look at the world as a whole, it is expected that irrigation expansion will continue at a rate of 4 million to 5 million ha a year or a little less up to the year 2000. About half the expansion will take place in India and China.

The expansion of irrigated areas is not sufficient in itself, and as stated earlier in this paper, of equal or greater importance is the need to increase productivity of the existing irrigated lands. In many developing countries crop yields from irrigated land are only about one-third of those obtained in developed countries. There must be greater emphasis on the rehabilitation and modernization of existing irrigation systems. The sociological, technical, and institutional problems are severe, but there are signs that a vigorous and objective approach to them is being adopted.

In drainage there will be a new focus on the old established irrigation areas of the Indian subcontinent, Egypt, and the Middle East. In rainfed areas one of the larger programs of land drainage will take place in the Soviet Union. In flood control, the most urgent case in the world is that of Bangladesh, but there are many others such as Peru, India, and China, where the control of inundation is a prerequisite to most other forms of agricultural advancement, including irrigation.

As stated earlier in this chapter, two important developments in the last quarter of a century have strengthened the case for additional investments in irrigation and drainage.

The first is that the new crop varieties respond well only in good conditions of soil moisture control through irrigation or drainage or both. The second is because the high cost of agricultural inputs favors high-yielding land, and for many regions of the world this means not only land with good soils but also with irrigation and drainage and flood control.

Finally, it must be emphasized that better management of irrigation systems is a prerequisite to any real progress in the enhancement of agricultural productivity. The first priority is to raise management standards on the existing systems as they now occur, without modernization, because any form of remodeling is a slow, long-term process. To improve management, policies must be improved and the bureaucratic barriers in many irrigation authorities must be broken. An important element in any program to improve management is to establish a number of national and international training institutes. The international training centers should be created on a regional and perhaps also on a linguistic basis and should serve to give managers greater exposure to methods used in various countries and to introduce them to appropriate innovations. Over the next decade there should be a special endeavor to focus on the issues of irrigation management on a worldwide scale. A drive to raise irrigation management standards is the obvious complement to the very effective campaigns that have been pursued in agricultural research.

7. NEW TECHNOLOGY RELATED TO WATER POLICY—PLANTS

William L. Brown, Pioneer Hi-Bred International, Inc., Johnston, Iowa

"In culture after culture, from Sumeria to New Mexico, massive irrigation of arid lands follows a familiar pattern. First, there is prosperity, and the culture expands. But rather quickly, the mineral salts in the irrigation water increase the salinity of the soil, and food production drops. Farmers try to wash the salts out with even more water, and while there is some success, ground water levels rise, surrounding vegetation changes, and the soil erodes away. Cities and pueblos are abandoned, and civilizations which once flourished by irrigation vanish."

That is a quotation from the *Christian Science Monitor*. It obviously is not a completely accurate history of the effects of irrigation on society, and it may be overly dramatic, yet it does reflect, I think, the fears of a growing number of thoughtful people over a perceived impending U.S. water crisis.

That crisis, if indeed it occurs, will result not only from salinization, from depletion of some of the largest underground reservoirs of freshwater—the huge Ogallala aquifer, for example—but also from serious contamination of both surface and groundwaters by toxic chemicals, mutagens, and carcinogens. The Colorado River, whose water is used to irrigate more than 600,000 ha of prime farmland, is slowly becoming more saline. In the course of its flow from its headwaters in Colorado to the Mexican border, the river's salt content increases from about 50 mg/L to more than 800 mg/L. And we should be reminded that this concentration is well above the maximum safe level for drinking water, as established by EPA.

Because of the extensive use of irrigation in the west, we hear much about water problems in that part of the country. But water problems are not limited to the west. A study by the U.S. Army Corps of Engineers indicates that the increased drawing of freshwater from the tributaries of the Chesapeake Bay is dangerously increasing salt levels in that huge body of water.

Groundwater contamination has been found in almost every state in which it has been studied. And groundwater is estimated to be the sole source of drinking water for more than half of all Americans.

An excellent example of definitive research on agriculture's impact on surface and groundwater quality is an investigation now being conducted by the Iowa Geological Survey in collaboration with Iowa State University. Early stages of this work in northeastern Iowa document the relationship between rates of nitrogen fertilization and levels of nitrate in groundwater. The preliminary data suggest that in relatively wet years as much as 50 percent of the chemical fertilizer-N applied may be lost into groundwater and surface water. In the Big Springs watershed in northeastern Iowa, there appears to be a nearly linear relationship between rates of groundwater nitrate and nitrogen fertilization. (See also Lieth, this volume.)

It is becoming increasingly clear that fertilizers and pesticides may leach through the soil profile, eventually reaching even deep groundwater aquifers. And although several decades of use may be required for an agricultural chemical to reach groundwater, once there, it could remain for decades.

It is estimated that about 83 percent of the water consumed is used in farming. The water problem, therefore, is largely an agricultural problem, and it was this recognition, no doubt, that led to this conference.

Many of the problems relating to the conservation and more efficient utilization of water in agriculture are hydrological and physical in nature and can be dealt with best by the engineers. They will be covered in other chapters in this volume. But there is also a genetic component—that dealing with the genetic manipulation of plants in ways which, if successful, could generate new genotypes with improved efficiency of water utilization, with the capacity to produce satisfactorily with reduced amounts of available water, or with the capacity to utilize saline water.

Suffice it to say that despite the fact that plants have been subjected to selection by man for centuries and have been exposed to scientific breeding technologies for more than half a century, very little breeding for drought tolerance per se has been attempted. This neglect has persisted despite the constant occurrence of drought stress in the arid parts of the country and the occurrence of drought stress in July or August of most years even in the U.S. Corn Belt. This has been clearly demonstrated by the Palmer Drought Index as reported by the National Climatic Center. Indeed, it has been suggested by Jensen and Cavaliera (1983) "that soil water deficits, especially when accompanied by excessively high temperatures, are probably the most common limiting factors in maize production."

This is not to suggest a complete lack of progress in improving the drought tolerance of crop plants. There has been progress, but with very few exceptions, it has occurred as a by-product of selection for higher productivity and for consistency of performance over an array of environments. For example, Russell (1974) reported results of a study in which the performance of a number of maize hybrids used in the Corn Belt in the 1930s were compared with more modern hybrids. Russell's data show that the relative performance advantages of the more modern hybrids was greater at drought stress locations than at more favorable test sites, indicating some indirect progress. However, in a similar experiment conducted by Duvick (1977), the modern hybrids demnonstrated their greatest superiority at the highest rather than the test sites having the lowest yield.

Using regression analyses to estimate yield stability, Jensen and Cavaliera (1983) compared the performance of 339 maize hybrids in tests located in most of the important maize-growing regions of the United States and Canada. The tests were conducted over a three-year period. To the extent that yield reductions at some locations in some years were due to drought, the differences in performance should, to some extent, indicate differential response to drought conditions. Although the hybrids used in this experiment were all commercial or experimentals of potential commercial value, considerable variability in yield stability (b values) was shown to exist among them, i.e., b values fluctuated both above and below 1.0. These results can be taken to mean that, even in highly select maize hybrids of the Corn Belt, considerable genetic variation exists with respect to those genes that code for response to stress conditions. In this experiment, there were more hybrids with b values significantly lower than 1.0 than with b values greater than 1.0. On this basis the authors concluded that selection in modern maize has indeed been for hybrids that are stable and stress resistant and not solely for high yield potential. Based on these results, Jensen and Cavaliera (1983) concluded that conventional breeding programs will continue to improve drought tolerance in maize. While this seems to be a reasonable conclusion, it tells us nothing about the relative merits of conventional breeding programs versus others specifically designed to address drought tolerance directly.

In recent years, there have been a number of studies that deal with the physiological response of plants to drought stress. Many of these studies have been reviewed in an excellent paper by Jordan, Dugas, and Shouse (1983). The thrust of most of these studies has been to identify individual physiological processes that influence drought tolerance and to evaluate the relative importance of each of a number of such processes. From the standpoint of genetics and breeding, this approach seems to make sense. Because of the multiplicity of processes involved in a plant's response to water stress, field experiments to study the end result of those processes—yield, harvest index, or whatever—are fraught with innumerable potential sources of error. Because of the difficulty of controlling all variables, genotype x environment interactions are frequent and highly significant, and error variances are usually discouragingly high under drought conditions. Because of its complexity, the inheritance of so-called "drought tolerance" is probably so complicated as to be difficult if not impossible to effectively manipulate genetically even when it can be identified. Yet to my knowledge, there is also little known about the inheritance of any of the individual physiological processes that contribute to drought stress response. But it is reasonable to assume that the genetics of these individual components will be much simpler than that of total drought response and, if so, will be much more amenable to genetic application.

A recent study on the physiological response of plants to water stress is that of Seropian and Planchon (1984).

They used three varieties of both bread wheat (*Triticum aestivum* L.) and durum wheat (*T. durum* L.) as experimental materials. The three cultivars for bread wheat were Baalback, Capitole, and Sakha. The durum varieties were Bidi 17, Haurani 24, and Jori. Baalback and Haurani 27 are considered highly drought resistant, Capitole and Sakha are susceptible to drought, and Bidi 17 and Jori are considered intermediate in their response to drought stress. Using three parameters—leaf water potential, photosynthesis, and stomatal behavior—Seropian and Planchon observed the highest leaf water potential in Haurani 27 and Bidi 17, a highly drought-resistant and an intermediate variety, respectively. The lowest leaf water potentials occurred in Sakha and Jori, representing drought-sensitive and intermediate varieties. Photosynthesis was altered least by water stress in the most drought-resistant varieties and was altered most in the drought-susceptible varieties. The varieties that kept their stomata opened at low leaf water potentials exhibited the highest photosynthetic tolerance to internal water stress. On the basis of these observations, Seropian and Planchon concluded that "for the cultivars investigated, the ability to keep their stomata opened in spite of internal water stress, is an agronomic form of drought tolerance."

The observed intervarietal variation in physiological response to water stress in these studies should be of particular interest to the breeder. It suggests that commercial cultivars are usable sources of genetic variability in physiological traits that influence the response of wheat plants to drought stress. This is a most fortunate circumstance since the use of such varieties as sources of drought-tolerant traits avoids or greatly reduces the many problems encountered when the only sources of desirable genes are wild relatives, land races, or primitive cultivars. Noncommercial varieties always embody many undesirable traits. Eliminating such traits through backcrossing requires much time and, depending on the effects of linkage, may be nearly impossible to achieve.

There are, of course, numerous other physiological components of drought resistance under investigation, many of which have been listed by Blum (1983). These include osmotic adjustment, plant recovery from dehydration, tolerance in enzyme activities, tolerance in translocation, stability of cellular membranes, and proline accumulation.

Blum (1983), however, played down the value of such traits when used as selection criteria in breeding for drought tolerance. He reasoned that the physiological methodology, while accurate, is too slow to be applicable to routine screening. He also felt that little information was available on the relationship between physiological traits affecting drought response in plants and economic yields of those plants when grown within stress and nonstress environments.

It is certainly unrealistic to assume the practical application of precise physiological methodology to large populations of plants. However, if drought tolerance and susceptibility can be broken down into their several more important components, and if through physiological studies the presence of these components can be identified in certain genotypes, then this provides the breeder with information and sources of building blocks with which to establish populations known to carry genes that code for high photosynthetic activity, desirable leaf water potential, stability of cellular membranes, etc. With this knowledge and with materials of known genetic constitution, populations can be developed that should exhibit marked differences in tolerance to drought. With the use of such experimental materials, we are in a position to begin to understand the basic mechanisms through which plants respond to water stress. Until this knowledge is available, applied genetics will continue to contribute in an empirical way only to the further improvement of drought tolerance in crop species.

In choosing materials with which to work in attacking the problems of drought tolerance, one should, in my opinion, range freely among the species of the plant kingdom and search for those organisms that respond in unique ways to drought stress. Many of the most drought-tolerant plants are not cultivated but have adapted in ways that permit their survival under extreme water deficiency. For example, photosynthesis in desert plants often occurs at much higher temperatures than in other species. Leaves of such plants often have thicker cuticles and fewer stomata per square centimeter than nondesert species.

Should it ever become possible to snip and paste genes at will, gene transfer may no longer be confined to members of the same species or closely related species. Some scientists have even suggested that molecular biology may ultimately make possible the movement of any gene from any organism into any other organism. Should that goal ever be realized, the entire plant kingdom could become the gene pool for any given species. I expect, however, that biological conservatism developed over millions of years of natural selection may place many unanticipated constraints on the achievements of such lofty goals. Yet the breeder must find attractive even the remote possibility of being able to transfer to the soybean, for example, a useful component of drought tolerance from a desert *Euphorbia*. Or the possibility that salt tolerance in the halophytic mangrove or wild tomato thriving on the salty shores of Isla Isabella of the Galápagos may in time provide the genes needed for maize to continue as a profitable crop in the irrigated valleys of California.

Yet no matter how intriguing in theory the use of exotic genes for stress tolerance may be, there are other less exotic and more compatible sources of potential stress tolerance that have been largely ignored even to this day. Permit me to give an example: Some thirty years ago in the course of a study of the evolution of American maize, I investigated the origin, evolution, and culture of some of the important crops that furnish the major sources of food for certain native Americans of the desert southwestern United States. In parts of what are now Arizona and New Mexico, a number of Indian tribes and their ancestors learned and practiced with a high degree of success the art of dryland agriculture. Outstanding among these tribes are the Hopi and Papago. The typical Hopi farm lies at the base of one of the many mesas from which seep limited amounts of moisture. Any rain that falls during the growing season is a bonus that cannot be counted on. A Hopi cornfield would hardly be recognized as such by the modern corn farmer, but the way in which it is planted and cared for is planned and purposeful and based on centuries of desert living.

The corn is planted in hills about 2 m apart. The hills are in rows, which also are equally widely spaced. Each hill contains not two or three plants but ten to a dozen plants. The Hopi have learned that the clumping of plants within a relatively small space apparently reduces the desiccation of the foliage, the anthers and silk thereby allowing normal fertilization to occur in that extremely arid environment. Moreover, the kernels of maize when planted are placed not 5 to 7.6 cm below the surface of the soil but as much as 25 cm, where there is usually adequate moisture to support germination and the growth of the seedling. Of course, normal maize so planted would never reach the soil surface because of genetic limitation on the maximum length of hypocotyl extension. Yet natural selection over centuries under these conditions has resulted in the evolution of genotypes whose hypocotyls are almost invariably of sufficient length to fully emerge from that depth.

It would be most interesting and perhaps instructive to subject such materials to the modern laboratory techniques of the plant physiologist and compare their responses with respect to stomatal activity, leaf water potential, stability of cellular membranes, etc., to those of modern cultivars.

Though I have described in some detail only the drought-tolerant Hopi maize, those same primitive but highly observant and intelligent desert farmers have learned to adapt to their use other food plants, including beans, sunflowers, and a number of fruits. These possibly useful genetic materials are still available. They should, I think, offer some attraction to physiologists investigating the biochemical and physiological basis of drought stress.

Plants have an enormous capacity to adapt to environmental change, including temperature. Bjorkman and Berry (1983, 37–38), for example, showed that under conditions of extreme temperature change, a plant's photosynthetic activity responds by increasing at high temperatures and declining at low temperatures. The increase at high temperatures has been shown to result from changes in the chloroplast membranes, which cause the membrane to be more stable at high temperatures. Who is to say that this trait, when better understood, cannot be transferred to cultivated plants? Or, more importantly, do we know that the trait does not now exist in some cultivated species?

High concentrations of salt ions in soil water seem to have similar osmotic properties and similar effects as those caused by reduced water availability. These similarities, it would seem, may provide additional opportunities to utilize modern cell culture techniques to study variability in response to salinity (and drought) in cellular populations of cultivated species. Results with tobacco suggest that these techniques may have important practical application.

Regulation of the opening and closing of stomates, perhaps by substances that control plant growth, and greatly influenced by water stress, varies in both wild and cultivated species. If the variation is genetic in nature, as it probably is, the trait is amenable to improvement through selection. Osmoregulation continues to be recognized as an important mechanism in a plant's response to salt and drought stress.

Yet our understanding of the biochemistry and genetics of this and other physiological processes involved in water stress must be enhanced before they can be effectively utilized by the breeder. And this requirement holds regardless of the breeding methodology involved, be it classical or some version of biotechnology.

I am inclined to think that the early and perhaps more important contributions of biotechnology to the solving of these problems may be in providing much of the new knowledge required rather than in transforming traits, once they have been identified. It is encouraging to note, for example, that in bacteria, use of the lactose (*lac*) and histidine (*his*) operons may serve as probes for studying intracellular changes in solutes when these organisms are subjected to salt or drought stress (Rains and Valentine, 1980). The extent to which model systems based on prokaryotes have application to higher plants is yet unclear. Nonetheless, Boyer and Meyer (1980) reported the results of an experiment utilizing soybean seedlings in which it was observed that in response to moisture stress, "soybean seedlings are capable of internal osmotic compensation for changes in water potential caused by the external water supply." Remarkably, the adjustment is thought not to depend on the presence of salts in the external medium and, according to the authors, is capable of occurring under natural conditions. These, it seems to me, are the kinds of data needed if we are ever to understand drought stress mechanisms and if those mechanisms are to be manipulated genetically. The chances of accumulating this knowledge will be greatly enhanced by closer integration of technologies from a number of biological disciplines than is now evident in many research institutions. Unfortunately, the multifaceted aspects of what has come to be known as biotechnology have too frequently been isolated in the organization of research laboratories. This, it seems, is particularly disadvantageous since the most promising areas of application of biotechnology to agricultural problems are extremely difficult to predict, and many costly mistakes will likely occur in the absence of close integration with related disciplines. Among the many important techniques of biotechnology is that of isolating a single DNA fragment or gene from a complex genome and then transferring it to a new organism. But these techniques can be applied only after the gene in question has been identified and characterized in some way. So, partly as a result of progress in biotechnology, there is perhaps even greater need today for continued support for the more traditional disciplines such as biochemistry, physiology, classical genetics, etc., and the integration of these with emerging new technologies.

Perhaps the first constraint—the first bottleneck—we may encounter in attempts to apply molecular genetics to plants may result not from a failure of molecular biologists to deal effectively with the complexities of higher organisms, but rather from a lack of knowledge of the basic genetics of those traits of crop plants which are of significant agronomic and economic importance, including drought tolerance.

Let me explain a bit further, again using maize as an example. I expect we know as much about the genetics of maize as any other plant. More than 250 genes have been identified in maize. The inheritance of each is understood, the chromosomal location of each is known, and there is a considerable body of knowledge relative to the linkage relationships of these 250 genes. Yet, despite this knowledge, very little is known, even today, about the inheritance of those traits that code for performance of the maize plant—those traits of agronomic and physiological importance with which breeders endeavor to improve maize cultivars. So, even if the tools were available for moving genetic material from one plant to another by nonconventional means, we would not know how many genes govern the expression of important agronomic traits, let alone knowing where such genes are located with respect to individual chromosomes. Until that knowledge is available, it becomes very difficult, if not impossible, it seems to me, to move genes about in higher plants, even if the techniques for doing so were known.

Planners of this conference suggested that projects or programs be identified in the various topics covered which justify further review, analysis, and possible action recommendation. One could name many, of course, but under technologies applicable to plants, I suggest that the following points be considered:

1. Research aimed at identifying, understanding, and evaluating the more important mechanisms involved in the plant's response to drought stress should receive greater emphasis. These approaches to gaining fundamental knowledge about the basic life processes associated with stress response should be interdisciplinary and fully integrated.

2. Known and newly discovered stress response mechanisms should receive timely genetic analysis in order to determine how such traits are inherited and how they may best be manipulated in breeding populations.

3. In the field of biotechnology, current research on the protection of plants from stress imposed by pathogens and arthropod pests should be expanded to include stress resulting from water deficiency and increased salinity.

4. In the search for additional sources of traits which may be used to enhance more efficient water utilization by plants, particular attention should be given to sources of germplasm known to have evolved during centuries of evolution under domestication in highly water-deficient environments.

REFERENCES

Bjorkman, O., and J. Berry. 1983. Washington, D.C.: Carnegie Institute Year Book 83.

Blum, A. 1983. Genetic and physiological relationships in plant breeding for drought resistance. *In* J. F. Stone and W. O. Willis (eds.), Plant production and management under drought conditions. Amsterdam: Elsevier Science Publishers.

Boyer, J. S., and R. F. Meyer. 1979. Osmoregulation in plants during drought. *In* D. W. Rains, R. C. Valentine, and A. Hollaender (eds.), Genetic engineering of osmoregulation. New York: Plenum Press.

Duvick, D. N. 1977. Genetic rates of gain in hybrid maize yields during the past forty years. *Maydica* 22:187–96.

Jensen, S. D., and A. J. Cavaliera. 1983. Drought tolerance in U.S. maize. *In* J. F. Stone and W. O. Willis (eds.), Plant production and management under drought conditions. Amsterdam: Elsevier Science Publishers.

Jordan, W. R., W. A. Dugas, Jr., and P. J. Shouse. 1983. Strategies for crop improvement in drought-prone regions. *In* J. F. Stone and W. O. Willis (eds.), Plant production and management under drought conditions. Amsterdam: Elsevier Science Publishers.

Rains, D. W., and R. C. Valentine. 1979. Biological strategies for osmoregulation. *In* D. W. Rains, R. C. Valentine, and A. Hollaender (eds.), Genetic engineering of osmoregulation. New York: Plenum Press.

Russell, W. A. 1974. Comparative performance of maize hybrids representing different eras of maize breeding. Proceedings Annual Corn and Sorghum Research Conference. Washington, D.C.: American Trade Seed Association.

Seropian, C., and C. Planchon. 1984. Physiological responses of six bread wheat and durum wheat genotypes to water stress. *Euphytica.* 33:757–67.

8. NEW TECHNOLOGY RELATED TO WATER POLICY—ENGINEERING

Marvin E. Jensen, Water Management/Salinity, Agricultural Research Service,
U.S. Department of Agriculture, Fort Collins, Colorado

ABSTRACT

Although water management technology is evolving at an accelerating pace, implementing these new technologies may require decades. Additional investments in physical and supporting infrastructure usually are required. National water policies that are constrained by traditional systems and practices may hinder the implementation of new technologies. Major advances in science and technology are being made, but basic crop production–water relationships still govern the fundamental processes.

This paper summarizes some relationships between water use and crop production. Most agricultural technologies have evolved over decades with periods of acceleration following major breakthroughs in related fields. Examples of technological evolution and implementation in agriculture illustrate that long times are required to develop and implement many technologies. Examples of irrigated land development in three regions of the United States with different characteristics and over different time periods show that physical features of land, the availability of water supplies, and available technology affect the rate of development. Policy implications related to the development of improved technology for water management for increased food production are listed.

INTRODUCTION

New technology for water management can significantly affect food production, but plant growth and water use are still governed by physical and biological principles. Implementation of water policies intended to improve efficiency of food production should be based on proven or evolving technology, not on potential scientific "breakthroughs." National water policies, tied to constraints of traditional systems and practices, may hinder the adaptation of new technology.

Users must be trained to successfully adapt and continuously use new technology. Finally, and equally important, incentives are essential to achieving effective implementation of new technology. Unfortunately, some policies do not create needed incentives. Some policies destroy the incentives that may have existed. Low prices paid to farmers for agricultural products are a disincentive.

In this chapter I summarize some relationships between water and crop production that govern food production, as well as review some basic terminology relating dependent and independent variables. I briefly describe the impacts that some recent advances have had in improving agricultural technologies and in increasing food production. I conclude with a list of policy concerns that need to be considered.

TERMINOLOGY—CONCEPTS AND MISCONCEPTIONS

Manageable Water Supplies for Agriculture

Total, long-term annual national water supplies are essentially fixed. Water supplies that can be managed for irrigated agriculture include surface flow that is related to the water requirements of crops, or flow that can be stored in surface or groundwater reservoirs and released or pumped as needed. As populations continue to increase, water supplies for agriculture will decrease as competitive domestic and industry demands increase. While groundwater must be used to create aquifer space to enhance annual recharge, groundwater use in excess of annual recharge, or mining, should be considered only to meet supplemental or emergency needs. Some groundwater supplies are vast, but they can be depleted beyond economic pumping levels for agriculture in just a few decades.

Assessment of national agricultural water supplies must include water that is available to rainfed agriculture. Water available for use in rainfed agriculture may be much greater than that used in irrigated agriculture. For example, in the United States, the annual consumption (evapotranspiration) of water by irrigated crops is about 115 km^3 ($115 \times 10^9 \text{ m}^3$) (Solley et al., 1982). Although irrigated agriculture is the major consumer of water withdrawn (over 80 percent of total U.S. withdrawals), water consumption by rainfed crops is about 12 times that amount (Jensen, 1984). Assessment of water supplies for food production also must consider new technologies for conserving water and increasing food production on both rainfed and irrigated agricultural lands.

Irrigated agriculture can stabilize national food production, and, in some countries, it may be the major source of food production. The role of irrigated agriculture depends on the relative production from irrigated lands versus that from rainfed lands. Drought frequency analyses, the magnitude of variations in rainfed crop production, and carryover food storage requirements should be part of national food production–water supply planning. National food security and foreign exchange also are important factors.

Irrigation Efficiency

The general public and many knowledgeable professionals misuse or misunderstand the concept of irrigation efficiency. This misuse typically leads to the conclusion that agriculture wastes water. Misuse also may adversely affect water/food policies and major decisions about irrigation projects.

Irrigation efficiency (E_i) is the ratio of the volume of irrigation water beneficially used by a crop as evapotranspiration (ET) in a specified area (V_{et}) to the volume of irrigation water delivered to this area (V_d).

$$E_i = V_{et}/V_d \qquad (1)$$

The term E_i by itself is not adequate to estimate or predict available water supplies because potentially usable return flows are not included. When considering water supplies or water balance, a change in irrigation efficiency, as it has been defined and used for more than a half century, does not result in a proportional increase in water supplies because return flow is not considered. Major improvements in irrigation efficiency in an upstream project may have little effect on the water supply within a river basin because of return flows.

Drainage Requirements

The most common problem encountered in irrigation projects is a rising water table and eventual waterlogging and salinization of the soils. Waterlogging and salinization of irrigated soils are not inevitable, however. Basic hydrologic principles must be recognized and projects designed and properly managed to avoid these problems. The drainage requirements and capacities, including both natural and artificial drainage, often are ignored in project development until the water table approaches crisis levels. Drainage requirements must be considered during the initial stages of project planning. There are many factors involved and natural drainage capacity may be difficult to quantify. Artificial drainage may not be needed immediately in new projects because several decades may be required for water tables to rise to critical levels. The excess irrigation water that eventually must be removed from the project by drainage (V_{dr}) to prevent waterlogging if there is no reuse within the project is linked to the overall project irrigation efficiency.

$$V_{dr} = (1 - E_i)V_d \qquad (2)$$

Eq. (2) clearly shows that if the drainage capacity is limited or if the rate the water level rises because of irrigation must be decreased, project irrigation efficiency must be increased. This may require improving the water distribution system to reduce seepage losses and to permit timely water deliveries and upgrading the irrigation systems on farms and the manner in which they are operated. When water is reused within a project, the absolute minimum volume of excess irrigation water that must be removed from the project is:

$$V_{dr} = L_r(V_d) \qquad (3)$$

where L_r is the minimum leaching requirement within the project that is necessary to control salinity. The L_r is based on each crop's salinity tolerance, the salinity of the irrigation water, and annual ET. The drainage system also must be able to control the level of the water table so that soil salinization does not occur during nonirrigated periods. During fallow periods, capillary flow of water and salts from the saturated zone to the surface of the soil leaves salt near the surface as water evaporates.

In some areas, excess precipitation also must be considered. The timing of precipitation excess relative to irrigation excess is an important factor.

Water Use Efficiency

The production of the marketable unit of a crop per unit of water consumed in ET is called "water use efficiency" (WUE) (also called water utilization efficiency). WUE indicates the effectiveness at which water is used in agricultural production. WUE assessment should be an integral part of both rainfed and irrigation project evaluations.

The most common WUE expression relates crop production to the water consumed in ET from planting to harvest. I have defined this term as net WUE.

$$WUE_{net} = \text{(yield in kg)/(ET in cubic meters)} \qquad (4)$$

For rainfed crops it is more common to relate crop production to water consumed from the harvest of one crop to the harvest of the next crop. I have defined this term as gross WUE (WUE_{gross}) because the total water consumed includes the amount evaporated during the fallow period between crops).

A term defined to evaluate the increase in irrigated crop production over rainfed production relative to the increase in ET resulting from irrigation is called irrigation water use efficiency (Bos, 1980). Example values of net WUE for a grain crop are presented later in this chapter along with some general yield-ET relationships.

CROP YIELD–WATER USE RELATIONSHIPS
Yield-ET Relationships

Extensive research has shown that when available soil water limits transpiration and the stress periods are distributed throughout the season, the yield (Y) of the marketable component of most crops decreases linearly with the decrease in water consumption (ET) within a climatic regime. The relationship between aboveground dry matter (DM) production, and transpiration (T) is linear for all crops when soil water limits T and ET. Howell and Musick (1984) summarized DM-T and DM-ET relationships for several major crops clearly illustrating the linear relationships. DM must be multiplied by a harvest index (HI) to obtain the marketable yield ($Y = HI \times DM$). The HI is the ratio of marketable yield to dry matter production.

A general empirical relationship of marketable yield to ET where maximum ET is limited by climate can be expressed as:

$$Y = a\,ET - b \qquad (5)$$

where a and b are constants. The relationship of WUE to ET based on Eq. (5) is:

$$WUE = Y/ET = (a\,ET - b)/ET \qquad (6)$$
$$= a - b/ET$$

With Y in tons per hectare (t/ha) and ET in millimeters (mm), WUE in kg/m^3 is:

$$WUE_{net} = 1000\,a - 100\,b/ET \qquad (7)$$

Data from Stewart et al. (1983) were selected to illustrate the typical characteristics and magnitudes of these relationships. For grain sorghum grown on the high plains of Texas they found:

$$Y = 0.0154\,ET - 2.20,\ \text{for } ET > 225\ mm \qquad (8)$$

Using this relationship, WUE_{net} becomes:

$$WUE_{net} = 1.54 - 220/ET \qquad (9)$$

There are several important characteristics of Eqs. (5) through (9):

1. When soil water limits ET, yield decreases as ET decreases.

2. When soil water limits ET, the yield per unit of water increases as ET and Y increase. The highest WUE occurs at the highest yield. A threshold amount of ET is required before the first increment of marketable yield is produced.

3. Eqs. (5) through (9) do not include economic aspects. From an economic viewpoint, if water is not limiting, it should be applied up to the point where the price of the last unit of water applied is just equal to the revenue resulting from its application (Vaux and Pruitt, 1983).

Coefficients a and b in Eqs. (5) through (9) can be developed for most major crops and current cultivars using existing research data. Eqs. (5) and (6) are valuable in evaluating the productivity of projects and the probable increase in yield to be expected from allocating water obtained through conservation. They also can be used to evaluate the net economic return to be expected from increasing usable water supplies. A summary of WUE values to be expected and the relative yield response for various crops is presented in a Food and Agriculture Organization (FAO) publication (Doorenbos and Kassam, 1979).

As new cultivars with higher yields and new cultural practices are developed, the a and b coefficients may need to be updated. During the past few decades, the higher yields of new cultivars have resulted primarily from increases in the HI. New cultivars do not use less water if they have similar growing periods. For example, Musick et al. (1984) summarized ET and WUE values for winter wheat reported by investigators over the past three decades at Bushland, Texas (Table 1).

The total ET and DM produced have not changed significantly over three decades, but WUE values have doubled because of increased HI involving plant density, nutrition, water, and partitioning of photosynthates. Further increases in HI of this magnitude are not expected because HI may be near the optimum, i.e., the proportion of straw cannot be

Table 1. ET and WUE values for winter wheat reported at Bushland, Texas.

Researchers	Years	(ET) (mm)	(WUE) (kg/m³)
Jensen and Sletten	1956–59	645	0.44
Schneider et al.	1966–67	735	0.53
Musick et al.	1979–82	698	0.89

reduced much more and still provide the strength needed to support the grain and the length needed to permit combine harvesting. Current cultural practices also may be optimal. Studies of old and new cultivars of other crops show similar results (Donald and Hamblin, 1976; Wells and Meredith, 1984).

Yield–Applied Water Relationships

There is no similar, linear relationship between the amount of irrigation water applied and the yield increase except for the first few increments of applied water. Stewart et al. (1983) reported the following increase in ET in millimeters above rainfed values for grain sorghum versus irrigation water applied (W_i) with a furrow system.

$$\Delta ET = 139(\ln W_i) - 545 \qquad (10)$$

Eq. (10) indicates that ET increased linearly for the first 100 to 200 mm of irrigation water applied. As more water was applied, a larger proportion either became runoff or deep percolation. Stewart et al. (1977) presented a detailed analysis of this relationship for maize, and Vaux and Pruitt (1983) presented a detailed analysis of several crop-water production functions.

Yield–Salinity Relationships

Crop yields tend to decrease linearly as soil salinity increases above threshold values in the following manner:

$$Y = 100 - b'(EC_e - a') \qquad (11)$$

where a' is the threshold salinity value, b' is the yield decrease per unit of salinity increase, and EC_e is the electrical conductivity of a saturated soil paste extract expressed in decisiemen per meter ($dS \cdot m^{-1}$) corrected to a temperature of 25°C. A summary of a' and b' values can be found in several publications (Maas and Hoffman, 1977, and Hoffman et al., 1983).

Yield–Excess Water Relationships

The relationships between crop yield and excess water are more complex than effects of limited water because more variables are involved. For example, in cool, humid climates, poorly drained soils do not warm up as fast in the spring as well-drained soils, and poor trafficability shortens the potential growing season. Heavy rains during the growing season can depress yields as a result of poor soil aeration. Late fall rains can delay or prevent harvest.

In irrigated areas the benefits of drainage are primarily related to salinity. Benefits of deep drainage of fine-textured irrigated soils on crop yields have been documented (Johnston et al., 1982).

TECHNOLOGY—AN EVOLUTIONARY PROCESS

Today, many articles on scientific breakthroughs and revolutionary progress in agriculture are carried in the news media. Breakthroughs do occur, and many have had major impacts on agricultural technology during the past few decades. However, we cannot assume that future problems in food production will be solved by hoped-for breakthroughs. We must consider the current state and rate at which agricultural technology is evolving. Scientific breakthroughs, or technological breakthroughs in related fields can hasten the evolutionary process. We need to continuously assess breakthroughs in other fields for possible adaptation to agricultural technology.

Improved technology is primarily the result of evolutionary steps rather than breakthroughs. Decades may be required to develop sophisticated technology. Breakthroughs can greatly advance technology or lower costs. For example, development of the transistor had a major impact on the development of computer technology (Gomory, 1983).

Everyone is familiar with the Green Revolution in agriculture, but most major improvements in agricultural technology have evolved slowly during the past century. The trend in future technology development is not expected to change dramatically regardless of the many hopes that are expressed. Also, some new technologies are very easy to implement, while others require major capital investments and supporting software infrastructure. For example, to change cultivars, only the seed source is changed along with some adjustments in cultural practices. Even this may require a few years for adoption. In contrast, decades may be required to develop or to modernize an irrigation project.

Large changes in production systems are not apt to occur quickly where water is the primary limiting variable because in many developing countries the physical infrastructure is not in place to implement the new technology on a large scale. Developing the necessary infrastructure and the necessary supporting software will require careful planning, design, operation, maintenance, and management—and time.

Examples of Technological Evolution in Agriculture

I will mention a few examples of technological evolution in agriculture to illustrate the effects of advances on the evolutionary process that eventually results in improved technology for water and food production.

New crop cultivars. Donald and Hamblin (1976) reviewed the biological yield (dry matter produced aboveground, DM), the harvest index (HI), and grain yield for cereals of cultivars developed in this century. Many factors are involved in yield increases (plant density, ears, stems, leaves, nutrition, and water), but there has not been a significant change in DM. Most of the increases in grain yields have resulted from increases in the HI.

Wells and Meredith (1984) evaluated twelve obsolete and modern cotton cultivars. They found that net assimilation rates were not higher in new cultivars. The new cultivars produced more lint because more DM was partitioned to the reproductive organs. There also was an increase in the number of reproductive organs.

Rainfed agriculture. Rainfed, semiarid agriculture technology has slowly evolved over the past century, and in the United States, it has become very effective. For example, furrow damming, which was initiated in the 1930s in Texas, rapidly expanded in the 1970s because improved farm equipment was available and herbicides could replace cultivation for weed control. Research results clearly demonstrated that crop yields benefited from furrow damming to prevent runoff from intense summer rains. Development of mulch tillage started in the 1940s. Today, no-till systems can double the amount of water stored during the fallow period (Unger, 1978). But no-till practices still have not been implemented on a large scale by U.S. farmers in the semiarid Great Plains. Gerard et al. (1984) and Jones and Hauser (1975) summarized experimental results that clearly show the benefits of using various conservation practices. Other rainfed practices are described in a monograph edited by Taylor et al. (1983).

Drainage. The development of corrugated plastic tubing in the 1960s greatly changed subsurface drainage technology. About 90 percent of the drain tubing being installed today is plastic instead of clay tile. The adaptation of laser control to drain installation in the 1960s also advanced this technology. Advances in drainage technology have greatly reduced the cost of drainage, but design techniques and criteria for subsurface drainage of irrigated land have not changed. Today, new techniques are being initiated in humid regions. These techniques include controlling drainage outflow and using the same system for subirrigation.

Sprinkler irrigation. A farmer invented the center-pivot sprinkler system and obtained a patent in 1952 (Splinter, 1976), and industry then developed this technology into a commercial system. The development of electronics in the 1960s and microprocessors in the 1970s advanced this irrigation method to one of the most efficient and reliable irrigation methods available today. Further improvements using the concepts of low-pressure drop tubes and microbasins developed by Lyle and Bordovsky (1983) are under way. For example, with these improvements they reported irrigation efficiencies of greater than 95 percent with a linear-move system. Heermann et al. (1984) adapted computer control and optimization technology to center-pivot systems. Similar advances have been made in water distribution, measurement, and technology for system control, but it has taken years to perfect such technology. In developing countries, most irrigation projects still perform well below their potentials (Plusquellec, 1985). Improvements can be made without highly sophisticated technology. For example, Plusquellec emphasizes that not all automation of water control needs to be computerized.

Surface irrigation. Surface irrigation has been used for centuries. Major technological advances in other fields have been used to improve technology for surface irrigation. For example, the adaptation of laser controls to land leveling equipment in the mid 1970s had a major impact on technology for leveling basins. With laser-controlled equipment, 4- to 8-ha basins can be leveled so that 85 percent of the soil surface is within 15 mm of the mean elevation. Irrigation efficiencies of 70 to 100 percent are now being achieved with level basins (Dedrick et al., 1982).

Surge flow, or cycling the flow to irrigation furrows, is a technique developed in the late 1970s to increase the advance of water in furrows with a given amount of water. It has made it possible to reduce runoff and improve irrigation uniformity on many soils. The commercial development of automatic equipment using low-cost valves and electronic controllers has played a major role in the development of this technology (Stringham and Keller, 1979). Another new method of controlling water delivery to furrows is a method called "cablegation" (Kemper et al., 1981). It has enabled automatic and more uniform distribution of flow to individual furrows.

Trickle (drip) irrigation. Trickle irrigation technology, often called drip irrigation or microirrigation, has advanced greatly during the past two decades (Bucks et al., 1982). These systems, when properly designed, installed, and operated, can provide excellent control of irrigation water. Plugging of emitters has been a major problem, but filtration and chemical treatment of water minimize these problems. ET for most close-growing crops is essentially the same with these systems as with other systems. However, decreases in seasonal ET of 10 to 15 percent can be achieved with buried, widely spaced trickle lines because of reduced evaporation. Trickle irrigation is used on only about 3 percent of the irrigated lands in the arid southwestern United States and about 5 percent in the humid southeastern states, where soils are very sandy.

Artificial intelligence and expert systems. Artificial intelligence (AI) is the second computer revolution. AI computers can be used to develop expert systems for assisting in the planning, design, and operation of irrigation systems. An expert system is a problem-solving computer program that uses judgmental and formal reasoning in solving problems. Building an expert system can require several years and cost several hundred thousand dollars. Once developed, expert systems can be adapted to mini- and microcomputers. This is an emerging technology that can be used to improve irrigation systems and water management.

Irrigated agriculture infrastructure. How rapidly can irrigation be developed to a fully productive system? Table 2 summarizes data on irrigation development from three regions in the United States. Each region has distinctly different features. The period selected in each region represents the most rapid period of development based on the U.S. Census of Agriculture data (USDC, 1981, 1984). Different time periods were used to illustrate that advances in technology played a role. Most important, the physical infrastructure and supporting systems did not develop rapidly even with adequate available technical and financial resources. A1 and A2 in the following data are the land areas irrigated at the start and end of the period in thousands of hectares.

The average annual rate of expansion of irrigated land in the Pacific Northwest (PNW) from 1944 to 1982 was only 1.67 percent per year compounded annually. The PNW is characterized by a steady increase in irrigated land since 1944. Most of the water is pumped from rivers with highlifts, and costs for electrical energy, which was readily available until recently, have been low. Sprinkler irrigation was used extensively. In the southern plains (SP), irrigation with groundwater began expanding rapidly during the drought years of the 1950s. Furrow irrigation could be used without land leveling because of ideal topography, and the costs for energy, primarily natural gas, were very low. Development of irrigation in this region increased at an annual rate of 4.36 percent per year. In the central plains (CP), groundwater was the primary water source, and the advanced center-pivot sprinkler system was the main irrigation method used. This system made it possible to irrigate land that was not otherwise suited for irrigation and to do it as soon as a source of water was available. This combination of readily available water and a modern, efficient system of applying it resulted in an annual increase of 5.77 percent per year. These data show that regardless of scientific or technical breakthroughs that occurred during the past four decades, and under favorable cost-price conditions and tax laws, the annual rate of expansion of irrigated lands ranged from 2 to 6 percent per year. Expansion of irrigation in developing countries is not expected to occur at faster rates.

POLICY IMPLICATIONS
Food Production–Water Assessments

National food production related to water and water policy must be based on long-term projections of food production per capita. Two variables are involved in per capita projections: production and population. This chapter considers only the first variable—production.

Food aid is only a temporary, but meaningful solution to hunger and famine. Food production, when limited by water, can be increased by applying current technology in most developed and developing countries. If water is the limiting variable, the current production levels and water use efficiencies for rainfed and irrigated agriculture must be evaluated. What are the relative contributions to food production from each area, their expected variations, and the food storage–transportation requirements needed to level out the annual food supply? An assessment of this type is needed to determine where the greatest potentials and opportunities lie in developing food/water priorities and policies. It also is needed to assess the relative cost and benefits

Table 2. Data on irrigation development.

Region	Period	Years	A1	A2	A2/A1	Annual Rate (%)
Pacific Northwest	1944–82	38	1,487	2,791	1.887	1.67
Southern plains	1949–69	20	1,278	2,227	2.347	4.36
Central plains	1964–82	18	1,284	3,527	2.747	5.77

of investing in research to improve rainfed or irrigated agricultural technology.

Issues and Policies

1. Water is a natural resource and generally renewable. The efficiency at which water is used is linked to its cost to the user or the value placed on water. Water, as a primary resource needed for food production, should not be provided at little or no cost to agricultural users. Free or low-cost water leads to waste, as well as additional or indirect costs like those resulting from waterlogging and salinity. The prices paid for farm products must be adequate to offset these costs.

2. Increasing food production with existing water supplies requires incentives for all involved individuals. The impacts of positive incentives to increase food production have been demonstrated. For example, major agricultural policy changes introduced in China in 1978 greatly increased wheat and rice production.

3. The design, construction, and management of the physical infrastructure is a critical factor in the productivity of irrigation projects. For example, salinity control involving the disposal of saline effluent to sinks or the ocean is essential to the long-term productivity of irrigated agriculture. The volume of saline wastewater can be reduced and economic returns can be gained by reusing moderately saline drain water on salt-tolerant crops, or by using it during noncritical periods of crop growth followed by using good-quality water. However, the salt load cannot be allowed to accumulate in the soil if productivity is to be maintained. Projects constructed without ensured long-term drainage and outlets or sinks for saline effluent are subject to failure.

4. Advanced biotechnologies cannot be substituted for improved technology for water management and associated physical infrastructure. They can supplement improved water management to achieve increased food production.

5. Adaptation of new technology for water management is largely an engineering effort. For a country with limited resources, proven or established technology should be given higher priority than untried technology because the evolution of new technology is expensive. Adaptation and effective use of improved, proven technology generally will require increased training and user skills.

6. Delivering limited water supplies at predetermined and hydraulically efficient rates and schedules may not meet water requirements for crops. To assume that farmers will automatically optimize the use of limited water supplies delivered at arbitrary schedules ignores the real problems limiting food production in many irrigated areas. Even well-trained engineers and scientists are not able to optimize water use with the constraints under which many farmers must now operate. Farmers must be accepted as partners in decision making that affects the productivity of projects.

7. The long delay in developing an irrigation project and the long life expectancy needed to return the capital costs of a project require project flexibility. We do not know the future requirements of a system even after one decade. They certainly will be much different in the next three to five decades from those that exist today.

8. Investments in many irrigation projects are not producing expected returns today. This is due to many factors. Although drainage requirements must be established early, the installation of the drains may be delayed. Policies that reduce the risk of low productivity or failure are needed.

9. Some new technologies for water management may be too energy intensive for use in developing countries. Current and future energy resources must be evaluated in planning and designing future irrigation projects.

REFERENCES

Bos, M. G. 1980. Irrigation efficiencies at crop production level. *International Commission on Irrigation and Drainage Bulletin* 29(2):18–25, 60.

Bucks, D. A., F. S. Nakayama, and A. W. Warrick. 1982. Principles, practices, and potentialities of trickle (drip) irrigation. Pp. 219–98. *In* D. Hillel (ed.) Advances in irrigation, vol. 1. New York: Academic Press.

Dedrick, A. R. 1982. Level-basin irrigation. Pp. 105–45. *In* D. Hillel (ed.) Advances in irrigation, vol. 1. New York: Academic Press.

Donald, C. M., and J. Hamblin. 1976. The biological yield and harvest index of cereals as agronomic and plant breeding criteria. Pp. 361–405. *In* N. C. Brady (ed.) Advances in agronomy. vol. 28. New York: Academic Press.

Doorenbos, J., and A. H. Kassam. 1979. Yield response to water. FAO Irrigation and Drainage paper no. 33. Food and Agriculture Organization.

Gerard C. J., P. D. Sexton, and D. M. Conover. 1984. Effect of furrow diking, subsoiling, and slope position on crop yields. *Agronomy* 76:945–50.

Gomory, R. E. 1983. Technology development. *Science* 220:576–80.

Heermann, D. F., G. W. Buchleiter, and H. R. Duke. 1984. Integrated water-energy management system for center pivot irrigation: implementation. *In* Transactions of the American Society of Agricultural Engineers. 27:1424–1532.

Hoffman, G. J., R. S. Ayers, E. J. Doering, and B. L. McNeal. 1983. Salinity in irrigated agriculture. Pp. 145–85. *In* M. E. Jensen (ed.) Design and operation of farm irrigation systems, Revised Printing.

Howell, T. A., and J. T. Musick. 1984. Relation of dry matter production of field crops to water consumption. *In* Proceedings of the crop water requirements conference. Paris: International Commission on Irrigation and Drainage (In press).

Jensen, M. E. 1984. Water resource technology and management. Pp. 142–66. *In* B. C. English, J. A. Maetzold, B. R. Holding, and E. O. Heady (eds.) Future agricultural technology and resource conservation. Ames: Iowa State University Press.

Johnston, W. R., B. C. Steinert, and C. M. Stroh. 1982. Benefits from drainage of heavy irrigated soils. Pp. 171–77. *In* Proceedings of the advances in drainage conference. Chicago: American Society of Agricultural Engineers.

Jones, O. R., and V. L. Hauser. 1975. Runoff utilization for grain sorghum production. Pp. 277–83. *In* Proceedings of the water harvesting symposium. Phoenix: USDA-ARS-W-22.

Kemper, W. D., W. H. Heinemann, D. C. Kincaid, and R. V. Worstell. 1981. Cablegation: I. Cable controlled plugs in perforated supply pipes for automatic furrow irrigation. *In* Transactions of the American Society of Agricultural Engineers. 27:1526–32.

Lyle, W., and J. P. Bordovsky. 1983. LEPA irrigation system evaluation. *In* Transactions of the American Society of Agricultural Engineers. 26:776–81.

Maas, E. V., and G. J. Hoffman. 1977. Crop tolerance-current assessment. *In* Proceedings of the American Society of Civil Engineers, *Journal of the Irrigation and Drainage Division.* 103(1R2):115–34.

Musick, J. T., D. A. Dusek, and A. C. Mathers. 1984. Irrigation and water management of winter wheat. American Society of Agricultural Engineers paper no. 84-2094.

Plusquellec, H. 1985. The silent minority. *World Bank* 4(1): 13–15.

Solley, W. B., E. B. Chase, and W. B. Mann IV. 1982. Estimated use of water in the United States in 1980. Geological Circular 1001.

Splinter, W. E. 1976. Center-pivot irrigation. *Scientific American.* 234:90–99.

Stewart, B. A., J. T. Musick, and D. A. Dusek. 1983. Yield and water use efficiency of grain sorghum in limited irrigation-dryland farming. *Agronomy* 75:629–34.

Stewart, J. I., R. E. Danielson, W. T. Franklin, R. M. Hagan, R. J. Hanks, E. B. Jackson, W. O. Pruitt, and J. P. Riley. 1971. Optimizing crop production through control of water and salinity levels in the soil. Utah Water Research Laboratory PRWG151-1.

Stringham, G. E., and J. Keller. 1979. Surge flow for automatic irrigation. Pp. 132–42. *In* Proceedings of the 1979 Irrigation and Drainage Specialty Conference, Albuquerque, N. Mex. American Society of Civil Engineers, Irrigation and Drainage Division.

Taylor, H. M., W. R. Jordon, and T. R. Sinclair (eds.). 1983. Limitations to efficient water use in crop production. Madison, Wis.: American Society of Agronomy.

Unger, P. 1978. Straw-mulch rate effect on soil water storage and sorghum yield. *Soil Science Society of America Journal.* 42:486–91.

U.S. Department of Commerce. 1981. 1978 Census of agriculture. vol. 1. Summary and state data. Washington, D.C.: Government Printing Office.

U.S. Department of Commerce. 1984. 1982 Census of agriculture. vol. 1. Summary and state data. Washington, D.C. Government Printing Office.

Vaux, H. J., Jr., and W. O. Pruitt. 1983. Crop-water production functions. Pp. 61–97. *In* D. Hillel (ed.) Advances in agronomy, vol. 2. New York: Academic Press.

Wells, R., and W. R. Meredith, Jr. 1984. Comparative growth of obsolete and modern cotton cultivars: I. Vegetative dry matter partitioning; II. Reproductive dry matter partitioning; and III. Relationship of yield to observed growth characteristics. *Crop Science* 24:858–72.

9. WATER, FOOD, AND THE CHALLENGE OF DEVELOPMENT IN LATIN AMERICA

Michael E. Curtin, Inter-American Development Bank, Washington, D.C.

I am very happy to have this opportunity to convey to you President Ortiz Mena's best wishes for a fruitful meeting. Being very deeply interested in water resource issues, he had hoped to be able to attend this conference. Unfortunately, the pressure of other commitments did not permit him to do so. He asked me, however, to outline to you some of our recent experiences and to share with you some of our concerns about this vital resource.

Most of you have devoted many years to the study or the practice of managing water resources, the key factor in any attempt to achieve food security. Your expertise and the themes being discussed here are of special importance to the countries of Latin America and the Caribbean whose development is the preoccupation of our bank. We congratulate Texas A&M University for its foresight in arranging this timely conference, and we welcome the chance to exchange insights and conclusions derived from dealing with problems of water management in diverse parts of the world. I am confident that all of us will benefit from this experience and that our experts, present among you, will return from Texas imbued with new enthusiasm and fresh ideas that we will try to apply in our operations.

Twenty-five Years of Development, Financing, and Progress

In prefacing my remarks, I would like to say a few words about the Inter-American Development Bank, which is celebrating its twenty-fifth anniversary this year.

The creation of the bank brought a new dimension to international cooperation: the participation of the beneficiary countries in decisions on the use of external financing. The direct participation of Latin American countries in the conduct of the bank's affairs, not only in policy formulation but also in the day-to-day technical and operational tasks, made possible the flowering of a viable regional development institution, one molded by cultural values peculiar to our peoples. This institution was born with the participation of the United States and nineteen Latin American countries. Its constituency grew to a family of nations that now embraces eighteen industrialized countries and twenty-five member countries of Latin America and the Caribbean.

During the first twenty-five years, the bank's actions took place within the framework of a truly extraordinary age for Latin America and the world, one characterized by high rates of economic progress, rapid advance of technology, and profound transformations in social and political realms, both national and international.

After 1974, however, the direction of these trends began to change, with major setbacks suggesting that the industrial economies may be in the process of transition from a phase of dynamic expansion to one of slow, long-term growth. The real growth rate of the gross domestic product of the industrialized economies, taken as a whole, declined from an average of 4.9 percent per annum between 1960 and 1973, to 2.8 percent during the 1973 to 1979 period, and to 1.9 percent in the last five years. This last period has been marked by a spreading pattern of high unemployment, protectionism, and monetary change. A decline in the rate of growth of world trade and a state of uncommon rigidity in certain other economic variables compounded these difficulties.

Latin America's gross domestic product grew vigorously until 1973, picking up speed as time went along and climbing from an average of 4.8 percent per annum in the 1950s to nearly 6 percent in the 1960s and a truly exceptional 7.4 percent between 1970 and 1973. In the second half of the 1970s, despite the unstable condition of the world economy, output continued to grow at a relatively satisfactory rate of 5.1 percent per annum. The following years, however, from 1981 to 1984, ushered in the most acute, prolonged, and widespread economic crisis that the Latin American countries have experienced since the 1930s. The region's total product suffered successive declines in 1981, 1982, and 1983. By 1984, its per capita product slumped to levels first attained seven years earlier.

Since 1982, most of the Latin American countries have exerted extraordinary efforts to realign their economic and financial situations. The focus of their adjustment measures has been to safeguard their capacity to pay the interest on external debt by expanding exports and curbing imports. Private international banks have cooperated in this adjustment effort by postponing the payment of overdue financial commitments and through a marginal supply of new lending. The International Monetary Fund, in addition to its conventional functions, has played the role of an intermediary between debtors and creditors. The cost of the adjustment process has been high, particularly in terms of the stagnation of economic growth and its accompanying effects, including a sharp decline in per capita income levels and a substantial rise in unemployment. Adjustment measures have been fraught with difficulties for all of our countries, both the relatively less developed ones as well as—and perhaps more intensely—those which had achieved higher levels of economic development and social well-being. After more than three years of adjustment, therefore, our countries are searching for a new approach that could give greater weight to the goal of revitalizing long-term economic growth, together with careful discipline in the monetary and fiscal areas, and compliance with external financial commitments.

It is within the context of this desire for a new approach that we must view the future contribution of agriculture.

During its first twenty-five years, the Inter-American Development Bank has actively promoted investment in Latin America's development. Through its lending operations, which totaled nearly $28 billion by December, 1984, the bank has made possible new investments amounting to approximately $100 billion, in other words, more than four times the value of its own lending. The bank has strived to develop agriculture in Latin America through a wide range of projects, ranging from increased direct investment and global agricultural credits to more complex rural development and research and extension programs. Agriculture receives about a quarter of our total lending and a major element of this, about 30 percent, has been for irrigation and drainage projects, which have brought improved agricultural techniques to a large area of highly productive land. Just as important, the bank's technical cooperation has fostered institutional development, the training of middle-level and senior technicians, and the strengthening of the region's capacity to analyze and carry out investment projects.

Besides industrializing rapidly, the Latin American countries have exerted tremendous efforts to cope with the growing demand for social services. Between 1960 and 1980, water-supply services were extended to 75 percent of the urban population, with the number of beneficiaries increasing from 40 million to 168 million. With the help of improved sanitary conditions and extended health-care programs financed by our bank, the average life expectancy in the region rose by six years. The bank also devoted a major effort to education. While the total population of Latin America increased by 70 percent between 1960 and 1980, enrollment in the primary schools has doubled, in secondary education nearly quadrupled, and in institutes of higher education, increased eightfold.

RECENT TRENDS IN LATIN AMERICAN FOOD AND AGRICULTURE

Within this framework, the performance of agriculture has been a disappointing element. During the decade of the seventies, value added by agriculture increased at an average rate of 3.6 percent in real terms, well below the 6.0 percent rate at which gross domestic product expanded. Thus, the sector continued the long-term decline in its share in value added, dropping from an average of 15 percent in the decade of the sixties to 11 percent in the period from 1976 to 1980. The sector did, however, meet the challenge of population growth by providing an annual per capita increase in output of 1.2 percent.

Accompanying the growth of output were changes in resource use, especially in land and labor, and their productivity. In the 1960s and 1970s, agricultural output grew by about 40 percent in each decade. During that twenty-year period, employment in agriculture rose by less than 10 percent as the cities absorbed most of the increase in the rural population. Since cultivated land areas expanded by 22 percent in the sixties, and only 11 percent in the seventies, farm-yield increases were achieved largely through the use of improved production techniques.

Disturbing trends were also in evidence in the area of international trade in agricultural products. Between the mid-seventies and the present, worldwide agricultural exports outpaced the growth of production, with production increasing 12 percent and exports 35 percent. But in Latin America, a 20-percent increase in output over the same period was accompanied by a more modest, 24-percent increase in the export volume and a near doubling of imports. Thus, in spite of Latin America's superior performance in the production area, our region has lagged behind the world in export expansion and greatly increased its dependence on imports, especially imports of food and food-related products.

The recent international recession had a greater impact on Latin America in terms of prices than in physical output, as our agricultural export and domestic prices failed to keep pace with those for manufactured goods and petroleum. The trade situation began to improve in 1983 and 1984, probably as a consequence of the initial adjustment measures, including currency devaluations and import restrictions. While the improvement in the trade balance was desirable from the standpoint of our region's external debt, it occurred during a year when Latin America experienced a further decline in per capita agricultural output. Without a strong recovery of output, efforts aimed at increasing agricultural exports and reducing imports may meet with difficulties.

PROBLEMS IN FOOD, AGRICULTURE, AND WATER DEVELOPMENT

I have attempted to review the national and sectorial economic trends in Latin America because of their importance as a backdrop for improving regional food security and because they will inevitably shape the future of water resource use and management. Now I would like to turn to an issue closer at hand: How can water resources be managed to meet the key development problems of Latin America and to ensure an acceptable level of regional and national food security?

During past periods of relative economic growth in Latin America, as domestic economies expanded, bolstered by favorable international markets, the region was able to invest heavily in small, medium, and large irrigation and drainage projects. As the economic crisis intensified in the early 1980s, however, these countries have had to bring to a halt, or to delay, many important irrigation investments—investments which, in an earlier period, would have raised agricultural productivity and cushioned the rising urban food demands. And the challenge of creating viable water resource institutions—which the chapters in this volume will consider in more detail—now tests the ingenuity of scientists and policy makers alike.

Currently, the region faces a complex challenge—to use the existing resources more effectively and to assign limited investment funds to the highest priority activities. This is a very difficult task because the economic, social, and political demands which confront Latin America today are many and often in conflict with each other.

The first issue which confronts the region is how to sustain food security in a time of financial and economic crisis. We refer to this as the food gap. You may ask—particularly those of you dealing with the human anguish and food problems in Africa—why would a food gap be relevant in this region, which is so often called "middle income"? Why should food security be a problem in Latin America? In fact, the absence of food security is partly a consequence of the region's success in development. Growing incomes have meant improved diets and, since the domestic agricultural system responds slowly to changes in local food demand, rising food imports. Diets changed as our population urbanized, with people increasing their protein consumption and using more nutritious foods, while traditional food staples began to fade from the consumer's diet. This experience has been repeated over and over again in countries of Latin America that became more urbanized. With the urban transition nearly complete, this means that agricultural investments—and the management of water resources—must be designed to meet such dietary needs in urban centers five to ten years in the future. Consequently, food security in Latin America cannot be seen only in terms of protecting traditional food production but of meeting the changing requirements of a rapidly growing and diversified diet.

The second major problem which affects the future of agriculture has been magnified by the economic and fiscal crisis. Until recently, agriculture and water resources development have benefited from extensive public investment programs. Countries such as Brazil, Mexico, Peru, and Venezuela have invested large sums in irrigation projects. These programs and their associated incentives were introduced, in part, to compensate agriculture for the favorable treatment given to other sectors, especially industry. Fiscal constraints currently require that we make established irrigated agriculture much more productive and efficient, rather than spend money on new works. Water resources will have to be used to maximize production, which fits in with the expected national imperative of food security through the end of this century.

The region's third problem arises from the fact that virtually all of the member countries are facing severe social strains. The social costs of the economic adjustment policies are reflected in employment and income drops, in lower spending on health and education, and in rising social tensions. Governments may well be setting future limits to social progress by restraining social programs now. In Latin America, public policy today involves a choice between long-term productive investments in fixed plant and equipment, such as irrigation works, as opposed to short-term investment in human resources and living standards. In making choices, we should be aware of the costs incurred by putting scarce financial resources into investments which can only yield returns some years ahead. I trust, therefore, that as scientists, engineers, and administrators, you will strive for effective low-cost technical solutions to agricultural development.

I have mentioned three critical problems that are likely to shape the evolution of agriculture in Latin America and determine how water resources might fit into our region's future investment plans.

THE NEED FOR NEW APPROACHES, POLICIES

Now I want to refer to the role of international financial and technical assistance agencies, universities, individual scientists, and students in helping to promote viable agricultural and water resource development in the years ahead in Latin America. I will be selective because this conference is covering many of these and other topics very comprehensively. From the experience of the bank, we wish to emphasize three major development themes: (1) project preparation and financing; (2) institutional development, both for project administration and building up technology, and (3) national and sector policy formulation and application. I will mention each of these very briefly.

We have learned that the process of resource development, especially of water, proceeds best within an investment project framework. In the past, projects have referred mainly to investment in fixed infrastructure with their associated operating services. We should now rethink our perception of exactly what a project is. In particular, we believe that the rehabilitation and better management and use of existing irrigation systems should be given similar weight in the region's plans and studies as that accorded to new and costly additions to irrigated areas. This does not mean that we should suspend needed irrigation and drainage investments; it means that in times of fiscal scarcity, we should first think hard about how to maximize the benefits from the existing infrastructure.

The second developmental theme relates to the need to improve the capacity of our national institutions to serve agriculture and water resource management. The bank has provided substantial support for these purposes in the past and continues to provide such assistance. Several of the member countries, like Mexico, have made great institutional progress, while others such as Costa Rica are embarking on an intensive new program of improvements. There is an opportunity for cooperation among countries and among institutions, such as universities, to establish effective communication networks. These research networks, which we currently support with technical cooperation, have been effective vehicles for the interchange of technology among countries. We recommend that Latin America's national administrators and scientists be better integrated into existing international and regional networks; Latin America can both contribute to and learn from this exchange. The Inter-American Development Bank (IDB) stands ready to support this process.

The third theme that concerns us is the application of appropriate national, sectoral, and regional economic policies. The IDB has long believed that the formulation of national or sectorial policies is a matter for a country's own economic authorities. This does not mean, however, that we view such policies as being unimportant; rather, we feel that we are less able to say what might be the "best" policy at any particular moment in history. But we should not neglect the significant function that policies play in supporting agricultural development. It is increasingly clear that, in many member countries, agriculture has not been provided with appropriate economic incentives during the past twenty-five years. This has occurred because of the way national and sectorial policies were designed to favor industry over agriculture, and urban centers over rural regions. To some extent these policies—aimed, for example, at industrial import substitutions—have been modified by recent national economic adjustments. But it seems that there is still a place for countries to increase the contribution of agriculture by applying policies that increase agricultural incentives. Other structural measures, such as improving technology, strengthening institutions, and training people, are also essential elements in agricultural development.

While the bank does not feel that its function is to define national policy since we work through individual projects, we do stand ready to assist governments to clarify the consequences for water resource development of different economic policies. National economic policies create favorable or unfavorable markets for agricultural products. Sectorial policies, such as water pricing and subsidies, will likely determine how irrigation is organized and what types of commodities are sold locally or exported. Therefore, we suggest that as scientists, administrators, and educators in the field of water resources, you give greater attention to economic policies and their impact on the sector's future.

I would like to conclude with some thoughts about the future. What has occurred in Latin America in the last twenty-five years—with rapid economic growth, urbanization, and disappointing agricultural performance—suggests that in tandem with national economic adjustments, the agricultural sector requires its own adjustments. Looking ahead, the opportunities lie in better use of the existing infrastructure and resources and a search for lower-cost solutions via more effective technology, institutions, and economic policies. We hope that in your deliberations, you will look for the new approaches that are so urgently needed. I wish you the greatest success in these endeavors.

PART III. WATER SUPPLY

10. ATMOSPHERIC ASPECTS OF VARIATIONS IN GLOBAL WATER SUPPLIES: PREDICTABILITY, RAINMAKING, AND PRACTICAL USES OF METEOROLOGICAL INFORMATION

Thomas D. Potter, World Climate Programme, World Meteorological Organization, Geneva, Switzerland

ABSTRACT

Less than one-thousandth of 1 percent of the total amount of water on the Earth is contained in the atmosphere. Yet this small amount of water is crucial for food production because most of the total water on Earth exists in saline oceans or in inaccessible polar ice caps. Water requirements for rainfed crops depend largely on past rainfall and on evaporation. For irrigated crops, the water requirements depend mostly on past irrigation, which itself is related to past rainfall and evapotranspiration. For both rainfed and irrigated crops, the water supplies depend ultimately on rainfall. Thus the atmospheric aspects of water supplies for crops are a crucial aspect of the entire crop-water issue.

The basic problem is that large variations in rainfall and evaporation occur from season to season and from year to year, especially in the regions where there is barely enough rain to grow crops. Hence, farmers and the entire agricultural community are faced with great uncertainties about water supplies from rainfall.

This chapter will explore the atmospheric aspects of these variations in global water supplies for crops—their predictability, prospects for rainmaking, and finally some practical uses of meteorological information in this important problem.

BACKGROUND

The Global Water Balance

At any given location, the law of conservation of mass (in this case water mass) means that over the long term, precipitation (P) equals evaporation (E) plus runoff (R): P = E+R. The standard picture of the hydrologic cycle is shown in Fig. 1A, along with a schematic diagram (Fig. 1B) giving numerical values of P, E, and R for the land and the oceans. Fig. 2 shows the average annual latitudinal distribution of precipitation and evaporation for the entire globe and for land and sea areas as well. From Fig. 2 we see that a water surplus (P>E) exists in the equatorial latitudes (about 15°N to 8°S). The subtropical regions in both hemispheres have water deficits (E>P), with the Southern Hemisphere having a more pronounced deficit. From 40° to 90° lat., precipitation exceeds evaporation so a surplus exists; in these latitudes the Southern Hemisphere has a larger surplus than the Northern Hemisphere. In the polar regions, both P and E are small and nearly in balance.

For the globe as a whole, precipitation equals evapora-

The views expressed in this paper represent solely those of the author and do not necessarily represent the position of the World Meteorological Organization or any other organization involved in the World Climate Program.

tion, about 1 m per year on the average. Over land, it is found that evaporation is about 62 percent of precipitation, which gives an average runoff of 38 percent of P. Over the oceans, E is about 10 percent greater than P, with the excess supplied by runoff from the land. The total runoff from land has been found to be about 37,000 km^3.

Continental Water Balance

These latitudinal distributions are interesting and important, but they do not give us the information we need about the distribution of precipitation and evaporation on the continents where food crops are grown. These required patterns (Baumgartner and Reichel, 1975) result from global atmospheric circulations and the interactions with the oceans, the cryosphere, and land surface processes (including the biota) to form the complex climate system shown schematically in Fig. 3. A summary of values of P, E, and R is shown in Table 1. From this table we conclude that South America is the best endowed continent for potential water resources, with Africa and Australia the least well endowed. Some differences exist among various investigators on the relative positions of the remaining continents.

Variations in Precipitation and Evaporation

The average values of P, E, and R are important, but as noted earlier, it is their variations that cause problems for farmers and national decision makers in agricultural policies and ultimately for the consumers. The variations of mean precipitation with latitude are shown in Fig. 4 for January, July, and the entire year. The maximum variation in mid-latitudes is more pronounced in the Southern Hemisphere than in the Northern Hemisphere. The variation of mean annual precipitation is shown by month in Fig. 5 for the continents, the oceans, and the entire globe. The oceans receive by far the larger total quantity of precipitation, but the within-year variability is more marked over land than over the oceans. These variations of rainfall within a given year are very important for rainfed agriculture. Results from a computer model (Mitchell, 1981) give the distribution of P, E, P-E (atmospheric supply to the ground), and R by latitude throughout the year. Precipitation was at a maximum during the summer months. The seasonal variation of evaporation was large outside the tropics. In middle and high latitudes, the seasonal variation of evaporation was greater than that of precipitation, so P-E was at a maximum in winter when E was smallest. In low latitudes, the

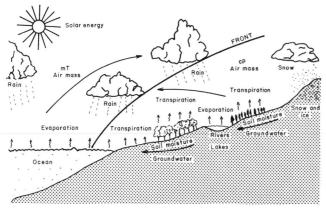

Fig. 1A. The hydrologic cycle. (Redrawn from Mather, 1984).

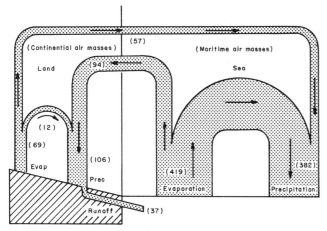

Fig. 1B. Schematic representation of the hydrologic cycle. The width of each tube is proportional to the volume of water involved in that phase of the hydrological cycle. The values are water volumes in 1,000 km³. (Redrawn from Mather, 1984).

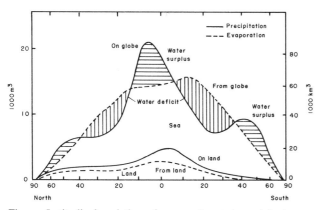

Fig. 2. Latitudinal variation of evaporation and precipitation on the globe as well as on the land and sea areas. (Redrawn from Mather, 1984).

Table 1. Summary of continental values of precipitation, evaporation, and runoff (km³/yr).

Values in km³/yr	P	E	R
Africa	21,450	17,590	3,860
Asia	30,390	18,440	11,950
Australia	3,560	2,830	730
Europe	6,380	3,730	2,650
North America	15,550	9,430	6,120
South America	27,030	15,470	11,560
Antarctica	1,890	1,110	780
Total	106,250	68,600	37,650

SOURCE: Mather, 1969.

variation in P was greater, so P-E was at a maximum in summer corresponding to the maximum in precipitation. The water balance at the surface is completed by the runoff. Runoff was greatest near the equator and in the middle and high latitudes where P-E was greatest. Snowmelt produced the large runoffs in high latitudes in the Northern Hemisphere at the end of spring. Shorter-term variations in rainfall also occur, ranging from an hour or so, to days, weeks, and months, which significantly affect soil moisture and hence, crop growth.

Droughts

Droughts are extreme variations in water supply for a region, often being defined as a significant reduction in normal rainfall for an area that results in a significant decrease in crop yields or other economic activities in the region. Drought is a recurring but noncyclic phenomenon that appears most frequently in the arid and semiarid subtropical latitudes from about 20° to 40°. Much is known about the general atmospheric conditions that produce droughts. Also, modeling efforts are under way to try to determine the effects of mankind's activities (e.g., overgrazing) on the development or prolonging of drought. Unfortunately, such studies have not yet produced firm conclusions that are accepted by all meteorologists.

The most extreme drought in recent times began in the Sahel in 1968 and has continued up to the present (1985), with only minor improvements in some areas in some years; rainfall reductions of 50 to 60 percent or higher have occurred in some areas in some years and sometimes lasted for several successive years. Other recent droughts have occurred in eastern and southern Africa, in northeastern Brazil, in Australia, Indonesia, the Indian subcontinent and other parts of Southeast Asia, in the Great Plains in North America, as well as in the Soviet Union, China, and many other locations. Droughts occur commonly in all of these areas, and sometimes they persist for years. Agricultural production systems must be designed to be flexible enough to survive such persistent droughts.

Climatic Changes

Much publicity has been given in recent years to the possibility of significant climatic changes, both natural or man-

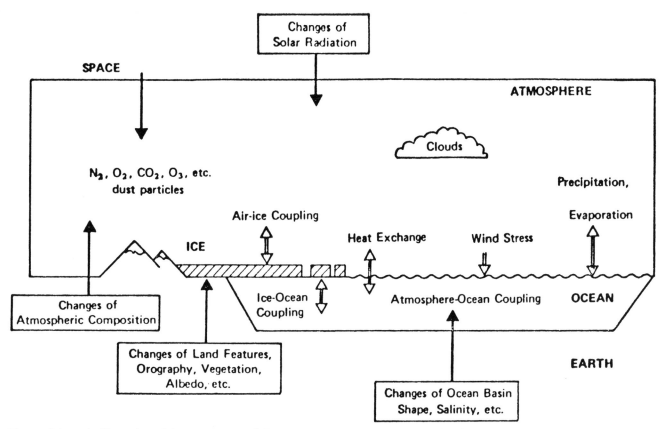

Fig. 3. Schematic illustration of the components of the coupled atmosphere-ocean-earth climatic system. The full arrows are examples of external processes, and the open arrows are examples of internal processes in climatic change. (*Understanding Climatic Change, A Program for Action*. Washington, D.C.: National Academy of Science, 1975).

made. One reads of impending ice ages or, on the other hand, of impending "heat deaths," such as the "greenhouse effect." Most climate investigators take the position that to date, there is no clear evidence that either of these fates is in store for the planet Earth in the foreseeable future, let alone demonstrated evidence that such events are now under way even in places like the Sahel where drought has persisted for sixteen years. There is great concern, however, for the possibility that increasing amounts of carbon dioxide in the atmosphere from burning fossil fuels will cause long-wave radiation from the earth to be trapped by the lower atmosphere, resulting in significantly warmer temperatures in middle and high latitudes and probable changes in global precipitation patterns as well. Such climate changes are not likely to take place until about the middle of the next century or later, and the possible effects on agriculture and other activities are not known at this time. Similar effects on the climate will arise from other radiatively active gases, which collectively will produce warming comparable to that of carbon dioxide. Active research is under way to study the effects of CO_2 and other radiatively active gases.

Conclusions on Variations in P, E, and R

The information contained in previous sections (and additional information not explicitly discussed there) shows that significant variations in P, E, and R exist regularly, on time scales ranging from an hour to seasons to interannual periods and even to decades or longer. These variations significantly affect crop yields and are designated by many investigators as having the single largest effect on year-to-year variations in crop production. The question arises: What can be done about these variations to permit better planning and better day-to-day operations? Can we predict the variations? Can we artificially stimulate rainfall? Can we make better use of existing information on the effects of weather and climate on crop production? The remainder of this chapter will review answers to these questions.

CAN WE PREDICT SIGNIFICANT VARIATIONS IN PRECIPITATION AND EVAPORATION A MONTH OR MORE IN ADVANCE?

Prediction Capability

The atmospheric sciences have made great progress over the past twenty-five years in better understanding of the atmosphere and in developing an improved capability to predict short-term atmospheric circulation patterns out to seven days or so. But the capability to predict even general patterns of temperature and precipitation for a month or a season has not significantly improved during this period. The capability to predict departures from normal conditions a

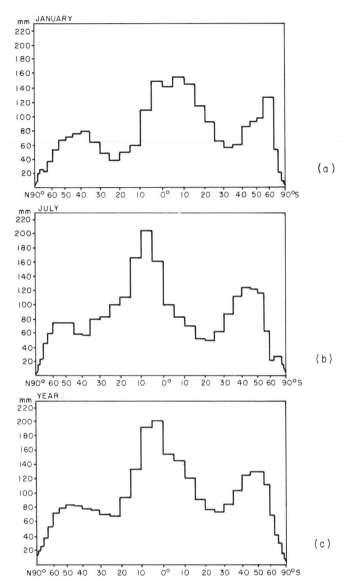

Fig. 4. Variation of mean precipitation with latitude: (a) January, (b) July, (c) annual. (Redrawn from Jaeger, 1981).

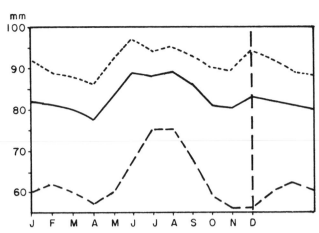

Fig. 5. Variation of mean annual precipitation over: . . . oceans, --- continents, ⎯⎯ the globe. (After Jaeger, 1981).

near the year 2000 before significant advances are made in this difficult science.

Statistical Probabilities

Despite the fact that we cannot yet make accurate predictions for time scales of one month and beyond, some useful information can be provided in the form of statistical probabilities that certain events will occur. These probabilities can be developed from past records of climate observations, from computer simulations of climate variations, or from the limited but still useful skill in prediction. The probabilities can be given to decision makers in the same format as, for example, predictions of future economic conditions. A specific example could be that there is a 65 percent chance that sufficient rain will fall during a specified growing season to ensure a successful crop. Even such a slight edge over blind chance can be very useful, especially where it is combined with information on past rainfall that is reflected in soil moisture conditions that persist for extended periods and largely determine the future crop yields.

CAN WE MAKE RAIN OR SNOW, ESPECIALLY IN A DROUGHT?

Artificial weather modification, more popularly known as rainmaking, would seem to be a ready-made solution to water shortages, especially in extended dry periods. A very few experiments have demonstrated that rainfall can be increased in certain special circumstances, but even here the evaluation process is long and difficult, and the results are not unanimously accepted. The capability to increase rainfall in droughts or chronically dry areas has not been conclusively demonstrated. The conclusion of many meteorologists is that expensive operational rainmaking programs are not yet justified, especially in drought areas. But the potential benefits are so great that research into rainmaking must be continued. Also, pilot experiments should be performed to determine the feasibility of conducting operational rainmaking in a specific area. Such pilot experiments must be carefully designed and conducted under strict procedures to ensure that the evaluations have scientific credibility.

month or a season in advance remains low, in the range of 55 to 60 percent accuracy; flipping a coin would give a 50 percent accuracy. No attempt is made in these predictions to try to give specific daily or even weekly conditions, but rather, general categories of below or above normal or near normal for a month or season. For longer periods of interannual variations, the capability for credible predictions is even lower. The meteorological community currently has essentially no capability to accurately predict interannual or decadal variations in temperature or precipitation or evaporation (despite the fact that one often sees such predictions). Nor can we currently predict the onset, duration, cessation, or recurrence of drought. Active research is ongoing to increase our capability to predict climate variations on time scales of a month or more, but the climate system is highly complex so it very likely will be

BETTER USE OF EXISTING METEOROLOGICAL INFORMATION

As stated above, we cannot yet accurately predict climate variations or changes nor can we ensure that we very definitely can increase rainfall in all conditions, especially during severe droughts. What then can the meteorologist do *now* to help alleviate water shortages? The answer is that we can make better use of existing meteorological information to help avoid wasting water and to help increase crop yields, both in planning and in daily farming operations. Many practical methods exist for different types of climate and different crops that have been used in both developing and developed countries. Methods to be used in droughts will be stressed here because drought is the most critical period of water shortage.

The first thing we can do is calculate statistical probabilities of the most critical conditions, such as the probable beginning and duration of rainy seasons or the statistical likelihood that a drought will continue for a specified period. Such knowledge is useful in planning the introduction of drought-resistant seeds, for the introduction of new crop-rotation systems, for the selection of appropriate farm machinery, and to establish practices to combat desertification.

Next, running observations of rainfall, temperature, humidity, and wind combined with knowledge of soils, sowing dates, and crop calendars for each specific crop throughout a growing season can give probability estimates of the water balance of crops throughout the growing season. This information can be immediately applied to give advice on timing farming operations such as weeding, thinning, ridging, application of fertilizers, and harvesting operations. Similar information can be used to estimate crop yields a few months before harvest. Note that these procedures do not depend on accurate long-range weather forecasts but only the weather *observations* (especially precipitation and temperature). These weather factors largely determine soil moisture, which in turn is a key factor in final crop yields. Thus we can successfully estimate crop yields over a growing season from weather & agronomic observations even though we cannot yet predict the long-term weather variations.

Third, we can make a rapid analysis and dissemination of observations of recent past (four or five days) weather, as it affects the development of agricultural pests and diseases. Prompt spraying actions can then be taken which will avoid many of the current losses of up to 30 percent from pests and diseases.

Fourth, information on crop water requirements of irrigated crops can now be supplied with a precision comparable to that for application of water, thus avoiding gross overirrigation and maximizing agricultural yield per unit of scarce water.

Finally on this brief list, an early warning system can be developed using the techniques listed above to detect the early signs of meteorological drought that often precedes the agricultural drought responsible for decreasing crop yields. These techniques should be supplemented by operational satellite data to determine a vegetative index, which estimates the health of crops and rangeland vegetation. Measures can therefore be taken in time to prevent damage.

These and other fairly simple techniques based on existing information have been tested in both developing and developed countries with good results, e.g., Mali, where such information helped farmers to increase production by about 25 percent during the Sahel drought. It is clear that something useful can be done now with existing information, provided we organize it properly and disseminate the results promptly to farmers and decision makers. All of this work is clearly an interdisciplinary effort among farmers, agriculturalists, water managers, meteorologists, and decision makers.

KEY ISSUES

For the atmospheric aspects of global water supplies, the key issues are:

1. Recognizing that large variations in rainfall and evaporation occur regularly, especially in chronically dry areas, and that droughts are an extreme example of these variations, which often lead to decreases in agricultural productivity and other economic difficulties.

2. Recognizing that currently we cannot accurately predict climate variations (including rainfall) a month or more in advance.

3. Recognizing the lack of a current operational capability to artificially increase rainfall, especially in droughts.

4. Recognizing that methods are available now for better use of existing meteorological information to help avoid wasting water and to help increase agricultural production. These methods should be widely disseminated, and relevant training and pilot projects should be supported by governments and funding agencies.

REFERENCES

Baumgartner, A., and E. Reichel. 1982. Water balance. Land surface processes in atmospheric general circulation models. P. S. Eagleson (ed.) Cambridge, England: Cambridge University Press.

Jaeger, L. 1981. Monthly and areal patterns of mean global precipitation. Variations in the global water budget. Dordrecht: D. Reidel Publishing Company.

Mather, J. R. 1969. The average annual water balance of the world. Pp. 29–40. *In* Proceedings of the Symposium on Water Balance in North America. American Water Resources Association, Series 7. Banff, Canada, June 23–26.

Mather, J. R. 1984. Water resources. Distribution, use, and management. New York: J. Wiley and Sons.

Mitchell, J. F. B. 1981. Hydrological cycle modeling. Variations in the global water budget. Dordrecht: D. Reidel Publishing Company.

National Academy of Sciences. 1975. Understanding climatic change. A program for action. Washington, D.C.

11. WATER SUPPLY IN AFRICA—A CASE STUDY

John F. Griffiths, Department of Meteorology, Texas A&M University, College Station, Texas

ABSTRACT

The distribution of precipitation and its large, but natural variability are illustrated. The use of probability estimates of threshold rainfall amounts is shown, but it is suggested that soil moisture probability values give more useful information. The problems associated with drought and rainmaking are discussed, followed by sections on excessive moisture and evaporation. Finally, the methods taken in West Africa to reduce the impact of rainfall variability are reviewed.

INTRODUCTION

Africa is the second largest of the continents. It covers an area of over 30 million km² (about 20 percent of the world's land surface), is very symmetrically located (37°N to 35°S), and has almost equal extent east-west (7,200 km) and north-south (8,000 km). It is the home of about 350 million people distributed very unevenly among more than fifty independent countries. There is an old saying that goes: "Geographers on Africa maps make lions and tigers fill the gaps, and o'er the uninhabited downs put elephants in place of towns." Even now there are large almost uninhabited areas, while some regions have very great population density.

Precipitation is by far the most important climatic element in Africa. Unfortunately, it exhibits appreciable year-to-year variation and, in most places, a large season-to-season (or month-to-month) variation also. Examples of these are seen in Figs. 1 and 2.

During the past fifteen to sixteen years large areas of the continent have suffered from below-average rainfall, and some two-thirds of the countries are feeling the effects of the drought. It is therefore very pertinent to consider the water situation of Africa as a case study.

ATMOSPHERIC CONSIDERATIONS

Over nearly all of the continent the movement of the Intertropical Convergence Zone (ITCZ), the region at the surface where the trade winds of the two hemispheres meet, is the major determinant of the precipitation patterns—in both amount and duration. The ITCZ follows the sun's seasonal movement, with a lag of about one month (Fig. 3). This generally means that stations on the extreme edge of the ITCZ get only one rainfall season.

It is said that there are three rules concerning rainfall in Africa.

1. The yearly amount increases as one approaches the equator, from north or south.

2. The duration of the rainy season increases as one goes towards the equator.

3. Do not place too much reliance on the previous two rules.

The picture is complicated by high mountains. For example, note the break in the wet equatorial belt when it reaches eastern Africa (Fig. 4). Because warm air can hold much more moisture than dry (the water-holding capacity approximately doubles for every 11°C increase in temperature), most of the air over the continent can hold a lot of moisture. Even the searing hot air over the Sahara in summer contains much moisture, generally more than the humid air over the North Atlantic in winter. Put another way, air at a temperature of 50°C and a relative humidity of 10 percent, contains about 1.6 times as much moisture as saturated air at 6°C.

From past records, average rainfall amounts are often calculated for weekly, monthly, and annual periods. But what do these averages mean? The average of 0, 10, 0, 10, 16, 1, 3, 0 is the same as that of 4, 6, 5, 5, 6, 6, 4, 4. Makindu has a mean of 611 mm, but the range is from 1,964 mm to 67 mm. In Africa the variability is as important as the average.

Although the idea of calculating the probability of receiving chosen amounts during a selected time interval, usually a month or year (Fig. 5), was introduced more than thirty years ago, it appears that most planning is still made using averages only. This is most unfortunate because in many areas of the continent, the chance of exceeding the average is only half that of getting less than the average (Fig. 6). This fact is of great importance in agriculture.

The first step toward a more realistic approach is to think in terms of three scenarios: too much rain, an acceptable amount (includes ideal or optimum), or too little. These terms have to be defined according to the crop and its stage of development.

Let us turn to a specific area to understand the complexity of the atmospheric situation. In eastern Kenya there is an ingrained concept of the "long" and "short" rains, occurring March–May and November–December, respectively. However, a detailed study conducted at Texas A&M University shows how in reality, over much of the region, the short rains exceed the long rains in duration, reliability, and often in amount. This means that the thinking, and the planning, of most farmers is incorrect at an early stage.

Other studies have shown how the rainy seasons are very variable: sometimes they are prolonged, sometimes curtailed or nonexistent, and occasionally fragmented. These points are made clear in Fig. 7. Of course it may be argued from a practical viewpoint that it is soil moisture values that are important, not the rainfall. Using a reliable empirical method of estimating soil moisture, Fig. 8 results. This il-

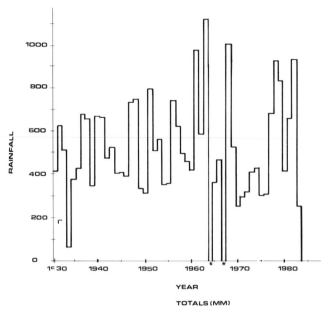

Fig. 1. Annual rainfall totals (mm) at Makindu, Kenya, 1930–1983. *1964 and 1967 missing.

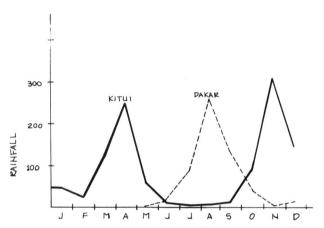

Fig. 2. The mean monthly rainfall at Kitui (Kenya) and Dakar (Senegal).

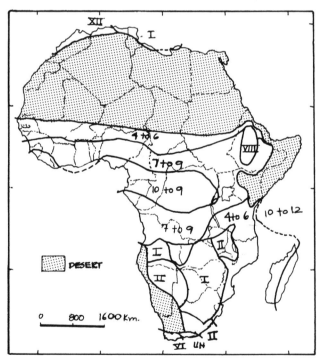

Fig. 3. Approximate positions of the Intertropical Convergence Zone in January and July.

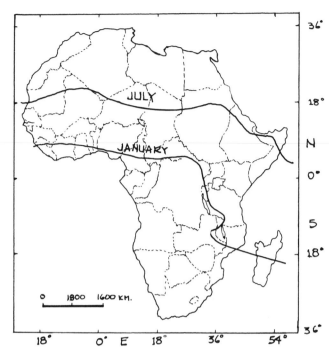

Fig. 4. Rainfall distribution. Arabic numerals refer to the number of months with at least 50 mm. Roman numerals identify the central month of the wettest quarter (I = January, XII = December). UN refers to uniform rainfall through the year.

lustrates perfectly the variable nature of the rainy seasons and allows one to make probability estimates.

From methods such as these, and similar techniques, the probability (based on past records) of the "too much," "acceptable," or "too little" scenarios can be calculated, once they are defined by the agriculturalist.

DROUGHT

Of the three scenarios it is the too little (i.e., drought) situation that receives the greatest attention. First, what can one say about drought? A real, and basic, problem is the absence of a uniform definition of the word. On reflection it is clear that no single definition can exist since the word is

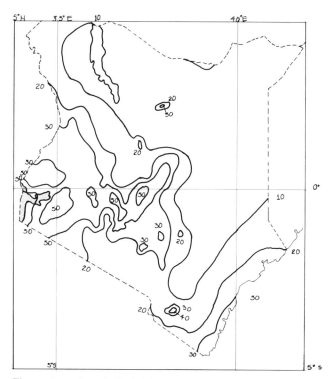

Fig. 5. Annual total of rainfall (inches) likely to be exceeded four years in five (80 percent probability).

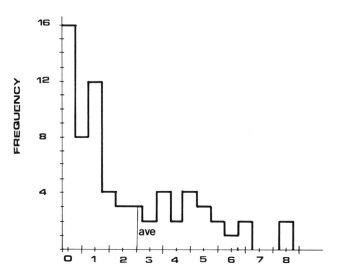

Fig. 6. Frequency distribution of rainfall amounts, February, Machakos, Kenya.

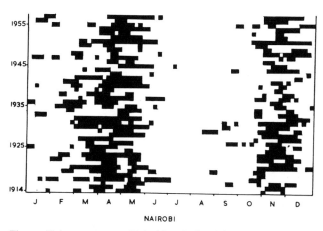

YEARLY DISTRIBUTION OF 'RAINY' PENTADES.

NAIROBI

Fig. 7. Rainy seasons at Nairobi, calculated by pentad. A black shaded pentad denotes the center one of three pentads totaling more than 75 mm. Long rains are March–June, short rains, October–December.

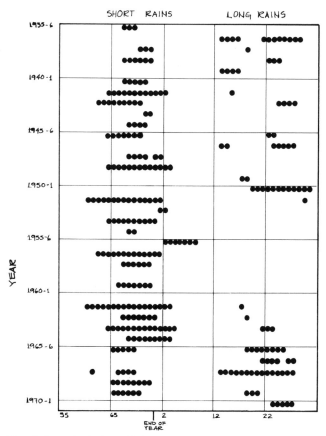

Fig. 8. Pentads during which soil moisture is sufficient for good plant growth, Makindu, Kenya.

problem specific; any definition must include the dimensions of both time and area. Meteorological drought occurs when the rainfall is well below expectations in a large area for an extended period.

Studies of past records would show, in all of Africa, variability in precipitation is to be expected (and planned for), and every site experiences periods in which there is too

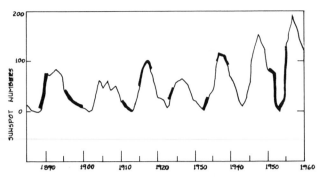

Fig. 9. Drought years in Texas and sunspot numbers (Schematic). Broad lines indicate periods of drought.

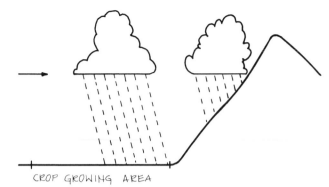

CROP GROWING AREA

Fig. 10. Cloud seeding may cause precipitation to start earlier than would occur naturally.

little precipitation for the regular agricultural practices of the region—a qualified drought. If the times of these dry spells are plotted, it is noted that drought is a recurring phenomenon, but that at any one place it does not exhibit a periodic pattern. This means that drought cannot be predicted accurately by the use of cycles or trends in the climatic pattern. A World Meteorological Organization (WMO) Expert Group concluded recently that no known method exists to predict reliably the onset, cessation, or recurrence of drought in Africa.

If you will permit a digression, take the case of droughts in Texas. These are represented in Fig. 9, against the sunspot number of each year. It is clear that droughts can occur at any time in the sunspot cycle and no simple cyclic pattern can be deduced.

RAINMAKING

If it is accepted that at present no way exists of forecasting droughts with sufficient accuracy to be of much practical use, then it is natural to consider the possibility of rainmaking. One can hardly do better here than to quote from a statement of the Secretary-General of the WMO to the Conference of Ministers, Economic Commission for Africa.

Rainmaking has been successful only in very few special cases. The experts on weather modification within the WMO state quite clearly that the evidence of success is so limited that no operations to produce rain artificially should be attempted at this time. They feel that only scientific experimentation is presently justified in order to improve our insight into the process of rain formation and its possible modification.

I would like to point out that unless it can be proven by a proper experimental layout that a certain rainmaking activity has been successful, it should not be undertaken. Time and again weather modification activities all over the world have been stopped because users and governments have started to ask the question of success and could not find an answer. The reasons for some initial successes of rainmaking are easy to understand. A drought means a meteorological situation with precipitation below the average. Normally weather adjusts itself over the years and produces years with more rain and years with less. Thus the starting of seeding during a drought has been seemingly successful because the weather adjusted itself closer to the average with more natural rain. And it was the weather

turning to more "normal" which caused the rain increases and not necessarily the effects of the seeding.

This may all sound very pessimistic. But the complexities of the scientific and technical problems are not allowing quick success.

Let me just summarize the rainmaking methods. In the tropics, where most of the cloud is at a temperature above freezing, a good nucleation material is finely ground, dry common salt (NaCl). This, or another substance, has to be injected into the cloud to induce precipitation. For this there are three ways: ground generators (sending up the nuclei on warm air currents), rockets, and aircraft. The degree of uncertainty in positioning when using generators is very great, and so the latter methods are usually employed. In East Africa in the late 1950s and 1960s it was found that aircraft were superior because one could judge exactly when in the updraft to seed. The findings, more correctly suggestions since the experiments were controlled by government orders and not scientifically designed, were that it was likely that efforts caused the rainfall to begin some fifteen to thirty minutes earlier than it would have under natural causes. This change in time often led to rainfall on the coffee or maize fields of the plains and not on the forested mountain slopes (Fig. 10).

EXCESSIVE MOISTURE

Another of the three scenarios is almost as devastating as the drought but is often given only cursory attention. This is the "too much" situation.

Excessive rainfall for an area is very undesirable. Many of the lateritic soils of the tropics become compacted readily so that intensive rains lead to heavy runoff with associated soil erosion and flash flooding. The recent acceleration in deforestation in many African countries resulting from the need for fuel and/or farm land compounds the problem. It is a most dispiriting sight to stand on river banks in east, west, or southern Africa and see so much of the continent's natural resources being carried away to the oceans.

Probabilities of occurrence of the "too much" condition, once defined, can be calculated in the same manner as the "too little" situation.

EVAPORATION

So far the emphasis has been on the water gain from the atmosphere, but water supply studies must also be concerned with the water loss. From the atmospheric viewpoint this involves evaporation from water surfaces (rivers, lakes) and the soil, plus the transpiration loss from vegetation. The general term *evapotranspiration* will be used to express the total water loss in this manner.

True evapotranspiration has not been measured at sufficient places in Africa for an accurate estimate of the loss to be made. Often evaporimeters are used and their water loss converted to an estimate of evapotranspiration. This method is very approximate, and many measurements of evapotranspiration need to be made as soon as possible. In Africa, annual evaporation rates (E_0) vary between about 1 m and 4 m. A very rough approximation for the potential evapotranspiration (E_T) is $0.7E_0$. It is clear that under dry farming conditions, E_T cannot exceed the rainfall amount.

AGRICULTURAL OBSERVATIONS

A pronounced and serious lack of observations concerning agricultural data is prevalent in nearly all countries. This needs to be rectified because such information is needed in the development of crop-yield models. For this development to occur, accurate values of the yields in various regions are necessary. This allows the appreciation of the impact of the wide-ranging weather and climate conditions prevalent in Africa. At the same time, full phenological observations are required so that the role of weather during the various developmental stages of the crops can be estimated. These types of observations should be made at agroclimatic stations, which are best located at agricultural research institutions. In addition, these institutions need to take microscale climatic measurements within and around growing crops.

MEASURES, NEEDED TO COMBAT EFFECTS OF RAINFALL VARIABILITY

Before considering measures and recommendations it is necessary to identify where the problem areas lie. From the atmospheric viewpoint, these are in three categories: (1) inadequate public and political awareness of the benefit of meteorological and hydrological services in the role of socioeconomic development, (2) inadequate liaison between the meteorological and hydrological services and the user community, and (3) inadequate meteorological and hydrological data combined with insufficient methods of dissemination.

The solutions to the above, within any country, are clear, but all require adequate funding. Because of the continuity of the atmosphere there is a tendency for groups of countries to suffer similar stresses at the same time. Therefore, a regional approach is often more relevant, more effective, and less costly in the long run.

With these ideas in mind the Agrhymet Program has been developed in western Africa. This is concentrated in the area south of the Sahara that receives from 250 to 800 mm of rainfall annually. It is an outcome of the Inter-State Committee for Drought Control in the Sahel (CILSS, in the French acronym), with assistance from the UNDP, some donor countries (Belgium, West Germany, France, the Netherlands, Switzerland, and the United States), the Sahel Club, WMO, and the Food and Agriculture Organization (FAO). The aim of the program is to assist decision makers and users by keeping them informed of the current situation, collecting and analyzing data, and creating national agrometeorological services. A keystone in the work has been the creation of the Regional Centre for Training and Applications of Agrometeorology and Operational Hydrology in Niamey, Niger.

At this stage national meteorological services have been reinforced, agrometeorologists have been trained, data processing and telecommunications equipment has been installed, and selected students have been instructed in data processing. In addition, historical meteorological data have been collected. A pilot experiment entitled the Mali Pilot Project has been set up near Bamako with the short-term objectives of monitoring the water balance and crops, improving water management, establishing crop calendars (including sowing dates), assessing the impact of climatic factors on production, and training the project's farmers in the basic methods for taking observations and using agrometeorological information efficiently.

The concept of the Agrhymet Center is an excellent one, and attempts should be made to establish similar units in, for example, Nairobi and Harare. It should be ensured that the personnel who will staff these offices have been trained in their field and have practical experience.

Finally, it should be iterated that, with water being such a precious commodity, it is essential to ensure accurate water budgets on all scales, regional, national, and local. Without these, the efficient distribution and use of water cannot be achieved.

REFERENCES

Carr, John T., Jr. 1966. Texas droughts. Report 30, November. 58 pp. Austin: Texas Water Development Board.

Griffiths, John F. 1972. Climates of Africa. Vol. 10, 604 pp. *In* World survey of climatology. Amsterdam: Elsevier.

12. MANPOWER FOR WATER RESOURCES DEVELOPMENT

L. J. Mostertman, International Institute for Hydraulic and Environmental Engineering, Rotterdam, The Netherlands

ABSTRACT

Engineering for water resources development used to depend mainly on the transfer of practical experience from one generation to the next. With the growing urgency of water resource development, scientific methods were introduced. The required professional training could not sufficiently be provided by standard civil engineering curricula. Hydraulic engineers should be trained at the postgraduate level. Because of the particular circumstances of the Netherlands, much experience on water resources development was accumulated in that country. The country wished to share this with others. For this transfer, the International Course in Hydraulic Engineering was founded in 1957. Increasing demands led to a greater variety of program offerings. They are now given by the International Institute for Hydraulic and Environmental Engineering at Delft. The specific difficulties of such a program are described, with methods for overcoming them. A description is made of more recent developments, with an outlook to the future.

THE ART OF HYDRAULIC ENGINEERING

For many centuries hydraulic engineering was an art rather than a science. Relevant know-how was transmitted from generation to generation. Hydraulic works were adapted to the characteristics of the location, the morphology of a river or a coastline, and the materials that were locally available. Each part of the world had its own type of hydraulic structures, and one can even observe marked differences within a country from river basin to river basin. At some times in history, the need of a growing population or the vagaries of nature made it necessary to leave the familiar practices behind. New solutions had to be invented. Outstanding persons, often without a formal scientific education, combined logical thinking with local experience and proposed solutions far advanced for their time. By their diplomacy and persuasiveness, they got their proposals accepted. Some of these projects were successful; in other cases, considerable later adjustments were needed for the works to perform as required. In this way, projects were executed that are landmarks in the history of hydraulic engineering. Some of these classical works in which new technological ground had been broken, involved the taming of large rivers. Others were directed at the reclamation of new land, at irrigation, or at the protection of settlements from floodwaters.

When the need to predict the future behavior of a new project was perceived, one tried to make numerical calculations even where theory was not yet well developed. In other cases water flow was measured, and there are even old examples of small-scale experiments. The mathematical theory of the movement of fluids was derived in the first half of the nineteenth century, and engineers hesitantly started to apply it.

Where, because of local circumstances, several works of a certain kind were executed, specialized knowledge accumulated. A call was issued to the engineers involved to serve as consultants elsewhere, even abroad. Many of the waterworks and sewerage systems in continental Europe were built by British engineers. German engineers were consulted in connection with river-training problems. The accumulated experience of the Dutch with land reclamation and the protection of low-lying areas against the sea was used by many other countries. Reclamation experts from the Netherlands obtained concessions to reclaim land as far away as Russia and France, and Dutch farmers settled on the land that they had previously reclaimed.

INTRODUCTION OF SCIENTIFIC METHODS

The growth of population in virtually all countries called for better use of farmland and required improved flood protection. This resulted in an increase in investments for water resources development. As these funds should be spent in the most effective and efficient way, higher standards were set for design studies and for the execution, operation, and maintenance of the works. There was now a need for scientifically trained staff with a specialization in some aspect of hydraulic engineering. Many civil engineering departments of universities started to take more interest in this field. Eminent professors lectured on the mechanics of fluids and soils, and in some places hydraulic engineering was even taught in separate lecture series. The hydraulics and soil mechanics laboratories became important tools. These efforts had an important impact on practice. Gradually, scientifically based methods replaced the empiricism. Experience and engineering judgment remained essential, however, where available data was insufficient and where there were gaps in theory.

The last forty years have shown an almost tempestuous development. In the beginning of this period, because of the bulk of numbers, numerical calculations in this field were hardly feasible, and one had to make do with coarse approximations. The computer now makes it possible to make a numerical study of even complicated cases. New subjects such as computational hydraulics, water waves, and soil dynamics were rapidly developing. The economic and social dimensions of water resources development became of direct concern to the engineer. Multidisciplinary approaches were introduced. As a result it is no longer possible to deal even with the most important aspects of water resources development in an undergraduate civil engineering curriculum. Any civil engineer should have a firm grasp of applied mechanics and its application to concrete, steel, and timber structures. This already occupies so much time on the student's schedule that not much time is left for hydraulic engineering. A more complete education for the water resources specialist must therefore be deferred to the postgraduate level. Even at the postgraduate level it is not possible to treat fully the various specialized fields of water resources development. The student should work out specific design assignments so that he will gain sufficient self-confidence to work with a certain independence. In most countries the newly graduated engineer was not considered or even allowed to perform tasks of responsibility for some time. He or she was required to work for a number of years under the guidance of an experienced colleague before being recognized as a full member of the profession. For developing countries where there is no long tradition in hydraulic engineering, this system does not work. The experienced engineers who would have supervised their younger colleagues were nonexistent. Many trained engineers had left the country, and the few experienced engineers that were available were needed for higher management and political functions. There was apparently a gap to be bridged.

THE SITUATION IN THE NETHERLANDS

The Netherlands are situated on the delta of three important rivers. The country borders the North Sea opposite Great Britain. The shortest connection by waterway from the most densely inhabited parts of Germany, Switzerland, and eastern France to Great Britain passes through this delta.Therefore, inland navigation is well developed, and there are a few very big ports. Heavy storm winds over the shallow North Sea will at irregular intervals cause storm surges, menacing the coast and estuaries. The western and northern parts of the country have a soft subsoil consisting of peat and marine clays. Because of a coincidence of geologic features and land-use patterns, the major part of the land is below sea level, at some parts more than 6 m. Mastering hydraulic engineering is a necessity for this country. It must be protected against floods from the sea and rivers; its soil must be drained artificially; its rivers must be developed for navigation. The high value of the land makes it worthwhile to reclaim new land from the sea. The planning and execution of major new hydraulic works, together with innovations in the operation and maintenance of existing hydraulics systems, have drawn worldwide attention. There are many deltas in the world where conditions are similar to those in the Netherlands, and the methods developed here can be applied in many other countries. Therefore, a demand for advice and instruction was directed at the Netherlands. International organizations and foreign governments requested that our country receive their trainees for observation periods. In some cases students wished to come for a few days only, in other instances for several months. With the growing international cooperation after the year 1950, the number of these requests increased. These observation periods often did not yield the expected results. The theoretical background required to appreciate the observed solutions was lacking. Our personnel engaged in water resources development activities were in danger of becoming overburdened by the number of visitors from abroad who were often in need of detailed instructions and briefings in a foreign language. As the people of our country feel obliged to share their know-how and experience with others, it became necessary to create a special mechanism for this transfer.

AN INTERNATIONAL COURSE IN HYDRAULIC ENGINEERING

This led to the establishment of the International Course in Hydraulic Engineering, preparations for which began in 1955. The transfer of recent developments in technology in such a way that they can be applied elsewhere is only possible where there is a sound theoretical background. This made it necessary to design the course for participants who had already obtained an engineering degree elsewhere. The course would thus have to be at the postgraduate level. The minimum requirement for admission is a civil engineering degree from a recognized university followed by at least three years of practical experience. The optimal duration of the course has been carefully studied. A program of only a few months duration cannot cover sufficient ground to enable the participants to carry out a responsible technical assignment independently. It would be quite difficult for a practicing engineer, however, to leave a job for more than a year. A course duration of eleven months seems to fit the requirements as well as possible. As the fieldwork must be performed in the open air, the summer period with fair weather should be utilized. Therefore, the course starts in October and ends in September.

Each participant has personal requirements. It is not possible to fit the program perfectly to the needs of every individual. In order to achieve the best fit, however, there are various branches of study from which the student can choose. Today there are six branches: hydraulic engineering in upland areas, hydraulic engineering in lowland areas, land and water development, experimental and computational hydraulics, port engineering, and coastal and offshore engineering. For the first few years, the course content was derived almost entirely from conditions occurring in the Netherlands. After the course was well established, many students came from countries with mountainous areas. At their request parts of the program were reoriented so that subjects like mountain-torrent control and construction of high dams would also be treated. In conformity with the philosophy of the courses, teachers were not recruited from academe but preference was given to engineers engaged in the practice of the profession. When no teacher from the Netherlands was available for a specific course, experts from other countries were invited to lecture.

THE FORMATION OF AN INSTITUTE

The first course, in 1957, was a success. There were forty-four participants, and many of them already occupied important positions in their fields. Although the program was initially intended to meet the needs of developing countries many engineers from industrialized countries attended the program. Before the end of the first year, there were already requests to organize similar courses in other subjects related to the water sciences. As a result, a course in sanitary engineering, organized along the same lines as the hydraulic engineering course, was offered in 1960. Later, other programs followed suit. From the outset, hydrology was an important component of the hydraulic engineering course. After the number of participants in this course had grown to such an extent that it threatened to become unmanageable, the branch in which hydrology was the major subject was removed and developed into a separate course for hydrologists. Its content was developed in line with the findings of the International Hydrological Program. When the demands for sanitary engineering education outgrew available laboratory space, a second sanitary engineering course was organized. After close consultation with the World Health Organization, the program of the first sanitary engineering course was redirected to conditions in urban areas and the second course was focused on improvements of sanitation in rural areas. The increased awareness of environmental problems led to the establishment of an international course in environmental science and technology in 1969. This program was not destined for engineers but for chemists and biologists. The expansion of the scientific staff kept pace with the increase in the number of programs offered. Most staff members also do research or serve as consultants abroad. There was a need for consolidation, however, and for this purpose a new organization was created—the International Institute for Hydraulic and Environmental Engineering (IHE), in the town of Delft.

Some demands for training in water resources development could not be met sufficiently by the existing courses. Governments and international organizations asked for training activities adapted to their specific needs and circumstances. IHE was prepared to organize such courses. Some of them were held at Delft; in some cases, however, shorter programs were offered overseas. There is a growing interest among international organizations to have special training programs organized by IHE in the last few years. (The working language of the Institute is English. On special request, arrangements can be made for activities in other languages.)

COURSE POLICY

The basic objective of the course is the transfer of knowledge and not the preparation for academic degrees. The participants' work was checked and corrected, but no provisions were made for formal examination and the issuing of a certificate at the termination of the studies. In the first year (1957–58) of the course, it had already become clear, however, that the majority of the participants did not agree with this policy. After a year of intensive study they wanted to be able to take home a certificate or a diploma. A system of examinations was therefore improvised so that participants with good results could obtain a diploma. In this situation an important issue is the wide variation in backgrounds of the participants. Some already have upon arrival a sound knowledge of such fundamental subjects as advanced hydraulics, soil mechanics, and theory of constructions; on the other hand some participants have deficiencies in such subjects. Therefore, in the beginning of the academic year an opportunity for intensive instruction in fundamental subjects was offered.

Crossing the oceans for education entails heavy sacrifices for the participants who have responsible jobs at home. A prolonging of their studies in case they achieved less than satisfying results would be highly impractical. Failure for them has much graver consequences than for a regular university student, who may always have the opportunity to repeat a course. Course participants drawn from other cultures need a great deal of adaptation to the different styles of living, weather conditions, and a curriculum differing from what they knew at home. One should not let a person study for eleven months, subject him or her to an examination, and then conclude that the diploma cannot be awarded. It is necessary to evaluate individual results much earlier and to leave opportunities for prompt remedial action. Many examinations and exercises are therefore given in the first semester of the course. This is followed by an evaluation of individual performances at the end of the fourth month of the course. The student will then get advice on further studies. Those who have done well can take a somewhat expanded study program; those with less satisfactory results will have to restrict themselves to the minimum requirements for the diploma; those whose results are unsatisfactory can decide to withdraw early from the program or to continue with a free curriculum not leading to a diploma.

The second semester is used mainly for design work and fieldwork, which should resemble actual practice as closely as possible. Toward the end of the course field trips are made to important hydraulic works in Europe. The program is concluded with an oral final examination in which the content of the entire course is reviewed. Around 80 percent of those who arrive at the beginning of the year will leave with a postgraduate diploma. Although the university system in the Netherlands does not use the expression "master's degree," the IHE diploma is widely recognized as being equivalent to such a degree.

The total number of graduates of IHE courses in water and environmental sciences is now around 4,600. The number of those who took special short-term courses is around 2,100. Although the course was designed to serve developing countries, many participants from industrialized countries enrolled. Regular working relations developed with a number of organizations who regularly sent their engineers to take courses. An example is our relation with the U.S. Army Corps of Engineers, which is interested in programs on coastal engineering and dredging. Several professors from American universities also came; they wished to take the course in order to observe the practice of hydraulic engineering in Europe. The results of the research by the IHE staff in subjects like computational hydraulics drew wide attention. Some Americans come in order to become more familiar with the application of computers to hydraulic engineering.

OUTLOOK FOR THE FUTURE

Many developing countries wish to obtain, in addition to fellowships, financial help to create or strengthen their own institutions. In order to help them, the government of the Netherlands made funds available to institutes of international education for the execution of projects abroad. Also, IHE was given funds for such projects. International organizations gave IHE similar assignments. Within this framework, IHE undertakes manpower studies for water resources on behalf of international organizations or governments. The institute is also engaged in the creation of new institutes or the strengthening of existing ones in developing countries. Examples of such projects that are now under way, include a common hydrological survey for the fourteen English-speaking countries of the Carribean and an institute for postgraduate courses in water sciences at the University of Moratuwa in Sri Lanka. It is expected that IHE and with the government of Indonesia will start a postgraduate institute for water resources toward the end of 1985 at Bandung.

The training of high-level personnel is a key component of any water policy for world food supplies. The experience gained by IHE may convince other institutes to organize similar activities in order to contribute to the welfare of the peoples of the world.

13. OBSERVATIONS FROM THE U.S. DEPARTMENT OF THE INTERIOR EXPERIENCE IN WATER DEVELOPMENT

Herbert H. Fullerton, Utah State University and U.S. Department of the Interior, Washington, D.C., and K. Mitchell Snow, U.S. Department of the Interior, Washington, D.C.

ABSTRACT

The U.S. Department of the Interior (hereafter, Department) has been involved with planning and developing water projects for nearly a century. Almost since the beginnings of the department itself, irrigated agriculture has been central to our water resource program. For those who work for the Department, water policy and food supply are inseparable terms. The objective of this chapter is to provide a selection of observations from the Department's experience in water development. Because constraints and opportunities for water development differ so much from one area to another, these observations are offered as tentative hypotheses to be tested and reformulated in the light of better and more complete information.

There are two interrelated bureas of the Department that are involved in water resources work: the U.S. Geological Survey (Survey), which oversees data collection and water research work, and the Bureau of Reclamation (Reclamation), which is the water development agency. Originally, Reclamation was part of the Survey, but as the program grew it was established as a separate agency.

RECLAMATION'S OBJECTIVE AND SCOPE

Reclamation was originally created to encourage the establishment of family-owned and operated farms on arid land in the sparsely populated western United States. In this respect, Reclamation has clearly been successful. Tens of thousands of family farms now stretch across the seventeen states of the American West. The productive farmlands that were created by Reclamation projects have given rise to growing population centers. Small communities and businesses serving farmers and their families have emerged and grown. Clearly, the benefits of a secure supply of water for agriculture created other opportunities for economic development reaching far beyond the basic issue of food.

An idea of the magnitude of development that has been sponsored by Reclamation in the United States is best conveyed by reviewing a few major project statistics:

- Reclamation has in operation 336 storage reservoirs; 349 diversion dams; 24,865 km of canals; 1,802 km of pipeline; 401 km of tunnels; 56,480 km of laterals; 25,639 km of project drains; 215 pumping plants of more than 1,000 HP each; and 49 hydroelectric powerplants.
- More than 22 million people use Reclamation water.
- In 1981, Reclamation delivered more than 33.5 billion cubic meters (BCM) of water for agricultural use.
- Irrigation service is available to nearly 12 million acres (roughly 4.8 million ha).
- Nearly $7 billion in crops are harvested from lands served by Reclamation water each year. The 55.5 million tons of crop would meet the annual food requirements of 42 million people, nearly the combined populations of the 30 largest cities in the United States. Food processing activities add nearly $4 billion in value after the harvest.
- Estimated flood-control benefits, which are associated with irrigation projects, amount to well over $100 million each year.
- Power plants at Reclamation dams have a total installed capacity of 12.3 million kilowatts (kW) generate nearly 50 billion kWh of electricity annually. The production of an equivalent amount of power would require 85 million barrels of oil or 23 million tons of coal per year.

Currently, Reclamation water irrigates about 3 percent of the nation's croplands, yet the value of the crops harvested from Reclamation lands represents about 10 percent of the nation's crop output. Clearly, there is a close association between success in the Reclamation program and our ability to produce food. Because of a relative abundance of food, less than 15 percent of an average American's income goes toward food supplies. Although much of the food exported from the United States is produced on rainfed farms, our ability to produce more than enough food to meet our own needs provided more than $43 billion in export income in 1981. Agriculture accounts for 20 percent of the total value of our exports.

Since 1902, Reclamation has spent about $11 billion in building and operating its water supply facilities. About one-fifth of that amount has already been repaid by those who receive direct benefits from Reclamation's water development projects. Eventually, almost all of the capital costs of building these projects will be repaid to the U.S. Treasury, in some cases with interest. The investment has been large, but the returns have clearly justified this action.

OBSERVATIONS FROM RECLAMATION'S EXPERIENCE

The International Food Policy Research Institute (IFPRI) estimated that the capital costs of producing the additional food crops to feed the developing world in 1990 would be $98 billion. More than half this investment would be required for irrigation project development. What are the prospects? The cost is high, but the evidence suggests that the potential returns could be greater than those experienced with irrigation in the United States for a number of reasons. First, many of the world's developing countries lie in tropical regions, where both the climate and the soils are well suited to year-round production—if water is controlled. Second, the costs of land and labor for agricultural production in those countries are generally not as great as those in the United States. Third, labor, which is frequently one of the most expensive elements in building a water supply, is available at lower rates than in the United States. Finally, the number of high-yield storage and irrigation sites which may be developed at reasonable cost is more plentiful.

The world has more than enough freshwater to meet both its agricultural and municipal and industrial needs well into the next century. As a planet, we have an estimated 1.36 billion km³ of water that nature is constantly recycling for our use. If we had no mountains, the entire surface of our planet would be covered with water. The problem, then, is not strictly supply. In the United States, as in most countries of the world, the water simply isn't where we need it, in the quality we need it, at the time we need it. The question boils down to the economic issues associated with water development. Water is available virtually any place at any time if we are willing and able to pay the costs.

Our experience in the United States shows that people are willing to pay a wide range of prices for water, depending on the purpose for which the water will be used. Irrigators generally can pay anywhere from $5 to $50 an acre-foot. Water for residential use ranges from $50 to $300 an acre-foot, with the higher end of the scale reflecting the costs of desalting supplies. Industry has been willing to spend several thousand dollars per acre-foot in securing water supplies for developing its products.

Agriculture currently consumes the greatest amount of water in the United States, but the limits on developed supply pose some interesting questions for irrigators and those who would develop water for irrigation. Clearly, municipal and industrial users can afford to pay more than irrigators for a water supply in a market economy. Under these conditions, should irrigation be maintained and expanded at public expense? Should irrigation water supplies be protected from those other economic activities with greater ability to pay? Are the answers to these questions the same in Southeast Asia or in Saudi Arabia as in the United States?

There are still several developing areas in the United States which do not have an adequate supply of water, most of them are in the so-called "Sun Belt," which includes much of the arid Southwest. In the past, major water development projects were planned and built to meet the needs of those states. For a number of reasons, the processes used in the past are changing. Because Reclamation has been so successful in developing water resources, most of the economically attractive sites suited for major dams and reservoirs have already been used. An increasing number of environmental concerns are entering into project planning requirements. The major issue which confronts us, however, is still the increasing cost of water projects.

Whereas increases in water demand were at one time met with new supplies from new projects, today we must also look to conservation and management initiatives to get more water out of existing projects. In some cases, we are also encouraging changes in the way water resources are allocated within a given area. We are now using a combina-

tion of new construction, improved management, and voluntary reallocations to meet increases in water demand.

As a result of the situation just outlined, changes are being made in water use in the United States. The lessons we have learned as these changes have taken place can be of use to countries which are in the beginning stages of water development.

Central to any understanding of the water development process in the United States is the concept of water rights. These rights differ somewhat from the ownership rights to other real property. For example, an individual may own a piece of land and sell or use it with minimal restriction, while water rights typically do not involve actual ownership of water at all. Instead, water rights grant an owner only the right to use water subject to a statutory definition of permissible uses.

The concept of water rights is simple enough in and of itself. There are basically two systems of water law which have developed to meet the needs of different regions within the United States: the riparian and appropriative doctrines of state water law. With the exception of certain federally declared rights which apply throughout the United States for such areas as national parks and Indian reservations, primacy in allocation and control of water rests with the states—not with the federal government. The common purpose of water rights under state law is to provide security of tenure and continued access to a supply of water.

The eastern states have historically had a relatively ample supply of water. In these states, almost exclusively, the riparian principle of water rights is recognized. Riparian rights are tied closely to the land, and the right to use the water is based on ownership of land next to the water source.

In the western states a much more complex system of rights has evolved. Generally, the western states use appropriative rights. Under the appropriative rights system, the first person to put water to beneficial use gains a right to that water in perpetuity. In some states, however, if that right is not used, it may be revoked. Differences exist in the ways which the individual states determine exactly what "beneficial use" means. There are also a number of differences in the laws that permit the transfer of water rights and define the consequence of a sale of right or a change in use. A recent Supreme Court decision declared water to be an article of commerce that could not be restricted in commerce between individuals in different states. This prompted several states to reexamine present transfer policies that might be restraining interstate transactions.

It is also critical to recognize that this system of water law and institutions governing water management and use developed well before there was major federal involvement in irrigation development. Small, private water developments and mutual irrigation companies had been established in one form or another for well over a century before Reclamation was created. Much of our current water law is based on the needs and problems that were identified and resolved on a local level. When the Federal Government did begin developing large projects that sometimes involved water rights administered by more than one state, compacts were required to delineate the various rights to the water such projects would develop. The Colorado River provides a classic example of this approach. Before Hoover Dam could be built, the states had to agree to a division of waters along the Colorado River and Congress had to ratify the agreement. Later court cases have further clarified those water rights.

The concept of water rights provides the security which is needed to carry out water development. Unless an individual, a community, or a bank has the assurance that potential returns from investments made in securing a water supply can be protected, there is no incentive for the private sector to undertake the long-term effort of securing those water supplies.

Providing and protecting a manageable system of water rights is necessary if development work is to be successful. While cultural considerations should be respected in the development of water rights provisions for any country, some viable method for securing continued access to the benefit of individual and communal investment in the development project itself will be necessary. Unless security of tenure is ensured, the costs and responsibility for planning, building, and maintaining water projects will rest with the Treasury and will not produce the desired results.

Where a workable base of property rights in land and water can be established, the developing world offers great potential to meet its food needs through increased irrigation. An irrigated acre of land can produce two to four times the amount of food that an equivalent amount of nonirrigated land can produce. Proper water development can, in fact, mitigate losses in productivity from desertification and erosion by providing alternative sources of food and feed supply.

On the subject of project planning, it is critical to recognize that the assumptions used in North America don't always hold for major infrastructure developments in other parts of the world. There are distinct differences in local cultural traditions, availability of private capital, input and product markets, transport facilities, and management. The sudden need for a large quantity of concrete and steel to complete a large water project, for example, could place a strain on the economy of a developing country if such construction commodities are not readily available. If major construction components such as steel or concrete must be imported, heavy demands are placed on foreign-exchange credits as well.

Because water development has proved to have a leading effect on other areas of the economy, decisions regarding water projects should take the broader infrastructure needs of an area into account. In Malaysia, for example, the incomes of 51,000 farm households nearly doubled in seven years after a large irrigation project was completed. Much of this additional income was spent on local goods and services and other related enterprises. Under such conditions, it is logical that an area will draw population from less developed regions. It is also reasonable to expect that the development of a major water project will result in the need for new roads, schools, and hospitals. Water development

should be understood and initiated as a tool in increasing the effectiveness of other forms of infrastructure development.

THE DEPARTMENT OF THE INTERIOR'S FOREIGN ACTIVITIES

The water programs undertaken by Reclamation and the Survey are not limited to the United States. Currently, representatives from the Department are working in cooperation with more than a dozen countries in addressing their water information and development needs.

In fact, before Reclamation was created, the Survey sent scientists to Egypt and India to study the irrigation systems that had been developed in those countries. Those studies provided a guide for Reclamation's earliest projects. Cooperative assistance programs have been a tradition since that time. Both agencies operate foreign activity programs.

The Survey offers hydrologists for assessments of resource potential, most frequently in support of initiatives of the Department of State, U.S. Agency for International Development, U.S. Office of Foreign Disaster Assistance, and other international development organizations.

The Survey's activities in Saudi Arabia illustrate the kind of expertise that the Department has available. In Saudi Arabia, where there are no perennial streams or lakes, water for agriculture is of prime concern. The Survey began work in Saudi Arabia in January of 1945 as part of a U.S. Agricultural Mission for the purpose of evaluating the irrigation potential of several groundwater sources.

Extensive programs began in 1975 as part of the U.S.–Saudi Arabian Joint Commission on Economic Development. One of the Survey's major efforts has been in the Agriculture and Water Project, in conjunction with the U.S. Department of Agriculture. The Survey provided technical support for establishment of a national water-data bank, development of digital models to maximize output and reduce impacts on water supply, and organization of data network programs.

The Survey has also been involved in a number of food-related water resources investigations in other countries. In Pakistan, the Survey did an extensive evaluation of the surface waters and groundwaters in irrigated areas and prepared a recommendation that tubewells be used to lower the water table, enhance soil drainage, and restore soil fertility. In Paraguay, work was done on a flood forecasting system that was specifically geared to protecting agricultural productivity in the flood plain of the Paraguay River. Tests to determine the suitability of aquifers for agricultural use are under way in Uruguay and Senegal. The project in Senegal is focused on the development of a groundwater computer model which will allow Senegalese hydrologists to design an optimal groundwater withdrawal scheme for crop production. Landsat images are being used in addressing land classification and associated issues in the Sahel region of Africa.

While the work of the Survey is generally centered around gathering the basic hydrologic data necessary for project planning, Reclamation's foreign activities work usually deals with the more specific aspects of project planning, design, and economic evaluation. Reclamation has also been heavily involved in project rehabilitation, dam safety, and desalting and salinity control. Although Reclamation does no actual construction overseas, Reclamation is frequently called on to oversee the contractor's work.

Reclamation recently completed a project in Peru that is typical of the assistance that is available. At the request of the Peruvian Ministry of Agriculture and Food, a detailed technical feasibility review was conducted on eight projects scattered throughout Peru. These projects ranged from the rehabilitation and betterment of existing dams and canals to the opening of new irrigated lands. Because of the variety of projects and the diverse geography and economic conditions of the country, a new set of cost/benefit analyses had to be prepared and applied.

Working with their Peruvian counterparts, a Reclamation review team prepared guidelines relating to specific needs and conditions of that country. Training in economics, hydrology, soil science, and construction engineering was also given by team members while the project was under way.

Reclamation is providing technical assistance for the Fourth Drainage Project in the Faisalabad section of the Punjab province in India. Reclamation will assist with designs for subsurface drainage, supervise construction, and prepare operation and maintenance strategies. At the request of the government of Sudan, a review of the irrigation projects along the Blue and White Nile rivers was recently completed. This review will serve as the basis for a ten-year rehabilitation and modernization program sponsored by the World Bank. Reclamation is also cooperating with the Agency for International Development (AID) in preparing a master plan for land development in Somalia.

Because proper management of a project is just as vital to its success as proper planning and design, many of our overseas programs include on-site training in operations and maintenance. Reclamation also sponsors long-term and short-term programs to provide technical experience and education for engineers and administrators in every phase of water resources development, use, and management.

The training program is headquartered at Reclamation's Engineering and Research Center in Denver, Colorado, where individually tailored instruction is available from the center's staff. Participants can also learn the skills required to build and manage projects through direct field experience at Reclamation projects located throughout the western United States. One- and two-week seminars on specific water development and management areas are also presented periodically. These seminars offer the most current information available in the fields of engineering, project planning, system operations and maintenance, and safety.

However, neither the Survey nor Reclamation receives direct funding to operate their overseas programs. All of the costs of assistance must be reimbursed by the host country or be included as part of a larger package offered by other lending or development agencies. This raises the critical question of finance. As I noted above, water can always be available at any time or place if we are willing and able to pay the price.

A report at the State of the World Conference sponsored by the World Resources Institute last year described the value of water pricing to relieve the water-shortage problems that are encountered throughout the world. A representative from Africa stood up following presentation of that report and said, "We need water. I see the women digging in the sand to grow a few vegetables, and I see the wells too dry to moisten the crops. And I don't hear you tell me how we are going to do it." Possibly we are looking at the wrong projects?

Historically, water development in the United States has been financed by the beneficiaries of water development. Even for irrigation, small, private water development companies had been in existence for decades before the Reclamation program was initiated. Tolls, operations charges, and "sweat equity" were generally used to cover the costs of building and running projects. When the federal government did step in to develop large-scale projects, it came at the invitation of local and state constituencies and it built on the incentive structure and organizational base provided by these private operations. The Reclamation program was developed to provide a revolving fund to finance continuing water development. Originally, the proceeds were to come from the sale of public lands. The proceeds would then be repaid, over time, by the beneficiaries of the projects. Although this concept has been changed and expanded over time, the basic principles of repayment are still maintained in Reclamation law. The people who have requested a project organize as a public district, agree to be taxed if revenue from project activities proves insufficient to meet contract obligations, and make the necessary arrangements to pay their own operations and maintenance costs. This attitude of self-responsibility at the local level has been critical to the productivity, the longevity, and the general success of the Reclamation program.

We recognize that similar opportunities and attitudes do not always exist in other countries, but we believe that fostering strong local support and organization is a necessity if a project is to provide any real benefit. Small, locally oriented projects may actually provide more benefits than large projects that result in artificially imposed management schemes.

Rather than seeking funding for large projects, it might be useful to consider seeking a pool of funds that would be available to smaller projects, similar to the money available through the Reclamation Small Project Loan Program. In this program, initiative rests solely with groups of privately organized farmers outside federal water service areas who wish to expand or improve their facilities. In establishing the Small Project Loan Program nearly thirty years ago, Congress set aside $600 million for small water development projects to be loaned to individual water districts outside federal project boundaries. These districts are responsible for planning and designing the project as well as proposing the manner in which the loan will be repaid. After plans for a project are certified by Reclamation and submitted to Congress, a contract which ensures repayment of the capital lent is drawn up and funds become available to the individual district to proceed with construction. Reclamation assists with construction contract oversight to ensure that a quality project is built. The local water users are then responsible for repayment and operations and maintenance. Again, the concept is one of beneficiary pay, but it does provide for flexibility to meet local needs.

A similar program could help foster local organizational and management skills, as well as provide employment and experience for waterworks engineers. Such a program might also encourage development of projects that are more closely attuned to the resources and the social structure of an individual community. The standards for planning and design, which are centrally administered, ensure that the projects are economically sound and properly engineered.

The United States has been able to provide a number of programs to assist in bringing water to agricultural lands. Much of the success we have experienced can be related to secure water rights and the concept of placing responsibility for operation, maintenance, and energy costs with project beneficiaries. Individuals have the assurances that water supplies they develop or finance are secure for their use.

Once that security is given, they have shown a willingness to invest, to maintain, and to manage the water supplies they need. All this translates into more efficient use of human, natural, and economic resources.

Throughout our history, government and the people have worked together to develop America's water resources. The government provided the security needed to encourage water development, through the granting of water rights and providing assurance that economic gains from water development would continue to accrue to project beneficiaries. Farmers have been free to manage water and land resources to their best individual advantage. This has been a mutually supportive relationship, but we have placed our reliance on private initiative. However, without the assurance that access to developed water can be maintained, there is no incentive for either private investment or efficient management. Without the effective participation of the private sector in the form of investment, management, and markets, we have no guarantees that a project will produce the food supplies or the related development we desire.

14. WATER AND FOOD PRODUCTION IN DEVELOPING NATIONS: ROLE OF WATER SUPPLY

Warren A. Hall and Neil S. Grigg, International School for Water Resources, Colorado State University, Fort Collins, Colorado

INTRODUCTION AND SCOPE OF PROBLEMS

The food production problems in developing nations continue to be with us. For example, in recent months there have been many accounts of severe famine in Africa. Feeding the hundreds of millions in the growing populations of the world will continue to pose a serious challenge. Indeed, we expect the statistics of the food problem to be repeated many times during this conference. The purpose of this chapter is to highlight some of the lessons learned by development specialists at Colorado State University in alleviating these problems, with emphasis on the role of water.

In its most fundamental dimensions, resolving the food production problem is really only a means to achieve a hoped-for end. The resources needed for food production, although possibly renewable and expandable, to some extent are still finite. At the same time populations continue to grow, in some cases as fast or even faster than food production resources can be provided. With the grim shadow of Malthus over our shoulders, we are engaged in a race to prevent far more serious disasters than would have occurred had the food-production problem been ignored. We are desperately trying to buy sufficient time to be able to resolve population-control problems before food production resources are outstripped by that population growth. If we fail in either task, then the number of human beings who will suffer from famine and starvation will be several orders of magnitude greater than that which would have been experienced had no effort been made at all.

The latter course of action was and remains untenable. The challenge has been accepted. The race is on, and it must be won. Significant progress has been made in improving technologies to increase food production. Some progress has also been made in technologies for population control, but the population-control methods proposed have frequently proved to be socially unacceptable in many parts of the world.

Many "explanations" for this social infeasibility have been advanced, from placing the blame on religious tenets to ignorance of the probable consequences, the latter due to unsatisfactory educational opportunities. Some believe it is caused more by the historical role of children in the individual's concern for reliable social security. While not the focus of this conference, nor of this presentation, this problem must be given much more attention.

The food production problem has two basic strategies for its resolution. First, we could increase food production po-

tential through a well-planned program of productivity research. Although clearly the basis for the quantum jump of the past two to three decades, research on agricultural productivity was effectively curtailed some fifteen years ago by those who control budgets because the research was too successful, creating severe problems of local surplus production.

The lead time between initiation of production research and the implementation of the findings is measured in decades (three decades for the Green Revolution *after* all the basic research was done). The long moratorium on production research makes it unlikely that the results from this strategy will appear in time to resolve the problems faced.

This leaves us with the strategy of technical assistance through "technology transfer." Although very remarkable gains from previous research have been made, we are still far from obtaining the full potential implid by that research. Achieving a much greater fraction of that full potential can be considered to be the only effective strategy in sight, and technical assistance-technology transfer apparently represents the most effective means of implementing that strategy. Unique approaches to using field-based "adaptive research" are the approaches favored by Colorado State University (CSU), due to the differences between and among the developing countries.

In this paper we will attempt to describe some of the activities undertaken by Colorado State University that have been directed toward technical assistance and to present some possible conclusions this experience would appear to support.

EXPERIENCE OF COLORADO STATE UNIVERSITY

Colorado State University (CSU) has been heavily involved in international work since the 1950s and has a great deal of institutional experience in providing assistance to development projects, especially those concerned with irrigated agriculture. In this report on the university's experience we must point out in advance that it is impossible to cover all of the international programs and expertise available at the university in a single paper, and with this in mind, what we offer is a combination of fact and considered opinion regarding our accomplishments.

The experience of CSU has been in a number of development sectors. The first comprehensive project was assistance to the University of Peshawar in the mid to late 1950s. Corollary relationships have continued to recent years, and

CSU's influence has been felt in the educational experiences of that university for almost thirty years. In 1958 a program of support for the Southeast Asia Treaty Organization (SEATO) graduate school was begun. This institution is now known as the Asian Institute of Technology. In 1960 CSU studied the feasibility of the Peace Corps concept and delivered a report that was influential in establishing this agency. By the mid-1960s CSU was working on water management projects in Pakistan and had a new project of assistance to the University of Peshawar. By this time it also had established the International School for Water Resources and Associated Programs, designed to supplement regular graduate programs as needed.

By the 1970s the university was firmly entrenched in the international development arena and had a number of efforts under way, financed by different agencies. CSU had a large number of staff serving as individual consultants to agencies as well as overseas projects of its own. Some of the projects of particular note in food production and water development have been those that were aimed at improving irrigation practices in developing countries in most parts of the world. In recent years these have been mostly in Pakistan and Egypt. In addition, the university has been an active participant in the Title XII program of the Department of State and was the first university to sign a Memorandum of Understanding with the Agency for International Development (AID) for enhancing the institutional capability in this area.

There also have been a number of projects that related to food production without direct water management components. For example, there was a university effort to assist Kenya with their veterinary medicine programs and another to assist Nigeria in their agricultural research, both in the 1960s. In recent years there have been projects to assist Gambia with mixed farming and resource management and Lesotho with improved management in the agricultural sector. Although these projects were not primarily directed at water management, they have increased the university's experience in the problems related to food production in other social and physical environments, and thereby improved the capabilities of both individuals and CSU programs to respond to development needs of all kinds.

Several recent activities should be highlighted as having especially enhanced the university's capability and experience in water management for agricultural production. These include the on-farm water management programs in Pakistan and Egypt, the Water Management Synthesis Project (WMS), and the experiences of individual professors working as consultants.

The projects for improving on-farm water management in Pakistan and Egypt have greatly added to the experience of the university and of individuals in solving the real practical problems of water management. This is especially important since so many of the difficulties in water management are at the farm level where the professional expertise necessary to take initiatives and solve problems is often missing. Both of these projects led to findings that have been embodied in the Water Management Synthesis Project, which seeks to transfer some of the findings of the several field projects that have been conducted in on-farm water management abroad. It focuses on the interdisciplinary and systemic nature of the problems inhibiting effective water management.

One result has been the development of a diagnostic analysis course to teach water managers how to identify the complex causes of problems throughout an irrigation system, including the farm level and the supply systems at higher levels. The WMS staff have reported that it is often the tough and nitty-gritty problems of motivation and incentive at all economic and governmental levels that are the major problem elements rather than technical or training problems alone. These can sometimes be helped by better organization or other means that require the interactive participation of farmers, water managers, and extension personnel together.

As individual consultants, CSU professors have been involved literally around the world in practical optimization analyses for water projects, water resources planning problems involving hydraulic structures, river mechanics (with particular reference to sediment transport and deposition), hydrologic data analysis and interpretation, mathematical models of water and groundwater systems, etc., in addition to those involved in the larger CSU projects cited above.

Universities have historically been involved in research, education, and technology transfer, and CSU has been no exception, particularly with respect to the disciplines concerned with the problems of economic develpoment in general and food production in particular. At the present time, students from developing nations constitute a majority of those enrolled in postgraduate programs of study in water resources (planning and management, hydrology, hydraulics, groundwater, and environmental and agricultural engineering) and constitute significant numbers in the water-related areas of study in agronomy, economics, watershed management, political science, and sociology.

Although indispensable for accomplishing a permanent technology transfer, these research-oriented degree programs still leave major education requirements unfulfilled. One of these is a need for intensive "advanced professional education" programs directed toward bringing the professional engineers, economists, and other professionals of a developing country up-to-date in their respective disciplines and/or to complement their own disciplinary knowledge with some of the essential ideas of other disciplines, relevant to water resources and agricultural development in developing nations.

To meet the requirement, CSU established the International School for Water Resources and Associated Programs in 1967. In the intervening years it has attracted from almost all developing nations professionals with educational backgrounds ranging from the Ph.D. to the S.H.K. (School of Hard Knocks). By 1982 it appeared that "associated programs" did not convey an appropriate sense of the range of studies available, and the International School for Agriculture and Resource Development was established, emphasizing the agronomic and economic aspects of development. Most recently, an International School for Natural Resources was created to provide an emphasis on forestry and watershed management. While overlap obviously exists, it is not a serious problem, as the objective is to offer a more complete display of the diversity of professional education programs available at CSU.

The International School for Agriculture and Resource Development (ISARD) has initiated programs in three main areas: training, technical assistance, and action research projects. It operates the Hubert H. Humphrey North-South fellowship program, which has been in operation at CSU since 1980, having begun under the Department of Economics, but now administered by ISARD. The school has several special-purpose courses under way at the present time, including agricultural marketing, farm management, and project analysis. It complements the International School for Water Resources quite well in many programs, such as a special course in irrigation management for Indian trainers that has just been completed.

These programs still have deficiencies. It is difficult for a developing nation to send substantial numbers of key staff to a program abroad for the period of training. To meet this deficiency in part, the International School for Water Resources and ISARD have developed a number of "mobile short courses" which can take specific instructional units to the country. This permits far greater numbers to participate, thus increasing the probability of creating the necessary critical mass necessary to implement new technologies on a permanent basis.

Other nonuniversity education and training requirements remain. These are not addressed as yet by CSU because they are outside the province of university education. This by no means minimizes the importance of these requirements, which must be met if supporting services are to be provided as needed for the process of permanent development.

SOME CONCLUSIONS

In writing about development, it is tempting to try to take on some of the complexities of the overall problem rather than restrict the subject to a specific focus, and the authors are impressed that many of the necessary lessons about land and water management needs are tied up with the larger problems of development. In making our conclusions here, however, we try only to report some of the important lessons that are apparent from the water management work we have surveyed.

Four categories of these lessons seem apparent. The first is that interdisciplinary teams are necessary to diagnose problems and to develop procedures in order to have any hope of success in improving water management. Scond, it is important to have a collaborative approach to problem solving and research. Third, a comprehensive model of the development process is required to identify what the effects of interventions will be on other parts of the system. Finally, the importance of training must continually be stressed.

The use of interdisciplinary teams has become an institution at CSU because of the necessity of understanding the complex technical-social systems that underlie irrigation management. Normally they will have agronomic, engineering, economic, and sociologic components, with the possibility of additional inputs such as special management or other technical skills. The interdisciplinary training courses in diagnostic analysis have been judged to be particularly necessary.

The collaborative approach—recognizing the value of each point of view and contribution—is one of the lessons of development that has really endured. There are some variations on the approach, such as the recommendation from the on-farm water management project in Pakistan that there be not a single counterpart agency but that the collaboration be diffused. Actual recommendations would appear to be somewhat site specific, since the governmental structure as well as the problems addressed differ from place to place.

The need for a model of the development process is consistent with the observations of a longtime CSU development specialist, Maurice Albertson, who has been developing such a model for the village level. The model is called the "development wheel" and recognizes the many social interactions and complexities of the development process. If the potential for increased food production is to be realized, all of these elements must be involved in the technology transfer process with appropriate coordinated levels of attention.

Finally, the need for training is evident everywhere, and this has been one of the principal experiences of CSU. Training is needed from the executive levels down to the individual, and it must be continuous and backed up with the right incentive structures. In many developing countries the main resource is the human resource, and the way to utilize it best is through better education and training.

Within these four categories several basic problems have been encountered with frequencies which suggest that they be given special consideration in programs of technical assistance, particularly those related to food production.

First, there is the problem of motivation. The food production problem involves many of the elements of Garrett Hardin's *Tragedy of the Commons*. In one sense it is no one's problem. In another sense, it is everyone's problem. Implementation of any program requires independent decision making on the part of the farmer, the primary producer. Yet the farmer is seldom the primary beneficiary even though he is commonly asked to accept all the risk involved. For every program designed as an incentive to him, there is at least one other whose effect is counterincentive.

Governments are necessarily structured into mission-oriented agencies, yet, as indicated earlier, all are essential actors for this problem. That does not mean that all are primarily directed to this problem. In many cases, agencies tend to maximize some indication of their "success," which is seldom, if ever, synonymous with the basic objectives. Water agencies like to brag about the number of thousands of cubic kilometers of water provided. Land-reform agencies brag about the number of hectares of land reallocated to the landless. Both are critical contributors to increasing food production, but neither index reflects the necessities for that purpose. There is little or no incentive for agencies to accept lower values of their own performance measure just to help another agency look better.

A common joke concerns the boss who said "We have

been doing it this way for forty years. If there was a better way we would have found it by now!" It is human nature to resist change and to resent criticism. None of us are immune. Even when criticism is valid and change would be a definite improvement, what are the incentives to ensure the criticism will be accepted and/or the changes needed implemented? Whether the action agent is the farmer or the agency sponsoring technical assistance or any unit in between, there appear to be more disincentives to change than incentives. What is even nicer is that in this system one can always blame someone else. Finding a whipping boy to blame for your failures is a time-honored technique used by those responsible for problem solving.

A second basic problem that has surfaced is a continuing need for research. Unfortunately, most officials of agencies involved in technical assistance (givers and receivers) appear to have a strong aversion to that word. Problems are solved using a combination of knowledge and understanding of the nature and interactions of the systems involved plus a goodly amount of "judgment" (alias "guesswork"). The more knowledge and understanding is brought to bear, the greater the probability of success. The more guesswork, the greater the probability that more problems will be created than solved.

Research is nothing more or less than the process of gaining knowledge and understanding. One can spend considerable time and money gaining knowledge and understanding of interesting phenomena that do not appear to be related to the systems or the problems involved. Such research is not required in the technical assistance process.

On the other hand, technology transfer is not a simple process of taking useful technology as implemented in one country and bolting it into place in another, any more than a mechanic can transfer a piston from one make of automobile and bolt it into the engine of another. If the transfer is to be effective, considerable "adaptive research" will be necessary, followed by modifications of either the technology or environment into which it is to be introduced so as to ensure compatibility and proper functioning. This as-

pect must be given appropriate attention (and credit—see incentives) as an integral and essential component of the technology-transfer process.

The last problem is a touchy one. One might call it "preservation of appropriate humility." To alleviate it will require a healthy dose of this characteristic on the part of all concerned, but particularly on those of us who are considered the experts on the technologies to be transferred. We are, of course, expected to be experts on the technology proposed for transfer. We are seldom, if ever, experts on the environment into which the technology is to be transferred. As a rule of thumb, if the "expert" on the technology does not learn far more than he presents, the transfer will be a failure. In fact, most, if not all, failures of technology transfer in the past can be attributed directly to this deficiency.

When a farmer doesn't want to risk his practice to something the expert considers better, there is an outside chance he simply doesn't want to change, but much more likely, there are good reasons, which he understands even if he cannot articulate it in the form of an explanation to the expert. A group of farmers in Peru refused to use (free of charge) water brought to their lands by a government ditch, even though it would obviously increase the productivity of their land by a factor of three or four. Their reason was quite valid. With the higher productivity, their land would be confiscated under land-reform laws. Farmers in many countries were reluctant to use high-yielding varieties. Why? Because they had to rely for water, fertilizer, and other essential inputs on government agencies whose personnel could not care less whether the farmer got the water and fertilizer when he needed it or when it was too late to do any good.

In most technical assistance situations those involved as the recipients of assistance are just as much experts, if not more so, than those who are expected to provide the assistance. Any individual, any discipline, any organization or other entity involved that does not understand this fact and does not reflect it in their conduct will place a thousand artificial obstacles in their path, making it difficult if not impossible, to accomplish the objectives.

15. WATER: CRITICAL AND EVASIVE RESOURCE ON SEMIARID LANDS

Gerald W. Thomas, New Mexico State University, Las Cruces, New Mexico

SUMMARY

Over the long term, water will be a more critical resource for food production than either land or energy. There are ample sources of renewable energy in our ecosystem *if* we can capture it and make it available to mankind in a usable and economical form. As new technology develops and crop and livestock yields increase, the amount of land needed per person decreases, leaving some flexibility in this basic resource. However, water, as a renewable but limited resource, is becoming more critical with time, particularly because of our dependence on irrigated agriculture.

An examination of the "desertification" issue as an international concern indicates the necessity for separating geologic and climatic trends from the impact of man. Nevertheless, mankind is the "great accelerator of change" on vast areas of arid and semiarid lands. Proper range management and conservation cropping are essential to the reduction of desert encroachment.

The pressure to import water into areas of deficiency will continue in the arid zones. However, importation schemes for surface water in the United States have been virtually halted because of economic and environmental considerations. On the other hand, a more subtle development is occurring—the transfer of water from underground aquifers. Data indicate that virtually all of these aquifers are being depleted with little planning beyond a forty-year time frame.

To an increasing extent, water is becoming the subject of litigation. There are now more than 150 Supreme Court decisions relating to water issues. The food sector can lose water through the courts as well as through the evaporation/transportation stream.

There are many opportunities for improvement in the efficiency of water for food production. Conservation offers the most immediate, and in most cases, the most economical hope for improving the productivity per unit of water. However, an accelerated research effort is a high priority. More emphasis should be placed on "systems research" to point to the most appropriate ways to tap the complicated hydrologic cycle for food production and economic development.

INTRODUCTION

It is an honor to be invited to address this International Conference on Food and Water at Texas A&M University. I am particularly pleased to be back on the campus where I received graduate training and where I launched my professional career in teaching and research. I remember that on this campus over thirty years ago, Dr. Rex Johnston, under the direction of Chancellor Gibb Gilchrist and Dr. R. D. Lewis, developed the first statewide water budget for Texas. The results were startling when we estimated the waste and dissipation of water in our system. These first calculations were admittedly very rough, perhaps accurate only to several hundred thousand acre-feet (or several hundred million cubic meters). Nevertheless, Chancellor Gilchrist, with his engineering background, asked Dr. Johnston, as I remember it, to publish the figures to the nearest acre-foot because, "No one will believe the data unless you show the figures to the nearest decimal point."

Chancellor Gibb Gilchrist demanded accuracy. But we all know how difficult it is to define precisely the complicated pathways of water as it moves through the hydrologic cycle and leaves in its wake the variable environment and the multiplicity of living organisms that inhabit this wonderful planet.

I have had a long and continued interest in water. When I was a young boy living on a farm on Medicine Lodge Creek in Idaho, I remember the fights over the limited water supply in the stream. The lack of water on our old farm in Idaho served as one good reason for me to join the Navy during World War II. For nearly four years, I saw plenty of water as I served on three aircraft carriers in the North Atlantic and South Pacific—frequently seasick. I was forced to ditch my plane in the South China Sea which gave me another perspective on water. But while saltwater was abundant in every direction, I well remember the orders to conserve freshwater on board the U.S.S. Essex and the limitations in the showers and mess hall. "Water, water everywhere, but not a drop to drink." Even now, good economical techniques for saltwater conversion are not within our grasp.

After World War II I left the farm, but two of my brothers tried to salvage the old home place by digging a well for supplemental irrigation. My older brother cut a limb from an apple tree in our yard and "waterwitched" the first hole. It turned out dry so he moved closer to the creek. A second well did hit water, but the cost and erratic supply never made an economic operation. The old home place was later abandoned.

There is something both nostalgic and sad about an abandoned, formerly irrigated farm gone to weeds. My story has been repeated in many areas of the west. A *Newsweek* report called this "The Browning of America," stating that ". . . the water wars have erupted once again. . ." (*Newsweek*, 1981).

My early work with the Soil Conservation Service in Idaho from 1946 to 1950 was aimed at developing one of the first systems for contour irrigation of potatoes in the United States. At Texas A&M, my interest in water was heightened by research on the dry rangelands of the Edwards Plateau of Texas. As I moved into the dean's position at Texas Tech University, my interests shifted from specific concerns about water conservation and range management to the larger issue of world food production. It became increasingly clear from these later studies that water was a limiting factor in food production and water use was critical to world food supplies. Also, since the economy of the High Plains of Texas is sustained from water stored in the Ogallala formation, the wise use of this depletable underground resource was of utmost importance to our future. Consequently, I helped organize the West Texas Water Institute at Texas Tech and argued for a share of the Water Research funds through the Department of Interior. Later, we formed Water, Inc. as a means of organizing support for possible water importation into the High Plains of Texas and eastern New Mexico.

When I accepted the presidency of New Mexico State University in 1970, I found in place one of the strongest water resources research institutes in the nation and a faculty and staff dedicated to solving problems on arid and semiarid lands.

With that historical background, I now want to develop my remarks around five topics relating to food production on arid lands: (1) water as the most critical resource, (2) the evasive nature of the water resource, (3) a perspective on the "desertification" issue, (4) social and ecological implications of water importation into arid lands, and (5) the conservation and research imperative.

WATER: OUR MOST CRITICAL RESOURCE

How important is water, as a resource, in comparison with other basic resources, such as land and energy? It is my belief that for the next two, perhaps three decades, energy (its cost and availability) will remain the most critical factor in food production and economic development both at home and abroad. But energy is different from the other resources in that there is an adequate supply of energy in our system, if we can capture it and make it available to people in a usable and economical form. Some of the new research on energy alternatives looks promising, particularly the developments in solar, geothermal, and bioconversion. If we can gear up our research effort, which should be multiplied by a factor of 10, we can find solutions to the energy problems and design systems for food production and industrial development based on renewable rather than depletable energy supplies.

The second important resource, then, is land. While I am concerned about land, and particularly about the rapid transfer of good cropland to other purposes such as buildings, asphalt, and concrete, I believe that land will not become limiting in the United States and many other countries for many years into the future. At the present time, we are losing well over 3 million acres (1.2 million ha) of agricultural land in the United States each year to other pur-

poses. The recently released National Agricultural Lands Study (National Association of Conservation District, 1980) points to this loss in America's agricultural land base. Dr. David McClintock, in a technical paper supporting the National Agricultural Lands Study, stated it this way:

> International relations in the 1980's and 1990's are likely to be influenced by resource scarcities to a considerably greater extent than in the past. These, rather than conventional rivalries, will pose increasing dangers to global security. . . . American cropland must be perceived as a global as well as a national resource (McClintock, 1981).

The loss of cropland is a problem not only in the United States, but also worldwide; it is a phenomenon associated with industrial development and population growth. Society must become more concerned about this loss of land to irreversible transfers and to erosion. Nevertheless, as new technology develops and crop yields increase, the amount of land required to sustain each person will decrease. The world still has some flexibility in the land resource.

That means, then, that water is more critical in the long term than either land or energy. We can, and must, find solutions to the energy problem; we can, and will, determine ways to operate with a smaller relative land base; but the amount of water in our system is fixed. There is no substitute for water. Water is a renewable resource. Man uses it as it moves through the hydrologic cycle, usually pollutes it to a certain extent, and feeds it back into the system. While we can reduce the dependence on water by increasing the efficiency of water use, there is a very limited supply which must be husbanded with great care as the world population increases.

A few years ago scientists were talking about the great potential for food production in the higher rainfall zones of the tropics. Much of this optimism has disappeared as we have learned more and more about the sensitivity of the tropics and the difficulty in producing food under extremely high rainfall situations. The arid and semiarid lands—the vast moderate- to low-rainfall areas—will remain the major regions for world food production.

Irrigated agriculture is becoming much more important with time, as the world's growing population increases the demand for food and fiber. The recent growth in irrigated land has been not only in the traditional irrigated areas but also in the moderate- to high-rainfall zones as a risk-reducing factor. For example, in the United States, Nebraska has become the fifth most irrigated state in the nation. Also, irrigation is becoming more important in the less developed areas of the world—perhaps the major hope for many of these poor countries.

On a global basis, the major increase in total food output in recent years has been associated with expanding the area under cultivation—particularly the irrigated sector. Roughly 40 percent of all increases in developing country food production in the last two decades has come from expanded irrigation (McNamara, 1980). Since 1950, the irrigated acreage worldwide has increased from 94 million to 261 million ha (Postel, 1984). Approximately a third of the total world food harvest now comes from the 17 percent of the cropland that is irrigated. The trends toward more irrigated cropland will likely continue in spite of the increased energy costs, the problems of underground depletion, and serious problems of salinity and other forms of pollution.

THE EVASIVE NATURE OF THE WATER RESOURCE

The evasive nature of water as a resource is emphasized by the highly variable patterns of precipitation (in time and space) and the complicated pathways of water as it passes through the hydrologic cycle—from ocean to land and back to the ocean. While water is, in a very real sense, a renewable resource, the use of this water as it moves through the cycle is the basis for life itself.

Water can be transferred in *space* from so-called surplus areas to water-short regions by water diversions or interbasin construction facilities, or, to some extent, by weather modification techniques. Water can be transferred in *time* by constructing storage facilities along streams or by variable withdrawals and variable recharge of underground aquifers. Desalinization can also be considered as a technique for transferring water in time. As our standard of living rises so does our per capita use of water for domestic, industrial, and agriculture purpose. An individual needs only about 2L daily for drinking, but water use rises rapidly with the level of income. My study in Sub-Saharan Africa indicated that the average water consumption from wells was 10 to 15 L per person per day for home use, about 20 L for cattle and about three 3 L for sheep and goats. In the United States, our home use is about 681 L (180 gallons) for personal use. However, to sustain our present lifestyle for industrial purposes, the average American uses over 2,500 gallons (9,463 L) per day (Council on Environmental Quality, 1980).

Our largest per capita water requirement is for food. For example, we spend about a metric ton of water to produce a pound of bread, and on some of our southwestern rangelands more than 100 tons of water are used to produce a pound of beef (Thomas, 1977). Much of the water associated with the production of meat is dissipated by undesirable weeds and brush or evaporates from the unprotected soil surface. Such statistics provide a convincing argument for better water management in the food sector. "It is time to assemble better data on such water use and to design systems for food production which value water with the concern of the desert Nomad" (Thomas, 1980).

Agriculture cannot compete for water against municipalities, business, and industry. These other uses can afford to pay more for water and will continue to purchase water rights away from the food sector. We see this transfer every year in New Mexico and in other agricultural states, and this moves land out of food production just as surely and as effectively as direct transfer to housing or highway construction. Dawson states that water is a marketable quantity and "*water flows uphill to money.*" Dawson further stated that "short-run economic returns will continually guide the resource allocation decisions. . . . therefore, agriculture will be the residual economic user of water" (Dawson, 1981).

From a world perspective, it is not possible to separate the water resource from climate, since evaporation, transpiration, and precipitation are a part of the climate complex. Decisions made in this decade about our energy options will have a profound effect on future climate and water supplies. There is increasing evidence that coal, if used in large quantities, may be our most hazardous future fuel option from the environmental standpoint. A gradual warming of the climate will increase drought and water shortages in the United States and most semiarid parts of the globe. To me, an ecologist, this problem of climatic change is further reason for increasing our research on non-fossil-fuel energy options, particularly solar, geothermal, wind, and bioconversion. Even the nuclear option may be preferable to massive uses of coal. There is no doubt that our water future and our energy future are inseparably intertwined.

To an increasing extent, water is becoming the subject of litigation. I purposely list litigation under the subtitle "The Evasive Nature of the Water Resource" because the food sector can lose water through the courts as well as through the evaporation stream. There are now more than 160 Supreme Court decisions relating to water issues. Steve Reynolds, the state engineer for New Mexico, stated that a Supreme Court justice told him recently that because of his association with water, he was the most "litigious S.O.B." in the history of the state. There have been about sixty Supreme Court opinions involving the New Mexico state engineer alone in the last twenty-five years. The El Paso challenge to New Mexico's underground water, which I will mention later, will now be added to the list. Personally, I am very leery about decisions involving water that have been relegated to the courts, but this trend will continue.

A PERSPECTIVE ON THE DESERTIFICATION ISSUE

"Desertification is probably the greatest single environmental threat to the future well being of the earth" (Thatcher, 1979). This quotation is from P. S. Thatcher, deputy director of the United Nations Environmental Program. In my opinion, this is an overstatement, particularly when one considers the recently identified concern about climatic change from increased carbon dioxide levels in the upper atmosphere or the depletion of the ozone from chlorofluorocarbons (Sagan, 1985). To put the desertification problem in world perspective, it appears more likely that the activities of highly developed countries, with their large appetites for fossil fuels and other resources, along with their sophisticated technologies, pose more of a potential threat to the world's environment than the poor people in the underdeveloped world who unknowingly are contributing to the progress of the deserts. However, there is ample cause for concern on both fronts.

In most of the recent literature, humankind has been uniformly condemned for the "advance of the deserts" (Sabadell, 1982). While the opinions of the experts vary, the geological and ecological evidence indicates that there is an element of the desertification movement in Africa and the American southwest that is geologic, that is, associated with natural climatic fluctutations or long-term climatic change (Thomas, 1983). Also, the effects of "normal" periodic drought can be very pronounced on soils and vegetation even under complete protection from domestic livestock or farming operations. For example, the occurrence of drought at the time of an explosion in certain insect populations could be just as devastating as drought combined with overgrazing.

In the African study entitled, "Profile of a Fragile Environment," I cited more than sixty references and interviewed more than forty scientists working in Sub-Saharan Africa (Thomas, 1980). I will quote only two references which illustrate differences of opinion on this subject:

> The Sahara became dry in the course of the Neolithic age. . . . There has been continued degradation for about 500 years, which must be attributed to rainfall, therefore, in the first place to climatic causes (Kaki, 1977).
> The main cause of desertification is the interaction between man and a fragile environment in dryland ecosystems: man is the initiator and the victim of desertification (Tolba, 1978).

I also found in the literature a most interesting observation made by Napoleon Bonaparte in the year 1799. This statement is still appropriate in 1985: "Under a good administration, the Nile gains on the desert; under a bad one, the desert gains on the Nile."

These quotes from the African study are not too different from those found in the literature on the American Southwest. Recent research on the Chihuahuan, Sonoran, and Mohave deserts in the United States has produced a number of new reports since the 1977 Nairobi conference on desertification. I will cite only a few of these as they relate to the question of natural vs. man-caused desertification, starting first with some geologists and soil scientists. I should point out here that geologists are usually hesitant to talk about time spans of less than 10,000 years. The discussions of change within the last few centuries have been left largely to the biologists and ecologists.

The geologic evidence indicates that there was a marked change in climate about 10,000 years ago. Since that time the change has been more gradual, but we may still be in a warming trend—difficult to measure in only a few centuries. If we add to this the increasing evidence of warming due to the increased levels of carbon dioxide in the upper atmosphere, the climatic factor will continue to have a background effect on the desertification process. To identify and isolate the climatic variable is difficult but very important to our understanding and management of desert and semidesert ecosystems.

A few citations on climatic change in the American Southwest are appropriate to this discussion since most of these also contain a comprehensive review of literature to support the generalizations:

> . . . radiocarbon-dated pack rat middens document woodland communities in the deserts of the southwestern United States less than 10,000 years ago. A synchronous change from woodland to desert or grassland occurred about 8,000 years ago in the Chihuahuan, Sonoran, and Mohave Deserts (Van Devender, 1977).

> —The transition from glacial conditions was not complete until 7,000–8,000 B.P. (Before Present). Since that time, long-term (100 years or more) mean annual precipitation has varied by less than 40 percent in most desert regions (Earl, 1983).

The Sonoran and Chihuahuan deserts of the American Southwest are probably a million years old as deserts, and yet they have become perceptibly more barren during the past 100 years (Sheridan, 1981).

Given that there have been, and perhaps continue to be, changes associated with long-term climatic trends, there is still a question as to whether or not vegetation has come into equilibrium with the present climate. In other words, under a fixed desert-type climate, with immature soil development, is natural plant succession continuing toward a more xeric composition? Is the erratic nature of the desert climate, with periodic severe droughts and more years below normal than above, still causing vegetation change regardless of man's influence? These questions remain unanswered to my satisfaction.

Some of the most comprehensive studies of vegetation change on semidesert range lands have been conducted in Arizona, New Mexico, and Texas. Access to territorial survey records dating back to 1858 has been valuable for reference vegetation studies. The Jornado Experimental Range, in the Chihuahuan Desert, initiated range research in 1935. Also near Ozona and Sonora, Texas, some vegetation transects were laid out in the 1930s as a basis for comprehensive range management research.

In evaluating these vegetation studies, it is important to recognize that domesticated livestock were introduced into the southwestern United States in the sixteenth century. Many areas were subjected to extremely high rates of stocking by horses, sheep, and cattle from about 1840 to the 1930s. In many cases, these rates were 5 to 10 times the recommended carrying capacity used by today's range scientists. With the removal of public lands from open grazing by the Taylor Grazing Act in 1934 and, with the interest in soil conservation, which peaked during the dust bowl period, stocking rates were reduced and initial approaches were taken to sustained grazing management.

Although it is impossible, after the fact, to isolate the effects of the period of extreme overgrazing with the more recent moderate rates of stocking, it is my belief that the earlier pressure by livestock, combined with drought and other factors, created environmental instability and accelerated the desertification process.

In the 1940s, range management emerged as a science—a hybrid combination of animal husbandry, agronomy, botany, and basic ecology. Through education and technical assistance programs, most U.S. ranchers have became aware of the importance of proper range conservation. According to Soil Conservation Service estimates, the percentage of private range in "good" to "excellent" condition increased from 17 to 40 percent between 1963 and 1977 and this trend is continuing (Harris, 1980). Similar changes have been reported on most federal lands—although improvement in the more arid lands has been very slow and difficult to document, and obviously, some areas are continuing to retrogress—even under moderate stocking rates. *Overall, the western range in the United States has improved markedly since the 1930s.* These changes were well documented at the 1984 National Conference celebrating the fiftieth anniversary of the Taylor Grazing Act (Heady, 1984).

Good range management is good water management. The focus on both is the maintenance and manipulation of the vegetation cover on the land. Therefore, management directed toward quality vegetation is the key to both livestock productivity and environmental stability.

The value of sound range management should be obvious, but I must tell you that range conservation is difficult to sell to both the U.S. ranching community and Third World countries—primarily because overgrazing sometimes yields short-term economic gains, while the payout for many range conservation practices cannot be realized in less than a decade.

I can predict, with some certainty, that in Sub-Saharan Africa as this drought cycle ends, both the developing nations and the donor nations will slip into the traditional pattern of measuring progress by the rapidity with which livestock numbers (and people) can be "added back" to the drought-stricken areas, rather than face the politically sensitive issue of rebuilding the area according to the sustainable carrying capacity of the land. In the African Sahel, as well as other arid lands, periodic drought is normal and must be considered as a part of the environmental complex. Yet, we continue to be surprised when a drought occurs.

One technique that I found useful for selling water conservation in Texas was to try to convince ranchers that overgrazing was reducing the amount of water available for plant growth and that, if they continued to mismanage the resource, they were effectively, "moving the ranch toward El Paso—the driest part of the state." I have seen livestock operations in an 800'mm rainfall zone mismanaged to the extent that they were operating in the equivalent of the 200-mm zone.

In spite of the influence of climate, the activities of civilized man have accelerated the desertification process. In the Sahelian/Sudanian zones of Africa, four major activities of man leading to desert encroachment were identified. These are: (1) cultivation of marginal and submarginal lands, (2) overgrazing or mismanagement of livestock, (3) overharvesting of brush and tree species for wood, and (4) irresponsible or haphazard buring of vegetation. Notice that I purposely used the terms *over*grazing, *over*harvesting, *irresponsible* burning, and *submarginal* lands. This again reinforces my assumptions that, by proper management, man can operate in arid and semiarid lands without contributing to desert encroachment.

SOME ECOLOGICAL IMPLICATIONS OF WATER IMPORTATIONS INTO ARID LANDS

In the book *Arid Lands in Perspective,* published in 1969, Dr. Thadis Box and I developed a chapter on the social and ecological implications of water importation into arid and semiarid lands. The conclusion we drew from our research in 1969 are significantly different from the conclusions that I will now make nearly twenty years later. We stated at that time that "large-scale water movement to the arid zones appears to be inevitable." We cited several reasons for this generalization: (1) Large-scale water transfer projects are technologically possible; (2) many water transfer projects are economically feasible, particularly if adequate consideration is given to the "multiplier" effects on the economy and the added value of water-based recreation; (3) water movement into the arid zones may be necessary for society to grow and survive. Here, we cited the growing demand for food and technology development as population increases; (4) political pressures will be brought to bear to move water to arid and semiarid lands. For example, we stated that some areas, such as the Texas High Plains, were at the height of economic development, and the aquifer depletion would have to be answered with some form of water augmentation.

Obviously, these predictions were wrong. Three very significant developments since 1969 have forced a reevaluation of interbasin, interstate, or intercountry water-transfer projects.

First, the energy crisis and other economic developments made most of the plans unrealistic. Second, the environmental movement went much faster and much further than we expected. Not only can one endangered species slow or stop a project, but a small minority of people can override the wishes of the majority. And, third, our political structure has changed. The 3 percent of our population in agriculture has lost political clout. Politicians from the water-short areas of the United States cannot get the automatic support they need for expensive and "long-term-payout" water projects.

However, while Box and I were wrong in the predictions that large-scale water projects were inevitable, we were right about the social and ecological implications of these types of water transfers. Additional data are now available on the effects of water impoundment and diversion on the distribution of aquatic populations, on terrestrial plant and animal communities, on humans and our living environment. There *is* evidence of significant change in certain ecosystems as water projects are developed. There *is* evidence of loss of habitat for certain biota. There is also evidence of changes in the local environment that call for new approaches to wildlife and plant management. Ecological understanding may indeed override political, social and economic considerations for water transfer projects.

In the past two decades, surface water transfer schemes in the United States have virtually come to a screeching halt. In today's environment, California could not have constructed the largest water movement scheme in our history. The Central Arizona Project would be difficult if not impossible to sell to Congress. We have stopped talking about the multibillion-dollar NAWAPA concept involving Canada, Mexico, and thirty-three states. We have almost forgotten about CNAWP—the Central North American Water Project—and several other schemes to move water into the

Great Plains and the southwest through the "Rocky Mountain Trench."

I should point out, however, that the people benefiting either directly or indirectly from the rapidly depleting Ogallala Aquifer have not given up on some water augmentation plans. One of the major objectives of the High Plains study was to examine various plans to import water into the area. The U.S. Army Corps of Engineers conducted this part of the study and reported on several possible transfer projects to bring water from the tributaries of the Missouri and Arkansas rivers (High Plains Study Council, 1982). The costs of the projects were out of reach for most agricultural purposes. But even if the water transfers had been economically feasible, environmental concerns would become an awesome hurdle. Add to this the firm belief by many people that there is no "surplus" water in these rivers if adequate consideration is given to the freshwater inflow requirements at the ocean estuaries.

> The zone of interplay between the margins of the sea and the land is the environment for a remarkable assemblage of terrestrial and aquatic life. . . . Fish (and fowl) that divide their lives between freshwater and salt . . . pause for a sojourn between coastal waters and upstream souces (Carn, 1966).

In spite of the slowdown of U.S. water projects, a status report by Postel (1984) in a *Worldwatch* paper shows the following data on selected major world river diversion programs:

1. The decision to begin construction on the North China Plan for the Chang Jiang River to divert 15.0 km³ per year was made in 1983.

2. Construction of the Caspian Sea Soviet Union project to divert 20.0 km³ per year is scheduled to start in 1986.

3. Engineering designs have been completed on the Central Asia Soviet Union project for the Siberian rivers, involving 25 km³ per year.

Major projects planned for South America, Africa, and Australia are in a holding pattern and will probably not receive serious consideration until an abundant, cheap source of energy becomes available.

MINING UNDERGROUND AQUIFERS IN ARID LANDS

A significant fraction of the world's irrigated agriculture is based on the development of underground water sources. Most, if not all, of these aquifers are being depleted—mined just as surely as we mine copper and silver. In the United States, the best known of these depletable aquifers is probably the Ogallala, which underlies parts of the states of Nebraska, Kansas, Colorado, Oklahoma, New Mexico, and Texas. For our purposes today, I will mention only that the Ogallala supplies water for approximately 14.3 million acres (5.8 million ha) and is tapped by more than 150,000 irrigation wells (Barh, 1984). Nearly half of the available water has already been utilized, and the recharge rates are only a fraction of the annual withdrawals.

But, while many people know about the Ogallala depletion problem, few realize that most other underground aquifers are also being depleted. I am on a statewide water study committee in New Mexico. We have looked at the statistics on every underground basin in the state. Although the data are admittedly incomplete, several observations can be made about these studies:

1. If we continue the present rates of withdrawals in New Mexico, some declared basins will be exhausted in thirty to fifty years while others may last seventy-five or more years. "Economic" exhaustion will be reached long before total depletion occurs.

2. After an underground water basin has been declared "closed" by the state engineer, depletion can continue. The commonly used forty-year time frame for future planning should be extended to protect the coming generations for at least one hundred to two hundred years.

3. Most underground aquifers have a direct, or at least indirect, relationship with surface water even though part of the water may be identified as "fossil" water stored over many centuries in the past.

4. There is a need to clarify the term "unappropriated water." There is no "unappropriated" water in New Mexico—if one considers the well-being of future generations. Therefore, no interbasin or interstate transfers should be considered except under extreme circumstances.

I make these observations about underground aquifers in the midst of a legal controversy involving the state of New Mexico and the city of El Paso, Texas. This case illustrates several of the points I have tried to make in this paper about the competition for water in arid lands and the evasive nature of the resource. Since I am now a confirmed New Mexican, my comments on the El Paso water suit will obviously carry the bias illustrated by a former territorial governor when he made this statement about our state: "New Mexico is so far from Heaven and so close to Texas." Many bumper stickers in our state now carry the slogan, "Thou shalt not covet thy neighbor's water."

The basis for this concern dates back to September 5, 1980, when the El Paso Public Service Board filed suit in federal district court seeking to overturn a New Mexico law that prohibited anyone from drilling a well in New Mexico and transporting the water for use in another state. The thrust of El Paso's argument was that the New Mexico statute was unconstitutional because it represented an impermissible burden on interstate commerce.

The New Mexico state engineer, caught by surprise and concerned about a surge in speculative drilling as a result of the lawsuit, immediately declared the Lower Rio Grande underground water basin and the Hueco underground water basins as "closed basins"—with further drilling under the control of the state engineer. El Paso then filed for 326 well permits in the two basins seeking to be "first in line" over any further New Mexico or Texas permits. The irony of this situation is that New Mexico historically has had fairly good water laws with some protection for prior users, whereas in Texas the landowner also owns the water under the land and the state has limited control over allocations.

From the 326 well permits, El Paso is proposing to produce 290,000 acre-feet of water (0.3575 km³). This is

100,000 acre-feet more than the current consumptive use within the entire Elephant Butte Irrigation District (Bahr, 1984).

About two years after El Paso filed suit to challenge the New Mexico Water Export Law, the court held that groundwater is an article of commerce and as such the state boundary could not be used to stop the movement of water. In addition, a year later, Judge Bratton ruled that the Rio Grande Compact is not relevant to the case. This later ruling came in spite of the belief by many hydrologists that there is a relationship between the "Rio Grande Underground Basin" and the surface flow controlled by the Rio Grande Compact, which involves three states and two countries.

In the meantime, the state engineer has been ordered to process the El Paso permits, Fort Bliss has also filed for water, and New Mexico has again revised its water laws. We are back on the courthouse steps, illustrating again that water is an important, but "evasive" resource. According to one of our state leaders who has a unique way with our language, the city of El Paso has, through the filing of this lawsuit, "opened up a box of Pandoras."

THE CONSERVATION AND RESEARCH IMPERATIVE

This overview of the water problems on arid and semi-arid lands points to the need for two action programs—conservation and research. Immediate attention must be given to both.

Conservation offers the best short-term opportunity and in most cases, the most economical hope for increasing the efficiency of water use in the food sector. Conservation practices can extend the life of our valuable underground aquifers and offer the equivalent in water savings of many multimillion-dollar water importation schemes. Water conservation practices on rangelands can slow the desertification process and increase productivity. With a 10 to 15 percent savings in the agricultural sector enough water could be released for most of the expanded needs created by industrial and municipal development in the western United States.

I was pleased to see that the new Texas water plan, released in June, 1984, defined specific action plans for municipal and commercial water conservation, as well as recommendations for industry and agriculture. This new plan, with much more accuracy than the first one we developed under Chancellor Gilchrist, projected savings in the agricultural sector through conservation practices alone, of over 1,450,000 acre-feet (178,784 km^3) water annually.

An accelerated research effort should parallel the conservation thrust on semiarid lands. We must learn to measure everything we do in units of water and become more conscious of water in all aspects of our daily life. Unfortunately, too much of our research is not designed with water as a constraint. If we ask ourselves the right questions and design our research properly, we can increase the efficiency of water use in all aspects of food production, processing, and distribution. Research must provide the answers and the alternatives.

Research on photosynthesis shows great potential to capture more energy from the sun. Research can point to more effective ways to increase the efficiency of water in a soil medium. More emphasis must be placed on plant breeding and genetic engineering using water as the prime measurement unit. Some of our research already indicates that by selecting plants for various water regimes, we can increase the production potential in excess of 200 percent.

Finally, it is imperative that we design sophisticated "systems research" programs to examine the total hydrologic cycle, including climatic variables. Only then can we see the best opportunities for increasing the efficiency of water use. Only then can we best determine how and when to tap this solar-powered water cycle for man's welfare. Only when we better understand the total system can we determine the impact of our individual and sometimes contradictory tamperings with the natural order. More than forty years ago, the astute ecologist Aldo Leopold stated it well: "Thus, men too wise to tolerate hasty tinkering with our political constitution accept without a qualm the most radical amendment to our biotic constitution" (Leopold, 1941).

REFERENCES

Bahr, Thomas G. 1984. Legal, hydrological, and environmental issues surrounding the El Paso water suit. *In* Water law in the West, Proceedings of the 29th annual New Mexico water conference.

The browning of America. 1981. *Newsweek,* February 23.

Carn, Stanley A. 1966. Coordination of fish and wildlife values with water resource development goals. *In* Proceedings of the second annual American water resources conference. Chicago: University of Chicago.

Council on Environmental Quality and the Department of State. 1980. The global 2000 report to the president. Washington, D.C.: U.S. Government Printing Office.

Dawson, George R. 1981. Water for agriculture is a competitive environment. *In* Proceedings of the 26th annual New Mexico conference, New Mexico State University Water Resources Research Institute Report No. 134.

Earl, Richard A. 1983. Correspondence on climatic change. New Mexico State University, April 15.

Harris, Robert. 1980. State of the range resources. *In* Proceedings of the national conference on renewable natural resources. Washington, D.C.: AFA.

Heady, Harold F. 1984. Range management from 1934 to 1984. *In* Proceedings of the national celebration of the fiftieth anniversary of the Taylor Grazing Act.

High Plains Study Council. 1982. A summary of the results of the Ogallala aquifer regional study. August 12.

Kaki, Ibrahima Baba. 1977. Where are the rains of yesteryear? *In* CERES FAO Review of Agriculture and Development. March–April.

Leopold, Aldo. 1941. Lakes in relation to terrestrial life patterns. Prepared for a symposium on hydrobiology. Madison: University of Wisconsin Press.

McClintock, David. 1981. The global importance of American cropland availability. National Agricultural Lands Study paper no. 12.

McNamara, Robert S. 1980. Food as a determinant of world development. Congressional roundtable, March 4. Washington, D.C.

National Agriculture Lands Study. 1980. National Association of Conservation Districts.

Postel, Sandra. 1984. Water: Rethinking management in an age of scarcity. *Worldwatch* paper no. 62. December.

Sabadell, J. Eleonora. 1982. Desertification in the United States: Status and issues. Washington, D.C.: U.S. Department of the Interior.

Sagan, Carl. 1985. The warming of the world. *Parade,* February 3.

Sheridan, David. 1981. Desertification of the United States. Council on Environmental Quality.

Thatcher, P. S. 1979. Desertification: The greatest single environmental threat. *UNWP Desertification Control Bulletin* 2 (no. 1) June.

Thomas, Gerald W. 1977. Environmental sensitivity and production potential on semi-arid range lands. *In* Frontiers of the semi-arid world. Lubbock: Texas Tech University.

———. 1980. The Sahelian/Sudanian zones of Africa: Profile of a fragile environment. Report to the Rockefeller Foundation. 1983.

———. Desertification: Some progress—much confusion. AAAS symposium on desertification. Detroit.

Thomas, Gerald W., and Thadis W. Box. 1969. Social and ecological implications of water importation into arid lands. *In* Arid lands in perspective. Tucson: University of Arizona Press.

Tolba, M. K. 1978. *Desertification Control Bulletin* 2 (no. 1), June.

Van Devender, Thomas R. 1977. Holocene woodlands in the southwestern deserts. *Science* 198 (October 14).

16. THE MANAGEMENT OF WATER DEVELOPMENT FOR LIVESTOCK IN DRY ZONES OF AFRICA

Stephen Sandford, International Livestock Centre for Africa, Addis Ababa, Ethiopia

ABSTRACT

This chapter draws attention to issues that policy makers should bear in mind in the development of water supplies for livestock in dry zones of Africa. It identifies areas that should be the main concerns of policymakers. These include increased productivity coupled with stability, and environmental conservation and equity. Also presented are the issues concerning the number of water sources, their type, who controls them, and on what financial terms water is provided. It contrasts traditional strategies for overcoming water shortages for livestock with modern ones. Traditional strategies do not depend on inputs and skills endogenous to Africa, five traditional strategies are distinguished. These can do only little to supply more water; they are focused on alleviating the problem rather than overcoming it. They can do little to correct weather-induced instability but are not very prone to administrative or technical breakdowns. Their performance in relation to conservation is ambiguous. As for equity, they do not present opportunities for outsiders to exploit pastoralists, but pastoralists may exploit each other. Modern strategies are dependent on exogenous inputs, and two main ones are distinguished. One seeks to open up previously inaccessible areas and to reduce the amount of energy wasted trekking to water; the second aims to use water supplies as a mechanism for controlling grazing. The performance of modern strategies has tended to be disappointing partly because modern water supplies have proved very vulnerable to technical and administrative breakdowns, partly because governments have often not been able to control water supplies, with consequent bad effects on productivity, stability, and equity.

INTRODUCTION

This chapter draws attention to the issues that policymakers should bear in mind in the development of water supplies for livestock in dry zones, with particular reference to Sub-Saharan Africa. The chapter identifies the main options available, highlights the main strategies that have been followed, and draws lessons from the experience gained.

Domestic livestock need water, and unless it is provided in adequate quantities, their output is reduced and they may die. It is not always possible to provide a water supply wherever it is wanted, and in dry areas water will always remain a scarce or expensive resource. A number of different strategies have been used to overcome or alleviate this shortage of water for livestock. Some of these strategies focus on management of the livestock herd; others on management of water supplies. The latter serves not only the purpose of overcoming water shortage, it can also be used in dry zones more positively as a tool for ensuring optimum use of rangeland vegetation.

CONCERNS OF POLICYMAKERS

In considering livestock water supplies, producers as well as policymakers, both in government and in local communities, normally have a number of major concerns. First, they are interested in the current productivity of the system: how many and what kinds of livestock water supplies will yield the greatest benefits? What capacity and spacing of water supplies will give the best access to forage and reduce the time and energy of watering? In addition to average short-term or long-term productivity, producers and policymakers will be concerned with the stability of income and production and, therefore, with ensuring a reliable water supply. Unreliability may be brought about by seasonal and interannual variations in weather, by administrative or technical breakdowns in the water supply, or by disruptions of a social or political nature.

Policymakers' second major concern tends to be the conservation of the natural environment. What will be the effect of changing the number, capacity, or mode of use of livestock water supplies on the surrounding vegetation, on soil erosion, and on the availability and quality of water for other purposes?

The third major concern of policy makers tends to be with what are called equity issues. Who are the major gainers and losers from the way water supplies are contained, used, and maintained? For example, some technically sophisticated kinds of water supply, e.g., deep boreholes, can be constructed or maintained only by special equipment or skills drawn from outside pastoral areas, often from outside Africa. Other kinds, e.g., open wells, can be dug and maintained by the pastoralists themselves or their neighbors, with domestically manufactured tools. In the one case there is a leakage of income from the area in order to finance the work. In the other case it is retained. In the former case there is also a loss of control by pastoralists, making them dangerously dependent on the goodwill of others. But a more important equity issue is usually the one of who will be allowed access to a water supply and the forage within reach of it, and on what terms (e.g., payment or limits on the number of livestock they may water).

THE MAJOR OPTIONS

Decision makers have an enormous number of choices to make concerning water development, the choices being governed by the place or time. It is possible, however, to classify them in four groups: the number or spatial density of water supplies, the type of supply, who controls the supply, and the financial terms on which water for livestock is to be supplied. Decisions falling under each of these four main classes will sometimes have unexpected effects in terms of the productivity, environmental, and equity concerns previously mentioned. For example, a decision to increase substantially the density of water supplies in an area may suddenly make accessible for the first time to a tribal group that raises cattle an area that could previously be used only by a tribal group owning camels. The former thus gains at the expense of the latter.

A decision made in one of these areas is not entirely independent of one made in another area. For example, the decision to install a water supply of a very sophisticated type may, because of its expense, imply that the number/density of such water supplies must be very low, and that their control be vested in government rather than in the hands of a local community who are not accustomed to such sophistication. A decision that the costs of water supply shall be fully recovered from the user may, in turn, require that ownership and control over it be vested in the hands of an individual because only in this way is there any likelihood of user fees being properly collected.

LESSONS FROM THE PAST

In drawing lessons from the past and extrapolating therefrom, it will be useful to distinguish between what we can call "traditional" and "modern" strategies for overcoming water shortages in dry zones of Africa. A traditional strategy is defined as one which does not require large inputs of money, equipment, or skills from outside Africa. A modern strategy, in contrast, does require such exogenous inputs. The crucial difference between the two is that under a traditional strategy there is extremely little choice, because of technical constraints, about where to locate a water supply and what its capacity should be. Under a modern strategy the choices are much wider because the technology exists to find or bring water almost anywhere it is needed. The primary constraint is that of cost.

TRADITIONAL STRATEGIES FOR OVERCOMING WATER SHORTAGES

We can distinguish five traditional strategies, three of which essentially involve the management of livestock herds and two, the management of water supplies. We shall describe herd management strategies first.

Adjusting the Species, Age, and Sex Composition of Herds

This "composition" strategy involves adjusting the species, age, and sex of livestock holdings. Livestock owners react to relative water shortages by adjusting the species composition of their holdings. In drier areas there tend to be more camels; in wetter areas, more cattle. Because various species differ in ways other than their adaptability to water shortages (e.g., in the frequency, timing, and duration of lactation, and in the amount of labor required to tend them), pastoralists will often try to keep more than one species, but the overall balance between species will differ between drier

Table 1. The relative proportions of livestock species in the herds of two Somali clans in southeastern Ethiopia.

Clan	Approx. Density of Dry-season Water Points (No. per km²)	Proportion of Total Livestock (% Total Biomass)			
		Camels	Goats	Sheep	Cattle
Habar Awal	0.04	72	4	15	9
Abaskul	2.57	27	9	33	31

SOURCES: Cossins, 1971a, and Watson, 1973.

areas and wetter ones. This is well illustrated by the example of two neighboring Somali clans whose animals graze in southeastern Ethiopia. These clans' territories differ in their levels of water resources, and so, in consequence, does the balance between species in the two clans' livestock holdings. Table 1 gives the evidence. Livestock owners also adjust the age and sex composition of individual herds within their total holdings in accordance with water requirements and adaptability to water shortages.

Positioning Livestock and Conserving Feed and Water

This "positioning" strategy involves two elements. One of these is the careful adjustment in space and time of different species and classes of livestock in relation to water supplies. This adjustment depends on the relative water requirement of each class and species and on the availability of forage areas in the quantity and quality appropriate to those livestock. Where water is scarce, the total livestock holding will be split up into as many herds of relatively homogeneous livestock as the amount of labor available for herding permits, so that each herd can be managed in the most appropriate way (Swift, 1979, 144–158; Cossins, 1971a, 45; Dahl, 1979, 42). As a general rule in societies that split their holdings in this way, milk stock will graze closer to water and dry stock farther away. Camels will certainly graze the ring most distant from water, sheep and goats probably the intermediate one, and cattle the closest, although this depends on whether water can be transported to calves or not.

The Husbandry Strategy

Livestock owners engage in some other management practices—we can call them collectively the "husbandry strategy"—in order to overcome water shortages. For example, one Somali clan in southeastern Ethiopia (Cossins, 1971a, 70), and perhaps also some of the East African Maasai (Western, 1982), deliberately select for white- or light-colored cattle in their breeding practices because of their greater ability to withstand heat stress under conditions of water restriction (King, 1983, 34–37). In East Africa several pastoral groups alter the hours and length of daily grazing and trekking so as to maximize moisture intake from dew and to reduce water loss from movement in the heat of the day (Lewis, 1977, 41; Western, 1973; Branagan, 1962, 8; Dahl, 1979, 62). Another management variable is the duration and number of drinking episodes that take place at each visit to a watering point. For example, as the intervals between watering episodes rises from two to three days, pastoralists often allow livestock an opportunity to drink more than once at each visit to a water supply (Field, 1977; Bernus, 1981, 30; Marty, 1972, 27–29; Cossins, 1971b, 48; Torry, 1977, 10).

The Strategy of Investing in Water Supplies

This "investment" strategy is to construct new water supplies in water-deficit areas. In some parts of Africa this has been done on a considerable scale and with a high degree of skill. In arid southeastern Ethiopia, 41,000 water sources have been constructed in an area of 33,000 km², i.e., 1.2 per square kilometer (Watson, 1973). Traditional open wells in Niger reach a depth of 10 m (Swift, 1979). An alternative to investing in a water supply in order to gain access to grazing in a water-deficit area is to invest in a means of transport, such as a donkey or camel, which can carry water for the use of calves or small stock at camps located near good grazing but too far for these animals to trek to water themselves (e.g., see Swift, 1979, 147, and 154).

Managing and Controlling Water Points

The final traditional strategy we discuss is one for managing and controlling water points. By management we mean the organization of watering activities and maintenance in such a way that a minimum of time and water is wasted. Waste can be caused by slow rates of extraction due to insufficient labor or other forms of energy to draw water, through quarrels and fighting about turns for watering, through fouling of water by animals, or through losses from water sources or troughs. By control we mean the regulation of access to a water source and restricting this access to the number of people or livestock for which the water and surrounding grazing is adequate.

The rules and systems for managing and controlling water points differ from society to society and, within the same society, between different kinds of water sources, different seasons of the year, and sometimes between the same season in different years. The degree of management and control tends to vary with the scarcity of water, with the difficulty of extracting it, or with the amount of surrounding grass. Where neither water nor grass is scarce, management and control are often perfunctory, but becoming more strict as the dry season advances (Fortmann and Roe, 1981, 142 and 145). In areas where communal systems of land and grazing tenure apply, it is usual for water in ephemeral natural pans to be unmanaged and uncontrolled. The water in the pans is likely to dry up more quickly through evaporation and seepage than animals drinking there can exhaust the water or surrounding grazing, so that the water is not a conservable resource to be kept from the livestock.

However, in dry areas most societies control (i.e., regulate access to) permanent water. In some cases the power to do this is vested in individuals through a concept of private property, and this power can be bought, sold, or inherited. In some cases ownership is vested in the society as a whole that grazes in that area, and in others ownership is vested in only one section of that society. In some cases different

rules apply to different kinds of water supply within the same area and society (e.g., see Cossins, 1971a).

Control of access to water usually only distinguishes persons with stronger or weaker claims to use a particular water point. It seldom, if ever, imposes a formal limit, by regulation, on how many stock each person may water in times of drought. However, other kinds of constraint may impose less formal limits. Foremost among these is the increased requirement in times of water scarcity for human labor to extract water from the source and to deliver it to livestock. Owners of herds with high stock family labor ratios will have to make arrangements to hire labor or to entrust their animals to the care of those whose herds are smaller. Such arrangements are expensive, and in times of water shortage owners of large herds will have to either de-stock or remove their animals to less labor-intensive watering points (Asad, 1970, 24–25; Helland, 1980, 63–71).

Management of watering points is designed to ensure that these are efficiently used. It includes a number of activities that require a degree of coordination and organization of effort between different individuals or groups. Wells and, to an extent, dams and ponds need annual maintenance to remove silt and sand, repair structures, and replace the equipment, e.g., wooden frames or windlasses, by which water is drawn (Holy, 1974, 107). Either daily or at the watering of each herd, minor repairs must be made to watering troughs, and dung and other refuse removed so that they do not contaminate the source (Helland, 1980, 66–67). Watering and labor rosters have to be drawn up so that each herd or type of animal is allocated an appropriate frequency of watering and a place in the order of watering for that day, and so that adequate labor is there when cooperation between different herding units is required. Some further rules may be needed, for example, to prevent the mixing up of herds (Lewis, 1978, 48) or trampling of smaller animals, or to segregate sick animals (Chambers, 1969, 15).

In some pastoral areas specialist institutions have evolved to perform these management activities. Among the better known of these is the system of "well master" and "well council" among the Borana of Ethiopia (Helland, 1980). But where water is not scarce, management tends to be minimal. In regions where water is relatively abundant, specialist traditional institutions for water management may not exist. In regions where water is scarce only in some seasons, specialist organizations may exist but operate only at the season of scarcity.

However, in regions where water is extremely scarce, specialist water management institutions do not seem to have evolved. In areas used by Somali pastoralists in the Horn of Africa—areas adjacent to but more arid than those of the Borana—no specialist institutions for water management have evolved. In southeastern Ethiopia informal councils of Somali elders from among those who expect to use a well may meet to work out watering schedules (Cossins, 1971a, 39). But among the Somali of northeastern Kenya even such informal councils appear to be lacking (Chambers, 1969).

How do these traditional strategies measure up to policymakers' concerns with productivity, stability, environmental conservation, and equity? As we shall see later, a key factor in improving productivity is reducing the distance livestock have to travel in search of water. In this respect, traditional strategies, because of the low level of technology inherent in endogenous supplies, can make little progress in tackling the issue directly by placing new water supplies in water-deficit areas. Instead, as we have seen, a variety of approaches are adopted to get around or alleviate the problem rather than to overcome it directly. As far as unreliability is concerned, again, because of technical limitations, little can be done under traditional strategies to reduce weather-induced instability. On the one hand, their independence from exogenous inputs makes traditional strategies much less prone to instability induced by administrative or technical breakdowns. On the other hand, politically or socially induced breakdowns, e.g., fighting by rival pastoral groups over water supplies, are fairly common.

As far as environmental conservation is concerned, two points can be made. First, traditional strategies are heavily dependent on human labor to extract water from its source, e.g., from deep wells, and the shortage of labor, therefore, effectively acts as a brake on excessive water depletion. At the same time, the extraction techniques involved—buckets, direct contact between animals and water source—provide ample opportunity for severe pollution of the source. Second, the fact that traditional strategies are so dependent on human labor is an indication of the degree of close herding, and while this degree of close herding results in a much more even distribution of grazing pressure compared with situations when animals are roaming free, this even distribution also permits a higher overall intensity of exploitation of soil and vegetation.

In terms of equity the picture is mixed. Traditional strategies, being independent of exogenous and complex inputs, present fewer opportunities for outsiders to exploit pastoralists through control of their water supplies. The higher labor requirements of large herds under traditional stategies also provide an opportunity for those with surplus labor to profit at the expense of the rich with large herds. On the other hand, the extreme scarcity of water supplies under traditional strategies provides many opportunities for those pastoralists who control access to the water supplies to exploit their neighbors.

MODERN STRATEGIES FOR OVERCOMING WATER SHORTAGES

A modern strategy uses inputs exogenous to Africa. It therefore has access to the skills and resources of the developed world with a consequent enormous increase in ability to locate new water supplies in the places and of the capacity needed. The main modern strategy is, therefore, to open previously inaccessible water-deficit areas to grazing and to achieve a density of watering places that provides an optimum balance between the increased output resulting from reducing the distance trekked by animals in search of water and the increased cost resulting from investment in new water supplies.

Table 2. How multiplying the number of watering points increases output by saving energy spent by livestock on trekking to water.

Spacing between water points (km)	20	10	5	2.5
Increase in output per head compared with next widest spacing (%)[a]	—	34	5	2

[a]Output per head of livestock at spacing A less output at next widest spacing B as a proportion of output at spacing B is given by
$$\frac{A - B}{B} \times 100.$$

Hard evidence of differences in output arising, *ceteris paribus,* from differences in access to water is still lacking, although the International Livestock Center for Africa (ILCA) is currently experimenting in this area. It is, however, possible to put all the existing scattered, incomplete, and indirect evidence into a "simulation model" that estimates, on the basis of certain assumptions, the effect on output of reducing the distance animals have to travel in search of water. Table 2 presents the results (reported in detail in Sandford, 1983) of such a model for range areas, and indicates, for example, that halving the spacing between water points from 20 to 10 km (which involves quadrupling the number of watering points) leads to an increase in output per beast of 34 percent; but that halving the spacing again from 5 to 2.5 km will lead to only a further 5 percent increase in output per head.

The second main modern strategy is to use water points as an instrument to control the intensity, uniformity, and period of grazing in a way that increases the productivity of pasture and minimizes soil erosion. The density of water points, their location in relation to natural features such as hills, and to periods of the day or year in which they are open, influence the distribution and movement of livestock in space and time. On unfenced rangelands in Australia, unherded cattle can be redistributed between different areas simply by closing one water point and opening another (UNESCO, 1979, 469). Where livestock are herded, the opening and closing of water points, and limitations (in theory, at any rate) on the supply of water from them, can be used to enforce pasture rotations and stock limitations against the wishes of the herdsmen.

Naturally, the distance that livestock will graze out from an isolated watering point (and thus the location of any stress they exert, through grazing and trekking, on soil and vegetation) varies by species and class of livestock, from place to place and season to season, and according to vegetation type and whether or not the animals are herded. For example, around one watering point in Central Australia the grazing distance from the watering point of the majority of cattle (unherded) varied from 1 km to 13 km, depending on season and grazing abundance (Hodder and Low, 1978). At another watering point in the same general area, faced with similar conditions of feed scarcity, at no time did the majority graze more than 8 km.

A spatially even distribution of pressure on vegetation, soil, and water can be brought out by adjusting the density and location of water points so that the whole area is brought within the usual range that livestock will graze out from water. The overall pressure of grazing will be greater in this way, but more evenly distributed. However, a high density of watering points, perhaps in combination with fencing, is not the only way to achieve an even distribution. Herding is an alternative to extra watering points (or fencing) as a way of obtaining a more spatially even distribution of livestock.

There can be little doubt that, in the past, water development has contributed significantly to African livestock output by opening up for more intensive use areas that, prior to water development, could only be used by a few livestock, or for short periods of the year, or could not be used at all. For example, between 1965 and 1976 the area of land in Botswana accessible to livestock approximately doubled as a consequence of borehole drilling (Sandford, 1977). There has almost certainly also been an impact in terms of increased output resulting from the reduction in energy wasted by livestock in trekking to water, although the partitioning of the increased output between these two causes, increase in accessible area, and reduction in energy wastage is difficult.

Whereas in principle modern technology, albeit at some cost, can provide water wherever it is needed, in practice its performance is often dismal. Frequently, water supplies of an inappropriate type are put in the wrong place and they either never function properly, or function only sporadically, as a consequence of technical or administrative breakdowns. For example in Botswana 40 percent of boreholes drilled never operate, and one survey found that only 65 percent of watering points (85 percent of these were boreholes) were operating, 19 percent had been abandoned, and 16 percent were temporarily not functioning for some reason (Hitchcock, 1978, 143–57). Boreholes probably have a worse performance than other types of water sources, but these too have their problems. For example, in the northern rangelands of Tanzania a development project constructed or rebuilt twenty-five major dams in the early 1970s. By mid-1977 all of these had been destroyed by heavy rains (Jacobs, 1980).

These defects come about for a number of reasons. Modern technology requires for its installation expensive equipment and staff which have to be used intensively if unit costs are to be kept down. As a consequence modern water development tends to be rushed, without leaving adequate time to consult users or to accumulate enough years of climatic and hydrologic data. Modern technology often depends on imported spare parts and fuel, which in turn require foreign exchange and complex procurement channels. They also require hard cash for their purchase rather than reciprocal services within a community, and this cash is difficult to collect, to account for, and to keep safely. Any enterprise, whether owned by a government or individual, finds it difficult to recover the cash costs of water supplies in pastoral areas, particularly the overhead costs, because of the fluctuating nature of demand, but governments probably have greater difficulty in handling the cash thereafter. It is also easy for the disgruntled or suspicious to sabotage modern

technology. A final problem lies in the fact that modern water technology is often financed from aidsources, and then the choice of water supply type, e.g., borehole or dam, often becomes as much a question of what the donor concerned wants to provide as of what is more appropriate. It is for all these reasons that modern technology has proved so unreliable.

Modern strategies have been disappointing in another way. It was expected that new water supplies would be a means whereby use of the surrounding grazing could be controlled, thereby ensuring higher productivity and less environmental damage. Both the technology involved, e.g., mechanical power which can be switched on and off, and the fact that the new supplies would be administered by government officials, appeared to provide the necessary mechanisms whereby the identity of the users, the numbers of their animals, and the period of grazing could be controlled in a grazing area dependent on a water supply. In practice these expectations proved wide of the mark (Bernus, 1977, 63; Eddy, 1979, 16; Bourgeot, 1981, 174). Governments have been reluctant to make politically unpopular decisions and operators at watering places have been terrorized into doing what they should not do and to demand bribes for doing what they should.

Therefore, in terms of policymakers' three concerns— productivity with stability, environmental conservation, and equity—modern strategies have a rather mixed record. New water supplies have been constructed, and as a result, productivity, on balance, has increased. But any decline in weather-induced instability has often been counterbalanced by increased unreliability owing to technical and administrative factors. The increased complexity of exogenous technology over indigenous provides more scope for breakdowns. The exploitation of pastoralists by private owners of water supplies in traditional systems may be no worse than the exploitation that occurs when government functionaries find themselves, in modern systems, in control of publicly owned water essential for the survival of people and herds.

CONCLUSIONS

Modern strategies for overcoming shortages of water for livestock in dry areas are capable of very greatly increasing productivity. However, these overall increases in productivity may not be accompanied by any increase in stability of output (indeed the reverse may occur) since unreliability resulting from technical and administrative breakdowns often increases, offsetting any reduction that modern technology may bring about in weather-induced instability. The scope for managing modern water supplies in such a way as to conserve and increase the productivity of the surrounding grazing has been overstated.

In contrast, traditional strategies have much less scope for placing water supplies where they are needed, and they have instead sought other means to overcome water shortages. The high labor requirements of implementing many traditional strategies have imposed some limits on the number of livestock kept, and, in this way, rather than through anything more deliberate, traditional strategies have avoided putting so much pressure on the environment as have modern strategies. There is nothing inherently equitable about traditional strategies.

A major reason why modern strategies have not achieved all that was expected is that choices about the number, density, and location of watering points have become entangled with other choices about the type of supply, about who controls it, and on what terms its operations should be financed. Some of this entanglement is inevitable and is derived from the nature of modern technology; some of it can be avoided, and policy makers should consider their water development programs carefully to ensure that each of the kinds of choices is, as far as possible, made separately. The overall concerns of policymakers, for productivity with stability, for environmental conservation, and for equity, must be kept constantly in mind.

REFERENCES

Asad T. 1970. The Kababish Arabs. Power, authority and consent in a nomadic tribe. London: C. Hurst and Co.

Bernus, E. 1977. Case study on desertification. The Eghazer and Azawak region, Niger. United Nations Conference on Desertification (A conf74/14). Nairobi.

Bernus, E. 1981. Touareg nigériens: Unité culturelle et diversité régionale d'un peuple pasteur. Paris: ORSTOM.

Bourgeot, A. 1981. Pasture in the Malian Gourma: habitation by humans and animals. In J. G. Galaty, D. Aranson, P. C. Salzman, and A. Chouinard (eds.) The future of pastoral peoples: Proceedings of a conference held in Nairobi, Kenya, August 4–8, 1980. Ottawa: International Development Research Centre.

Branagan, D. 1962. A discussion on the factors involved in the development of Maasailand. Unpublished report.

Chambers, R. J. H. 1969. Report on social and administrative aspects of range management development in the northeastern province of Kenya. Unpublished report.

Cossins, N. 1971a. Pastoralism under pressure: A study of the Somali clans of the Jijiga area of Ethiopia. Unpublished report.

Cossins, N. 1971b. People and their cattle in the Shire lowlands. Unpublished report.

Dahl, G. 1979. Suffering grass: Subsistence and society of Waso Borana. Stockholm: Department of Social Anthropology, Stockholm University.

Eddy, E. D. 1979. Labor and land use on mixed farms in the pastoral zone of Niger. Ann Arbor, Mich.: Center for Research on Economic Development.

Field, C. R., 1977. Progress report for the first quarter of 1977, UNESCO-UNEP Arid Lands Project, Mount Kulal Field Station. Unpublished report.

Fortmann, L., and E. Roe. 1981. The water points survey. Gaborone, Botswana: Ministry of Agriculture.

Helland, J. 1980. Five essays on the study of pastoralists and the development of pastoralism. Bergen, Norway: Socialantropologisk Institutt, Universitete i Bergen.

Hitchcock, R. K. 1978. Kalahari cattle posts. Gaborone, Botswana: Ministry of Local Government and Lands.

Hodder, R. M., and W. A. Low. 1978. Grazing distribution of free-ranging cattle at three sites in the Alice Springs district, Central Australia. Australian Rangelands 1(2):95–105.

Holy, L. 1974. Neighbours and kinsmen: a study of the Berti people of Darfur. London: C. Hurst and Co.

Jacobs, A. H. 1980. Pastoral development in Tanzania Maasailand. Rural Africana 7, new series (Spring, 1980):1–14.

King, J. 1983. Livestock water needs in pastoral Africa in relation to climate and forage. ILCA research report no. 7. Addis Ababa, Ethiopia.

Lewis, J. G. 1977. Report of a short-term consultancy on the grazing ecosystem in the Mount Kulal region, northern Kenya. UNEP/MAB/IPAL technical report E. 3.

Marty, A. 1972. Les problèmes d'abreuvement et le fonctionnement des stations de pomages vus par les eleveurs de l'arrondissement de Tchin Tabaraden. Unpublished report.

Sandford, S. 1977. Dealing with drought and livestock in Botswana. Unpublished report.

———. 1983. Organization and management of pastoral water supplies in tropical Africa. International Livestock Centre for Africa research report no. 8. Addis Ababa, Ethiopia.

Swift, J. J. 1979. The economics of traditional nomadic pastoralism. The Twareg of Adrar N Iforas (Mali). Ph.D. diss., University of Sussex.

Torry, W. I. 1977. Labor requirements among the Gabbra. In East African pastoralism: Anthropological perspectives and development needs. Addis Ababa, Ethiopia: ILCA.

UNESCO (United Nations Educational, Scientific, and Cultural Organization). 1979. Tropical grazing lands ecosystems: a state of knowledge report prepared by UNESCO/UNEP/FAO. UNESCO: Paris.

Watson, R. M. 1973. Aerial livestock and land-use surveys of the Jijiga Area. Ethiopia, January, 1973, and final unpublished reports.

Western, D. 1982. The environment and ecology of pastoralists in arid savannahs. Development and Change 13:183–211.

17. RANGE MANAGEMENT IN ARID REGIONS AS RELATED TO WATER CONSERVATION AND USE

Martin H. González, Ecoterra International, El Paso, Texas

ABSTRACT

To make the most efficient use of the limited rainfall in arid and semiarid rangelands is the greatest challenge facing range managers. Large water losses occur because of runoff and evaporation in most range ecosystems, and by undesirable vegetation utilizing it so, the actual net rainfall remaining for desirable forage species is only between 20 and 40 percent of the total precipitation recorded.

This dramatic reduction in the availability of water for good forage plants shows the importance of establishing, as priority, the range improvement actions involving vegetative modifications to control runoff and reduce evaporation; soil and water conservation practices and structures; and design of the adequate grazing systems with balanced intensities of use that good management demands for each particular situation. Evidence is presented on the positive improvements obtained when one or more of these practices are implemented, in terms of better forage and animal production.

The influence of the vegetative type and of the condition of the range on infiltration and runoff; the effects that grazing has on water conservation; and different methods of modification of the vegetative cover to improve water use, mainly through brush control and reseeding, are discussed.

INTRODUCTION

The greatest challenge that range managers in arid and semiarid regions of the world face is to understand how to live with and make the most efficient use of limited water resources in these areas. These include both surface and underground aquifers.

According to the Society for Range Management, 40 percent of all land on our planet is classified as rangeland. This type of land includes most of the great deserts and the arid, semiarid, and temperate grazing lands in the world, in more than fifty-two countries.

Nature has blessed, nevertheless, most of these lands with a great variety of plants adapted to these relatively unfavorable climatic conditions. These plants have served, through milennia, as forage for animals and some for humans, as fuel, for shelter, for working tools, and for medical purposes, among other uses.

However, man has not been able to manage and preserve on a sustained basis, the productivity of those resources. An almost continuous abuse has occurred in many regions of the world, which has a direct relation to the acceleration of desertification—a process that seems to be affecting more areas on several continents even today.

With depleted vegetative resources; with erratic and low precipitation patterns; with a scarcity of subterraneous aquifers; and in many areas, with erroneous governmental programs and political decisions, mankind has been forced to fight back and face the challenge before him, to take some definitive actions in trying to improve and conserve this diminishing resource, adopting a series of agronomic practices and systems for animal management in order to return to an adequate ecological equilibrium.

This chapter presents different examples about some of these practices that tend to accelerate secondary plant succession and the rehabilitation of degraded soils.

RAINFALL USE AND LOSSES IN RANGELANDS

Any range improvement in arid rangelands should be associated with water conservation practices if satisfactory results are to be obtained (González, 1973, Javalera et al., 1976; Fierro et al., 1979; Sierra, 1982). This is based on the fact that most of northern Mexico rangelands (and some of the southwestern United States) are in a condition between fair and good, that is, that only from 26 to 75 percent of the vegetative cover is desirable forage species. The remaining species of vegetation are undesirable shrubs, forbs, trees, cacti, or annual invaders, which use the same amount or even more of the available water in the soil than the desirable species.

Fig. 1 illustrates for northern Mexico, for example, how annual rainfall is used by plants and what losses occur during the year in short grass-shrub communities where annual average precipitation is 340 mm. The frost-free period is 237 days, and 88.23 percent of the total precipitation falls during this period. Potential evaporation is 11 mm/day.

Information for similar grassland and mixed-shrub ranges indicate that evaporation averages 13 mm and evapotranspiration 220 mm (Branson et al., 1970). These high rates of evapotranspiration are confirmed by Langbein et al. (1949) and Busby (1966), indicating that 80 to 90 percent of the total annual precipitation in the western United States is used in evapotranspiration.

Regarding runoff, water losses are usually high in arid and semiarid rangelands, and this is distinctly related to the type of vegetative cover and range conditions (Leithead, 1959). Studies in Sonora, Texas, by Blackburn (1983) mention surface runoff being 25 percent of total rainfall for a bunchgrass vegetative type, and 50 percent for sod grass, with soil losses of 783 and 2,150 kg/ha, respectively.

In Fig. 1, from an average total precipitation in central Chihuahua of 340 mm recorded annually, 40 mm (11.76 percent) falls as rain or snow during the winter months, long before the beginning of the growing season. From the remaining 300 mm, an estimated 172 mm (50.59 percent of total) is lost as runoff and surface evaporation, leaving

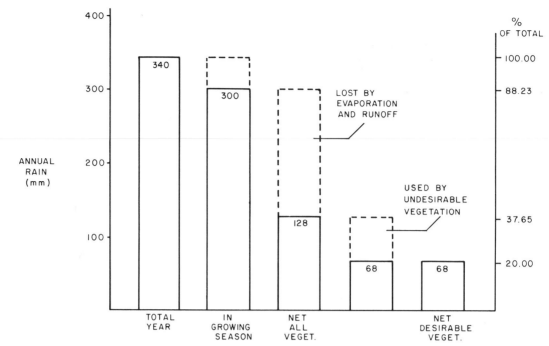

Fig. 1. Rainfall losses and use by plants in rangelands of central Chihuahua. Average range conditions fair to low to good. (Modified from González, 1983).

128 mm to be used by all vegetation; that is only 37.65 percent of all the recorded precipitation in a year. But since most of the rangelands in the area are in fair to slightly good condition, this means that only around 50 percent of the vegetation in those ranges consists of desirable species, and the balance left for these is only 68 mm, equivalent to 20.0 percent of the total rainfall.

This dramatic reduction in availability of water for desirable forage species shows the importance in establishing, as priority, the range improvement actions involving vegetative modifications to control runoff and reduce evapotranspiration, water and soil conservation practices and structures, and design of the grazing systems and intensities that good management demands for each particular situation.

Specifically, water conservation, control of undesirable plants (mainly woody species), revegetation of denuded areas, and well-balanced grazing systems may account for very significant increments in water, forage, and animal production. Evidence of the benefits obtained with some of these actions are discussed in the following pages.

RANGE IMPROVEMENT FOR WATER CONSERVATION AND USE

The level of degradation of a given range ecosystem will determine how much improvement it needs to integrate it again into a productive process. Potential to achieve success, feasibility, costs, climate, and edaphic conditions are some of the most important considerations in trying to implement any improvement program. One other decision to make is the adoption of one or various improvement practices, combined in order to accelerate the rehabilitation process in the secondary succession.

Through selected examples, this chapter illustrates how rangeland vegetation and its management affects water management and use, and their impact in soil stabilization, modifications in the vegetative cover, and forage production.

Influence of Vegetative Type and Range Condition on Infiltration and Runoff

Numerous factors influence infiltration of rainfall into the soil. These include intensity and duration of the storm, topography, vegetative cover, rock cover, soil texture, litter accumulation, and range condition, among others (e.g., Slayter and Mabbut, 1964).

Comparing infiltration rates for those vegetative types under different conditions in rangelands in central Chihuahua, Sanchez (1972) found a directly proportional relation between condition of the range and infiltration for shortgrass plains, for oak-grassland foothills, and for alkali flats, as shown in Table 1. Vegetation inside a thirteen-year exclosure protected from grazing had the highest infiltration rates in the three vegetative types, averaging 20.8 liters (L) in 105 minutes, compared with averages of 16.2, 11.5, and 7.7 L for pastures in good to fair condition, in poor condition, and for bare ground.

These results are in accordance with those found by González (1964) in earlier infiltration tests at Rancho Experimental La Campana, in Chihuahua, where protected Bouteloua-Aristida pastures accounted for an increase in infiltration of 96.3 percent over denuded areas; moderately grazed pastures had 61.5 percent more and heavily grazed areas 27.4 percent more water infiltrated than denuded soil.

The effect of intensity and system of grazing over infiltration, losses of soil, and standing crop production was dem-

Table 1. Influence of range condition on water infiltration in three vegetative types in Chihuahua.

Condition	Short-grass Plains	Oak-bunchgrass Foothills	Alkali Flats	Mean
	(Liters in 105 minutes)			
Excellent	32.5	22.5	7.5	20.8
Good to fair	24.0	18.7	6.0	16.2
Poor	19.0	11.5	4.0	11.5
Bare ground	10.0	9.5	3.6	7.7

SOURCE: Sanchez, 1972.

Table 2. Precipitation and runoff in different vegetative communities in New Mexico.

	Creosote Bush	Semiarid Grassland	Mountain Grassland
Altitude, m	1,400 to 1,940	1,590 to 2,800	2,540 to 3,500
Precipitation, mm	208	305	575
Runoff, mm	1.25	2.40	150.0
Runoff as percentage of precipitation	0.6	0.8	26.0

SOURCE: Adapted from Dortignac, 1956.

onstrated by McGinty et al. (1978), at the Sonora Experimental Station in West Texas. They studied those effects under heavy continuous grazing, heavy grazing in a deferred-rotation four-pasture system, and inside a twenty-eight-year livestock exclosure. Infiltration rates were higher in the exclosures (10.24 cm/hr) and the rotated pastures (10.40 cm/hr) than in the continuously grazed pastures (4.4. cm/h4). Soil losses were 134, 160, and 211 kg/ha under rotation grazing, exclosure and continuous grazing, respectively, and this same trend occurred on the yield of standing crop, with 2.56, 1.91, and 1.27 ha DM.

Also in Sonora, Texas, Blackburn (1983) demonstrated the influence of the type of grass cover on runoff and soil loss. Surface runoff was 25 percent of recorded rainfall in a bunchgrass vegetative type, while in the sod-grass areas runoff was 50 percent of rainfall. Similarly, soil losses were 783 kg/ha for the bunchgrass type and 2,150 kg/ha in the sod-grass area. These results are based on an average 100 mm simulated rain in thirty minutes, applied twenty-two times over a four-year period.

Table 2 presents data obtained by Dortignac (1956) in studies in the upper Rio Grande basin in New Mexico, comparing runoff in three vegetative communities: mountain grassland with 575 mm rainfall; semiarid grassland with 305 mm, and creosote bush range with 208 mm rainfall. Runoff was 150 mm (25 percent of rainfall) in the mountain grassland, 2.5 mm (0.8 percent) in the semiarid grassland, and 1.25 (0.6 percent) in the drier creosote bush community.

In general, numerous studies have demonstrated how infiltration increases and runoff decreases as the condition of the range improves. Leithead (1959) concluded that a range site in Texas in good condition absorbed moisture five to six times faster than the same range in poor condition. For semiarid rangelands, this trend was found also by González, Martinez, and many others.

INFLUENCE OF GRAZING ON WATER CONSERVATION

When measuring infiltration under different grazing intensities, there is some tendency to show that, in general, undergrazed areas absorb more water than those under any type of grazing. However, light grazing seemed to produce a lower infiltration capacity than moderate grazing, at least in short-grass ranges of Colorado. Some other examples of these relationships exist but on the other hand, there is abundant evidence that infiltration rates are inverse proportional to grazing intensity and that in semiarid rangelands, more effective use of rainfall can be achieved if grazing is managed to allow for the accumulation of grass litter; retarding runoff affords greater opportunity for infiltration of rainwater (Rauzi and Hanson, 1966; Hendricks, 1942).

In a pine-bunchgrass range in Colorado, Dunford found that erosion, measured in kilograms of soil per hectare, was 100, 107, and 204 for nongrazed, moderately grazed, and heavily grazed areas. In this same study, soils in areas before grazing had an erosion of only 79 kg/ha.

When the intensity of grazing resulted in removal of more than half the herbage, there was a significant impact on surface runoff and soil losses, as demonstrated by Dunford (1954) and Currie (1975), in the Manitou Experimental Forest in Colorado. Data from their investigations indicate that for the summer rainfall season, in plots of 4 m², the no-grazing treatment had a runoff of 26 L containing 0.25 kg of soil, equivalent to soil losses of 7 t/km²; moderate grazing (one-third of herbage removed) produced 136 L of runoff with 0.27 kg. of soil, equivalent to 7.5 t/km²; and heavy grazing (two-thirds of herbage removal) produced 227 containing 0.58 kg of soil, which is equivalent to a soil loss of 16.0 t/km².

Average erosion rates of surface runoff for open timber and grassland combined, as determined by Smith (1967), were 6 to 7 kg/m² in a twelve-year previously ungrazed range for light, moderate, and heavy grazing, respectively, and 12, 16, and 46 kg/m² in a grazed range under the same grazing intensities.

For the Edwards Plateau in Texas, Wood and Blackburn determined the mean infiltration of the midgrass community for various grazing practices. The heavily stocked, continuously grazed site and two grazed and rested sites under HILF grazing had the lowest rates of infiltration (8.2, 8.3, and 9.6 cm/hr, respectively), while two exclosures and both the rested and the grazed deferred-rotation sites accounted for the higher rates, from 12.95 to 16.50 cm/hr.

Several factors interact to determine the hydrologic impact of grazing animals: climate; vegetation type and density; topography and soils; and, of course, intensity and duration of grazing by livestock and fauna. Therefore, grazing impacts will vary naturally from area to area because of normal variability of these factors.

There is a great deal of information still needed in order to arrive at definitive conclusions on the effects of grazing in water conservatism and use, particularly in arid and semiarid rangelands, where ". . . so many million hectares owe so much to so few mm of rain."

MODIFICATIONS OF THE VEGETATIVE COVER TO IMPROVE WATER USE

As was indicated in Fig. 1, great parts of the North American rangelands are now invaded by brush and need vegetative modification to control runoff and improve infiltration, so, in turn, the infiltrated water can be used by as many desirable plant species as possible. Techniques for vegetation control and other improvement practices in rangelands are basically planned to expedite secondary succession, that is, the return from woody plants to grasses. Successful brush control, reseeding, or other range improvement actions are not one-shot affairs but must be integrated into an overall program of land management based on in-depth understanding of plant ecology and principles of herbicide use (Scifres and Merkle, 1975).

Satterlund (1972) and Wood and Buckhouse (1983) agree that removal of woody plants reduces evapotranspiration and increases groundwater recharge, and also that spring flows will increase if evapotranspiration is reduced more than infiltration.

Increases or decreases in spring flow and runoff are the result of removing woody plants and of subsequent land use. Favorable conditions for infiltration must be maintained after the woody plants are removed (Wood and Buckhouse, 1983). Mechanical treatment of soil is important in converting shrub-infested ranges to grass and is a prime consideration in controlling runoff and erosion and reducing sediments (Tromble and Wood, 1981). An example of this was found by Tromble (1981) when infiltration increased and runoff and erosion decreased about four years after land was root plowed and reseeded in New Mexico.

Brush control can be obtained with mechanical and biological methods. Availability and cost of equipment, materials, and herbicides influence the type of control to use. All of them have their advantages and disadvantages. For instance, Vallentine (1980) indicates that defoliation following chemical brush control added more litter to the soil, which increased soil aggregation and water infiltration. Similarly, Hoffmann (1968) reports for Central Texas a forage production increase of 500 percent after brush was controlled by chemicals.

Responses in forage production to brush control are very satisfactory most of the time. Gomez and González (1976) treated *Eysenhardtia spinulosa, Mimosa biuncifera,* and *Microrahmnus ericoides* (totaling over 27,000 plants per hectare) with foliar applications of six herbicides at different dosages. An increase in forage production of 283 percent with applications at early flowering, and of 84 percent with application at maturity are reported. On the average, all treatments produced 598 kg/ha DM, compared with 171 kg/ha DM for the untreated plots.

Combining Improvement Practices

The combination of mechanical and chemical controls has proved very successful, although sometimes more expensive. Cholla cactus (*Opuntia imbricata*), was treated with chaining, shredding, and foliar and basal applications of herbicides and their combination, in a heavily infested area in Buenaventura, Chihuahua (Ibarra and Prieto, 1983). Forage production increased from 16 percent (basal applications of petroleum) to 141.7 percent (chaining and raking), and the basal cover of the principal perennial grasses increased an average of 27.6, 9.8 and 34.8 percent for the mechanical, for the chemical, and for the combined effect of both treatments, respectively.

In some developing countries one has to consider the relatively low cost of rural labor for mechanical control of undesirable plants, the high costs of machinery, and the high cost and erratic availability of herbicides, particularly the delay with which the new products reach those countries. Under these conditions, a detailed evaluation of mechanical control "by hand" is necessary if time is also a limiting factor.

Literature related to vegetation modification by the different methods is abundant for most of the arid and semiarid rangelands of the world (Wood and Buckhouse, 1983; Branson et al., 1970). But the selection of the proper control method must be a very well planned decision on the part of the range manager, based on his particular problem and condition.

Seeding is a practice often associated with brush control, especially in those areas where the forage potential of the site is low. On the other hand, where the potential is high, natural grasses will prosper after removal of the woody species, as demonstrated by Hoffman (1968) in the Edwards Plateau of Texas.

Under less favorable climatic conditions, seeding with native or well-adapted introduced grasses appears to be necessary for seeding or recovery of the treated area. Hydrologic responses depend on quantity and rate of establishment of the plants, and the subsequent management of the treated areas is as important as the seeding itself (Wood and Blackburn, 1983).

Sometimes, mechanical brush control may provide an adequate seedbed, like roller crushing, root plowing, disking, and others; if not, a seedbed preparation is necessary in order for the very small and expensive grass seeds to have adequate contact with the soil. Seedbed preparation is the beginning of a successful seeding operation.

Hydrologically, any degree of seeding establishment is preferred over bare ground conditions, except in situations where soil particles are so large that wind erosion is not a problem and no runoff occurs under any circumstances.

Seeding alone, in denuded, overutilized areas where brush infestation is not a problem, provides an easier site for this practice. Also, in these areas, seeding is recommended when there is no possibility for the natural vegetation to come back for a significant number of years.

In arid rangelands, seeding is generally not recommended when annual rainfall is less than 280 to 300 mm. However, seeding combined with water catchment and conservation "structures" have proved successful in areas with precipitations well below those figures. Rainfall distribution in these cases is as important as the total volume recorded.

Subsoiling, pitting, contour furrows, low retention fences, and terracing are some of the most commonly water conservation practices used with positive results in rangelands.

Seeding native and introduced grasses in different models of micro-watersheds in a Larrea-Flourensia site in northern Chihuahua with less than 240-mm rainfall increased forage production from 73 kg/ha to an average of 680 kg/ha DM using *Eragrostis chloromelas, Leptochlea dubia, Sorghum almum,* and *Bouteloua curtipendula* (Fierro et al., 1979).

Adaptation of buffel grass (*Cenchrus ciliaris*) and sand lovegrass (*Eragrostis lehmanniana*) in southwestern Arizona, and northern Sonora, Mexico, have been successful for several years and are the basis now for most revegetation and grazing programs in those extensive areas, where rainfall is well below 250 mm (Velazquez et al., 1979; Servin et al., 1983).

Many more examples could be cited in relation to seeding or reseeding of arid rangelands but space is limited. However, one that deserves to be mentioned because of its extension and social impact is the rehabilitation of nearly 3,000 ha in four rural locations in eastern Zacatecas, a state in central Mexico (González, 1973). Traditionally, what once were productive native grasslands have been plowed and converted to rainfall agriculture, through decades of monocropping with corn and using almost rudimentary cultivation systems, these lands became unproductive, since the fertile topsoil was carried away by strong winds. This conversion from productive rangeland to unproductive agricultural area in arid and semiarid environments is a classic example of an accelerated desertification process in developing countries.

A rehabilitation program was initiated in 1970 with the objective of restoring a permanent grass cover in those grass-depleted areas through reseeding and soil and water conservation. Terracing and contour furrowing were constructed to hold rainwater, and seedbed was prepared with disk harrows. A mixture of five grasses, three native and two introduced previously and tested in other states, was used. The natives were *Leptochloa dubia, Setaria machrostachya,* and *bouteloua curtipendula,* and the introduced were *Panicum antidotale* and *Sorghum almum,* the latter serving also as a nurse crop.

With an annual rainfall of 310 mm the first year and 296 mm the second year (1972), forage production after two years averaged 1,072 kg/ha DM in the four locations. *S. almum* and *L. dubia* accounted for 67 percent of this yield; *B. curtipendula* for 17 percent and *P. antidotale* and *S. machrostachya* combined for the remaining 15 percent. But the most important long-term benefit is the stabilizaton of the soil bringing back its productivity, and above all, the stabilized settlement of numerous rural communities who have learned the tough lesson that, in working with biotic resources one has to work with, and not against, nature (González, 1973).

REFERENCES

Alvarez, G. Angel. 1985. Informacion del servicio meteorologico de SARH y gobierno del estado. Chihuahua, Mexico.

Blackburn, W. H. 1983. Livestock grazing impacts on watersheds. *Rangelands* 5:123–25.

Branson, F. A., R. F. Miller, and I. S. McQueen, 1970. Plant communities and associated soil and water factors on shale-derived soils in northeastern Montana. *Ecology* 4(6):311–19.

Busby, M. W. 1966. Annual runoff in the conterminous United States. *U.S. Geological Survey Hydrologic Investment Atlas* HA-212.

Currie, P. O. 1975. Grazing management of ponderosa pine-bunchgrass ranges of the central Rocky Mountains: the status of our knowledge. Forest Service Research Paper Rm-159.

Dortignac, E. J. 1956. Watershed resources and problems of the upper Rio Grande basin. U.S. Forest Service Rocky Mountain Forest and Range Experiment Station Paper.

Dunford, E. G. 1954. Surface runoff and erosion from pine grassland of the Colorado Front Range. *Journal of Forestry* 52:923–27.

Fierro, L. C., J. Javalera, M. H. González, and F. Ibarra, 1979. Comparacion del establecimiento de cuatro mezclas de zacates nativos e introducidos en cuatro tipos de cama de siembra. *Pastizales* 10:6. Rancho Experimental La Campana, INIP-SARH. Mexico.

Gomez, F., and M. H. González. 1976. Evaluacion de cinco mezclas de herbicidas y dos epocas de aplicacion en el control de chaparrillo (*Eysenhardtia spinosa*). *Pastizales* 8:2. Rancho Experimental La Campana, INIP-SARH. Mexico.

———. 1978. Effecto del chapeo mecanico en el incremento de la produccion forrajera de un pastizal invadido por arbustivas indeseables. *Pastizales* 9:5. Rancho Experimental La Campana, INIP-SARH. Mexico.

González, M. H. 1964. Influencia del pastoreo en la infiltracion de agua en suelos de un pastizal mediano abierto. Informe Anual, Rancho Experimental La Campana, INIP-SARH. Mexico.

———. 1973. En Plan Zacatecas de mejoramiento de pastizales. Mimeo. Informe a gobierno del estado de Zacatecas.

Hendricks, B. A. 1942. Effect of grass litter on infiltration of rainfall on granitic soils in a semi-desert shrub grass area. U.S. Forest Service. Southwest Forage and Range Experiment Station Research Note 9 b.

Hoffman, G. H. 1968. Maintenance control for mesquite. Texas Agricultural Extension Service. Fact Sheet 766.

Ibarra, F., and S. Prieto. 1983. Metodos de control de cholla (*Opuntia imbricata*) en pestizales de Chihuahua. *Pastizales* 14:1. Rancho Experimental La Campana, INIP-SARH. Mexico.

Javalera, J. V. Ortiz, and F. Gomez. 1976. Effecto de la fertilizacion en el establecimiento de dos zacates nativos y cuatro introducidos en microcuencas. *Pastizales* 8:3. Rancho Experimental La Campana, INIP-SARH. Mexico.

Langbein, W. B., et al. 1949. Annual runoff in the United States. U.S. Geological Survey, Circular 52.

Langbein, W. B., and S. A. Schumm. 1958. Yield of sediment in relation to mean annual precipitation. American Geophys. Unim. Trans. 39:1076–84.

Leithead, H. L. 1959. Runoff in relation to range conditions in the Big Bend–Davis Mountains section of Texas. *Journal of Range Management* 12:83–87.

Lusby, G. C. 1970. Hydrologic and biotic effects of grazing vs. nongrazing near Grand Junction, Colorado. *Journal of Range Management* 23:256–60.

McGinty, W. A., F. E. Smeins, and L. B. Merrill. 1979. Influence of soil, vegetation and grazing management on infiltration rate and sediment production of Edwards Plateau rangelands. *Journal of Range Management* 32:33–37.

Rauzi, F., and C. L. Hanson, 1966. Water intake and runoff as affected by intensity of grazing. *Journal of Range Management* 19:351–56.

Rich, L. R., and H. G. Reynolds. 1963. Grazing in relation to runoff and erosion of some chaparral watersheds of Central Arizona. *Journal of Range Management* 16:322–26.

Sanchez, A., and J. Valdez. 1975. Infiltracion de agua en cuatro tipos vegetativos y relaciones suelo-vegetacion. *Pastizales* 6:4. Rancho Experimental La Campana, INIP-SARH, Mexico.

Satterlund, D. R. 1972. Wildland watershed management. New York: John Wiley and Sons.

Scifres, C. J., and M. G. Merkle. 1975. Herbicides and good management improves range pastures. *Weeds Today* (Spring).

Servin, C. M. Ramirez, and C. Alcala. 1983. Prueba de tres densidades de siembra de zacate africano (*Eragrostis lehmanniana*) en el desierto de Sonoyta, Sonora. Memorias Dia de Campo. CIPES, INIP-SARH, Mexico.

Sierra, J. S. 1982. Establecimiento y productivadad de cuatro mezclas de gramineas en la region centra de Chihuahua. *Pastizales* 8:4. Rancho Experimental La Campana, Mexico.

Slayter, R. P., and J. A. Mabbut. 1964. Hydrology of arid and semiarid regions. Ven Te Chow Handbook Applied Hydrology. New York: McGraw-Hill.

Smith, D. R. 1967. Effects of cattle grazing on a ponderosa pine–bunchgrass range in Colorado. United States Department of Agriculture Technical Bulletin 1371.

Tromble, J. M. 1981. Precipitation interception by creosote bush. *In* Rangelands improvements for New Mexico. New Mexico State University Special Report 41, Las Cruces, N.Mex.

Tromble, J. M., and M. K. Wood. 1981. Arid rangelands treatment effects on the control of erosion and sedimentation. *In* Rangelands improvements for New Mexico. New Mexico State University Special Report 41, Las Cruces, N.Mex.

Vallentine, J. F., 1980. Range development and improvements. Provo, Utah: Brigham Young University Press.

Velasquez, J., V. del Cid, E. Medina, and R. Lopez. 1979. Establecimiento, manejo y utilizacion del zacate buffel (*Cenchrus ciliaris*). Memorias Dia de Campo. CIPES, INIP-SARH, Mexico.

Wood, M. K., and J. C. Buckhouse, 1983. Technologies for capturing and detaining water on rangeland. New Mexico Agriculture Experiment Station Special Report 52.

PART IV. SALINITY

18. SOIL SALINITY, SALT COMPOSITION, AND WATER QUALITY

Pieter Buringh, Wageningen, The Netherlands

Soil salinity of cultivated land was already investigated and described by Urukagina some 4,400 years ago near Lagash in Mesopotamia. Since then, salt-affected soils have been found in many countries in coastal areas, where soils are influenced by seawater, and in inland areas of arid and semiarid regions, particularly in land that is influenced by groundwater containing highly soluble salts. These salts are mainly sodium, magnesium, and calcium chlorides; sodium and magnesium sulfates; sodium carbonates and bicarbonates; nitrates, and borates.

The processes of salinization and sodication in soils are often complicated. Much land is affected by salts under natural conditions; moreover, other land has become saline because of mismanagement by man. The latter type is particularly the result of irrigation of land in regions with a low precipitation, a high rate of water evaporation, and without artificial leaching or drainage. The result is a rather rapid accumulation of highly soluble salts, which influence the growth of crops. The effects are mainly physiological drought, disturbance of the ion balance in the soil solution, or the degradation of the structure and permeability of the soil. Moreover, there is an important decrease in the biological activity in the soil. The final result is poor growth of disease-prone crops, giving a low yield of poor quality. The intensity of crop damage depends on the quantity and combination of salts in the soil solution, the soil management system, and the crops' tolerance of saline and sodic conditions.

The presence of highly soluble salts in the soil solution, which determines the effect on crop growth, depends on the water content of the soil and on the quantity and type of salts in the capillary zone and in the groundwater as well as of the salts present as crystals.

Some crops have a somewhat higher salt tolerance than others. The critical values for most crops, however, are rather low. Even a very low salt content in the soil may harm crop growth, and the range in salt content that is acceptable for crops is very small.

There are several methods of soil analysis to determine the salt content. Most of them, however, are insufficient for characterizing the salinity status, because for purposes of desalinization and knowledge of the influence of the salts in crop growth we must know at least: (1) the composition and properties of the various soil layers and horizons; (2) the seasonal variations of the capillary zone and the depth of the groundwater, together with the composition and content of salts in the groundwater; (3) the soil temperature and its seasonal variations, because some salts are more soluble at a high than at a low temperature, e.g., sodium sulfate is 10 times more soluble at 34° C than at 0° C, and consequently, leaching of such salts is much more effective in the hot than in the cold season; (4) the stage of development of crops, because most crops are less salt tolerant in young stages of development than in older stages.

It is evident that within the critical range of soil salinity, the normal analyses made and expressed in EC_e-values are a poor representation of what has to be known. Such analyses are made on a saturated soil extract and expressed at a temperature of 25° C. The real soil solution is not a saturated extract, the soil temperature can be much higher or lower than 25° C, and the EC-value does not indicate which salts are present. Moreover, it has to be realized that salinization and sodication are dynamic processes, changing with time and varying at short distances, vertically and horizontally, within soils. There is a continuous change in salt concentration and salt composition as a result of dilution, migration, diffusion, accumulation, crystallization, and ion exchange on the absorption complex.

It is a pity that soil scientists are more interested in soil with a high salt content than in soil with a salt content in the range of critical values for crops. The latter is of the greatest importance for agriculture.

My experience is that we are analyzing far too many soil samples for salt content without knowing enough about the properties of soils, the groundwater, and the soil salinity where these samples were obtained. Most analyses of soil salinity are useless, not only because of what I stated before, but also useless for planning leaching and desalinization by drainage because very often the time lag betwen analyzing soil and land reclamation is several years. During that period the situation in the field might have changed drastically. Instead of doing just a routine analysis, which often even does not include chemical groundwater analysis, I prefer to study carefully and in a detailed way the salinity status of a number of soils that represent the area to the investigated, in order to get at least an idea of what is happening in these soils, which effects this might have on crop production, and how such soils might be improved.

In this connection one has to realize that salinization and sodication are natural processes governed by a number of factors, and all measures to be taken imply a fight against nature. This also means that once the soils have been desalinized, they need continuous care, or they will become saline again within a few years.

There are many systems of soil classification. The classification of salt-affected soils has always been a difficult and controversial problem. Many soils have been formed by normal soil-forming processes but have become saline because of human activity. Therefore, some soil scientists prefer to classify according to the characteristics of the original soil, adding that the soils are saline. Other soil scientists consider salt-affected soils to be special units in the higher categories of soil classification, which means that they are set apart because of the effect of salinization or sodication.

Textbooks on soil science present systems of soil classification in which salt-affected soils are classified on the basis of chemical properties, salt content, agro-physical characteristics, pedogenesis, morphological characteristics, and so on. These classifications, however, are insufficient when dealing with salt-affected soils in a specific area that must be reclaimed for agriculture. On small-scale soil maps made for a general inventory of the main soils, the four types of solonchaks and the three types of solonetz (as well as the saline and sodic phases of other soils, shown as mapping units of the new Soil Map of the World, scale $1:5,000,000$, made by the Food and Agriculture Organization [FAO]), may present enough information to get a general idea of soil conditions of very large areas.

For practical purposes, more detailed information is needed, particularly in relation to soil reclamation and amelioration. Farmers almost everywhere, where salt-affected soils occur consider soils to be saline if crop yields are less than three times the quantity of seed planted. This often means that some salt crystals can be observed on the land surface. It is very interesting to learn how some farmers have developed special types of management for growing vegetables on small plots of extremely saline land.

My experience is based on investigations of salt-affected soils in agricultural development projects in a number of countries. Investigations in such areas are carried out in cooperation with agronomists, irrigation and drainage engineers, project planners, and economists. Units on soil maps must have a meaning for reclamation purposes, and for agriculture; therefore, various types of salt-affected soils must be distinguished. The most important ones and their characteristics are listed below.

SALT-AFFECTED SOILS

Salt-affected soils contain highly soluble salts in the rooting zone. EC_e is more than $4 \, dS \cdot m^{-1}$ ESP is less than 5, and the pH is lower than 8.2. The highest annual groundwater depth is mostly within the upper 3 m, and the capillary zone is within the rooting zone.

Marine Salt-affected Soils

Marine salt-affected soils are soils in coastal areas that are influenced by seawater or groundwater with a composition similar to that of seawater. Crystals of halite and hydrohalite occur only when the salt content is very high.

Hygroscopic Salt-affected Soils

Hygroscopic salt-affected soils do occur in arid regions. The main salts are magnesium and calcium chlorides, both are hygroscopic salts and very harmful to plant growth, particularly bishofite ($MgCl_2 \cdot 6H_2O$). The soil surface has the color of the moist soil, is gluey, and there are bubbles at the surface. The capillary zone reaches almost to the surface.

These soils are called "Sabakh soils" in Mesopotamia, where they occur widely. They are present in several other countries as well, and they often indicate the presence of mineral oil deep underground. These soils can easily be leached under all circumstances. They are generally very permeable and they will never become sodic.

Fluffy Salt-affected Soils

Fluffy salt-affected soils occur in arid regions. They have a grayish white, loose, powdery, dusty surface layer with long needle-shaped crystals of sodium and magnesium sulfates, mainly as mirabilite ($Na_2SO_4 \cdot 10H_2O$), thenardite (Na_2SO_4), and epsomite ($MgSO_4 \cdot 7H_2O$), the last being the most harmful to crops. These salts are highly soluble, but the solubility is much higher at high temperature than at low temperature, and consequently, leaching during the summer is much more effective than during winter. They generally occur in areas with permeable soils.

Speckled Salt-affected Soils

Speckled salt-affected soils look like normal soils. However, they have some glittering gray and white salt crystals, and many crystals appear on soil profile walls that dry out. Most salt crystals are sodium and magnesium chlorides and sulfates of varying mineral composition and structure.

White Salt-affected Soils

White salt-affected soils have a surface layer of white salt crystals. This layer may vary in thickness from several millimeters to several centimeters. Salt crystals are mainly a mixture of halite ($NaCl$), hydrohalite ($NaCl \cdot 2H_2O$), thenardite, mirabilite, epsomite, leonardite ($MgSO_4 \cdot 4H_2O$), and hexahydrite ($MgSO_4 \cdot 6H_2O$). Some of these soils have a glassy surface crust of bloedite. Such a glassy salt crust is often overlying an anaerobic soil horizon, having a bluish black color and a smell of hydrogen sulfide, which is produced as a result of reduction of sodium sulfate in the presence of organic matter. These soils, which mainly occur in large depressed areas, have a high groundwater table. They generally cannot be reclaimed because of the very high salt content and the low permeability of soils.

Crusty Salt-affected Soils

Crusty salt-affected soils have a variable salt composition and salt content. The main characteristic is a dense, hard, thin surface soil layer, with a curling (feuilleté) structure. The permeability of these soils is generally low. Possibilities of soil improvement depend mainly on soil structure and permeability.

Vertic Salt-affected Soils

Vertic salt-affected soils are a kind of saline Vertisols with a high clay content; low permeability, particularly in the subsoil; and with swelling and shrinking smectite clays, occurring in arid and in some semiarid regions where the groundwater table is deep. They can be reclaimed for special crops, such as cotton, if these soils are carefully irrigated, if rainfall is enough to leach the annually accumulated salts, and if it is cultivated only once in three years.

Internal Salt-affected Soils

Internal salt-affected soils have a deep groundwater table. There are no highly soluble salts in the surface layer; however, salts do occur in or near the rooting zone of the subsoil. There are salts of varying composition, depending primarily on the type of salts occurring in the groundwater. Such soils may occur in semihumid and semiarid regions. Soils with favorable properties can be cultivated; however, they have to be drained to a great depth or they will become saline.

Potential Salt-affected Soils

Potential salt-affected soils are nonsaline soils that, without adequate artificial drainage, will become saline as soon as they are irrigated. Even when the groundwater level is at a depth of several meters below the land surface, these soils will gradually become saline because of the continuous rising groundwater level as a result of irrigation practices.

SODIC SOILS

Sodic soils of this group are characterized by the presence of sodium carbonates and sodium hydrocarbonates in the soil solution, and by crystal soda ($Na_2CO_3 \cdot 10H_2O$), thermonatrite ($Na_2CO_3 \cdot H_2O$), trona ($Na_2CO_3 \cdot NaHCO_3 \cdot 2H_2O$), and nahcolite ($NaHCO_3$) in the crystal phase. These salts are very harmful, particularly if the soil does not contain gypsum. The solubility of these salts is low at low temperature, and high at high soil temperature. The physical properties of these soils change gradually as a result of the formation of sodium clay. There is a migration of clay and organic colloids. Peds in the subsoil are covered by argillans, reducing permeability and rooting volume. Finally a natric horizon is formed. Magnesium carbonate may have a similar effect as sodium carbonate, and therefore magnesium adsorption has to be determined as well. Sodic soils have an ESP of more than 6 and a pH of more than 8.2.

Initial Sodic Soils

Initial sodic soils have the characteristics as described above, except for the natric horizon, because its formation is not yet completed. There are many subtypes. Soil improvement is possible by adding gypsum in order to exchange the sodium on the exchange complex by calcium. As the sodication is still in an initial stage, most soils can be improved considerably.

Natric Sodic Soils

Natric sodic soils are soils in which the physical degradation processes have continued for a long time and a natric horizon has been formed. In arid regions natric horizons may be present at a shallow depth; in subhumid regions they occur at a depth of some decimeters. Some soils can be improved by mixing gypsum with the soil by deep plowing. This is very expensive, however.

Potential Sodic Soils

Potential sodic soils are nonsodic soils, often salt-affected, that may become sodic soils as a result of irrigation practices during which sodium bicarbonates are formed. They have to be recognized by a careful study of the processes that take place.

Pseudo Sodic Soils

Pseudo sodic soils are nonsodic soils with a high ESP, often more than 50 when analyzed according to the normal methods. There is, however, no formation of sodium clay. The soil analysis is influenced by weathering products of sodium silicate, and consequently the ESP is high. However, only thin silica skins, not sodium clay, are observed under the microscope. Crops develop normally in these soils.

Solodic Planosols

Solodic planosols are soils in the final stage of degradation from sodication and solodication. The destruction of clays in the upper soil layers is completed. Soils are strongly leached. A real aerobic horizon and a dense B-horizon has been formed. Such soils can hardly ever be improved.

The soils described above are the main types. There are several subtypes, including combinations of some of them. The gypsiferous soils and the acid-sulfate soils, which also are a kind of salt-affected soil, are not discussed. Reclamation of these soils is very difficult, and generally impossible.

It should be realized that, as mentioned before, soils are units that occur in the field and can be recognized by using simple tools. They can be shown on soil maps to be used for land reclamation purposes. They do not represent taxa of any soil classification system. It is of great importance to select a number of spots where soils must be studied in detail. They should represent the most important soils of the area to be investigated. Samples of representative soils must be analyzed in the laboratory, both chemically and mineralogically. Groundwater samples should be analyzed as well, not only for salt content, but also for the presence or absence of the various cations and anions. The analytical data must be studied carefully. In addition to the study of soil profile pits, deeper soil layers must be examined to a depth of approximately 5 m below the land surface, and permeability tests of all horizons and layers must be made in order to calculate drainages.

The following considerations are important when salt-affected soils are to be improved or reclaimed.

1. It is necessary to distinguish various types of salt-affected soils because: (a) the various highly soluble salts have different influences on plant growth, e.g., chlorides are more harmful than sulfate, magnesium sulfate is worse than sodium sulfate, magnesium chloride is more toxic than calcium chloride, and borates are highly toxic; (b) some salts, like sodium carbonate and bicarbonate, have an irreversible effect on physical soil conditions, and consequently on plant growth; (c) various types of salt-affected soils need a different land reclamation procedure, e.g., those soils with sodium sulfate should be leached during the hot season, others like those with hygroscopic salts can also be leached during the cold season; gypsum as an additive is necessary for some types of salinity, while others such as the Sabakh soils do not need gypsum.

2. The main purpose of investigating salt-affected soils

for land reclamation is to determine how, when, and by which means the productive capacity of the soil can be improved. Salts have to be removed and measures taken to avoid resalinization. Drainage requirements of salt-affected soils, therefore, are completely different from those of non-saline soils whose groundwater level is too high.

3. It is much better and less costly to reclaim small areas of land with a high potential productive capacity, which can be intensively cultivated, than to reclaim larger areas of land with a rather low potential productive capacity. Almost all agricultural development projects in salt-affected areas include too many soils that cannot be reclaimed efficiently and therefore should be excluded from the projects. Unfortunately, this important fact is not always understood by irrigation engineers and planners.

4. Many land reclamation specialists do not realize that the quality of irrigation water that penetrates the soil is different from the quality of the irrigation water, as measured in a river or in a main canal, because a great deal of water evaporates during transport to the field and when it stands on the land.

5. Highly saline soils can be leached by brackish water during the first stages of desalinization if the composition and quantity of salts, both in the brackish water and in the soil, are well known. The salts in the more concentrated leaching water will have a composition different from that of the brackish water or of the soil. Leaching with brackish water means that sometimes groundwater or water that has already been used to leach the last salts from an almost reclaimed area can be used. This may contribute to a more efficient use of irrigation water of good quality. Soil permeability often does not decrease considerably during leaching with brackish water in the first stages of desalinization.

6. Agronomists should pay more attention to various farm management procedures after reclamation is completed. For example, preparation of seedbeds, application of organic and inorganic fertilizers, quality of seeds, plant protection, breeding, etc., have now become important. One has to know how newly reclaimed land will react; therefore, no reclamation project should be started without collecting in advance all necessary information in pilot schemes.

7. Farmers must be taught management procedures to ensure that they can get good yields and that reclaimed land remains nonsaline. Most farmers cannot handle land with salinity in the critical ranges. As even a very low salt content in soil decreases crop yields considerably, the farmer should be given truly nonsaline land on which he can obtain yields that are high enough to pay the production costs and to get a reasonable profit.

8. The project authority should farm newly reclaimed land for at least five years before the land is handed over to private farmers, in order to ensure that land reclamation has been carried out in a proper way and that the farmer and his family can make a living on it. Most farmers are poor and cannot afford a crop failure. The risks of farming in new project areas are extremely high during the first years.

9. Much more attention should be given to the biology of salt-affected soils and to promoting biological activity in newly reclaimed soils. The biological activity of salt-affected soils is very low, and it is even lower after intensive leaching. It should therefore be activated.

10. A final remark will be on the quality of irrigation water in the future. Irrigation, leaching, and drainage of agricultural land will become much more complicated when cities and industries are expanding near rivers that now provide most irrigation water, which is still of good quality at present. New industries and the sewage systems of the expanding cities surely will pollute the river water. New and very serious problems will arise for irrigated agriculture. I am often thinking of what might happen if the highly polluted water of the Rhine River were to be used for irrigation of agricultural land. This water contains, besides various salts, heavy metals, chemicals used by industry and hospitals, and various complicated organic compounds.

I have tried to get an idea of what would happen to soils in the valleys of India, Pakistan, Mesopotamia, and in the Nile Delta if water of a composition similar to that of the Rhine had to be used for irrigation. Unfortunately, I did not succeed; the problem was too complicated. However, it is certain that irrigating land with such water will cause serious problems for agriculture. All countries with large areas of irrigated land and that promote industrial development should be aware of problems that might arise in the future.

19. SALINITY AND FOOD PRODUCTION IN THE INDIAN SUBCONTINENT

I. P. Abrol, Central Soil Salinity Research Institute, Karnal, India

INTRODUCTION

According to current assessment, the present population of India, estimated at 700 million, will reach 1 billion by A.D. 2000. An annual food grains production of 230 million tons would be required to feed this population; at present, production is 150 million tons. This would imply that while an increase in the annual food grains production over the past fifteen years has been only 45 million tons, an increase of about 75 million tons must be achieved over the next fifteen years. The situation is similarly serious in neighboring Pakistan. To achieve these production goals would require a tremendous effort and a multipronged approach. As in the past, increases in food production are likely to be achieved both by bringing additional areas under cropping and by increasing the per-hectare yields of the existing cultivated area. The possibilities of bringing more land under cultivation are limited because more than 85 percent of the potentially arable land is already under cultivation. Thus, the National Commission on Agriculture (1976) estimated that the net cropping area may increase from 140.4 million ha in 1970–71 to 145 million ha in 1985 and 150 million ha in A.D. 2000. An increase in area is therefore likely to contribute only marginally to increased production, and a major effort will be needed to increase the yields in areas already under cultivation. Soil salinity is a major constraint in obtaining increased production through either of the above two approaches in the subcontinent. Soil salinization, alkalinization, and waterlogging are the major desertification processes the world over. Realizing this, the United Nations Conference on Desertification held in Nairobi in 1977 adopted the following recommendations:

> It is recommended that urgent measures be taken to combat desertification in the irrigated lands by preventing and controlling waterlogging, salinization and alkalinization; by reclaiming deteriorated lands; by improving irrigation and drainage systems; by modifying farming techniques to increase productivity in a regular and sustained way by developing new irrigation and drainage schemes where appropriate, always using an integrated approach; and through improvement of the social and economic conditions of people dependent upon irrigated agriculture (United Nations, 1977, 448).

The objective of this chapter is to draw attention to the magnitude of the salinity problem, current programs for mitigating these problems, and the future efforts required for maintaining high productivity of the land.

EXTENT AND NATURE OF SALINITY PROBLEMS

Salinity problems are widespread in the subcontinent. Salt-affected soils are known to occur in almost all climatic conditions ranging from humid to arid. Along the coastal areas excess salts affect crop growth because of the ingress of seawater through estuaries, creeks, and rivers; because of groundwater flows, and because of inundation during high tides. By far the most serious problems of salinity are in the arid, semiarid, and subhumid regions. Available estimates of the extent of salt-affected or waterlogged soils are largely tentative, and very little effort has been made to map these on a national scale. According to El Gabaly (1977), out of a total of 15 million ha of irrigated land in Pakistan, nearly 11 million ha or 75 percent of the irrigated land suffers to varying degrees from salinity, waterlogging, or both, with a pronounced reduction in the yield of most crops. In India nearly 7 million ha of salt-affected lands have reached a level of zero productivity (Abrol, 1982). In another 20 million ha of land irrigated by canals, the productivity has been reduced to varying degrees because of salts. The 7 million ha now lying unproductive constitute about 5 percent of the potentially arable land but are otherwise a part of the most productive terrain, and accumulation of excess salts is the sole reason for their unproductivity.

Processes leading to land degradation because of salts may vary depending on the nature of soluble salts involved. Two chief processes are recognized: salinization and alkalinization. Salinization is the major process; soils are influenced by excess neutral soluble salts, including the chlorides and sulfates of sodium, calcium, and magnesium. Alkalinization results in the formation of alkali soils, also termed sodic soils, and is due to the influence of salts, for example, sodium carbonate, that are capable of raising the alkalinity of soil. It is important to distinguish between these two categories because efforts to control these processes and to reclaim the deteriorated lands are likely to require specific approaches. These two groups of salt-affected soils differ not only in their chemical and physical characteristics but also in their geographical distribution. While saline soils tend to dominate the arid and semiarid regions, alkali soils are widespread in the subhumid regions.

THE CONTRIBUTING FACTORS

The processes leading to salt accumulation in the root zone of soils, and rendering them partially or completely unproductive, are largely the result of human intervention in one form or another.

Rise in the Groundwater Level

The subcontinent experiences a monsoon-type climate in which the major portion of rainfall is received in a brief period of two to three months. Both the total amount of rain and its distribution are highly variable, making crop production very unstable. Data in Table 1 are an example of the rainfall pattern in a medium rainfall (700 mm) area of India. These data show that, for a two-year return period, two-day maximum rainfall may be up to 155 mm accompanied by a dry spell of twenty-eight days. Since evapotranspiration is high during the rainy season, raising rainfed crops is risky. Irrigation, is therefore the most effective means of stabilizing agricultural production in the subhumid and semiarid regions and of having any production in the arid regions. For this reason, the Indian government has made huge investments in creating a large irrigation potential in the postindependence era.

Before the introduction of irrigation into an area a water balance exists between the rainfall on one hand and the stream flow, groundwater table, evaporation, and transpiration on the other. This balance is seriously disturbed when large quantities of water are introduced artificially for growing crops, introducing additional factors of groundwater recharge from seepage from canals, distributaries, and unlined field channels from the irrigation water released onto the fields over and above the quantities actually utilized by the crops. As a result of these, the groundwater table rises. Several studies (Gardner, 1958; Khosla et al., 1980) have shown that once the groundwater table is close to the soil surface, within 2 m, there is an appreciable upward movement of groundwater because of evaporation from the soil surface (Fig. 1), resulting in accumulation of salts in the root zone. Since the groundwaters in most arid and semiarid regions contain appreciable quantities of soluble salts, soil salinization is further aggravated. Some examples follow.

The water from the Bhakhra canal system was introduced in parts of the Hissar district in Haryana in northern India in 1963. Fig. 2 shows the rise in water table in twenty years following the introduction of irrigation. Large areas irrigated by canals are already salinized, and the problem is becoming more serious each year.

The left bank canal of the Tungabhadra irrigation project in Karnataka state was commissioned in 1953. A study

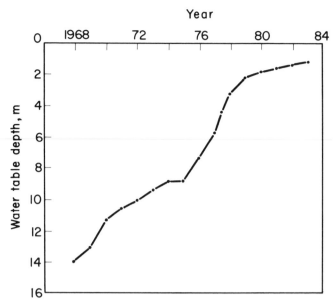

Fig. 1. Schematic relationship between the depth of water table and evaporation from the soil surface.

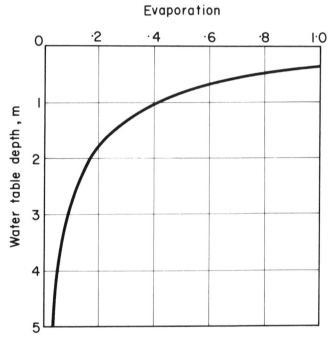

Fig. 2. Changes in water table at the experimental farm of Haryana Agricultural University at Hissar following introduction of irrigation from the Bhakhra canal system in 1963.

Table 1. Frequency analysis of maximum rainfall (mm) for one, two, and three days, and the length of dry spell at Karnal, India.

Event	Return Period (years)				
	1.01	2.33	5	10	100
One day's rainfall	41	120	152	183	289
Two day's rainfall	51	155	201	238	355
Three day's rainfall	61	171	219	258	381
Dry spell (days)	15	28	34	39	54

SOURCE: Dhruva Narayana et al., 1978.

made thirty years later showed that about 33,000 ha had been severely affected by waterlogging and salinity. It was further estimated that this area was expanding at the rate of 6,000 ha annually. Production from about 20,000 ha had already reached a zero level, forcing the cultivators to abandon their lands. In three years this area is likely to double. In the initial years of soil degradation, the cultivators tend

Table 2. Impact of waterlogging and salinity on the yield of rice in the Tungabhadra command area.

Period	Rice Yield (t/ha[a])
Before the rise of groundwater table	2.28
After the rise of groundwater table	1.65

SOURCE: Bowonder and Ravi, 1984.
[a] Average of seventeen farms.

to switch to more tolerant crops such as rice, but even the production of the tolerant crops is substantially reduced (Table 2) apart from accelerating the degradation of additional areas because of inefficient water use.

In the Nagarjunsagar project command area, nearly 25,000 ha of the 140,000 ha in irrigation have been affected by salinity and waterlogging in a period of only fourteen years.

Such examples could be enumerated one after another. A rise in water table and consequent soil degradation are the natural corollary to irrigation introduction, and, for any long-term success in maintaining land productivity, preventive and/or corrective measures become a necessity.

Inadequate Drainage Measures

It has long been recognized that for lasting success in irrigated agriculture, adequate provisions must be made in the system for the drainage of excess water. However, this has rarely been done. There is often a tendency, for political and socioeconomic reasons, to find only the money required for rapid establishment of irrigation facilities to grow food crops quickly and to defer or omit the drainage works in the hope that either they will not be required or that the necessary funds would be found when the project is producing a profit. Unfortunately, the cost of providing drainage and reclamation when the lands have already become waterlogged and salinized is much higher, apart from the huge losses already suffered through partial or complete loss of production of the affected areas. As early as 1928 the report of the Royal Commission on Agriculture in India stated:

> It would appear that many of the troubles which have arisen in the irrigated tracts of India in regard to waterlogging and formation of salty lands have been due to failure to properly correlate a new irrigation system with the natural drainage of the tract. *We have little doubt that the lesson has been learnt* and that where this is not already the practice a careful drainage survey which could include estimates for drainage construction will, in future, form an integral part of all new irrigation projects."

In practice this aspect has been grossly neglected such that problems of salinity and waterlogging continue to increase. Although the subcontinent can be proud of having the largest amount of irrigated area in the world, it is doubtful if even a few square kilometers have a well-planned drainage system. The existing drainage provisions, if any, are largely intended to remove water stagnation caused by excess rain, and thus the attempt is to divert the excellent quality rainwater to the sea—a policy which needs serious reconsideration.

Table 3. Approximate order of losses and utilization of irrigation water in some northern India canals.

Particulars	Approximate value (%)
Losses in the main canal and branches	15 to 20
Losses in the major and minor distributaries	6 to 8
Losses in the field channels	20 to 22
Losses during application, including deep percolation, evaporation, etc.	25 to 27
Utilization by crops via evapotranspiration	28 to 29

SOURCE: Gopinath, 1976.

Faulty Water Management Practices

In the early stages of irrigation development, it was considered sufficient to deliver water to blocks of 100 to 150 ha through pipe outlets from canals and distributaries. How the farmers within these blocks, each farmer holding only a few acres, shared the water, equitably or otherwise, was left to the farmers. The development of agriculture was considered automatic once water was delivered at an outlet. In recent projects the block was reduced from 100 to 150 ha to about 40 ha. Clyma and Corey (1974) made several measurements on the field application efficiencies of irrigation water in traditionally farmed fields at several locations in Pakistan. Their studies showed that almost three-fourths of the measurements indicated efficiencies of less than 30 percent and over half of the measurements showed efficiencies of less than 20 percent. Table 3 presents the results of some measurements on the magnitude of water losses in some northern India canals. A discussion of factors responsible for low efficiency utilization of the available water potential follows.

Excessive irrigation. For practical reasons, head reaches of a canal become fit to receive water much earlier than the tail ones. The work of constructing field channels and of leveling land for water application is slow, often resulting in a gap of several years between development of head and tail reaches of a canal project. During early stages of development, demand for water in the lower reaches is low; therefore, much more water is available to the farmers in the upper reaches than is their due. For this reason the farmers start consuming large amounts of water by irrigating such areas and growing such crops as are otherwise prohibited in the project. The farmers also tend to overirrigate their fields because of the uncertainty of getting the next irrigation at an appropriate interval.

Unscheduled cropping patterns. At the project planning stage, water deliveries to an area are planned with definite cropping patterns in mind. In practice, however, these are rarely adopted. In the Tungabhadra project command area, only 13 percent of the irrigated area was planned for heavily irrigated crops, the remainder being for light irrigation. A study in 1971–72 and again in 1981–82 (Table 4) showed that there was much more area under heavily irrigated crops. This coupled with low application efficiencies has accentuated the increase in water table and salinity problems in many areas.

Table 4. Area planned and actually covered under heavy and light irrigated crops.

Irrigation Type	Area Planned (ha)	Area Covered (ha)	
		1971–72	1981–82
Heavy	30,000 (13%)	37,616 (32%)	60,389 (25%)
Light	2,02,000 (87%)	78,135 (68%)	1,86,675 (75%)

SOURCE: Bowonder and Ravi, 1984.

Inadequate land development. Inadequate land leveling resulting in nonuniform water application is the single most important factor contributing to low water use efficiency, nonuniform leaching of salts, and soil salinization.

Fallowing. Spreading limited quantities of water over a wide area is yet another factor responsible for speeding up the rate of soil salinization. This is so because insufficient water is available to meet both the crop water requirements and the water needs to meet the leaching requirements for the control of salts in the root zone. For this reason, even within the command of an irrigation project, crops are grown in large areas under unirrigated conditions or the land is left fallow. Fallowing encourages salt accumulation in the root zone, and salinization may be severe if the fallow period is long, if evaporative demand is high, and if the groundwater is shallow and saline.

Social factors. Land fragmentation and associated difficulties in the transport and application of water result in inefficient water use and in the spread of salinity. The system of land tenure whereby the cultivators may be share-tenants who are often moved from one area to another is yet another factor that encourages land degradation. Existing water laws and pricing systems are also not conducive to efficient water use.

CONTROL OF SOIL SALINITY

Maintaining the long-term productivity of irrigated lands using salinity control is a complex process. The complications arise because of the large number of factors involved as well as our limited understanding of the way they interact under natural conditions. There is an urgent need to develop appropriate technologies for reclaiming lands that have gone out of cultivation and to prevent additional areas from being affected by the salinization processes. The term "technology" refers to these areas. These include: the method of land preparation, selection of the best-suited crops, varieties and sequences, fertilization, irrigation, drainage, and farm water-management practices, etc. The technologies developed must be relevant and adaptable to the farmers' level and needs. Thus, efforts must be made simultaneously to:

1. Enhance our understanding of the basic principles involved in the management of our resources. These will cut across several different disciplines, including soil-water-plant-climate relationships, surface and subsurface hydrologies, and geohydrology. An enhanced understanding will provide us with the capability to predict, in a quantitative manner, the changes in time and space consequent upon imposition of a set of practices like the effects of a change in cropping pattern on the water balance of an area, and the results of providing drainage in an area with regard to its salt and water balance.

2. Develop and improve upon practices that will result in:
   (a) efficient on-farm water use. This will require efforts to define optimum water needs of crops, water delivery regulation according to the crop requirements, optimum methods for land preparation, etc.
   (b) efficient drainage of the irrigated areas. Efforts must be directed at defining the optimum methods of drainage of surface water and groundwaters, practices for controlling the quality of drainage flows and their environmental impact, maintenance of drains including control of weeds, etc.
   (c) Optimum conjunctive use of surface water and groundwaters with a view toward controlling the water table, maintaining a favorable balance of quantity and quality of water, conserving rainwater, etc.

3. Develop an infrastructure for the transfer of technologies to the farmers through continuing education programs and pilot and demonstration projects.

4. Provide a mechanism for constant review, change, and implementation of legal provisions, water laws, pricing systems, etc., to bring about a disciplined use of soil and water resources.

SOME ACCOMPLISHMENTS

The intent here is not to convey that efforts to find solutions to the problems have been lacking. In recent years implementation of the "on-farm water management" improvement programs has been considerably strengthened by setting up Command Area Development Authorities in nearly eighty irrigation projects. Technologies developed for the reclamation of alkali soils (Abrol, 1983) occupying nearly 2.5 million ha in the Indo-Gangetic plains have found wide acceptance by the farmers, and in the past seven to eight years, more than 300,000 ha of barren alkali soils were reclaimed in the states of Haryana, Punjab, and Uttar Pradesh, resulting in more than 1.5 million tons of food grains production annually. Over the next ten years reclamation of nearly 1.5 million ha of alkali lands, which will contribute more than 8 million tons of food grains annually, is proposed. In Pakistan several salinity control and reclamation projects (SCARP) were launched and have yielded good results (Rathur, 1982). These successes, notwithstanding the urgent need for accelerated efforts to solve salinity problems on a sound scientific basis, cannot be overemphasized.

CONCLUSIONS

The problems of salinity control are indeed complex. There appear to be no simple and straightforward solutions. Our ability to deal with these effectively will require in-depth understanding of the widely different disciplines involved, including soil-water-plant-climate relationships, surface- and groundwater hydrologies, geohydrology, etc., and their interactions in an integrated manner. A very sound research base, equally strong field monitoring programs, and vigorous field implementation programs based on well-tested technologies are the only answer. Shortcuts to success have proved very costly in the past. Research programs of the appropriate magnitude must be organized to define and to improve upon ways of managing our water resources at distribution and "on-farm use" stages. A continuous effort to improve upon the efficiency of water use, installation of drainage systems as an integral part of any irrigation system, together with increasing the level of education of the farming community, will help in better utilization of scarce soil resources while preventing their degradation.

REFERENCES

Abrol, I. P. 1982. Reclamation of wastelands and world food prospects. Pp. 317–37. *In* Transactions of the 12th international congress of soil science. New Delhi.

Abrol, I. P. 1983. Salt affected soils and their management. Pp. 221–33. *In* Isotope and radiation techniques in soil physics and irrigation studies 1983. Vienna: International Atomic Energy Agency.

Bowonder, B., and C. Ravi. 1984. Waterlogging from irrigation projects: an environmental management problem. p. 41. (Mimeographed) Hyderabad: Center for Energy, Environment and Technology, Administrative Staff College of India.

Clyma, W., and G. L. Corey. 1974. The importance of farm water management in Pakistan. Field Report No. 2. Fort Collins: Colorado State University.

Dhruva Narayana, V. V., S. K. Gupta, and A. K. Tiwari. 1978. Rainfall and runoff analysis for rainwater management in agriculture. Proceedings of symposium on hydrology of rivers with small and medium catchments. *New Delhi, Central Board of Irrigation and Power* 130 (2):43–58.

El Gabaly, M. M. 1977. Problems and effects of irrigation in the near east region. Pp. 239–49. *In* E. E. Worthington (ed.) Arid land irrigation in developing countries. Elmsford, N.Y.: Pergamon Press.

Gardner, W. R. 1958. Some steady state solutions of the unsaturated moisture flow equation with application of evaporation from a water table. *Soil Science* 85:228–32.

Gopinath, C. 1976. Problems and concepts in irrigation use. Pp. 10–15, 201. *In* Role of irrigation in the development of India's agriculture. Bombay: The Indian Society of Agricultural Economics.

Khosla, B. K.; R. K. Gupta, and K. L. Chawla. 1980. Evaluating the field hydraulic conductivity and soil salinization under conditions of high water table. Pp. 256–64. *In* Proceedings of the international symposium on salt affected soils. Karnal, India: Central Soil Salinity Research Institute.

National Commission on Agriculture. 1976. Abridged Report. P. 748. New Delhi: Ministry of Agriculture and Irrigation, Government of India.

Rathur, A. Q. 1982. A review of salinity and waterlogging in the Indus basin area of Punjab, Pakistan. Pp. A15.1–15.16. *In* Proceedings of the first international symposium on soil geology and landforms: impact on land use planning in developing countries. Bangkok: Asian Institute of Technology.

Royal Commission on Agriculture in India. 1928. Bombay: Government Central Press.

United Nations. 1977. Desertification: its causes and consequences. Elmsford, N.Y.: Pergamon Press.

20. SALINITY MANAGEMENT IN NILE DELTA FOOD PRODUCTION

Yehia Barrada, Faculty of Agriculture, University of Cairo, Giza, Egypt

ABSTRACT

The population of Egypt is increasing at an annual rate of 2.8 percent, and the per capita area of cultivated land decreased from 0.214 ha in 1897 to 0.05 in 1985. The number of holdings, 2.9 million, has an average size of 0.84 ha. Egypt's average annual share of the Nile water at Aswan is 55.5×10^9 m^3. Much water is wasted, and the irrigation efficiency ranges from 44 to 58 percent. Water balance studies of the aquifer under the Nile valley show 2.9×10^9 m^3 per year. Overirrigation; inefficiency of drainage; and seepage from head regulators, canals, and relatively higher, newly reclaimed land caused a gradual rise in the water table. Waterlogging, salinity and hardpan formation are the cause of deterioration of about 50 percent of the total area under cultivation.

One of the world's biggest projects aimed at providing 2.1 million ha with drainage networks is under way and will be completed by 1990. Reducing water conveyance and distribution losses, improving the efficiency of water use, providing an effective drainage system, and applying appropriate soil amelioration techniques are essential for increasing food production. Establishing an experimental farm on sandy soils, more effective extension service, and better coordination of applied research are also badly needed.

INTRODUCTION

The cultivated area of Egypt is about 2.4 million ha or about 2.49 percent of the total area. The area under cultivation consists of the irrigated Nile Delta and the narrow strips on either side of the river, as well as a small rainfed area covering the north desert coast of Alexandria to about 15 km from the sea. Rainfall averages 192 mm per year, mostly during the winter months (November to March). The rapidly growing population of Egypt and the improvement of the standard of living challenge agriculture with a continuously increasing demand for products. Great efforts are being made to increase food, feed, and fiber production through increasing yields per unit area, intensifying the cropping patterns to achieve a cropping index higher than 2, and bringing new land areas under cultivation. During the past five decades, about 0.44 million ha of new land were brought under cultivation (Table 1). However, the expansion of villages and urban centers, as well as various other nonagricultural developments, consumed an appreciable area of fertile land. A conservative estimate indicates that more than 15,000 ha per year are lost from agriculture. Table 2 shows that since 1897, the per capita area of cultivated land decreased and the population increased.

A rather optimistic estimate for the per capita area of cultivated land by the year 2000 is 0.043 ha. This is based on the assumptions that the population of Egypt will continue to increase at the same rate observed in 1984−85 (2.8 percent), thus reaching 72.6 million by 2000, while 0.945 million ha of new land will be brought under cultivation (0.063 million ha per year), and only 0.189 million ha are used for various nonagricultural developments.

The system of inheritance coupled with the rigid laws of land reform, which limit the ownership of land to a maximum of 21 ha per person and make land rent permanent and inheritable, contributes to the fragmentation of land. Hindi (1983) stated that the number of holdings exceeds 2.9 million. The average size is about 0.84 ha, which is very small as a production unit. The number of parcels making up a holding varies from one to ten. Each parcel may be cultivated with a different crop according to a specific rotation. The final result is a dispersed system of land use, which makes the application of adequate management practices difficult in many respects.

Reclamation of new lands at higher levels adjacent to the delta and the Nile valley, the availability of greater amounts of water after establishing the Aswan High Dam, land fragmentation, and inadequate management practices, caused an appreciable deterioration of over 1 million ha of old fertile land. Of the area now under cultivation in Egypt, 16 percent is newly reclaimed land. Its production, however, is less than 3 percent of the total national agricultural production. In view of the high cost of land reclamation and the long period of time needed to reach production potential, Hindi (1983) states that higher priority should be given to investing funds for the amelioration of deteriorated old land, the development of better soil and water management practices, and soil consolidation programs, as the returns will definitely be quicker and higher than those anticipated from investments on reclamation of new land.

With the rapidly and continuously increasing demands for food and fiber, agriculture has a long way to go in making more rational use of its limited water and land resources.

WATER RESOURCES

Agriculture in Egypt depends on Nile water. The Aswan High Dam allows for complete control of the Nile water and makes storage of water from one year to another possible. The total storage capacity is 164×10^9 m^3. The average annual flow arriving at Aswan is 84×10^9 m^3, which consists of:

Sudan's share	$= 18.5 \times 10^9$ m^3/yr
losses in Lake Nasser	$= 10 \ \ \times 10^9$ m^3/yr
available in Egypt	$= 55.5 \times 10^9$ m^3/yr

Between 1968 and 1978, the amounts of water flowing annually through the High Dam ranged from 53.8 to 62.2×10^9 m^3.

Table 1. Areas of reclaimed soil.

Period	Area (ha)
Before 1952	68,000
1961–1965	210,000
1966–1970	105,000
1970–1984	58,000
Total	441,000

Table 2. Decrease of per capita area of cultivated land in Egypt since 1897.

Year	Population (millions)	Area under Cultivation (million ha)	Average per Capita Area under Cultivation (ha)
1897	9.717	2.076	0.214
1907	11.190	2.257	0.202
1917	12.817	2.230	0.174
1927	14.178	2.238	0.158
1937	15.921	2.231	0.140
1947	18.967	2.420	0.128
1960	26.085	2.478	0.095
1966	30.075	2.520	0.084
1970	33.200	2.520	0.076
1976	38.228	2.574	0.067
1985	48.000	2.394	0.050

SOURCE: Adapted from "Plan for Irrigation Development in Egypt," Ministry of Irrigation, 1979.

During 1978 and 1984, 3.5 and 4×10^9 m^3 of water, respectively, were allowed to pass through the dam to cover the needs of navigation and electricity production during the closure of canals (January and February) and between crops (September and October) (Ministry of Irrigation, Cairo, 1979). As Sudan does not use all of its share of the Nile water, the available water to Egypt often exceeds its average annual share.

Irrigation as practiced in Egypt today makes inefficient use of available water resources. Huge amounts of water are wasted and contribute to a rising water table, waterlogging, and salinity problems. A study of the water released from the Aswan High Dam and the recoverable losses for the 1974 water year (USDA, 1976), indicated that irrigation efficiency ranges from 44 to 58 percent. This is a low figure for a river system such as the Nile, from which many of the losses are recoverable. Further, the amount of water remaining in the system and potentially contributing to raising the water table is estimated at 10×10^9 m^3, equivalent to 0.42 m of depth over the total irrigated area in 1974 (USDA, 1976).

Table 3 shows the quantities of irrigation water, the quantities of drainage water (in the delta) and the percentage of drainage water to irrigation water during the period 1970–78 (El Quesy, 1983). El Quesy (1983) indicated that the rate of drainage in the delta is about 3 mm per day. The leaching requirement ranges between 1 and 1.5 mm per day,

Table 3. Quantity of irrigation and drainage water for the delta.

Year	Quantity of Irrigation Water ($\times 10^9$ m^3)	Quantity of Drainage Water ($\times 10^9$ m^3)	Drainage to Irrigation Water (%)
1970	26.990	14.025	51.9
1971	30.054	14.386	47.0
1972	32.003	14.847	46.3
1973	29.173	16.020	54.0
1974	29.731	15.528	52.2
1975	30.246	15.941	52.6
1976	31.178	16.238	52.4
1977	32.175	16.261	50.5
1978	32.591	15.989	49.6
Average	30.460	15.471	50.8

SOURCE: El-Quesy, 1983.

so the remainder is considered to be excessive and could be saved if the appropriate management practices are applied. Therefore, 7.75 to 10.32×10^9 m^3 of water are wasted annually as excessive irrigation water.

If the existing water supply is to be utilized for development of additional new lands or increased cropping index on old lands, this water must come from one or more of the following sources: (1) improved irrigation efficiencies through the development of better water management practices, (2) reduction of canal losses by lining areas of high seepage, (3) increasing the amount of reuse from the drainage system, (4) increased use of groundwater, (5) reuse of municipal and industrial wastewater, and (6) modification of cropping patterns.

About 3.6×10^9 m^3 of water now used to meet the navigation, barrage safety, and hydropower demands could be utilized. Hefni (1983) indicated that the water balance studies of the aquifer under the Nile valley show an increase of recharge to the sum of losses and extractions which exceeds 2.9×10^9 m^3 per year showing a general trend of increases in the groundwater levels. The Drainage Research Institute, which carried out the aforementioned studies, estimates the amounts of usable groundwater resources to be up to 5×10^9 m^3 per year. These data show clearly that for the time being, and at least for the coming two decades, enough water is available for all planned developments, including increasing the cropping index and new land reclamation. In fact, water management is a major constraint for agricultural production while water availability is not, at least for now and in the near future.

Projects to add irrigation water by increasing the annual flow into Lake Nasser are being pursued. Egypt's share of the water anticipated from the planned Upper Nile projects is estimated at 9.5×10^9 m^3 per year.

LAND RESOURCES

The total land area of Egypt is 100 million ha. Despite the large amount of available area, suitable land for crop production is scarce. The best cropland is in the Nile valley downstream from the Aswan High Dam and in the delta downstream from Cairo. The delta comprises 68 percent of the total cultivated area in Egypt.

The major part of the delta is made up of alluvial plain sediments deposited by seven main branches. Only two remain today. Under natural conditions, water overflowed the banks, and the changes in water velocity resulted in the deposition of sediments in a soil sequence composed of relatively narrow, coarse-textured strips of higher elevation running adjacent to the channels, gradually dropping to broader and finer textured strips with increasing distance from the channels. Thus, interrelated texture-relief soil catinas were formed along each channel. These merge in the middle of the delta, producing depressions of heavy clay soils between the channels. Around the borders of the delta, alluvium merges with soils of different parent materials, producing interference zones in which the properties of one soil gradually change into those of the other. The resulting microrelief of the delta is summed up as fingerlike projections of higher land joined at the base and spreading fan-shaped into the lowlands of the north with depressions appearing in between.

From the present 2.4 million ha surveyed as cultivated land in Egypt, the productivity of only 5 percent is classified as excellent, 40 percent as good, and the remaining 55 percent as either fair or poor. This limitation in productive land resources is holding back the effect of any other agricultural improvement or additional inputs on increasing agricultural production in Egypt. The deterioration of soil productivity of the present cultivated land is often reported as being caused by soil salinity, alkalinity, waterlogging, subsoil compaction, and hardpan formation.

Massoud (1983) stated that the role of groundwater as a factor in salt-affected soil formation depends on salt concentration, depth, and motion of the water. Generally, a water depth of 1 to 3 m is considered critical, especially under high evaporation demand and where movement of fresh irrigation water is limited by restricted internal drainage conditions. On the other hand, the mineral concentration of the groundwater is considered critical if it is 2 to 3 $g \cdot L^{-1}$ for Cl or SO_4 type or 0.7 to 1.0 $g \cdot L^{-1}$ for soda waters.

Mineralized groundwater is also a source of salinity and sodicity when used for irrigation. The extent of its effect depends on the salt concentration and composition, quantity, method of application, and the soil properties. The drainage water which is partially reused for irrigation in the delta contains on the average only 700 to 1000 $mg \cdot L^{-1}$ total salts, because of the important dilution with unused water which passes directly from the ends of conveyance canals to the drainage network. However, its salt content should be periodically monitored. It should also be used with caution, preferably after mixing with freshwater, only at times of water shortage, or when no other source is available.

Variation of macro and micro relief also contributes to soil degradation in different ways. Changes in elevation even of a magnitude of 2 to 3 m result in salinization of the lower parts where the water table is closer to the surface. On the other hand, changes in the micro relief on the order of less than 30 cm result in increasing salt content on the raised spots and better leaching in the low areas, which may explain the spotted nature of salinity observed in poorly leveled fields.

A gradual rise in the water table has occurred during this century as a result of overirrigation; inefficiency of drainage; and seepage from head regulators, canals, and relatively high, newly reclaimed land. Both the intensity of groundwater evaporation and the salt accumulation process increase as the groundwater level approaches the surface.

Mashali (1983) stated that under the arid climatic conditions of Egypt where the total evaporation ranges from 1500 to 3000 mm per year, the salt accumulation processes attain their maximum when the groundwater level reaches a depth of 2 to 3 m or less. The capillary flow of the groundwater is affected by evaporation, soil texture, porosity, water-holding capacity, permeability, and available moisture content.

The most common observation is the salinization of soil strips running parallel to irrigation canals. Canals are invariably placed in old river channels or on land of relatively high elevation and, consequently, with coarser soil texture. Thus, seepage has caused severe damage to the productivity of adjacent soils. Also, the general seepage from higher land has compounded the salinization problem in the depressions. In the soils of the northern delta, the problem of salinity is grave. With the approach to northern lakes, the soils become heavier, the elevation decreases, the groundwater becomes more saline (due to contamination with seawater), and the water table approaches the soil surface.

Saline and salt-affected soils in Egypt make up about 840,000 ha and are concentrated mainly in the northern part of the delta. In addition, salinity has been noted in another 400,000 ha in sufficient levels to affect crop production.

SALINITY MANAGEMENT

Improving the productivity of saline and salt-affected soils in the Nile Delta should be based on the results of sound applied research programs aimed at investigating the causes of soil deterioration, finding out the most appropriate means of recovery, setting preventive measures, and maintaining high soil productivity levels. Research should be planned and implemented by interdisciplinary teams of scientists, including irrigation, drainage, and farm mechanization engineers, as well as specialists in soils, agronomy, and agricultural economics. Also, extension service specialists must be involved in the planning and execution of research.

Institutes active in applied agricultural research in Egypt are numerous and belong to different ministries. The universities, the Executive Authority for Land Improvement Projects (established in 1971), the National Research Centre, the Soil and Water Research Institute of the Agricultural Research Center of the Ministry of Irrigation and its various Institutes (irrigation, drainage, and groundwater research institutes), and the Desert Institute are among the active organizations in research aimed at improving soil productivity. However, the level of cooperation between the research institutes and the coordination of their research programs have much room for improvement.

By far, irrigation and drainage are the most important practices that contribute to both the solution or creation of salinity problems in soils. Using furrow irrigation (long furrows), together with land leveling and the reshaping of fields, would improve water use efficiency by increasing uniformity of water distribution, reduce water consumption, decrease the load on drainage networks, and prevent spot salinization. Improvement of the physical environment of the root zone, proper soil and water management, subsoiling, and applying gypsum also contribute a great deal to improving the productivity of saline and salt-affected soils.

During the past two decades, great effort was made and sound applied research programs were performed to improve the productivity of saline and salt-affected soils. Some major activities and a few research results are discussed below.

Recognizing that effective drainage is the key to improving productivity of saline and salt-affected soils, the Egyptian government in 1970 started one of the world's largest irrigation projects. It was planned to provide approximately 0.42 million ha in the Nile Delta with covered field drainage systems (Abdel Deim, 1983). By 1984, the Egyptian Public Authority for Drainage Projects provided 1.092 million ha with a drainage network. An additional 1.008 million ha will be provided with a drainage system to be completed by 1990.

Abu-Zeid (1983) discussed the possibility of using vertical drainage, especially in low-lying lands close to newly reclaimed high lands and along the Nile in areas just upstream from existing or new barrages. Vertical drainage appears to be promising because of the very large existing underground water reservoir, the good quality of groundwater (200 to 500 mg·L^{-1} total salts), and the need for water resources for future agricultural expansion.

Research to develop the design criteria for drainage systems and to evaluate the effect of drainage on soil productivity is very active. For example, El-Guindy (1983) found that the dry matter production of Berseem (*Trifulium alexandrium*) increased on heavy clay soils in the northwest and northeast delta by 36 and 18 percent, respectively, as a result of the introduction of drainage.

Mashali (1983) stated that a 58 percent increase in cotton yield was achieved in Kalioubia in 1968 as a result of plowing, subsoiling, gypsum application, and establishing open drains with suitable slopes at a depth of 100 cm. Similar experiments at various locations in the delta gave similar results with other crops. As a result of the success achieved, the Executive Authority for Land Improvement Projects was established in 1971. It has the overall responsibility for land improvement projects in Egypt.

Genet and Malik (1978) recommended the maintenance of the water table following an irrigation application at least 1 m below the surface for areas west of Noubaria Canal. This criterion is slightly stricter than the provisionally applied salinity control criterion. They also recommended a spacing of 50 m at a depth of 2 m for the field tile drain in the North Tahrir pilot area.

Table 4. Cotton and wheat yields as affected by different drainage treatments.

Drainage Treatment		Seed Yield Cotton (Giza 70/89)		Wheat Yield (Sakha 69)	
(Depth, cm)	(Spacing, m)	(ton/ha)	(%)	(ton/ha)	(%)
90 to 120	50	1.470	100	3.541	100
	25	2.351	160	4.262	120
	12.5	2.846	194	4.487	127
120 to 150	50	1.927	100	3.616	100
	25	2.220	115	4.371	121
	12.5	2.944	153	4.718	131

SOURCE: USDA, 1984.

A comprehensive research program was initiated in 1975 to develop a drainage guide for soils that includes depth and spacing requirements at two locations, one representing fine-textured soil (clay) in the northern delta region and one for loamy soils (clay loam) in Upper Egypt (USDA, 1984).

The results obtained during 1983–84 in Mehallet Mousa Farm (clay soil) are given in Table 4. The increase in production is closely tied to the decrease in drainage spacing. Amer (1979) discussed the development of drainage projects since their initiation in Egypt in 1938 and compared the different techniques and materials used in the implementation of subsurface drainage networks, and the plans of the Egyptian government for providing most of the land under cultivation with drainage systems. He indicated that soil deterioration was stopped, and the yields of the main-field crops were increased by 20 to 30 percent on the average as a result of introducing effective drainage systems.

Irrigation as practiced in Egypt today makes inefficient use of its water resources. Huge amounts of wasted water contribute to a rising water table, waterlogging, and salinity problems, in addition to leaching of nutrients and yield reduction. El-Khadi (1979) indicated that some farmers use twice as much water as that applied by others for irrigating the same crop during the same season at a given location. She also stated that the actual irrigation efficiency is, on the average, 42 percent. The major causes for wasting water are given below.

1. Farm irrigation openings are greater in number and larger in cross section than should be. This causes unfairness in water distribution, as water often does not reach fields at the end of the canal.

2. Private conveyance canals are not properly maintained and are full of weeds, have a cross section much larger than needed, and are connected to the drainage system.

3. There is no water use coordination among farmers using the same canal.

4. As farmers get the water free of charge, they have no incentive to give the necessary effort or make the required investment to save water.

5. The rotation system makes farmers fear that water stress may take place while water is unavailable in the canal, and thus they irrigate at the beginning and the end of the same rotation period.

6. At the early stages of plant growth, farmers use much more water than the plants need.

7. Lack of adequate leveling and inclination, which causes uneven water distribution and great waste of water when using small irrigation basins, is common.

The Irrigation Research Institute of the Ministry of Irrigation (1979) indicated that water consumption in Giza was 129 m³ per hectare per day when water was delivered at the field level. This amount was reduced to 106 m³ per hectare per day when water was delivered at a level 0.5 to 1 m below field level. An increase in yields of wheat and maize by 15 and 20 percent on the average, respectively, was associated with the water savings. This shows clearly that when farmers had to pump irrigation water, they had an incentive for reducing water consumption and avoided wasting it.

Further investigations are needed for determining the optimum depth and spacing of drains, as well as the most appropriate amelioration techniques required in salt-affected soils. Also, improving the efficiency of irrigation and water use on the farm is essential for increasing food production.

Demonstrating research results on a pilot scale on farmers' fields while adopting an integrated approach of the optimum soil, water, and crop management practices is very effective in convincing farmers of the benefits of improved agricultural practices.

RECOMMENDATIONS AND SUGGESTIONS

It is believed that the proper implementation of the following suggestions and recommendations would greatly contribute to increasing feed, food, and fiber production in Egypt and would thus help agriculture cope with the rapidly and continuously increasing demand for its products.

1. Higher priority should be given to investing funds in improving the productivity of deteriorated soils, as this would give higher and quicker returns than funds invested in reclamation of new lands.

2. Avoiding land fragmentation in newly reclaimed areas and encouraging land reconsolidation on established cultivated land by revising the prevailing land reform laws and supporting concentration and specialization in agricultural production on relatively large areas.

3. Increasing crop index up to 2.5 would lead to an appreciable increase in agricultural production. This, however, requires:

(a) Reducing the time necessary for harvesting and removing a crop from the field, as well as that required for soil preparation for the following crop, through intensifying the use of machines to overcome labor shortage at periods of peak demands.

(b) Developing or introducing early maturing, disease-resistant, and high yielding varieties of the main field crop.

4. Highest priority should be given to the following applied research topics, which would provide the basic information necessary for increasing yields, reducing water losses, avoiding soil deterioration, and the hazard of soil salinity and alkalinity:

(a) Determination of water requirements of the main field crops as a function of weather conditions while taking soil properties and quality of irrigation water into consideration.

(b) Improving the efficiency of water use on the farm in order to obtain the highest return in monetary terms for each cubic meter of irrigation water. Precision land leveling and the use of furrow irrigation on old land, as well as using sprinkler or trickle irrigation on the coarser textured soils in the newly reclaimed areas, are likely to contribute to the achievement of this goal. Since agriculture practices that increase dry matter production, reduce yield losses, or conserve water would increase the efficiency of water use, the cooperation of an interdisciplinary team of researchers is needed.

(c) Improving the efficiency of irrigation. It requires large investments, great effort, and many investigations and economic considerations to estimate the cost of a certain improvement and the anticipated benefits in terms of saving water, avoiding soil deterioration, increasing yields as a result of lowering the water table, reducing expenses of pumping drainage water, and the greater possibilities of agricultural expansion through land reclamation (Ministry of Irrigation, Cairo, 1979). Improving the efficiency of irrigation involves mainly the following:

(i) improving the control of water delivery and distribution, and reducing the amounts of irrigation water flowing from the ends of conveyance canals to drainage networks. This requires recalibration of water flow through barrages, revising cross sections of canals, and providing entrances and ends of all canals with adequate gates which allow water flow to be determined.

(ii) controlling weeds in canals. A combination of mechanical and biological control (Chinese mabrouk fish) appears to be very effective (Ministry of Irrigation, Cairo, 1979).

(iii) making water available to farmers at all times at a level about 1 m lower than the fields. The abundance of water rotation would make farmers feel secure, and they would not be tempted to irrigate their fields at the beginning and end of rotation. Also, pumping the water to his field will discourage excessive water application.

(iv) expansion of pipe conveyance systems, periodic cleaning of private canals, and lining canals in high seepage areas would appreciably reduce water losses.

(d) Improving the productivity of deteriorated soils. This requires an effective drainage system, application of various soil amendments (mainly gypsum and organic matter), and subsoiling. Research would address:

(i) determination of adequate spacing depth, length, diameter, material, and inclination of field drains so that the water table is kept at a level which would ensure satisfactory yields and avoid the danger of salinization.

(ii) the need for and amount of gypsum and the best application method.

(iii) the effect of farm yard manure, green manure, and organic matter from other sources on soil properties and crop yields.

(iv) the effect of subsoiling on the physical properties of soil and on crop yields.

5. More support should be given to institutes performing applied research aimed at increasing agricultural production. Closer cooperation between these institutes and better coordination of their research programs should be encouraged. As these institutes belong to different ministries, either a special authority or committee should be established for this purpose, or the Academy of Science may be asked to take up this role.

6. A master plan should be prepared for all possible areas of future agricultural expansion. The plan should indicate priority areas for land reclamation and should be consulted when preparing to reclaim a given land area.

7. Farmers should pay for the water they use for irrigating their fields, as this will provide an effective incentive for them to spend the time, effort, and money necessary to avoid waste. They also should be involved in water management and should cooperate in suggesting and implementing the necessary activities which would ensure proper distribution and minimizing water losses.

8. Extension service should play a more effective role in improving the productivity of deteriorated soil. To achieve this goal, demonstration plots should be established to train farmers and the quality of village extension agents should be elevated.

REFERENCES

Abdel, Diem Safwat. 1983. Field drainage design, construction and maintenance in Egypt. Pp. 72–75. Proceedings on amelioration and development of deteriorated soils in Egypt. FAO Technical Report EGY/79/020.

Abu-Zeid, M. 1983. Vertical drainage in Egypt. Pp. 76–79. *In* Proceedings on amelioration and development of deteriorated soils in Egypt. FAO Technical Report EGY/79/020.

Amer, M. H. 1979. Development of techniques and projects of subsurface drainage. Symposium proceedings on soils and water in food security projects. Egyptian Society of Soil Scientists, Cairo.

El-Guindy, Samia. 1983. Economic evaluation of tile drainage projects. Pp. 186–202. *In* Proceedings on amelioration and development of deteriorated soils in Egypt. FAO Technical Report EGY/79/020.

El-Khadi, M. 1979. Water distribution and food security. Symposium proceedings on soils and water in food security projects. Egyptian Society of Soil Scientists. Cairo.

El-Quesy, Dia. 1983. Hydrological aspects of re-use of drainage water in Egypt. Pp. 108–118. *In* Proceedings on amelioration and development of deteriorated soils in Egypt. FAO Technical Report EGY/79/020.

Genet, W., and M. B. Malik. 1978. Control of waterlogging and salinity in the areas west of the Noubaria Canal. UNDP/FAO Technical Report 4. Rome.

Hefni, Kamal. 1983. Groundwater resources in Nile valley and delta. Pp. 99–104. *In* Proceedings on amelioration and development of deteriorated soils in Egypt. FAO Technical Report EGY/79/020.

Hindi, Kamel. 1983. Economic aspects of water and land resources in Egypt. Pp. 173–84. *In* Proceedings on amelioration and development of deteriorated soils in Egypt. FAO Technical Report EGY/79/020.

Mashali, Amin. 1983. Soil deterioration and role of the Executive Authority for land improvement projects in its control. Pp. 16–31. *In* Proceedings on amelioration and development of deteriorated soils in Egypt. FAO Technical Report EGY/79/020.

Massoud, Fathi I. 1983. Salt affected soils and concepts of control. Pp. 31–42. *In* Proceedings on amelioration and development of deteriorated soils in Egypt. FAO Technical Report EGY/79/020.

Ministry of Irrigation, Cairo. 1979. Plan for irrigation development in Egypt. *In* Proceedings on amelioration and development of deteriorated soils in Egypt. FAO Technical Report EGY/79/020.

Tayel, M. F. 1983. Agricultural extension in Egypt. Pp. 202–10. *In* Proceedings on amelioration and development of deteriorated soils in Egypt. FAO Technical Report EGY/79/020.

U.S. Department of Agriculture. 1976. Egypt's major constraints to increasing agricultural productivity. Foreign Agriculture Economic Report No. 120. Washington, D.C.

U.S. Department of Agriculture. 1984. Criteria for design of drainage systems—depth and spacing requirements of subsurface drains for proper soil drainage. 9th Annual Res. Prog. Rep. US PL 480. Washington, D.C.

Zein, El-Abedin I. 1983. General characteristics of Egyptian alluvial soils. Pp. 13–16. *In* Proceedings on amelioration and development of deteriorated soils in Egypt. FAO Technical Report EGY/79/020.

21. SALINITY AND FOOD PRODUCTION IN AUSTRALIA

A. R. Aston, CSIRO, Canberra, Australia

ABSTRACT

Salinity is both a natural and a man-induced problem in Australia. It is a major area of concern as it affects urban, industrial, and rural growth and development. This chapter is an overview of the salting problems of nonirrigated and irrigated land in Australia and the effects of salinity on food production. Apart from the degradation of a major valuable land resource, the annual cost effect on Australian agricultural productivity is small. However, in certain areas of Australia and rural enterprises in particular, the reductions are significant and there is potential for increased impact in the future. The effect of the predicted carbon dioxide enrichment of the atmosphere on salinity problems is discussed. Suggested management, policies, research, and investigation requirements are outlined.

INTRODUCTION

Salinity is a natural and a man-induced problem in Australia and is an increasing area of concern. Many Australian soils are naturally saline as a result of their hydrogeological development. However, since European settlement, man has upset the balance between water and salt movement in many of these soils and, as a result, has increased the extent of land and stream salinity. A direct consequence of increased salinity is reduced food production.

This chapter is an overview of salinity and food production in Australia and summarizes mainly two reports, to which the reader is referred for further information (Peck et al., 1983; SCSC, 1982).

SALINITY IN AUSTRALIA

Salinity refers to the total concentration of the major ions (Na^+, K^+, Ca^{++}, Mg^{++}, Cl^-, HCO_3^-, $CO_3^=$ and $SO_4^=$) in a solution as measured by the electrical conductivity (EC) of that solution. Conductivity relates to the total soluble salt concentration (TSS) at $25°$ C as

$$TSS = 6.5 \; EC$$

where EC is in $mS·m^{-1}$ and TSS is in $mg·L^{-1}$ (Brown, 1983). The Australian Water Resources Council (AWRC, 1981) classified water on the basis of total dissolved solids concentration (TDS) where $TSS = 1.05 \; TDS$ (Brown, 1983). The AWRC describes water quality as follows:

	TDS $mg·L^-$
Fresh	< 500
Marginal	500–1,000
Brackish	1,000–3,000
Saline	> 3,000

The salinity of a soil is commonly defined as the weight of soluble salts or Cl^{-1} (expressed as NaCl) in a unit weight of dry soil. Surface soils are said to be saline when NaCl content exceeds 0.1 percent for loams and coarser soils or 0.2 percent for clay loams and fine-textured soils. Subsoils are saline when NaCl concentrations exceed 0.3 percent. Northcote and Skene (1972) point out that sodicity and alkalinity in association with excess soluble salt are also characteristic of salt-affected land.

Soil salting is due to the accumulation of soluble salts in parts of or in the total soil profile. These salts come from many different sources. Such sources are weathering of soil and rocks, sea spray, terrestrial salt in dust and rain, periodic marine inundation and other sources such as run-on, seepage, saline irrigation waters, and saline groundwaters. The relative importance of each of these sources depends on the regional climate, topography and land use.

Salts can be accumulated over different time periods. The input of salt in rainfall and dust is very slow, typically 10^{-3} to 10^{-2} $kg·m^{-2}$ per year and can give rise to an increase in soil salinity of the top meter of soil at a rate of around 0.0001 percent per year. However, this low accumulation over millennia has led to significant salt levels within the profile in some areas. Natural weathering of soil and rocks varies considerably, and it is believed that rates are around 10^{-5} $kg·m^{-2}$ per year, which are much less than the content in rain and dust.

Irrigation and/or the movement of salts upward to the soil surface from deeper strata can add salt to the top meter of soil much more rapidly than can rainfall, dust, and weathering. Salt addition to soil by irrigation is a direct result of human activity, but other activities can indirectly result in a flow of groundwater to the surface or an enhancement of existing discharge to streams and rivers. The activities include the storage, conveyance, and disposal of surface water—works which impede natural drainage patterns and cause vegetation and land-use changes.

Salting of Nonirrigated Land

Salts are stored either in the unsaturated zone above the water table or within the saturated zone in aquifers that are either unconfined or confined and under pressure.

Water that has infiltrated the soil surface dissolves stored salts not already in solution. The dissolved salt then moves with the transport of water either back to the soil surface to the sites of root water uptake or by gravitational flow below the rooting zone to lower positions in the profile or laterally downslope.

Saline seepages are produced following the removal of forests and other deep-rooted perennial natural vegetation as originally proposed by Wood (1924). Shallow rooted annual crops with fallow reduce the total annual water use of a particular area, and this leads to higher soil moisture levels and increased movement of water down through the profile. The extra water movement through the soil and weathered mantle dissolves more salts (Jenkin, 1980), increasing the salt flow to the groundwater. Where impervious layers are present, the water with dissolved salts may move laterally downslope as perched groundwater (Conacher, 1979).

Water tables rise, particularly after a succession of wet seasons, and eventually reach the surface, where they emerge as hillside seepage (Smith, 1962). Quite often the seepage first appears at the break of slope, or if not, it will emerge in the valley floor. After first emergence, the seepage may then extend upslope. Surface runoff or excessive rainfall can then transport these emerged salts downslope. In the low-lying areas where waterlogging can occur, contact is made with pre-existing saline groundwater, which then results in the whole profile becoming saline (Bettenay et al., 1964).

The parts of southern Australia with a Mediterranean-type climate with long dry summers and cool wet winters have not experienced significant levels of soil leaching. The water balance of these areas is particularly sensitive to the amount and extent of water loss by plant water uptake and transpiration. The removal of the deep-rooted perennial vegetation in these areas has upset the hydrologic balance, as indicated by the extent of salt seepage and increasing stream and groundwater salinities following man's changing land-use patterns.

Overgrazing and other forms of land disturbance in other areas of Australia have resulted in the loss of surface vegetative cover, thus allowing erosion of the topsoil and exposure of the originally saline or sodic soil layers below, giving rise to areas known as scalds.

Farther inland, in salt flats, the water table of salty groundwater is sufficiently close to the surface for periods long enough to affect vegetation. Salt pans represent the more or less permanent outcrop of the saline water table. In the dry saline soils of arid areas, salts have accumulated in the subsoil, which has become sodic and alkaline. In these areas, rainfall has been insufficient to leach the salts from the profile.

Types and Distribution of Nonirrigated Salt-affected Land in Australia. Eight identifiable types of salt-affected land have been defined (SCSC, 1982), and these are described in Table 1. Estimates of areas of each of the types for each state in Australia are shown in Table 2.

Generally salt marshes are along the coast mostly in regions where the tidal range is large. Salt pans and flats are found in areas where the potential and actual evaporation greatly exceeds the amount of rainfall and where the drainage is slow. In other areas with a net evaporative loss of water, dry saline land, either loams or clays, occurs over parent material containing soluble minerals and salts.

Man is responsible for the other types of salt-affected land. Saline seepages are restricted to agricultural areas where there has been extensive clearing of the natural vegetation. In these areas, annual rainfall is generally more than 300 mm, and the majority of saline seepages occur in Western Australia, with its Mediterranean-type climate. Dry, salinized lands occur where the clearing of native vegetation

Table 1. Brief definitions of types of salt-affected land.

Type 1: *Salt marsh.* Coastal land with water table (i.e., the upper limit of that part of the soil that is saturated with groundwater) at or near the surface, naturally saline in the subsoil or throughout the soil, and carrying salt-tolerant plants.

Type 2: *Salt pan.* Land with water table intermittently at the surface and naturally too salty throughout to support plant growth (shown as "salt lakes" on many maps).

Type 3: *Salt flat.* Land with water table not at the surface, naturally saline in the subsoil or throughout, and carrying salt-tolerant plants.

Type 4: *Saline seepage.* Land with water table, and which has become saline as a result of land use changes since European settlement.
   a. *topsoil saline seepage.* water table periodically within capillary range of soil surface; soil saline throughout.
   b. *subsoil saline seepage.* water table below capillary range; saline in the subsoil only.

Type 5: *Dry saline lands (saline loams).* Land without water table, naturally saline in the subsoil or throughout, and with uniform or gradational light-textured soils in areas with less than 375 mm average annual rainfall.

Type 6: *Dry saline lands (saline clays).* Land without water table, naturally saline in the subsoil or throughout, and with uniform heavy soils or duplex soils in areas with less than 300 mm average annual rainfall.

Type 7: *Scalds.* Land where erosion of soil from the surface has revealed a naturally saline or sodic horizon and is largely bare of vegetation.
   a. *saline scalds.* whole soil saline and sodic.
   b. *saline scalds.* subsoil saline and sodic.
   c. *non-saline scalds.* soil non-saline but sodic.

Type 8: *Dry salinized lands.* Land without water table and which has become saline in the subsoil or throughout, possibly as a result of land use change since settlement.

SOURCE: SCSC, 1982.

in agricultural areas with low rainfall has resulted in the movement of salts from lower in the profile to the soil surface. Scalds are prevalent in the semiarid and arid areas where grazing has removed the surface vegetation, which allows wind erosion of the topsoil and leads to the exposure of saline and/or sodic subsoils.

Salting of Irrigated Land

The area of land irrigated in Australia in 1980–81 was approximately 1.65×10^6 ha, and this was about 9 percent of the total area under crops but only 0.3 percent of the total area of agricultural establishments (Year Book, 1984). The areas of different crop and pastures irrigated in 1980–81 are shown in Table 3. The total use of irrigation water estimated in 1977 was $13,300 \times 10^6$ m^3, and 87 percent of this was supplied from surface water resources. Total per capita water consumption in 1977 in Australia was about 3500 L per day. Of this consumption 75 percent or 2590 L per day was used for irrigation, 630 L per day for urban and industrial use, and the remaining 8 percent for other rural water use.

The variability in stream flow and seasonal rainfall requires adequate water storage for successful irrigation using surface water resources. As a consequence, most irrigated areas in Australia are supplied with water by a state authority. Expansion of irrigation has been due mainly to pub-

Table 2. Areas of nonirrigated salt-affected land in Australia ($\times 10^3$ ha).

Type	Queensland	New South Wales	Victoria	Tasmania	South Australia	Western Australia	Northern Territory	Australia
1. Salt marsh	620	n.e.[a]	n.e.	3	108	1,150	620	2,501
2. Salt pans	950	450	100	0.5	1,800	3,450	500	10,915
3. Salt flats	8			6	50	3,600	nil	
4. Saline seepages	8	4	90	5	55	264	nil	426
5. Dry saline lands (saline loams)	n.e.	2,364	n.e.	nil	n.e.	2,800	n.e.	14,780
6. Dry saline lands (saline clays)	285		—	—	5,100	351	3,880	
7. Scalds	582	920	60	—	1,200	335	680	3,777
8. Dry salinized land	n.e.	n.e.	nil	nil	n.e.	8	2	10
All nonirrigated salt-affected land	2,453	3,738	250	14.5	8,313	11,958	5,682+	32,409

SOURCE: SCSC, 1982.

[a]n.e. = not estimated.

Table 3. Areas of irrigated and nonirrigated crops and pastures in Australia 1980–81 ($\times 10^3$ ha).

Crop	Irrigated	Nonirrigated	Total
Cereals	383	16,684	17,064
Vegetables	70	69	139
Total fruit	55	142	197
Grape vines	46	24	70
All other crops	232	568	800
Sown pastures and grasses	868	24,032	24,900
Grazing, with fallow, etc.	0	452,300	452,300
Total	1654	493,819	495,473

Table 4. The areas of irrigated land, salinized irrigated land, and land with a water table <2 m from the surface (1980–81).

	Area Irrigated ($\times 10^3$ ha)	Salinized Irrigated Land ($\times 10^3$ ha)	Area of Land with Water Table <2 m ($\times 10^3$ ha)
Queensland	255.7	0.6	0.2
New South Wales	714.6	8.4	85.0
Victoria	546.5	92.0	425.0
Tasmania	32.7	n.s.[a]	n.s.
South Australia	79.5	21.5	14.0
Western Australia	24.7	0.5	n.e.[b]
Northern Territory	n.e.	0	n.e.
Australia	1653.7	123.0	524.2

SOURCES: Year Book: Australia, 1984; Peck et al., 1983.

[a]n.s. = not significant.

[b]n.e. = not estimated.

lic investment in the building of dams and reservoirs and private investment by farmers in irrigation plant and earthworks (Year Book, 1984).

Irrigation can increase soil salinity in a number of ways. The use of saline water for irrigation from either streams or groundwater increases salinity directly. As pointed out by Peck et al. (1983), by way of an example, 1 m of irrigation water with 1,000 mg·L^{-1} TSS infiltrating to a depth of 0.5 m increases soil salinity by about 0.1 percent. As time progresses, this added salt concentrates at the root water uptake surfaces and at the soil surface. Saline water flowing from below also adds to the salt levels at the uptake and evaporation sites. To prevent this salt concentration in the upper layers, a continual movement of water through the root zone is required. This extra water then causes water tables, which are usually saline, to rise. As water tables approach the surface, there is direct injury to plant roots, increased soil salinity, and/or waterlogging.

From a management point of view, there is a balance between the amount and frequency of irrigation and accession to the water table. The balanced irrigation regime depends on many site and crop factors, quality of irrigation water, and climate. Direct injury to plants can also be caused by foliar applications of saline irrigation waters. The extent of salinized soil as a result of irrigation practices in the Australian states is shown in Table 4.

In Queensland the use of poor-quality groundwater as a result of seawater intrusion causes most of the problems, although overall, the small area affected is not considered to be a major problem. New South Wales irrigated lands amount to 714.6 $\times 10^3$ ha, of which only 1 percent is salt affected. This affected land is usually associated with a water table within 2 m of the surface. By far the greatest problems occur in Victoria and South Australia, where the percentages of salt-affected land to total irrigated land are 17 percent and 27 percent, respectively. These problem areas are nearly all associated with a water table within the upper 2 m of the soil. In South Australia the problem is increased by the use of poor-quality irrigation water. In Western Australia the salt-affected irrigated land is due also to poor quality irrigation water and rising water tables.

Stream and Groundwater Salinity

The salinity of a stream at any point is a measure of the amount of dissolved salts in a given flow of water. Clearly, any changes in either the water flow or the salt load will change stream salinity. Such activities as water pumping or diversion for irrigation or other rural or urban and industrial uses, storage in reservoirs, weirs, etc., and land use changes can all influence streamflow. The salt load in a stream is also affected by diversions and return flows, as well as inputs from groundwater.

The salinity of groundwaters can be increased by disposal of saline liquid and solid wastes. Groundwater extraction may lead to an inflow of saline water from the sea or adjacent saline aquifers. When groundwater is used for irrigation, surface evaporation concentrates the salts, which may then recharge the aquifer below. Land-use changes modify the natural recharge rate, which can affect the level of the water table and sometimes increase groundwater salinity.

The River Murray flows between New South Wales and Victoria and then into South Australia where it enters the Southern Ocean. Water diversions around $184 \times 10^6 \, m^3$ per year are transferred by pipeline to serve urban and industrial areas of South Australia. Unfortunately, the water is of low quality. Median salt loads of 1400×10^6 kg per year have been estimated; these give rise to salinity values in excess of $500 \, mg \cdot L^{-1}$ for periods up to nine months per year. Of this total estimated salt load, it has been further estimated that 40 to 50 percent of this load is man-induced. (Maunsell and Partners, 1979; River Murray Commission, 1979, 80, 81; Engineering and Water Supply Department, 1981; and Peck et al., 1983). Also in New South Wales in the Hunter River there are increases in stream salinity as a result of rising groundwaters in saline strata, causing increased saline inflow to the river (Garman, 1980). Storage and diversion of good-quality water in the upper reaches substantially reduce river flow farther downstream, where tributaries, irrigation return flows, and groundwater inflows contribute to increased salinity. In southwestern Victoria, 48 percent of total annual streamflow of $4160 \times$ $10^6 \, m^3$ per year is salt affected with salinities exceeding $1000 \, mg \cdot L^{-1}$ TDS.

In Western Australia 35 percent of conventionally divertible surface water resources are now saline or brackish as a consequence of dryland agricultural development (Sadler and Williams, 1981) and a further 16 percent are considered to be of marginal salinity.

Seawater intrusion is a significant problem in coastal areas of all states where groundwaters are pumped for irrigation. Elsewhere there is a wide range of salinities in groundwater resources. In the Murray-Darling basin there are reports of some local changes of groundwater salinity associated with irrigation, but they are not considered to be a serious problem. In South Australia the salinity of groundwaters is a major problem which restricts potential uses. In Western Australia it is estimated that there are 16,000 borehole wells providing on-farm water supplies, but water from 25 percent of these has become too salty for use.

THE EFFECT OF SALINITY ON AGRICULTURAL PRODUCTION

In Australia, about 42.4×10^6 ha of land has been affected by enough salt to restrict agricultural production (SCSC, 1982). This represents about 4.3 percent of the total area of Australia. Most of this (87 percent) is, however, naturally salty land that was present before European settlement.

The extent of salinization as a result of man's activities in Australia is summarized in Table 5. For nonirrigated land, 4213×10^3 ha or 0.85 percent of agricultural land is salt affected. The majority of these areas are scalds that are restricted to the arid and semiarid regions. The rest of the salt-affected lands involve saline seepages, for which most concern is expressed. Nearly all saline seepages are in the southern fringe of the mainland and, in extent, are about twice the area of irrigated salt-affected land. Of particular concern is the fact that saline seepages occur almost entirely on the better arable or potentially arable agricultural land.

The areas of irrigated and nonirrigated crops and pastures in 1980–81 in Australia are given in Table 3. The total

Table 5. The areas of man-induced salt-affected agricultural land in Australia (1980–81).

	Nonirrigated			Irrigated		
	Land Area 1980–81 ($\times 10^3$ ha)	Salt-affected Area ($\times 10^3$ ha)	(%)	Land Area 1980–81 ($\times 10^3$ ha)	Salt-affected Area ($\times 10^3$ ha)	(%)
Queensland	157,244	590	0.38	255.7	0.6	0.2
New South Wales	64,485	924	1.43	714.6	8.4	1.2
Victoria	14,154	150	1.06	546.5	92.0	16.8
Tasmania	2,167	5	0.23	32.7	0	0
South Australia	62,321	1,255	2.01	79.5	21.5	27.0
Western Australia	115,775	607	0.52	24.7	0.5	2.0
Northern Territory	77,600	682	0.88	n.a.[a]	n.a.	n.a.
Australia	493,746	4,213	0.85	1,653.7	123.0	7.4

SOURCES: Year Book: Australia, 1984; SCSC, 1982; Peck et al., 1983.

[a] n.a. = not available.

area irrigated (1654×10^3 ha) was only 0.3 percent of all agricultural land. The irrigated cereal area was 2.2 percent of the total land sown to cereals in 1980–81. Of land producing vegetables, fruit, and grapes, the percentage areas irrigated were 50, 28 and 66 percent, respectively.

The application of saline irrigation water may decrease agricultural productivity by directly affecting the plants. Indirect effects may also occur, for example, the requirements of more elaborate and costly methods of water application or increased water applications to induce leaching of salts from the soil profile. The need for and installation of agricultural drainage also reduce economic returns to the farmer.

Peck et al. (1983) were the first to assess, for Australia as a whole, the extent of crop and pasture yield reduction as a result of increasing salinity of irrigation water. Much of available data on yield response is based on data from the United States and may not apply to Australian conditions even though allowances have been made for differences in the chemical composition of applied water. Also, as pointed out by Peck et al. (1983), it is possible that crop yield responses could be different in Australia because of differences in the chemical and physical properties of the soils. Assessment of productivity losses due to salinity is also complicated since economic surveys of relevant crops are infrequent. Consequently, any estimate of the effects of salinity on crop and pasture yields in Australia is tentative. The findings of Peck et al. (1983) are summarized and are combined with those of SCSC (1982).

Crops and Pastures

Very little irrigated cereal and pasture production is currently at risk from increasing salinity of applied irrigation water. The three main crops (wheat, barley, and rice) are grown largely in the upper Murray and Murrumbidgee basins where the salinity of irrigation water has been within the tolerance of the crops. There has been no evidence of reduced pasture yield at current levels of salinity in irrigation water within Australia. Other crops, including sugarcane, tobacco, and cotton, have been little affected.

Most irrigation salinization caused by high water tables occurs in Victoria. It is difficult to assess the overall reduction in agricultural productivity because statistical trends between salt-affected land and farm incomes do not exist. This is due to the manner in which farmers adapt to local conditions. It is not uncommon to find profitable farms with severely salt-affected land. In these instances farmers work mainly on the better-quality land of the farm. Cary et al. (1982) estimated the cost of irrigation salinization in Victoria but only on the grazing land because apparently, adequate control is achieved in other enterprises using groundwater pumping and tile drainage. The cost of salinization in irrigation areas was estimated to be 6 M$ per year.

Salt-affected nonirrigated land at present is around 4213×10^3 ha. The economic cost of this salinization is a decline of approximately 157 M$ in capital value and a loss of approximately 21 M$ in annual productivity (SCSC, 1982).

Vegetables, Fruit and Grapes

These crops are relatively intolerant of salinity in irrigation water and significant decreases in yield may occur. An approximate estimate was made of the incomes of the Australian vegetable-, fruit-, and grape-producing sectors, which are at some risk from increasing salinity of irrigation water. Local values of production were decreased in proportion to the potential decline in crop yield for increasing salinity. Farm income per hectare was then calculated, and this was applied to an estimate of the area of irrigated production that was judged to be at risk from rising salinity above a threshold level. Using this procedure, Peck et al. (1983) estimated potential losses in fruit production of 1.2 M$ per year in areas subject to risk where total productivity was 50 M$. The potential loss could be as high as 13 M$.

Grapes apparently exhibit a greater salinity tolerance than citrus and stone fruits. Irrigation water has generally been of sufficient quality not to affect yields in the major irrigated vineyard regions. The area of irrigated vegetables was 70×10^3 ha in 1980–81, and about 20 percent of this area was at some risk of salinity problems. Income earned in these areas at risk was about 40 M$. Using the procedure outlined earlier, a potential loss of income of 2 M$ per year is possible with an increase in irrigation water salinity of 100 mg·L^{-1}.

The total estimated cost of salinization on combined annual agricultural productivity in Australia is around 30 M$ per year, which is about 0.26 percent of the gross value of agricultural commodities produced in Australia in 1980–81.

CURRENT TRENDS AND FUTURE DEVELOPMENTS

There has been a general increase over the last three decades in the area of scalds and saline seepage–affected land by around 2 to 5 percent per annum (SCSC, 1982). In some states, particularly New South Wales, it is anticipated that the development of scalds will cease since scald development is closely related to land management practices. In other states (e.g., Queensland), there is, however, greater fear for future development of scalds. According to SCSC (1982), opinions differ about the possible future development in seepage salting and suggest that over the next 20 years the extent of induced seepage salting will double.

Peck et al. (1983), have stated that the bulk of land irrigated with surface water is likely to develop a shallow water table in the long term unless some form of drainage is incorporated. Depending on soil drainage characteristics, these areas may or may not become salt affected. In the Murrumbidgee irrigation area of New South Wales an area of 750 km^2 could develop a shallow water table over the next twenty-five years, but only 150 km^2 could become salt affected. Increases are expected in the other states; for example, in Victoria about 10 km^2 is expected to develop a shallow water table, and around 35 km^2 will develop in Queensland. Soil salinity problems in South Australia are expected to be reduced by increasing the area drained from 30 to 50 percent.

THE EFFECT OF ENRICHED ATMOSPHERIC CARBON DIOXIDE

There is a potential for atmospheric carbon dioxide to rise, and at some time in the foreseeable future a doubling of stomatal resistance seems to be inevitable. Aston (1984) simulated the effects of a changed stomatal resistance on streamflow. His results indicated that we can expect streamflow to increase from 40 to 90 percent as a consequence of a doubling of atmospheric carbon dioxide concentration. Soil moisture levels were also increased, and this would lead to more water movement through the root zone and more leaching, and elevated water tables and increased recharge of the groundwater would result.

Land clearing, in certain areas, also causes similar hydrologic changes which result in the development of saline seepages. It is therefore possible that the carbon dioxide–enriched atmosphere of the future will also induce seepage salting similar to land clearing. Furthermore, existing saline seepages may be exaggerated by the lower plant water transpiration losses in the recharge areas.

MANAGEMENT AND POLICIES

In Australia, with nonirrigated soils there are no generally accepted management techniques or policies for the prevention and control of salt-affected land. Various methods are practiced, but these all depend on the local conditions and are subject to varying environmental and economic constraints. Methods, both proved and unproved, include: the withholding of Crown land; the requiring of a license to clear land; the introduction of salt-tolerant vegetation; the use of appropriate stocking rates and grazing management; the construction of earth banks and shallow ditches to restrict lateral flows of surface and shallow subsurface water; the installation of ditch, mole, and tile drainage; the growing of trees and crops that consume water at a much greater rate than the present vegetation; and reforestation.

With irrigated soils a combination of methods is used to manage salinity. These methods are well established and are used in many other countries. In areas where salinity problems are associated with the water distribution systems and with saline irrigation water, the methods include: the lining of water distribution channels, the conversion of above-canopy sprinkler systems to below-canopy application when irrigation water is saline, modifying time and rate of application of saline irrigation water, the application of gypsum to improve soil permeability, and the selection of crop varieties that are salt tolerant.

Where shallow water tables are the main cause of soil salinity levels that lead to lower food production, a variety of techniques is used. As mentioned earlier, the actual method or combination of methods used depends on the different conditions prevailing in each region and on each farm. Options available to reduce the amount of water being added to the groundwater system include: cancellation of water entitlements, reduction of water deliveries, reduction of channel leakages, regrading of land to improve application efficiency, and planting of deep-rooted vegetation.

Shallow water tables may also be lowered by drainage via open ditch drains, tile drainage, or groundwater pumping.

RESEARCH AND INVESTIGATION REQUIREMENTS

The Standing Committee on Soil Conservation (1982) recommended a number of programs to facilitate the development of land-use policies for the prevention and control of induced dryland salting. These are also appropriate to salting problems associated with irrigated agriculture as noted by Peck et al. 1983. The programs are as follows:

1. Determining the extent of the problem with more accuracy and to monitor changes in the future by developing and using more precise mapping techniques using remote sensing.

2. Investigating processes in order to provide more detailed information of the basic causes of salting. These studies should include local hydrological investigations, salt and water balances, soil hydrological parameters, water use of particular plant species under various conditions, and groundwater recharge.

3. Determining the consequence of land-use options involving an estimation of future trends and modeling of water and salt flows in surface and groundwater systems and in rivers.

4. Developing salinity standards for irrigation water and Australian conditions.

5. Finding the best treatment for affected sites by investigating appropriate salt-tolerant plant species and techniques of rehabilitation.

6. Conducting economic studies of salting on regional and national scales to guide funding policies. These include assessments of disbenefits of salt-affected land, costs/benefits of various strategies, rehabilitation methods and regional land-use policy options, and the identification of suitable methods of funding.

7. Identifying distinct strategies and preventative land use policies as a prerequisite of a works program.

8. Undertaking work projects in local salt-affected areas according to the prescribed district strategy.

9. Incorporating preferred preventative land-use policies into state and commonwealth strategies or legislation.

PERSPECTIVE

In the future, most of the productive land in Australia will not be salt affected (SCSC, 1982); however in Western Australia, South Australia, and Victoria at least 2 percent of the wheat land and sheep range will have been ruined by seepage salting. In the hardest-hit districts in southwestern Western Australia and northwestern Victoria, according to SCSC (1982), the land most affected will be the better, more productive land. Dryland and irrigated agricultural development has and will continue to cause a reduction in stream water quality which will no doubt cause an increase in the costs of providing and using water.

The overall reduction of Australia's total food production due to salinity is small. However, in particular areas with certain irrigated crops where individual farm incomes are substantial, production losses caused by salinity would be significant both in terms of lower farm incomes and in increased social costs to the local district. Added costs to household, industry, commerce, and government are significant (see Peck et al., 1983).

There is no doubt that salinity is a real problem and is increasing. To minimize losses, concentrated efforts must be carried out at all levels, from the individual farmer to governments. Only by such integrated, interdisciplinary cooperation will Australia be able to preserve and maintain two of its most valuable resources, land and water.

ACKNOWLEDGMENTS

The author gratefully acknowledges the work of Drs. Peck, Thomas, and Williamson of CSIRO Division of Groundwater Research and also the Working Party on Dryland Salting in Australia for their comprehensive reports.

REFERENCES

Aston, A. R. 1984. The effect of doubling atmospheric CO_2 on streamflow: A simulation. *J. Hydrol.* 67:273–80.

AWRC. 1981. The first national survey of water use in Australia. Aust. Water Resources Council Occasional Papers Series No. 1. Canberra: Aust. Govt. Publishing Service.

Bettenay, E., A. V. Blackmore, and F. J. Hingston 1964. Aspects of the hydrological cycle and related salinity in the Belka valley, Western Australia. *Aust. J. Soil Res.* 2:187–210.

Brown, J. A. H. (1983). Australia's surface water resources: an assessment of the quantity of Australia's surface water resources. Water 2000 Consultant Report. vol. 1. Canberra: Aust. Govt. Publishing Service.

Cary, J. W., J. O. Ferguson, and P. Belin. 1982. Economic and social costs of salinity. Proceedings Symposium on salinity in Victoria. La Trobe University, Department of Agriculture Economics. Bundoora, Canada:

Conacher, A. J. 1979. Water quality and forests in south-western Australia: review and evaluation. *Aust. Geog.* 14:150–59.

Engineering and Water Supply Department. 1981. Salinity in the River Murray. Information Bull. 15. Adelaide: Public Relations Branch, E & WS Dept.

Garman, D. E. J. 1980. The Hunter River valley—water quality present and future. *In* Hunter environment–proceedings symposium in honor of A. D. Tweedie. Newcastle: University of Newcastle.

Jenkin, J. J. 1980. Terrain, groundwater and secondary salinity in Victoria, Australia. *Agric. Water Management* 4:143–71.

Maunsell and Partners 1979. Murray valley salinity and drainage. A report for development of a co-ordinated plan of action. Canberra: Maunsell and Partners.

Northcote, K. H., and J. K. H. Skene. 1972. Australian soils with saline and sodic properties. Soil Pub. No. 27. CSIRO, Australia.

Peck, A. J., J. F. Thomas, and D. R. Williamson. 1983. Water 2000: Consultants Rep. No. 8. Salinity issues. Effects of man on salinity in Australia. Canberra: Aust. Govt. Pub. Service.

River Murray Commission. 1969–81. Annual reports, Canberra: River Murray Commission.

Sadler, B. S., and P. J. Williams. 1981. The evolution of a regional approach to salinity management in Western Australia. *Agric. Water Management* 4:353–81.

Standing Committee on Soil Conservation [SCSC]. 1982. Salting of non-irrigated land in Australia. Report by working party on dryland salting in Australia for standing committee on soil conservation.

Smith, S. T. 1962. Some aspects of soil salinity in Western Australia. M.Sc. thesis, Univ. of Western Australia.

Wood, W. E. 1924. Increase of salt in soil and streams following the destruction of native vegetation. *J. R. Soc. West. Aust.* 10:35–47.

Year Book: Australia No. 68. Canberra: Australian Bureau of Statistics.

22. SALINITY PROBLEMS IN FOOD PRODUCTION OF THE MEXICAN IRRIGATION DISTRICTS

Everardo Aceves-Navarro, Colegio de Postgraduados, Chapingo, Mexico

INTRODUCTION

World hunger is increasing every day, mainly in the undeveloped countries, despite programs carried out by international organizations. The problem in these countries is that production is increasing at an annual rate that is lower than the population growth rate. This situation implies that more food must be produced if we are going to meet world food demand.

In Mexico, we are importing food, mainly grains, to cover the country's needs, but government policies are oriented to satisfy our own needs by more efficiently using the available resources.

Mexico has about 5.0×10^6 ha under irrigation using both surface- and groundwater sources (See Fig. 1). In these irrigated areas, about 10 percent of the soils have different degrees of salinity problems. Salinity effects range from land abandonment to moderate yield decreases. Around 500,000 ha in the Mexican irrigation districts are not producing at optimum yield, and in part of this area, about 55,000 ha, there is no production because of high salt concentrations. Distribution of salt-affected soils under irrigation is shown in Fig. 2. The higher percentage of these soils is located in the northwest region, where the mean annual precipitation is less than 500 mm. In the southeast region, where annual rainfall is less than 1,500 mm, the area of salt-affected soils is very low.

Chemically, all Mexican rivers have good water quality. A representative concentration range varies from 1,000 ppm of total dissolved salts for the Colorado and Grande rivers in northern Mexico to 300 ppm for the southeast Mexican rivers.

We are also using groundwater with salt concentrations up to 2,000 ppm for crop irrigation. This amount of dissolved salts suggests that soil salinity problems are not caused by water quality, but by water management.

WATER MANAGEMENT AND SALINITY CONTROL

Water Availability and Irrigation Systems

Mexico has a total area of approximately 2 million km². About 31 percent is arid, 36 percent is semiarid, and 33 percent is humid and subhumid. The mean annual precipitation is equivalent to a water depth of 780 mm. This calculates to a mean annual volume of precipitation in the whole country of 1560×10^9 m³ (see Table 1). It is important to note that 50 percent of the runoff in Mexico occurs in 20 percent of the territory and the other 50 percent in the remaining 80 percent that is arid and semiarid. This arid and semiarid region is where 97 percent of the Mexican irrigated agriculture and soil salinity problems exist.

The areas irrigated by different systems are shown in Table 2. As we can note, 96 percent of the irrigated area uses surface systems, and only 3.3 percent are sprinkler or trickle systems.

This implies that because of the irrigation system used, farmers generally do not have high water application efficiency, and starting from this point, I would comment that the scientific and technical literature usually indicates that farmers must irrigate crops to meet evapotranspiration needs and to control salt in the root zone. This can be accomplished more or less efficiently using sprinkler or trickle irrigation, but not using surface irrigation systems. For surface irrigation systems in Mexico, it does not make sense to recommend application of water to meet the leaching requirement because the farmers are already applying excess water for leaching salts from the crop root zone. Actually, the problem is to convince them to increase the water application efficiency. So in the Mexican districts, rather than speak about a leaching requirement or a leaching fraction, we have to speak to the farmers about increasing the water application efficiency at least for reaching crop evapotranspiration plus a mean leaching fraction.

Actually, the mean water application efficiency in the Mexican irrigated areas is 66 percent, and the conveyance mean efficiency is 70 percent. These two percentages make the mean irrigation efficiency percentage equal to 46 percent, i.e., for each 100 m³ diverted from dams, 54 m³ are lost in different ways.

Drainage Systems

The Mexican irrigation districts lack complete drainage systems. This results in a rise in the water table and subsequently, the appearance of soil salinity problems. Soil salinity problems in Mexico are not caused by poor water quality but by lack of drainage and deficient irrigation water management in arid regions.

When irrigation areas were opened, farmers believed that as more water was applied, a higher yield was obtained. This thought led to serious seepage and salinity problems in the Mexican irrigation districts.

SALINITY PROBLEMS IN FOOD PRODUCTION

Of the 500,000 ha with salinity problems, 55,000 ha have already been abandoned, and the remaining areas have

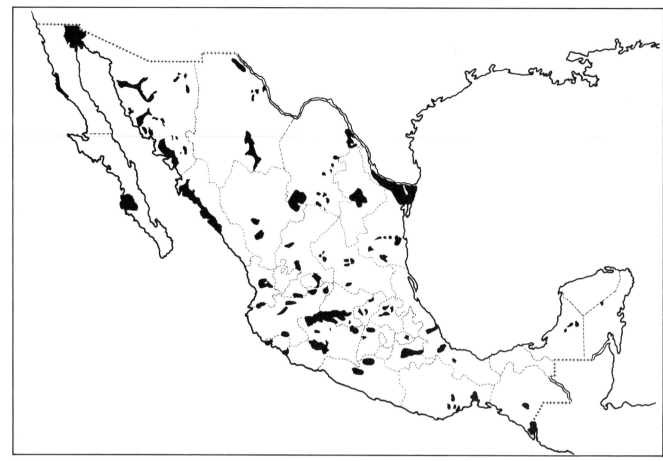

Fig. 1. Distribution of irrigated areas in Mexico.

Table 1. Availability, distribution, and use in agriculture of the water resources of Mexico.

Total area of Mexico	2,000,000 km²	100%
Arid and semiarid area	1,340,000 km²	67%
Humid and subhumid area	660,000 km²	33%
Mean annual precipitation in Mexico	1560×10^9 m³	100%
Mean annual runoff[a]	410×10^9 m	26%
Actual annual water storage capacity in dams and reservoirs for irrigation	49×10^9 m³	12% (Runoff basis)

[a]Fifty percent of the runoff occurs in 20 percent of the territory, mainly in the southeast region.

Table 2. Areas and main irrigation systems used in Mexico.

Irrigation System	Area (ha)
Furrow	3,059,000
Border	1,350,000
Flat-topped	166,000
Sprinkler	150,000
Trickle	15,000
Other systems	260,000
Total	5,000,000

Table 3. Estimation of land area with different salinity levels in the active root zone.

Salinity Levels ($dS \cdot m^{-1}$)	Land Area (ha)	Percent of the Affected Area (%)
4.0 to 8.0	180,000	36.0
8.1 to 12.0	135,000	27.0
12.1 to 16.0	85,000	17.0
16.1 to 20.0	45,000	9.0
Greater than 20.0	55,000	11.0
Total	500,000	100.0

problems in different levels, generally ranging from 4 to 20 dS·m⁻¹ of the soil saturation extract.

Estimations of areas with different levels of salinity in the active root zone are shown in Table 3.

For estimating the food production decrease in these areas, the following basic accumptions were made: (1) the crops are exposed to the mean salinity range; (2) soils with a

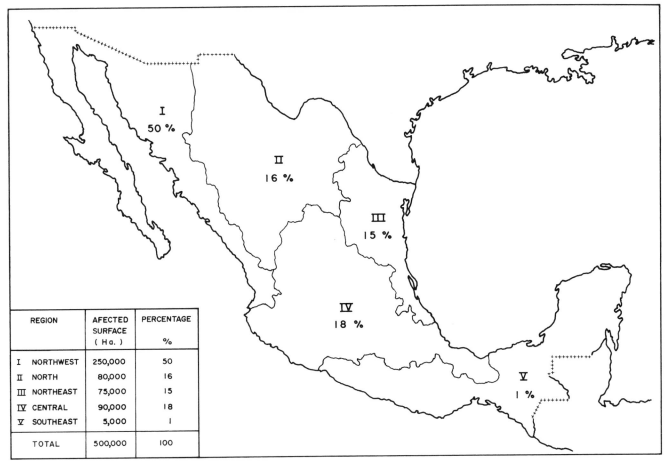

Fig. 2. Regional distribution in Mexico of irrigated areas affected by salinity.

REGION	AFECTED SURFACE (Ha.)	PERCENTAGE %
I NORTHWEST	250,000	50
II NORTH	80,000	16
III NORTHEAST	75,000	15
IV CENTRAL	90,000	18
V SOUTHEAST	5,000	1
TOTAL	500,000	100

salinity range from 4.0 to 8.0 dS·m^{-1} are cultivated with soybeans and corn, half and half; (3) soils with a salinity range from 8.1 to 12.0 dS·m^{-1} are cultivated with sorghum; (4) soils with a salinity range from 12.1 to 16.0 dS·m^{-1} are cultivated with wheat; (5) soils with a salinity range from 16.1 to 20 dS·m^{-1} are cultivated with barley; (6) soils with a salinity level greater than 20 dS·m^{-1} are abandoned, and the food production lost is estimated for wheat.

The salt crop tolerance evaluation and yield decrease are made following Maas and Hoffman (1976) and according to a general response curve of crops as a function of soil saturation extract mean salinity level in the active root zone, as shown in Figure 3.

From this curve, the mean yield decrease per hectare for a given crop and a given mean soil salinity level can be calculated with the equation

$$Y_{100} - Y_x = \frac{ECy_x - ECy_{100}}{ECy_0 - ECy_{x100}} \qquad (1)$$

where:

Y_{100} = optimum yield per hectare for a given crop without salinity problems in the root zone

Y_x = expected yield per hectare for a given crop with mean soil electrical conductivity in the active root zone equal to ECy_x

ECy_{100} = threshold soil electrical conductivity after which yields per hectare decrease approximately linearly as salinity increases

ECy_x = given mean soil electrical conductivity in the crop active root zone

ECy_0 = given mean soil electrical conductivity in the active root zone at which the yield per ha for a given crop is zero.

The crop yield loss caused by salinity for each considered surface is shown in Table 4.

This estimation shows that more than 1 million tons of food are lost per year in the Mexican irrigated areas due to salinity. Solution alternatives to these problems follow.

SOIL RECLAMATION

As noted, the salinity problems were produced by lack of drainage and poor water management. The main Mexican irrigation districts are located in the coastal plains where drainage may be technically feasible but very expensive. When reclaiming a salt-affected soil, two conditions must be met: First, the water has to pass through the soil profile, and second, after the water passes through the soil profile and leaches the salts, it must be drained from the reclamation area. If either of these conditions is not met, it is impossible to reclaim the soil.

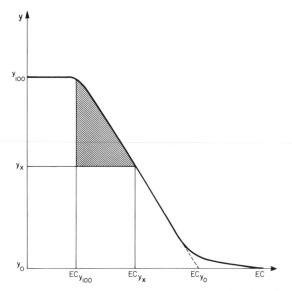

Fig. 3. Yield/general response curve of crops as a function of soil saturation extract mean salinity in the active root zone.

Soil reclamation in Mexico has been done where possible, as soon as the drainage systems have been constructed, following the methodology indicated in USDA Handbook 60 (USDA, 1969).

WATER QUALITY IMPROVEMENT

Generally speaking, we have good water quality in the irrigation districts, but there are some irrigation return flows that can be used when mixed with canal waters. Following the same principle, actually, we are mixing canal water with brackish water from wells in several irrigation districts to help to produce more food, mainly during dry periods.

MANAGEMENT PRACTICES

The key in producing food under saline conditions is soil, water, and plant management practices. The main problem in Mexico, and maybe in other countries, is that farmers still use the traditional methods after they have developed salinity in their soils, thus producing low yields.

If this situation is to be changed, a wide campaign must be initiated to convince farmers to follow these recommen-

dations: (1) select salt-tolerant crops, (2) plant under dry soil conditions and then irrigate, (3) use at least twice the seeding rate recommended for nonsaline conditions, (4) use flooding, border, or sprinkler irrigation systems rather than a furrow system, and (5) irrigate more frequently.

For greater success, other factors have to be taken into account. These include type of soil, climatic conditions (mainly precipitation, temperature, and relative humidity), and drainage systems. All factors must be integrated in management practices to avoid salt accumulation in the soil profile. In other words, the cultivation practices have to be changed, which requires a change in the farmers' minds.

USE OF HALOPHYTES FOR PRODUCING FOOD

In the arid regions of Mexico, water is scarce. Instead of using the water for reclaiming saline soils, it has to be used in food production. This implies that an alternative crop must be found for using saline soils and water in food production; in other words, we must find ways to live with the salinity problems, perhaps by cultivation of native plants tolerant of high salt concentrations or to develop salt-tolerant new crop varieties for food production. Development of salt-tolerant plants will take time.

One recently explored alternative is the use of halophytes, which grow in soils with very high salinity. These plants can be domesticated and cropped for producing food or forage. In the basin of the former Texcoco Lake, salty grass (*Distichlis spicata*) (L) Green, is cropped in soil with electrical conductivity ranging from 50 to 70 $dS \cdot m^{-1}$, pH of 9.3, and a groundwater with salinity concentration higher than the ocean, near the soil surface.

Under these conditions managers have five cows per hectare, each cow weighing 200 kg. Gains are 413 g per day per animal during the four-month rainy season; the rest of the year weight gains are lower.

In Mexico there are several thousand hectares outside irrigation-district perimeters that have high water tables and salinity. These areas can be cropped with salty grass or other halophytes for feeding cattle and producing food.

CONCLUSIONS

Relative to salinity problems and increasing food production in Mexican irrigation districts, the following policies are recommended:

Table 4. Total yield decrement for some given crops in areas affected by different salinity levels in the Mexican irrigation districts.

Crop	Affected Surface (ha)	Y_{100} (ton/ha)	EC_{y_x} (dS · m⁻¹)	$EC_{y_{100}}$ (dS · m⁻¹)	EC_{y_0} (dS · m⁻¹)	$Y_{100} - Y_x$ (ton/ha)	Total Yield Decrement (ton)
Corn	90,000	3.5	6.0	2.0	10	1.75	157,000
Soybean	90,000	2.3	6.0	5.0	10	0.46	41,400
Sorghum	135,000	5.0	10.0	5.0	14	2.78	375,300
Wheat	85,000	4.4	14.0	6.0	20	2.51	213,350
Barley	45,000	3.5	18.0	8.0	28	1.75	78,750
Wheat[a]	55,000	4.4	20.0	6.0	20	4.40	242,000

[a] Assumed mean yield in the abandoned areas.

1. Reclaim soil with salinity problems in the irrigation districts.

2. Encourage the farmer to plant salt-tolerant crops when salinity problems exist, and to manage irrigation systems, soil, water quality, and drainage according to climatic conditions, and in general, to apply all management practices that will enhance crops' tolerance of salt.

3. Change cropping patterns and diversify and change crops according to the productive potential of the soil and the needs for food production.

4. Establish training programs for technicians and engineers working in soil-water-crop management in the irrigation districts.

5. Apply the most recent findings of research programs to crop and halophytes management and food production under saline conditions.

Finally, it is very clear that in the Mexican irrigation districts, more food can be produced with more effective water management and by increasing irrigation efficiency.

REFERENCES

Aceves, N. E. 1979. El ensalitramiento de los suelos bajo riego. (Identificacion, Control, Combate y Adaptacion) Colegio de Postgraduados.

Maas, E. V., and G. J. Hoffman. 1976. Managing saline water for irrigation. Pp. 187–98. *In* Proceedings of the International Salinity Conf., Texas Tech University, Lubbock, Tex.

Secretaria de Agricultura y Recursos Hidraulicos. 1981. Plan Nacional Hidraulico 1981.

U.S. Department of Agriculture. 1969. Saline and alkali soils. Diagnosis and improvement of alkali soils. Agriculture Handbook No. 60. Washington, D.C.: U.S. Government Printing Office.

23. SALINITY AND FOOD PRODUCTION IN SOUTH AMERICA

José F. Alfaro, Alfaro and Associates, Walnut Creek, California

ABSTRACT

Food production is a priority—a major concern and cause for dependency in Latin America. Prior to the Spanish conquest, food production was sufficient for most of the population of the region, which produced many of the agricultural products found today on most North American and European tables. Inca agriculture in particular was ecologically balanced and provided sufficient food. The decline of large portions of the Inca population was partly due to the chaotic effects of the Spanish conquest. In addition, agricultural decline in some regions could have been caused by salinization and waterlogging resulting from prolonged use of irrigation with inadequate drainage.

South American agricultural systems include both capital-intensive farming, which utilizes modern technology for the production of export products, and subsistence-oriented farming. Paradoxically, food production for the mass population has traditionally been in the hands of peasant agriculture, which has not been successful in achieving its goals. Salinity in the arid lands of Peru, Argentina, Chile, and Brazil constitutes a major obstacle to obtaining adequate crop yields, particularly in the Peruvian coastal region, where about 90 percent of the population lives in the arid zone.

To alleviate food supply problems and other common problems of the region, Latin America should make a concentrated effort to search for solutions. This action should be directed toward pooling resources for the study and solution of problems. Furthermore, industrialized nations should dedicate a small portion of their capital resources to develop non-patentable technologies applicable to the socioeconomic conditions of most of the population of Latin America to promote food self-sufficiency and political and economic independence.

HISTORICAL DEVELOPMENT

When Pedro de Cieza de León described the way of life of natives in South America, he recalled "plains and sand wastes" of Peru where it "never rained" and where the natives did not "build covered houses like those of the highlands." For their agricultural fields, "conduits leading from the rivers" watered the valleys, and were "so well built and so carefully planned that all the land is watered and planted, and nothing is lost. These irrigation ditches are very green and gay, lined with orchards of fruit trees of Spain and those native of the country. And at all seasons in these valleys fine crops of wheat and corn and all that is sown can be harvested" (Cieza de León). Their agriculture was ecologically balanced and supplied sufficient food. Many agricultural products found on North American and European tables today originated in Latin America and other regions of the developing world (Mooney, 1983). In particular, as in industrialized countries today, the potato was the Indians' staple foodstuff, together with corn and yuca (*Manihot esculenta*), from which tapioca is made.

Agriculture became established with the domestication of corn early in the first millennium B.C. Diversion of streams for irrigation probably originated in the early centuries of the first millennium B.C. as indicated by findings in the Viru valley of Peru (see also Bennet, 1949).

Improvement of agriculture and the spread of irrigation continued during pre-Inca and Inca periods. Evidence of irrigated agriculture and the magnitude of know-how is represented by the Viru valley canal system; the Ascope canal; irrigation in the valleys of Chilca, Mala, and Chala near Lima and those farther south in Ica, Nazca, Atico, and Arequipa. The Viru canal system irrigated 9,800 ha of land versus 7,000 in 1953 (Willey, 1953). The 1,400 m Ascope canal follows the base of the hills and was constructed with approximately 785,000 m^3 of earth and adobe (Bennet, 1949, and Willey, 1953).

Crops found growing by Cieza de León in the "oases" of the Peruvian coast included those native to the country and many introduced by Europeans—wheat, grapes, bananas, and citrus. The decline of Indian agriculture and decimation of large portions of the population were partly due to "the astonishingly disastrous effects of the Spanish conquest . . ." and the "social chaos brought about by the faction wars between the conquistadores" (Armillas, 1961, 270). Agricultural decline of these civilizations could very well have been caused by improper soil and water management, namely soil salinization and waterlogging due to prolonged use of irrigation with inadequate drainage.

Colonial and post-colonial periods of South America were characterized by the slow introduction of techniques, developed mainly outside the region, and spread, in controlled doses by the owners of this technology, to large holdings of land. For the most part, market-oriented agriculture was (and is) practiced. Thus, South America emphasized export agriculture for the direct benefit of the colonizers during the colonial times, and of the European descendants during the post-colonial period. Maximum profits have been the main goal of this market-oriented agriculture. This has had some positive effects, but negative effects arise too frequently. Salinity, at least in South America, is perhaps one of the least evils.

PRESENT STATUS

The Region

General. The outlook for the region of South America is not promising. Numerous studies and reports forecast a grim future for this area. Although most of these accounts have little to do with management of the land and water resources for salinity control, they have a great deal to do with causes and constraints which make these and other agricultural problems unsolvable and ever-present despite the existence of feasible technical solutions. A Food and Agriculture Organization (FAO) report (1984) states that "the basic problems faced by the region [Latin America] are socioeconomic rather than technical." To this statement, it should be added that omnipresent political problems, of international scale, control the economic growth and the people's social well-being. As the FAO report indicates, the agriculture in the region has a dualistic nature "consisting of a modern, capital-intensive sector producing for the market, and a traditional sector that is partly subsistance oriented. . . ."

Peasant agriculture has been neglected in modern times. This neglect is the primary cause of poverty and the exodus from villages, which leads to overcrowding in the cities. The distribution of land holdings in Latin America is uneven, and the situation as a whole has deteriorated (FAO, 1984, 11). Marshall and Esfandiary (1979) concluded that most countries in South America, with the possible exception of Argentina and Colombia, will find it impossible to become self-sufficient in food production by the end of the 1980s. This, or a worse situation, unfortunately could be the case by the beginning of the twenty-first century.

As is pointed out by Marin-Villegas (1982), the most important problem in Latin America is increasing unemployment coupled with the relatively high population growth (about 2.8 percent annually) and the exodus of the rural population. If these ciphers continue to represent the population changes in Latin America, the region is expected to double its population every twenty-five years, and by the end of the twentieth century it would have an urban population of 475 million instead of the present 220 million (Interamerican Development Bank, 1979, cited by Marin-Villegas, 1982). In addition, this growing population is young, with little training or education. To solve the problem of unemploy-

ment, jobs would have to be created at a rate of 4.5 million per year, which is equivalent to 40 percent of the global population growth (Marin-Villegas, 1982).

Irrigation and salinity. Houston (1975, cited by Kovda, 1980), estimates that 15 to 20 percent of the arable lands in the world are under irrigation at present and that 30 to 40 percent of the world's agricultural production is obtained from these irrigated lands. Half of the irrigated lands are located in developing countries, and this amount should double by the year 2000 (Kovda, 1980). Table 1 shows the arable, irrigated, and potentially irrigable lands in various South American countries. The arable lands include those with perennial and annual crops as well as cultivated and fallow lands.

Of the approximately 102 million ha of arable land in South America, 6.6 million ha (6.5 percent) correspond to irrigated lands, of which 75 percent are in four countries (Argentina, Brazil, Chile, and Peru). South America has 3 percent of the total irrigated lands in the world, and Latin America, as a whole, has about 5 percent of these lands (Interamerican Development Bank, 1983).

Argentina, with approximately 1.5 million ha under irrigation, has 23 percent of the irrigated lands of South America, followed closely by Chile with 1.32 million ha. The principal irrigated crops are grapes (209,000 ha), irrigated pasture (230,000 ha), vegetables (208,000 ha), and fruit trees (130,000 ha). Problems in the irrigated districts include poor water management and operation of irrigation systems, inadequate and obsolete irrigation structures, and improper or insufficient preparation of land for irrigation. To alleviate some of these pressing problems, the Interamerican Development Bank approved, in 1981, a substantial loan ($48 million) for a program of rehabilitating irrigation systems (Mathison, 1985).

Water pollution in Argentina is a major problem, particularly in the northeastern region, and industry is the primary cause. The magnitude of the problem is such that the enor-

Table 1. Arable, irrigated, and potentially irrigable lands in South America (millions hectares).

Country	(1) Arable[a]	(2) Irrigated[b]	(3) Potentially irrigable[a]	(2)/(1) (%)	(2)/(3) (%)
Argentina	34.42	1.54	2.400[c]	4.5	64.2
Bolivia	1.10	0.125	0.600	11.4	20.8
Brazil	38.803	1.050	2.964[d]	2.7	35.4
Chile	5.742	1.320	1.300	23.0	102.0
Colombia	5.090	0.295	N/A[e]	5.8	N/A
Equador	4.324	0.520	"	12.0	"
Guiana	0.845	0.120[a]	"	14.2	"
Paraguay	0.970	0.050[a]	"	5.2	"
Peru	2.880	1.180	1.733	41.0	68.1
Uruguay	2.252	0.045[a]	N/A	2.0	N/A
Venezuela	5.214	0.360	0.727	6.9	49.5
Total	101.640	6.605		6.5	

[a] Interamerican Development Bank, 1983.
[b] FAO, 1980.
[c] Estimated by the author.
[d] Includes only the land in the São Francisco valley.
[e] N/A: not available.

mous flow of the La Plata River is not sufficient to dilute the pollutants constituting the country's most severe case of water pollution (Llop, 1978).

One of the most productive areas of South America is the northern Mendoza basin in Argentina, with an area of about 1.5 million ha, of which more than 210,000 are under intense agriculture. The Mendoza basin contains about 75 percent of the vineyard lands of Argentina, and its fields are irrigated with waters from the Mendoza River, the lower Tunuyan River, and two aquifers. The Mendoza River carries about 1.3 million tons of salts per year, which are applied to the land by irrigation and to the ground aquifers through the recharging surfaces. The main aquifer contains water of low salinity but is subjected to salinization by irrigation return flows, excess pumping, and inadequate drainage. A second aquifer contains mostly seepage waters from the canal system and deep percolation losses from irrigated lands, thus increasing the salinity to an extremely high level for agricultural use (Llop, 1978).

In the region of Patagonia, about 40,000 ha irrigated in the nineteenth century were 50 percent salinized in 1971 because of overirrigation, the loss of large amounts of water from the canals, and insufficient drainage (Bergmann, 1971).

Irrigation development of the Rio Negro basin in Argentina began in the 1890s with 5000 ha in the Choele-Choel area, developed by a community of Welsh farmers. In 1951 3,000 ha were lost to severe salinization. By 1967 the irrigated area in this basin totaled about 83,000 ha. Up to 24,000 ha, located in the upper Rio Negro, required corrective measures for salinity control, including intensive leaching. Salinization became more serious in the lower portions of the basin. In general, the main causes of the salinization and waterlogging problem can be attributed to inefficient irrigation practices, high water losses from canal seepage, inadequate natural drainage, and insufficient artificial drainage. Although the solution of salinization and waterlogging problems might be technically feasible, institutional, managerial, and political constraints, as well as lack of economic and other incentives, present serious obstacles to controlling the aforementioned problems (Novara, 1969).

Brazil ranks fourth in irrigated land among South American countries, and its potential for expansion is tremendous. The potentially irrigable land in the São Francisco valley alone surpasses the present irrigated area of every country in the region, as well as each country's potential (see Table 1). Total possibilities for irrigation are in the magnitude of 48 million ha. Irrigation efforts started in 1877. The total irrigated area in the northeastern region reached 500 ha by 1940 and is estimated to be 71,000 ha today (Marin-Villegas, 1982).

Although there are no available data on the magnitude of land salinization in the northeast, preliminary studies indicate that relatively young irrigation projects are being affected by salts as a result of improper project planning and management. These lands have been irrigated for ten to thirty years with waters from the São Francisco River, small reservoirs (açudes), or from small streams of nonperennial flow.

The waters from the São Francisco River are of good quality. However, some irrigated perimeters have developed saline spots which should be considered warnings of possible development of more serious problems, justifying the revision of present water management practices. In a preliminary study (Vadivieso and Cordeiro, 1983), the origin of salinization is traced to the water storage in the açudes. Water accumulated in the catchment picks up salts on its way to the açudes, where it is further concentrated by the intense evaporation characteristics of the region (a maximum of 10 mm per day). Lands located at a level below these reservoirs are affected not only by the quality of the irrigation water but also by water seepage. Relatively newly irrigated lands are being abandoned after a few years of operation because salinization and/or waterlogging have made them unproductive. This, in turn, is creating an additional problem of neglected irrigation and drainage structures.

Estimates are that 20 percent of the land under irrigation in northeastern Brazil is affected by salts (Cordeiro and Millar, 1978). Some of the projects are under-utilized. In the São Gonçalo project, for example, of 4,100 ha, only 1,300 ha are actually under irrigation. In addition, 24 percent of the area in operation corresponds to sodic soils (Cordeiro et al., 1982). Social and economic losses resulting from these problems are substantial considering the poverty of northeastern Brazil and the unproductive capital invested, including the cost per irrigated hectare—$8,000 (Marin-Villegas, 1982, 11).

The Case of Peru

Estimates are that the Incas had 2 million ha under irrigation when the Spanish conquistadores arrived in Peru. With implantation of the colonial governments, large areas of land with infrastructure for irrigation were abandoned. Agriculture was given low priority by the governments to give way to a more profitable activity, namely mining. The 2 million ha were reduced to 100,000 ha, poorly utilized and with productivity at the subsistence level, which continues to this day (Marin-Villegas, 1982).

Today Peru has approximately 1.2 million ha in irrigated agriculture, which represent only 41 percent of its estimated potential (see Table 1). The country has the highest yields in rice (4,460 kg/ha) and sugarcane (126,400 kg/ha), grown totally under irrigation, and in cotton is second only to Mexico (FAO, 1980). On the other hand, Peru, the source of the potato, is now importing them. This situation worsened with the disastrous effects of the El Niño current. Production of most crops decreased, with potatoes declining 600,000 tons and grains falling 12 percent. In addition, droughts in the south and torrential rains in the north caused a 12 percent decline in real income and three-digit inflation—the "worst economic situation of the century" (U.S. Department of Agriculture, 1984, 10).

Most of the coast of Peru is arid, or extremely arid, like the Sahara region. About 90 percent of the population resides in the arid zone. The mean temperature is between 18° and 24° C, with the maximum reaching 38° C. Precipitation, ranging from 0 to 300 mm, is poorly distributed and averages 25 mm along the extremely arid coastal strip. Paradoxically, it is here that one finds land with the most agricultural potential and soils producing almost 50 percent of the agricultural gross product. There are fifty-two valleys, traversing the coast from east to west, where most of the agricultural activity take place. The main crops are cotton (133,000 ha), rice (88,000 ha), corn (109,000 ha), sugarcane (48,000 ha), alfalfa (41,000 ha), beans (22,000 ha), potatoes (8,000 ha), and sorghum (7,000 ha) (Estrada Ancajima, 1983, and Masson, 1974).

Irrigation along the coast is practiced on about 700,000 ha. Nevertheless, only 20 percent of the 40 million m^3 of surface water is utilized. Most of this water (70 percent) is lost to the ocean by the rivers carrying the water originating from heavy rains in the sierras mainly during the months of January through March (Estrada Ancajima, 1983).

Most of the Peruvian coastal soils are affected by salinity. The salinity problem has been identified and classified by ONERN (National Office for Evaluation of Natural Resources). Of the fifty-two coastal valleys, thirty-nine have been studied, as have two hundred pampas. Although studies are not complete, it is estimated that out of 800,000 ha of cultivated coastal lands, 250,000 ha are affected by salinity and 150,000 ha have associated drainage problems. In addition, ONERN estimates that natural salinity exists in the desert or pampas on 2 million ha (out of 3.5 million ha of potentially irrigable lands (Masson Meiss, 1974).

Some of the soils of the Peruvian coast have high concentrations of boron, mainly in the southern coast (Masson Meiss, 1974). Nevertheless, crops such as alfalfa, cotton, and corn showed little or no effect when grown in soils with concentrations ranging from 5.2 to 115 ppm (Fox, 1968).

Most of the saline soils of the lower coast are Solonchaks, in association with Regosols and Fluviosols, formed from recent alluvial deposits. Salts are present below 1.50 m depth, and electrical conductivities are above the level of 15 dS·m^{-1}. A cemented Solonchak hardpan layer is commonly found at a depth of 1 m. These soils are quite extensive, representing more than 1 million ha (Zamora, 1975).

Salinity in the semiarid region of the Peruvian highlands (the Sierra) offers no major obstacles to agricultural development. On the other hand, the salinity of the arid coast affects the irrigated valleys and the uncultivated virgin desert, called "pampas," as well. In the irrigated valleys the scarcity and irregularity of water supplies have caused problems of drainage and salinity associated with excess water application during the months of water abundance, which coincide with high crop water demands and evaporation. Irrigation of the upper portions of the valleys has had considerable effect on older irrigation developments in the lower lands, which are in most cases well prepared, more productive, and of better quality. In the pampas the salinity has been traced to the marine origin of the soils or of their substratum (Masson Meiss, 1973).

The impact of salinity on the economy of Peru is great. Data presented by Estrada (1984) indicate that the annual loss in agriculture traceable to salinity is about $190 million. Total losses are about $400 million when effects of the drought of 1980–81 are added. Estrada points out that "existing data indicate that salinization has increased in the last 15 years." He explains that the reasons for this are poor planning in the implementation of new irrigation schemes and lack of coherent and continuous programs to develop intermediate technologies adaptive to particular conditions. Irrigated agriculture on the coast reached a high level of technology, which was promoted and maintained by private enterprise, but was practically destroyed by political actions in the 1970s. As a consequence, the recently redistributed land and its water were poorly managed; salinization and waterlogging followed. Some of this land was later abandoned, leaving behind useless irrigation infrastructure and unproductive land (Estrada Ancajima, 1984).

DISCUSSION AND CONCLUSIONS

When one considers the vast knowledge that exists as a result of worldwide experience and scientific work, salinity and related problems in irrigated agriculture should be minimum. Well-planned, executed, and managed irrigation schemes should last for centuries for the use of future generations as highly productive, well-balanced, and controlled ecological systems. In reality the opposite occurs. Too often, productive irrigated lands are progressively deteriorated due to salinization and the buildup of toxic elements contained in the irrigation water or in the ground.

Although this is happening in both developing and industrialized countries, the economic and social consequences are, in many instances, catastrophic for a developing country. In general, salinization problems, like many others in agriculture, have their main roots outside the technical field. In a market-oriented economy, planning does not evolve spontaneously to maintain and perpetuate the proper ecological balance. On the contrary, there exist political short-term and myopic goals and always a discrepancy between the administrative planning phase and the strategy that would ensure proper management of the nonrenewable resources involved. The institutional framework in too many instances is guided by purely political considerations, which in most cases have little to do with the preservation of a well-balanced ecosystem.

Increased food production is essential for maintaining political and economic independence of South America. Crop yields in many countries of the region are unacceptably low and could be much higher if soil salinity were eliminated and proper agronomic, conservation, and irrigation practices together with highly water-responsive cultivars, were introduced.

In South America all available lands for irrigation are potentially subject to salinization, particularly those of the arid regions, and maintaining productivity is crucial for the much-needed food. Nevertheless, political, budgetary, institutional, and many other constraints prevail over the prevention and control of salinization and the execution of properly planned agricultural programs to ensure and maintain food self-sufficiency.

The lack of sufficient numbers of scientific and technical personnel and the similarity of problems in the Latin American nations more than justify the search for solutions in an all-out action. This action should pool resources for the study of and solution to common problems, such as land salinization, directed toward a common goal, i.e., sufficiency in food production. With the participation of international agencies and inputs from industrialized nations, research and learning centers and programs at the regional level should be created.

In addition to the foregoing, industrialized nations should dedicate a small portion of their capital resources for research aimed at nonpatentable technology to increase food production. This technology should be readily available and applicable to the conditions of Latin America, thus promoting economic and political independence of the region.

REFERENCES

Armillas, P. 1961. Land use in pre-columbian America. Pp. 255–76. *In* L. D. Stamp (ed.) A history of land use in arid regions. Paris: UNESCO.

Bennett. W. C. 1949. Andean culture history. Handbook series No. 15. New York: The American Museum of Natural History.

Bergmann, J. F. 1971. Soil salinization and Welsh settlement in Chibut, Argentina. vol. 5, Pp. 361–69. *In* Cahiers de geographie de Québec.

Cieza de León, P. The Incas of Pedro de Cieza de León. Translated by H. de Onís. 1969. Norman: University of Oklahoma Press.

Cordeiro, G. G., and A. Millar. 1978. Problemas de sais nas areas em operacão agricola de projeto de irrigacão de São Gonçalo. Paper presented to the 1978 Irrigation and Drainage Congress. Salvador, Bahía.

Cordeiro, G. G., G. Zylstra, and A. A. Millar. 1982. Influencia da irrigacão na salinizacão e sodificacão dos solos do projeto de São Gonçalo. Unpublished mimeographed report. Petrolina, Brazil: EMBRAPA/CPATSA.

Estrada Ancajima, J. 1983. La agricultura de la costa. Lima, Peru: Universidad Agraria.

Estrada Ancajima, J. 1984. La technologia edafica en el agro peruano: situacion actual y perspectivas. Pp. 367–95. Seminario nacional de agricultura peruana. Lima.

Food and Agriculture Organization [FAO]. 1980. Anuario de producão 1979. vol. 33. Rome.

———. 1984. World food report. Rome.

Fox, R. H. 1968. Tolerancia de las plantas de maiz, algodon, alfalfa, y frijol a concentraciones altas de boro soluble en agua en los suelos de la costa sur del Peru. *Anales Cientificos* 34:185–97.

Houston, C. E. 1975. Irrigation development in the world. *In* E. B. Worthington (ed.) Arid land irrigation in developing countries. London: Pergamon Press.

Interamerican Development Bank. 1979. Socio-economical progress in Latin America. Annual report. Washington, D.C.

Interamerican Development Bank. 1983. Progresso socioeconomico na America Latina: Recursos naturais. Relatorio de 1983. Washington, D.C.

Kovda, Victor A. 1980. Land aridization and drought control. Boulder, Colorado: Westview Press.

Llop, A. A. 1978. Economics of irrigation under salinity conditions: the case of Mendoza, Argentina. Ph.D. diss., University of California, Davis.

Marin-Villegas, J. 1982. A agricultura irrigada como estrategia de desenvolvimento regional. Instituto Interamericano de Cooperacão para a Agricultura—Ministerio do Interior. Brasilia, D. F. Brazil.

Marshall, A. M., and A. N. Esfandiary. 1979. The potential for self-sufficiency in food production in six Latin American countries: some projections for 1985 and 1990. Paper presented at the American Agricultural Association meeting, July 29–August 1. Washington State University, Pullman, Washington.

Masson Meiss, L. 1973. Evaluacion de la salinidad en el Peru. Pp. 363–84. *In* Grupo de trabajo sobre evaluacion y control de degradacion de tierras en zonas aridas de America Latina. Proyecto Regional FAO/PNUD. Lima.

Masson Meiss, L. 1974. Problemas de la zona arida peruana, con especial referencia a la incidencia de la salinidad sobre su desarrollo economico. Primer seminario nacional de sistemas ecologicos—recursos naturales y medio ambiente. Lima.

Mooney, P. R. 1983. The law of the seed—another development and plant genetics resources. Development dialogue. Uppsala, Sweden: The Dag Hammarskjold Foundation.

Novara, J. J. 1969. An economic analysis of salinity and waterlogging in irrigation: a study of the Rio Negro basin in Argentina. Research essay. Department of Agricultural Economics. University of California, Berkeley.

U.S. Department of Agriculture. 1984. Latin America—Outlook and situation report. Economic Research Services. RS-84-9. Washington, D.C.

Vadivieso, C. R., and G. G. Cordeiro. 1983. Drenagem e salinidade nos perimetros irrigados do nordeste do Brasil. Parte I: relatorio de identificacão e reconhecimento. Unpublished report. IICA-EMBRAPA.

Willey, G. R. 1953. Prehistoric settlement patterns in the Viru valley, Peru. Bulletin No. 155. The Smithsonian Institution, Bureau of American Ethnology. Washington, D.C.

Zamora, C. 1975. Los suelos de las tierras bajas del Peru. Pp. 45–60. *In* E. Borneisza and A. Alvarado (ed.) Manejo de suelos en la America tropical. University consortium on soils of the tropics. Raleigh: North Carolina State University.

24. PRINCIPLES AND PRACTICES OF SALINITY CONTROL ON FOOD PRODUCTION IN NORTH AMERICA

James D. Rhoades, U.S. Salinity Laboratory, Riverside, California

ABSTRACT

This paper presents some of the important principles and practices in controlling salinity in irrigated lands. Approaches are presented and some needs are identified to improve our ability to deal with major salinity problems in North America.

SALINITY EFFECTS ON SOILS AND PLANTS

Salts exert both general and specific effects on plants, thus influencing crop yields. Salts also affect soil physiochemical properties, which could in turn reduce the suitability of the soil as a medium for plant growth.

Effects on Plants

Excess salinity (essentially independent of its composition) in the irrigated root zone adversely affects plant growth by a general reduction in growth rate. The hypothesis that seems to best fit observations is that salt stress increases the energy that must be expended to extract water from the soil and to make the biochemical adjustments necessary to survive under stress. This energy is diverted from the processes which lead to normal growth and yield.

The salt tolerances of crops are expressed, after Maas and Hoffman (1977), in terms of their threshold values and percentage decreases in yield per unit increase of soil salinity in excess of the threshold (the preferred unit of soil salinity is the electrical conductivity of the extract of a saturated soil paste, σ_e in dS·m^{-1}). Salt tolerance data cannot indicate accurate, quantitative crop yield losses from salinity for every situation, since actual response to salinity varies with growing conditions, including climate, agronomic management, crop variety, etc. Salt tolerance data are useful, however, to predict how one crop might fare relative to another under similar conditions of salinity. Plants are generally most sensitive during the seedling stage; hence, it is imperative to keep salinity low in the seedbed. When salinity reduces plant stand, potential yields are decreased far more than that predicted by the salt tolerance data.

Typically, salt tolerance data apply most directly to surface irrigated crops and conventional irrigation management. Sprinkler-irrigated crops may also suffer damage from foliar salt uptake and "burn" from contact with the spray. The available data base predicting yield losses from foliar spray effects is limited (Maas, 1984). The degree of foliar injury depends on weather conditions and water stress; for example, visible symptoms may appear suddenly when the weather becomes hot and dry.

Certain salt constituents are specifically toxic to some crops. Boron is highly toxic to many crops when present in the soil solution at concentrations of only a few parts per million (Maas, 1984; Bingham et al., 1985). In some woody crops, sodium and chloride may accumulate in the tissue to toxic levels (Bernstein, 1974). These toxicity problems are not major in North America. The effects of salinity and toxic solutes on the physiology and biochemistry of plants are reviewed by Maas and Nieman (1978) and Maas (1984).

Sodic soil conditions may induce calcium and various micronutrient deficiencies by the associated high pH and bicarbonate conditions repressing their solubilities and concentrations. Sodic soils can be improved with amendments such as gypsum and sulfuric acid (Rhoades, 1982). Sodic soils are less extensive than saline soils in the *irrigated* lands of North America.

Effects on Soils

The suitability of soils for cropping depends appreciably on the readiness with which they conduct water and air (permeability) and on aggregate properties which control the friability of the seedbed (tilth). In contrast to saline soils, sodic soils have lower permeabilities and poorer tilth, causing problems in some irrigated lands of North America.

Because of negative electrical surface charges, clays adsorb positively charged ions (cations), such as calcium, magnesium, and sodium, by electrostatic attraction. These cations can be replaced or exchanged by other cations that are added to the soil solution. Each soil has a measurable capacity to adsorb and exchange cations (the cation exchange capacity). The percentage of this capacity satisfied by sodium is referred to as the exchangeable sodium percentage, P_{Na}. The percentage is approximately numerically equal to the proportion of sodium relative to calcium plus magnesium present in the soil solution referred to as the sodium adsorption ratio ($R_{Na} = Na^+/((Ca^{++} + Mg^{++})/2)^{1/2}$, where the concentrations are expressed in mmol (+)/liter). Thus, R_{Na} can be used essentially interchangeably with P_{Na} over the normal range of P_{Na} encountered in irrigated soils.

The adsorbed ions in the "envelope" around colloidal clay are subject to two opposing processes: (1) They are attracted to the negatively charged clay surface by electrostatic forces, and (2) they tend to diffuse away from the surface of the clay under a concentration gradient. The two opposing processes result in an approximately exponential decrease in adsorbed-ion concentration with distance from the clay surface to the bulk solution. Divalent cations, such as calcium and magnesium, are attracted to the surface with a force twice as great as monovalent cations, like sodium, for example. Thus, the "envelope" in the divalent system is more compressed toward the clay surface. The "envelope" is also compressed by an increase in the electrolyte concentration of the bulk solution.

Short-range adhesive forces, called van der Waals forces, are involved in the particle-to-particle associations that bind the clays into aggregates. The net forces, which result in the formation of aggregates, are diminished when the cation "envelopes" are extended and are enhanced when they are compressed. This occurs because the relatively long-range electrostatic charged "envelopes" around adjacent clay particles repel one another. With compression of the cation "envelope" toward the clay surface, the overlap of the "envelopes" of two adjacent particles is reduced for a given distance between them, the repulsion forces between the like-charged "envelopes" is decreased, and the particles can approach sufficiently close to permit the van der Waals forces to come into play. The resulting aggregate structure is more porous, resulting in enhanced permeability and tilth. When repulsion between clay particles is predominant, more solution is imbibed between clay particles, causing swelling. Such swelling reduces the size of the interaggregate pore spaces in the soil and hence reduces permeability. Swelling is primarily important in soils that contain expanding layer phyllosilicate minerals (smectites like montmorillonite) and P_{Na} values in excess of about 15. For such minerals, exchangeable sodium is initially preferentially adsorbed on the external clay surfaces. These external surfaces make up about 15 percent of the cation exchange capacity (CEC). Only with further "buildup" of adsorbed sodium does it enter the interlayer position between the parallel platelets of the oriented and associated clay particles of the subaggregate assemblages, called domains, where it creates the repulsion forces that lead to swelling. Dispersion (release of individual clay platelets from aggregates) and slaking (breakdown of aggregates into subaggregate assemblages) can occur at P_{Na} values lower than 15, providing the electrolyte concentration is sufficiently low. Dispersed platelets or slaked subaggregate units can lodge in pore interstices, also reducing permeability. Soil solutions composed of high solute concentrations and calcium and magnesium salts produce good soil physical properties. Conversely, low concentrations and sodium salts adversely affect permeability and tilth.

When water infiltrates the soil surface, the soil solution of the topsoil is essentially that of the infiltrating water, while the exchangeable sodium percentage is essentially that preexistent in the soil (since P_{Na} is buffered against rapid change by the soil CEC). All water entering the soil must pass through the surface; hence, the stability of the topsoil aggregates influences the water entry rate of the soil. Therefore, soil permeability and tilth problems must be assessed in terms of both the salinity of the infiltrating water and the exchangeable sodium percentage of the topsoil. Representative guideline threshold values of R_{Na} ($\sim P_{Na}$) and the electrical conductivity of infiltrating water for maintenance of soil permeability are given in Rhoades (1982). Significant differences exist among soils in their susceptibilities, and this relation should be used only as a

guideline. Effects of salts on soil properties are reviewed by Keren and Shainberg (1984), Shainberg (1984), Shainberg and Letey (1983), and Emerson (1984).

SALINITY-RELATED PROCESSES OPERATIVE IN SOIL-PLANT-WATER SYSTEMS

Salinity management requires an understanding of not only how salts affect plants and soils but also of how cropping and irrigation affect soil and water salinity.

Irrigation-Evapotranspiration-Leaching-Drainage Interactions

The concentration of soluble salts increases in soils as the applied water, but not salts, is removed by evaporation and transpiration. Evapotranspiration (ET) can cause an appreciable upward flow of water and salt into the root zone from lower soil depths. By this process, many soils with shallow, saline water tables become salinized. Soluble salts will eventually accumulate in irrigated soils to the point that crop yields will suffer unless steps are taken to prevent it. To prevent the excessive accumulation of salt in the root zone, irrigation water (or rainfall) must be applied in excess of that needed for ET and must pass through the root zone to leach out the accumulating salts. This is referred to as the "leaching requirement" (L_r, U.S. Salinity Laboratory Staff, 1954). Once the soil solution has reached a salinity level compatible with the cropping system, subsequent irrigations must remove at least as much salt from the root zone as is brought in with irrigations, a process called "maintaining salt balance." In fields irrigated to steady-state conditions with conventional irrigation management, the salt concentration of the soil water is essentially uniform near the soil surface regardless of the leaching fraction (L, the fraction of infiltrated water that passes through the root zone) but increases with depth as L decreases. Likewise, average root zone salinity increases and crop yield decreases as L decreases. Details on methods to calculate the leaching requirement and salt balance are given by Rhoades (1974, 1982).

Adequate drainage is mandatory to handle the leachate needed to achieve the leaching requirement and salt balance. In addition, the water table depth must be controlled to prevent any appreciable upward flow of water and salt into the root zone. This water table depth is irrigation management dependent and not single valued as is commonly assumed (van Schilfgaarde, 1976).

Soil Salinity–Plant Interactions

The time-averaged root zone salinity is affected by the degree to which the soil water is depleted between irrigations (Rhoades, 1972). As the time between irrigations is increased, the matric potential decreases as the soil dries, and the osmotic potential decreases as salts concentrate in the reduced water volume. Crop yield is closely related to the time and depth averaged *total* soil water potential, i.e., matric plus osmotic (Ingvalson et al., 1976). As water is removed from a soil with nonuniform salinity distribution, the total water potential of the water being absorbed by the plant tends to approach uniformity in all depths of the root zone (Rhoades and Merrill, 1976). Following irrigation, plant roots absorb water in soil depths of low osmotic stress rather than regions of high osmotic stress. Normally this means that most of the water uptake is from the upper, less saline soil depths until sufficient water is removed to equalize the total water stress with depth. After that, salinity effects on crop growth will be magnified. In summary: (1) plants can tolerate higher levels of salinity under conditions of low matric stress (e.g., high-frequency forms of irrigation, like drip), and (2) high soil-water salinities occurring in deeper regions of the root zone can be significantly offset if sufficient low-salinity water is added to the upper profile fast enough to satisfy the crop's evapotranspiration requirement. Research results tend to support these conclusions (van Schilfgaarde et al., 1974). Thus, irrigation management affects permissible levels of salinity of soils and irrigation waters. A typical deficiency of prevalent classification schemes of water quality for irrigation is that they exclude irrigation management effects. For methods of assessing water suitability for irrigation, see Rhoades (1972, 1982, 1984) and Rhoades and Merrill (1976).

Soil Salinity–Irrigation System Interactions

The distribution within and the degree to which a soil profile becomes salinized also are functions of the degree and manner of water application and leaching. More salt is generally removed per unit of leachate with sprinkler irrigation than with flood irrigation. Thus, the salinity of water applied by sprinkler irrigation could be higher than that applied by flood or furrow irrigation with a comparable degree of cropping success, provided foliar burn is avoided. There is evidence that trickle irrigation, in which water is applied steadily at a rate slightly in excess of ET, permits crops to be grown more successfully with saline waters than otherwise possible. With this method, the high matric potential resulting from the high soil water content and limited drying between irrigations minimizes time-averaged soil-water salinity. Crop salinity tolerances determined under flood and furrow irrigation may not be directly applicable to trickle irrigation because of the higher water potential achieved with the latter form of irrigation; however, substantial data are lacking in this regard.

As noted above, the salt-removal efficiency with sprinkler irrigation tends to be substantially higher than with flood and trickle irrigation. Solute transport is governed by the combined processes of convection (movement with the bulk solution) and diffusion (movement under a concentration gradient); convection is usually the predominant process. Differential velocities of water flow normally occur within the soil matrix (dispersion) because the pore size distribution is typically nonuniform. Dispersion is appreciable when flow velocity is high, and diffusion often limits salt removal under such conditions. Soils with large cracks and well-developed structure are especially variable in their water and solute transport properties because the large "pores" are preferred pathways, as are earthworm channels, old root holes, interpedal voids, etc., and most of the flow in flooded soils occurs in them. Much of the water and salt in intra-aggregate pores is "bypassed" in flood-

irrigated soils. Flow velocity and water content are typically lower in soils irrigated with sprinklers; hence, bypass is reduced and efficiency of salt leaching is increased. For a more quantitative description of effects of convection and dispersion on solute transport in soils see the review of Wagenet (1984).

Salinity-Soil Interactions

Other soil-related processes also affect salt concentration and transport during the irrigation and leaching of soils. In most arid land soils, the clay particles are dominated by negative charges, which can retard cation transport through exchange processes. Simultaneously, anions are effectively excluded from part of the pore solution adjacent to the negatively charged clay surface, accelerating their transport. Boron also undergoes adsorption reactions that retard its movement. These reactions are reviewed by Wagenet (1984).

Dissolution and precipitation of salts and mineral weathering significantly affect the composition of the soil solution and salt-loading contributions from irrigation. Studies by Rhoades et al. (1973, 1974) have shown that the effects of salt precipitation are generally insignificant at leaching fractions of 0.2 and higher with irrigation waters of less than about 1.0 dS·m^{-1} electrical conductivity (σ_{iw}). At leaching fractions of 0.1 or less, salt precipitation is frequently significant, depending on the composition of the irrigation water. For waters with a σ_{iw} of less than ~0.4 dS·m^{-1}, the dissolution of minerals is often more important in controlling the level of soil water salinity than is the salt content of the irrigation water. Models of soil chemistry have been developed and coupled to descriptions of solute transport (Wagenet, 1984). These models are primarily based on chemical *equilibrium* concepts and seldom include silicate mineral weathering. Furthermore, many salt dissolution/precipitation reactions are *kinetically* controlled in soil systems. Lack of appropriate descriptions of mineral weathering and other kinetically controlled reactions in irrigated soils are major factors limiting the validity of prevalent chemistry models (Jurinak, 1984).

The hydraulic properties of the soil depend upon total salt concentration of the percolating water and the nature of the adsorbed cations. The sodium adsorption ratio of the soil water (R_{sw}) is a good estimate of the exchangeable sodium percentage of the soil, as discussed earlier, and is frequently used for diagnosing sodicity problems. However, R_{sw} is related to but is not the same as that of the irrigation water (R_{iw}). Changes in R_{iw} occur as the irrigation water infiltrates the soil because of concentration by ET, the accumulation of salts in the seedbed because of evaporation, and the decomposition of plant residues near the surface. Other factors affecting R_{sw} are the loss or gain in Ca and Mg salts due to precipitation of alkaline earth carbonates present in the irrigation water and the introduction of Ca, Mg, and HCO_3 into the soil water from the dissolution and weathering of soil minerals. These effects limit the applicability of R_{iw} as a suitable index of R_{sw} to relatively saline, low-carbonate waters. For *sodic* waters, the more generally applicable adjusted sodium adsorption ratio should be used in its place. The adjusted R_{sw} may be calculated by either of two methods, which give essentially equivalent results, as described elsewhere (Rhoades, 1982, 1984; Suarez, 1981, 1982; Oster and Rhoades, 1977). Soil permeability will be reduced if the adjusted $R_{sw} - \sigma_{iw}$ combination lies to the left of a threshold relation between adjusted R_{sw} (ordinate) and σ_{iw} (abscissa). The threshold relation curves downward below adjusted R_{sw} values of 10 and intersects the σ_{iw} axis at a value of about 0.3 because of the dominating effect of electrolyte concentration on soil aggregate stability, dispersion, and crusting at such low salinities. A representative $R_{sw} - \sigma_{iw}$ threshold relation is given in Rhoades (1982) as a guideline for arid-land soils. There is a lack of sufficient quantitative information to assess clearly the sodicity hazard of an irrigation water for different soils. Mineralogy is one cause of substantial variation in response among soils. Additional variations may be caused by the effects of cementing materials such as organic matter and calcareous, siliceous, and oxide coatings, which tend to stabilize soil aggregate stability. Additional complications include the effects of tillage and other cultural practices, such as sprinkler water impact, which enhance disaggregation and the associated problems of sodicity.

In many semiarid regions the irrigation season is followed by a rainy season. During the irrigation season the salinity of the irrigation water usually prevents excessive aggregate slaking, soil swelling, and clay dispersion. When the irrigation water is displaced by rain water, a $R_{sw} - \sigma_{iw}$ situation conducive to disaggregation, dispersion, and crusting can result. Insufficient research has been directed toward prediction of this type of response, with resulting limitations in the management of salt-affected soils. Indeed, it is a function not only of soil sodicity but also of other soil properties, including the rates of soil mineral weathering, salt dissolution and transport, and cation exchange. For more information on this topic, see Shainberg (1984).

Adsorption by the soil of some solutes like boron also occurs with the irrigation process. Plants respond primarily to the boron concentration of the soil water rather than to the amount of adsorbed B (Keren et al., 1985a, b; Bingham et al., 1985). Some boron added with the irrigation water will be adsorbed by the soil, but boron still concentrates in the soil water. For some transitional period of time, the degree to which boron is concentrated in the soil water will be less than that of non-adsorbed solutes like chloride. The time required to reach a state when boron concentration in the soil water reaches its maximum is typically three to five years but varies with soil properties, amount of irrigation water applied, leaching fraction, and concentration of B in the irrigation waters.

The prevalent models of solute reactions and transport in irrigated soils suffer the deficiency of not appropriately representing the large variations in the above described processes that often occur under field conditions. Only recently has this problem been approached directly by measuring, on a large scale, solute distributions in field soil profiles. The results to date indicate that we do not yet have a suitable method to summarize and to integrate the processes opera-

tive on a field basis (Jury, 1984). It is probable that alternative modeling approaches, like that proposed by Corwin et al. (1984), may help in this regard.

SALINITY-RELATED PROCESSES OPERATIVE IN IRRIGATION PROJECTS AND GEOHYDROLOGIC SYSTEMS

Some unique effects of irrigation are operative at the scale of whole projects and entire geohydrologic systems; hence, some management practices for salinity control should address this larger scale. The control measures for minimizing the impacts of irrigated agriculture should be coordinated with overall water resource development programs.

Irrigation Return Flow

The primary sources of irrigation return flow are bypass water, canal seepage, deep percolation, and tailwater or surface runoff. Bypass water is often required to maintain hydraulic head and adequate flow through the canal system. It is usually returned directly to the river, and few pollutants are picked up in this route. Canal seepage may contribute to high water tables, increase groundwater salinity and phreatophyte growth, and generally increase saline drainage from irrigated areas. Law et al. (1972) estimated that 20 percent of the total water diverted for irrigation in the United States is lost by seepage from conveyance and irrigation canals. If the water passes through salt-laden substrata or displaces saline groundwater, the salt pickup from this source can be substantial. An example is the Grand Valley of Colorado. Canal lining can reduce such salt loading. Evaporation losses from canals commonly amount to only a small percentage of the diverted water. Closed conduit conveyance systems can minimize both seepage and evaporation losses and ET by phreatophytes. The closed conduit system also provides the potential for higher project irrigation efficiency and lower salt loading (van Schilfgaarde and Rawlins, 1980).

Salt Loading from Irrigation and Drainage

Irrigation water may contain from 0.05 to 3.5 tons of salt per 1,000 m³. With crops requiring annual irrigations of 6,200 to 9,300 m³ water per hectare to meet ET, from 0.3 to 32 tons/ha of salt may be added to irrigated soils annually. Reducing the volume of water applied will reduce the amount of salt added and the amount to be removed by leaching. Minimizing the leaching fraction maximizes the precipitation of applied Ca, HCO_3, and SO_4 salts as carbonates and gypsum minerals in the soil, and it minimizes the "pickup" of weathered and dissolved salts from the soil. The salt load from the root zone can be reduced from about 2 to 12 tons/ha per year by reducing L from 0.3 to 0.1 (Rhoades et al., 1973, 1974; Rhoades, 1977; Oster and Rhoades, 1975).

Minimizing leaching may or may not reduce salinity degradation where the drainage water is not intercepted and is returned to the associated surface or groundwater. A reduction of degradation will generally occur where saline groundwaters with concentrations in excess of those of the recharging drainage waters are displaced into the surface water. Many such situations occur in the upper Colorado River basin. Reduced leaching will also reduce the salinity of receiving surface waters, if they are undersaturated with $CaCO_3$ and/or gypsum and the drainage water becomes saturated with one or both of these minerals. Reduced leaching will not reduce salinity of the receiving water if it is already saturated with these constituents. Rivers unsaturated with gypsum but essentially saturated with $CaCO_3$ will not benefit from reduced leaching unless salts other than those derived from the diverted water or from soil mineral weathering and dissolution in the root zone are encountered in the drainage flow path or a "foreign" saline groundwater is displaced by the drainage water to the river. The Colorado River in its lower basin is probably of this type.

Like surface waters, groundwater receiving irrigation drainage water may not benefit from reduced leaching. With no sources of recharge other than drainage return flow, the groundwater eventually must come to the composition of the drainage water, which will be more saline with low leaching. However, the groundwater salinity may be lower with reduced leaching for an interim period of time. For groundwater being pumped for irrigation with no recharge other than by drainage return, the short-term limitations are the same as described above. Groundwater undersaturated with $CaCO_3$ (unlikely in arid lands) will show a slight benefit under low leaching, groundwater saturated with $CaCO_3$ will show no benefit under low leaching, and groundwater saturated with $CaCO_3$ and nearing saturation with gypsum will show substantial benefit from low leaching. Low leaching management can continuously reduce degradation of the groundwater, only if other sources of high-quality recharge into the basin exist and if flow out of the basin is high relative to drainage inflow. If a fixed volume of saline water is disposed of in a closed basin by irrigation, groundwater salinity will usually be lower with high leaching (Rhoades and Suarez, 1977).

The extent to which leaching can be minimized is limited by the salt tolerances of the crops being grown. In most irrigation projects, the currently used L's can be reduced appreciably without harming crops or soils, especially with improvements in irrigation management (van Schilfgaarde et al., 1974).

PRACTICES TO CONTROL SALINITY IN THE ROOT ZONE

Management practices for the control of salinity and sodicity include: selection of crops or crop varieties that will produce satisfactory yields under the existing conditions of salinity or sodicity; use of land-preparation and tillage methods that aid in the control or removal of salinity; special planting procedures that minimize salt accumulation around the seed; irrigation to maintain a relatively high level of soil moisture and to achieve periodic leaching of the soil, and special treatments (such as additions of chemical amendments, organic matter, and growing green manure crops) to maintain soil permeability and tilth. The crop grown, the quality of water used for irrigation, and soil properties determine to a large degree the kind and extent of management practices needed.

Growing Suitably Tolerant Crops

Where sailnity cannot be entirely eliminated, the judicious selection of crops that can produce satisfactory yields under moderately saline conditions is required. In selecting crops for saline soils, particular attention should be given to the salt tolerance of the crop during seedling development, because poor yields frequently result from failure to obtain a satisfactory stand. Some crops that are salt tolerant during later stages of growth are quite sensitive to salinity during early growth. Among the highly tolerant crops are barley, sugar beets, cotton, Bermuda grass, Rhodes grass, western wheatgrass, bird's-foot trefoil, table beets, kale, asparagus, spinach, and tomatoes. Crops having low salt tolerance include radishes, celery, beans, clovers, and nearly all fruit trees (Maas and Hoffman, 1977).

Managing Seedbeds and Fields to Minimize Local Salinity Accumulation

Failure to obtain a satisfactory stand of furrow-irrigated row crops on moderately saline soils is a serious problem in many places. The failures usually are due to the accumulation of soluble salt in raised beds that are "wet-up" by furrow irrigation. Modifications in irrigation practice and bed shape may reduce salt accumulation near the seed. The tendency of salts to accumulate near the seed during irrigation is greatest in single-row, flat-topped beds. Sufficient salt to prevent germination may concentrate in the seed zone, even if the average salt content of the soil is moderately low. With double-row beds, however, most of the salt moves into the center of the bed, which leaves the shoulders relatively free of salt, thus enhancing seedling establishment. Sloping beds are best on saline soils because the seed can be safely planted on the slope below the zone of salt accumulation. Planting in furrows or basins is satisfactory from the standpoint of salinity control but is often unfavorable for the emergence of many row crops because of crusting or poor aeration. Pre-emergence irrigation by sprinklers or by special furrows placed close to the seed may be used to keep the soluble salt concentration low in the seedbed during germination and seedling establishment. After the seedlings are established, the special furrows may be abandoned and new furrows made between the rows, or sprinkling may be replaced by furrow irrigation.

Careful leveling of land makes possible a more uniform application of water and, hence, better salinity control. Barren or poor areas in otherwise productive fields often are high spots that do not receive enough water for good crop growth or for leaching purposes. Lands that have been irrigated one or two years after initial leveling often need to be replaned to remove the surface unevenness caused by the settling of fill material. Annual crops should be grown after the first leveling so that replaning can be performed before a perennial crop is planted.

Irrigating to Maintain High Soil Water Potential and Periodically Leach Salts

The method and frequency of irrigation and the amount of irrigation water applied may be managed to control salinity. The main ways to apply water are basin flooding, furrow irrigation, sprinkling, subirrigation, and drip irrigation. Flooding the entire surface is suitable for salinity control if the land is level, though aeration and crusting problems may occur. Aeration and crusting problems are minimized with furrow irrigation, but salts tend to accumulate in the beds. If excess salt does accumulate, a rotation of crops and periodic irrigation by flooding is a possible salinity-control measure. Alternatively, cultivation and irrigation depths can be modified, once the seedlings are well established, to "shallow" the furrows so that the beds will be leached by later irrigations. Irrigation by sprinkling may permit better control of the amount and distribution of water. The tendency is to apply too little water by this method, and leaching of salts beyond the root zone is accomplished only with special effort. Salinity is kept low in the seedbed during germination, but crusting may be a problem. Subirrigation, in which the water table is maintained close to the soil surface, is not generally suitable when salinity is a problem unless the water table is lowered periodically and leaching of the accumulated salts is accomplished by rainfall or by surface applications of water. Drip irrigation, if properly designed, minimizes salinity and matric stresses because the soil water is kept relatively high and salts are leached to the periphery of the wetted area. As noted earlier, higher levels of salinity in the irrigation water can be tolerated with drip as compared with other methods of irrigation.

Because soluble salts reduce the availability of water in almost direct proportion to their total concentration in the soil solution, irrigation frequency, irrespective of method of irrigation, should be increased so that the moisture content of saline soils is maintained as high as is practicable, especially during seedling establishment and the early stages of vegetative growth.

Managing Soils to Sustain Tilth

Sodic soils are especially subject to puddling and crusting. They should be tilled carefully, taking care to avoid wet soil conditions. Heavy machinery traffic should also be avoided. More frequent irrigation, especially during the germination and seedling stages of plants, tends to soften surface crusts on sodic soils and encourages better stands. Amendments such as gypsum, organic matter, and animal and green manures may be used to maintain permeability and tilth.

PRACTICES TO CONTROL SALINITY IN IRRIGATED LANDS

Improvements in the efficiencies of the delivery and application systems will appreciably facilitate salinity control in irrigated lands. Overirrigation contributes to the water table and salinity problems and increases the amount of water that the drainage system must accommodate. Therefore, a proper relation between irrigation, leaching, and drainage must be maintained in order to prevent irrigated lands from becoming salt affected. The amount of water applied should be sufficient to supply the crop and satisfy the leaching requirement but not enough to overload the drainage system. Overirrigation is a major cause of salinity buildup in many irrigation projects of North America.

Operating Delivery Systems Efficiently

Excessive loss of irrigation water from canals constructed in permeable soil is a major cause of high water tables and saline soils in many irrigation projects. Such seepage losses should be reduced by lining the canals with impermeable materials or by compacting the soil to achieve a very low permeability. Because the amount of water passing critical points in the irrigation delivery system must be known in order to provide water control and to achieve high water-use efficiency, provisions for effective flow measurement should be made. Unfortunately, many current irrigation systems do not use flow measuring devices and, thus, the individual farmers operate their own turnout facilities with limited control of the amount diverted to the farms. In addition, many delivery systems encourage overirrigation because water is supplied for fixed periods, or in fixed amounts, irrespective of seasonal variations in on-farm needs. Salinity and water table problems often are the result. Increasing the efficiency of the distribution system to provide water on demand and in metered amounts facilitates salinity control.

Irrigating Efficiently

Improvements in salinity control will come from improved on-farm irrigation efficiency. The key to effective irrigation and salinity control is to provide the proper amount of water at the proper time. The optimum irrigation scheme provides water continuously to keep the soil water content in the root zone within narrow limits, although carefully programmed periods of stress may be desirable to obtain maximum economic yield with some crops; cultural practices also may demand periods of dry soil. Thus, careful control of timing and amount of water applied is a prerequisite to good water use efficiency and to high crop yield, especially in saline soils. As mentioned above, this requires water delivery to the field on demand which, in turn, requires close coordination between the farmer and the entity that distributes the water; it calls for devices to measure water flow (rates and volumes), and feedback devices that measure the water and salt content in the soil.

Automated solid-set and center-pivot sprinklers systems are conducive to good control and distribution; in principle, trickle irrigation is even better. Gravity systems, if designed and operated properly, can also achieve good control. Laser-controlled precision land leveling allows better areal water distribution over the field and smaller water applications; combined with automation, it has led to high irrigation efficiencies for dead-level, flooded systems (Dedrick et al., 1978). Using closed conduits rather than open waterways for laterals has the advantage of effective off-on control, in addition to capturing gravitational energy for pressurizing delivery systems or controls. In furrow-irrigated areas, furrow length can be reduced—and thus intake distribution is improved and tail water eliminated—using a system such as

Worstell's (1979) multi-set system. Surge irrigation can improve irrigation uniformity in graded furrows (Bishop et al., 1981). For tree crops, a low-head bubbler system that provides excellent control while minimizing pressure requirements has been developed (Rawlins, 1977). Drip systems, of course, are increasingly being used for permanent crops and high-value annual crops. Numerous opportunities exist for modifying existing irrigation systems to increase the effectiveness of water and salinity control.

A frequent constraint in improving on-farm water use is the lack of knowledge of just when irrigation is needed and of how much capacity for replenishment is available in the root zone. Ways to detect the onset of plant stress and to determine the amount of depleted soil water are prerequisites to supplying water on demand and in the amount needed. Prevalent methods of scheduling irrigation usually do not, but should, incorporate salinity effects on water availability (Rhoades et al., 1981). Irrigation management for salinity control is the subject of reviews by van Schilfgaarde (1976) and van Schilfgaarde and Rawlins (1980).

All irrigation projects, if they are to remain viable, must be accompanied by drainage, which must remove seepage and leaching water, as well as water that invades the area from the surrounding fields and lands. This water should be reused to the extent possible and the residual disposed of at a suitable site. Tailwater recovery and reuse for irrigation will help in this regard. If natural drainage is insufficient, it should be supplemented by artificial drainage (van Schilfgaarde 1974, 1984).

PRACTICES TO CONTROL SALINITY IN WATER RESOURCES

Irrigated agriculture is a major contributor to the salinity of many rivers and groundwaters in North America. The agricultural community has a responsibility to protect the quality of these waters. It must also maintain a viable, permanent irrigated agriculture. Irrigated agriculture cannot be sustained without adequate leaching and drainage to prevent excessive salination of the soil, yet these processes are the very ones that contribute to the salt loading of our rivers and groundwaters. River and groundwater salinity could be reduced if salt loading were minimized or eliminated. The protection of our water resources against excessive salination, while sustaining agricultural production through irrigation, will require a comprehensive land and water use policy that incorporates the natural processes involved in the soil-plant-water and associated geohydrological systems.

Strategies to consider in coping with increasing salinity in receiving water systems resulting from irrigation include: (1) eliminating irrigation, (2) intercepting point sources of drainage return flow and diverting them to other uses, and (3) reducing the amount of water lost in seepage and deep percolation.

Minimizing Deep Percolation and Intercepting Drainage

Deeply percolating water often displaces saline groundwater of higher salinity or dissolves additional salt from the subsoil. Reducing deep percolation will reduce the salt load

returned to the river (or groundwater) as well as reduce water loss. The adoption of the "minimized leaching" concept of irrigation which reduces deep percolation should be of appreciable benefit for reducing salination of our water resources, especially in the upper Colorado River basin (van Schilfgaarde et al., 1974). In addition, the interception of saline drainage water should likewise be beneficial. Intercepted saline drainage water can be desalted and reused, disposed of by pond evaporation or by injection into some isolated deep-aquifer, or it can be used as a water supply where use of brackish waters is appropriate.

Isolating and Reusing Drainage for Irrigation

While there is an excellent opportunity to reduce the salt load contributed by drainage water through better irrigation management, especially through reductions in seepage and deep percolation, there are practical constraints which limit such reductions. But the ultimate goal should be to maximize the utilization of an irrigation water supply in a single application with minimum drainage. To the extent that the drainage water still has value for use by a crop of higher salt tolerance, it should be used again for irrigation.

Drainage waters are often returned by diffuse flow or intentional direct discharge to the water course and automatically "reused." Dilution of return flows is often advocated for controlling water salinity. This concept has serious limitations when one considers the effect on the true volume of usable water, and it should not be advocated as a general method of salinity control. Diversions in excess of crop needs often provide return flows for irrigation downstream and help modulate the river flows. However, as already noted, such return is the mechanism by which much of the salt loading of rivers occurs, which, in turn, limits the kind of crops that can be grown. More significant is the fact that if the water being returned to the river is so saline that its use for crop production is nil, then dilution with purer water and using the mix for irrigation of crops of the same or lesser salt tolerance does not add to the *usable* water supply. One has, in this process of mixing, simply utilized the river as a combined "delivery and disposal" system and mixed the usable and unusable waters into one blend, which is separated again by plants for their use. In an irrigated soil, the plant, through transpiration, "distills" out the usable fraction of the mix (expending bioenergy to do so) and the "unusable" fraction passes through the profile again and in the process displaces or "picks up" more salt in its flow path. Greater flexibility for crop production results if the drainage water can be intercepted and isolated. Then the waters can be blended or used separately for irrigation or other uses. Once the drainage is mixed in surface waters, these alternatives are lost.

Strategy for salinity control of river systems is to intercept drainage before it is returned to the river and to use it for irrigation by alternating it with the river water normally used during certain periods in the growing season of selected crops. When the drainage water quality is such that its potential for reuse is exhausted, then it is discharged to evaporation ponds or other appropriate outlets. This strategy will conserve water, sustain crop production, and minimize the salt loading of rivers. It will also reduce the diversion of river water for irrigation. The feasibility of reusing drainage waters for irrigation is facilitated using the "dual-rotation" management system of Rhoades (1984a, b, c). In this system, sensitive crops (lettuce, alfalfa, etc.) in the rotation are irrigated with "low salinity" river water, and salt-tolerant crops (cotton, sugar beets, wheat, etc.) are irrigated with drainage water. For the tolerant crops, the switch to drainage water is usually made after seedling establishment, preplant irrigations and initial irrigations being made with river water. The feasibility of this strategy is supported by the following:

1. The maximum possible soil salinity in the root zone resulting from continuous use of drainage water does not occur when the water is used only for a fraction of the time.

2. Substantial alleviation of salt buildup resulting from irrigation of salt-tolerant crops with drainage water occurs during the time salt-sensitive crops are irrigated with river water.

3. Proper preplant irrigation and careful irrigation management during germination and seedling establishment leaches salts out of the seed area and from shallow soil depths.

4. Data obtained in modeling studies and in field experiments support the credibility of this "cyclic" reuse strategy (Rhoades 1977, 1984c).

Desalination of agricultural drainage waters for improving water quality is not economically feasible even though it is to be implemented for the return flow of the Wellton-Mohawk project of Arizona. The high costs of the pretreatments, maintenance, and power are the deterrents. Only in extreme cases, or for political rather than technical reasons, is desalination advocated (van Schilfgaarde, 1979).

ACTIONS NEEDED TO IMPROVE SALINITY CONTROL IN NORTH AMERICA

A number of needs for salinity control through management have been identified in the preceding sections. Yet other control possibilities exist, some of which await advancements in knowledge and technology. Some of these needs are outlined below.

Expansion of Basic Research of Plant Response to Salinity and Development of Tolerant Varieties

In spite of all the effort expended, the specific effects of salt on plants are not sufficiently understood. An expanded study is needed to make greater progress in this area. A companion effort should be undertaken to improve the salt tolerance of crop varieties. Research on the genetics of salt tolerance has not been adequately supported, and intraspecific differences in salt tolerance should be exploited so that progress can be achieved in the form of more salt-tolerant cultivars. Because phenotypic symptoms of salinity stress are vague, physiological and biochemical mechanisms of salt tolerance must be identified to provide the geneticist with specific selection criteria. Rapid screening techniques to evaluate these criteria are needed to select genotypes with heritable salt-tolerant traits. As proposed by

Shannon (1984), a plant breeding program for the development of salt-tolerant species should be undertaken and should include (1) identifying varieties with superior salt and boron tolerance and crossing them with high-yielding, adapted varieties; (2) screening segregated generations for increased tolerance in controlled stress conditions, such as greenhouse; and (3) testing advanced generations in the field.

Claims have been made of the potential for genetically engineering crops capable of being grown using seawater. Researchers at the U.S. Salinity Laboratory believe, however, that the extent of such improvements will be modest—10 percent or, at most, 20 percent increases in permissible salt levels being more likely—and question claims or implications of breakthroughs leading to commercial yields using seawater or even half-strength seawater for irrigation. They are not aware of any success to date in selecting or developing plants that are significantly more salt tolerant by means of any such techniques (van Schilfgaarde, 1983).

Although increased efforts in genetics and breeding for greater salt tolerance are needed, we must be cautioned against the false premise that management research is outdated and should be minimized. The needed conservation of soil and water resources still demands breakthroughs of equal magnitude if a permanent, viable irrigated agriculture is to be sustained.

Another approach for overcoming salinity restraints is to introduce new crops that grow well under saline conditions. Halophytic species, by definition, are tolerant of high salinity. Unfortunately, though they thrive in adverse environments, they tend to grow much more slowly than conventional crops. It is likely that those genetic mechanisms that protect the halophytes against stress are, at the same time, the ones that restrict growth rate. As in the case of breeding, the development of new crops (including halophyte culture) is an area that deserves more attention, but it also is an area prone to false hopes, sometimes kindled by reports from prestigious institutions. The fact that a plant is native to, and survives in, saline environments does not mean it can be cultivated successfully as a crop, since biomass production tends to be proportional to transpiration (van Schilfgaarde, 1983).

Our ability to improve salinity control in crop production could increase if we better know how to relate crop tolerances to field conditions. Though an extensive literature exists on salt tolerance of crops (Francois and Maas, 1978), there exists rather limited knowledge of how management and climate, as well as their interactions, affect salt tolerance and crop growth. Our knowledge of crop water use as affected by salinity and stage of plant growth is insufficient, though recent gains have been made in this regard (Letey et al., 1985). The salt tolerance of various crops under a variety of farm water management practices should be thoroughly investigated. The studies should include short-term effects of high salinity at various stages of growth. The long-term effects of recommended irrigation and agronomic practices for salinity control also need to be more thoroughly evaluated. Rather than using only crop yield as a measure of success of salinity control management, evaluations should also include effectiveness in the protection of the quantity and quality of our water resources.

Since crop salt tolerance and soil salt balance are intrinsically related, better techniques for determining optimum leaching requirements are needed, especially for dynamic situations. A serious limitation in this regard is the lack of quantitative knowledge of how plants respond to varying salinity and matric stresses, according to time and space, within the root zone. Another deficiency in this regard is the lack of adequate knowledge, on a field basis, of solute transport phenomena, which influence variability of salinity and which affect minimum leaching requirements. Most of our present knowledge regarding leaching requirements and the movement of water and salts has been developed in laboratory-soil columns and lysimeters. The results obtained usually cannot be applied under natural field conditions.

Development of Models for Predicting Irrigation Effects on Water Quality

Quantitative prediction techniques that will describe the quantity and quality of subsurface return flow from irrigation are needed. These models must be capable of predicting long-term changes in the quantity and quality of subsurface return flows under a variety of water management alternatives. To fully evaluate chemical quality changes, the models should be capable of handling salt precipitation, minimal weathering, and cation exchange reactions, which take place as water moves through the soil profile. Critical limitations of such models will be in defining the pathway(s) of subsurface return flows and the chemical and physical properties of the substrata in the pathway(s) within large hydrogeologic systems, i.e., irrigated valleys or large basins. In studying such large areas, a balance must be reached between the sophistication of the model and the cost of collecting the required physical data. Because of the current lack of such models, the problems resulting from the development of new irrigation projects, particularly those involving lands not previously irrigated, are usually confronted after the fact.

Development of Models for Assessing Economic Impacts of Salinity Control Measures

There is a need to delineate the wide variety of benefits and damages that occur as a result of salination of soils and waters. In assessing costs and benefits associated with salinity control and effects, the development of crop production and crop damage functions caused by salinity are requisites for making more accurate economic evaluations and for the decision-making process. However, such economic studies should also consider effects on our water resources, including the local, state, regional, and national benefits that would accrue from the implementation, either in an irrigated valley or river basin, of a salinity control program. For example, a control measure implemented in a particular valley has direct benefits to the local area, including nonagricultural sectors and downstream water users. Benefits that accrue to both upstream and downstream users result from increased crop yields, reduced need for fertilizer, reduced drainage, savings in water costs, etc.

Improved methods are needed for making area-wide investigations to define the need and potential benefit of salinity control measures. These studies should pinpoint the sources and causes of salinity and provide background information to select the most appropriate control measures. Once the sources of salts are defined, more detailed studies should be undertaken to specify how those sources may best be controlled. Demonstration projects and extensive educational programs should be carried out to demonstrate and accomplish implementation of selected programs.

Development of Soil Salinity Inventory

Proper operation of a permanent irrigated agriculture, which uses water efficiently, requires periodic information on soil salinity. Only with this information can the effectiveness of irrigation project operations be assessed with respect to salt balance and water use efficiency. Suitable inventories of soil salinity do not now exist in the United States, nor are there monitoring programs to document the salinity status of our soils and to assess the adequacy of our irrigation and drainage systems on a project-wide basis. National or state programs to monitor soil salinity are likewise nonexistent. Currently used methods based on "salt balance" calculations are inadequate (Kaddah and Rhoades, 1976). The need for monitoring will increase, since less water will be available for leaching as the competition increases for water now used in irrigation. In addition, more restrictions are expected to be placed on the discharge of salt from irrigation projects. With less leaching, there will be a corresponding increase in soil salinity. The inventorying and monitoring of soil salinity is complicated by salinity's spatial variability. Monitoring is influenced by salinity's dynamic nature because of the impact of changing weather patterns, management practices, water table depth, etc. When the need for repeated measurements is multiplied by the extensive requirements of a single sampling period, the need for simple, practical methods for measuring field salinity is obvious. Procedures for delineating representative monitoring areas within irrigation projects are also needed, as are procedures for rapidly producing soil salinity maps. New instruments for measuring soil electrical conductivity, coupled with computer mapping techniques, have the potential for meeting salinity monitoring and mapping needs. These methods need to be integrated with computer-aided mapping techniques to develop a geographic information system for salinity. A network of representative soil salinity monitoring stations should be established in irrigation projects, especially those projects undergoing changes in operation. It would be appropriate for a governmental agency to assume this responsibility. The fact that no agency is now monitoring salinity on irrigated land is a major concern from the standpoint of land and water degradation. For more discussion of salinity inventorying and monitoring, see Rhoades and Corwin (1984) and Corwin et al. (1985).

Expansion of Adaptive Research and Implementation of Existing Technology

Much more is known about salinity and its control than is currently being used. Known principles should be adapted to existing field circumstances. Much progress can be made simply by the transfer of existing technology and by innovative adaptive research. The present approach to salinity research, where studies are carried out in artificial, small, controlled, and relatively simple systems, which exclude much of the reality of irrigated agriculture and the larger hydrological system, leaves much to be desired.

We must keep a proper balance between basic and applied research and not expect accomplishments in basic biotechnologic, genetic engineering research to supplant the need for research and improvements in management and engineering. Nor should we forget the real goal for our research—to feed people while conserving our dwindling soil and water resources and to avoid increasing the literature with more reports of studies that are irrelevant or of academic interest only.

REFERENCES

Bernstein, L. 1974. Crop growth and salinity. *In* Jan van Schilfgaarde (ed.) Drainage for agriculture. *Agronomy* 17:39–54.

Bingham, F. T., J. D. Rhoades, and R. Keren. 1985. Effects of salinity and varying boron concentrations on boron uptake and yield of wheat. *Soil Sci. Soc. Am. J.* (submitted)

Bingham, F. T., J. D. Rhoades, and R. Keren. 1985. An application of the Maas-Hoffman salinity response model for boron toxicity. *Soil Sci. Soc. Am. J.* 49:672–74.

Bishop, A. A., W. R. Walker, N. L. Allen, and G. J. Poole. 1981. Furrow advance rates under surge flow systems. *J. Irrig. and Drainage Division, ASCE,* 107 (IR3): 257–64.

Corwin, D. L., J. W. Werle, and J. D. Rhoades. 1984. The use of computer aided mapping techniques to delineate potential areas of salinity development in soils: a conceptual introduction. *Geoderma* (submitted)

Dedrick, A. R., J. A. Replogle, and L. J. Erie. 1978. On-farm level-basin irrigation—save water and energy. *Civil Engineering* 48:60–65.

Emerson, W. W. 1984. Soil structure in saline and sodic soils. Chap. 3.2, pp. 65–76. New York: Springer Verlag.

Francois, L. E., and E. V. Maas. 1978. Plant response to salinity: An indexed bibliography. USDA, ARM-W-6.

Ingvalson, R. D., J. D. Rhoades, and A. L. Page. 1976. Correlation of alfalfa yield with various indices of salinity. *Soil Sci.* 122:145–53.

Jurinak, J. J. 1984. Thermodynamic aspects of the soil solution. Chap. 2.1, pp. 15–31. New York: Springer Verlag.

Jury, W. A. 1984. Field scale water and solute transport through unsaturated soils. Chap. 4.2, pp. 115–25. New York: Springer-Verlag.

Kaddah, M. T., and J. D. Rhoades. 1976. Salt and water balance in Imperial Valley, California. *Soil Sci. Soc. Am. J.* 40:93–100.

Keren, R., and I. Shainberg. 1984. Colloid properties of clay minerals in saline and sodic solution. Chap. 2.2, pp. 32–45. *In* I. Shainberg and J. Shalhevet (eds.) Soil salinity under irrigation. New York: Springer Verlag.

Keren, R., F. T. Bingham, and J. D. Rhoades. 1985. Plant uptake of boron as affected by boron distribution between the liquid and the solid phases in soil. *Soil Sci. Soc. Am. J.* 49: 297–302.

———. 1985. Effect of clay content in soil on boron uptake and yield of wheat. *Soil Sci. Soc. Am. J.* 49:1466–70.

Law, J. P., J. D. Denit, and G. V. Skogerboe. 1972. The need for implementing irrigation return flow quality control.

Pp. 1–17. *In* Proceedings of National Conference on Managing Irrigated Agriculture to Improve Water Quality. Washington, D.C.: Graphics Management Corp.

Letey, J., A. Dinar, and K. C. Knapp. 1985. Crop-water production function model for saline irrigation waters. *Soil Sci. Soc. Am. J.* 49:1005–1009.

Maas, E. V., and G. J. Hoffman. 1977. Crop salt tolerance—current assessment. *J. Irrig. and Drainage Division, ASCE* 103 (IR2):115–34.

Maas, E. V., and R. H. Nieman. 1978. Physiology of plant tolerance to salinity. Chap. 13. *In* G. A. Jung (ed.) Crop tolerance to suboptimal land conditions. ASA Spec. Publ. 32:277–99.

Maas, E. V. 1984a. Salt tolerance of plants. *In* B. R. Christie (ed.) Handbook of plant science in agriculture. CRC Press Inc. (in press).

———. 1984b. Crop tolerance. *California Agriculture* 38:20–21.

———. 1984c. Crop tolerance to saline sprinkling waters. (submitted)

Oster, J. D., and J. D. Rhoades. 1975. Calculated drainage water compositions and salt burdens resulting from irrigation with river waters in the western United States. *J. Environ. Qual.* 4:73–79.

———. 1977. Various indices for evaluating the effective salinity and sodicity of irrigation waters. Pp. 1–14. *In* Proceedings Intl. Salinity Conf., Texas Tech University, Lubbock, August, 1976.

Rawlins, S. L. 1977. Uniform irrigation with a low-head bubbler system. *Agric. Water Mgmt.* 1:167–78.

Rhoades, J. D. 1972. Quality of water for irrigation. *Soil Sci.* 113:277–284.

———. 1974. Drainage for salinity control. *In* Jan van Schilfgaarde (ed.) Drainage for agriculture. *Agronomy* 17:433–61.

Rhoades, J. D., R. D. Ingvalson, J. M. Tucker, and M. Clark. 1973. Salts in irrigation drainage waters. I. Effects of irrigation water composition, leaching fraction, and time of year on the salt compositions of irrigation and drainage waters. *Soil Sci. Soc. Am. Proceedings* 37:770–74.

Rhoades, J. D., J. D. Oster, R. D. Ingvalson, J. M. Tucker, and M. Clark. 1974. Minimizing the salt burdens of irrigation drainage waters. *J. Environ. Qual.* 3:311–16.

Rhoades, J. D., and D. L. Suarez. 1977. Reducing water quality degradation through minimized leaching management. *Agric. Water Mgmt.* 1:127–42. Santa Barbara, Calif. Calif. Water Resources Ctr. Rept. No. 38:93–110.

Rhoades, J. D., and S. D. Merrill. 1976. Assessing the suitability of water for irrigation: Theoretical and empirical approaches. *FAO Soils Bulletin* 31:69–109.

Rhoades, J. D. 1977. Potential for using saline agricultural drainage waters for irrigation. Pp. 85–116. *In* Proceedings Water Mgmt. for Irrigation and Drainage, ASCE/Reno, Nevada, July, 1977.

Rhoades, J. D., D. L. Corwin, and G. J. Hoffman. 1981. Scheduling and controlling irrigations from measurements of soil electrical conductivity. Pp. 106–15. *In* Proceedings, ASAE, Irrigation Scheduling Conference, Chicago, Dec. 14, 1981.

Rhoades, J. D. 1982. Reclamation and management of salt-affected soils after drainage. Pp. 123–97. *In* Proceedings of the First Annual Western Provincial Conf. Rationalization of water and soil res. and management. Lethbridge, Alberta, Canada, Nov. 29–Dec. 2, 1982.

———. 1984a. Reusing saline drainage waters for irrigation: a strategy to reduce salt loading of rivers. Chap. 43, pp. 455–64. *In* Richard H. French (ed.) Salinity in watercourses and reservoirs.

———. 1984b. Using saline waters for irrigation. *In* Proceedings

Int'l Workshop on Salt Affected Soils of Latin America, Maracay, Venezuela, Oct. 23–30, 1983.

———. 1984c. New strategy for using saline waters for irrigation. *In* Proceedings ASCE Irrigation and Drainage Spec. Conf., Water today and tomorrow, July 24–26, 1984, Flagstaff, Arizona (in press).

———. 1984d. Principles and methods of monitoring soil salinity. Chap. 5:1, pp. 130–42. *In* Soil salinity and irrigation—processes and management. Berlin: Springer Verlag.

Rhoades, J. D., and D. L. Corwin. 1984. Inventorying soil salinity: use of instrumental and mapping methods. *J. Soil and Water Conserv.* 39:172–75.

Shainberg, I. 1984. The effect of electrolyte concentration on the hydraulic properties of sodic soils. Chap. 3.1, pp. 49–64. New York: Springer Verlag.

Shainberg, I., and J. Letey. 1983. Response of soils to sodic and saline conditions. *Hilgardia* vol. 52, No. 2.

Shannon, M. C. 1984. Breeding, selection and the genetics of salt tolerance. Pp. 231–54. *In* R. Staples and G. H. Toenniessen (eds.) Salinity tolerance in plant strategies for crop improvement. New York: Wiley International.

Suarez, D. L. 1981. Relationship between pH_c and SAR and an alternative method of estimating SAR of soil or drainage water. *Soil Sci. Soc. Am. J.* 45:469–75.

———. 1982. Graphical calculation of ion concentrations in $CaCO_3$ and/or gypsum soil solutions. *J. Environ. Qual.* 11:302–308.

United States Salinity Laboratory Staff. 1954. Diagnosis and improvement of saline and alkali soils. U.S. Department of Agriculture Handbook 60.

van Schilfgaarde, J., L. Bernstein, J. D. Rhoades, and S. L. Rawlins. 1974. Irrigation management for salt control. *J. Irrig. and Drainage Division, ASCE,* 100 (IR3): 321–38. Closure: 102 (IR4): 467–69.

van Schilfgaarde, J. (ed.) 1974. Drainage for agriculture, Agronomy 17, American Society of Agronomy, Madison, Wis.

van Schilfgaarde, J. 1976. Water management and salinity. *FAO Soils Bulletin* 31:53–67.

———. 1979. Water conservation potential in irrigated agriculture. *In* Proceedings Soil Conservation Society of America's 34th Annual Mtg., Ottawa, Canada, July–Aug., 1979.

van Schilfgaarde, J., and S. L. Rawlins. 1980. Water resources management in a growing society. *In* T. R. Sinclair (ed.) Efficient water use in crop production. Am. Soc. Agron. 12: 517–30.

van Schilfgaarde, J. 1983. Abstract. Managing limited water supplies. AAAS Symp., Whatever happened to desertification? Detroit, Mich., May 25–31, 1983.

———. 1984. Drainage design for salinity control. Chap. 6.2, pp. 190–97. New York: Springer Verlag.

Wagenet, R. J. 1984. Salt and water movement in the soil profile. Chap. 4.1, pp. 100–14. New York: Springer Verlag.

Worstell, R. V. 1979. Selecting a buried gravity irrigation system. Transactions of the American Society of Agricultural Engineering 22 (1): 110–14.

25. MANAGEMENT SOLUTIONS FOR SALINITY CONTROL IN AN IRRIGATION DISTRICT

Lowell O. Weeks and Thomas E. Levy, Coachella Valley Water District, Coachella, California

ABSTRACT

Coachella Valley, California, began irrigated agriculture in the 1870s using groundwater. Increased demand resulted in the lowering of water tables and the need for an additional source of water. Water was imported from the Colorado River through the All-American and Coachella canals, and an underground distribution system was constructed to deliver water to the farms. Before importation of water began, it was recognized that drainage of the irrigated land would be required, and an extensive investigation of salinity control by drainage was undertaken. Implementation of procedures based on the findings has resulted in the construction of an on-farm and district-wide drainage system. In conjunction with the research, adequate irrigation water, a depository for drainage water, and enlightened farmers have produced high crop yields and no effects of salinity on agricultural productivity in the valley.

INTRODUCTION

The production of food by the use of enterprise is the most important industry in the world. Agriculture is one of the oldest endeavors of man and probably began about 6,000 years ago (Garbrecht, 1981).

For hundreds of years people lived by fishing, hunting, and gathering wild plants and seeds. They had to look for food continually, which left little time for any other activities. Early civilizations began to develop an agricultural society where fewer people were required to produce the needed food. This left time for the non-farmers to develop arts, crafts, and to engage in trading, which all led to the establishment of towns, cities, and countries.

Food development occurred in the great river valleys where soil and water were abundant. Thus, the farmers soon learned the primitive art of irrigation.

Irrigation probably started in the Nile River valley more than 4,000 years ago. Nile valley farmers soon learned they could grow two and three crops a year in the warm, rich soils (Said, 1981). Thus began the first major world power. However, irrigation brought problems that continue throughout the world even today. Problems of poor land and water management have resulted in farms becoming waterlogged, with increased salinity that has curtailed crop production. Correcting these conditions requires good drainage of all irrigated crop lands. Drainage is essential for removal of excess water and salts. Whenever irrigation facilities are constructed to water land, a drainage system must be installed. In Coachella Valley, California, this resulted in a management solution for salinity control by the Coachella Valley Water District (CVWD).

COACHELLA VALLEY

Coachella Valley, in southeastern California, is situated in eastern Riverside County, within a basin that was called the Salton Sink around the turn of the century. This valley is some 80 km long and from 8 to 16 km wide. As shown in Fig. 1, it lies between the coastal range on the west and the Little San Bernardino Mountains on the east. The Salton Sea forms the valley's southeastern boundary.

The climate of Coachella Valley consists of long, extremely hot summers (with occasional high temperatures throughout the year), mild winters, and a low relative humidity. The skies are almost cloudless, with an annual average rainfall of 66 mm since 1877. Killing frosts are rare, but when one does occur it is generally in December, January, or February. Every month has had a temperature of at least 32°C (National Oceanic and Atmospheric Administration). Thus evaporation is very high during every month of the year and the need for irrigation is year round.

The average rainfall is so slight in Coachella Valley that it is disregarded, and all water for crops is from irrigation. There are two sources of water for irrigation: deep wells fed by rainfall and melting snows on the mountains surrounding the valley, and since 1949, water diverted from the Colorado River at Imperial Dam upstream from Yuma, Arizona, through a 258-km canal system that distributes it to the farms.

The dominant soils are of recent valley alluvium eroded from granitic mountains to the east, west, and northwest, and grade in texture from coarse and fine sands to clays. The clays occur predominantly in the lower trough of the valley and are of alluvium of the Colorado River deposited while the Grand Canyon was developing. The soil gradation is not uniform. Because of the extremely variable capacity of floodwaters to carry suspended material and because of progressive movement of part of the deposited materials from flood to flood, there is a mixture of materials. Deposits of sands, silts, and clays are found throughout the valley. In addition, seasonal high winds have redistributed some sediments. Therefore, the soils are highly stratified with layers of less than 25 mm to more than 0.3 m thick (USDA, 1980).

The coming of the railroad in 1877 was an important factor in opening the desert to settlement. The discovery of a water-bearing sand and gravel stratum in 1888 was the beginning of irrigation. During the first years of farming, nearly all the wells had an artesian pressure that produced sufficient flow for domestic and urban needs, as well as

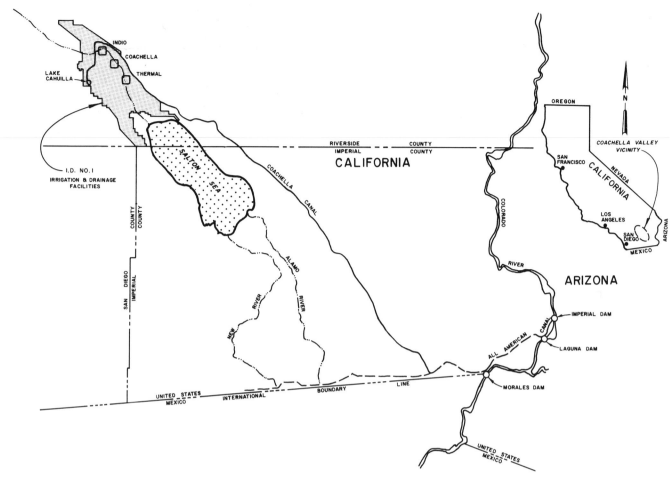

Fig. 1. Location map.

small irrigation requirements. As the increased acreage required more water, many of the wells ceased to flow or the flow was so greatly decreased that water users began to employ pumps. Thus it became evident at an early date that additional water must be found and brought to Coachella Valley if its agricultural base was to continue to expand.

COACHELLA VALLEY WATER DISTRICT

The Coachella Valley Water District was formed in 1918, under the County Water District Act of the state of California, for the purpose of protecting and furthering the water rights of the people in the area, to invoke and maintain water conservation principles and practices, and to seek additional sources of water for the region. These continue to be the responsibility of the CVWD.

All of the lands within the district are desert lands, and the district now contains approximately 2600 km². Most of the agricultural land is below sea level.

Since its establishment, the district has continuously functioned as a public agency of the state of California. All its authorized functions and duties are governmental in nature. In 1937, by special act of the legislature, the Coachella Valley Storm Water District was merged into the Coachella

Valley Water District. Present activities are all water related and include: (1) water conservation and underground recharge and replenishment; (2) irrigation water delivery; (3) installing and maintaining an agricultural drainage system; (4) installing and maintaining domestic water production, storage, and delivery facilities; (5) providing wastewater collection and sewage reclamation facilities; (6) construction and operation of stormwater protection works; and (7) providing recreation facilities.

WATER SUPPLY CONTRACTS

Since 1918 the district has entered into eight separate and distinct contracts with the U.S. government, all dealing with water supply from the Colorado River. In the early contracts of 1920, 1921, and 1929, the district made contributions to the federal government for its early surveys, investigations, and reports relating to the construction of Hoover Dam and the building of the All-American Canal to deliver water into Coachella and Imperial Valleys.

The district has also entered into five separate repayment contracts with the federal government, incurring repayable obligations that totaled $80 million. These contracts are: (1) 1934, for delivery of water and capacity in the Imperial

Dam, and All-American and Coachella canals; (2) 1947, for construction of an underground pipeline distribution system for 300 km^2; (3) 1958, for construction of an irrigation system and drainage works for 42 km^2 of Indian lands; (4) 1963, for rehabilitation and betterment of works that were constructed under the 1934 and 1947 contracts; and (5) 1978, for lining the first 80 km of the Coachella Canal for saving 150,000 dkm^3 of water per year. Repayment of all contracts was over a forty-year payout period and is current.

On March 29, 1963, the district entered into a contract with the state of California for a water supply from the California Water Project. The cost of this water supply makes it uneconomical for agricultural use, but it will be used exclusively for domestic and municipal purposes.

IRRIGATION

The combination of a climate characterized by hot summers, mild winters, almost negligible rainfall, and good soils has given Coachella Valley a distinct advantage in the growing of many specialty crops. This area has a 365-day growing season. Field crops include carrots, sweet corn, many kinds of leaf lettuce, and asparagus, and its citrus fruits and table grapes are among the finest produced anywhere. This area has the largest acreage on the North American continent where dates are grown.

The methods of irrigation in Coachella Valley are similar to those used in other irrigated regions. In the valley, much thought and effort have been given to the most efficient way of handling water. The district's distribution system consists of 800 km of underground concrete pipelines. By reducing water loss due to evaporation, underground lines maintain water quality while making valuable land useful instead of covering it with open canals and ditches. All water delivered through lateral turnouts to the farmer is measured through a meter. Detailed records of the quantity of water delivered to the farm are kept by both the farmer and the district.

MANAGING SALT IN AN IRRIGATION DISTRICT

Through many years of technical studies, observations of farm results, and ideas ranging from ridiculous to very conservative, the district is firm in its opinion that managing salt in an irrigation district requires six major items: (1) knowledge of the hydrologic and subsurface profile characteristics, (2) adequate supply of irrigation water, (3) on-farm drainage collection system, (4) district-wide drainage collection system, (5) depository for saline drainage waters, and (6) informed farmers.

Knowledge of the Hydrologic and Subsurface Profile Characteristics

Drainage of irrigated land throughout the world is required unless optimum soil, water quality, rainfall, and crop conditions occur naturally. Drainage improvement may be required because: (1) poor water and land management has resulted in waterlogging and high salinity, (2) the area is low and swampy, and (3) the soils may be saline. Under arid conditions, such as these which prevail in Coachella Valley,

salts accumulate if they have not been leached or dissolved from the soils. Coachella Valley soils are high in soluble salts such as sodium chloride, sodium sulfate, sodium bicarbonate, and calcium chloride.

Because of the properties of the soil in Coachella Valley, it was believed that farm drainage would be needed. In 1927, the district installed a number of shallow groundwater observation wells called "alkali wells." The water levels were recorded for several years, but because of the great economic depression of the 1930s and diminishing water levels in the irrigation wells as the result of an overdraft, interest in the "alkali wells" was lost, and by 1940, most of them were lost or damaged beyond repair.

As long as farming, then confined to approximately 69 km^2, was dependent on groundwater as its source of irrigation water, drainage was not an important problem. This was because of the effect of heavy pumping on artesian pressures, using water containing low total dissolved solids (TDS), and only the less saline soils were being farmed. There was evidence that with the widespread use of newly imported Colorado River water, less groundwater pumping would take place and water tables would rise, causing serious drainage problems in the future. In addition, the more saline soils would be irrigated, and the higher TDS of the imported Colorado River water would require drainage for salinity control.

In 1945, a Memorandum of Agreement was signed by the University of California Experiment Station, the U.S. Salinity Laboratory, and the district, relative to "Investigations on Salinity Removal and Control by Drainage." In 1948, the U.S. Bureau of Reclamation also joined in this agreement. The memorandum set forth three objectives: (1) to observe groundwater conditions, (2) to develop techniques for land reclamation of salt-affected soils, and (3) to obtain information for the practical design of on-farm drainage systems. In order to achieve these objectives, it was necessary to obtain a thorough understanding of the hydrologic and stratigraphic conditions of the valley. This included information regarding: (1) changes in water table levels with increased use of Colorado River water for irrigation; (2) changes in groundwater quality with time, as influenced by the use of Colorado River water, which had different chemical characteristics as compared with natural groundwater; and (3) the direction of groundwater flow. More than 1300 piezometric wells ranging from 3 to 47 m in depth were drilled. This investigation was unique since an intensive study was initiated before any significant drainage problem existed in the area, and basic data were obtained prior to the importation of water. Investigations are usually made after crops have been damaged and soils made saline because of high water tables.

An Adequate Supply of Irrigation Water

Colorado River water has been imported to Coachella Valley since 1949 through the canal and distribution system, as previously noted. Farmers order water for next-day delivery up until 5:00 P.M. the day before. With few exceptions, such as unexpected frost conditions or exceedingly hot periods, water has always been available. With the water storage fa-

Table 1. Water requirements and land area for crops grown in the Coachella Valley.

Crop	Consump-tive Use[a]	Land Area				
		1975	1977	1979	1981	1983
	Meters	Hectares				
Alfalfa	1.71	4,514	3,698	3,981	3,885	3,832
Misc. field	1.20	1,180	442	330	1,304	323
Cotton	0.95	567	2,185	1,416	1,943	699
Asparagus	1.36	215	121	231	386	743
Corn, sweet	0.67	1,934	2,458	1,986	2,362	1,866
Carrots	0.52	2,150	2,142	2,107	1,380	1,150
Vegetables, all	0.94	1,775	1,862	2,709	2,699	3,879
Dates	2.29	1,579	1,656	1,824	1,839	2,202
Grapes	1.28	2,986	2,917	3,205	3,856	3,973
Citrus	1.31	7,066	6,562	6,318	6,085	5,967
Non-harvested	1.43	1,464	1,393	1,482	816	1,170
Total hectares of crops		25,431	25,439	25,589	26,553	25,805
Less double crop		3,023	2,933	2,840	2,998	3,197
Total hectares irrigated		22,408	22,506	22,749	23,555	22,608
Water received through Coachella Canal (cubic dekameters)		523,411	47,006	457,153	530,402	430,114
Irrigation requirement in meters per year		1.47	1.41	1.43	1.43	1.49

[a] $U = KF$, Blaney-Criddle formula from United States Department of Agriculture Technical Bulletin No. 1275, "Determining Consumptive Use and Irrigation Water Requirements," page 1. Where U = consumptive use requirement; K = empirical seasonal coefficient; F = sum of the monthly factors (f) for the season (sum of the products of mean monthly temperature (t) in degrees Fahrenheit and monthly percentage of annual daytime hours (p).

cilities located behind the many dams on the Colorado River and the water priority of this district, it is anticipated that there will continue to be an adequate supply of irrigation water.

The annual consumptive use of crops grown in Coachella Valley as calculated using the Blaney-Criddle formula (USDA, 1962) and updated by the district to reflect irrigation practices in planting and growing crops in Coachella Valley is shown in Table 1. The cropping pattern of Coachella Valley for the last ten years is also shown on Table 1. The average annual water requirement is 1.44 m. The diversions from the Colorado River for the last ten years are also shown on Table 1.

On-Farm Drainage and Collection System

Successful agricultural activity in arid regions such as Coachella Valley requires a method of land drainage for the removal of excess soluble salts from the root zone. In this valley the choice was made to do this with a system of underground pipe drainage lines. This decision was based on effectiveness of drainage, better use of land, and the cost of installation.

The farm tile drainage system is laid out in a grid arrangement with a base of collector lines of 200 mm in diameter with laterals of either 100-, 127-, or 152-mm diameter pipe, depending on the length of the lateral. A typical farm system is shown on Fig. 2. The drainpipes were originally made of red clay tile or concrete, but today most of the new pipe is plastic. The drainpipe is laid in a continuous gravel filter envelope, which increases the drainage efficiency and keeps fine soil particles from entering and plugging the drainage lines. Installation involves trenching, pipe laying, and backfilling, all in a continuous operation. The cost today to drain a hectare of land is approximately $1,200. The maintenance of a proper salt level is probably the most important function for economic success in an agricultural endeavor in Coachella Valley and would be impossible without these systems, which discharge water and salts into the outlet system provided by the district

District-wide Drainage Collection System

The main outlet collector drains for all on-farm drainage systems are constructed and maintained by the district. The policy of the district is one outlet for each 0.32 km² or to within 400 m of each 0.16 km² parcel.

The outlet drains are either open drains or underground pipe drains. The open drains are used in the area between the agricultural lands and the Salton Sea and as a large valley-wide collector drain that also conveys floodwaters. In the rest of the valley, underground pipe drains from 0.3 to 0.6 m in diameter are used as the outlet system. All drainage waters discharge into the Salton Sea, which is the drainage depository for both the Imperial and Coachella valleys.

Depository for Saline Drainage Water

The U.S. Geological Survey in the mid-1920s undertook an investigation of the Salton Sea as to its importance as a depository for agricultural wastes and to predict the future ele-

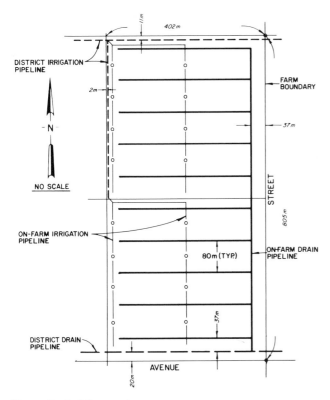

Fig. 2. Typical farm system.

vations of the surface of the sea. With the completion of this report, the federal government by executive order in 1928 withdrew from all forms of entry the public lands of the United States in the Salton Sea area lying 74 m or more below sea level. These restricted lands were set aside for the drainage of all waters into this natural drainage basin. In addition, the Imperial Irrigation District and the CVWD undertook to acquire private lands under and around the Salton Sea. Thus, a large area in the bottom of the old Salton Sink is now available for the discharge and depository of agricultural wastes from Coachella Valley.

Informed Farmers

It has been said that an informed farmer can be successful on poor land and an uninformed farmer will not be successful on good land. As to drainage and salinity, it can be restated that the best farmer cannot be successful on lands of inadequate drainage and the worst farmer will have a disaster on good land.

The original studies in Coachella Valley determined that approximately 2000 m^3 of water per hectare applied by ponding would be required for leaching the soil for reclamation (CVCWD, 1953). Additional leaching would occur in conjunction with the irrigation of crops. If soil tests in later years indicate that salt buildup was taking place in the soil, then additional leaching by ponding would be needed for short periods of time. This information is made available to the farmer by the district, the University of California Extension Service, and the Soil Conservation Service. The farmers have taken advantage of this knowledge. Today the farmers of Coachella Valley are among the most progressive in the world.

CONCLUSION

Experience of the district in a half century of involvement in drainage of agricultural lands indicates that management of salt to increase food supplies takes cooperation, knowledge of soil salinity, and the facilities of water agencies and farmers. Without an engineered drainage system, Coachella Valley could not produce an average crop value of $11,200 per irrigated hectare as it did in 1983. The drainage and salinity problems threatening agricultural productivity are practically nonexistent in the district because of (1) comprehensive drainage investigations and research, (2) an adequate supply of irrigation water, (3) a farm drainage system, (4) a district-wide collection system, (5) a depository for saline waters, and (6) informed and cooperative farmers.

REFERENCES

Coachella Valley County Water District. 1953. Ordinance No. 871. *In* Proceedings of the July 1, 1953, Board Meeting. Coachella, California.

Garbrecht, Gunther. 1981. Keynote lecture. Special session on the history of irrigation, drainage and flood control. Pp. 8–10. *In* Proceedings of the Eleventh Congress. Grenoble, France: International Commission on Irrigation and Drainage.

National Oceanic and Atmospheric Administration. Climatological Data—California Series. Asheville, North Carolina: National Climatic Data Center.

Said, Naguib F. 1981. The history of irrigation in Egypt. Special session on the history of irrigation, drainage and flood control. Pp. 13–28. *In* Proceedings of the Eleventh Congress. Grenoble, France: International Commission on Irrigation and Drainage.

U.S. Department of Agriculture. 1962. Determining Consumptive Use and Irrigation Water Requirements, Technical Bulletin No. 1275. Washington, D.C.: Government Printing Office.

U.S. Department of Agriculture. Soil Conservation Service, 1980. Soil Survey of Riverside County, California, Coachella Valley Area (1979-230-732/17). Washington, D.C.: Government Printing Office.

PART V. WATER MANAGEMENT

26. IRRIGATION AND THE LAND-POOR

Jael Silliman, Columbia University, New York, New York and Roberto Lenton, Ford Foundation, New York, New York

ABSTRACT

This chapter analyzes the available information on irrigation research and action undertaken on and for land-poor rural people in developing countries and helps identify those irrigation planning, design, and management interventions that can improve their lives. First, we present some background information on those who constitute the land-poor and give an overview of the principal types of irrigation systems found in different parts of the world. We will then review the ways in which irrigation can indirectly assist the land-poor, particularly through the generation of employment opportunities. Third, we discuss experience with direct attempts to assist land-poor people through irrigation, using land- and water-allocation approaches. Finally we analyze irrigation research, policy, and action that can be undertaken to address the needs of the land-poor.

Nature has enough to sustain all, but nothing to satisfy the need of a few.

—M. Gandhi

INTRODUCTION

It is now generally accepted that in many developing countries irrigation has great potential for improving food production and enhancing rural incomes. In much of the world the scope for the expansion of irrigation facilities is vast, and many developing countries are investing heavily in irrigation to meet their production needs.

Policymakers in most developing countries would agree that the fundamental objective of irrigation is the alleviation of rural poverty. Thus from a social and economic standpoint irrigation must necessarily be viewed in the context of the rural poor, large numbers of whom do not own land or do not own enough to make a difference. Yet from a physical point of view irrigation is inextricably linked to land and has thus generally been viewed by engineers and scientists in the context of the landed—as projects undertaken by or for those who own land to which irrigation water can be applied. Consequently, the very people who are generally implicitly or explicitly the "target group" of irrigation programs are often not taken into account in the planning, design, and management of irrigation projects. Furthermore, they are all too frequently bypassed in the setting of irrigation and water-management policy. Even irrigation research studies and pilot projects that focus on those who own little or no land—the "land-poor"—are few and far between.

The purpose of this chapter is to help reverse this trend. Approaching irrigation from the perspective of the land-poor, the chapter has as a principal objective to begin to analyze the available information on irrigation research and action undertaken on and for this target group of people and to help identify those designs and management interventions that can increase their livelihoods.[1] The chapter also attempts to develop a better understanding of the relationship between irrigation and the land-poor, so that policies and planning, design, and management criteria that take them into account may ultimately be developed and utilized.

This chapter is divided into four sections. In the first section we present some background information on those who constitute the land-poor and give an overview of the principal types of irrigation systems found in different parts of the world. In the second section we review the ways in which irrigation can indirectly assist the land-poor, particularly through the generation of employment opportunities. In the third section we discuss experience with direct attempts to assist land-poor people through irrigation, using land- and water-allocation approaches. Finally we analyze research, policy, and action that can be undertaken to address the needs of the land-poor.

Two caveats are in order. First, irrigation is but one of several alternative approaches to enhancing incomes and employment among the land-poor, and the economics of achieving these objectives through irrigation should be compared with those of other forms of investment to achieve the same objective. Second, the dual importance of both landlessness and irrigation in south and southeast Asia undoubtedly biases much of this paper, and some of the material may be less relevant to those parts of Latin America, Africa, and Asia where the landless and near landless are not a significant proportion of the rural poor, or to areas characterized by labor scarcity.

SUMMARY BACKGROUND INFORMATION

In this section we provide a summary description of the "target group" of landless and near-landless people and of the different types of irrigation systems prevalent in much of Asia and other parts of the developing world. An understanding of both is required if better irrigation policies and priorities that directly address the land-poor are to be developed and implemented. Inclusion of this material is an attempt to begin to overcome the gaps in the existing literature on irrigation. Much of this literature does not focus on the characteristics of the land-poor, and that which does tends not to pay attention to the characteristics of the irrigation system.

1. Following Chambers (1984a), in this chapter we use the term "livelihood" to denote a level of wealth and of stocks, flows of food and cash which provide for physical and social well-being, and security against impoverishment.

The Land-Poor

In most developing countries the rural poor are generally small and marginal farmers, small cultivator tenants or part tenants who cannot derive livelihoods from their land, or households of agricultural laborers with little or no land who rely on casual agricultural labor for their livelihoods. A working definition of the land-poor thus includes (1) those who own no land, (2) those who operate no land, and (3) those whose major source of income is wages derived from agricultural employment (Singh, 1981, 1982). Many small and marginal farmers are included in this extended definition. Since their holdings[2] are too meager to produce enough food and income to sustain them, they periodically join the agricultural labor force to supplement their agricultural earnings. Their livelihoods from their land are so precarious that unforeseeable circumstances, or even slight perturbations, easily push them off the land to join the completely landless.[3]

In this chapter we distinguish between the term "landless," which is applied only in the strict sense to those who own absolutely no agricultural land, and the term "landpoor," which is used to refer to the landless in the extended sense described above. Differentiation between the two is required because the term "landless" has often been used loosely in the literature, resulting in conceptual confusion and (in some cases) large variations in statistical data.

The numbers of land-poor have reached alarming proportions in several countries; in Bangladesh, for example, 50 percent of all rural households are land-poor, while in India they account for 40 percent of the rural labor force (Singh, 1981, 1982). In Indonesia and the Philippines the proportion of land-poor rural households has been steadily increasing because of pressure on land and "proletarianization" caused by eviction and technological displacement (Gooneratne, 1982). In much of Asia fragmentation of landholdings because of increasing population pressures has led to landlessness. The subdivision of holdings into small shares which are no longer viable result in land transactions by which the land sellers join the ranks of the landless. In much of Africa people who own land are effectively landless because the land they own is of such poor quality that it does not generate enough food or income for subsistence.

Women make up a significant (and growing) proportion of the land-poor. The rates of unemployment for women in Asia are two to three times higher than those of men (Singh, 1981, 1982). This is a particular burden for agricultural laborer families, who rely heavily on the women's wages for survival, and spells disaster for those households headed by women.

It is important to recognize that landlessness or "land-

poorness" is not necessarily associated with poverty. Lack of land becomes a serious problem only when no alternative employment opportunities exist and when people are forced to perform relatively unproductive and poorly remunerated labor to survive. For instance, landlessness occurs in agriculturally dynamic regions as rural people move away from agricultural occupations toward a growing nonfarm sector (Singh, 1981, 1982).

The land-poor are usually also asset-poor. Among their major assets are livestock and the household plots they own. Because of the seasonal nature of the agricultural demand for labor, the land-poor must rely on several sources of income besides wages for agricultural labor. By engaging in several income-generating activities, they are able to maximize income from available resources and skills and minimize risk.

In Asia, where the problem of landlessness is most severe, the land-poor are employed mainly as casual laborers; in agriculturally stagnating areas and in areas where agricultural growth is not keeping pace with population growth, they face declining real wages and are increasingly indebted (Singh, 1981, 1982; Briscoe, 1984). In many areas living standards have deteriorated because of the depletion and commercialization of forests and other natural resources to which the land-poor traditionally had access. The breakdown of traditional institutions, which gave some security in times of stress, has in some instances worsened their situation (Wood, 1984; Gooneratne, 1982).

The nature of the relationship between landowners and the land-poor can have an important bearing on rural employment. In areas where the rural community is relatively socially homogeneous and where good relationships exist between cultivators and agricultural laborers, as in much of southeast Asia, there is a tendency to hire laborers to meet increased labor demands (Hayami, 1981). The picture is often different in those areas where the relationship between the two groups is conflict-ridden, as in several Indian states (Hayami, 1981). There, cultivators and agricultural laborers typically belong to different castes, and the relationship between the two groups is often impersonal, marketlike, and subject to caste prejudice. Under these circumstances, and especially where costs of labor transactions are high, increased labor demands are more likely to induce mechanization, thereby reducing employment opportunities. Thus, similar interventions in regions with different agrarian structures may have opposite outcomes.

The introduction of intensive agricultural practices has in some instances altered traditional institutions governing labor-hiring systems, often adversely affecting the employment and wages of the land-poor. For instance, commutation of customary payments in kind to cash has made agricultural laborers more vulnerable, especially in periods of inflation and drought, for they are forced to purchase a greater portion of their food requirements from farmers, weakening their bargaining position in the market (Clay, 1978). Similarly, increased yields have sometimes led to a decline in the customary harvest share paid to agricultural laborers (Critchfield, 1982; Gooneratne, 1982). Overall, agricultural intensification has widened the gap between

---

2. Depending on a number of factors, the most important of which are soil and water, the size of a viable holding differs from region to region. For example, in much of south Asia a holding of less than 0.81 ha is considered inadequate.

3. Wood (1984) has described the landless as "a group with no control over the means of production and distribution, landless or marginal farmers with no assets, fishermen with no implements, rural artisans who lack working capital or raw materials, families who sell their manual labour."

middle to upper peasants and land-poor laborers, principally because the increase in the return to land has been greater than the increase in the return to labor (Hayami, 1981).

Irrigation Systems

To better understand the opportunities for interventions that benefit the land-poor, it is important to distinguish between different kinds of irrigation projects. Although it is beyond the scope of this chapter to present a full analysis of alternative designs for irrigation systems, we briefly discuss the principal characteristics of different projects in terms of who owns and administers them (public, communal, or private systems), their scale (large or small), and their source of water supply (groundwater or surface water).

Publicly administered projects include large and small irrigation systems. An important subset comprises large-scale projects in which water flows by gravity from a reservoir or river diversion through a network of distributory canals that may extend over vast areas. Large-scale publicly administered systems are a dominant form of irrigation in many parts of the world, including India, Pakistan, Sudan, and Egypt. Partly because of their size and complexity their management is often poor. Typically they have low levels of performance, which lead to low crop productivity and inequitable water distribution, particularly to tailenders (see, for example, CGIAR, 1982). Many governments are now paying increasing attention to improving large-scale irrigation management on the assumption that this can lead to substantially higher levels of productivity and returns on investment. Higher productivity, in turn, can generate significant increases in employment for the land-poor.

Privately owned and operated systems are mostly groundwater lift projects, usually consisting of an open well or tubewell from which water is pumped by means of electric, diesel, animal, or human power, and are widespread in areas of northern India, Bangladesh, and Pakistan (IDS, 1980). Where both energy and groundwater recharge are plentiful, private groundwater irrigation can yield two to three high-productivity crops a year—primarily because owners of private wells can control the amount of water supplied to crops and because aquifers permit the storage of monsoon water for use in the dry season. Private groundwater systems have several inherent problems, however, including (1) inadequate supplies of electricity or diesel fuel; (2) the danger of groundwater mining (i.e., when extraction exceeds replenishment); (3) the widespread use, by affluent farmers in some areas, of deep wells and powerful pumps which lower the groundwater table, making ineffective the shallower wells on which smaller farmers often depend; and (4) the lack of technology for lifting water for very small farms. It should be noted that governments can and do exert considerable influence over private irrigation development, both through policies controlling groundwater extraction and through systems of incentives and subsidies which can induce or constrain groundwater development by different categories of rural people.

Communal irrigation systems are those owned, operated, and maintained by farmers and their local associations. They account for a significant proportion of total irrigated areas in parts of southeast Asia, including the Philippines and Indonesia. Many communal systems, which usually consist of small diversion structures coupled with earthen distribution channels, have existed for considerable periods of time. Extensive governmental programs are under way in parts of southeast Asia to extend and enhance communal irrigation schemes to improve water supply and distribution. Because these programs have often been conducted without close collaboration with farmers, they have met with mixed results.

In sum, as this brief description shows, the term "irrigation" covers a range of projects with widely varying levels of performance.[4] Project performance, in turn, has substantial bearing on employment potential and other factors which have an impact on the land-poor. In the next two sections we review both the indirect ways, including employment, through which irrigation projects affect the land-poor and the direct ways in which irrigation projects can be designed, constructed, and operated so that they have a positive impact on land-poor people.

INDIRECT APPROACHES

Irrigation affects the land-poor in a number of indirect ways, shaping the lives of more people than those within its command. Undoubtedly the key indirect way in which land-poor men and women gain from irrigation is through employment—increases in the number of days employed in agriculture, increases in the wage rates for agricultural labor, and leveling off in the seasonality of agricultural employment. As illustrated in Table 1, the land-poor also gain through nonagricultural uses of irrigation water, which benefit both landed and landless people with access to the water (this includes uses of water that improve health conditions); through secondary growth in nonfarm employment; through lower food prices; and through return migration.

Although the emphasis in this section is on land-poor gains, it is necessary to recognize that some groups, landless as well as landed, lose as a result of irrigation. These include (see Table 1) those whose health is adversely affected by irrigation-induced increases in the prevalence and morbidity of waterborne diseases, particularly laborers such as water tenders who work to control water flow and are thus directly exposed to disease, landless tenants and marginal farmers affected by market competition with newly irrigated farmers, female agricultural wage workers faced with increased unpaid workloads, and agricultural workers and farmers whose livelihoods are affected by reductions in farm productivity as a result of irrigation-induced salinity and waterlogging (see Lenton, 1984, for further examples).

Since employment is undoubtedly the key indirect way in which the land-poor may gain from irrigation, in this section we explore this subject further, reviewing the available information on the relationships among irrigation, employment, and the land-poor. At the end of this section we also

---

4. For example, areas irrigated by groundwater projects with good storage capacity and good water control can yield two to three crops a year with high productivity, whereas areas irrigated by poorly managed projects are often only marginally better off than rainfed areas.

Table 1. Indirect gains and losses to the land-poor.

Type of Gain	Who Gains	Under What Conditions
1. Increase in employment in construction of irrigation projects	Male and female agricultural laborers	Labor-intensive construction methods
2. Increase in number of days of employment, and leveling off of peaks in agricultural employment	Male and female agricultural laborers	Irrigation-induced agricultural intensification
3. Increase in wage rates for agricultural labor	Male and female agricultural laborers	Irrigation-induced agricultural intensification; no surplus labor to keep wages from rising
4. Growth in nonfarm employment	Male and female agricultural laborers	Irrigation-induced agricultural intensification
5. Return migration	Male and female agricultural laborers	Irrigation-induced agricultural intensification
6. Lower food prices	All sections of rural society but particularly the poor (who spend a disproportionate percentage of their income on food)	Payment in cash rather than kind
7. Nonagricultural uses of water, including uses that improve health	Those living close to major canals and distributaries	Year-round irrigation, with access by villagers to canals or groundwater

Type of Loss	Who Loses	Under What Conditions
1. Increase in land prices	Marginal farmers pushed off land. Landless tenants	Actual or anticipated irrigation-induced agricultural intensification
2. Market competition between irrigated and rain-fed farmers	Marginal rain-fed farmers	Irrigation-induced agricultural intensification
3. Displacement because of irrigation construction	Those located in areas marked for reservoir sites etc.	Inadequate compensation structures
4. Increased unpaid workloads for women	Women	
5. Increase in waterborne diseases	Particularly agricultural workers	Presence of endemic waterborne diseases; lack of preventive health measures
6. Labor displacement	Agricultural workers displaced by mechanical threshing, herbicides, etc.	Effect of irrigation-induced mechanization greater than that of increased productivity
7. Waterlogging and salinity	Small farmers, sharecroppers displaced by induced waterlogging and salinity	Irrigation-induced waterlogging and salinity

Note: Certain groups of people may be doubly or triply disadvantaged.

briefly analyze the information available on nonagricultural uses of water.

Employment

In analyzing the relationship between irrigation and employment it is important to distinguish between employment opportunities generated by the construction of new irrigation projects and those generated by irrigation-induced intensification of agricultural operations. We will analyze the latter first.

A substantial body of empirical evidence has emerged on the relationship between irrigation- and employment-induced agricultural intensification. For example, a search undertaken by the authors revealed a total of 45 microstudies based on primary data on the subject. (Most of these were from Asia. A disproportionate share—25—was from India, the remainder being from Bangladesh, Indonesia, the Philippines, Pakistan, Thailand, and Nepal.) These studies will not be described in depth here, since many of the most significant studies and their findings have been summarized by Laureto (1982) in a review of the literature on the eco-

nomic impact of irrigation. Nevertheless, it is important to note that, with few exceptions, the studies confirm the positive relationship between irrigation and employment, while indicating that much of the potential of irrigation to increase yields and cropping intensities has not been realized. Most studies conclude that it is cropping intensity, which is largely a function of good irrigation- and water-control facilities, that can have the greatest employment impact. Similarly, most studies conclude that the employment gains made possible by the introduction of new varieties of crops have been disappointing, though the evidence consistently shows that high-yield varieties (HYVs) can increase labor absorption and productivity.

To better understand the relationship between irrigation and employment generated by irrigation-induced agricultural intensification, the impact of irrigation on employment should be singled out from the cluster of other associated variables that lead to high agricultural growth but may have different effects on employment. It is also necessary to understand what other conditions, along with irrigation, are necessary to produce a positive relationship between irriga-

Table 2. Labor-intensive and labor-displacing practices and technologies associated with irrigation.

Labor-intensive	Comment	Selected References
Cropping intensity; multiple cropping	Great potential to further increase demands for labor; mostly a function of good irrigation and water-control facilities. Most employment gains from increased cropping intensity.	Narain and Roy (1980); Anderou et al. (1982); Aiyaswamy and Natarajan (1980).
Choice of labor-intensive crops (e.g., rice), horticulture	Choice of crop affects particular sections of the rural labor force. Women traditionally hired for crops like tea, cotton, and silk.	Ghate (1984); Ahmed (1981); Ghodake and Ryan (1981).
Adoption of modern varieties	Modern varieties positively associated with labor because of increased weeding, fertilizer, and water-control and maintenance activities. Hired labor positively associated with percentage of area under HYVs.	Lee, in AREP (1980); Mehra (1976); Raju (1976); IRRI (1980).
Small farm size	Small farms use more labor-intensive methods than do large farms.	Ahmed (1981); Parikh (1980)
Choice of lift-irrigation technology	Intensity of labor use positively associated with the use of hand tubewells, powered tubewells, and indigenous methods.	Ahmed (1981); Clay (1975); Ishikawa, in AREP (1980).
Use of draft animals	Quite often, because of incentive structures favoring tractors, draft animals have not been used.	Bala and Hussain (1978).

Labor-displacing	Comment	Selected References
Mechanization	Mechanization of operations (e.g., tilling, threshing, and weeding) has reduced employment of laborers.	Ghate (1984); Singh (1982); Agarwal (1983); Clay (1975); Gopinath (1977).
Large farms	Farm size has an inverse relationship to both labor use and productivity. On an individual basis farms hire more agricultural labor. However, the spread of HYVs and mechanization assumes a certain complementarity with an increase in farm size. The income effect on farms often leads to mechanization.	Ghodake and Ryan (1981); Mehra (1976); Ahmed (1981).

tion and employment, since there have been instances where extensive irrigation and/or agricultural growth rates associated with irrigation have not shown correspondingly high growth rate for the labor force (ARTEP, 1980; Naseem, 1980).

It is useful to make a distinction between labor-intensifying and labor-displacing mechanization practices (Singh, 1981, 1982). Land-intensifying mechanization includes such equipment as low-lift pumps and shallow tubewells, which lead to increased cropping intensities. Though they may displace task-specific labor, they increase the demand for labor in other tasks and thus, in the final analysis, have a net positive effect on labor use. Labor-displacing mechanization includes use of tractors and harvesting equipment such as threshers, combines, cotton pickers, and vegetable harvesters which have a negative net effect on employment. Likewise, the practices and technologies associated with irrigation can either generate or displace labor, as can be seen in Table 2.

In analyzing the available information, it is important to recognize that the studies conducted to date fall far short of providing a complete and satisfactory understanding of the relationship between irrigation and employment. Some of the principal weaknesses of these studies are as follows:

1. Most studies fail to specify the type of irrigation system analyzed and its performance level. This is a severe limitation because the quality of irrigation determines cropping intensity, type of crop grown, and yields, all of which significantly affect the labor used per unit of cultivated area.

2. Most studies fail to extricate the impact of irrigation from other variables that affect employment because they fail to recognize explicitly the complementary nature of the relationship between irrigation and the use of modern technology and HYVs. An important exception is Mehra (1976).[5]

3. Many studies have overlooked irrigation as a necessary precondition for using modern seed varieties. As a result, undue emphasis has been placed on the contributions of technology, fertilizer, or cropping to increases in employment.

4. With notable exceptions (Gooneratne, 1982; Agarwal, 1981) most studies fail to establish which sections of the rural population, in terms of both class and gender, have benefited from the increased employment opportunities. The few studies that have disaggregated the effect of irrigation and the HYV package on labor use by gender indicate that there has been an increase in demand for female casual labor (see Agarwal, 1981). Most of the labor increases are

5. This study set out to ascertain quantitatively the increase in labor when an unirrigated hectare is converted to an irrigated hectare by studying the employment situation before and after the advent of the Green Revolution. The study, conducted in Ferozepur, Punjab, compared overall labor input per cultivated hectare in the 1950s with the periods 1966–67 and 1969–70 for irrigated and unirrigated areas. The study showed that total labor input in crop production measured in man-days per hectare of cultivated area was 150 percent greater for irrigated areas and that the contribution of HYVs toward increased labor input was of a smaller order than that of irrigation.

operation-specific (weeding, transplanting, etc.). Thus the type of labor demanded varies according to cultural norms governing the sexual division of labor. Similarly, in some areas in-migration resulting from new irrigation-induced employment opportunities has caused women to lose their jobs to male agricultural laborers coming from elsewhere (Agarwal, 1981). Few studies take into account the specific categories of workers that either benefit from increased employment opportunities or are displaced.

5. Most studies do not identify those design and management interventions that could lead to greater employment benefits to land-poor women and men. There is a lack of research and field experimentation on such issues as the relationship between irrigation intensity and employment and the employment impacts of alternative interventions to improve the performance of irrigation systems such as those which involve modification in the cropping pattern (e.g., from paddy to nonpaddy crops; see Lenton, 1985).

6. Most studies do not address the economics of generating employment through irrigation development and management and do not evaluate this approach against other methods of generating employment.

Although much of the literature on irrigation and employment has focused on employment generated by irrigation-induced agricultural intensification, it is important to recognize the importance of employment created through the construction of large irrigation projects. According to rough Food and Agriculture Organization (FAO) estimates developed on the basis of the Indian experience, for every irrigated hectare some four person-years of employment can be generated during the construction phase, as compared to 25 person-years for agricultural activities during the life of the project (Sagardoy and Farago, 1976).

As yet labor-based construction techniques have not been used extensively to increase employment opportunities, although many large irrigation projects in India and China have successfully implemented labor-intensive practices (Biswas, 1980). Earthworking and spreading is often the most labor-extensive component in irrigation works, and masonry and concrete work are labor-based construction techniques. For example, to rebuild the earth-filled Kuochuang Dam, on the Sungi River in China, a labor input of 1.05 million man-days was required (Henle, 1974; Biswas, 1980). Labor-intensive methods employed in the construction of the Nagarjunasagar Dam, in India (the highest masonry dam in the world), resulted in savings estimated at about $4 million as a consequence of reductions in machinery costs (Bliss and Reddy, 1974; Biswas, 1980).

In closing, it is useful to note that rural people's perceptions provide evidence of the perceived impact of irrigation on employment. This is well illustrated by the Cavite Community Irrigation Project in the Philippines (Dozina et al., 1978), where several agricultural laborers from the area participated in the rehabilitation of the irrigation system on a voluntary basis, in anticipation of increased employment opportunities in the dry season as a result of irrigation. Follow-up studies showed that the benefits in terms of substantial increases in income were widely distributed among the participants. Hired laborers received the largest relative gains from the increased employment opportunities, and the estimated daily return to communal labor was 10 times the prevailing farm wage rate.

National Policies on Irrigation-induced Employment

Irrigation employment policies differ significantly from country to country. Three Asian countries—China, Taiwan, and Japan—are of particular interest in this context.

In China the employment potential of irrigation, both for agricultural practices and for construction, appears to have been realized. It is estimated that agricultural employment in irrigated areas is as high as 1,000 to 1,500 man-days per hectare per year, half of which is involved in land-development practices. China has absorbed employment in the agricultural sector despite pushing for rapid mechanization. Labor is absorbed in planting and transplanting of rice seedlings. The use of traditional methods to hull and thresh grain, farm-management tasks, the building of small irrigation works, multiple cropping and intercropping, new crops adopted, and the development of animal-husbandry practices are all labor-intensive practices that China has implemented. Mass mobilization campaigns for irrigation control and maintenance, for construction and reconstruction, and for control of plant and animal pests are undertaken in the slack season. What is especially remarkable is that the steady increase in the size of the labor force has been achieved without a decline in productivity per unit of labor. China has also shifted the demand for labor upward, from less to more productive and remunerative tasks (Critchfield, 1983; Kitching, 1982).

In Japan and Taiwan considerable emphasis was placed on minor irrigation and drainage works in the early stages of land development. These practices, coupled with the mixed use of farmyard manures with chemical fertilizers and wide use of traditional farm implements with continuous improvements, along with the adoption of modern equipment, have led to high levels of labor input in agriculture (Ishikawa, 1980).

Nonagricultural Uses of Irrigation Water

The most far-reaching indirect contribution that irrigation can make to the land-poor is undoubtedly through employment generation. However, irrigation also indirectly benefits the land-poor by providing water for nonagricultural purposes.

Nonagricultural uses of irrigation water include the following:

Domestic uses:

1. Drinking water, food washing and preparation, washing of utensils.

2. Washing and bathing.

3. Homestead plots, both for consumption and for income generation (e.g., horticulture).

4. Sewage disposal.

Animal uses:

1. Drinking water for animals. (Small ponds sometimes built to provide access to water without destroying channels. Irrigation canals sometimes used by buffaloes for bathing; canals lined and steps built for easy access.)

2. Fish and bird habitats. (Fish raised in irrigation reservoirs, tanks, channels, and rice paddies. Ducks, which use irrigation channels freely, are part of the farming system of many rural families.)

Power:
Water-powered grain milling etc.

Transport:
Transport of people and goods on irrigation channels.

Nonagricultural uses of water in irrigation systems have been extensively studied by Yoder (1981), who has summarized the experience to date and outlined some measures which might be taken to facilitate nonagricultural uses of irrigation systems. These uses have also been discussed by the Agricultural Development Council (ADC, 1980). A number of practical measures to meet rural community needs have been suggested by these and others (see, for example, Jones, 1981). It should be recognized, however, that local communities and organizations have often ingeniously tapped irrigation systems to meet their particular requirements and conditions. For example, villagers have lined canals near villages and have constructed steps for easy access to canals for washing and bathing purposes. They have made provisions for animals to drink water. Ponds off the main watercourse have been constructed strictly for this purpose. In several parts of India and Pakistan canals near a village are diverted through a pond to reduce the velocity of the water and to facilitate silt settlement, thus allowing drinking water to be better drawn (Yoder, 1981).

Experience with government action to provide irrigation water for nonagricultural purposes has often not been satisfactory. For example, the Gal Oya Project in Sri Lanka, which had a mandate to supply water for domestic purposes, has not fulfilled this mandate despite considerable expenditure. Although there have been serious bottlenecks in water supply, the practice of supplying domestic water continues because settlers expect it and have no alternative water supply. These villagers have failed to make the same efforts other villagers have made to meet their water needs, and thus are increasingly dependent on an irregular source (Yoder, 1981).

DIRECT APPROACHES

Irrigation projects can be designed, constructed, and operated in a number of ways to have a direct impact on the livelihoods of those with little or no land. These include (1) employment-intensive irrigation construction, operation, and maintenance practices (referred to in the previous section); (2) approaches that allow landless people to own irrigation projects and sell water for profit; (3) water-distribution procedures that allocate water rights to landless people; and (4) planning, design, and settlement practices that allow for allocation of land to the land-poor when irrigation is introduced.

In the following pages we explore the experience with each of these three approaches in some detail. Two cautions are in order, however. The first is that the experience to date with these approaches is so limited that it is not possible to draw any conclusions of widespread significance. At best the experience is helpful in illuminating the range of possi-

bilities available for exploration and in pointing the way toward needed research, field experimentation, and action. Second, most of the approaches have been tried on only small-scale systems by nongovernment organizations. Experience with large, publicly administered irrigation systems is lacking. Nevertheless, some of the experimental approaches described below are attracting attention and are helping irrigation professionals consider how lessons learned might be transferred to larger government schemes.

Water Allocation to the Land-Poor

In most irrigation systems water is allocated to farmers on the basis of landholdings. Typically the ratio between water supplied to the farm and the size of landholding is constant and based on crop water requirements. Thus a 4-ha holding requires, and is entitled to, twice as much water as a 2-ha holding.[6] On this basis the landless are not entitled to water.

Despite the almost universal acceptance of this physically based approach to water allocation, a number of pioneering pilot projects are under way in several countries that are experimenting with alternative, nonland-based approaches to water allocation. These experiments do not allocate water on the basis of landholding and thus hold promise for landless and land-poor people. Two such projects are described below.

Although both of these pilot programs involve small-scale systems and have been implemented by nongovernment organizations, some experience is available for large-scale systems. For example, the West Banas Medium Irrigation Project in Rajasthan, India, allocates water in proportion to holdings only for farms up to 2.03 ha. Larger farms are supplied with a fixed amount of water equal to that supplied to a 2.03-ha farm (Bottrall, 1980). And the Bhakra and Western Yamuna irrigation projects in northwest India allocate water to village tanks used by landless and landed people on the basis of need rather than landholding size.

The Sukhomajri Project: Sukhomajri, a small village in Haryana, India, is situated in now-barren hills. Traditionally the villagers' livelihood was rain-fed agriculture and livestock grazing, but since 1979 about 12.15 ha of village land have been irrigated by a small dam installed at the foot of an extensively eroded ravine immediately above the village. The irrigation system is the result of a project initiated by the Central Soil and Water Conservation Research and Training Institute to check the silting of a lake some distance away. Once the dam was built, it was realized that the soil erosion caused by overgrazing could best be halted through an irrigation development program that would provide villagers with an alternative grazing area for their cattle. The irrigation program enabled the village to meet its fodder requirements, check soil erosion, and increase income and on-farm employment (Seckler, 1980; Seckler and Joshi, 1982; Franda, 1983; Government of India, 1984).

The allocation of water in the Sukhomajri Project is of specific interest because it embodies a "water-to-the-

6. In practice there are often large variations in water received by farmers, particularly between head- and tailenders, as a result of poor irrigation management (see, for example, Wade and Chambers, 1980).

people" philosophy. Every bonafide family—that is, any group eating from a common hearth—receives a water coupon entitling it to a given quantity of water. The amount is the same for all families. With the approval of the Village Users Association, which manages the project, any family can give, sell, or trade its coupons. For example, a large farmer has two small farmers working his land. They provide the labor and water, he provides the land, and the crop is divided equally.

Irrigation not only has increased agricultural production and spawned some household and cottage industries but has helped increase the supply of fodder from crop residues. This in turn has reduced grazing pressures on nonagricultural land, thereby arresting the process of deforestation that was occurring on an unprecedented scale. The reservoir is used as a supplemental source of drinking water. Because of the water-allocation system all villagers benefit from the project in a relatively equitable manner. Since everyone has a vested interest in the system, animals are kept out of the watershed.

The approach taken in this pilot project is now being used as a model for microwatershed management elsewhere in India and in Nepal. In Nepal, for example, the Adhi Khola Irrigation Project (Pradhan, 1985) is being developed on similar lines. Water will be provided to all the workers in the command of the project, whether or not they hold land. Moreover, the management of water will be organized by members elected by the water shareholders. This project is thus dealing with the issue of landlessness at the inception of the project itself.

The Pani Panchayat Program. The Pani Panchayat Program (Chambers, 1981; Morehouse, 1981; Parulker, 1982; Shenoy and Rao, 1983) is a small-scale irrigation development program run by a nongovernment organization, the Gram Gourav Pratisthan (GGP). The projects are situated near Pune, in the Indian state of Maharashtra, a poor area where traditionally low-yielding crops have been cultivated by rainfed agriculture. Until the advent of GGP only large farmers had wells and pump sets. Under the GGP's Pani Panchayat Program groups of small and marginal farmers come together, subscribe shares, and with the help of the Panchayat, develop and manage a source of water using pumps. The size of each project varies, and each group makes its own arrangements for distribution within the main framework of rules set by the Panchayat. Many of the groups are homogeneous; for example, there are women's, shepherds', and liquor makers' groups.

Though the Pani Panchayat Program does not yet work with the completely landless, but only with small and marginal farmers, it is of interest here because of its innovative water-allocation system. The key feature of this system is that the amount of water allocated to each farm is related not to the size of the landholding but to the number of persons in the family. Specifically, the amount of water allocated to each family is equal to that required to irrigate approximately 0.2 ha per person in the family, adult or child. Water rights thus calculated, which are embodied in a stamped legal document, are attained after a member pays the subscription, which is proportional to the individual's water right. Member subscriptions cover 20 percent of the capital costs of the project, and the remainder is provided by the Gram Gourav Pratisthan and through government subsidies.

At the present time thirty-four such projects are fully operational, seven more are complete and ready except for electric connections, and nineteen are in various stages of planning and preparation. Although no further projects in the area are currently being commissioned, the GGP has helped in the development of at least one project elsewhere—the Bhima Command Area Lift Irrigation Scheme No. 3. The GGP has also started a training center through which training, visits, and dissemination of information to other interested parties are taking place (Chambers, 1985).

Water Ownership for the Land-Poor

As described earlier, many irrigation systems are communally or privately owned and managed. Virtually all communal or private irrigation systems are owned and managed by farmers owning land irrigated by such systems. However, a number of experimental programs currently under way in Bangladesh (and perhaps elsewhere) are indicating that it is feasible for landless people to own and manage small-scale irrigation projects that supply water that can be sold to farmers. One such program has been organized by Proshika, a Bangladeshi nongovernment organization (Ahmed, 1983; Wood, 1983, 1984; Bottrall, 1984).

Proshika was established in 1976 to organize and assist land-poor laborers and other poor peasants in rural Bangladesh. In 1980, Proshika initiated a pilot project to organize land-poor groups to purchase and manage irrigation pumps and to establish water rights. The objectives of Proshika were (1) to facilitate the acquisition and use of lift pumps and shallow tubewells by land-poor groups and enable them to sell water to owners or cultivators of land, (2) to develop a source of income and purchasing power for these groups; and (3) to ensure that the land-poor share in the benefits from multiple cropping and enhanced productivity of land, to which they would contribute if they provided the source of water.

By 1984, Proshika had organized 104 groups of 15 to 25 men each, in each instance negotiating a line of credit with the Bangladesh Krishi Bank to underwrite loans for both equipment and operations (Bottrall, 1984). Irrigation water is provided by the landless for a fee, on the basis of a prearranged share of the total yield. Although Proshika has faced some difficulties, including inefficient pump management, inadequate identification of good pump sites, and unsatisfactory contracts with farmers, three-fourths of the groups have made a profit, and the loan repayment rate is 75 percent after operating costs and loan payments are deducted. Eventually, it is hoped, the landless will provide farmers with a complete package of inputs and be responsible for maintenance of facilities.

The land-poor, by asserting control over a newly emerging resource, have thus been able to obtain supplementary income, increase the demand for employment during the second crop, and gain secondary benefits though the whole cycle of construction, operation and maintenance, and support services (e.g., pump repairs). Their involvement in water delivery is expected to enhance their bargaining position in other transactions with landowners, especially those concerning agricultural labor wages, local moneylending rates, and sharecropping terms. The project has also helped increase the access of the land-poor to government subsidies. Land-poor peasants now have access to substantial government subsidies available for irrigation equipment which previously was purchased only by those farmers who owned considerable land and had investable surpluses. However, the success of the scheme will ultimately depend on the ability of the land-poor to organize, negotiate, and reach agreements to extract timely payments from farmers.

A number of such groups are now operating in Bangladesh, through organizations like the Bangladesh Rural Advancement Committee (BRAC) and the Grameen Bank (Wood, 1984). The Bangladesh Rural Development Board has also initiated a pilot program with format and objectives similar to those of Proshika (Bottrall, 1984). The Proshika projects have also attracted substantial interest outside Bangladesh. In India, for example, the Tata Steel Corporation is considering a pilot project with similar characteristics (Levine, 1985).

Land Allocation to the Land-Poor

The introduction of irrigation into an area can be seen as an opportunity for reallocation of land to the land-poor. This can occur in resettlement schemes such as the Mahaveli Irrigation Project in Sri Lanka or the Rajasthan Canal in India. Typically these schemes involve the allocation of small plots of land to both landless and landed people brought in from other parts of the country. In some schemes, such as the Gezira and others in the Sudan, land-use rights are allocated to settlers, who then become long-term tenant farmers (see Scudder, 1981, for an extensive review of experience with settlement projects).

Chambers (1984b) notes that a potentially feasible approach to providing land to the landless is simply for the state to buy land on a willing-seller basis and then parcel it out to the landless. Since this approach depends very much on farmers' willingness to sell at reasonable prices, it may be easier to implement as part of an irrigation program, taking advantage of existing land-ceiling legislation in countries like India, which specifies lower ceilings for irrigated as opposed to rainfed land. To our knowledge, however, there is no experience with this approach when combined with irrigation, though Chambers (1984b) notes that experience with the provision of land and its settlement by landless families has been gained by two nongovernment organizations in Tamil Nadu and Karnataka, in India.

Land may also be allocated in conjunction with the allocation of water rights to the land-poor. In the Adhi Khola Irrigation Project in Nepal referred to earlier, for example, the landless and the land-poor will be given previously procured land in exchange for their work in the construction of the project (Pradhan, 1985).

RESEARCH, POLICY, AND ACTION NEEDS AND OPPORTUNITIES

The foregoing sections have demonstrated that a fairly substantial body of research on indirect approaches to the land-poor through irrigation now exists and that a beginning is being made in developing experience with direct approaches to the land-poor based on water and land allocation. Nevertheless, significant gaps in our understanding of the relationship between irrigation and the land-poor remain, and there appears to be substantial room for gains for the land-poor through the formulation of better policies and through action on several fronts.

In this section we analyze some of these research, policy, and action needs and opportunities. To facilitate the discussion, we address these first in the context of employment generation, nonagricultural uses of water, and other indirect, irrigation-based approaches. In the latter half of the section we discuss these needs in the context of direct approaches.

In what follows, it is possible to differentiate between needs and opportunities that relate to existing irrigation systems and those that relate to future systems. The first category involves improvements in the management of existing systems and is of particular importance in Asia, where over 100 million ha of land are served by existing canal and groundwater irrigation systems, and where the potential for expansion of irrigation, though larger in absolute terms, is relatively constrained. The second category involves primarily changes in policy and/or design procedures and is of greater significance where current irrigation is limited relative to the potential—as, for example, in most countries of sub-Saharan Africa.

Indirect Approaches

Four principal needs can be identified:

Information on overall indirect impacts. There appears to be a clear need for better information on actual costs and benefits to the land-poor of new or improved irrigation. Detailed empirical research is needed to assess the various impacts of present irrigation systems on the land-poor and to identify the likely key remedial actions, in particular actions at the policy level.

Employment research. Although a substantial body of literature on the employment impacts of irrigation is available—the cumulative impact of which indisputably suggests that irrigation has a positive effect on employment—there remain substantial gaps in our understanding of the relationship between irrigation and employment. To help in the formulation of better decisions, various types of irrigation should be subjected to detailed empirical research which (1) extricates the impact of irrigation from other variables that affect employment; (2) differentiates between different sections of the rural population, in terms of both class and gender, that have benefited from increased employment opportunities; (3) identifies design and management interventions that could lead to greater employment benefits to the landless; (4) addresses specific design and management issues, such as the relationship between irrigation intensity and employment and the employment impact of alternative management interventions; and (5) relates all these variables to the physical design and managerial characteristics of irrigation systems and their performance level. Better understanding of these issues may help in addressing whether and how employment criteria may be used in making planning and design decisions, such as the choice of groundwater versus surface-water development or intensive versus extensive irrigation.

Employment economics. A better understanding of the economics of employment generation through irrigation and improved irrigation management is needed. In particular, irrigation as a means of providing employment opportunities should be compared with alternative forms of investment to achieve the same end.

Trade-offs between uses: Empirical research is needed on trade-offs between different uses of water in irrigation systems and their impact on the land-poor. In particular, better understanding of the costs of adding facilities for nonagricultural uses of water is required, to permit the evaluation of trade-offs between the costs and benefits to the land-poor from these kinds of interventions, in comparison with the costs and benefits to the land-poor in extending or improving the delivery of irrigation water for agricultural purposes.

Direct Approaches

Research, policy, and action should include the following:

Field experimentation and research. Far more experience is needed on direct approaches to assist landless and near-landless people through the allocation of water and land. More approaches should be developed and tested under a broader range of conditions, with particular attention to detailed documentation of both processes and outcomes. In addition, further studies on ongoing pilot projects should be undertaken. For example, for those strategies involving ownership of irrigation assets by the landless, estimates are needed of employment benefits, other secondary benefits, and administrative costs if implemented on a wider scale.

Policies. Irrigation policies relating to the land-poor should be formulated. These include policies for (1) locations of irrigation facilities, so that areas characterized by great poverty and unemployment and/or small landholdings can be given priority; (2) construction methods for irrigation projects so that labor-intensive methods can be accepted as an integral part of overall socioeconomic and technical criteria by which alternative plans are judged and selected; (3) technology development, so that irrigation technologies that are relatively labor-using and/or readily accessible to the poor can be given priority; (4) the incentive structures for groundwater development, so that greater numbers of the land-poor will have access to groundwater; and (5) land distribution and settlement, so that the introduction of irrigation can be used for targeting benefits for the landless.

Action. Much can be done, even without improvements in our understanding of the relationship between irrigation

and the landless and without changes in policy, to ensure that the landless gain more and lose less from irrigation. Although specific construction, design, and management interventions will vary from place to place, examples include (1) making landlessness a precondition for settlement in newly irrigated areas; (2) considering nonland-based criteria for water distribution in the design of new irrigation projects; (3) designing particular interventions at the design and implementation stage of new irrigation projects to help make irrigation more useful to the land-poor by providing for nonagricultural uses of water; and (4) implementing available design procedures to help prevent the occurrence of water-related diseases.

Extension to large systems. Lessons learned from small-scale experimental projects need to be extended to large-scale, publicly administered projects. For this to occur, attention must be given to training programs, visits, workshops, and other forms of information dissemination.

ACKNOWLEDGMENTS

This paper has its origins in an internal Ford Foundation staff meeting on irrigation held in Dhaka, Bangladesh, in April, 1984. We would like to acknowledge the many direct and indirect contributions made by the participants at this meeting, particularly by Robert Chambers, Anthony Bottrall, Adrienne Germain, Gil Levine, and Fran Korten. Katharine McKee and Phil Oldenberg also significantly contributed to the ideas outlined in this chapter. Sidney Jones was particularly helpful in developing the material on employment, and Susan Newman was of invaluable assistance in the library search.

REFERENCES

ADC [Agricultural Development Council]. 1980. Background material for workshop Irrigation: making it useful for disadvantaged groups, held in Salisbury, Conn., June. New York.

Agarwal, B. 1981. Water resource development and rural women. Mimeographed. New Delhi: Ford Foundation.

———. 1983. Mechanization in Indian agriculture: an analytical study based on the Punjab. New Delhi: Allied Publishers.

Ahmed, I. 1981. Technical change and agrarian structure: a study of Bangladesh. Geneva: International Labour Organization.

———. 1983. Irrigation projects for the landless in rural Bangladesh. *ADAB News.* January–February.

Aiyaswamy, and B. Natarajan. 1980. Labour use patterns on small farms in Tamil Nadu. Coimbatore, India: Tamil Nadu Agricultural University.

Anderou, A., F. A. Haj, and M. I. Hussain. 1982. Deep tube-well irrigation and adoption: certain practices for rice cultivation in Bangladesh. Agricultural Mechanization in Asia, Africa and Latin America.

ARTEP [Asian Regional Employment Programme]. 1980. Employment expansion in Asian agriculture: a comparative analysis of south Asian countries. Bangkok: Asian Regional Employment Programme.

Bala, and M. I. Hussain. 1978. Farm size, labour employment and farm mechanization in Bangladesh. Agricultural Mechanization in Asia.

Biswas, A. K. 1980. Labour based technology for large irrigation works: problems and prospects. Working paper. Geneva: International Labour Organization.

Bliss, C., and J. H. Reddy. 1974. Appropriate technology in civil engineering works in developing countries: an exploratory appraisal of the state-of-the-art. Cambridge, Mass.: Arthur D. Little.

Bottrall, A. F. 1980. Comparative study of the management and organization of irrigation projects. Washington, D. C.: World Bank.

———. 1984. Personal communication. Dhaka, Bangladesh.

Briscoe, J. 1980. Energy use and social structure in a Bangladesh village. *Population and Development Review* 5 (4).

CGIAR [Consultative Group on International Agricultural Research]. 1982. Report of the Study Team on Water Management and Training. Rome: Technical Advisory Committee, CGIAR.

Chambers, R. 1981. Gram Gourav Pratisthan: notes and reflections on a field visit. Mimeographed. New Delhi: Ford Foundation.

———. 1984a. Employment: income-generation or livelihood? Mimeographed. New Delhi: Ford Foundation.

———. 1984b. To the hands of the poor: water, trees, and land. Discussion paper series. New Delhi: Ford Foundation.

———. 1985. Personal communication, March 19.

Clay, E. 1975. Equity and productivity effects of a package of technical innovations and changes in social institutions: Tubewells, tractors and HYVs. *Indian Journal of Agricultural Economics.*

———. 1978. Environment, technology and the seasonal patterns of agricultural employment in Bangladesh. Revised version of paper presented at Institute of Development Studies, Sussex, England.

Critchfield, R. 1983. Villages. New York: Anchor Press, Doubleday.

Dozina, G., H. Kikuchi, and Y. Hayami. 1978. Mobilizing local resources for irrigation development. *In* D. Taylor and T. Wickham (ed.) Irrigation policy and the management of irrigation systems in Southeast Asia. Bangkok: Agricultural Development Council.

Franda, H. 1983. Voluntary associations and local development in India. New Delhi: Young Asia Publications.

Ghate, P. 1984. Direct attacks on rural poverty: Policy, programmes and implementation. New Delhi: Concept Publishing Co.

Ghodake and Ryan. 1981. Human labour availability and employment in semi-arid tropical India. *Indian Journal of Agricultural Economics.*

Gooneratne, W. 1982. Labor absorption in rice-based agriculture: case studies from S.E. Asia. Geneva: International Labour Organization.

Gopinath, C. 1977. An analysis of factors affecting output and employment of selected crops in tractor and non-tractor farms. Paper presented at Harvard University, Center for Population Studies, Cambridge, Mass.

Government of India. 1984. Hill resource development and community management: Sukhomajri and Dasholi Gram Swarajya Mandal. *In* Report to planning commission's working group on hill area development. New Delhi: Planning Commission.

Hayami, Y. 1981. Agrarian problems of India: an east and S.E. Asian perspective. *Economic and Political Weekly,* special articles.

Henle, H. V. 1974. Report on China's Agriculture. Rome: Food and Agriculture Organization.

IDS [Institute of Development Studies]. 1980. Who gets a last rural resource? The potential and challenge for lift irrigation for the rural poor. Sussex, England.

IRRI [International Rice Research Institute]. 1980. Rice production in the Teral of Kosi Zone. Nepal Research Series, No. 54. November. Manila: International Rice Research Institute.

Ishikawa. 1980. *In* ARTEP. 1980.

Jones, B. J. 1981. Non-agricultural uses of irrigation systems: Household water supplies. New York: Agricultural Development Council.

Khan, H. H. 1975. The economics of the Green Revolution in Pakistan. New York: Praeger.

Kitching, G. N. 1982. Development and underdevelopment in historical perspective. New York, London: Methuen.

Laureto, A. S. 1982. Economic impact of irrigation in Pakistan. *Journal of Agriculture, Food and Nutrition.*

Lee. 1980. In ARTEP.

Lenton, R. L. 1984. Irrigation and disadvantaged groups. Mimeographed. New York: Ford Foundation.

———. 1985. A note on employment effects of crop diversification. Mimeographed. New York: Ford Foundation.

Levine, Gil. 1985. Personal communication.

Mehra, S. 1976. Some aspects of labour use in Indian agriculture. *Indian Journal of Agricultural Economics.*

Morehouse, H. 1981. Technology and social justice: defying the law of gravity. Mimeographed draft.

Narain, D., and S. Roy. 1980. Impact of irrigation and labour availability on multiple cropping: a case study of India. Washington, D.C.: International Food Production Research Institute.

Naseem, I. 1980. In AREP.

Parikh, J. 1980. Impact of technical change on employment in Indian agriculture. University of East Anglia economics discussion papers.

Parulker, V. 1982. Pani Panchayat can save Bombay. Imprint Business Press Publication, Vol. 22, April.

Pradhan, P. 1985. Research status report on irrigation: Nepal, Kandy, Sri Lanka. Paper presented at the IIMI/WMS II workshop on research priorities for Asia, January.

Raju, V. T. 1976. The impact of new farm technology on human labour employment. *Indian Journal of Industrial Relations.*

Sagardoy, J. A., and G. Farago. 1976. Labour-intensive irrigation construction methods: identification of research. Report TF-RAS 18 (SWE). Rome: Food and Agricultural Organization.

Scudder, T. 1981. The development potential of new lands settlement in the tropics and subtropics: A global state-of-the-art evaluation with specific emphasis on policy implications. Pasadena: Institute for Development Anthropology, California Institute of Technology.

Seckler, D. 1980. A rural development programme in India. Mimeographed. New Delhi: Ford Foundation.

Seckler, D., and D. Joshi. 1982. Sukhomajri: water management in India. *Bulletin of Atomic Scientists,* March.

Shenoy, P. D., and S. Rao. 1983. Pani Panchayat—A new philosophy of rural development. *Wamana* (Indian Institute of Management, Bangalore), October.

Singh, J. 1981. Small farmers and the landless in south Asia. Washington, D.C.: World Bank.

———. 1982. The landless poor in South Asia. Invited paper, July. Washington, D.C.: World Bank.

Voder, R. 1981. Non-agricultural uses of irrigation systems, past experience and implications for planning and design. New York: Agricultural Development Council.

Wade, R., and R. Chambers. 1980. Managing the main system: canal irrigation's blind spot. Sussex, England: Institute of Development Studies.

Wood, G. D. 1983. The socialization of minor irrigation in Bangladesh. *ADAB News* 10(1), January–February.

———. 1984. Provision of irrigation services by the landless—an approach to agrarian reform in Bangladesh. *Agricultural Administration*, No. 17.

Naseem, I. 1980. In AREP.

Parikh, J. 1980. Impact of technical change on employment in Indian agriculture. University of East Anglia economics discussion papers.

Parulker, V. 1982. Pani Panchayat can save Bombay. Imprint Business Press Publication, Vol. 22, April.

Pradhan, P. 1985. Research status report on irrigation: Nepal, Kandy, Sri Lanka. Paper presented at the IIMI/WMS workshop on research priorities for Asia, January.

Raju, V. T. 1976. The impact of new farm technology on human labour employment. *Indian Journal of Industrial Relations*.

Sagardoy, J. A., and G. Farago. 1976. Labour-intensive irrigation construction methods: identification of research. Report TF-RAS 18 (SWE). Rome: Food and Agricultural Organization.

Scudder, T. 1981. The development potential of new lands settlement in the tropcs and subtropics: A global state-of-the-art evaluation with specific emphasis on policy implications. Pasadena: Institute for Development Anthropology, California Institute of Technology.

Seckler, D. 1980. A rural development programme in India. Mimeographed. New Delhi: Ford Foundation.

Seckler, D., and D. Joshi. 1982. Sukhomajri: water management in India. *Bulletin of Atomic Scientists*, March.

Shenoy, P. D., and S. Rao. 1983. Pani Panchayat—A new philosophy of rural development. *Wamana* (Indian Institute of Management, Bangalore), October.

Singh, J. 1981. Small farmers and the landless in south Asia. Washington, D.C.: World Bank.

———. 1982. The landless poor in South Asia. Invited paper, July. Washington, D.C.: World Bank.

Voder, R. 1981. Non-agricultural uses of irrigation systems, past experience and implications for planning and design. New York: Agricultural Development Council.

Wade, R., and R. Chambers. 1980. Managing the main system: canal irrigation's blind spot. Sussex, England: Institute of Development Studies.

Wood, G. D. 1983. The socialization of minor irrigation in Bangladesh. *ADAB News* 10(1), January–February.

———. 1984. Provision of irrigation services by the landless—an approach to agrarian reform in Bangladesh. *Agricultural Administration*, No. 17.

Voder, R. 1981. Non-agricultural uses of irrigation systems, past experience and implications for planning and design. New York: Agricultural Development Council.

27. IRRIGATION INSTITUTIONS: THE MYTH OF MANAGEMENT

Daniel W. Bromley, Department of Agricultural Economics, University of Wisconsin, Madison, Wisconsin

ABSTRACT

Subsidized irrigation projects in the poor countries of the tropics continue to distort the social opportunity cost of irrigation water and so to undermine efforts at improving the management of irrigation systems. The poor management of irrigation systems precludes the realization of attainable increases in food production in most of these countries. Colonialism was the origin of many existing irrigation schemes, and the management of those systems was part of the larger colonial administration. With the emergence of independent nation-states there has been a persistent interest in continued construction of irrigation infrastructure, but no commensurate interest in the institutional arrangements that will ensure proper water management. The myth of management can be overcome only by a concerted effort to establish secure expectations by farmers with respect to water receipts. As long as new irrigation projects are available to countries, that management effort is undermined. A moratorium on new irrigation projects would properly concentrate the collective mind on improved management of existing systems.

THE MYTH OF MANAGEMENT

There seems to be widespread agreement among scholars of agricultural development that the general concept of management is central to any successful programs to overcome hunger in the tropics. Nowhere is this more evident than in the recent dialogue regarding the serious—and worsening—food problems in Sub-Saharan Africa (Delgado and Mellor, 1984; Eicher, 1982; Lele, 1981, 1984; Matlon and Spencer, 1984; World Bank, 1981, 1984). I pursue this matter of management here because I believe it to be the missing key ingredient in the successful operation of irrigation systems in the developing countries.

I suggest that irrigation management is a myth in most projects in the tropics and that this condition persists because host countries—and donor agencies—have not yet addressed the real market value of water. Part of the blame for this can be understood in the context of an unappreciated distinction between technique and institutions. Another part can be attributed to organizational divisions of responsibility. And a third part follows from an institutional vacuum that has existed in many countries since the demise of colonialism.

Technique and Institutions

Irrigation development in the tropics is, for the most part, a colonial legacy; colonial powers were interested in the tropics for the raw materials and plantation crops that could be exported. Irrigation techniques—that is, dams, ditches, and control devices—were developed for a particular economic and political purpose, and the careful administration of that infrastructure constituted an essential rationale for a continued colonial presence. With colonial administration there was little scope for—nor even a need for—the development of local-level institutional arrangements to manage water. It should come as little surprise that an indigenous "culture of management" failed to develop in an environment in which obedience to imposed management rules was expected.

This imposition of technique—physical capital—and water-management rules contributed to contemporary problems of irrigation mismanagement because of a persistent emphasis on yet more infrastructure while the institutional dimension remains ignored. Under colonial rule the physical aspect was easy to see, while the management aspect was simply implicit in the larger colonial administration that was taken for granted.

This division persists even today. Many countries are interested in yet more irrigation projects (technique) while largely ignoring the more critical need for enhanced management. Unfortunately, this preference reinforces the interests of the major development-assistance agencies who have a lot of money to spend on physical capital and who wish to avoid the more controversial aspects of influencing local-level management of water. For to manage properly is to confront existing water-allocation practices, and it often happens that powerful local interests have the most to lose should those practices be questioned.

Divisions of Responsibility

At the time they gained independence, many new nation-states adopted an organizational structure for irrigation similar to that found in the United States; in most instances the ministry of irrigation is separate from the ministry of agriculture. The problems of this distinction are well understood, so I will stress here only the obvious one that water deliveries may be quite unrelated to times of critical water stress for crops. Efforts to develop agricultural extension and research programs that are closely integrated with water management are seriously hampered when three distinct government agencies are involved.

This division of responsibility is particularly serious when local management arrangements have never existed and when the tradition of management does not exist.

Institutional Vacuum

The above conditions have combined to create an institutional vacuum at the project level with the result that there are few rules guiding the allocation of irrigation water and what rules exist are often ignored with impunity. This lacuna of behavioral norms, conventions, and parameters means that each irrigator is free to appropriate water as a fugitive resource and that collective maintenance needs are not met (Bromley, 1982b). Each irrigator can free-ride on the system and take any liberty with the beneficial aspects that water may provide. Unfortunately for those near the end of a system, the ability to free-ride on water deliveries diminishes as a function of one's distance from the head of that system (Bromley et al., 1980).

I use the term "institutional vacuum" to describe those situations in which there are no recognized—and adhered to—rules to guide the allocation of a valuable resource such as water. This aspect is elaborated on below.

INSTITUTIONS AND ORGANIZATIONS

Institutions are collectively derived rules that both constrain and liberate individual and group action. Institutions represent the essential structures of social interaction; institutions determine the essence of human interaction, and they are in turn determined by that action. The central issue here is one of transactions among individuals. Economists are ordinarily interested in transactions that entail the exchange of a good or service in return for money. Here we are interested in a broader connotation of the term "transaction" to include negotiated agreements among members of a group (society, village, irrigators) regarding accepted behaviors with respect to valuable community assets.

Some institutions are written down in the lawbooks or in village bylaws. Other institutions represent long-established norms and conventions regarding particular dimensions of group interaction. But the essence of institutions is to parameterize expectations among members of a group with respect to the behavior of others. By doing so, institutions also define the bounds of accepted behavior (Runge, 1984).

Institutions represent the "structural" dimension of human life in that they provide a constellation of rules. There are several types of rules, but the type of special interest to us here is the one that defines the organizations relevant to irrigation administration. That is, organizations—while usually regarded as "institutions" in popular usage—are in fact defined by institutions (rules). It is the institutional arrangements that define the behavior of a ministry of irrigation both with respect to, say, the ministry of agriculture and with respect to the farmers on an irrigation project. These institutions, by establishing the norms of behavior for individuals within the irrigation organizations, influence the culture of management both within that organization and also among the farmers on an irrigation project.

We say that institutions define opportunity (or choice) sets for individuals or groups. By that is meant that the choice domain of the individual is defined by institutions. If the choice domain of one farmer on an irrigation system is constrained, then by definition the choice domain of another is expanded. It is essential to understand this dual nature of institutions since the conventional wisdom is that institutions constrain only individuals.

Consider the example of water allocation along a canal. If the individual at the head of the system is free to take as much water as he likes—regardless of the interests of the other farmers on the system—then that individual's choice set is unaffected by the actions of those downstream, and the only effective constraint is the physical availability of water. But consider the downstream farmers. Their choice domain is directly influenced by the actions of the individual at the head of the system in that his excessive withdrawal of water prevents the rest of them from having as much water as they like—and when they need it.

An institutional arrangement that constrained the greed of the upstream farmer would, at the same time, liberate the downstream farmers. All institutions possess this dual nature; in a world of scarcity, constraint for one is liberation for another.

In the absence of parameterized expectations for all farmers on an irrigation system, the water becomes an open-access resource subject to all the well-understood problems that inhere to such resources (Bromley, 1982a). But when well-understood institutions are present, both with respect to the government agencies pertinent to irrigation and with respect to the farmers on an irrigation system, then behavior with respect to the valuable resource is brought under the domain of the collective good as opposed to individual prerogatives.

Institutions define limits on individual behavior and at the same time can be thought of as enhancing the welfare of the group. Many individuals confuse the concept of laissez-faire with the absence of parameters on the behavior of individuals. In fact, market processes representing the very essence of choice and discretion are highly structured modes of human interaction. Commodities, property, contracts, and price are all defined in markets, and in fact markets could not exist in the absence of these aspects. Thus it is the range of individual choice that is defined by institutional arrangements—rules that both liberate and constrain individual behavior.

THE CONCEPT OF MANAGEMENT

By management I mean both the development of institutional arrangements to guide water allocation among farmers on a system—as well as among systems—and also the dimension of compliance with those evolved structural parameters. The goals of management ought to be several.

First, the nation as a whole will have an interest in the productive efficiency of the irrigation investments, by which I mean the overall productive efficiency. The evidence is clear that systems with better overall water allocation among all irrigators are also the most productive systems (Bromley, 1982b). Hence, implicit in the concept of overall productive efficiency is some concept of equity among irrigators on a system. Not only will irrigators have an interest in an equitable water allocation, but at the national level equity will show up in terms of productivity. The second goal of management is, therefore, an equity goal.

A third goal of management is order and predictability among irrigators over time. That is, while efficiency can be thought of in the short run, a more compelling notion of efficiency concerns the long-term enterprise implications of secure water deliveries. Because the modern high-yield varieties are more demanding of precision in the application of water and fertilizers, overall production will be enhanced to the extent that farmers can develop secure expectations regarding the timely availability of water and purchased fertilizers. Established institutional arrangements that parameterize expectations bring order to the rural countryside and so help determine a more predictable agricultural environment. Institutions help minimize the social costs of "strategic uncertainty," by which I mean the random influence on one farmer by others.

At the same time that a goal of management is to create order in the daily economic life of irrigators, it is also imperative that institutional arrangements exist to facilitate necessary change. There is a critical distinction between an institutional vacuum—a situation in which no rules exist—and one of parameterized expectations (order) yet with the provision for considered change when new conditions warrant. Just as there are rules (institutions) to guide daily behavior, there must be rules for changing rules. This aspect of institutional change must not be so easy that the situation resembles one of "no rules." Yet neither can change be so difficult that rigidity precludes wise adjustments to meet new conditions and imperatives. Hence, the ability to permit change is the fourth goal of management.

We thus have efficiency, equity, order, and adaptation as four possible management goals for irrigation systems, and suggested measures of success in achieving these four goals follow.

Efficiency would be measured in conventional economic terms in that the value of the marginal unit of irrigation water is the same across all irrigators on a system (and indeed among systems). As long as this marginal condition does not occur, water reallocation would represent a gain to the nation.

As for equity, I repeat several conditions from an earlier paper on water-management institutions (Bromley et al., 1980). We there proposed, first, following Rawls (1971), that each participant in an irrigation system possess an equal right to the most extensive liberty (regarding water receipts) compatible with similar liberty for others. Second, we argued that the prevailing institutional system must be fully understood by all participants. Third, we proposed that there must be a shared concept of justice so that a situation in which a few irrigators were continually favored in water receipts would be widely viewed as being "unfair." Fourth, we argued that a system of formal enforcement must exist in which there is consistent and impartial administration of the prevailing institutional arrangements governing water allocations, maintenance, and other activities that have joint benefits and costs. Finally, we suggested that the prevailing institutional arrangements should be designed to reinforce the basic self-interest of the participants in the system. While this goal may not be universally attainable, it is possible to seek opportunities to create behavioral norms and rules that reinforce certain natural instincts of the irrigators.

I want to point out that equity does not mean exactly the same quantity of water per hectare or per farmer. That would be an outcome measurement that would likely result in important inefficiencies. Recall that efficiency is ensured by a consideration of the marginal value of another unit of irrigation water to each farmer's situation. Equity is ensured by a set of procedures and behaviors, not by water receipts. We must be careful to avoid confusing process criteria with end-result criteria.

The measurement of order is a little more difficult for the economist. I would suggest, however, that order can be considered a function of the number of disputes that arise from the operational system over a specific period of time; the fewer the disputes, the greater the order. This performance indicator assumes, of course, the existence of an institutional structure that meets the efficiency and equity criteria spelled out above. Given those conditions, an orderly system is characterized by few confrontations and disputes. The economist considers transaction costs to consist of the costs of gaining information, the costs of reaching agreements, and the costs of enforcing those agreements. An irrigation system with a high degree of order will have low information costs, very low bargaining costs, and—ideally—zero enforcement costs.

Finally, the measurement of change can be thought of in terms of the transaction costs described above. For issues of institutional change the relevant components of transaction costs are concerned with information and bargaining. Irrigation systems in which information is very costly—and in which negotiation is difficult or impossible—will not be systems in which incremental adjustment to new conditions and needs is likely to be forthcoming.

Management is, therefore, the establishment of a structure of institutional arrangements that defines the rights and duties of the farmers on an irrigation system. No group of individuals can thrive and prosper in a setting of chaos and anarchy. Access to water is no different from access to a number of other important economic inputs. The economist would be inclined to suggest that what is needed is a pricing scheme for water so that it might be allocated efficiently. But a pricing scheme assumes the presence of an institutional structure of the sort discussed above. No market process can function without well-established rules defining rights and duties and in the absence of an enforcement mechanism that ensures that one gets what one has paid for. To jump immediately to a recommendation for water pricing is to ignore the logically prior condition of an institutional structure that will allow atomistic decision making with respect to water use whereby each individual equates its price to his own perceived marginal value.

REHABILITATING IRRIGATION INSTITUTIONS

With the exception of a few places in southeast Asia the performance of irrigation systems in the tropics—performance here referring to agricultural production per unit of land or per unit of water or per unit of labor—is very poor (Bromley et al., 1980; Bromley 1982a). A reasonable hypothesis would be that irrigation systems experience high performance when national policymakers conclude that the market value of water is high enough to justify taking the necessary action. The scarcity value of water in Taiwan and Japan is such that poor irrigation performance cannot be tolerated.

In the rest of the world this realization is slow to come. My second hypothesis is that the continued availability of development assistance funds for yet more irrigation projects is a major part of the reason for this failure to understand the true scarcity value of water. By continuing to subsidize more irrigation projects—and so by reinforcing the desire in many countries for the government to show a commanding physical and political presence in the rural countryside—we simply put off the day of this recognition. Development assistance funds distort the shadow price of water and so undervalue the benefit-cost perception of addressing existing performance problems.

A moratorium on new irrigation investments would do several things. First, it would focus attention on solving problems on existing systems. Second, it would eliminate high-status jobs of a cadre of engineers in these countries by terminating the continued construction of new concrete edifices. Third, these engineers would instead be reallocated to the less glamorous task of making existing systems work better. Fourth, we could expect such a moratorium to reinforce the need for closer integration among ministries of agriculture, among extension services, and among the irrigation administrations. Finally, it would increase the demand for social scientists when it was suddenly realized that, in addition to the engineering dimensions to irrigation, it is the transactions among individual farmers that determine the performance of irrigation systems.

Irrigation institutions have been ignored because of the myth of management that derives from the commanding presence of physical infrastructure. Investments of this sort have the aura of Pareto safety in that one is led to believe that everyone can be made better off without making anyone else worse off. In fact, irrigation works that deliver water in the absence of secure expectations regarding timing and quantity of those receipts for all irrigators are anything but Pareto-safe. The food-producing performance of most tropical countries will suffer until this essential aspect of water management is understood.

REFERENCES

Bromley, D. W. 1982a. Land and water problems—An institutional perspective. *American Journal of Agricultural Economics* 64:834–44.

———. 1982b. Improving irrigated agriculture: institutional reform and the small farmer. Working paper 531. Washington, D.C.: World Bank.

Bromley, D. W., D. C. Taylor, and D. E. Parker. 1980. Water reform and economic development: institutional aspects of water management in the developing countries. *Economic Development and Cultural Change* 28:365–87.

Delgado, C. L., and J. W. Mellor. 1984. A structural view of policy issues in African agricultural development. *American Journal of Agricultural Economics* 66:665–70.

Eicher, C. K. 1982. Facing up to Africa's food crisis. *Foreign Affairs* 61:154–74.

Lele, U. 1981. Rural Africa: modernization, equity, and long-term development. *Science,* February 6, p. 547–53.

———. 1984. The role of risk in an agriculturally led strategy in Sub-Saharan Africa. *American Journal of Agricultural Economics* 66:677–83.

Matlon, P. J., and D. S. Spencer. 1984. Increasing food production in Sub-Saharan Africa: environmental problems and inadequate technological solutions. *American Journal of Agricultural Economics* 66:671–76.

Rawls, J. 1971. A theory of justice. Cambridge, Mass.: Harvard University Press.

Runge, C. F. 1984. Institutions and the free rider: the assurance problem in collective action. *Journal of Politics* 46:154–81.

World Bank. 1981. Accelerated development in Sub-Saharan Africa. Washington, D.C.

———. 1984. Toward sustained development in Sub-Saharan Africa. Washington, D.C.

28. MANAGING WATER MANAGERS: DETERRING EXPROPRIATION, OR, EQUITY AS A CONTROL MECHANISM

Robert Wade, World Bank, Washington, D.C., and Institute of Development Studies, University of Sussex, Sussex, England

ABSTRACT

The performance of canal irrigation systems depends, in part, on trust by farmers in the good faith and abilities of irrigation officials. In India this trust is typically lacking; there is, instead, a "syndrome of anarchy" under the canals: farmers lack the confidence that if they refrain from taking water out of turn they will get water on time, and officials lack confidence that if they work conscientiously to get the water on time farmers will refrain from rule breaking. To break the syndrome, changes need to be made in the relationship between operation and maintenance (O&M) and construction, in the source of the O&M budget, and in the geographical scope of the O&M organization. The East Asian Irrigation Associations provide an example of the direction in which institutional changes might sensibly be made. Changes in physical design can also help, particularly the punctuation of the hydraulic system at a point within the ken of farmers.

The expression "deterring expropriation" seems to invite us to consider how irrigation lawbreakers can be more effectively punished.[1] It is understandable that canal managers, faced with irrigators who steal water or break the structures, should respond by demanding more powerful deterrents. That response fails, however, because it misses the deeper problem of which the lawbreaking is a symptom and because in any case the law as a mechanical barrier can be effective only when a tiny minority of the population is likely to break it. Most of the observance of rules has to be more voluntary, because the cost of enforcement when large numbers of the population comply involuntarily (through a calculus of evasion and punishment) is likely to be prohibitively high. What, then, are the conditions in which a group of people will voluntarily subscribe to a rule of restrained access to irrigation water?[2]

My context is surface irrigation systems for which public officials operate the higher levels of the distribution network and farmers take over below a certain point. Here the question becomes, What are the conditions in which *trust* by farmers in the good faith and abilities of irrigation officials can be sustained?

THE NEED FOR TRUST IN AUTHORITY

Whenever water is scarce in relation to demand, there is a rationing problem. Even in those rare canal systems in which water is sold in a market (as in the Alicante canals of southern Spain; Maass and Anderson, 1978), and where price is thus the principal means of rationing, an organization to administer and sanction the rationing is needed. In the usual situation, in which water is not priced volumetrically, the "load" on the rationing organization is heavier, and it increases as water becomes scarcer in relation to demand. More and more farmers will want to take water they are not entitled to.

The situation from the viewpoint of an individual irrigator (or small group or irrigators) can be likened to a Prisoners' Dilemma game. Each individual has a clear preference ordering of options. The first preference is for everyone else to abide by a rule of restrained access while the individual enjoys unrestrained access—while he "free-rides"; the second preference is for everyone, including himself, to follow the rule; the third preference is for no one to follow the rule—for everyone to grab what he can; and the worst outcome of all is for everyone else to grab while he follows the rule. Given that this is the order of preferences, the stable outcome (in the absence of careful institution design) is likely to be the third alternative: unrestrained access. From the more socially desirable second alternative (restrained access by all), each individual has an incentive to cheat and go for his own first preference (restrained by all except him), with the result that the aggregate situation deteriorates to the outcome of the third alternative. In other words, mutual rule-bound restraint is not necessarily a stable situation because from that position each individual can be immediately better off by cheating—provided he thinks the others will not also immediately cheat. But the third preference implies that unless water is very abundant, many farmers will get little or unreliable water supply because their own supply is a function of the unrestrained access of those higher up the distributory system. They will in turn struggle to obtain better supplies by stealing water, breaking the gates, breaching the banks, bribing the officials, and even committing murder (Maass and Anderson, 1978, 2), thus compounding the overall problem.

Many theorists of Prisoners' Dilemma have concluded that the socially desirable outcome of restrained access by all can be sustained only by the imposition by an external authority of powerful penalties against rule violation. If so, the conclusion is a counsel of despair, because in most Third World countries legal mechanisms and the authority of government are simply not powerful enough to make a sufficiently plausible threat access myriad microsituations.

But the conclusion is too strong. Prisoners' Dilemma is useful in drawing attention to the point that just because a set of individuals have a joint interest in a certain outcome does not mean that the outcome will be forthcoming. Beyond this point, however, Prisoners' Dilemma is misleading

---

[1] The views expressed here are my own and must not be attributed to the two organizations with which I am affiliated. Acknowledgments: Ron Dore, Herve Plusquellec, Richard Reidinger, Gabriel Tibor, and Ronald Ung.

[2] The same question can be asked about other common property resources, such as grazing land and trees.

for the irrigation case. It makes good sense to suppose that in many situations individual irrigators will restrain their water rule breaking *if* they are confident that others will also refrain and *if* they are confident that they will still get as much water as they are fairly entitled to (even if not as much as they would like). They will more likely refrain from cheating if they are confident that by doing so they will not be the "suckers." Where people are motivated by an "I'll restrain if you restrain" calculation, then an institution (such as an irrigation department) that convinces them that these expectations are justified can promote voluntary compliance with the rules. The reason is that the rational individual will not free-ride regardless of what others do, as the Prisoners' Dilemma game assumes. He will calculate the likelihood that his own free riding will encourage others to do so and how much their free riding will reduce the benefits that he gets from doing so. It must be remembered that the individual's first preference is to free-ride while others do not free-ride, so that he continues to get the collective benefit which their restraint produces. If that collective benefit might not be forthcoming because his free riding encourages others to do the same, it may be rational for him to comply with the rule. Free riding remains a possibility, but not an imperative (Runge, 1984; Kimber, 1981).

This argument is hypothetical. But there is a growing body of experimental evidence—admittedly about contexts rather far from what we are discussing here—which suggests that ideas about "fairness" are important factors in individuals' choices about whether to free-ride and that the strong version of the free-rider hypothesis (that individuals will voluntarily contribute very little of their resources toward the provision of a public good) is very implausible (Runge, 1984; Marwell and Ames, 1981).

Or consider the converse. Hart identifies a "syndrome of anarchy" at work under Indian canals, which is, he suggests, a major factor in their underperformance (1978). The syndrome of anarchy grows out of and reinforces a basic lack of confidence, of trust in good faith and on both sides of the irrigator–irrigation official line. The farmers lack the confidence that if they refrain from taking water out of turn (refrain from stealing it, breaking the structures, bribing the officials), they will nonetheless get water on time. The officials for their part lack the confidence that if they do work conscientiously to get the water delivered on time, farmers will refrain from rule breaking. It is a "syndrome" in that the behavior of each party to the relationship now tends to confirm the negative expectations held by the other. Each is the other's headache. (The syndrome may operate within a given village between individual farmers who behave anarchistically toward each other over water matters; or, given the capacity of some villages to organize canal-water distribution within the village [Wade, 1985c], it may operate only between village units, each village unit struggling to get more water than it is entitled to against other village units).

Breaking this syndrome has to be achieved primarily from the government side by means of a sustained demonstration of the ability to deliver reliable and expected amounts of water if the farmers do not interfere. Our question then is, How can public officials assure farmers that if they restrain their taking of irrigation water they will get the expected amounts?[3]

Part of the answer is to be found in the physical design of the system, to make the dependence of farmers on irrigation officials less critical, to make it less necessary for farmers to trust their good faith day by day. I come back to some of these physical features later. Another part of the answer is to be found in the design of the irrigation management organization.

ORGANIZATIONS AND TRUST

Political theorists generally stress two elements as preconditions of authority. First, the person given decision-making power should have some competence which makes such a division of labor sensible. Second, he should evoke trust in his good intentions—his use of power should not be seen as being predatory and self-interested but concerned with the welfare of the larger whole of which both he and his subordinates or clients are part.

Compare against these preconditions the situation under Indian canals, as seen from the farmers' perspective. The members of the immediate field staff—those who are responsible for actually opening and shutting gates, doing minor maintenance, etc.—are recruited from among landless laborers and carry little respect in rural society. The officers typically have little prior experience of canal O&M—the size of O&M divisions compared with other divisions of the irrigation department is so small that any one person normally spends most of his career on things other than canal O&M, in particular on construction (if O&M posts account for only, say, a tenth of the total number of professional posts, and if there is no career specialization, any individual can expect to spend only about a tenth of his career on O&M work). No training is available for prospective O&M managers.[4] Their competence in O&M will thus frequently be more striking by its absence than by its presence. In practice, of course, farmers will typically not be in a good position to assess competence directly; and as the judgment of competence becomes more difficult, so the trust element becomes more important. Typically, the officers have no identification with the area or the farmers they are responsible for, and they typically are rotated in and out of any one posting every fifteen to twenty months or less (Wade 1982c, 1985b). Other than at the bottom field-staff level, there is no stable core of people who are associated with a particular canal. Transport facilities are poor and the distances large, so officers are rarely seen on the canals (Hart, 1978, A-126). Such conditions are almost guaranteed to create a situation in which the legitimacy of the pub-

---

[3]Irrigation engineers in India, talking about how they try to manage water allocation, commonly stress the need to create trust: "You have to build up affection," explained one. Another remarked that "water management is 25 percent water and 75 percent soothing." The India side of my remarks in this chapter is based on detailed fieldwork carried out between 1976 and 1982, which included long periods of residence in one canal command area, as well as trips to several others.

[4]Only in the 1980s has this surprising state of affairs begun to change, and then because of pressure from foreign-aid donors (Sundar, 1984, 22).

lic officials who allocate water is always close to being questioned, whether by their own subordinates within the irrigation agency or by the farmers.

The conditions that keep competence and trust at low levels are themselves the results of three basic structural features of the organization. The first is that canal O&M is carried out by an organization whose primary function has been construction. That is why few of the professional staff members on a particular canal will have had much prior experience of O&M. It is also why they are not especially interested in O&M, because the O&M budget will be a tiny part of the overall irrigation department budget, and its allocation will be given little attention. Also, because professional reputations will be anchored firmly in construction, officers will then tend to behave while doing O&M work in the top-down hierarchical control mode that is appropriate for construction but inappropriate for O&M. The second important structural feature is the lack of connection between the budget of the irrigation department and the collection of water rates. Water rates are normally collected by a separate department, and in those few states where rates are collected by staff attached to the irrigation department, the department's budget is still entirely unrelated to what it collects. Lacking a revenue base of its own, it must depend on the government budget. The third feature is the almost complete absence of contact with, let alone coordination between, the irrigation staff and the staff of other agencies that provide important inputs into irrigation agriculture (for example, irrigation water might be released into the canal at the start of the season in complete ignorance of whether farmers are ready to use it; if there have been delays in the disbursements of credit, farmers may not have been able to buy the inputs needed to make prompt use of the water). The lines of authority run parallel, from the top of each department in the state capital right down to the lowest rank of field staff. At each level the staff of each department goes its own way.

Compare now the irrigation associations (IAs) of Japan, Taiwan, and South Korea (in South Korea they are called farmland improvement associations).[5] All three countries use a basically similar form of organization, which is a watershed-based parastatal. In South Korea and Taiwan the term "association" is misleading in that it suggests democratic control by farmers' representatives, whereas in fact there is no such mechanism of accountability. (In Taiwan the irrigators' council of each association—which in any case had fairly circumscribed powers—was abolished between 1975 and 1982.) However, each parastatal has considerable autonomy within its geographic jurisdiction.

The primary function of each parastatal is canal O&M, not construction. Construction is carried out by a separate national-level organization that undertakes the design and construction (supervision of construction carried out by private contractors) of all sizable structures in the country.

So the staff members of each IA do not have their incentives constantly tipped toward construction, nor is their behavior constantly shaped by the control mode appropriate to construction tasks. They are O&M professionals. What is more, they have their own independent revenue base: the IA itself collects water fees from farmers (so much per irrigated hectare), and this revenue meets (most of) its operating costs for staff salaries, routine maintenance, etc.[6] So the staff has a direct sense of dependence on the prosperity of farmers in the aggregate. In addition, South Korea's IAs provide some agricultural extension and land development; indeed, the same people who operate the canals provide the extension (though most of them do not much like having to do both). The ordinary extension service, organized in provincially based parastatals (one per province, which is much smaller than an Indian state), also provides extension in irrigated areas. In Taiwan the IAs do not provide extension—that is done by separate farmers' associations. The jurisdictions of the IAs and farmers' associations are not congruent, but the key point is that a stable set of officials is engaged in the same small area, some of the officials providing O&M, others providing extension, and informal coordination develops between them. In South Korea's IAs the coordination between the water-supply function and the extension function is built into the organization. In none of the three countries are the IAs involved in input supply or marketing or in other than minor construction.

A higher level (provincial and/or national) agency monitors the performance of each agency against various kinds of financial and physical targets and lays down general regulations about, for example, salary scales, staffing densities, and ratios of administrative to operational expenses. The east Asian form of irrigation association is thus quite different from the Indian pattern of a centralized irrigation department (at state level), with a chief engineer general at the top of the pyramid in the state capital and a hierarchy of regional and project offices stretching out beneath him, the same department attending to construction, investigation, design, and O&M across the entire jurisdiction of the state (which may have a population of 40 million or more).

Organizational structure is only one determinant of how organizations perform; the same structure can be activated in different ways. But one can see, just from the structure, how trust between farmers and irrigation staff and within the irrigation hierarchy itself is easier to maintain in the east Asian type of organization.[7]

Several other features of the east Asian type also help. The staff members are locals; they tend to be recruited locally and spend most of their career within the same IA. There is limited movement by irrigation staff from one IA to another. This helps promote an identification of interests between the staff and the farmers. With respect to South Korea's IAs (Wade, 1982a), the "patroller," who bicycles

[5]My statements on South Korea are based on three months of field research on irrigation organization in 1979 (Wade, 1982a); for Taiwan, on short visits in 1979 and 1983 and on Moore (1983). The east Asian form is similar to that used in Italy (Wade, 1979).

[6]The South Korea IA that I studied in detail covered about 80 percent of its recurrent costs with water charges (Wade, 1982a, 42).

[7]In the interests of brevity I hedge on the distinction between trust in relations between farmers and the agency and trust between hierarchical levels of the agency.

around a 100-to-150-ha jurisdiction twice a day opening and shutting gates, is nominated each year by the headmen of the villages within his jurisdiction. He must be a farmer himself, with land to irrigate, so that he experiences the problems firsthand. If the headmen are unsatisfied with his performance, they nominate someone else. At the top level the senior employees are mostly promotees (in South Korea and Taiwan the most senior official of each IA is appointed by the government). Virtually all the senior employees will have spent years on the project scheme before they make it to the senior positions. Moreover, the IA is not a launching pad for a career in the central government. In all these ways the eyes of the officials are kept firmly on the locality, and an identification between their own welfare and that of the farmers is further encouraged.

This identification is strengthened in still other ways. The contractual nature of the employment relation between the IA and individual staff members is obscured, or replaced by, a sense of common membership in a corporate entity which has objectives that can be shared by all members. Various methods are used to build up this corporate sense within the association itself; these include competitions between the field stations (in quality of canal maintenance, collection of water charges, volleyball, even having the staff process farmyard manure to spur farmers to do the same); once-a-week joint exercise sessions for all the staff; or weekly planning meetings for all field-station chiefs. Most important, all the staff (other than the patrollers) are paid on rising seniority scales, so that pay is not closely tied to the job they do; all the staff expect to have lifetime employment; and the lower ranks in each IA identify more closely with their IA than with lower ranks in other IAs, which helps avoid the ingrained conflictualism found between lower and higher staff in Indian irrigation departments and which erodes any sense of common purpose and pride in work.

Staff involvement with farmers is promoted by such devices as a monthly newsletter and, more important, by the constant presence of irrigation staff along the canals. This last is a function of a particular method of supervising the patrollers, whose responsibilities have already been noted. Every staff member, even the clerks (males only), has the responsibility of supervising one patroller in addition to his other duties. At least once every two or three days he must go to his patroller's beat and make sure that he is on the job. He is provided with a small motorcycle for the purpose. The supervisors are expected to, and in any case are inclined to, stop and chat with farmers whom they pass along the canals. The intensity of this sort of local, dyadic contact helps make up for the paucity of more formal channels of communication between farmers and staff, which is in turn an expression of the authoritarian character of the South Korean political regime (Wade, 1983).

Thus, the IA structure encourages a local identification. Local identification is important because it gives both sides a set of shared experiences. This directly assists a sense of mutual obligation between them and also provides a basis for a shared set of beliefs according to which the existing order is fair and just and every betrayal is perverse and unjust—including betrayal of the irrigation agency's rules.

This is a much more cost-effective method of avoiding free-rider problems than relying on a calculus of punishment.

At the same time, pressures and incentives bear down on individual staffers, and on the IA in general, to perform. For individual staffers, promotion is decided by means of a complex formula. The formula includes, very importantly, seniority (length of service) but also includes a weighting for performance in the regular training sessions organized by a national training agency, and for superiors' judgments on such things as diligence, willingness to take responsibility, and loyalty (Wade, 1982a, 112). The performance is monitored from above, within the Ministry of Agriculture, by means of various criteria, such as staffing density, revenue collection, and ratio of expenditure on administration and expenditure of maintenance. In addition, each IA can expect to have a team arrive from the ministry at least once a year to make an inspection that may last several days and includes not only the financial accounts but also the state of the physical structures. Prizes are awarded to IAs for good performance.

I would not wish to be seen as starry-eyed about the IA form as it works in South Korea. Indeed I have elsewhere argued that canal operation in South Korea is not very proficient for the simple reason that land being normally more limited than water, good supplies can be delivered to the crop (which is rice) without any degree of finetuning of supply to demand (Wade, 1982a, 26, 58). I think it is clear, however, that the IA structure does offer big advantages over the irrigation department structure in terms of its capacity to include O&M officials to do their jobs conscientiously and to evoke in farmers a countertrust in authority.

PHYSICAL STRUCTURES AND TRUST

The need for trust, and the likelihood that it will be forthcoming, is also related to the physical structure. The larger the system, the more difficult it is for individual farmers to understand how it operates and the constraints under which the canal staff work. The more difficult it is for the farmers to understand, the more crucial is the trust element (as opposed to the element of understanding) in the acceptance of authority. And the more than active act of faith is needed, so the more those given authority must be seen to be using their power in a benevolent, not a predatory, way, in good faith for the common good, not merely for personal aggrandizement.

Compare now the typical Indian canal (Wade, 1982b, 1985a). It has a command area of 50,000 to 100,000 ha or more. It has a single source of water and no intermediate storage. The water may take a week or more to travel unimpeded from head to tail. From the viewpoint of the farmer the rest of the system outside his immediate locality is a mystery. He simply has to take the word of the irrigation staff about the overall water-supply situation. He and his village neighbors have no stock of water that they can call their own. Their "own" water begins at the outlet, but significantly more water may be available in the distributary on the other side of the outlet. They can go at night with a spade, take water against the rules, and leave little trace of their action behind.

Moroever, the design of the typical Indian system itself makes it necessary that irrigators have a high degree of trust in the irrigation officials if they are to refrain from grabbing. The typical Indian system is *not* the kind found in the northwest (Punjab and Haryana), with its ungated outlets and rotational delivery rule in the main system (Malhotra, 1982; Reidinger, 1974). The typical design uses (more or less) continuous flow in the main system and gated outlets, with few cross regulators. Here, water levels in the main system vary greatly, and to maintain constant discharges through the outlets, it is essential that an irrigation official run around raising and lowering his gates; but the raising or lowering of one gate typically sets up changes in upstream levels, requiring further gates changes there. In theory, then, the system contains a high level of water-control capacity, despite the lack of cross regulators. In practice, of course, the irrigation staff rarely shows the required devotion to duty and technical skills needed to carry out the required routines, and the unadjusted gates discharge fluctuating amounts. But farmers usually want constant, not fluctuating, discharges and take whatever defensive action is needed to smooth out the fluctuations—perhaps by adjusting the gates themselves in line with their local interest. The failures of the irrigation staff force the farmers to compensate, but in ways that make the situation worse overall (Wade, 1982c).

Compare the east Asian canals. They are typically much smaller (few canal systems in South Korea command over 10,000 ha, while Taiwan has a few of more than 50,000 ha but fewer than 100,000 ha). The larger ones are generally linked agglomerations of smaller subsystems, each with its own water supply but capable of feeding into one or more of the other networks. Thus it is less likely that the whole area will run short of water at any one time, and lags in the adjustment of supply to demand are shorter than in areas where water can be brought from only one source. The South Korean canals, like the typical Indian canals, also require frequent adjustment of gates to maintain a constant discharge (I am not sure how the Japanese and Taiwanese compare on this score). But because the systems are smaller, the lags in the adjustment for supply to demand are shorter, and because the wider political structure makes for a more disciplined administration at field level, this particular design requirement does not have the trust-eroding consequences that it has in India.

So the design of the Indian canals requires that the farmers have more trust in public officials than is needed in east Asia, while in Indian conditions that trust is more difficult to create and sustain.

IMPLICATIONS

Large-scale systems are a given in Indian conditions. But within that constraint performance might be improved by changes in both the organizational and the physical design. The guiding principal of these changes should be both to reduce the need for farmers to trust the staff and to increase the likelihood that the needed trust will be forthcoming. Changes that meet this criterion have a chance of breaking the damaging "syndrome of anarchy."

The basic way to reduce the need for trust is to reduce the farmers' dependence on the allocation decisions of officials. For this, two conditions are necessary: first, an "inventory" of water, so as to buffer fluctuations in water supply and water demand; second, a clear hand-over point where the officials' jurisdiction ends and the farmers' jurisdiction begins. One design feature that seems promising from this point of view is the breakpoint reservoir. The breakpoint reservoir does not have to be between the outlet and the farmers' fields; it can be at a higher level of the system, serving more than one outlet or village. The important point is that it be at a low enough level, first, to permit water to reach all the fields within a few hours; second, to allow farmers to see the stock of water that is "theirs"; and, third, to ensure that they have a large (legitimate) hand in how it is allocated. The breakpoint reservoir also has major drawbacks, however; water losses are often very high (efficiency very low); land acquisition commonly is difficult and costly; siltation may be high; there are health hazards; and the storage capacity—and so the ability to buffer—is typically small. It is interesting that in Taiwan the same Japanese engineers who put breakpoint reservoirs into the Taoyuan system during the colonial period did not put them into most of the other systems on the island, partly because the flatter slopes of most of the other systems made breakpoint reservoirs much more expensive. In practice, more use of within-canal storage can substitute for a breakpoint reservoir in terms of the "inventory" condition, though within-canal storage does not provide for such a clear hand-over point between officials' and farmers' jurisdictions.

Thus, there are trade-offs. One wants to aim at a physical design that will help create an organizational distinction between the task of water conveyance, which is properly the concern of experts in hydraulics, and that of irrigation, which should be the concern primarily of agricultural experts. The design should permit the water-supply agency to deliver plugs of water according to simple, transparent rules.

Simple operating procedures help make the system more transparent; the more transparent the system and its operating principles, the more easily farmers can judge the competence of the irrigation staff and so, by hypothesis, the less needed is trust in their good faith for the legitimacy of their allocation decisions to be respected.[8]

Also, the simpler and more transparent the operating pro-

---

[8] The argument for simplicity of operating procedures means that the demand to which water supply is to be adjusted must be considered at a relatively high level of aggregation, rather than at the level of the individual needs of each person or microlocation served by the system. One reason is the limited information-processing capability of most bureaucracies (and the unreliability of computer technology in most rural Third World conditions). This applies even without the second reason, which greatly reinforces the point. Where high margins of discretionary control over water allocation are available to irrigation officials and where water is scarce, corruption is likely and may reach the point where irrigation officials have an incentive to act so as to reduce farmers' confidence in the reliability of water supply because this enhances the protection money the officials are able to extract from particular groups of farmers in return for increasing their confidence about their own supplies (Wade, 1982c).

cedures, the easier it is for the officials to be competent at performing them, and the more farmers will acknowledge their legitimacy. This competence-legitimacy causation can then be reinforced by the more powerful trust-legitimacy causation if the irrigation agency is structured in the IA rather than irrigation department form, for where the water-supply agency is structured along IA lines, it is more likely that the behavior of staff members will be trustworthy, because of their (1) O&M orientation, (2) sense of dependence on farmers' prosperity, (3) local identification, supplemented by (4) the sorts of promotion incentives, and (5) monitoring pressures described earlier.

Of course, it is easier to introduce more inventory capacity and simpler operating procedures than it is to switch from a centralized irrigation department to an IA form. To a degree the breakpoint reservoir could be a substitute for that more difficult organizational change, since the centralized irrigation department could continue to run the main system, as now, but down only as far as the breakpoint. If the breakpoint came relatively high in the system, one could imagine an IA, covering the whole command area or major portions of it, taking over responsibility for water allocation from the breakpoint reservoirs down to small outlets; or, if the breakpoint came lower, farmers might do it themselves in less organized ways.

But even without going as far as the widespread use of breakpoint reservoirs and an IA form, valuable but less far-reaching changes in the same direction could be made and, in a few places in India, are being made. In the state of Maharashtra, for example, responsibility for the operation and maintenance of tertiary distributaries has been taken from the irrigation department and given to new project-specific command-area development agencies, which combine a staff of irrigation engineers with agricultural specialists. But the command-area development agency is still vulnerable to one of the main problems, which is rapid transfer of officials in and out of posts, with trust-eroding consequences.

Another experiment, in Gujarat, India, which is promising in terms of the argument made here, involves the sale of bulk amounts of water to a tertiary distributary—to all the farmers under that distributary as a unit. The farmers themselves then organize the distribution of water and the collection of the fee. This experience deserves particular study, because it seems to provide a method of gaining many of the benefits of the breakpoint reservoir without the costs (in land removed from production, for example). It must be noted, however, that the area of the tertiary is only about 162 ha and the crop is sugarcane, a high-value, low-risk crop. Extension of the idea to larger units and other crops may be more difficult.

Similarly, the type of canal design used in France and Morocco—which combines hydromechanical automatic gates plus constant-discharge modules—looks promising from a trust perspective, primarily because it greatly reduces the dependence of farmers on the irrigation staff and greatly simplifies what the irrigation staff has to do. But there are problems with this technology, especially its cost, dependence on reliable supply at the head, rigorous design and construction standards, etc.[9] Again, there are trade-offs.

CONCLUSIONS

I have taken the question of how to deter expropriation—how to stop farmers from stealing or bribing for more water than they are entitled to under some general rule of water delivery—back to the question of how to enhance the legitimacy of the authority of irrigation staff. Given that factors like the degree of water scarcity are constant, legitimacy depends on farmers' judgment of how competent the staff is and how much they trust its good intentions. Given that competence is often difficult to judge (especially when the system is large and the farmers' knowledge of it is confined to the locality), trust becomes the crucial factor. If the "syndrome of anarchy" under the canals is to be reduced, farmers must be confident that if they restrain their own individual (or small-group) access to water they will still get enough water, or at least that if they do not get enough water there are good reasons beyond the control of the staff, and the shortage is being shared "fairly." I have then suggested first, that the amount of trust or confidence needed can be reduced by features of the physical design, such as punctuating the hydraulic system at some point within the ken of farmers, and, second, that features of the organizational structure can make it more likely that trust-evoking behavior by the irrigation staff will be forthcoming. I have emphasized the importance of separating the O&M organization from the construction organization; providing the O&M organization with a revenue base to ensure some link between what is collected in water rates and what the organization can spend; and shaping the O&M organization into a geographically circumscribed parastatal.

What I have not talked about are management techniques—specific techniques for monitoring and controlling the performance of irrigation staff. Management techniques, I suggest, are an important but auxiliary issue that can too easily occlude the more basic issues addressed here. Or, in the words of a noted Indian irrigation specialist:

> Management is based on the premise that things can be done better, which in turn means that one wants better performance. In a socio-political situation where what is legitimate is what one can get away with, can there be any concern about public system performance? And if there is no desire to manage, what can management techniques do? "In the land of nudists, what can a washerman do?" [Sundar, 1984, 22]

REFERENCES

Hart, H. 1978. Anarchy, paternalism, or collective responsibility under the canals? *Economic and Political Weekly* (Bombay) 13 (51–52). Review of agriculture.

[9]Cost comparisons between this type of technology and the more conventional type are exceedingly difficult to make. The gates and modules are said to be about twice as expensive as conventional ones; but if, as I have heard said, this adds only another 5 to 10 percent to total cost, compared to the costs of the same canal with conventional technology, this might be offset by the extra benefits of more reliable water supply.

Kimber, R. 1981. Collective action and the fallacy of the liberal fallacy. *World Politics* 33:178–96.

Maass, A., and R. Anderson. 1978. And the desert shall rejoice: Conflict, growth, and justice in arid environments. Cambridge, Mass.: MIT Press.

Malhotra, S. 1982. The Warabandi system and its infrastructure. Publication No. 157. New Delhi: Central Board of Irrigation and Power.

Marwell, G., and R. Ames. 1981. Economists free ride, does anyone else? Experiments in the provision of public goods IV. *Journal of Public Economics* 15:295–310.

Moore, M. 1983. Irrigation management in Taiwan. Mimeographed. Sussex, England: Institute of Development Studies, University of Sussex.

Reidinger, R. 1974. Institutional rationing of canal water in northern India: conflict between traditional patterns and modern needs. *Economic Development and Cultural Change* 23 (1).

Runge, C. F. 1984. Institutions and the free rider: the assurance problem in collective action. *Journal of Politics* 46:154–81.

Sundar, A. 1984. Modern techniques for management of irrigation systems: what can they do in the absence of commitment to manage? *Wamana* (Indian Institute of Management, Bangalore), July.

Wade, R. H. 1979. Collective responsibility in the construction and operation of irrigation canals: The case of Italy. *Economic and Political Weekly* (Bombay) 14 (51–52): 22–29. Review of agriculture.

———. 1982a. Irrigation and agricultural policies in South Korea. Boulder, Colo.: Westview Press.

———. 1982b. Employment, water control and irrigation institutions: South India and South Korea. Working paper, Asian Regional Employment Program, ILO, and IDS discussion paper No. 182. Sussex, England. Institute of Development Studies, University of Sussex.

———. 1982c. The system of political and administrative corruption: canal irrigation in South India. *Journal of Development Studies* 18 (3).

———. 1983. South Korea's agricultural development: the myth of the passive state. *Pacific Viewpoint* 24 (1).

———. 1985a. On the sociology of irrigation statistics: how do we know the truth about canal performance? *Agricultural Administration* 19 (2).

———. 1985b. The market for public office: why the Indian state is not better at development. *World Development* 13 (4).

———. 1985. Common property resource management in South Indian villages. Discussion paper ARu 36. Washington, D.C.: Agriculture and Rural Development Department, World Bank.

29. WATER POLICY AND LAW: THE MISSING LINK IN FOOD PRODUCTION?

George E. Radosevich, Agricultural and Natural Resource Economics, Colorado State University, Fort Collins, Colorado

ABSTRACT

Increasing food and fiber production has been a major objective of many nations since the beginning of time, but the key components which contribute to reaching this objective have varied. Most often the solution consists of employing appropriate technologies. What is frequently overlooked is the institutional framework—the role of water policy, law, and organizations and the process of implementation. The lack or inadequacy of the elements within this framework often constrains or prevents development. Three key legal questions emerge: Who owns the water? How is it allocated and distributed? and What means are available to avoid or resolve conflicts? Relevant policies, laws, and regulations address these central questions. In addition, the process of implementation within the framework often lacks the capability of monitoring and evaluating the process and results and, through appropriate feedback, either continuing or adjusting the process and its components to achieve the desired objectives. The value of this "missing link" has received global recognition in the last decade but needs to be carefully analyzed and properly employed.

All law is a response to social needs, and because of the essential similarity of those needs in human society, the various legal systems provide comparable solutions to similar problems.
—Badr, 1985

THE INSTITUTIONAL FRAMEWORK

Fifteen years ago, suggesting that part of the solution to managing water and increasing food production in many countries lay in the institutional arena was like proposing a cure for an unknown disease. Few nations really gave more than casual recognition to the role of laws in the development and utilization of natural resources. Policy and law were considered a political or legal drafting exercise even though the results often constrained the operation of implementing agencies. This is not to say that significant changes in water and other resource laws did not take place before or during that time. In fact, it appears that historically, legal interventions for water development and control have been cyclical. Many water codes and special laws were adopted during the 1860s, in the 1900s, and from 1950 through the 1960s. Generally these changes were brought about as a result of crises or when legal and organizational impediments were obvious.

In the last ten years, however, we have realized that the old geometry rule—that the sum is equal to the total of its parts—applies universally to water management and the achievements of national goals and objectives. The real question or issue is, When and how do we examine all of the "parts"? This chapter addresses the issue of devising legal approaches to facilitate achievement of the national goal of increasing food production, irrigated agriculture, or, rhetorically, Is water law the missing link in the chain of food production?

At the outset it is important to have a basic understanding of a few key terms. Throughout this chapter the term "institutional framework" refers to policies, laws, rules and regulations, government and nongovernment organizations, and the interactive process of implementation that results in the allocation, distribution, utilization, management, and control of water resources. "Water law" refers to the policies, rules, and regulations pertaining to the development, use, conservation, and management of water.

The evolution of the institutional framework in any country is a product of many factors or components. The first factor is the general legal system of the country. Fig. 1 identifies ten legal systems with distinct historical, national, or political roots. David and Brieley (1968, 14–20) have condensed this classification into four general families of law. They point out that each political society has its own law and that in fact several systems may coexist within the same state. Because of this grouping they prefer to use the term "legal families" instead of "legal systems." The four families are (1) the Romano-Germanic family, (2) the common-law family, (3) the family of socialist laws, and (4) the philosophical, religious, and traditional laws.

One element of law unique to other disciplines is that of "jurisdiction," or venue, of the subject matter. A law is limited to the territorial or administrative boundary and its enacting body. Thus, water laws generally do not follow hydrologic boundaries. Primary jurisdiction over water may be a national or subnational (state or provincial) issue, creating problems of administration between regions or political subdivisions where lack of uniformity in the law or rate of development exists.

Focusing directly upon water laws, a factor that significantly influences the type of system of any particular country or segment thereof is the geoclimatic conditions. Humid areas tend to produce laws that provide greater emphasis on control of drainage, floods, and water quality. Arid areas tend to emphasize allocation distribution and management of water put to many and often conflicting uses. Even in areas of what might be considered excessive rainfall, recent trends indicate that legal interventions are necessary when overall demands or conflicts between uses occur, particularly during dry seasons.

The third component is the state of national development. The technical, socioeconomic, and institutional status of a

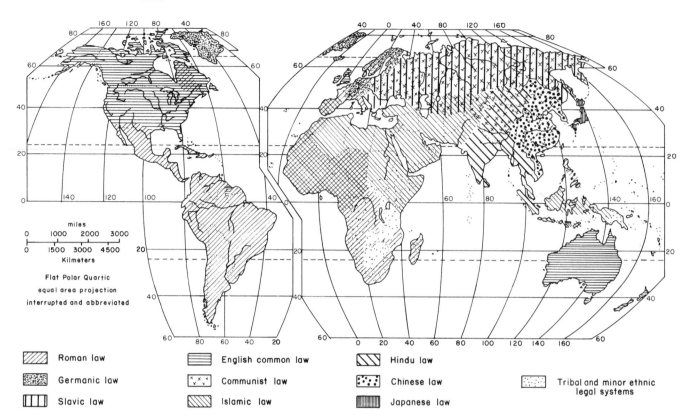

Roman law   English common law   Hindu law

Germanic law   Communist law   Chinese law   Tribal and minor ethnic legal systems

Slavic law   Islamic law   Japanese law

Fig. 1. In the major legal systems of the world there has been considerable blending of legal tradition. This blending is partly because European powers established overseas empires. (In part, after John H. Wigmore, "A Map of the World's Law," *Geographical Review*, 19 (1929): 114–20).

country, or region within a country, tends to regress, remain static, or progress depending on the level of national development. Influencing this state of development is the historical role of irrigated agriculture in the country, as well as the potential for reclamation of new lands and improvement of existing systems.

The demand for water, even in humid environments vis-à-vis the spatial and temporal availability of the source and supply, is another major component affecting the type and form of water law system. Conflicts and complementarity may exist or be created as a result of demands. Some demands are natural: maintenance of aquatic estuarian and environmental conditions and intrusion and coastal zone management. Other demands are man-made: for domestic and municipal supply, irrigated agriculture, industry, power, transportation, fisheries, and recreation. These too may exacerbate problems in the natural environment by requiring steps to prevent saline intrusion and to establish programs of coastal zone management.

In 1975 the International Conference on Global Water Law Systems was held in Valencia, Spain. I was the principal investigator and coorganizer of the conference, which had as its major objective the identification of major water law systems, their attributes, and the role they play in developing a nation's water resources. A number of major legal systems, as well as their paths of influence in various parts of the world, were identified. These systems and their influ-

Fig. 2. A descriptive map of major legal systems and their paths of influence in the world. (After Radosevich, 1976).

ence are illustrated in Fig. 2. The major systems include those of the Soviets, two Chinese, Romans, Islam, the British, the Spanish, and the United States. A number of other unique systems were also identified, such as the system of water control in Israel and the Hindu-Bali systems in Bali, Indonesia. These legal sytems can be classified as customary, traditional, or modern (Radosevich, 1976). In any given country the water laws may consist of a general law or code and/or specific laws addressing a particular hydrologic characteristic, such as groundwater or surface water or some aspect of management and regulation.

All national water laws can be classified into one of two categories: national or federated. Under a national system the central government exercises primary jurisdiction, generally through a basic national water law such as exists in Spain, Mexico, and Egypt. Under a federated system jurisdiction over water is primarily a provincial or state matter, the central government retaining authority over such matters as interprovincial or interstate allocation, commerce or navigational uses of water, and water quality control, as found in the United States, Argentina, and India. Under the water law system written laws or the customary bodies of law are often referred to as the "substantive provisions," and the water and related organizations of both government and nongovernment types are referred to as the "structural components." The structural components generally consist of a lead government agency with responsibility over water, or particularly irrigation uses; examples are the Royal Irrigation Department of Thailand and the Irrigation Department in the Punjab Province of Pakistan. A hierarchy of offices exists from the central or provincial level to the local level. Quasi-government agencies such as river basin authorities, may also exist.

Many countries also have various types of nongovernment water-user associations (Radosevich, 1977). They range from informal to formal entities with simple to complex organizational structures. Their primary purposes are the distribution of water within the command area beyond the government outlet and the operation and maintenance of this distribution network. They often serve as the communication link between government and water users and are sometimes instrumental in resolving disputes and increasing water use efficiency.

EVOLUTION OF A PROBLEM: INSTITUTIONAL INADEQUACY

In theory, if not in fact, laws should not remain static. Laws need to be dynamic and progressive and to strive toward flexibility in meeting societies' needs and desires. Unfortunately, this is not always the case, particularly with water law. Technology, population increases and shifts, and the range of demands are changing too rapidly to remain constrained by concepts and interventions that were adequate when adopted but are limiting to the contemporary scene. Whether the law serves as a constraint or a facilitator, particularly in increasing food production from irrigated agriculture, depends on whether the action resulting from implementing the codes and regulations is repressive or responsive to needs of the water users, as illustrated in Fig. 3. It has been observed in many situations that the law tends to overregulate or otherwise repress the creativity of water users to improve their use of the resource and hence their production. This condition creates a serious problem, which unfortunately may not be immediately detected as an institutional constraint. And where the law is a recognized limitation, the agency charged with carrying it out may feel that it is easier to deal with the situation at the local level than to try to get the law changed. For example, in Pakistan

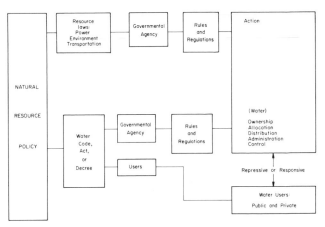

Fig. 3. Water law as a constraint to or facilitator of development. (After Radosevich, 1983).

the Punjab Canal and Drainage Act of 1863 prohibits the transfer of water among farmers. Most of the canal officers knew the rule but not its origin and do not question its validity. In field interviews it was found that farmers also knew the rule but quite frequently traded water turns to their advantage and hoped that their actions would not be detected.

Implementation constraints also often occur as a result of the difference between "responsibility" and "authority." In some situations canal officers are authorized but not required to perform certain tasks. In others they are responsible for certain tasks but lack the authority to carry them out fully. Such institutional inadequacy leads to mediocre conduct by government officers and personnel at all levels and a disrespect or mistrust of the system by the water users.

Another organizational constraint that occurs over time is the "functional" versus "objective" focus and orientation of the responsible agency. In most countries the agency mainly responsible for providing water to irrigated agriculture exists to perform the functions of construction, operation, and maintenance of the storage, delivery, and distribution system. Often greater emphasis is placed on constructing projects than on operation and maintenance. Further, operation and maintenance is usually a mechanical process of tasks to be performed without a clear explanation or application of the relationship between efficiency in carrying out these tasks and increased crop production. Examination of operation and maintenance activities in several countries clearly indicates that field personnel do not consider their role as significant in meeting national or water user objectives. Consequently, it can be readily understood why farmers are recalcitrant in paying water charges in those irrigation systems that fail to function properly by delivering timely and adequate quantities of water.

A related institutional inadequacy is the historical bias against water users found in many irrigation departments. Farmers are often viewed as ignorant and dependent on the government to provide water and other solutions to their problems. One can observe in many countries, however, that farmers' problems may begin when the government intervenes. Many examples exist in which farmers have demonstrated their ingenuity and independence in developing and operating fairly efficient irrigation systems, such as those in Bali; northeast Thailand; and Valencia, Spain. In most instances the irrigators have organized into some form of water user association. Study of these systems clearly indicates that farmers are in fact very competent and receptive to introducing new technologies where their benefits are increased and risks minimized. Research also demonstrates that a successful form of water organization in one part of a country or in a country cannot be directly transplanted elsewhere with the same results.

IMPROVING THE INSTITUTIONAL FRAMEWORK: DESIGNING LEGAL SYSTEMS

On several occasions I have been asked by a country or donor agency to send copies of water laws, policy statements, organizational diagrams, or rules on some particular aspect to be used as a solution to some problem or goal. On each occasion it became apparent after a brief inquiry that the answer could not be found in the requested materials. Recently I was asked to send a set of water quality standards to a Latin-American country. In this instance the water quality concern was not what is typically found in the Clean Water Act or the stream and drainage standards set out in regulations but was related to watershed management and erosion control. A legal solution in one country cannot be replicated as a solution in another.

Nor is the formulation of policies, laws, and implementation of rules the exclusive jurisdiction of lawyers, any more than is the designing of irrigation systems the jurisdiction of the engineer to the exclusion of local landowners and water users. In every situation some basic laws and procedures must be taken into account, even if they are customary and of only local significance. Formulating policies, laws, rules, and organizational structures is an interdisciplinary activity requiring a high degree of cooperation and coordination among officials in various departments and specialists in various fields. It is important to have an understanding of the hydrologic situation in the country, that is, the water supply and its sources, and temporal and spatial availability; the current use and systems of allocation and distributions; organizations and their areas of responsibility; and national and subnational goals and objectives. In the process of evaluating the institutional setting, the viewpoints of both water administrators and water users should be examined and taken into account. It is important to assess the direction, the objectives of the government, and the motives and capabilities of the major water agencies, particularly the agency responsible for irrigation development. Carruthers and Stoner (1982) note that when a legal framework for water management is being developed, no matter how well intentioned the legal intervention for public control may be, the framers should not overlook the inefficiency and cost of imposing more responsibility on an already overburdened bureacratic adminstrative process. Too often the panacea is thought to be simply delegating the responsibility to the irrigation department without considering its capacity for carrying out the additional assignment. Very

often the organization's constraint comes not from within but from the budget and personnel department's approval of needed resources.

For a water law specialist three basic and initial questions must be answered: (1) Who owns the water? (2) How is it to be allocated, distributed, and managed? (3) How does the law avoid or resolve disputes? To answer these questions, a thorough analysis must be made of existing water laws; related legislation, decrees, and orders; development plans and policy statements adopted by the government; and policies, rules, and regulations adopted by the water, agricultural, and other relevant agencies. Recommendations may include new or amended policies, laws, or codes and/or organizational additions or changes, as well as a blueprint for implementation outlining alternate courses of action, strategy, and schedule.

As a general rule, proposals for legal and organizational changes must take cognizance of the natural system. In its study on institutional constraints on alternative water for energy, the John Muir Institute (1980) described the interface between the natural and legal systems. Fig. 4 illustrates this relationship and notes that the legal system ranges from a segmented to an integrated treatment. The integrated treatment should also include an umbrella act, which may be described as a general water resources policy and management act, that sets out guidelines for communication, cooperation, and coordination by all government agencies charged with administrative aspects—responsibility for or authority over water resources. This act usually serves as the organic act for a national water resources council and provides the purposes, functions, and structural base for its implementation.

An analytical approach to formulating water laws is suggested, one that allows the draftsman to identify what exists compared with what may be necessary or desirable in the areas of (1) basic policy, (2) substantive provision, and (3) organizational structures. Fig. 5 illustrates this approach. In the figure the boldface inner squares represent the nonstructural components, and the outer squares represent the structural components. A missing link or potential problem area can be identified in a comparison of what exists with the results that are expected, needed, or desired. For example, one might find a lack of well-defined goals and objectives to which established policies might relate, or the failure to relate the policies, laws, and rules to the objectives. To assist those working in this area, I have prepared an extensive bibliography of legal material on drafting water laws, water law in general, and laws in select countries (Radosevich, 1985). It includes references to laws for surface water and groundwater allocation, distribution, administration, and enforcement, as well as provisions for conjunctive use of surface and groundwater, water quality legislation; integration of water quantity and quality control; special water control problems; river basin management; and interstate and international allocations, transfers, and sharing agreements.

The real focus of this chapter, however, is the key ingredient to a successful national program of developing and managing water resources for increased food production

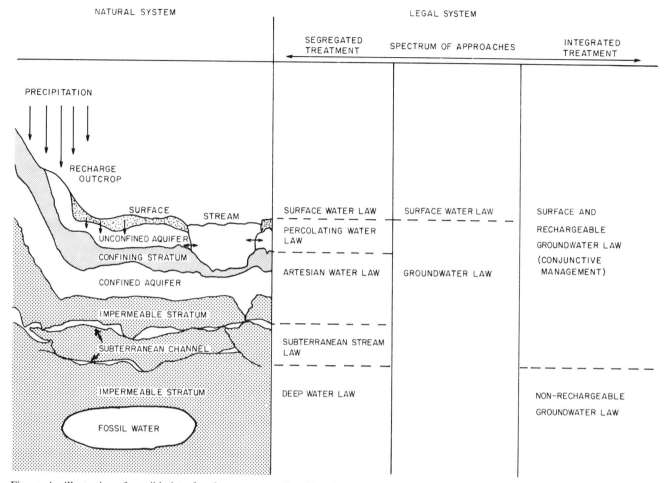

Fig. 4. An illustration of possible interface between natural and legal systems related to water.

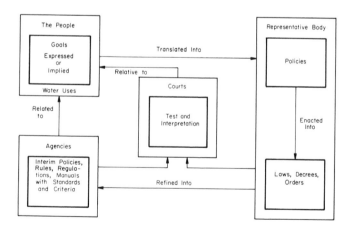

Fig. 5. The flow of information and action in the formulation of water law. (After Radosevich, 1985).

from irrigated agriculture. That ingredient is the body of water resources policy at the national and/or provincial state and basin levels. This is considered the key ingredient because what flows to and from policy is what should be accomplished in the process of managing the resource. Re-

peatedly in postproject reviews (sometimes cynically referred to as "postmortem evaluations"), the basic question is, Why did the project or program fail to reach its objectives?" A host of excuses can be identified, but in the "casket case" these reasons are not particularly satisfying. A close analysis frequently reveals a lack of guidelines by which to measure progress, guidelines which should have been established, at least in skeletal form, as policies.

Three common problems related to water policies have been identified. The first is when there are no policies at all. The second is that even when general development and water policies do exist they are not transmitted down the hierarchy to the local level. The third is that existing water policies are not implementable because they are vague or are laced with interagency constraints. For an understanding of the role of policy and its implementation a number of key questions must be asked: What is a water policy? Who makes water policy? Where is water policy located? What is the purpose of this policy?

Simply stated, water policy sets the framework for administration of the resource. In most countries it is readily understood that policies serve as guidelines for the nation (people), and particularly are the implementing agencies.

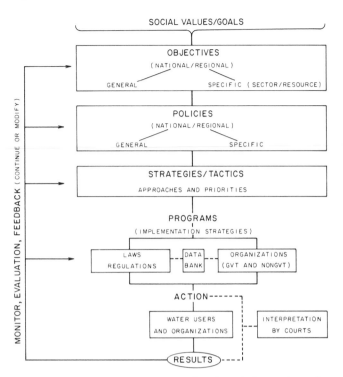

Fig. 6. National water resources policy formulation: a dynamic implementation process based on management by results. (After Radosevich and Vlachos, 1985).

One major distinction exists between policies and laws. The former are often made by the political process and found in such documents as five-year plans and as preambles to legislation or codes. Policies may change periodically with administrations, or new directions may be adopted by the government, whereas laws often remain the written and referenced authority for actions, interventions, or sanctions. The "emphasis" of implementation of the laws shift with the adoption of new guidelines.

The thrust of the argument for the role of policies in implementing a sound and successful water development and management program is best the process of management by results (MBR), not management by objectives. This places the tracking system on what is done, not what is planned. Fig. 6 identifies the key institutional elements and processes and serves as a benchmark for evaluating operational systems to identify problem areas and viable alternatives in the context of a particular nation. These elements consist of describing national and regional objectives in both general and specific categories based on social values and goals. The general objectives reflect societal goals in a comprehensive fashion, usually followed by specific objectives in vital areas of concern, such as agricultural production, rural power, navigation, industrial development, and environmental concerns.

Policies are written declarations of intent to carry out the goals and objectives and most often move from the general to the specific. For example, a general policy might be to increase national food production. A specific water policy would be directed toward increasing or improving irrigated agriculture, improving inland waterways to provide a transportation network for produce from rural to urban areas, or conjunctively developing and utilizing surface and ground water. These policies serve as guidelines not only for the implementing agencies but also for those affected by the programs and processes of government, such as the water user associations and cooperatives, and other elements of the private sector, such as local manufacturing enterprises. It is important that this component be written with clarity and commitment by the government. Implementation strategies and tactics based on these policies and the approaches and priorities to be employed need to be developed at the highest administrative level. Very often the aforementioned elements are difficult to identify. Most countries begin the process of water management with laws, regulations, and organizations. It may simplify the process, but it is not particularly advantageous to the nations, government agencies, or water users. In the United States, for example, questions have recently been raised about the adequacy of or need for a national water policy. Cordova (1982) wrote a series of articles on analyzing state water policy as it may affect the use and future development of water in the western United States.

Implementation through the operation of the law and the activities of the government causes an action on the water users and organizations, producing results that should relate back to the objectives and policies. On occasion the action and/or the results may be questioned through judicial or administrative interpretations.

It was previously stated that the institutional framework should be a dynamic process. To ensure that the process is dynamic and responsive to changing conditions, the action and results should be monitored and evaluated, and, depending on the results, a determination should be made whether the various components of the implementation process should be continued or modified. This is the dynamic process of MBR described by Seckler and Nobe (1983) as it applies generally to developing economics and by Fairchild and Nobe (1985) in a specific water management project in Pakistan. Fig. 6 is the macroapplication of both the role of policy and MBR in national water management.

A final element that is needed to achieve the desired results is accurate data upon which to base decisions. A data-bank and information-handling system is critical to responsible agency actions. In addition to conventional data-gathering techniques, the use of remote sensing and satellite imagery both for transmitting data through data-collection platforms (DCP), such as the system used by the U.S. Geological Survey and the State of Colorado, and for verifying and validating data enhances the decision-making capability of government officials. Satellite information has been instrumental in coping with drought problems in Africa (Edlin, 1985).

CONCLUSIONS

Experience gained in many countries and over many years of water resources research has shown that a good institutional arrangement for water resources policy and the basis for implementation is one that (1) ultimately facilitates social choice; (2) reflects in some reasonable way "political efficacy"; (3) facilitates decisions based on an understanding of the far-reaching consequences of a mix of social values and an expanded time horizon; (4) recognizes a decision-making process that takes into account the preferences and interests of those affected by the particular policy decisions; (5) produces decisions that are accepted as legitimate and are also the result of a balance between what is desirable and what is acceptable; and (6) places some constraints on the losses or restrictions that it imposes on individuals and on the cost required for its implementation. Further, a good institutional arrangement recognizes that to have a plan or program there must be a policy and that to have a policy there must be a reason. When the reason is vague or differs from desired goals and objectives, the results tend to be unsatisfactory. In essence, the water law system should facilitate rather than constrain change or improvement.

In many countries, and in fact in many of the United States, water policies and laws either do not exist or are antiquated, inadequate, or virtually unknown by field personnel. This missing link has no doubt cost millions of dollars in crop production and has often contributed to the mismanagement of national and donor funds. Heger (1972) and Howard (1976) have explored the role of law as an instrument or resource of development. In this regard, then, law, properly employed and enforced, becomes not the single solution to improving water use for increased food production but an essential ingredient of efficient and effective management.

REFERENCES

Badr, Gamal M. 1985. Arbitrations in the Sharia law. *U.S.–Arab Commerce,* January–February.

Carruthers, Jan, and Roy Stoner. 1982. What water management needs: A legal framework in the public interest. *CERES* (September–October): 15–18.

Cordova, Kathy. 1982. Analyzing your state water policy. *Irrigation Age.* (May–June), (July–August), (September–October).

David, Rene, and John E. C. Brieley. 1968. Major legal systems in the world today. New York: Free Press.

Edlin, John. 1985. Satellite helps Africa cope with drought. *Los Angeles Times.* May 12.

Fairchild, Warren, and K. C. Nobe. 1985. Improving management of irrigation projects in developing countries: Translating theory into practice. *In* Current issues in and approaches to irrigation water management in developing countries. Boulder, Colo.: Westview Press.

Heger, Michael L. 1972. The role of lawyers in developing countries. *American Bar Association Journal,* January.

Howard, John B. 1976. Law as a resource of development. *International Development Levian* 18 (1): 1–15.

John Muir Institute. 1980. Institutional constraints on alternative water for energy. Springfield, Va.: National Technical Information Service.

National Water Resources Council. 1982. Philippines Water Code and the implementing rules and regulations. Manila.

Radosevich, G. E., et al. 1976. Proceedings of the international conference on global water law systems. Summary and Vols. 1–4. Fort Collins, Colo.: Colorado State University.

———. 1977. Improvised agricultural water use: Organizational alternatives. Fort Collins, Colo.: Research Administration and Development.

———. 1985. Water policy and law bibliography of national and international sources. Fort Collins, Colo.: International School for Agriculture and Resource Development, Colorado State University.

Seckler, David W., and K. C. Nobe. 1983. The management factor in developing economies. *In* K. C. Nobe and R. K. Sampath (ed.) Issues in Third World development. Boulder, Colo.: Westview Press.

30. THE ROLES OF THE PUBLIC AND THE PRIVATE SECTOR IN WATER DEVELOPMENT

Anson R. Bertrand, Office of Agriculture, Bureau for Science and Technology, Agency for International Development, Washington, D.C.

ABSTRACT

There are no substitutes for water for human and animal consumption and for plant life. Water must be more effectively managed to meet health and food requirements. Water-management requirements differ from place to place, making necessary a variety of skills and capabilities. Some water-development and management requirements can be met most effectively by the public sector. Other needs are best handled by private entities.

In most developing countries both the private and the public sectors' practices in water development need strengthening. Experience indicates that water development is most effective when the public sector performs only essential activities that the private sector cannot or will not perform.

Most successful water-development projects have vigorous and continuing involvement of the private sector. Each sector usually has some strong capabilities to contribute to water development and management endeavors.

The public sector usually must carry out certain participant activities that are mostly related to financing and regulating. The public sector also has the responsibility of helping expedite educational and other activities. The private sector is most effective as a participant and as a local regulator.

In effective water projects both sectors work in harmony with a minimum of conflicts.

THE IMPORTANCE OF WATER

Water, a limited and indispensable resource in all aspects of human life and endeavor, is both a public and a private concern. On this planet we are surrounded by 326 million cubic miles (13.6 billion km³) of water. However, 97.2 percent is saltwater of the oceans and seas, and 2.15 percent is frozen in the polar caps and glaciers. Almost all (96.41 percent) of the remaining 0.65 percent is groundwater, leaving only 49,400 cubic miles (206,000 km³) of water for all lakes, rivers, soil, and atmosphere and the moisture contained in plant and animal tissues (Millbrook, 1981; Nance, 1982). Frequently the water is where people are not, and the water quality is not good even when it is available in adequate amounts. The United Nations Organization (UN) has declared the 1980s to be the International Drinking Water Supply and Sanitation Decade. Obviously water's importance to our future on earth is recognized, but we must do more than realize the worth of water; we must take major steps to make sure that there is water to meet all human needs (Hamilton, 1984).

"We are headed for a disaster much like the oil crisis of a decade ago. The main difference is that this crisis is a life threatening one," said Dr. Peter G. Bourne (1981), president of Global Water, Washington, D.C., an organization striving to educate people on water issues. Bourne also said he believes that "if people become aware of the problems they will begin working on them, and there are solutions, but we haven't got much longer to find them." Once found, the solutions must be implemented.

It is self-evident that water is essential for food production. During the past two decades increases in food production in the Third World have slightly surpassed the population growth. Between 1970 and 1982 the growth of major food crops in developing countries averaged 2.5 percent (FAO, 1982). This was just a little higher than the average population growth rate of about 2 percent for all developing countries. In the Third World the most rapid increase in food production among twenty-five developing countries was in Latin America, where food production outpaced population growth by 0.5 to 1 percent (USDA, 1982). The region with the slowest growth rate in food production was Sub-Saharan Africa, where production of major food crops lagged behind population increase by about 1.4 percent during the same years (Ho, 1984).

On a global basis food production is not critically short. However, the UN estimates that as many as 40 million people in twenty-eight nations in Africa are in danger of starvation, and massive food aid to avert starvation will be needed in nine African nations. This grim assessment might be considered an aberration: unfortunately, it is not. Although there is some evidence that frequency and duration may be increasing, drought is a natural phenomenon in Africa. The rapid growth in population is forcing large numbers of people to try to live in drought-prone areas historically shunned by farmers. Generally speaking, "The drought has not moved; the people have moved to the drought" (Stewart, 1984). The water problem has two basic aspects: quantity and quality. When either aspect becomes severely negative, the effects are deadly. In terms of quality, potable water is essential for life, and water that is essentially free of contaminants is equally essential for food production.

Inadequate water facilities can leave millions without readily accessible water, even in areas with enough water. Despite the hardship this can create, development of water-delivery facilities has lagged throughout the developing world. The UN estimates that only 2 percent of Africa's water resources have been developed, and Latin America fully utilizes only about 3 percent of its water resources. Even in many developed countries water use must be limited in specific locations from time to time.

Installing water-delivery systems is not all that is required. Operation and maintenance require natural and human resources. In the late 1970s the World Health Organization found that 80 percent of the village pumps were inoperative in three Asian countries, yet we are still not training nearly enough people in water management (McJunkin, 1982). UNICEF estimates that 100,000 people must be trained every year to meet the demand for potable-water delivery systems; to meet irrigation needs will require many more.

Having enough water and a reliable delivery system is not enough; the quality of the water supply must also be assured. In many countries water supplies may require removal of unwanted or harmful chemicals. For example, the government of India has identified 57,000 problem villages in which water from wells contains excess salt, iron, fluoride, and other chemicals. Untreated water often contains disease-bearing organisms and parasites. Unclean water often causes diarrhea, which may claim as many as 6 million lives a year. Other waterborne diseases are schistosomiasis, cholera, typhoid, onchocerciasis, guinea worm, and hepatitis. All these and other diseases are common in many developing countries in which water resource development is lagging. It is possible to cite example after example where progress is being made in providing safe and adequate water supplies for people in developing countries, but the pace is slow, and much remains to be done.

Every year throughout the world floods cause extensive human suffering and property loss. Sediment deposited by these floods can be either a blessing or a detriment. If high-quality sediment is deposited on fields where there are no standing crops, it can enhance potential agricultural productivity. But low-quality sediment deposited in homes, on city streets, or over a standing crop is a distinct detriment.

Structures such as dams are frequently constructed to reduce the chance of flooding. According to the International Commission of Large Dams, each year more than 350 dams higher than 15.25 m are built, joining a current inventory of more than 12,000 such dams. These large dams and thousands of smaller ones also provide essential energy as well as regulating flows to reduce the incidence of flooding. The continuing controversies over the relative merits of dams and drainageways produce no absolute conclusions. It is likely that water resource development will continue to include dams and drainageways for production of energy, flood control, and sedimentation reduction.

Because people now more than ever must live in drought-prone areas and because most food consumed must be produced where the people reside, development of indigenous water resources of Third World countries is essential. This development includes irrigation, which must expand and become more efficient. Irrigation not only is vital to the physical and financial survival of millions of subsistence farmers around the world but also is essential to meeting broader food requirements throughout the Third World. Irrigation is a technology available to the small farmer that can substantially increase the per-hectare output of a fixed quantity of land. Also it increases rather than decreases the demand for farm labor. Worldwide, irrigation is practiced on more than 200 million ha and accounts for more than 67 percent of all food production. This percentage must grow if food needs are to be met. Opportunities for irrigation abound throughout much of the Third World, where the bulk of the world's existing irrigated hectarage is situated and where most of the estimated 250 million to 300 million ha of potentially irrigable land can also be found.

Third World leaders often depend on their agricultural sectors to produce unique exportable products that can earn the needed foreign exchange. Irrigation is necessary to produce the needed quantity and quality of such potential exports.

Irrigation development is therefore important in most Third World countries for production of locally consumed food supplies and as a generator of foreign exchange. A formidable challenge faces efforts to meet these needs. Simply put, irrigation facilities must be expanded; existing and new facilities must be managed more effectively. Irrigation sectors in most developing countries perform at levels well below their potential. Their performance is also considerably lower than that needed to meet growing requirements and to justify additional investments. The causes of these substandard levels of productivity are varied, but, in general, they can be traced to poor system performance and poor management.

DEFINITION OF SECTORS

Experience has shown that water resource development is most effective where both the public and the private sectors participate in planning and execution. The public sector, consisting of government agencies with responsibility for resource development, must be involved in overall planning and financing. Private interests, consisting of water users' groups, individual water users, equipment supplies, technicians, and others who serve the water enterprise for profit, are essential and bring to the enterprise efficiency and stability that cannot be provided by the public sector alone. Not surprisingly, societies around the world in developed and developing countries alike have responded to the need for water development with a spectrum of public measures for conserving, developing, and managing water.

Given the range of mankind's needs for water and the range of conditions under which this valuable resource is found throughout the world, one might conclude that there is almost no role that the public sector could not have or has not had in water development. But because the public sector has been the predominant factor in water development, we should not assume that the private sector has no significant role to play in water concerns. On the contrary, some of the traditional public-sector roles might be more effectively and efficiently carried out by the private sector.

It is not an easy task to establish a set of criteria that applies to the respective roles of the public and private sectors. Observations have shown that public-sector involvement, particularly in the management of water projects, usually results in very high costs. This may be because the public sector usually lacks administrative ability and other more specific skills required for successful development and operation of water projects. On the other hand, the private sector frequently brings skilled management and efficient operating procedures to such endeavors. Private-sector entities involved in water projects are almost always closer to the users and, therefore, are more responsive to the needs and desires of water users.

It bears repeating: Successful planning and implementation of water development projects in Third World countries require the involvement of both the public and the private sectors.

APPROPRIATE ROLES

The U.S. Agency for International Development's (AID) years of experience in economic development have enabled a few general principles for water development to be identified:

1. *The public sector should perform only essential activities that the private sector cannot or will not handle.* Those things in which the public sector must become involved usually include large water development projects having major social as well as individual impacts.

2. *Public and private sector actions should be complementary.*

3. *In most developing countries both sectors need to be strengthened.*

Identifying and assigning specific public- and private-sector roles in the development and implementation of irrigation systems require early critical decisions. Decisions must be made about who will be responsible for the investment and the design. Coward (1984) points out that the single most critical and ambiguous issue is the optimum mix of state and local responsibilities in creating and sustaining small-scale irrigation facilities. Other critical decisions include identification of government agencies and local entities that will participate and the nature of their involvement, especially in such activities as program planning, monitoring, evaluation, and allocation of local resources. The most effective water projects result when the respective sector roles are clearly defined and carried out in an atmosphere of mutual respect and with adherence to territorial prerogatives.

THE PUBLIC SECTOR

As a Participant

Although there are essential participant-type activities that the public sector must fulfill (mostly related to financing and regulating), it usually functions least well as a direct participant. The roles of central and local government agencies and private organizations vary somewhat depending on the kinds of irrigation systems involved. Peterson (1984) describes irrigation systems in these dimensions: organizational structure, hydrologic, and technical. He identifies five possible organizational structures that are related to the size of the system: individual farmers, small partnerships or cooperative systems, village-owned and operated systems,

small-scale publicly operated systems, and medium- and large-scale publicly operated systems.

For large-scale national or regional systems requiring extensive capital investments and major engineering works, financing, planning, and maintenance are almost always in the hands of a government agency authorized to make and carry out major decisions. Economic considerations, such as the high cost of construction, maintenance, and operation and the slow rate of return from most major water projects, usually make government underwriting mandatory. For example, a $100 million irrigation project financed over forty years would require paying of interest and principal payment of about $8 million annually, assuming an annual interest rate of only 7.5 percent. It is no easy task for water projects to generate such revenues, especially in the early years.

The public-sector organizations have the responsibility of protecting society's interest relative to externalities. For example, only a government is in a position to ensure that the costs of capital and equipment are fair and that a water supply of high quality will remain available to the project area.

A basic choice to be made early in the planning process is between a direct and an indirect investment strategy. Direct investment is the dominant mode today. Government agencies use their own financial resources and staffs to design, construct, and operate irrigation systems. Through indirect investment the government makes resources available to the local sector for its use. Each of these strategies has potential advantages and disadvantages.

In a major study entitled "Improving Policies and Programs for the Development of Small Local Irrigation Systems," Coward (1984) concluded that indirect investment usually results in stronger local control and better management of resources. In addition, indirect investment usually produces systems that more closely fit local needs and conditions and precludes government assumption of a recurrent cost burden.

However, the public sector is of necessity responsible for participating in decisions that result in water allocation to public, private, and industrial users. Without public participation inequities can easily be built into a water project and can cause the system to fail when those who have been slighted take steps to gain their fair share.

Large-scale irrigation systems with their enormous budgets, complex engineering works, and visible bureaucracies tend to dominate water-management concerns. However, in many countries small-scale irrigation systems are significant in terms of total area served and persistence. The need for a government agency in direct involvement in small-scale projects is much less.

Small-scale systems can be defined in a number of ways (Coward, 1984; Wade, 1982; Underhill, 1983). However, "small-scale" usually identifies smaller systems in which a government agency has some responsibility contrast to traditional or indigenous systems, which are quite small and are independent of the state. Most often both types of systems are managed by a local entity that may take any of several forms. Government agencies will usually provide assistance to both small-scale and local systems. However, the local systems frequently must request help, while it may be automatically provided for small-scale systems.

As a Regulator

The public sector functions better as a regulator. Multiple private demands on water resources make necessary some type of neutral public arbitrator to protect public interests and ensure that the natural resource is not abused. There are many examples throughout the world in which failure to recognize potential problems and lack of regulation to protect long-term public interests have permitted individual and sometimes small groups to selfishly abuse and sometimes destroy a valuable resource. Public intervention is also essential to protect weak private-interest groups from more powerful ones to ensure equity of access to water resources.

As a Facilitator or Promoter

The public sector functions well as a facilitator or promoter. By adopting sound policies so that constructive economic signals and incentives are transmitted to private participants, the public sector can orchestrate private-sector water development and good management with minimal public investment and regulation.

Agenda for Public Programs in Water Development

Several measures that make up a constructive agenda for public programs are discussed in the following paragraphs.

Policies. Government policies that guide water development must be rooted in sound development principles that facilitate rather than hinder water development involving both public and private entities. This can usually be accomplished best by incorporation of incentives for effective and efficient use of water. Public organizations also have the responsibility of interpreting or establishing water codes and for designing and strengthening machinery for enforcement.

Water-resource inventorying. Water resources must be identified and inventoried, and technical features must be specified so that potential investors can accurately estimate development costs. Such accurate information is frequently unavailable in developing countries, and this deficiency has led to some serious failures stemming from such causes as improper dam construction, insufficient water, and excessive sediment. Shortcuts should not be taken in the inventory and planning phase.

Water-resource pricing. The public sector can also assist the marketplace by helping establish (but not independently fix) the price at which water will be supplied to users. Such assistance will increase investors' confidence that they will obtain adequate compensation for the financial and management investment and for the risks they are willing to take.

Water-development finance. Where major investments are required for economic exploitation of water resources, public sources of credit and investment guarantees can enable private investors—often grouped together as cooperatives of suppliers or users—to undertake water development schemes. Indirect financing such as subsidies, low-interest loans, grants, and tax abatement may be used effectively to accomplish overall economic or social policy objectives. For example, subsidies to selected users for the construction and maintenance of drainage works may give an entire water development project a longer and more viable life.

Private-sector procurement. Where the economically efficient scale of operation exceeds the existing private-sector capacity to undertake a water project, public-sector efforts can still tap private-sector talent and skills by subcontracting construction and jointly managing operations. Overseas a common pattern followed by AID-supported water projects is to team together officials and farmer-users to develop and distribute irrigation water.

Project design. Government agencies usually take the lead in designing projects. Most donors, including AID, insist that a responsible agency be accountable for the design work. However, the most successful projects are planned and designed with heavy local input. Local information is essential to ensure that the system meets the users' needs. Securing the right mix of agency and local input is usually difficult, but it is extremely important to strive for it.

Complementary services. The public sector should make sure that the required complementary services are provided. Without support in such areas as education, credit, extension, research, and marketing, irrigation projects are usually doomed to failure. Extension may be critical to introducing new soil-water relationships to farmers. It may also be critical in teaching farmers about long-term maintenance of the overall system and their individual farm-unit system.

THE PRIVATE SECTOR

As a Participant

According to Peterson (1984), "Irrigation system development is dynamic, passing through several phases: planning and design, construction, development, operation and maintenance, repair, and rehabilitation." Virtually without exception, planning for irrigation-system development assumes ultimate operation by the private sector.

Morris and Norman (1983) concluded that there are at least twenty-five essential functions that farmers in community organizations can effectively carry out in irrigation systems. These essential functions include decision making, implementation, benefits, and evaluation.

Plans are often quite specific about the type of participation expected. Frequently local interests are not consulted until after the plans are completed, although local interests will have the major responsibility for construction and maintenance, including clearing canals, making small repairs, and developing and maintaining facilities for conveying water from main-system canals to farmers' fields. This planning approach is usually a mistake because when ultimate water users are not involved in preconstruction decisions about investments, design, physical layout, and management plans, constructed facilities will frequently be wrong. Turnouts may be incorrectly situated, volumes of water may be insufficient, and management procedures that do not fit local capabilities may be required. Early participation of local interests will minimize postconstruction conflicts and result in irrigation systems that have a much better chance of success.

It is generally accepted that private-interest groups should be formed and strengthened to facilitate good irrigation management. Since such organizations do not normally exist before initial planning, the planning activity itself can be used as a vehicle for organizing farmers (Coward, 1984). Private voluntary organizations (PVOs) have been instrumental in helping organize irrigation user groups. Once organized, these local water-user organizations should participate in every phase of planning.

Often overlooked in planning water-management schemes is the willingness of potential water users to change their farming practices. Irrigated agriculture and rain-fed agriculture place entirely different demands on the farms and farmers. Many well-designed irrigation systems have failed because important sociological and cultural factors were overlooked. Well-founded judgments must be made about the genuine willingness and ability of farmers to work together and to make the collective and individual changes required for a successful irrigation project.

The desired relationship between the irrigation agency and local groups differs from situation to situation. One principle is clear, however: local groups should not be regarded as mere appendages of the agency. They function best when they have a high degree of autonomy and voluntarily cooperate with the agency. According to Coward (1984), most successful local groups have two important features: (1) they are accountable to the local people, are flexible, and can mobilize resources; and (2) they understand and can handle the distribution of rights in the localities of the project.

Involvement of the private sector as contractors or as managers usually results in more efficient operation than is possible when the agency operates directly. The private sector can usually secure more highly skilled technicians. Agency personnel, although most often sincere and dedicated, are usually generalists.

Another advantage of local groups' participation in water projects is that successful involvement will build confidence. Such groups are accountable to their neighbors rather than to an external agency. This local accountability increases the likelihood that performance will be acceptable locally. Too, such groups are usually more flexible than a large agency. They are able to act more quickly in allocating resources and implementing management decisions. The flexibility and accountability of local organizations enhances the odds for success.

As a Regulator

Four of the activities identified by Morris and Norman (1983) are regulatory in nature. Local organizations usually function more quickly and efficiently in resolving disputes among water users. They also effectively police members' obligations. Through peer pressure and penalties, when necessary, they can secure performance from users that meet the agreed-to guidelines, not the least of which are those related to conservation and protection of the natural resources. Local groups are also most likely to decide on

effective and enforceable rules—rules that dictate access to water, amount and time of water use, and circumstances under which water rights are transferred from one farmer to another.

As a Promoter and Facilitator

No irrigation system is likely to be 100 percent responsive to demand, but managers should strive for maximum system responsiveness at all times. Efficiency will depend on many factors, such as water supply, water quality, system design, system maintenance, and cooperation of all participants.

Local people and organizations can and should perform vital functions as promoters and facilitators. Local organizations can communicate with users more efficiently than can a remote government agency. Chambers (1984) makes the case that there are great opportunities for improving performance of irrigation systems and that most of these opportunities require communications that can best be carried out by the private sector. Opportunities identified by Chambers include scheduling and distribution of water; monitoring of information and actions; allocation of water within the system; water-saving measures; responses to rainfall, including rainfall probability; better information to users about water supplies; and better information and communications for managers about system operations and performance.

Peterson (1984) points out that local organizations can best promote understanding of the system's capabilities. He further states that they are also effective in "searching for cropping patterns and production sequences that more optimally match the real water delivery system."

Sometimes minor infrastructure improvements can produce major improvements in water systems. If farmers can be persuaded to contribute labor and equipment, financial resources can be saved and system performance improved. Only local organizations can effectively orchestrate such cooperation.

In many places PVOs are active participants in irrigation programs, especially in the local sector (Coward 1984). While PVOs are often viewed as technically weak, they are strong in stimulating local group involvement and participation. PVOs, indeed, have significant advantages. They can tailor their activities to local conditions, and they can afford to be flexible.

Where local private organizations do not exist, PVOs can be effective in catalyzing local interest and organizing representative bodies to participate in planning, design, and eventual operation of a water-development project. National water agencies and donor organizations would be well advised to consider involvement of PVOs in water-development projects where local participation is required for effective implementation.

COMPLEMENTARITY OF PUBLIC AND PRIVATE ROLES

Early planning decisions must identify which agencies and organizations will be involved, state essential functions, and determine which activities can best be carried out by government agencies and which activities can most effectively be accomplished by private-sector organizations. Such an analysis, if complete, will reveal that there are many complementary activities in which both public and private entities should participate.

Since early planning of most water-development projects is a responsibility of government agencies, it is incumbent on those planning agencies to identify and secure early involvement of the private sector. Where adequate private-sector organizations do not exist, provisions must be made for their creation. As previously stated, this is a role PVO often play.

Once essential functions are identified and agencies or organizations have been established to carry out these functions, the planning, design, construction, and operation of water projects largely depend on the care exercised by each organization to properly execute the functions in its area of responsibility. Where this occurs, water projects usually succeed. Where such collaboration does not occur in a cooperative atmosphere, water projects seldom attain their potential.

We have learned a great deal in recent years about what it takes to have a successful water-development project. Through projects such as AID's Water Management Synthesis II, and others throughout the world, we continue to refine the elements that are essential for success. As this new knowledge is put to work and we use the "comparative advantages" of the public and private sectors, future efforts will result in fewer disappointments and many more successes. The result will be greatly improved use of water resources throughout the world for meeting mankind's needs.

REFERENCES

AID [U.S. Agency for International Development]. 1984. Development experience. Abstracts, AID program evaluation report 8. Washington, D.C.

Bourne, Peter G. 1981. The United Nations international drinking water supply and sanitation decade. *Mazingna.*

———. 1983. Global water, Washington, D.C.

Chambers, Robert. 1984. Improving canal irrigation management: no need to wait. Paper presented at the national seminar on policies for irrigated agriculture. Administrative Staff College, Hyderabad, India.

Coward, E. Walter, Jr. 1904. Improving policies and programs for the development of small-scale irrigation systems.

FAO [Food and Agriculture Organization]. 1982a. Report: Farmers' participation and organization for irrigation water management. Rome.

———. 1982b. Food Production Yearbook. Rome.

Hamilton, Robert A. 1984. *Rotarian*, October.

Ho, Teresa J. 1985. Population growth and agricultural productivity in Sub-Saharan Africa. Presented at the Fifth Agricultural Development Symposium, World Bank, Washington, D.C.

Millbrook, G. T. 1981. Environmentally sound small-scale water projects. CODE 1/VITA.

Morris, John, Thom Derrick, and Roy Norman. 1983. Prospects for small-scale irrigation development in the Sahel: a report prepared for the Water Management Synthesis II Project. Washington, D.C.: Agency for International Development.

McJunkin, F. Eugene. 1982. Water and health. Washington, D.C.: Office of Health, Bureau for Science and Technology, Agency for International Development.

Nance, Raymond L. 1982. Water of the world. Washington, D.C.: U.S. Department of Interior, Geological Survey.

Paulina, Leonard A. 1984. Food in the Third World: past trends projections to 2000. Washington, D.C.: International Food Policy Research Institute.

Peterson, Dean F. 1984. Systems and technologies for improved irrigation water management. Prepared for the Agricultural and Rural Development Training Workshop, Washington, D.C., June 18–22.

Stewart, Ian J. 1984. Response farming: A scientific approach to ending starvation and alleviating poverty in drought zones of Africa. Paper presented at the conference on African agriculture development, California Polytechnic University, Pomona, May 28–June 2.

Underhill, H. W. 1983. Small scale irrigation in Africa guidelines. Rome: Food and Agriculture Organization.

Wade, Robert. 1982. Irrigation and agricultural policies in Korea. Boulder, Colo.: Westview Press.

USDA [U.S. Department of Agriculture]. 1982. World indices of agricultural production, 1972–1982. Statistical Bulletin No. 689.

31. PROSPECTS AND TRENDS OF IRRIGATION IN AFRICA: CONCEPTS FOR THE INVOLVEMENT OF PUBLIC AND PRIVATE SECTORS

H. M. Horning, T. H. Mather, and H. W. Underhill, Land and Water Development Division, Food and Agriculture Organization of the United Nations, Rome, Italy

ABSTRACT

The African food crisis, aggravated by recent droughts, has severely affected twenty-one countries of the Sahelian and Sub-Sahelian zones of the continent. Most of these countries will not be in a position to feed their increasing populations from their own resources if agricultural production remains at its present low-input level. The need to increase agricultural production by higher input use (fertilizers, improved seeds, pesticides, and better soil management) has also increased interest in expanding irrigation, which so far has played only a relatively minor role in Sahelian and Sub-Sahelian Africa. Different concepts for irrigation development have emerged:

1. Harnessing of the resources of major river basins.
2. Small-scale development that takes account of the physical, climatological, and demographic conditions in areas of water shortage.
3. Production-oriented projects.
4. Rural development–oriented projects.

These concepts take into account the need for surplus production of supplies to deficit areas, on the one side, and the broader objective of improving traditional agriculture in the context of improvement of rural life and society, on the other.

While these concepts are not mutually exclusive, they raise distinctive policy issues for government intervention and require different institutional support.

The inadequacy of institutional support to the rural and small-farmer sector is at present the retarding influence for more rapid expansion of small-scale irrigation development, thus the need for appropriate government and external support.

INTRODUCTION

The principles and general aspects of the involvement of public and private sectors and their application to the broader fields of water development are presented in the chapter by Anson R. Bertrand. Complementary to this, the present chapter is intended to demonstrate, on the specific subject of irrigation and drainage development in Africa, how the tasks assigned to the two sectors are determined by the concepts of agricultural development in general and irrigation development in particular.

The example of Africa—with particular focus on Sahelian and Sub-Sahelian Africa—was chosen in view of the present food crisis in this area, which has affected twenty-one African countries and has been caused by severe droughts and their effect in the low-rainfall belts. This has renewed interest in and discussion of the prospects and trends of irrigation development in Africa.

In the Sahelian and Sub-Sahelian zones irrigation so far has been of only marginal importance for food production. Its expansion, including reclamation of land for agriculture, requires the development of concepts appropriate to the given physiography, agricultural infrastructure, and social and economic development. The definition of the respective roles of the public and private sectors in irrigation development and land reclamation for food production and their complementarity are then a function of the chosen concepts and become a part of the water-development policies to be formulated at national levels.

This chapter is largely based on a policy paper that was discussed and endorsed by the Thirteenth Food and Agriculture Organization Regional Conference for Africa and is reflected in the "Harare Declaration on the Food Crisis in Africa by the African Ministers of Agriculture" adopted at that conference on July 25, 1984.

IRRIGATION IN AFRICA

For climatic and demographic reasons irrigation development in Africa has been concentrated in the north and northeast of the continent, and six countries in this zone account for 70 percent of all irrigation in Africa. Water control has been the basis of agricultural development in these countries, for some of which the entire economy depends on irrigation.

In Sahelian and Sub-Sahelian Africa, by contrast, water control has played a relatively minor part in agricultural development. It has been limited historically to traditional small-scale irrigation in drought-prone areas and the reclamation of small swamplands. In recent decades, however, there has been a move to develop larger schemes, usually for the commercial production of crops such as sugarcane, cotton, and rice.

THE FOOD SITUATION IN AFRICA

The food and agricultural situation in Africa gives cause for grave concern. Per capita food production has dropped by more than 10 percent in the past ten years, and the average dietary energy supplies have barely been maintained at 6 to 7 percent below nutritional requirements. Food imports have more than doubled in volume and have risen in cost five times. Africa is the only region of the world that is failing to keep food production ahead of population growth.

The recent droughts have aggravated the situation, and

Table 1. Projected growth of irrigation in two zones in Africa by the year 2000

Zone	Million ha 1980	Million ha 2000	Percentage of Growth
North and northeast Africa	5.9	8.3	41
Sahel and Sub-Sahel	2.6	5.0	92

SOURCE: FAO, 1981.

twenty-one countries in Africa have been declared "most affected," requiring substantive food aid. In the critical zones of Africa land resources cannot provide food for the population by the year 2000 under the present low-input level of the traditional production system (FAO, 1984). Thus the main efforts to improve the present situation of food production and food security must be directed toward raising the input level of production (soil management, improved seeds, and use of fertilizer and pesticides) on land with sufficient rainfall, irrigated land, and land brought under irrigation.

PROSPECTS OF IRRIGATION

In *Agriculture: Toward 2000* (FAO, 1981) the growth of irrigation from 1980 to 2000 was projected for two zones in Africa. These projections are shown in Table 1. Another important distinction between the two zones is that of cropping intensity. While the average for north and northeast Africa is currently about 130 percent, it is only about 110 percent in the other areas. This implies a need to intensify the use of irrigated land in the latter zone in addition to accelerating the rate of increase in area.

The history of irrigation in Africa, the available resources, and the predicted expansion of irrigated agriculture show that future development can be expected to take different directions in the two zones. In north and northeast Africa the natural-resources potential is known to be limited. This means that expansion must take place mostly within the existing infrastructure, as, for example, the Nile valley. The number of possible new developments will be restricted and can be expected to depend on approaches such as increased exploitation of groundwater, more intensive production through improved water management, water-saving technologies, and higher yields from better drainage. The present state of irrigation development in this area and the knowledge and skills already accumulated provide a sound base for future expansion and intensification.

In Sahelian and Sub-Sahelian Africa there is still a vast potential for water development for agriculture in the large river basins. On the margins of these basins and beyond are possibilities for many small developments that can ensure and stabilize production in areas affected by drought and irregular rainfall. In this part of the continent, water development is extremely important for future food production, but it also poses a variety of problems. There are, therefore, two trends in present irrigation development in the Sahel and Sub-Sahel: (1) harnessing the resources of major river basins and (2) undertaking small-scale development in areas of water shortage.

TRENDS AND NEEDS FOR IRRIGATION DEVELOPMENT IN SAHELIAN AND SUB-SAHELIAN AFRICA

Harnessing the Resources of the Large River Basins

In considering the development of the larger African river basins, it is important to recognize the variety of physical and climatological characteristics in the individual catchments, which tend to dictate both the possibilities and the limitations of major irrigation schemes. In some basins the highest rainfall areas are in the uppermost watersheds (Senegal River, South Chad Basin), and the drier zones could be supplied from reservoirs, using the rivers as conveyance channels for downstream projects. In other basins, however, the upstream parts are in the dry areas where irrigation is needed and abundant water is available only downstream, where rainfall is high (lower Niger basin, Zambezi). In many rivers low flows are only a few cubic meters per second, while flood flows may be 10,000 times greater, and the total annual flow in a wet year may be 10 times that of a dry year. For relatively small projects low flows may be adequate and reliable, but eventually, as already in the Senegal and Gambia rivers, base-flow extractions may cause intrusion of seawater into the delta and lower reaches, thus cutting off previously existing freshwater supplies.

It is uncommon to find inexpensive sites for large reservoirs on the major rivers, and the construction of numbers of smaller reservoirs on the tributaries will no doubt be more feasible. Large tracts of land suitable for irrigation near the main rivers require drainage and flood control, and costly water-conveyance systems are needed to supply extensive irrigation areas at a distance from the river. In the wetter parts of the large basins some swamps may eventually be controlled to increase agricultural production through major engineering works. In these wetter areas, however, health problems are often a major constraint.

The large-scale approach is usually intended to achieve a significant contribution to the national production of food and commercial crops, often combined with the earning or saving of foreign exchange. In the Sahelian zone modern irrigation farming now provides less than 5 percent of the total cereal production, but recent droughts have increased interest in hydroagricultural schemes to provide a high degree of water control and reliability.

Some African states envisage extensive agricultural development of the large river basins through an expansion of irrigation made possible by the building of huge infrastructural works. Such works are inevitably expensive, and, in addition to the need for thorough planning of the construction activities, they demand the establishment of institutional arrangements to ensure that the rate of development and the outputs from the scheme are compatible with the high investments.

Complex development programs of this type have a generally poor record of adhering to planned schedules and targets. Common causes are shortage of human, technical, and financial resources; problems of scheme management, organization of farmer groups, input supplies and services; and the need to revise and adjust original planning concepts to match national objectives.

Success in major irrigation schemes therefore depends on the removal of a number of institutional constraints that have too often been underestimated. It implies the need for complementary programs and services for the training, mobilization, and participation of peasant farmers; the creation of a skilled technical cadre; the application of an integral agricultural policy on prices, markets, and credit; the necessary infrastructure and storage and processing facilities; and supportive agricultural research into crop varieties and cultural practices.

In recent years there have been many reviews and analyses of irrigation costs in Africa and comparisons with costs elsewhere in the world. The unavoidable conclusion is that some of the highest costs, and consequently the poorest returns, are associated with major schemes in Sahelian and Sub-Sahelian Africa. This, however, tends to conceal the wide range of unit costs among schemes and to disregard the content and complexity of these schemes, many of which incorporate massive infrastructural costs that are unnecessary in other, more developed regions because the infrastructure is already there. Roads, bridges, power supply, and settlements do not then appear as project costs.

Small-Scale Development

Small-scale irrigation in a variety of forms has long been practiced in Africa where natural conditions provide easily obtainable water close to suitable land. Perennial streams are utilized through simple diversions in upland areas such as the slopes of Mount Kilimanjaro. In valley bottoms the use of simple structures and earth bunds gives a form of water control to extend the season of flood-recession cultivation, and in many instances shallow groundwater, accessible through small wells and pumps, offers profitable opportunities for vegetable crop production, especially on urban fringes or close to markets.

Recent droughts and an attempt to stabilize and improve productivity in rural areas of low rainfall have led to an increasing interest in this type of irrigation development. It can be expected, however, that areas suitable for small-scale irrigation development will usually tend to be scattered within particular zones and will provide a basis for improved self-sufficiency of remote rural communities rather than making a substantial contribution to national goals for food production.

The development of small-scale irrigation has an advantage in that it does not require heavy investments in infrastructure and water control of the large basins. Foreign-funding requirements for capital investments are therefore low, and gestation periods, that is, the time needed until full benefits can be drawn from the investments, are short. Farm-level investments are also below the requirements of large-scale, formal schemes if appropriate technologies are used, allowing a major share of the work to be done under farmers' self-schemes.

Great care should be taken in selecting the sites for small-scale development and the irrigation technologies to be used. Small, informal schemes must be founded on an abil-

ity to apply self-help measures to overcome problems and constraints imposed by water availability, land characteristics, and structural needs. By their very nature these schemes are not suited to massive injections of capital and imported technology in the form of sophisticated machinery and costly materials, because these, and the resulting works, cannot be sustained from within the project.

Some initial support will clearly be needed in the form of surveys, design, advice, and supervision of construction. This support could have a high cost per unit area if it is to be charged to individual, isolated schemes, but a phased approach to provide such support services to a group of schemes in a selected district can reduce the costs. Similarly, a program for financial support to a series of schemes will give continuity and momentum to development and will avoid the need for repeated budgetary allocations or loan negotiations that will retard progress, especially where there are foreign-loan components.

The concept of community initiative and involvement is basic to the success of small-scale, informal irrigation. There have been many instances of failure as a result of scheme planning, design, and construction from outside the community with little or no prior consultation with the affected farmers regarding their own needs, abilities, and customs. The unacceptability of this approach to the farmers is evident in schemes that are underutilized and badly deteriorated in the absence of regular maintenance. Occasionally this provokes a takeover by the responsible authority and subsequent operation under a formal administration; this in turn perpetuates the separation between scheme and community, suppressing farmer initiatives and at times even competing with the population it was intended to serve.

It is essential, therefore, to avoid excessive direction and investment from outside and to acquire instead an understanding of the cohesiveness and intricacy of existing farming systems in such matters as the seasonal labor pattern and differentiation of tasks between men and women. Assistance from designated authorities will be more effective if it is unobtrusive and encourages farmer and community initiatives.

In a region where irrigation forms only a part of a more complex farming system, aid to small-scale irrigation may be incorporated within a broader framework of rural development. In general, rural development programs are best suited for establishing contact with farming communities, and this approach is often used to advantage by local organizations and nongovernment organizations (NGOs). On the other hand, such organizations are frequently unable to provide sound technical advice and urgently call for government help when an ill-planned project is threatened with disaster.

To promote the extension of small-scale irrigation, these limited technical and financial support requirements must be recognized through the provision of a service that operates with local rural-development programs in scheme design and implementation. The staffing of this service will call for professional and technical personnel of a high caliber capable of working with the rural community. Their selection and training will be a matter of priority. The experience and knowledge they gain in their work will become an invaluable asset to future development programs.

Summary of Trends

Traditional irrigation based on simple technology has long been practiced in suitable locations, and in general, because population pressure on arable land is not as great in Africa as in other continents, peasant communities have been based on self-sufficient farming systems adapted to the local environments. Survival has therefore been more important than profit, and risk minimization has taken precedence over surplus production. On the other hand, the objective of recent large-scale formal irrigation in Africa has been the production of commercial crops by means of modern technology, supported by efficient management with adequate physical and social infrastructures, regular supplies of inputs, experienced farmers, and efficient marketing. The two types of irrigated agriculture have had very little in common. With a few exceptions the conditions required for successful commercial irrigation were absent from traditional irrigation. These conditions could be artificially created and imposed by a central authority, colonial or commercial, with a greater or lesser degree of success, but they did not grow out of the knowledge, experience, and skills of the traditional peasant farming system.

Given the appropriate conditions, both types of irrigation are valid. Indeed, they can and do exist successfully side by side in peasant communities and in commercial estates. The mistake has been in thinking that subsistence peasant irrigation could be rapidly transformed into competitive commercial farming by the massive injection of modern technology and capital. The transformation of subsistence into commercial irrigated farming is possible but can be achieved only by a process of growth from below, not by the imposition of an alien system from above.

The realization of the defects of the imposed top-down approach, the fact of the spontaneous growth of peasant irrigation, and the awareness of the potential of accelerated growth from below with judicious support from above indicate that irrigation development in Africa is at a turning point, with hopeful prospects if the opportunity can be grasped.

POLICY ISSUES

The concentration of effort and investment on large-scale irrigation projects in Africa, often modeled on similar schemes in other continents, has frequently failed to achieve the predicted goals of production or economic returns. A critical reappraisal of approaches is called for to find solutions that are better adapted to African needs. But any practical improvement will require the reorientation of policies for national development, investment, and technical assistance.

Among the many countries of the region is a diversity of type and degree in aspects and problems of irrigation development, reflecting the varieties of national political, social, and economic circumstances. At the same time it is possible to define and summarize some of the policy lines that can be

expected to lead most countries toward more effective and more productive irrigation:

1. In planning for future irrigation development, clear distinctions must be drawn between projects whose primary objectives are production-oriented and those intended to serve a broader role in the improvement of rural life and society. The objectives may not be mutually exclusive, but once the primary aim has been defined, the conceptual, physical, and institutional design must be entirely suitable to fulfill that purpose.

2. Proposed production-oriented projects must pass the test of technical and economic feasibility, and there must be a guarantee that the necessary management skills and material inputs will be provided. To ensure these initially, consideration may be given to external channels or local private enterprise in addition to government sources, but there should be an underlying, longer-term national policy for scheme management within general policies for manpower development and use.

3. Where existing schemes have performed badly, their rehabilitation should be a priority concern to derive maximum benefit from the sunken investment and from experienced human resources. Procedures for the evaluation of performance and subsequent redesign should extend beyond structural and technical changes to include the design of management systems with appropriate decentralization and delegation of authority and responsibility, ultimately reaching the farmers themselves.

4. Irrigation projects intended to form a component of more general programs for rural development and improvement should satisfy broader criteria than the typical economic analyses. They should offer scope for informal, small-scheme development through farmers' groups and water users' associations, place emphasis on self-help and self-sustainability, impose a minimum of external regulations, and offer attractive financial incentives through commodity pricing structures.

5. The human needs of rural development must always be kept in view, and this calls for the inclusion of policies to reduce the poverty gap and raise the quality of life in these communities through increased attention to disadvantaged groups, recognition of the particular role of women in agriculture, and incorporation of health measures through the provision of safe water supplies and protection against water-associated diseases.

INSTITUTIONAL NEEDS

The conversion of these policy lines into action calls for different institutions to be assigned responsibilities to the lowest possible level where such responsibility can be effectively carried out.

Development of the Infrastructure in Large River Basins

All major basins in Africa have more than one riparian state, and their development should be based on interstate agreements. For the most important basins interstate commissions have been established to plan the development and management of their resources, in most instances with assistance from the United Nations Development Program and the specialized agencies of the United Nations system (the Kagera, Niger, Gambia, and Senegal rivers and the Lake Chad Basin). Investments for major structures that are part of the basin development scheme, however, come under national jurisdiction (with the few exceptions of cross-boundary structures); they normally require substantive external financing through multinational or bilateral funding institutions and development funds.

Development at Scheme Level

While the allocation of land and water resources is the direct responsibility of the government, as is the allocation of investment funding, the responsibility for the schemes as such follows some different designs which can be classified according to the size of the schemes:

1. Very large schemes (over 10,000 ha) with full water control are entirely under government management. Examples are the gravity schemes from large river basins in Sudan (Gezira), Egypt, and Mali (Office du Niger) and pumped from large rivers in Senegal (SAED).

2. Large schemes (typically 1,000 to 10,000 ha) with full water control are generally under government or commercial management, the latter being usually found below the 5000-ha limit. Examples are Kenya (Bura Mwea), Tanzania (Mbarali), Zimbabwe, Cameroon, and Somalia (Shebelli).

3. Medium schemes (typically 100 to 1,000 ha) with full or partial water control are government-managed or government-assisted cooperatives or commercial estates. Examples are Niger (ONAHA), Senegal (SAED), Tanzania, and Malawi.

4. Small schemes (typically 1 to 100 ha) are single owners' (commercial) or farmers' groups or single small farmers. Examples are Kenya, Zimbabwe, Tanzania, and Madagascar for gravity systems from rivers; Nigeria (Fadama) for shallow groundwater; and Kenya and Tanzania for pumping from lakes.

Support Services

The support services to irrigated agriculture must provide—besides the usual services for extension, marketing, and credit—technical assistance to the schemes for construction, operation, maintenance, and eventually mecha-

nization. For large schemes the provision of such services is normally the responsibility of the scheme management. For medium and small irrigation schemes these services must be organized or provided by the appropriate government agencies, such as the agricultural extension service. They must operate at the district or local level to reach the farming communities and small farmers. While agricultural extension services are normally organized for the district and local level, the government services for technical support of irrigation development and management for medium and small schemes—if they exist at all—tend to be centralized in the ministry responsible for irrigation, which often is not even the ministry of agriculture.

It is now realized that the weakest point of institutional support to irrigation development and management is the provision of technical services to medium and small schemes, in particular those designed in the context of rural development. Action programs are called for—with external assistance as required—to help African governments establish and improve these irrigation services.

REFERENCES

Club du Sahel, CILSS. 1980. Stratégie de lutte contre la secheresse et de developement dans le Sahel—projet de version revisée, September.

Dudal, R., G. M. Higgins, and A. H. Kassam. 1982. Land resources for the world's food production. Twelfth International Congress of Soil Science, New Delhi.

FAO [Food and Agriculture Organization]. 1980. Regional food plan for Africa. Rome.

———. 1981. Agriculture: Toward 2000. Rome.

———. 1982a. Report of the Twelfth African regional conference. Rome.

———. 1983a. World food report. Rome.

———. 1983b. Conference document C 83/18. Twenty-second session. Rome.

———. 1984. Land, food and people. Rome.

Korten, F. F. 1982. Building national capacity to develop water users' associations. Staff working paper 529. Washington, D.C.: World Bank.

Sagardoy, J. A. 1982b. Organization and maintenance of irrigation schemes. Irrigation and drainage paper 40. Rome: FAO.

World Bank. 1981. Accelerated development in sub-Saharan Africa: An agenda for action. Washington, D.C.

32. MARKET VERSUS NONMARKET MANAGEMENT OF IRRIGATION WATER: A REVIEW OF THE ISSUES

Robert A. Young, Colorado State University, Fort Collins, Colorado

ABSTRACT

This chapter sets out some concepts and evidence relevant to the choice of market versus nonmarket institutions for managing irrigation water. Attributes of water and water-resource systems of interest from economic, political, and social perspectives are identified. Virtues and vices of market and nonmarket resource allocation systems are outlined. Incremental changes in both market and nonmarket institutions which have promise for improving system effectiveness are suggested.

The purpose of this chapter is to bring together a number of ideas and concepts which relate to the choice of market versus nonmarket management of water for irrigation. The chapter title reflects my belief that it is more fruitful to focus attention on rules for water allocation than on ownership of the system's resources. The assignment is a difficult one, as evidenced by centuries of ideological debates on the appropriate social, political, and economic forms for the organization of human affairs (Lindblom, 1977). In the brief space allotted here, one can only touch on the high points of this debate as it applies to irrigation water supply. The following remarks are aimed primarily at developing countries, but that is not to say that the discussion is irrelevant to the United States and other developed nations.

PRELIMINARIES

Prefatory to the policy analysis that follows, it is useful to identify society's goals with respect to water management, specify some assumptions about the behavior of the elements of an irrigation system, and indicate the range of available management alternatives.

Goals for Design of Water-Management Systems

Establishment of a water-management system involves compromises among several often conflicting goals. It is not surprising, then, that different cultures have chosen different institutional forms for managing water, the choice reflecting the relative importance placed by that culture on the various objectives.

The foundations of social organization are seen in the transcending values embodied in existing laws and institutions. Most of us would subscribe to such basic values as respect for the dignity of the individual, freedom, openness, and the rule of reason. At an operational level we find more tangible objectives. Economists emphasize economic efficiency, defined here as the maximizing of net value productivity for the resource base and level of technology. Also important is the effect of management systems on the distribution of income, since high on the list of objectives of most nations are equitable purchasing power among their citizens and balanced regional growth. Management rules should be fair, in the sense that equals are treated in equal fashion. Maass and Anderson (1979) note that desire for popular participation and local control also often plays an important role in shaping management institutions. They also emphasize the need for orderly processes of conflict resolution.

Institutional Arrangements

The human part of an irrigation system consists of the individuals who use the water and those who supply it. We can think of these people's activities as being coordinated by "institutional arrangements." As used by Fox (1976), this term refers to an interrelated set of *organizations* and *rules* that serve to coordinate activities to achieve social goals. Organizations to represent the interests of irrigators, establish and enforce the rules, and maintain the ditches are important at the local level, while large, hierarchical systems usually control the capture, storage, conveyance, and distribution of surface water.

Many forms of rules to allocate water among users are observed. These range from simple, informal systems, through the *warabundi* allocation (equal time of flow per unit land area) found in India and Pakistan to the elaborate volumetric pricing procedures found in Israel.

It is appropriate to point out here that the apparently clear distinction between market and nonmarket allocations in my chapter title begins to blur on closer examination. While many organizational forms have been formulated to deliver irrigation water, it is not always obvious how they should be classified. In Colorado alone, for example, Radosevich et al. (1976) identify a number of types. Primarily local organizations include unincorporated or incorporated voluntary associations, private or public mutual irrigation companies, and water users' associations. Organizations with broader jurisdictions include water conservation districts, water conservancy districts, irrigation districts, and groundwater augmentation organizations.

The Importance of Incentives

Policymakers would be well advised to better understand the characteristics and motivations of the human components of the irrigation system. These components include those people who provide the links between the source of the water supply and the growing crop and those who influence the incentives and constraints facing such people. The performance of the system depends on the incentives and disincentives for effective and timely execution of tasks. Policymakers can assume that both cultivators and public employees are self-interested; they will be motivated by income, work satisfaction, social and professional status, and peer approval. The well-functioning system will recognize these traits and capitalize on them, rather than ignoring them or trying to manage as though human nature were other than it really is.

THE SOCIOPOLITICAL-ECONOMIC NATURE OF WATER SUPPLY AND USE

The "water is different" concept refers to the special characteristics which distinguish water from most other resources or commodities (Kelso, 1967) and which are important in selecting management institutions (Bower, 1963; Young and Haveman, 1985). These unique attributes—supply, demand, and sociopolitical attitudes—are considered below.

Supply Characteristics

Mobility. Water, usually a liquid, tends to flow, seep, evaporate, and transpire. Its mobility presents problems in identifying and measuring the resource. The exclusive property rights which are the basis of an exchange economy are relatively difficult to establish and enforce.

Economies of large size. Surface water in particular exhibits economies of large size in storage, conveyance, and distribution, and the preconditions for a classic natural monopoly are present. (Groundwater seems to present a different story, since most size economies are achieved at relatively small outputs. Moreover, such size economies as are observed may be offset by conveyance costs and third-party spillover costs.)

Uncertainty in supply. Water supply is typically highly variable in time, space, and quality. At the extremes of the probability distributions of supply (floods and droughts) are the conditions that create problems for humankind. The solutions to such difficulties typically involve benefits which are nonrival in consumption and therefore have a public or collective good character.

Demand Characteristics

Relatively low economic value. A paradox arises in dealing with the value of irrigation water. The political and media rhetoric asserts its enormous economic importance. The conventional view, however, contrasts with the reality that the resource exhibits a relatively low economic value at the margin. Conceptually correct empirical estimates of the direct marginal value productivity of irrigation water for the most part fall in the range of $25 to $75 per acre-foot (Young, 1984; Hussain and Young, 1985; Bowen and Young, 1985). For most crops throughout the world the estimates are in the lower part of this range.

Put in other terms, resources devoted to irrigation water development, conservation, or management can justify a cost of only 1.5 to 3 cents a ton. While a substantial *total*

economic value may yet be implied for large water-supply projects, my point is that the *marginal* value of irrigation water to the user group is often insufficient to justify major water-saving technologies, or, more important, labor-intensive administrative and management procedures. (Compare irrigation water, for example, with other liquids important in modern economies. Gasoline retails in the United States at about $400,000 per acre-foot, implying that users are willing to pay 10,000 to 20,000 times per unit volume what they will pay for irrigation water.) Extensive water-conserving institutional arrangements (property rights and pricing policies) as well as technologies (closed conduits and metering) are currently found only where water is very scarce and valuable. This trend is only beginning to occur in economically developed arid regions such as the southwestern United States or Israel.

Many of the problems of management and technical efficiency discussed in this chapter would, I hypothesize, readily resolve themselves if the marginal value productivity were just two or three times higher. In such an event the incentives would be strong for capital or administrative effort to be substituted to save water.

Variability in demand. Demand for irrigation water tends also to be highly variable, depending on temperature and rainfall. This creates a peak-load problem, and institutions and storage and conveyance systems must be prepared to satisfy large demands in brief summer periods.

Pervasive interdependency among users. The physical nature of water mentioned above, combined with supply variability, causes a unique but unpredictable degree of interrelationship among water users. Water uses generally result in return flows to an aquifer or a stream. Downstream users are greatly affected (for good or ill) by the quantity, quality, and timing of releases or return flows by upstream users. This point is well illustrated by the effect on groundwater systems of conveyance and field seepage, which often result in rising water tables and waterlogging for downslope cultivators.

Social Attitudes toward Water

Conflicting social values. Goals other than economic efficiency play an unusually large role in the selection of water-management institutions. Boulding (1980) has observed that "the sacredness of water as a symbol of ritual purity exempts it somewhat from the dirty rationality of the market." Some cultures or religions (e.g., Islam) proscribe water allocation by market forces.

Unrealistic expectations about the regional growth-inducing role of water. A prominent article of faith, particularly in arid areas, is that water-resource developments yield large regional growth impacts. The direct evidence on this point, however, indicates that income and employment effects of irrigation in the United States are in fact modest (Young, 1984). While little evidence exists for other areas of the world, I would be surprised if public expectations are realized elsewhere.

Technical bias. Water management is typically viewed as a technical or engineering problem, even though a strong case can be made that the human components of the supply system should receive equal consideration. Most managers are engineers by training and experience and find more reward in solving the technical problems than the human ones. (My point here is nicely illustrated by the organization of this conference. Only one of the six technical themes deals directly with the human part of the system, and of the principal speakers invited for that one theme, barely half obtained advanced degrees in one of the human-oriented disciplines.)

OTHER FACTORS IMPORTANT IN THE DESIGN OF IRRIGATION MANAGEMENT INSTITUTIONS

A number of other considerations, in addition to the socio-economic attributes of water, are briefly touched on here.

Transactions Costs versus the Relative Scarcity Water

The term "transactions costs" refers to the resources required to establish, operate, and enforce a management or regulatory system. Transactions costs include costs of *obtaining information* (such as knowledge about the needs and attitudes of other participants), *contracting* (resources required to reach agreements), and *policing* (enforcing rules) (Dahlman, 1979).

Given the supply-and-demand characteristics of water noted earlier, transactions costs for water management and allocation tend to be relatively high. Where water is plentiful relative to demand, water laws tend to be simple and only casually enforced. Where water is scarce, more elaborate management systems have emerged. In many regions water supplies are only now becoming scarce enough to require formal management systems. Increased resource scarcity and technological advances which reduce the transactions cost of monitoring and enforcing regulations encourage innovations in allocative institutions to economize on the scarce resource (Ruttan, 1978).

Relative Complexity of Irrigation Distribution

Bromley (1982) has pointed out that the complexity of the institutional arrangements necessary to operate a water distribution system efficiently and equitably is not generally recognized, even among social scientists. (Recalling the evidence for low-value productivity cited above, I believe that the problem is to find institutions with low transactions costs as well as economical technologies.) To elaborate on this point, four different sources of this complexity can be identified.

Large-numbers problem. A typical irrigation system comprises many individuals. Because of varying physical production conditions (soils, microclimate, etc.), market situation, capital endowments, and personal preferences, these individuals will select somewhat differing cropping patterns and production practices and show varying water needs through the crop season.

System losses. Most water delivery systems are unlined and hence subject to varying degrees of seepage loss. When deliveries are not directly measured but are allocated on the basis of equal time per hectare, differing water supplies may be available to alternative locations unless this factor is recognized. Such systems tend to treat tail enders inequitably.

Upstream-downstream interdependence. Water supplies for downstream or downwatercourse users depend on the actions of upstream users. This physical interdependence results in differing degrees of concern for the system as a whole. Those close to the outlet have little interest in system maintenance and efficiency, while these are vital concerns to those separated from the water source by many people and much distance. These varying levels of concern compound the problem of achieving collective organization to operate and maintain an irrigation system.

Communication and information problems. Particularly in the larger-scale systems in developing countries, difficulties arise in accurately communicating water demands and availabilities among the various actors in the system. Farmers with specific water entitlements may be net demanders at one time and net suppliers soon afterward. The spatial distribution of producers and the absence of direct communication links (such as telephones) between individual farmers or farmers and system managers will hamper beneficial exchanges when excess water occurs at one place while unsatisfied needs exist elsewhere. Also, when several days may be required to move water from storage reservoirs to fields, unexpected weather changes can cause significant overshoot or undershoot from actual crop needs.

Flexibility versus Security

Ciriacy-Wantrup (1967) pointed out the conflicts between secure and "flexible" management systems. A secure set of water rights affords protection against legal, physical, and tenure uncertainties. Only when expectations are secure will irrigators find it profitable to undertake the long-term investments in land-leveling, conveyance, and application systems necessary to maximize water productivity. Flexibility refers to the ability to change at low cost the allocation of water between users, uses, and regions. From society's perspective flexibility is of great importance. Changes in demand can be accommodated, water being reallocated to more valuable uses as they arise.

Attention is now turned to the attributes of market versus nonmarket mechanisms for resource allocation. The advantages and disadvantages of each approach are briefly summarized with illustrations drawn from irrigation.

EVALUATING THE MARKET APPROACH

Any economic system must answer the questions: (1) What goods and services are to be produced? (2) What resources and technologies are used in producing them? and (3) Who is to enjoy the use of the products? The adoption of the market system to answer these questions is based on the premises that the personal wants of individuals should determine the employment of resources in production, distribution, and exchange and that the individuals themselves are the best judges of their own wants (consumer sovereignty).

Private-Sector "Virtues"

An idealized competitive market system (one that has many producers and consumers who are well informed, motivated by individual self-interest, and who individually own and control resources) can be shown to have certain desirable properties. One such desirable attribute is that the system will produce the maximum-valued bundles of goods and services, given the endowment of resources, the available technology, the preferences of consumers, and the distribution of purchasing power. Individual producers and consumers, acting in their own self-interest, will, in accordance with Adam Smith's "invisible hands," arrive at an allocation of resources which cannot be improved upon. Firms, encouraged by prospective profit, buy inputs as cheaply as possible, combine them in the most efficient form, and produce those things which have the highest value relative to cost. Consumers' tastes and preferences influence their expenditure patterns, thereby encouraging firms to produce the commodities people want. Prices are bid up for the commodities most desired, and the producers allocate resources in the direction of greatest profits. The firms most successful in the process, producing desired goods most efficiently, are rewarded by profit, and the unsuccessful are eliminated; thus production occurs at least cost.

A further desirable property of the market system is its ability to accommodate change in conditions of production and patterns of consumption. New knowledge and technology are rapidly reflected in the prices which producers are willing to accept for their products. On the consumer side, changes in income and preferences are soon reflected in expenditure patterns. Hence a market system yields maximum satisfaction in not only a static but also a dynamic context.

The actual market system may not always meet the precise preconditions of the idealized construct. Mixed capitalist systems are based on the assumption that for most goods and services the allocation resulting from the market processes sufficiently approximates the idealized system. Where this is not the case, regulatory processes or public production is provided to allocate resources.

Private-Sector "Vices"

The shortcomings of markets are encompassed in the theory of "market failure" (see, e.g., Haveman, 1976). Market failure is said to arise when the incentives facing individuals and groups in the economy encourage behavior that does not meet the appropriate efficiency or equity criteria. Several classifications of conditions which lead to market failure are found. They usually include externalities, public goods, increasing returns, market imperfections, and distributional inequity (Randall, 1983, sets out an intriguing alternative formulation).

Externalities. Externalities, also called spillover effects, are uncompensated side effects of individual activities. In such instances the full costs of economic activity are not recognized, and market outcomes will be inefficient. In irrigation systems an example is found in saline return flows detrimental to downstream water users, a cost unreflected in upstream water users' allocation decisions.

"Public" or collective goods. These goods are nonrival in consumption in the sense that one person's consumption does not preclude use by others. It is difficult to exclude

nonpayers and thus for the private producer to appropriate all the benefits provided. Water-storage projects often provide flood-control benefits that are a public good.

"Increasing returns." This term refers to the situation in which marginal costs are falling throughout the range of market demand. A firm that experiences continuously decreasing costs will take over the entire market and become a monopoly. The lowest-cost mode is by a single producer. An inefficient production situation will result, since monopolists will restrain production and have little incentive to innovate. Canal irrigation represents an example of such "natural monopolies," since more than one (competitive) supplier would present much higher distribution costs.

EVALUATING PUBLIC-SECTOR PERFORMANCE

Friedman (1962, chap. 2) envisions the role of the public sector as follows:

> A government which maintained law and order, defined property rights, served as a means whereby we could modify property rights and other rules of the economic game, adjudicated disputes about the interpretation of the rules, enforced contracts, promoted competition, provided a monetary framework, engaged in activities to counter technical monopolies and to overcome neighborhood effects widely regarded as sufficiently important to justify government intervention, and which supplemented private charity and the private family in protecting the irresponsible, whether madman or child, such a government would clearly have important functions to perform.

Public-Sector Virtues

The advantages of nonmarket allocation activities, as compared with those of the private market, for irrigation water include the following:

Reflect broader social goals. While the private market is seen as an efficient engine for producing the maximum-valued bundle of goods and services, public action may incorporate broader social goals of society. Primary among these might be the amelioration of inequalities in income and wealth among members of the society and perhaps among political subdivisions or regions.

Regulate externalities. Collective action to protect third parties from undesired third-party effects is a necessary role of the public sector. In irrigation protection against waterlogging or salinization from upslope farms is an example.

Regulate or supplant natural monopoly. The supplier of irrigation water has, as a natural monopoly, literal power to impose economic ruin on those served. Public regulation, or, more often, public supply, can in principle avoid the possible undesirable effects of a private, profit-oriented monopoly.

Public-Sector Vices: "The Theory of Nonmarket Failure"

Nonmarket responses to market imperfections may also lead to nonoptimal outcomes. Wolf (1979a, b) has formulated a model of nonmarket failure which focuses on those performance incentives in public agencies that result in divergence from socially preferable outcomes in terms of the criteria of allocative efficiency and distributional equity.

A general lesson here is that nonmarket solutions may not necessarily be superior to suboptimal market approaches.

Among the problems listed by Wolf are the following:

"Products" hard to define. The outputs of nonmarket activities are often difficult to define in practice and hard to measure independently of the inputs that produced them.

Evidence of quality elusive. Because consumer preferences transmitted by market prices are missing, it is difficult to know whether public performance is improving or deteriorating.

No single performance measure. Because there is no single "bottom line" for evaluating performance, the public cannot effectively determine the value of public action. Hence there is seldom a reliable mechanism for terminating unsuccessful programs.

The above points can be illustrated in public irrigation projects. The annual reports of the U.S. Bureau of Reclamation, as well as those of other irrigation ministries, document the number of hectares irrigated, the quantity of water stored or delivered, and the number of farms served or gross crop revenues. None of these directly answers the essential question about the actual economic return on the public investment. The most appropriate measure, the realized net social return on public investment, is so complex, requiring large annual sample surveys of farmer profitability (and not really desired by the agency), that it is attempted by only an occasional dissident academic. Even then there is disagreement on how to measure important elements of the formula, such as interest rates, prices for crops, and opportunity costs of labor and other inputs (Young and Gray, 1972; Young, 1979).

Private goals of public agents. Wolf refers to the internal goals of an organization as "internalities." These, in addition to the agency's public purposes, provide the motivations, rewards, and penalties for individual performance. Such internal goals are characteristic of any large organization, private or public, but the problem of performance measures noted above makes public inefficiencies less likely to be terminated.

Specific examples of counterproductive internal goals include budget maximization, overly expensive high-technology solutions, and outright nonperformance of duties. In the first example, when profit is not available as a performance measure, the budget often serves as a proxy. Agency heads are often, in fact, provided with staff and perquisites according to the size of their budget, reinforcing the incentive distortion. Second, high-technology solutions, or "technical quality," may become an agency goal. For instance, sprinkler or drip irrigation systems may be recommended when less expensive methods are to be preferred. Finally, agency personnel may be persuaded, by gifts or other inducements, to violate operating rules for a favored few (Wade, 1982).

Spillovers from public action. Public agencies, including irrigation projects, can also be a major source of third-party effects. Salinity on the Colorado River system, in the southwestern United States, and waterlogging of downslope lands from inappropriately managed public projects are ready examples. These problems are especially difficult to resolve when the third-party effects are registered in another country (Oyarzabal-Tamargo and Young, 1978).

Inequitable distribution of power. Public-sector responsibilities, however noble the intent, may not be exercised scrupulously or competently. Yet the monopoly control of water supplies by public agencies provides certain individuals with so much power over the economic welfare of farmers that procedures to protect those of limited influence must be of prime importance.

IMPLICATIONS FOR WATER ALLOCATION POLICY

Except in special cases I see no immediate need for major shifts in the present balance between market and nonmarket allocation of irrigation water, but a number of incremental changes would likely contribute to a more productive and economically efficient sector.

On-farm water allocation. Only the most radical central planning ideologues now disagree that economically efficient agricultural productivity and social stability are best served by leaving responsibility for production decisions to the individual cultivator on his own land. Decisions on when and how much to irrigate are best made by the private individual. The main role of the public sector here is to ensure secure and equitable rights to water and to avoid disincentive policies.

Groundwater supply. Aquifers can be effectively tapped by private initiative. On-demand water supply can optimize timing and quantity, and users have exhibited much more willingness to pay for groundwater than for surface water. The absence of scale economies removes the need for public supply. Where groundwater has been publicly supplied, as in Pakistan, unsatisfactory results have been reported.

Once groundwater extraction expands beyond natural recharge rates, allocation problems are likely to arise from interdependency (external) effects on neighboring users. These effects can include land subsidence, intrusion of adjacent poor-quality water, over-rapid depletion of water stocks, and depletion of flows in interrelated streams (Young, 1970). Public regulations will be required to ameliorate these difficulties and to protect the rights of affected third parties.

Surface water. Large-scale storage for canal irrigation is a classic natural monopoly. With few exceptions the returns on such investments are too low to attract private capital. Hence, nonmarket management of these systems is unlikely to give way to the market sector (though there is no technical impediment to a regulated private water utility, similar to those found in energy, transportation, or urban water).

Incremental changes to improve the performance of surface systems need to focus on the system's managers and personnel. A start would be to try to more closely associate the rewards received by the system agents with the ultimate profitability of their farmer clients. Wade (1982) has documented the heretofore anecdotal evidence of widespread payoffs in canal systems in one nation. These payoffs could be channeled productively by requiring them to be contingent on ultimate system performance. While space limits prohibit a full analysis, I am thinking of bonuses contingent on the cultivators served by an irrigation system achieving yields exceeding a moving average over seven (or five or ten?) years by a specified percent. The bonuses would be only a fraction of incremental farmer income but could be a substantial augmentation of the water managers' incomes.

CONCLUDING REMARKS

Two particular trends will continue to manifest themselves in the irrigated regions of the world. First, the pressures of growing demand for food against increasingly limited water supplies will likely cause an increase in the derived economic value of water. Increased scarcity begets a rising shadow price. Second, the increasing demands for water for energy production, urban uses, amenities, and waste disposal will bring about a rising incidence of interdependence and conflicts among users. Both of these trends will call for improved institutional forms for managing the water resource.

Where nonmarket processes are now dominant, we need to, first, learn how to make such processes work better (Bromley et al., 1980; Seckler and Nobe, 1983), and, second, open the way to doing with less nonmarket water management. There is a need to focus more attention on the incentives and disincentives facing the human components of the system. We must examine the tasks required to supply water to farmers when and where needed and to tilt incentives to reward those who contribute most to these tasks. At the same time we need to determine which activities are counterproductive and to what extent and then create disincentive or compensation schemes to help correct these difficulties.

Specific suggestions for a changing public role are as follows:

Agricultural price policies. Price-depressing marketing policies for crops in a number of countries (e.g., Egypt, Sudan, and Pakistan) may reduce the value productivity of water as perceived by the cultivator to half its value from the society's view (Bowen and Young, 1985). It is little wonder, that such governments have trouble interesting water users in improving technical efficiency of water use.

Research. Allocative institutions transfer much less readily to other cultures and economic systems than water management technologies. Developing countries and donor groups should spend relatively more, rather than less, on socioeconomic research.

A larger role for markets. Finally, after due consideration is given to the virtues and vices of each type of approach, I believe that, to meet future needs in a changing environment, market processes should play an increasingly greater role (see also Anderson, 1983.) The highest economic return for use of irrigation water will be achieved if water rights are clearly defined and exchangeable while third parties are protected. Exchanges, rentals, and sales of water between users and among user groups will help ensure that the resource is being used most efficiently and its allocation is responsive to changing conditions.

ACKNOWLEDGMENTS

Thanks are due Roger Mann and Ronald Griffin for helpful suggestions on earlier drafts. Support by the Colorado State University Experiment Station is acknowledged.

REFERENCES

Anderson, T. L., (ed.) 1983. Water rights: Scarce resource allocation, bureaucracy and the environment. Cambridge: Ballinger.

Boulding, K. E. 1980. The implications of improved water allocation policy. *In* Marvin Duncan (comp.) Western water resources: Coming problems and policy alternatives. Boulder, Colo.: Westview Press.

Bowen, R. L., and R. A. Young. 1985. Financial and economic irrigation net benefit functions for Egypt's northern delta. *Water Resources Research* 21.

Bower, B. T. 1963. Some physical, technological, and economic characteristics of water and water resource systems: implications for administration. *Natural Resources Journal* 3:215–38.

Bromley, D. W. 1982. Improving irrigated agriculture: institutional reform and the small farmer. Staff working paper 531. Washington, D.C.: World Bank.

Bromley, D. W., D. C. Taylor, and D. E. Parker. 1980. Water reform and economic development: institutional aspects of water management in the developing countries. *Economic Development and Cultural Change* 28:365–87.

Ciriacy-Wantrup, S. V. 1967. Water economics: relations to law and policy. *In* R. E. Clark (ed.) Waters and water rights, Vol. 1. Indianapolis, Ind.: Allen Smith Co.

Dahlman, C. J. 1979. The problem of externality. *Journal of Law and Economics* 22:141–62.

Friedman, Milton. 1962. Capitalism and freedom. Chicago: University of Chicago Press.

Haveman, R. H. 1976. Economics of the public sector. 2nd ed. New York: Wiley.

Hussain, R. Z., and R. A. Young. 1985. The economic value productivity of irrigation water in Pakistan. Submitted for publication.

Kelso, M. M. 1967. The "water is different" syndrome: or what is wrong with the water industry? Pp. 176–83. *In* Proceedings of the Third Annual Conference, American Water Resources Association.

Lindblom, Charles E. 1977. Politics and markets: the world's political-economic systems. New York: Basic Books.

Maass, A., and R. L. Anderson. 1978. And the desert shall rejoice: conflict, growth, and justice in arid environments. Cambridge, Mass.: MIT Press.

Oyarzabal-Tamargo, R., and R. A. Young. 1978. International external diseconomies: the Colorado River salinity problem in Mexico. *Natural Resources Journal* 18:77–88.

Radosevich, G. E., K. C. Nobe, D. Allardice, and C. Kirkwood. 1976. Evolution and administration of Colorado water law. Fort Collins, Colo.: Water Resource Publishers.

Randall, Alan. 1983. The problem of market failure. *Natural Resources Journal* 23:131–48.

Ruttan, V. W. 1978. Induced institutional change. Pp. 327–56. *In* H. Binswanger and V. W. Ruttan (ed.) Induced innovation. Baltimore, Md.: Johns Hopkins University Press.

Seckler, D. W., and K. C. Nobe. 1983. The management factor in developing economies. *In* K. C. Nobe and R. K. Sampath (ed.) Issues in Third World development. Boulder, Colo.: Westview Press.

Wade, Robert. 1982. The system of administrative and political corruption: canal irrigation in south India. *Journal of Development Studies* 18:287–99.

Wolf, Charles, Jr. 1979a. A theory of non-market failures. *Public Interest* 55:114–33.

———. 1979b. A theory of non-market failure: framework for implementation analysis. *Journal of Law and Economics* 22:107–39.

Young, R. A. 1970. The safe yield of aquifers: an economic formulation. *Journal of the Irrigation and Drainage Division, Proceedings, American Society of Civil Engineers* 96 (IR4): 377–85.

———. 1978. Economic analysis and federal irrigation policy: a reappraisal. *Western Journal of Agricultural Economics* 3:257–68.

———. 1984. Direct and regional economic impacts of competition for irrigation water. *In* E. A. Englebert and A. F. Scheuring (ed.) Water scarcity: Impacts on western agriculture. Berkeley: University of California Press.

Young, R. A., and R. H. Haveman. 1985. Economics of water resources: a survey. *In* A. V. Kneese and J. L. Sweeney (ed.) Handbook of natural resource and energy economics, Vol. 2. Amsterdam, Elsevier Science Publishers.

Young, R. A., S. L. Gray, R. B. Held, and R. S. Mack. 1972. Economic value of water: concepts and empirical estimates. Report to the National Water Commission, NTIS PB210356. Springfield, Va.: National Technical Information Service.

PART VI. INTEGRATED ECOSYSTEMS MANAGEMENT

33. ECOLOGICAL ASPECTS OF IRRIGATION

H. Lieth, University of Osnabrück, Osnabrück, West Germany

INTRODUCTION

Ecological aspects of irrigation, discussed by an ecologist, offer highly contrasting positions. On the one hand, irrigation has increased or permitted food and feed production in dry regions of the world and has made some regions habitable which otherwise would not be. On the other hand, throughout history large-scale irrigation systems have caused direct and indirect problems to such a degree that many have been abandoned. Many more must be abandoned if the major geoecological problems that have arisen or can be predicted cannot be solved. One special problem is that large-scale irrigation projects may cause heavy losses of highly fertile land inland and along coastal estuaries, which means that the net gain in biomass production for mankind may be zero. This problem contributes to the reason that freshwater irrigation systems may not be enough to feed the increasing world population. One possible solution is the use of high-salinity water, up to the strength of ocean water, to create new agricultural systems in suitable geographic regions.

Issues are presented in the following sequence: regional net primary productivity (NPP) and the availability of water, ecological problems generated with irrigation systems, and the agricultural potential of high-salinity irrigation systems. Many of the solutions proposed here should become subjects for future research. The options for future applications of new systems and approaches have been elaborated in theory and in pilot projects conducted by myself and other ecologists. Several unconventional projects discussed deserve financial support by international agencies because they promise great returns for populations living in semiarid or arid regions.

REGIONAL NPP AND THE AVAILABILITY OF WATER

Agricultural and forest production depends chiefly on factors that limit plant growth and control consumption of the biomass produced. Water is one of the most important growth-limiting factors. Its effect on plant production is greater when all other production controls are at optimal levels. This means that optimal fertilization is needed together with irrigation and optimum temperature. The global impact of these three production factors has been shown by my laboratory for natural systems. The set of equations describing these interrelations is

$$NPP/_{G^{-2}} \times A^{-1} = MIN \, (NPP_T, NPP_{Pp}) \times F_{(soil\ fertility)} \times F_{(CO_2)},$$

$$NPP_T = \frac{3000}{1 + E^{1.315} - 0.119\ T/_{0_C}},$$

$$NPP_{Pp} = 3000 \times (1 - E^{-0.000664\ Pp/mm}),$$

$$F_{(soil\ fertility)} = (see\ table\ 1),$$

$$F_{(CO_2)} = 3.6365 \times (1 - E^{-0.00134\ [CO_2/ppm - 80]})$$

in which NPP is in grams per year; T is average annual temperature (Celsius); Pp is the annual total sum precipitation in millimeters; and F(soil fertility) is the factor for the respective soil of the site as expressed in Table 1. The CO_2 factor takes into account the rising CO_2 fraction in the atmosphere. For the purpose of this chapter, the CO_2 factor is set for 340 parts per million (ppm).

The following three maps show the global pattern of natural NPP predicted for a 2.5 × 2.5-degree matrix. In Fig. 1, NPP is predicted by the above set of equations. In Figs. 2 and 3, NPP is predicted for temperature and precipitation, respectively. The difference between the predictions via temperature and precipitation is shown in Fig. 4, which demonstrates that much of the world's NPP is precipitation-limited. The higher the temperature, the larger the limitation, which means that much of the global solar energy untapped by biological energy fixation lies in tropical regions. Fig. 5 shows the general control of NPP by either temperature or precipitation across the geographical latitudes. It shows that 40° north latitude is about the turning point north of which temperature predominantly controls NPP and south of which precipitation mostly controls it. Fig. 5 was derived from an earlier model (Lieth, 1972) by Straškraby.

All the models presented are convenient to use for initial planning purposes. They provide total NPP figures which are in the realm of productivity of high-yielding crops as indicated in the International Rice Research Institute (IRRI) symposium on crop productivity.

ECOLOGICAL PROBLEMS GENERATED WITH IRRIGATION SYSTEMS

The productive benefit of irrigation systems is undisputed. In spite of that, however, the history of man shows that numerous cultures deteriorated after a period of apparently happy life that was supported by an irrigation system. Other cultures have lasted since the development of the first irrigation system and were interrupted by catastrophes not caused by faulty irrigation technique. Failures appear to be more numerous in dry than in humid climates.

The problems with irrigation systems may stem from the alteration of abiotic environmental conditions, cropping

Table 1. The factors for F (soil fertility) for the most frequent soils of the earth.

FAO Soil Units	Factor	Number of Data Points
Acrisols		
Ag	0.87	1
Ah	0.22	2
Ao	0.70	7
Other A	0.60	—
Cambisols		
Bd	0.94	10
Be	1.69	7
Bh	1.58	3
Bx	0.76	1
Chernosems		
Cl	0.99	1
Podsoluvisols		
Dd	0.83	1
Ferralsols		
Fx	0.55	1
Gleysols		
Gh	0.47	2
Gx	0.57	2
Other G	0.50	—
Lithosols		
I	0.52	7
Iy	1.14	1
Fluvisols		
J	0.49	1
Je	0.61	2
Other J	0.55	—
Kastanozems		
Kh	1.96	2
Kl	1.61	3
Other K	1.80	—
Luvisols		
La	0.34	1
Lc	1.04	2
Lf	1.65	1
Lg	2.78	1
Lo	0.85	4
Histosols		
Od	1.39	2
Podsols		
Ph	0.56	1
Po	0.61	7
Other P	0.55	—
Regosols		
Rc	1.61	2
Re	1.14	1
Rx	0.91	1
Other R	1.20	—
Solonetz		
So	0.59	1
Andosols		
Tv	1.65	1
Xerosols		
Xh	0.42	1
Yermosols		
Y	0.30	2
Yh	0.66	1
Yt	0.09	1
Yl	0.23	2
Solonchak		
Zo	0.44	2
Zt	0.03	1
Other Z	0.20	—

SOURCE: Adapted from Esser, 1984. The soil system corresponds with the classification of the FAO-UNESCO World Soil Map.

Table 2. Ecological problems with irrigation systems.

At the area of irrigation:

Soil conditions	Hardpan development
	High salinity
	Nitrate seepage
Water conditions	Breakage of dams
	Floods
	Stagnating waters
	Quality changes
Weather conditions	Extensive drought
	Sandstorms
	Torrential rains
Cropping system	Failure of growth because of environmental stress
Cash crops and bulk cereals	Failure of yield because of faulty management
	Pests, weeds, and diseases of crop plants
	Transportation problems
	Shortage of labor
	Marketing problems
Garden crops and vegetables	Growth failure because of various stress conditions
	Yield loss because of pests and diseases
Large-scale irrigation systems	Crop failure because of shortage of water
	Yield losses because of herbivorous insects and other small animals, including large bird populations
Impact on natural vegetation and wildlife	Replacement of natural ecosystems
	Unbalancing of animal populations; import of new species
Human health	Various waterborne diseases
	Morbidity or sickness because of airborne insects
	Possibility of epidemics

At areas geologically connected:

Abiotic environment changes	
Soil conditions	Loss of land for reservoirs
	Loss of land in the river delta
Water conditions	Alteration of sediment load downstream
	Erection of new barriers in rivers
	Alteration of floods
Cropping systems	
For agriculture, fisheries, and silviculture	Loss of farmland in delta areas
	Alteration of fisheries
	Loss of forest acreage
	Bridging of previously isolated productive systems
	Change of marketing chances for native products
Natural vegetation and wildlife	Unbalancing of wild-animal populations
	Reductions of natural vegetation
	Introduction of new species in area
	Bridging of previously isolated productive systems
Human health	Spreading of diseases over larger areas
	Generation of conditions for new diseases by creation of new habitats for their natural vectors

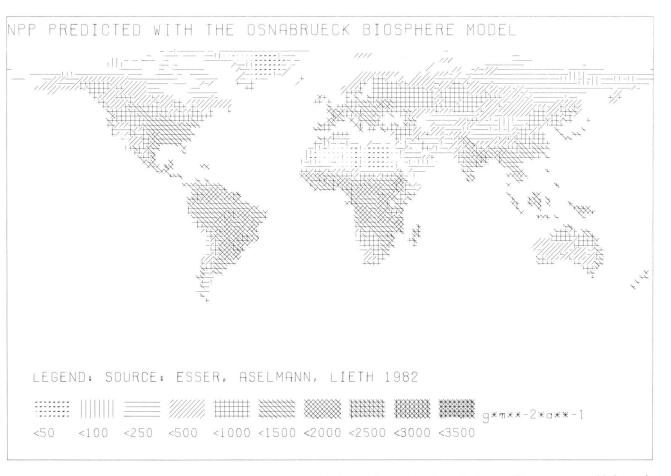

LEGEND: SOURCE: ESSER, ASELMANN, LIETH 1982

g*m**-2*a**-1

<50   <100   <250   <500   <1000 <1500 <2000 <2500 <3000 <3500

Fig. 1. Net primary productivity pattern of the world predicted with the set of equations shown in the text. The 2.5 × 2.5-grid size varies with latitude. The NPP values are divided from the environmental parameters averaged for each grid element. They are given in grams per square meter per year.

systems, and problems with human health. Table 2 shows some typical problem cases for each category. From the viewpoint of modeling an agroecosystem, note the last three problems mentioned under "Cash Crops and Bulk Cereals": transportation problems, shortage of labor, and marketing problems. An ecologist is usually not expected to deal with seed problems; however, as a systems analyst, I must include these aspects since all problems need ultimate consideration within a cost-benefit concept. In some instances we need to include legal and social aspects as well. This has a severe impact on the modeling strategy. I cannot deal with this problem here, however, and will only cite Thober et al. (1985). I select three problem cases from Table 2 only to demonstrate the seriousness of all points raised. They are: nitrate seepage, the loss of land in river delta areas, and the unbalancing of animal populations.

Nitrate Seepage

Advanced irrigation systems maximize crop productivity. Maximal crop production often requires high fertilizer inputs. When fertilizer is sprayed on irrigated fields, a certain amount will travel to the groundwater with the seepage water (as will various other chemicals). The groundwater is often the source of drinking water, especially where surface water is unavailable. If seepage water from irrigated fields

enters the drinking water, it may carry a substantial amount of chemicals used for the enhancement of crop production. I use nitrate as an example because it has become a great problem in countries with advanced, high-yield agriculture even without irrigation systems. Fig. 6 shows the nitrate amount found in seepage water under fields with different fertilizer applications. The high levels in this graph are from farm areas where either general-purpose liquid manure from feedlots or commercial nitrate fertilizer for sugar beets is applied. The ordinate of the graph shows the nitrate level in the seepage water in northern Germany and the abscissa the amount of nitrogen in the fertilizer from the two different sources. The graph shows that, with high but still productively and profitably used fertilizer levels, the nitrate content in the seepage water will exceed legal nitrate levels for drinking water. This problem is becoming more and more prominent in Europe. Fig. 7 shows the distribution of high nitrate levels in the groundwaters of the Federal Republic of Germany (see also Brown, this volume).

Loss of Land in River Delta Areas

Large-scale irrigation schemes in arid and semiarid countries are based on river water. Rivers carry large amounts of sediment eroded from higher elevations to the sea and deposit them near the shore. Part of the deposited material is

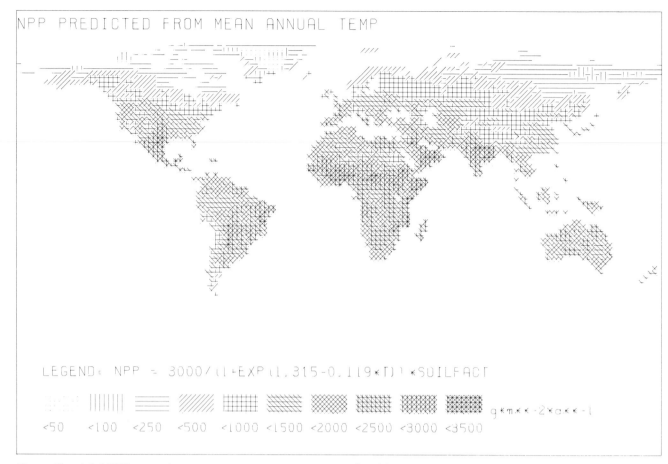

Fig. 2. The global NPP pattern in grams per square meter per year, predicted from average annual temperature and soil fertility only. All other conditions are as explained in Fig. 1.

carried away by wave action. The size of any delta area depends largely on the balance between these two forces. Large-scale irrigation projects interfere with this balance in two ways: they reduce the amount of water carried to the ocean, and, if dams are erected, they reduce the sediment load of the river. Together they have the affect that the land on the oceanfront is carried away by wave action faster than new material is deposited. This has been experienced on almost all rivers after large reservoirs were erected upstream. The example most often discussed is the Nile Delta area, which has lost several kilometers of land because of the Aswan Dam. In 1974, I saw the effects of the Kariba Reservoir on the delta of the Zambezi River, which at that time had lost about 1 km to the Indian Ocean (Lieth, 1974).

I mention these two examples because they demonstrate an additional problem. In the case of the Nile, the erection of the Aswan Dam, the benefit from it, and the loss of land to the ocean occurred in the same country. This makes it easier to provide relief to the population that must endure the loss of land. In the case of the Zambezi, however, one country, Zimbabwe, benefits from the reservoir, and another, Mozambique, endures the losses. International negotiations for compensation are necessary each time new losses occur at the seashore. On each large irrigation project

undertaken, the problems created on the site of the irrigation, together with the losses or changes generated at distant locations, require a thorough systems analysis to see whether the cost-benefit ratio justifies the expenditures.

The Unbalancing of Animal Populations

The ecological problems discussed so far affect the human population by the alteration of the physical environment. The alteration of the biological environment may, however, be more serious than the alteration of the physical environment.

Table 3 shows the major impacts of irrigation systems on plant and animal populations. These were mentioned in Table 2. Some of the entries in Table 3 are more harmful than others; some problems generated by the change of species populations are likely to make entire irrigation systems obsolete. I will discuss each group in Table 3 separately. Gifford's chapter in this volume will give more examples.

The interruption of normal population areas is mostly encountered in the rivers which supply the irrigation water. Dams often block the spawning grounds of fish. Frequently they separate upstream from downstream habitats and thereby offset the normal population growth of a large portion of the aquatic wildlife in general, not only fish.

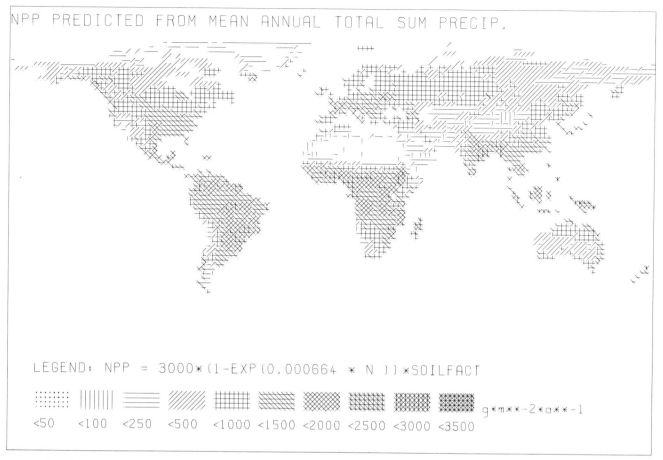

Fig. 3. The global NPP pattern in grams per square meter per year, predicted from average annual total sum precipitation and soil fertility only. All other conditions are as explained in Fig. 1.

Blocking the flow of natant plant species like *Eichhornia* sp., *Cyperus papyrus*, and others by dams has caused serious problems in several river reservoirs in dry areas; the Aswan Dam is only the most prominent example. There are ways to relieve problems caused by damming rivers; more difficult are the problems caused by new reservoirs and new irrigation systems that block migration routes for large-animal herds. Careful studies should be made before locations of future dam and cropping sites are determined so that new routes can be established for wildlife along the fields and across the rivers.

The second group of problems is caused by generating new habitats of high productivity in an area where little organic growth was encountered before. This is especially important since the sudden availability of open freshwater creates breeding grounds as well as ample feed.

Weeds and other pests are mainly problems for the cropping system. While several animal species also affect crops, others create numerous health hazards for the rural population working the irrigated fields. This problem requires careful studies about health hazards and also the provision of continued health care for each irrigation project.

The generation of new habitats makes possible the invasion of new species of plants and animals. Plants are dispersed conventionally as seeds as well as with commercial traffic to the irrigated area. Migrating animals like insects and birds invade in great numbers unless prevented from doing so by the managers of the irrigation system.

This problem may become especially severe if the irrigation site bridges natural barriers. Irrigation systems in arid lands appear basically as the most attractive improvements. They seem to be new oases in desert lands. The problem that may arise from constructing many systems in the same area, however, is that bridges are erected for arthropods, pathogens, or obnoxious pest species previously separated geographically. This fact is especially clear from the migratory locust problem in Arabian countries. Many other species can become potential problems if new crops are imported or common ones are spread over areas where they could not grow before. With our present knowledge we can only use chemical pesticides to prevent damage to plantations and crops. To determine whether this solution will remain feasible in the future or should be abandoned for economic or health reasons will require major research efforts.

The last entry in Table 3 deals with possible losses of plant or animal species in regions affected by irrigation projects. Endemic species are likely to be lost in areas that become submerged inland or are lost to the ocean. That this

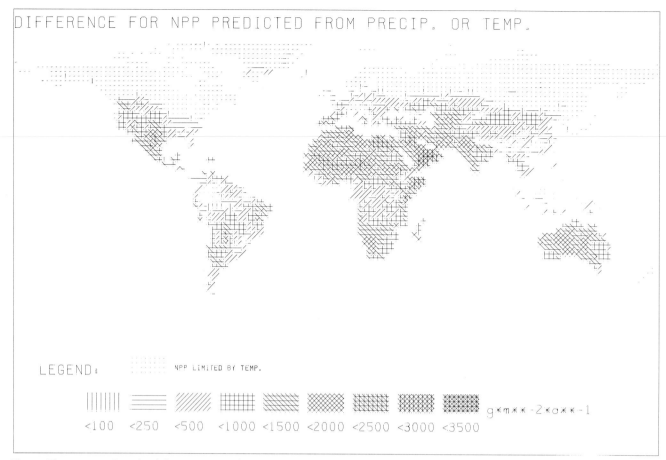

Fig. 4. The amount of productivity missing on the level predicted by the temperature because of a lack of rainfall for the individual grid elements shown in Figs. 2 and 3. The values are given in grams per square meter per year. The dotted grid elements are those in which temperature is limiting.

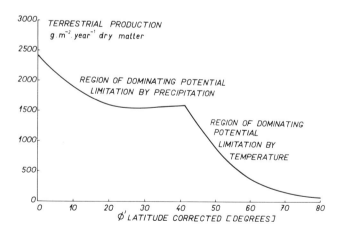

Fig. 5. The north-south profile of global NPP calculated with the Miami Model (Lieth, 1978) by Straškraby (unpublished) showing that north of 40° north latitude the NPP is primarily temperature limited, and that south of it, NPP is primarily precipitation limited.

Table 3. Possible impacts of irrigation systems on plant and animal populations.

Interruption of
   Travel routes for some fish species by dams
   Passage of floating plant species
   Travel routes of migratory land species with channels and fences
Generation of new habitats for
   Small mammals, migratory birds, snails, and insects
   Snakes and amphibians
   Weeds and other pests
Invasion of new species in
   Irrigated areas
   Reservoirs
Bridging of natural barriers against
   Weed and other pest species
   Migratory insects (e.g., locusts)
Loss of species in
   Areas under reservoir water
   Delta area

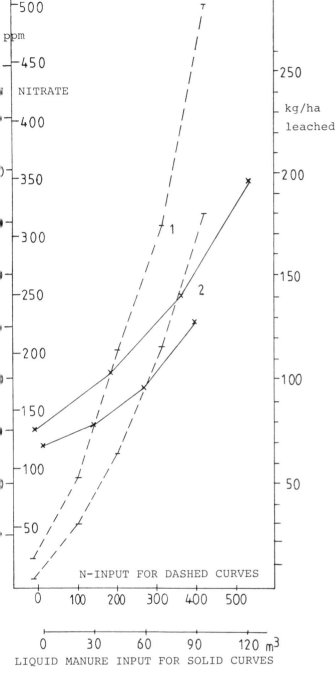

Fig. 6. The level of nitrogen and nitrate in seepage water under agricultural fields fertilized with commercial nitrate fertilizer (crop: sugar beets) and with liquid manure (crop: rye). In these instances the nitrate level in seepage water under the crop increases more rapidly when commercial fertilizer is added. The legal level of 50 ppm nitrate is reached well below the recommended maximum level of fertilization for each crop. This level is recommended for health reasons in drinking water. The farmers often tap the groundwater below their fields for their drinking water. Abscissa: Increasing amounts of nitrate; the scale for liquid manure is spread so that its nitrogen content per cubic meter fits the scale for commercial nitrate fertilizer. Ordinates: left, ppm nitrogen and nitrate in seepage water; right, amount of nitrogen lost per hour because of transfer into the aquifer. Thober, Lieth, and Fabrewitz, 1985.

is a realistic problem is demonstrated by the loss of all habitats for the Oconee bell (*Shortea robusta*) in the North Carolina mountains. The habitats were lost when a hydroelectric plant was erected. Similar conditions may arise when reservoirs are built for irrigation water.

All points raised in Table 3 are solvable, but it remains to be seen whether the solutions are economically feasible. Irrigation water is very costly and becomes increasingly rare with the growing world population and the growing amount of water demanded per person. It is worthwhile, therefore, to think about enlarging the water resources for irrigation with new alternatives.

THE "AGRICULTURAL POTENTIAL" OF HIGH-SALINITY IRRIGATION SYSTEMS

Today irrigation systems utilize freshwater and brackish water, primarily because all our crops are glycophytes, and the salt tolerance of most plants is restricted. Boyko (1966) made numerous experiments near Eilat, Israel, to learn how one could use ocean water for irrigation and which plants would tolerate it. Not much has come from these and similar experiments elsewhere, and yet the use of ocean water for irrigation systems should have the potential for new agricultural exploitation. As a matter of fact, several high-salinity-tolerant plants are already being used as animal fodder or otherwise in many coastal areas in Third World countries. In the United Arab Emirates, Lieth and Barth (1983) investigated the use of mangrove species, native as well as introduced, for agriculture. It was shown that such undertakings were possible, and subsequently it was found that subsistence agricultural practices around the Indian Ocean used mangrove shrub and tree foliage as feed to support cattle, goats, camels, and sheep. The general utilization of mangrove species had been shown by UNESCO (1979, 1981a, b, 1984), Chapman (1978), and Teas (1984).

In the context of water usage for irrigation the experience compiled in these reports needs to be recognized. The resource that can be tapped by using ocean water for the construction of productive ecosystems is potentially enormous. I have calculated the potential to be roughly 3.65×10^6 km² along arid and semiarid coastlines in tropical countries. Most of this area lies in countries with a strong need to increase agricultural land, being short of irrigation water and investment capital. International agencies should start or support already existing pilot projects in Africa, Arabia, and India.

CONCLUDING REMARKS

I have attempted to demonstrate the basic advantages and problems with irrigation projects from the viewpoint of an ecologist. It is obvious that such an introductory paper must be pragmatic. The main points may serve as a basis for further elaboration. Two points I would especially like to stress are the following:

1. We should seek optimal solutions for irrigation management considering all aspects, including ecological danger to wild species, rather than simply seeking to maximize agricultural productivity.

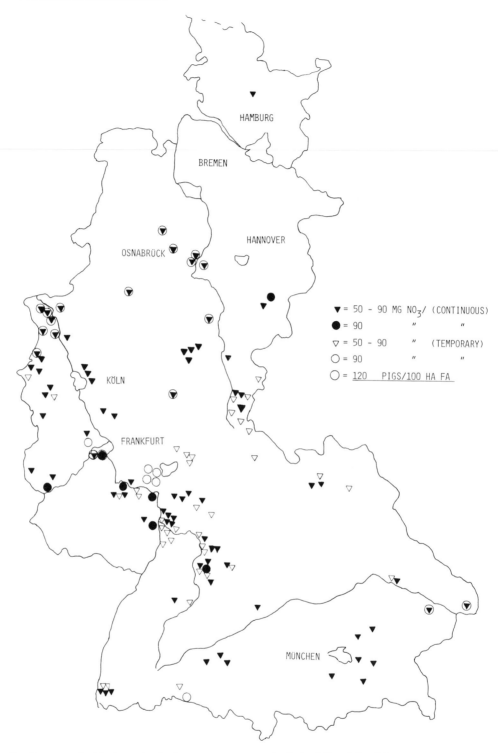

Fig. 7. The pattern of wells reported with nitrate levels above 90 ppm across the Federal Republic of Germany. High levels occur predominantly in regions with intensive agriculture (sugar-beet and vegetable crops) and intensive feedlot farming. After O'Hare, from Thober, Lieth, and Fabrewitz, 1985.

2. We should encourage research and pilot projects leading to agriculturally exploitable ecosystems based on irrigation with ocean water.

Whatever we do, we should not neglect the ecological balance of the entire irrigation system in its national setting.

REFERENCES

Boyko, H. 1960. Salinity and aridity. The Hague: Dr. W. Junk Publishers.

Chapman, V. J. (ed.) 1977. Ecosystems of the world. 1. Wet coastal ecosystems. Amsterdam, Oxford, and New York: Elsevier.

Esser, G. 1984. The significance of biospheric carbon pools and fluxes for the atmospheric CO_2: A proposed model structure. In H. Lieth, R. Fantechi, and H. Schnitzler (eds.), Progress in biometeorology, Vol. 3. Lisse, Netherlands; Swets & Zeitlinger.

FAO-UNESCO. 1974–. Soil map of the world. Vols. 1–10. Paris: UNESCO, IRRI [International Rice Research Institute]. 1983. Symposium on potential productivity of field crops under different environments. Los Baños, Laguna, Philippines.

Lieth, H. 1973. Primary production: Terrestrial ecosystems. *Human Ecology* 1 (4).

———. 1974. Cabora Bassa: Umweltschultz am Sambesi. *Umschau, Kurzberichte* 74:18.

Lieth, H., and H. Barth. 1983. Untersuchungen über die Möglichkeit zur Einrichtung von Mangrovenpflanzungen in Küstenwüsten. *Verhandlungen der Gesellschaft fur Okologie (Festschrift Ellenberg)* 11:265–75.

Teas, H. J. (ed.) 1983. Biology and ecology of mangroves: Tasks for vegetative science, Vol. 8. The Hague: Dr. W. Junk Publishers.

———. 1984. Physiology and management of mangroves. Tasks for vegetative science, Vol. 9. The Hague: Dr. W. Junk Publishers.

Thober, B., H. Lieth, and S. Fabrewitz. 1985. Modeling of the socioeconomical consequences of high animal waste application (MOSEC). Pp. 71–83. In D. O. Hall, N. Myers, and N. S. Margaris (eds.) Economics of ecosystem management. Tasks for vegetative science, Vol. 14. The Hague: Dr. W. Junk Publishers.

UNESCO. 1979. The mangrove ecosystem: Human uses and management implications. Report of a UNESCO regional seminar held in Dacca, Bangladesh, December 1978. Reports in Marine Science, Vol. 8. Paris.

———. 1980a. Coastal lagoon survey: Prepared by the SCOR/UNESCO ad hoc Advisory Panel on Coastal Lagoons, 1976–1978. UNESCO technical papers in Marine Science, Vol. 31. Paris.

———. 1980b. Marine and coastal progress in the Pacific: Ecological aspects of coastal zone management. Papers presented at a UNESCO seminar held at Motupore Island Research Center, University of Papua, New Guinea, July 14–17, 1980. Jakarta Pusat, Indonesia: Regional Office for Science and Technology for Southeast Asia.

———. 1981a. The coastal ecosystems of West Africa: Coastal lagoons, estuaries and mangroves. Workshop report, Dakar, June 11–15, 1979. UNESCO reports in Marine Sciences, Vol. 17. Paris.

———. 1981b. Coastal lagoon research, present and future. Proceedings of UNESCO/IABO seminar. UNESCO technical papers in Marine Science, Vol. 33. Paris.

———. 1984. Handbook for mangrove area management. L. S. Hamilton and S. C. Snedaker (eds.). Paris: Division of Marine Sciences.

34. MANAGING WATER, THE PLANT, AND THE ENVIRONMENT TO MAXIMIZE WORLD FOOD PRODUCTION

Glenn W. Burton, U.S. Department of Agriculture, Agriculture Research Service, University of Georgia Coastal Plain Experiment Station, Tifton, Georgia

ABSTRACT

Water, the earth's most abundant liquid compound, is necessary for all life on earth. The oceans occupying three-fourths of the earth's surface are the basic source of the earth's water. Each day the sun draws a trillion tons of water from the ocean, soil, vegetation, rivers, and lakes and returns a similar amount in rain to water food crops either directly or indirectly through irrigation.

Water is being conserved by the use of horizontal terraces, sod crops, rotations, and no-till to prevent runoff and by developing reservoirs for irrigation.

Choosing species that are drought and heat tolerant; have low water requirements, deep root systems, and efficient growth factor use; and have the ability to stay green under drought stress helps maximize world food production. Further yield increases can result from choosing or breeding cultivars or F_1 hybrids that are pest resistant, fit the rainfall pattern, have low straw per grain ratios if grown for grain or if used for forage, and grow full season; have high leaf percentage, digestibility, and palatability; and have good defoliation tolerance. Superior cultivars or hybrids can maximize world food production only if they are properly managed. Proper management consists of supplying enough of the other growth factors to make water the limiting factor.[1]

INTRODUCTION

Water is the earth's most abundant liquid compound. Its molecule, H_2O, is one of the simplest, but its properties and characteristics are unique. Water is the vital constituent of all living matter and is necessary for life. It is the dominant factor governing all aspects of the environment on the earth's surface.

WATER SOURCES

The oceans, occupying three-fourths of the earth's surface, are the basic source of the earth's water. Each day the sun evaporates an estimated trillion tons of water from the oceans, soil, vegetation, lakes, and rivers. Each day a similar amount of water is returned to the earth in the form of rain. The quantity of rainfall that waters the earth's vegetation ranges from a few millimeters a year in the deserts to more than 10,000 mm in some rain forests. Much of the earth's land mass experiences a rainy monsoon season of several months followed by several months with very little if any rainfall.

Some of the earth's rain falling on the land runs off or percolates to the groundwater. Most of it, however, infiltrates the soil to be returned to the atmosphere by evaporation or transpiration by plants. It is used directly to produce food, fiber, and wood to meet man's needs. Indirectly, controlled or otherwise, rainfall grows crops by flooding the land adjacent to rivers and filling reservoirs for irrigation.

The use of irrigation to grow crops is not new. Excavated ruins dating from centuries ago reveal that people in India, Assyria, Babylonia, Egypt, Israel, Greece, and Rome built irrigation canals and reservoirs to grow crops (Frank, 1955, 1). Today most of the world's rivers supply water for reservoirs that in turn irrigate crops. Wells, often tapping water sources that are centuries old, such as that in the Ogallala Aquifer, increase production of food and feed in semiarid parts of the world. Without irrigation much of the world would be hungry.

WATER CONSERVATION

Preventing runoff loss is one of the most effective ways of conserving rainwater for food production. Horizontal terraces can conserve most light and moderate rainfall. Furrow diking, developed on the Texas High Plains, has proved very successful in capturing low amounts of rainfall, stimulating water penetration, and producing almost zero runoff under clean cultivation.

Sod crops conserve water by slowing runoff and greatly increasing water penetration. Some conservation can be obtained by rotating clean-cultivated crops with small-grain or sod crops. No-till, like sod crops, slows runoff and conserves water.

Thousands of small reservoirs or ponds, built by damming a ditch or low land that carries runoff when it rains, conserve water. They also provide recreation and a source of water for irrigation.

WATER USE

The amount of food, feed, or fiber produced per unit of water is determined in part by the choice of plants. Characteristics that make for improved water-use efficiency were demonstrated in a field experiment designed to measure the drought tolerance and water use of eight southern grasses (Burton et al. 1954, 1957). The soil chosen for the experiment, located on a scrub-oak ridge, consisted of 95.3 per-

1. This chapter grew out of cooperative investigations by the U.S. Department of Agriculture, Agricultural Research Service, and the University of Georgia, College of Agriculture Experiment Stations, Coastal Plain Experiment Station, Agronomy Department, Tifton, Georgia.

cent sand, 1.5 percent silt, and 3.2 percent clay to a depth of 2.6 m, where the presence of small amounts of clay suggested the beginning of a B horizon. Physical studies indicated that at field capacity the soil would hold about 61 mm of available water per meter of depth. On March 20, 1951, eight grasses were planted in 5-m² plots arranged in a lattice square. Nitrogen at rates of 50, 100, and 200 lb/A (56, 112, and 224 kg/ha) plus primary, secondary, and minor elements were applied to subplots of each grass each year from 1952 through 1954. Dry-matter yields were taken every six to eight weeks during the growing season. Growing-season rainfall at the site in 1952, 1953, and 1954 was, respectively, 87, 135, and 47 percent of the long-term average. Droughts that occurred in the summer of 1952 caused carpet grass, *Axonopus affinis,* to turn brown and other grasses to wilt and fire except for Coastal and Suwannee Bermuda grasses, *Cynodon dactylon,* which showed very little evidence of injury. In the more severe 1954 drought carpet grass and Dallis grass, *Paspalum dilatatum,* died, while Coastal and Suwannee Bermuda grasses stayed green. The difference in the drought and heat tolerance of these grass species was well demonstrated.

The water use per kilogram of dry matter in 1953 and 1954 was 1,546 and 4,336 kg for common Bermuda, 803 and 641 kg for Coastal Bermuda, and 870 and 1,239 kg for Pensacola Bahia grass, *P. notatum.* The 1953–54 water-use ratios for common Bermuda grass, Coastal Bermuda grass, and Pensacola Bahia grass were 0.36, 1.25, and 0.70, respectively. It was interesting that coastal Bermuda grass used water more efficiently in the dry year than in a wet year. It is apparent that grasses can vary greatly in water requirement per unit of dry matter.

Coastal and Suwannee Bermuda grasses, the most drought-tolerant grasses, had root systems effective to a depth of 2.5 m. Carpet grass had practically no roots deeper than 1.2 m. In an experiment using P_{32} placed at various depths to measure the rate of root penetration, Coastal Bermuda roots penetrated twice as fast as common Bermuda roots and four times as fast as the roots of carpet grass (Burton et al., 1954).

Throughout the dry summer of 1954, Coastal and Suwannee Bermuda grass stayed green, whereas common Bermuda grass was brown most of the season. By staying green, Coastal and Suwannee were able to use light rains that evaporated from the brown common Bermuda grass before they could cause much growth. As a result Coastal and Suwannee Bermuda grasses were able to produce over half as much dry matter in 1954 as in 1953, whereas common Bermuda grass produced one-seventh as much dry matter in 1954 as in 1953.

Coastal and Suwannee Bermuda grasses were the only F_1 hybrids in this test. Selected F_1 hybrids usually outyield open-pollinated cultivars. When compared in the same yield trial where they have access to the same amount of water, the higher-yielding F_1 hybrids produce more than cultivars do per unit of water used.

In 1953, when the rainfall during the growing season was 35 percent above normal and well distributed, dry-matter yields were a good index of the efficiency of the eight grasses in using fertilizer. In 1953, Coastal and Suwannee Bermuda grass produced about twice as much dry matter as common Bermuda and three times as much as carpet grass when all received 200 kg/ha of N plus other primary, secondary, and minor elements (Burton et al., 1954).

CHOICE OF PLANTS FOR GRAIN

The production of grain and most other crops can be maximized by choosing crops that fit the rainfall pattern. In regions where most rain comes in the winter and spring and the summers are dry, small grains such as wheat, rye, oats, and barley will produce more food than summer-growing crops such as sorghum and pearl millet. In regions where much of the rain comes in the summer, warm-season food crops such as corn, sorghum, and pearl millet can maximize food production. Most farmers are well aware of this relationship and choose crops to fit the rainfall pattern.

Where grain is the food product sought, breeders are reducing the straw-grain ratio. This allows the plant to put a higher percentage of the photosynthate into the grain and increases the yield. By shortening the straw, breeders also reduce lodging, facilitate the harvest, increase grain yields, and help maximize grain production.

Pests (insects, plant diseases, and nematodes) that attack food crops usually reduce yields. To maximize food production, such pests must be controlled. When resistant germplasm can be found, breeding resistant cultivars is usually the best and cheapest way to control a pest. If resistant germplasm and support for plant breeding are not available, chemicals may be used to control the pests. The cost of the chemicals and the value of the crop determine the economics of such control measures.

Early flowering that reduces the time from planting to harvest reduces the water required to grow the crop and makes it better suited to regions with a short rainy season. Early flowering enables many crops to escape the summer heat that greatly increases daily water use. Early flowering also permits growing a crop following flooding in arid parts of the world.

In corn Troyer (1972) reported that selection against silk delay is the most effective method of breeding for drought tolerance. Hybrids selected to withstand stress from high plant density have less silk delay and less barrenness (more yield) under many forms of stress (Troyer and Rosenbrook, 1983). Troyer, who has spent many years breeding corn for heat and drought tolerance, described the ideal corn plant type of the future as follows: "It should silk before pollen shed; should flower early and have a relatively long grain filling period; should have erect leaves above the ear; have fast seedling growth; and have good 'stay-green' so the ear can fill longer" (Troyer, 1983).

CHOICE OF PLANTS FOR FORAGE

Forages are grown primarily to feed livestock. From 85 to 100 percent of the feed consumed by ruminants such as cattle, sheep, and goats is forage. These animals need feed every day of the year, and forages that can provide the greatest number of grazing days are the most useful. Perennials such as Coastal Bermuda grass that can utilize the full growing season can provide many more grazing days than annuals that must start growth from seed and usually terminate growth in late summer or early fall. Forages that use only part of the growing season waste rainfall that could produce forage with full-season perennials.

The leaves of forage plants are more palatable and nutritious than the stems. Increasing the leaf percentage of a forage can increase livestock produce per unit of water by increasing animal performance and reducing the forage that must be used for maintenance. Tifleaf 1 pearl millet, reduced 50 percent in height with the d_2 gene, is much leafier than Gahi 3 and produces higher daily gains and liveweight gains per hectare, even though it yields only 85 percent as much dry matter.

The performance of a ruminant consuming a forage is directly related to its digestibility. The higher the digestibility of a forage, the better the performance of the animal consuming it. Coastal and Coastcross-1 Bermuda grasses yield about the same amount of dry matter and use about the same amount of water, fertilizer, etc., to produce it. Coastcross-1, 12 percent more digestible than Coastal, enabled steers grazing it to make 39 percent better average daily gains and produce 42 percent more liveweight gain per hectare than Coastal (Utley et al., 1974). Thus the efficiency of water use was increased about 40 percent by planting Coastcross-1. Breeding forages for improved digestibility will help increase water-use efficiency and maximize world food production.

Palatability of a forage influences the amount of forage consumed daily and, together with digestibility, determines the production rate of animal products for food. Forage species and genotypes within species differ in palatability. Given free choice of duplicate 10 × 20-m plots of eight Bermuda-grass hybrids, milk cows consistently chose and grazed Coastal Bermuda grass (Burton, 1948, 6). Such "cafeteria" tests help determine the best forage, but they can be misleading. Bahia grasses ranking first in a cafeteria test have given no better daily gains when grazed in pure stand than others ranking significantly lower in the replicated cafeteria test.

Forages differ greatly in their tolerance of defoliation. To be persistent under most grazing systems, forages must be able to tolerate close grazing. Perennial grasses such as Bahia grass, Bermuda grass, and bluegrass can tolerate continued close grazing. On the other hand, kudzu, *Pueraria phaseoloides* (Roxb.), a good pasture legume if grazed lightly, can be killed in one season with close, heavy grazing. Droughts that slow growth of forages force livestock farmers to overgraze their pastures and cause them to lose interest in forages like kudzu.

CHOICE OF PLANTS FOR BIOMASS

Plants for biomass production must use the full growing season to maximize annual dry-matter yields. They need all the characteristics that make for more efficient water use, such as heat and drought tolerance, low water requirement, deep root systems, efficient growth-factor use, and ability to stay green during droughts. They must also produce biomass that can be harvested and processed at low cost. If the

conversion to energy can be made once a year so that the entire season's growth can be harvested at one time, Napier grass *Pennisetum purpureum,* will outyield most other species. If the plant must be harvested every four or five weeks, the hybrid Bermuda grasses will outyield Napier grass and persist much better (Burton, 1985).

CHOICE OF CULTURE

In regions where there is abundant water and irrigation can be practiced, solar energy can become the growth factor that limits yields. Here, to maximize food production, crops must be planted so as to capture all of the sun's rays striking a hectare of land. In New Jersey, for example, Flannery (1985) produced for five years an average of 15.3 t/ha (307 bu/A) of corn by planting, in a 30 × 30-cm diamond pattern, 107,590 plants per hectare (43,560 plants per acre) and using high fertility. Weeds must be eliminated so that all solar energy and other growth factors can be used by the food crop. Those species and cultivars capable of producing the maximum amount of food when grown in a closed canopy must be chosen. When these requirements have been met, the consumptive use or maximum "evaporation" of water from a hectare of land will depend largely on incident solar radiation and its effect on weather. At the Sixth International Grassland Congress, Schofield (1952) said that "maximum evaporation depends almost entirely on meteorological conditions and scarcely at all on the nature of the vegetation as long as it is green and effectively covers the soil."

In the rest of the world temperature or water or both will set the ceiling for food production. In regions where water sets the ceiling, cultural practices must ensure that water is the limiting factor if food production is to be maximized. Certainly cultural practices must be chosen that will best fit the expected weather pattern. Until meteorologists can accurately describe the weather, particularly the rainfall pattern for the growing season, species and cultivars must be flexible enough in their water demands to maximize yields under a range of weather patterns.

Plant breeding has developed cultivars that have increased water-use efficiency and food production per hectare. Adequately supported, it can continue to do so. Brief descriptions of some of the ways that plant breeding can realize this objective follow:

1. Breeding new cultivars capable of producing food where existing cultivars will not grow will increase world food production.

2. Water-use efficiency can be increased by breeding winter cultivars to replace spring cultivars. Several years ago, D. G. Hanway, chairman of the Agronomy Department, University of Nebraska, said, "At the turn of the century when we replaced spring wheat cultivars with winter cultivars, we essentially doubled wheat yields."

3. Breeding cultivars that can be grown in cooler regions where evapotranspiration rates are reduced may increase water-use efficiency. American and Canadian corn breeders have done this as they have made corn fit northern climates.

4. Small-grain breeders have increased yields of wheat, oats, and barley by breeding cultivars that mature earlier.

Reitz and Salmon (1959) reported that breeding earlier cultivars of hard red winter wheat afforded escape from rust, insects, and hot, dry summers and was worth over 60 kg/ha per day of earliness added.

5. Breeding cultivars resistant to diseases, insects, and other pests will increase yields and automatically increase the efficiency of water use.

6. Water-use efficiency can be increased by breeding cultivars resistant to lodging, which in turn reduces grain losses and increases the yield of harvested grain.

7. Breeding cultivars such as Coastal Bermuda grass that can remain green under high moisture stress and utilize every drop of rain for increased growth will increase yields and water-use efficiency. Light showers are lost through evaporation before new growth can be initiated when a grass like common Bermuda grass turns brown.

8. Yields and water-use efficiency can be increased by breeding cultivars that have deeper, faster-growing, more efficient root systems. Roots from plugs of sod of Coastal and common Bermuda grasses planted above P_{32} placed at depths of 0.3, 0.6, 1.2, and 2.4 m had reached depths of 2.4 and 1.2 m, respectively, after three months. The presence of P_{32} in the leaves was considered proof that roots had reached the depth of the P_{32} placement (Burton et al., 1954).

9. The best hybrids of a species usually outyield the best cultivars by a significant margin. In a letter of February 1965, K. O. Rachie, coordinator of pearl-millet improvement in India, reported that breeders of Indian pearl millet had agreed unanimously to release HB1, the first hybrid pearl millet, because in yield trials from 11° to 31° north latitude it had yielded an average of 88 percent more grain than the check cultivars. With the help of HB1 yields of pearl-millet grain in India increased from 3.5 million tons in 1965 to 8 million tons in 1970. Thus, breeding F_1 hybrids that carry the maximum amount of hybrid vigor can increase water-use efficiency and world food production.

Superior cultivars can maximize world food production only if they are properly managed. Water-use efficiency and yields can be maximized best with management systems that make water the limiting growth factor. Variations in rainfall from year to year may require that, for economic reasons, other growth factors must be applied at rates that may be limiting in the best rainfall year. For example, in 1953, with 35 percent more rain than average during the growing season, common Bermuda grass dry-matter yield was increased 4.9 t/ha by increasing the N rate from 50 to 200 kg/ha. In 1954 with 47 percent less rain than average in the growing season, increasing the N rate from 50 to 200 kg/ha increased the forage yield of common Bermuda only 0.5 t/ha. Choosing a drought-tolerant cultivar can help solve such problems. Increasing the N rate from 50 to 200 kg/ha for Coastal bermuda in the same test in 1953 and 1954 increased forage yields 8.3 and 3.7 t/ha, respectively. If such variations in rainfall occurred frequently, it would not be economical to apply 200 kg/ha of N to common Ber-

muda grass every year but would probably be economical for Coastal Bermuda grass.

For crops such as corn, plant populations have a significant effect on yields. In south Georgia in the 1930s, when corn received little if any fertilizer, single plants were spaced 1.2 m apart to give yields of 300 kg/ha (5 bu/A). Flannery (1985) found it necessary to increase plant population over twelve times to produce his record corn yield of 15.3 t/ha.

Weeds compete with food crops for water and all other growth factors. To maximize water-use efficiency and food production, weeds must be controlled.

Available water in the root zone at the time crop growth begins affects yields and must be considered in ascertaining the yield potential of an environment. Yields of rainfed corn in Illinois would be much less without the available water in 2 to 3 m of soil that accumulates from one growing season to another. Managing the soil to maximize the accumulation of water during the off-season can increase yields and world food production.

REFERENCES

Burton, Glenn W. 1948. Coastal bermudagrass. Georgia Coastal Plain Experiment Station Circular 10, rev. Tifton, Ga.

———. 1985. Biomass production from herbaceous plants. *In* Proceedings of the Third Biomass Energy Conference. In press.

Burton, Glenn W., E. H. DeVane, and R. L. Carter. 1954. Root penetration, distribution, and activity in southern grasses measured by yields, drought symptoms, and P[32] uptake. *Agronomy Journal* 46:229–33.

Burton, Glenn W., Gordon M. Prine, and James E. Jackson. 1957. Studies of drought tolerance and water use of several southern grasses. *Agronomy Journal* 49:498–503.

Flannery, Roy. 1985. Corn and soybean yields are 3 times the U.S. average. *FAR Letter* 1(1), February.

Frank, Bernard. 1955. The story of water as the story of man. Pp. 1–9. *In* Water: U.S. Department of Agriculture yearbook.

Reitz, L. P., and S. C. Salmon. 1959. Hard red winter wheat improvement in the plains. U.S. Department of Agriculture Technical Bulletin 1192.

Schofield, R. K. 1952. Control of grassland irrigation based on weather data. Pp. 757–62. *In* Proceedings of the Sixth International Grassland Congress, Pennsylvania State College, State College.

Troyer, A. F. 1983. Breeding corn for heat and drought tolerance. Pp. 128–43. *In* Proceedings of the 38th Annual Corn and Sorghum Research Conference. Chicago, Ill.

———, and W. L. Brown. 1972. Selection for early flowering in corn. *Crop Science* 12:301–304.

———, and R. W. Rosenbrook. 1983. Utility of higher plant densities for corn performance testing. *Crop Science* 23:863–67.

Utley, P. R., Hollis D. Chapman, W. G. Monson, W. H. Marchant, and W. C. McCormick. 1974. Coastcross-1 bermudagrass, Coastal bermudagrass, and Pensacola bahiagrass as summer pasture for steers. *Journal of Animal Science* 38:490–95.

35. PATHOGENS AS CONSTRAINTS TO CROP PRODUCTIVITY

R. James Cook, Root Disease and Biological Control Research Unit, U.S. Department of Agriculture, Agricultural Research Service, Pullman, Washington

ABSTRACT

Current cultivars of major crops would yield 25 to 50 percent and up to 100 percent more with the same water were it not for constraints of diseases and pests. The yield possible when the crop is healthy and pest free is at least as high as the best yield for the crop in a given area and year. In general, the higher the yield potential, the greater the range between poorest and best yield for that locality and year.

Yield increases of 25 to 50 percent and greater can be demonstrated routinely for most agronomic and horticultural crops by the combined use of soil fumigation, pathogen-free planting material, and full-season protection of the foliage with fungicidal sprays. It is not necessary to eliminate all microorganisms, only those that are pathogenic.

Root diseases and some virus diseases may occur so uniformly in fields as to lead scientists to accept the appearance and yield of diseased plants as the norm. The increased growth response of plants following soil fumigation is a glimpse of how plants with healthy roots are supposed to grow. In the Pacific Northwest yields of winter wheat are near or at potential only in areas with 25 to 40 cm annual precipitation. Wheat yields at only about 75 percent of potential in areas with 50 to 60 cm annual precipitation, but at potential if the soil is fumigated and foliage protected from rust. Under irrigation wheat in the Northwest is yielding at only 50 to 60 percent of potential set by the water and fertilizer applied.

INTRODUCTION

Present-day cultivars of major crops grown in modern farming systems commonly yield only 60 to 75 percent, and often only 50 percent or less, of their potential as set by their genetic makeup, available water, fertilizer, climate, and weather. This difference between the actual and potential yield results largely from constraints on the plants caused by diseases, arthropods, nematodes, and weeds. Crop yields are commonly 25 to 50 percent and sometimes 100 percent greater in fields in which (1) the soil is made disease and pest free by soil fumigation, (2) the field is planted with pathogen-free planting material, and (3) the foliage is protected through the season by fungicides. James (1980) estimated that crop productivity would be 35 percent greater were it not for diseases, arthropods, nematodes, and weeds.

Figures such as 50 to 75 percent of potential and yield gains of 100 percent because of disease and pest control may seem like exaggerations, but they are corroborated by the facts that major disease and pest problems continue to occur in the Third World and that developed nations are beginning to recognize the importance of chronic disease previously thought to be of only minor significance. The effects of a chronic disease may occur so uniformly across a given field and year after year as to lead to the acceptance of the diseased crop as the norm, e.g., when the planting material is uniformly virus-infected or where root hairs and the fine rootlets are destroyed rather generally by soilborne pathogens. The changes toward less rotation and conservation tillage have caused several previously minor or controlled diseases to become major constraints to achieving the high yields possible in these systems.

THE YIELD POTENTIAL OF PLANTS

As a general rule the average yield for a crop is only 50 to 60 percent of the best yield obtained for that crop, year, and locality. For example, the potential or attainable soybean yield in 1979 in Minnesota on the Waseca Agricultural Experiment Station was 5.5 t/ha (Zadoks and Schein, 1979), which is about 62 percent greater than the 3.4 t/ha actual yield on that station in 1979 and 120 percent greater than the 2.5 t/ha average soybean yield in Waseca County in 1979 (Teng and Shane, 1984). In general, the better the environment for a crop, the greater the spread between the poorest, average, and best yields for that crop. It is difficult to argue that the precipitation, temperature, and other weather or climatic factors limit the average yield of a crop to half or three-quarters of the best yield in that locality when all fields in the area are subject to more or less the same weather and climate.

The absolute yield potential is that yield possible with no limiting factors except the genetic and physiological traits of the cultivar itself and is at least as high as the world record yield for that crop (Cook and Baker, 1983). Record yields in tons per hectare of some important crops as of 1975 were maize, 19.3; wheat, 14.5; sorghum, 20.1; barley, 11.4; and soybeans, 7.4 (Wittwer, 1975). The potential yield (in contrast to the absolute potential) is that yield attainable under the local constraints of climate, weather, soils, and agronomic inputs (including irrigation). To achieve the potential requires only that the crop be disease and pest free (James and Teng, 1979) and that it be fertilized adequately to take advantage of available water. The difference between the actual and potential yield by these definitions is attributable to diseases and pests as yield-limiting factors.

Van der Zaag (1984) developed a method to estimate the potential yield of potatoes that relates dry-matter production of the crop under optimal conditions to total incoming radiation intercepted by the green foliage during the vegetative period. The highest potential was calculated for the state of Washington, where incoming radiation over the total vegetative period is sufficient to produce a tuber yield of 140 t/ha. The absolute potential for potatoes is thus at least as great as 140 t/ha. In 1975 the average yield in Washington, where potatoes are grown under intensive irrigation and nitrogen is added at 500 to 650 kg N/ha, was about 55 t/ha, but some fields yielded 95 t/ha, and some experimental plots yielded 118 t/ha (Kunkel et al., 1977). Values calculated by Van der Zaag (1984) for other countries were 100 t/ha for the Netherlands, 60 t/ha for Egypt, 70 t/ha for Tunisia, and 50 t/ha for Pakistan, and he determined that the best yields obtained in these respective areas are near or equal to the estimated potentials for those areas. However, average actual yields for potatoes in these same areas range between only 13 and 46 percent of the potential (Van der Zaag, 1984). Obviously, factors other than water, fertility, and incoming radiation limit actual yields to less than 50 percent of the attainable for potatoes.

In disease management it is common to make some change in the way the crop is grown so as to prevent a disease. A delay of two to three weeks in the seeding date for fall wheat in eastern Washington effectively controls *Pseudocercosporella* foot rot, but because a late-sown crop is less likely to take full advantage of available water, its yield is considerably less than the attainable or potential yield as set by available water. It makes little difference whether the yield is 60 to 80 percent of the potential because the crop was managed to prevent a disease, or if the crop was managed for maximum production but falls short in yield because of disease.

Boyer (1982), in attempting to determine why average yields for major crops are only one-fifth to one-seventh the world record yields of those crops, concluded that about 70 percent of the shortfall must be attributed to unfavorable climates, inappropriate soils, and competition from weeds. He allowed only 4.1 and 2.6 percent of the record yields as not being harvested because of damage from diseases and insects, respectively. This implies that yields of major crops could be elevated to within an average of 93 to 94 percent of their world-record yields only by eliminating weeds and if climate and soils (including available water) were not the constraints. Obviously water and climate are limiting to crop productivity over a vast area of the earth, but much of the earth would already be producing significantly more within existing water and fertilizer resources were it not for the constraints of diseases and pests. The higher the yield potential as set by edaphic and climatic factors and agronomic inputs, the more devastating are the pathogen and arthropod pests.

The USDA data (Handbook 291, 1965) used by Boyer (1982) gave estimates that are entirely too conservative compared with the demonstrated yield increases obtained when crops are grown as pathogen free as they can possibly be. In Illinois, Gray (1978) and Kittle and Gray (1982) obtained 20 to 35 percent greater yield of soybeans in each of five years, 1975–79, by soil fumigation alone or combined with a foliar fungicide spray. In the state of Washington, where average wheat yields are already two to three times the U.S. average, the yields are routinely 15 to 25 percent and sometimes 50 percent greater in plots with populations

of soilborne pathogens reduced by soil fumigation and foliage protected by fungicide sprays. These greater yields are obtained with no more added water or fertilizer. More will be said about the effects of diseases on Pacific Northwest wheat.

THE IMPORTANCE OF PATHOGEN CONTROL TO ACHIEVING THE YIELD POTENTIAL

Plants are subject to attack by pathogens from the day of seeding until the day the product is finally consumed by people or livestock. The agents responsible for plant disease include the same kinds of agents (but not the same agents) that affect human and animal health: fungi, bacteria (including mycoplasmas), viruses, and viroids. Plants may be attacked by viruses responsible for yellows and dwarfing or by bacteria and fungi that cause wilts, rust, mildew, leaf spots, and blights. Tissues may be rendered nonfunctional, or they may be destroyed completely, as with root rots.

Root Health

In modern farming systems of monoculture and conservation tillage, a major portion of the absorptive tissue of the root system and especially the rootlets and root hairs are destroyed by soilborne plant pathogens specialized in their ability to infect these tissues (Cook, 1984). The poor plant growth that begins in the seedling stage has been attributed to nitrogen tie-up by the crop residue and to phytotoxins released during decomposition of the residue, but in the Pacific Northwest the problem is eliminated by treatments that eliminate or inhibit *Pythium* species (Cook et al., 1980; Cook and Haglund, 1982). A plant without adequate absorptive capacity because of root disease can be likened to a human being whose lungs have no absorptive capacity because of emphysema. Just as some of the effects of emphysema can be overcome by increasing the supply of oxygen, so some of the effects of some root diseases can be overcome by applying more fertilizer. A better way is to keep the root (or lungs) healthy in the first place.

Pythium species are the most ubiquitous pathogens responsible for poor root health in our agricultural soils. They are responsible for destruction of root hairs and fine rootlets. Most cultivated soils have *Pythium* populations of 300 to 1,000 per gram, confined mainly to the surface, where most uptake of phosphorus, potassium, and trace nutrients is supposed to occur. Root pathogens such as *Rhizoctonia solani, Fusarium* species, and nematodes also destroy or prune roots. Plants with diseased roots resemble plants that lack needed mineral nutrients; the damaged root system does not take up sufficient nutrients for the tops. Plants with damaged or plugged water-conductive tissues tend to die prematurely.

The decline in yield and the associated nutrient deficiency symptoms of plants grown in fields where crop rotation is not practical are the direct result of root pathogens enriched by the monoculture of their host. Some alleged examples of allelopathy, where the only evidence for a "toxic" effect of one plant on another is stunting, lack of branching, and nutrient-deficiency symptoms in the tops of the sensitive plant, may actually be examples of damage from root pathogens. The absence of root infections should not be assumed.

There is no more spectacular evidence for the importance of root health to crop growth than the way plants grow in fumigated soil. The response manifests itself as taller, greener plants with more branches and an obviously healthier look, and the roots are white and dense with root hairs as they are supposed to be. It has been hard for plant and soil scientists to accept that eliminating root pathogens could result in such remarkable plant-growth responses. Chemical changes in the soil, including the flush of nitrogen and other mineral nutrients from the killed microbial biomass, cannot account for the effect (Aldrich and Martin, 1952; Wilhelm and Paulus, 1980; Cook, 1984). It is now clear that improved root health is the explanation for the increased growth response of plants to soil fumigation (Wilhelm, 1965; Wilhelm and Paulus, 1980; Cook, 1984).

Pathogen-free Planting Material

It does little good to eliminate pathogens from soil only to reintroduce them with the planting material. Hot-water treatment of planting material is one way to eliminate pathogens, including pathogens in vegetatively propagated material (Hollings, 1965). Potatoes, strawberries, and several ornamental plants were among the first crops to be grown from planting material derived from pathogen-free meristem cultures (Slack, 1980). The elimination of potato viruses S and X from seed was estimated to increase potato yields in British Columbia, Canada, and the Pacific Northwest by 2 to 9 percent, depending on the seed lot (Wright, 1970; Kunkel et al., 1977). In California the use of soil fumigation to eliminate weeds and soilborne pathogens, and meristem culture to eliminate pathogens carried with the planting material, resulted in two to three times the average yields of strawberries compared to yields before introduction of this technology (Wilhelm and Paulus, 1980). Many of the beautiful ornamental plants now available likewise are produced pathogen free; the application of this technology has revolutionized the ornamentals industry (Baker and Linderman, 1979).

In Taiwan the rearing of banana plants from plantlets derived from meristems resulted in a method to replant fields with *Fusarium*-free planting material (Huang et al., 1984). It is interesting, however, that such plants appear distinctly healthier in all respects, as evidenced by more vigorous growth, wider leaves, and better color than plants produced in the traditional ways. Possibly one or more undiagnosed systemic pathogens are also eliminated by establishing the banana plantations with plantlets.

Foliar Pathogens and Insect-vectored Viruses

Damage to plants caused by foliar pathogens is related to the duration of leaf wetness, and leaves in a dense canopy are likely to remain wet longer each day than leaves in a thin canopy. In addition, the larger, more vigorous plants tend to be more attractive or to present a better target to the sucking and chewing arthropods that transmit plant viruses than are small plants. Since plants grown from pathogen-free planting material in pathogen-free soil are the most vigorous, it

holds generally true that the practices aimed at control of these pathogens are likely to favor the foliar pathogens and arthropods that vector pathogens.

Historically the foliar pathogens have been the most destructive to food crops. The potato blight in Ireland in the mid-nineteenth century, wheat stem rust in North America in 1919 and 1952, and southern corn leaf blight in the United States in 1970 are examples of the kind of destruction possible from aerial pathogens. Local epidemics of rusts, mildews, leaf spots, and blights caused by fungi and bacteria continue to occur on most important crops. Rice blast, caused by *Pyricularia oryzae*, may be the most important foliar disease of grain crops worldwide at the present time.

Resistance of cultivars to foliar pathogens has been only temporarily effective, since each new source of resistance has eventually selected for races of the pathogen virulent on that cultivar. An alternative approach has been to select for those cultivars generally resistant to all strains of the pathogen, but unfortunately such "general" resistance has also been an incomplete resistance. Moreover, the defense reaction of plants to pathogens requires energy and may, of itself, be a yield-limiting factor (Smedegaard-Petersen, 1982). Aerial pathogens can often be escaped by delaying the seeding date, but if the late-planted crop is less likely to take full advantage of available water, the yield is still less than the potential.

Thorough burial of crop residue infested with leaf pathogens results in less disease caused by these pathogens, but such clean tillage is expensive and contrary to needs for erosion control. Fungicide sprays can be effective but are also expensive, and resistant strains of the pathogen may develop. Whether or not fungicides are used commercially, as with soil fumigation, they provide a tool to estimate what the crop should yield in the absence of the foliar pathogen (James and Teng, 1979).

Science has hardly begun to develop controls for the arthropod-vectored viruses. The problem is especially intractable because of the number of uncontrolled variables, usually a complex of genetically related strains of the virus reservoired in many hosts (some unknown) and carried by one or several biotypes or even species of arthropods. For example, barley yellow dwarf, a worldwide problem for wheat, is caused by any one of several serologically related viruses that multiply in plants of the grass family, including maize and all small grains (symptomlessly in some), and is carried to sensitive hosts such as wheat, barley, and oats by several species of aphids. Within vector-specific strains monoclonal antisera now reveal the existence of strains within strains. Most crops are susceptible to infections by the insect-vectored viruses, including several viruses of rice vectored by leafhoppers and aphids, depending on the virus.

PRODUCTION CAPABILITY OF A HEALTHY CROP ILLUSTRATED BY PACIFIC NORTHWEST WHEAT

The only area in Washington state where water is the limiting factor to wheat yields most years is where annual precipitation is 20 to 40 cm and wheat is grown in a fallow-wheat rotation (one crop every two years). The yield potential for soft white winter wheat in the Pacific Northwest is estimated at 0.5 to 0.7 t/ha for every 2.5 cm of available water above a base of 10 cm required to produce plants but not grain. The yield potential is about 3.8 to 4.3 t/ha with 25 cm annual precipitation, assuming that 30 percent of the total water available is captured in the fallow year and 80 percent in the crop year. In the past some growers managed their crop for a yield greater than that possible with available water by very early seeding and the application of heavy rates of fertilizer, but this only stressed the crop and favored *Fusarium* foot rot (Cook, 1980). This practice has now been discontinued, and *Fusarium* foot rot is controlled. Except in years when stripe rust and barley yellow dwarf occur, most growers today achieve the genetic yield potential of their crops as limited mainly by water in this dryland wheat-fallow area.

In the Palouse area of eastern Washington and adjacent northern Idaho, where soils are finer-textured, the yield potential for wheat after wheat with 50 cm of precipitation annually is 6.3 to 7.0 t/ha. The yield potential of wheat after peas in the same area is 7.8 to 9.2 t/ha, because peas leave 5 to 10 cm of unused water stored in the profile and available to a subsequent wheat crop. Field experiments with soil fumigation to eliminate root pathogens and foliar fungicides applied to protect against foliar pathogens and *Pseudocercosporella* foot rot have confirmed these yield potentials (Cook and Haglund, 1982). Actual yields with high fertility but without treatments to eliminate the pathogens is usually 5.6 to 6.4 t/ha after peas and 4.2 to 5.0 t/ha after wheat. These yields are only 60 to 75 percent of the potential for the area as set by available water.

In the irrigated Columbia Basin of Washington most growers apply 80 to 100 cm of water for the crop, sufficient, when combined with the 15 to 20 cm of natural precipitation, to produce 12.5 to 14 t/ha. One grower actually achieved a yield of 14.8 t/ha in 1961, but most fields today yield only 5.7 to 9.2 t/ha with the same or greater inputs of water and nitrogen used to produce that record yield. Because of the lack of adequate rotation root disease is the main yield-limiting factor for irrigated wheat. Current research programs are aimed at finding a control for these diseases other than by crop rotation or tillage and preferably without the use of soil fungicides or fumigants (Cook and Baker, 1983).

REFERENCES

Aldrich, D. G., and J. P. Martin. 1952. Effect of fumigation on some chemical properties of soils. *Soil Science* 73:149–59.

Baker, K. F., and R. G. Linderman. 1979. Unique features of the pathology of ornamental plants. *Annual Review of Phytopathology* 17:253–77.

Boyer, J. S. 1982. Plant productivity and the environment. *Science* 218:443–48.

Cook, R. J. 1980. Fusarium foot rot of wheat and its control in the Pacific Northwest. *Plant Disease* 64:1061–65.

———. 1984. Root health: importance and relationship to farming practices. Pp. 111–27. *In* D. F. Bezdicek et al. (eds.) Organic farming: current technology and its role in a sustainable agriculture. American Society of Agronomy Special Publication No. 46.

Cook, R. J., and K. F. Baker. 1983. The nature and practice of biological control of plant pathogens. St. Paul, Minn.: American Phytopathological Society.

Cook, R. J., and W. A. Haglund. 1982. Pythium root rot: a barrier to yield of Pacific Northwest wheat. Washington State University College of Agriculture Research Bulletin No. XB0913.

Cook, R. J., J. W. Sitton, and J. T. Waldher. 1980. Evidence for *Pythium* as a pathogen of direct-drilled wheat in the Pacific Northwest. *Plant Disease* 64:1061–66.

Gray, L. E. 1978. Effect of soil fumigation on soybean diseases and plant yield. *Plant Disease Reporter* 62:613–15.

Handbook 291. 1965. U.S. Department of Agriculture. Washington, D.C.: Government Printing Office.

Hollings, M. 1965. Disease control through virus-free stock. *Annual Review of Phytopathology* 3:367–89.

Hwang, S. C., C. L. Chen, J. C. Lin. 1984. Cultivation of bananas using plantlets from meristem culture. *HortScience* 19:231–33.

James, C. W. 1980. Economic, social, and political implications of crop losses: a holistic framework for loss assessments in agricultural systems. Pp. 10–16. *In* Crop Loss Assessment. E. C. Stakman Commemorative Symposium Miscellaneous Publication 7. St. Paul: Agricultural Experiment Station, University of Minnesota.

James, C. W., and P. S. Teng. 1979. The quantification of production constraints associated with plant diseases. Pp. 201–67. *In* T. H. Coaker (ed.) Applied biology. London: Academic Press.

Kittle, D. R., and L. E. Gray. 1982. Response of soybeans and soybean pathogens to soil fumigation and foliar fungicide sprays. *Plant Disease* 66:213–15.

Kunkel, R., N. M. Holstad, R. E. Thornton, and T. S. Russell. 1977. Potato seed source comparisons in Washington. College of Agriculture Research Center, Washington State University Bulletin 847.

Slack, S. A. 1980. Pathogen-free plants by meristem culture. *Plant Disease* 64:15–17.

Smedegaard-Peterson, V. 1982. The effect of defence reactions on the energy balance and yield of resistant plants. Pp. 299–315. *In* R. K. S. Wood (ed.) Active defence mechanisms in plants. New York and London: Plenum Press.

Teng, P. S., and W. W. Shane. 1983. Crop losses due to plant pathogens. *In* Proceedings of the Tenth International Congress of Plant Protection, Brighton, England. Suffolk: Lavenham Press.

Wilhelm, S. 1965. *Pythium ultimum* and the soil fumigation response. *Phytopathology* 55:1016–20.

Wilhelm, S., and Paulus, A. O. 1980. How soil fumigation benefits the California strawberry industry. *Plant Disease* 64:264–70.

Wright, N. S. 1970. Combined effects of potato viruses X and S on yield of netted gem and white rose potatoes. *American Potato Journal* 47:475–78.

Wittwer, S. H. 1975. Food production: technology and the resource base. *Science* 188:579–84.

Zaag, D. E. van der. 1984. Reliability and significance of a simple method of estimating the potential yield of the potato crop. *Potato Research* 27:51–73.

Zadoks, J. D., and R. D. Schein. 1979. Epidemiology and Plant Disease Management. New York: Oxford University Press.

36. WATER AND PLANT PRODUCTIVITY

J. S. Boyer, Department of Soil and Crop Sciences, Texas A&M University, College Station, Texas

ABSTRACT

Agricultural statistics show that large losses in crop yields are caused by unfavorable growth environments, particularly physicochemical environments. The most prevalent physicochemical environments causing the effect are those resulting in crop water deficiencies either because of inadequate soil water or excessive evaporative demand. Genetic variability exists for plant response to these forms of water deficiency. Use of this variability for selecting improved genotypes is most effective when the physiological mechanisms of adaptation are known and when selections are conducted under water-limited conditions. Recent advances in understanding plant osmoregulation and photosynthesis during water deficiencies has led to the development of new genotypes capable of improved yield.

INTRODUCTION

Agriculture has always relied on a steady source of water. Since the earliest efforts to grow crops, man has used irrigation and recognized its importance. In more recent times sophisticated means of water delivery have been developed, and new techniques of water catchment have come into use. These changes, together with advances in other aspects of crop production, have resulted in yields higher than those in the past. Consequently, we are compelled to question anew what factors control crop productivity and whether water remains a limitation.

Although irrigation is a prevalent means of eliminating water problems, high-quality water is essential if soil fertility is to be maintained. Water of high quality is increasingly scarce, and, as a consequence, only a small fraction of potentially irrigable land can be irrigated. In the United States, for example, approximately 5 percent of the land area is irrigated (U.S. Department of Agriculture, 1979). The availability of water limits future development to about double this amount (U.S. Department of the Interior, 1977). It seems inevitable that in the future, at least in the United States and probably in other countries as well, a large portion of agricultural production will remain unirrigated and will depend on natural rainfall.

This situation implies that crops will continue to rely on sporadic supplies of water during the growing season. Modern methods of water catchment and conservation can help alleviate the problem by evening out periods of surplus and scarcity. Even with successful catchment and soil-water management, however, there is the additional complication that plant shoots undergo daily water deficiencies that can inhibit yield (for example, see Boyer et al., 1980). The effect occurs because the rate of water loss by the crop exceeds the rate of water gain sufficiently to cause dehydration that inhibits metabolic processes. This form of water deficiency cannot be alleviated by additional rainfall or catchment systems. Rather, the plants must be modified or they must grow elsewhere to avoid excessive evaporation. Because of these kinds of mismatches between the crop and the evaporative environment, water deficiencies are more widespread than indicated by soil, rainfall, and irrigation data alone.

It is difficult to estimate crop loss and especially that caused by water deficits. Boyer (1982) attempted an analysis of the impact of unfavorable environments for agriculture in the United States, but it is not certain that the conclusions apply to world agriculture. In this chapter I extend that analysis to a global scale and explore opportunities for improving crop productivity in unfavorable environments, particularly where water is scarce.

IMPACT OF ENVIRONMENT

The maximum growth of plants is set by their genetic makeup, which can be fully expressed in optimum environments. For natural communities the environment is not managed, and many factors can suppress plant growth below the genetic potential. The impact can be measured as fitness—the ability of the plants to leave descendants over time. Individuals leaving the most descendants over time come closest to achieving maximum evolutionary success, reaching their genetic potential, at least in a given environment. Individuals leaving fewer descendants than other plants of the same species do not express their full genetic potential and are considered "stressed." Environmental stress is therefore a prime force in evolution.

In agriculture similar forces are at work. However, the test of fitness of a crop is not the same as in natural communities because the usual ability to leave descendants is not important in the same sense. Rather, the criterion is productivity per unit land area. Nevertheless, because crops are often grown for their reproductive propagules, there are similarities between factors affecting natural communities and crops.

Genetic potential for productivity in crops is probably best measured as the highest yield ever attained, that is, the record yield, because it is measured in the field under production conditions. Although this measurement does not ensure that environmental limitations are eliminated, they certainly are minimized.

Table 1 shows that the world record yields of eight major crops grown in tropical and temperate environments are high, indicating that the genetic potential is large. The grain crops have record yields of 4.8 to 22.2 t/ha. Potato and sweet potato yields are even higher, in part because of water content.

Table 1. Average and world record economic yields of crops from temperate and tropical areas.

Crop	Temperate Yields (t/ha)[a]		Tropical Yields (t/ha)[a]	
	Average	Record	Average	Record
Rice	4.1	10.5 (Japan)	2.0	7.4 (Asia)[b]
Wheat	3.0	14.1 (U.S.)	1.4	10.3 (Asia, Zimbabwe, Central America)
Maize	4.0	22.2 (U.S.)	1.4	12.9 (Zimbabwe)
Sorghum	2.3	20.1 (U.S.)	1.2	10.3 (Asia)[b]
Soybean	1.6	7.3 (Japan)	1.0	4.8 (Zimbabwe)
Groundnut	1.7	8.6 (U.S.)	1.0	9.6 (Zimbabwe)
Potato	18.1	126.0 (U.S.)	8.7	60.0 (Central America)[b]
Sweet potato	13.6	65.0 (U.S.)	6.9	—
Average percent of record yield	20.8	100	15.7	100

SOURCE: Haws et al., 1983.

[a]Subtropical and temperate zones are considered temperate, whereas the zones between 23.5° north latitude and 23.5°south latitude (excluding dry areas) are considered tropical.

[b]Asia is represented by the Philippines, Thailand, and India. Central America is represented by Mexico and Colombia.

Table 2. Record yields, average yields, and yield losses resulting from diseases, insects, weeds, and unfavorable physicochemical environments for major U.S. crops.

Crop	Yields (t/ha)		Average losses (t/ha)			
	Record	Average	Diseases	Insects	Weeds	Physico-chemical[a]
Corn	19.3	4.6	0.9	0.9	0.7	12.2
Wheat	14.5	1.9	0.4	0.2	0.3	11.7
Soybeans	7.4	1.6	0.3	0.1	0.4	5.0
Sorghum	20.1	2.8	0.4	0.4	0.5	16.0
Oats	10.6	1.7	0.6	0.1	0.5	7.7
Barley	11.4	2.1	0.4	0.1	0.4	8.4
Potatoes	94.1	28.2	8.4	6.2	1.3	50.0
Sugar beets	121.0	42.6	10.7	8.0	5.3	54.4
Mean percentage of record yield	100.0	21.5	5.1	3.0	3.5	66.9

SOURCE: USDA, 1965; Wittwer, 1975.

[a]Calculated as record yield − (average yield + disease loss + insect loss + weed loss).

Much of this potential is not realized, however. Average yields are substantially lower than record yields. For rice average yields are about 40 percent of the record in the temperate region and 27 percent in the tropics. For the other crops average yields are even lower. With but one exception average yields are more suppressed in the tropics than in the temperate regions. For all crops average yields are 15.7 percent of the record in the tropics but 21.4 percent in the temperate regions. Thus not only does the average agricultural environment greatly limit production, but the largest effect is in the tropics.

There are many reasons why average yields fall so far below the record. Crops are often grown in regions that are known not to provide maximum yields. Farmers may fail to use known management practices, either because of a lack of awareness or for economic reasons. In some parts of the world existing technology is simply not available because of political problems or inefficiencies in distribution. For all of these factors, however, the effect is translated into suppressed crop yield through unfavorable environments.

Clearly environment has a large effect on productivity, and it is important to ask what environmental limitations are most prevalent. Table 2 shows that in the United States the elimination of pests (diseases, insects, and weeds) would increase average yields about 43 percent. Thus pests are an important component of the environmental limitation of productivity, and major yield increases would occur if they were eliminated.

Even with the elimination of pests, however, environmental limitations would remain. The data show that without pests average yields would be about one-third of record yields (Table 2). Therefore, the largest yield suppression is caused by abiotic effects, that is, by the physicochemical environments in which the crops are grown.

This conclusion is supported by comparisons of experiment-station yields and record yields. In experiment sta-

Table 3. Experiment-station and world-record yields of maize and soybeans.

Crop	United States (t/ha)[a]	Japan (t/ha)[b]	Philippines (t/ha)[b]	World record (t/ha)
Maize	8.8 (Iowa)	7.7	6.0	22.2
Soybeans	4.0 (Illinois)	3.7	3.0	7.1

[a]Boyer, 1982.
[b]Haws et al., 1983.

tions the plots are free of pests insofar as can be determined. Table 3 shows these comparisons for experiment stations in the United States (Iowa and Illinois), Japan, and the Philippines (Boyer, 1982; Haws et al., 1983). The crops grown in the United States were not irrigated, whereas those in Japan and the Philippines were. In all but one instance yields were less than half the record yields.

These data, taken together, indicate that physicochemical factors account for the largest losses in crop yields. Thus improvements in plant productivity need to be based not only on increasing the genetic potential but also on bringing productivity closer to the existing genetic potential. In addition to pest management significant increases in production should be possible with improved plant performance in existing physicochemical environments.

PREVALENCE OF UNFAVORABLE PHYSICOCHEMICAL ENVIRONMENTS

The kinds of physicochemical environments that affect plants can be quantified even though they overlap and are often sporadic in their impact. A classification of soils in the United States indicates that those with low water availability occupy the largest fraction (44.9 percent) of the land area (Table 4, drought-prone and shallow soils). Soils that are too wet or too cold cover 16.5 and 15.7 percent, respectively, of the United States. Finally, saline soil, alkaline soil, and soil-less areas account for 7.4 percent. Only 12.1 percent of the land surface is relatively "free" from physicochemical problems. This area, when supplied with plant nutrients to replace those removed when crops are harvested, is the most productive.

Similar conclusions apply to the soils of the world (Table 5). The land area prone to drought is approximately 52.1 percent. Low temperatures affect 14.8 percent (shown separately in Table 5). About 22.5 percent is affected by mineral problems. Thus mineral problems are somewhat larger than those in the United States, probably because of low pH and aluminum toxicity, which affect large areas of the tropics. As in the United States, only a small fraction of the surface is free from physicochemical problems (10.1 percent).

The effects of unfavorable climates are as pervasive as those of unfavorable soils. As shown in Table 6, 40.8 percent of crop losses in the United States during a recent 40-year period were caused by drought. Flooding, cold, and hail accounted for 16.4, 13.8, and 11.3 percent of crop losses, respectively. The losses caused by insects and disease were 4.5 and 2.7 percent, respectively.

The similarity between climatic and soil data indicates that water problems dominate losses in agriculture. Not

Table 4. Area of the United States with soils subject to environmental limitations of various types.

Environmental Limitation	Percentage of Soil in United States Affected
Drought	25.3
Shallowness	19.6
Cold	16.5
Wet	15.7
Alkaline salts	2.9
Saline or no soil	4.5
Other	3.4
None	12.1

SOURCE: USDA, 1975.

Table 5. Area of total world soils subject to environmental limitations of various types. Soils characterized in nondrought categories also may be subject to periodic droughts. Area affected by unfavorable temperatures is indicated separately.

Environmental Limitations	Percentage of World Soil Subject to Limitations
Drought	27.9
Shallowness	24.2
Mineral	22.5
Excess water	12.2
Miscellaneous	3.1
None	10.1
Total	100.0
Temperature	14.8

SOURCE: Dudal, 1976.

Table 6. Distribution of insurance indemnities for crop losses in the United States, 1939 to 1978.

Cause of Crop Loss	Proportion of Payments (%)
Drought	40.8
Excess water	16.4
Cold	13.8
Hail	11.3
Wind	7.0
Insect	4.5
Disease	2.7
Flood	2.1
Other	1.5

SOURCE: USDA, 1979.

shown in these data are additional water problems caused by excessive evapotranspiration in areas supplied with adequate soil water. In these instances symptoms of water deficiency are often difficult to detect and may not be known until the end of the growing season. Many temperature effects are similarly elusive. Because these add to the already large losses documented above, the proportion of the total loss attributable to water and temperature is probably even higher. The magnitude of these losses has not been recognized until recently.

POTENTIAL FOR IMPROVEMENT

Advances in agricultural productivity have relied on the availability and low cost of environmental resources. Energy for irrigation has been cheap, plant nutrients have been abundant and inexpensive, and pesticides have been available. These factors have permitted the use of increasing plant populations adapted to high production in environments richly endowed with resources. The abundant resource approach will be less possible in the future, however, particularly where water is concerned. Not only is high-quality water less available, but energy costs are increasing. As the energy for pumping water causes a large fraction of the cost of irrigation, farmers are finding it increasingly difficult to justify irrigation. A greater emphasis on conservation and water catchment is likely, mostly for economic reasons. Therefore, methods of increasing productivity with lower inputs will be sought.

With this in mind it is important to note that genetic vari-

ability for water use exists in plants. This variability might be exploited to provide crops with higher water-use efficiency (more yield per unit of water used) than is currently available. Moreover, the simple existence of genetic variability implies that further variability might be found with additional germplasm exploration or by advanced genetic techniques such as mutation, insertion of foreign DNA, or somatic hybridization.

Fig. 1 shows the genetic variability that occurs between peanut and soybean growing with limited water. Seed yield is less inhibited in peanuts than in soybean when water is in short supply during the growing season (Pandey et al., 1984; Pandey et al., 1984).

Genotypic variation also exists within single crop species. Fig. 2 shows that sorghum genotypes differ in aboveground biomass and grain yield under limited water supply (Garrity et al., 1982). The tolerant genotype (RS626) yields more than the other genotype (NB505) under both high and low water supplies.

In both of these studies supplemental water was provided by irrigation throughout the growing season. Thus the responses are not attributable to delayed growth that is made

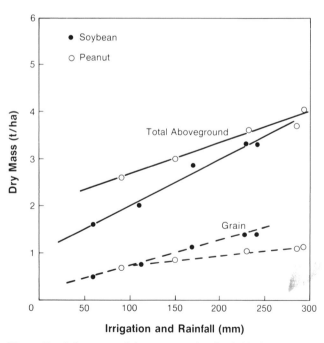

Fig. 1. Total aboveground dry-matter and grain yield of peanut and soybean crops grown on various amounts of water. Rainfall (shown by far left data points) was supplemented by irrigation from a line source. Pandey et al., 1984; Pandey et al., 1984.

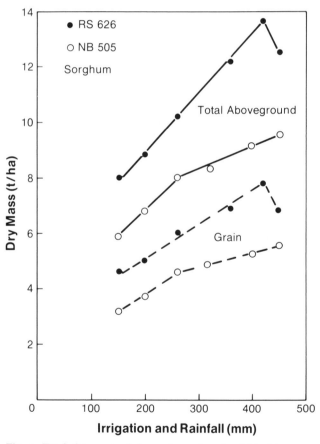

Fig. 2. Total aboveground dry-matter and grain yield of two sorghum crops grown on various amounts of water. Rainfall (shown by far left data points) was supplemented by irrigation from a line source. Garrity et al., 1982.

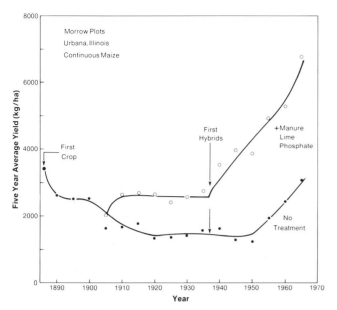

Fig. 3. Grain yield of maize grown continuously for eighty years on the Morrow Plots at the University of Illinois. No soil amendment was added (shown as "no treatment") to the plots except after 1905, when manure, lime, and phosphate were supplied to some of the plots. The effect of introducing the first hybrid maize is shown (1937). University of Illinois, 1969.

up at a later time when water is resupplied. Rather, the responses represent real differences in the crop's ability to yield with limited water supplies. Although some of the differences may be attributable to differences in rooting, the other mechanisms remain obscure.

A major question arising from the sorghum experiments and similar work is whether selection for high genetic potential protects crops against losses in unfavorable environments. A partial answer can be found in the historic yield data for hybrid corn. Fig. 3 shows that on the Morrow Plots at the University of Illinois the yield decreased when corn was grown year after year without additional nutrients or supplemental irrigation (University of Illinois, 1969). After years of continuous culture starting in 1887, yields were low and stable, sustained by low levels of nutrient input in rainwater and decomposition of organic matter and parent material in the soil. By the mid-1930s organic matter had declined to about two-thirds the level present at the beginning of the measurements. This resulted not only in nutrient

stress but also in low available water during the growing season.

Upon introduction of hybrid corn no improvement was observed initially (Fig. 3). The hybrids possessed a significantly increased genetic potential, as evidenced by the improved yields when nutrients were available and soil organic matter was high (Fig. 3). This behavior, which lasted fifteen years after the introduction of plants that had increased genetic potential for high yield, eventually improved when new hybrids were developed that could be used at higher populations. However, the fifteen-year period before the growing of these new genotypes shows that simply increasing the genetic potential will not necessarily improve yields per unit of land area under severe environmental limitations. Improved genotypes must be sought by testing under conditions in which the plants are expected to be grown.

MECHANISMS OF GENOTYPIC RESPONSE TO WATER LIMITATIONS

There is increasing awareness that an understanding of how plants cope with adverse environments may increase the rate at which crop species can be improved. When mechanisms of plant response are known, they may be specifically modified with rapid effects on productivity. Such knowledge might also suggest entirely different ways of increasing productivity in unfavorable environments.

That this kind of information can materially increase the effectiveness of crop-improvement programs was illustrated in 1972 when my laboratory (Meyer and Boyer, 1972) and an Australian group (Greacen and Oh, 1972) showed that plants can compensate osmotically for the onset of dryness in soils. This osmoregulation (osmotic adjustment) has a growth-maintaining effect under dry conditions (Meyer and Boyer, 1972; Michelena and Boyer, 1982). Morgan (1983), in an effort to determine whether the capability for osmotic adjustment differs among wheat genotypes, showed that a cultivar selected for this character outyielded other cultivars having a similar genetic background by 51 to 61 percent under dry conditions (Table 7).

It is important to note that conditions of adequate soil water gave yields that were comparable in all genotypes (Table 7), and the adaptation was called into play only under adverse conditions. This illustrates the advantage of understanding not only mechanisms of plant response to low water potentials but also the presence of mechanisms that express themselves only under adverse conditions. To ob-

Table 7. Average grain yields ($\pm$ s.e.) of F_4 and F_6 breeding lines in the field. High, medium, and low classes are based on selections for ability to osmoregulate when water was withheld in a controlled environment.

F_4 Class	F_4-droughted (g/plant)	F_4-watered (g/plant)	F_6-droughted (g/m^2)
High	2.16 ± 0.23	7.29 ± 0.49	44.32 ± 3.67
Medium	2.22 ± 1.17	6.72 ± 3.32	47.90 ± 3.32
Low	1.34 ± 0.18	6.80 ± 0.92	29.20 ± 2.64

SOURCE: Morgan, 1983.

tain an improved genotype, therefore, it was essential to select under the adverse conditions anticipated where the crop would be grown. Selection under favorable water conditions would have failed to identify the improved genotype.

This type of selection could not have been made before 1972 because until then it was not known that osmotic adjustment occurs in plants growing in dry soil. In this situation the new knowledge had a rapid impact on productivity; within ten years after the discovery of the basic mechanism a new genotype was available.

The mechanism of osmotic adjustment is worth noting. Most osmotic adjustment is caused by the accumulation of organic molecules, i.e., photosynthetic products, particularly in growing regions. The solutes are mostly sugars and amino acids (Morgan, 1984). They have the effect of increasing the concentration of the cellular solution sufficiently to generate additional force to bring water from the soil into the plant. As a result tissue water content is maintained, and cell turgor remains high and favorable for growth.

Because osmotic adjustment depends on photosynthesis, the response of photosynthesis is often important to the growth of plants under dry conditions. It is increasingly clear that the photosynthetic performance of plants under dry conditions can be modified by the environment the plant encounters before the onset of water limitation. Fig. 4 shows that sunflower plants previously grown under moderately dry conditions are able to acclimate so that they photosynthesize more rapidly under these conditions (Matthews and Boyer, 1984). This implies that, in addition to the osmotic adjustment of growing tissues to preserve growth, there can be acclimation of the solute-producing tissues to preserve the supply of solute. Because the solute for osmotic adjustment is mostly derived from photosynthesis, the acclimation of both the growing tissue and the photosynthetic tissue can have important regulatory consequences.

CONCLUSIONS

Taken together, these findings suggest that, with sufficient understanding of the response of plants to the environment, considerable improvements in plant productivity are possible under water-limited conditions. Investigations of plant response mechanisms show that specific processes are affected and that the plant has evolved ways to change these processes, leading to adaptation. More important, there is promise that these changes can be transmitted genetically.

There are beginning to be examples of physiological and metabolic features in plants that can be selected for specific drought tolerance under dry conditions. When this is possible, the rate of genetic improvement can be markedly enhanced. However, the lack of extensive knowledge of this kind often limits the use of advanced genetic techniques and selection procedures. Therefore, the genetic approach has not been as widely used as it might have been. While we may never be able to overcome the effects of water limitation completely by genetic means, there is reason to believe that modest increases in productivity are possible. The large impact of dry environments on plant productivity worldwide indicates that even modest genetic improvements could contribute significantly to agriculture under these conditions.

REFERENCES

Boyer, J. S. 1982. Plant productivity and environment. *Science* 218:443–48.

Boyer, J. S., R. R. Johnson, and S. G. Saupe. 1980. Afternoon water deficits and grain yields in old and new soybean cultivars. *Agronomy Journal* 72:981–86.

Dudal, R. 1976. Inventory of the major soils of the world with special reference to mineral stress hazards. Pp. 3–14. *In* M. J. Wright (ed.) Plant adaptation to mineral stress in problem soils. Ithaca, N.Y.: Cornell University, Agricultural Experiment Station.

Garrity, D. P., D. G. Watts, C. Y. Sullivan, and J. R. Gilley. 1982. Moisture deficits and grain sorghum performance: effect of genotype and limited irrigation strategy. *Agronomy Journal* 74:808–14.

Greacen, E. L., and J. S. Oh. 1972. Physics of growth. *Nature; New Biology* 235:24–25.

Haws, L. D., H. Inoue, A. Tanaka, and S. Yoshida. 1983. Comparison of crop productivity in the tropics and temperate zone. Pp. 403–13. *In* Potential productivity of field crops under different environments. Los Baños, Laguna, Philippines: International Rice Research Institute.

Matthews, M. A., and J. S. Boyer. 1984. Acclimation of photosynthesis to low leaf water potentials. *Plant Physiology* 74:161–66.

Meyer, R. F., and J. S. Boyer. 1972. Sensitivity of cell division and cell elongation to low water potentials in soybean hypocotyls. *Planta* 108:77–87.

Michelena, V. A., and J. S. Boyer. 1982. Complete turgor maintenance at low water potentials in the elongating region of maize leaves. *Plant Physiology* 69:1145–49.

Morgan, J. M. 1983. Osmoregulation as a selection criterion for

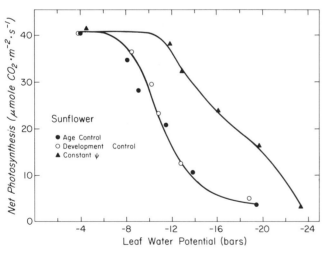

Fig. 4. Photosynthesis at various leaf water potentials for plants receiving different watering pretreatments. Plants grew in soil from which water was withheld. Controls received adequate water except when photosynthesis was measured. They were of two types, one of the same age (age control), the other of the same development (development control). Acclimated plants had been subjected to moderately low leaf water potentials (−7 to −11 bars) for two weeks before these measurements by maintaining soil at a low average water content. Matthews and Boyer, 1984.

drought tolerance in wheat. *Australian Journal of Agricultural Research* 34:607–14.

Morgan, J. M. 1984. Osmoregulation and water stress in higher plants. *Annual Review of Plant Physiology* 35:299–319.

Pandey, R. K., W. A. T. Herrera, and J. W. Pendleton. 1984. Drought response of grain legumes under irrigation gradient. 1. Yield and yield components. *Agronomy Journal* 76:549–53.

Pandey, R. K., W. A. T. Herrera, A. N. Villegas, and J. W. Pendleton. 1984. Drought response of grain legumes under irrigation gradient. 3. Plant growth. *Agronomy Journal* 76:557–64.

U.S. Department of Agriculture. 1965. Losses in agriculture. Agriculture Handbook 291. Washington, D.C.: Government Printing Office.

———. 1975. Soil taxonomy. Washington, D.C.: Government Printing Office.

———. 1979. Agricultural statistics. Washington, D.C.: Government Printing Office.

U.S. Department of the Interior. 1977. Estimated use of water in the United States in 1975. U.S. Geological Survey Circular 765. Arlington, Va.: U.S. Geological Survey.

University of Illinois. 1969. The Morrow plots. Urbana, Ill.: University of Illinois, Agricultural Experiment Station.

Wittwer, S. H. 1975. Food production: technology and the resource base. *Science* 188:579–84.

37. BIOLOGICAL CONSTRAINTS: THE IMPORTANCE OF PESTS

Michael J. Way, Imperial College, Silwood Park, Ascot, Berkshire, United Kingdom

ABSTRACT

Damaging organisms are estimated to cause about 35 percent crop loss worldwide. In the United States this loss has increased from about 31 to 37 percent (including 7 to 13 percent by insects) between the 1940s and the 1980s. This increase has occurred despite massive increases in chemical controls and is associated with pest-favoring, yield-increasing changes, including the development of high-yielding crop cultivars and greatly increased use of nitrogenous fertilizers. Irrigation has had complex effects, usually, though not always, making pests more damaging.

Overdependence on pesticides to counter the enhanced pest problems has induced pest resistance to pesticides and has also caused pest resurgences and created new pests in direct relation to intensity of pesticide use. A case is made for a more integrated approach, including careful analyses of interactions among different yield-increasing components, in order to manipulate them collectively against pests.

Temperate-climate high-yield technology creates serious pest constraints when applied in the tropics. A different path is urged for improving crop yields in the tropics, one aiming at production systems that put less emphasis on maximizing yields and more on attaining dependable immediate yields in conditions where pest avoidance is made more feasible through integrated cultural, biological, and chemical controls instead of overdependence on curative pesticides.

PESTS AND THE DAMAGE THEY CAUSE

Although the word "pests" is now commonly used to cover all forms of damaging organisms, this chapter is restricted to damaging animals. These include vertebrates, mollusks, nematodes, and arthropods, notably insects. Vertebrates may be locally very damaging and are sometimes major pests, for example, weaver birds, *Quelea* spp., on basic cereal food crops in parts of tropical Africa, and several species of rats, which can severely damage tropical rice. Moreover, it is often extremely difficult to combat such pests. Nematodes may also be difficult to control and are much more damaging than is normally appreciated, particularly in the tropics. However, of animal pests, insects are undoubtedly the worst worldwide hazard to agriculture in general. They are damaging in three main ways: (1) by directly feeding on crops, (2) by acting as vectors of plant pathogens, and (3) by indirectly limiting crop production through the harm they do to man and domestic animals. For example, the debilitating effects of mosquito-transmitted malaria have been a major cause of agricultural underdevelopment in much of the tropics, as has the tsetse fly, *Glossina* spp., in tropical Africa. Tsetse-transmitted trypanosomes harm man and especially domestic animals. Consequently, agriculture in much of tropical Africa has been deprived of intermediate technology based on domestic animal power, and, in particular, large areas of fertile, well-watered riverine parts of Africa remain unexploited because of human pathogens transmitted by insects.

In this chapter I use mostly insects to illustrate the role of pests as biological constraints on improved world food production.

ESTIMATES OF DAMAGE BY INSECTS

In an attempt to assess preharvest losses of major crops damaged by organisms, Cramer (1967) calculated that insects caused almost one-third of total preharvest losses by damaging organisms and decreased potential yield of some crops by more than 40 percent (Table 1). The Food and Agriculture Organization (FAO) (1975) subsequently estimated that 30 to 35 percent of crop losses were caused worldwide by damaging organisms. It is salutary to compare Cramer's figures with some later estimates for specific crops; for example, his estimate of about 9.4 percent insect-caused loss of corn in the United States compared with an estimate by the U.S. Department of Agriculture of 17.5 percent in 1973–74. Yet this apparent increase occurred during a period when the use of chemical insecticides for insect pest control was greatly intensifying. Table 2 shows also how estimated percentage losses of all crops in the United States have increased from the early 1940s to the present day (Pimental, 1982). During that period yields of some crops per unit of land have more than doubled. This means that the actual yield loss from insects, as distinct from the percentage loss, has approximately tripled between the 1940s and the 1980s, despite massive use of chemical insecticides. This evidence has serious implications for increasing world food supplies. It means that, as the inherent yielding capacity of the plant is increased, so, both potentially and actually, the biological constraints caused by insects and other damaging organisms may accelerate at a relatively greater rate despite intensified use of pesticides.

EFFECTS OF YIELD-INCREASING AGRICULTURAL CHANGES ON PEST INCIDENCE AND DAMAGE

In terms of their own strategies, plants in nature are well adapted to losses from "pests" that would be unacceptable if the plants were cultivated by man. Pests must therefore be recognized as fundamental biological constraints on human food production, predating agriculture, a situation which we now accept by using such terms as "pest management" rather than "pest control," the former implying that crop-protection practices must be based on learning how to live with pests rather than assuming that they can be obliterated.

Table 1. Estimates of world losses of major foodstuffs caused by damaging organisms.

Crop	Percentage of Losses Caused by	
	Insects	All Damaging Organisms
Cereals	14	34
Tuber and vegetable crops	17	42
Oil-protein crops	11	31

SOURCE: Cramer, 1967.

Table 2. USDA estimates of overall crop losses from insects compared with total losses from all damaging organisms in the United States.

Period	Percentage of Crop Losses	
	Insects	Total
1942–51	7.1	31.4
1951–60	12.9	33.6
1974	13.0	42.0
1980	13.0	37.0

SOURCE: Pimental, 1982.

So pest damage is inevitable even in the most primitive agriculture. Furthermore, in developed agriculture the drive for increasing yields of crucially important arable crops has involved changes that greatly influence pest incidence and damage. The major yield-increasing, pest-affecting changes are plant breeding, artificial fertilizers, changed cultural practices, irrigation, and pest control.

Plant Breeding

Breeding for increased yield and quality has almost invariably increased the sensitivity of plants to damaging organisms through inadvertent loss of resistance-conferring genes or because resistance is traded for increased crop yield. Where resistance has been retained or regained, as in rice against the brown plant hopper, *Nilaparvata lugens,* it may be unstable, like many disease-resistance mechanisms. Often resistance to animal pests involves diverting energy and nutrients otherwise devoted to crop yield. For example, in wild plants and in "traditional" grain crops energy is often used to maintain a high ratio of vegetative to reproductive structures. In contrast, the development of short-strawed cultivars of many cereals, which has been fundamental to yield increases in many modern cereal cultivars, is nearly always associated with increased sensitivity to insect pests and to diseases as well as lowered competitiveness with weeds. Host-plant resistance may also involve physical attributes such as hairiness or solid stems as well as chemical defenses, all of which divert energy from food production. Such plant resistance is therefore incompatible with maximizing potential yield.

Artificial Fertilizers

Fertilizers, particularly nitrogenous ones that are essential for high yields, exacerbate pest problems as they do for many other damaging organisms. This is illustrated later, especially for wheat.

Changed Cultural Practices

These have had complex effects. Simplification of crop production through monocultures, in both space and time, has made some pests worse but has decreased damage by others, depending upon the ecological conditions and the pest species (Way, 1977, 1979).

Irrigation

It is obvious that irrigation, which permits the growing of crops at times and in places where none grew before, will create entirely new pest problems. However, it has had other much more subtle effects. In general it increases pest problems in the overall agricultural system by permitting pest buildup in successive crops of the same or different species, whereas previously the life cycle of the pest was dislocated by the longer "off season." Case histories for rice and cotton given later illustrate this problem, which can create complex and very dangerous changes in the behavior of the pest and in the epidemiology of diseases it may transmit. For example, in Zimbabwe the irrigation of grassland and earlier sown cereal crops creates a situation where leafhoppers, *Cicadulina* spp., do not produce "high-mortality" long-distance migrants but continue building up on the irrigated crops and developing high levels of maize-streak virus infection, which is subsequently transmitted to maize that would otherwise be unharmed (Rose, 1978).

Finally, there are other unfortunate effects, such as the dispersal of soil pests, notably nematodes in irrigation water (Steadman et al., 1975; Tobar-Jiménez and Palacios-Mejía, 1976; Bos, 1978).

In contrast, irrigation or improved water supply in general can alleviate certain pest problems of particular crops during their growing season. Some pests, notably spider mites and some aphids and related species, can be controlled by the physical action of sprinkler-applied water. The control of cutworms, *Agrotis* spp., on irrigated potato crops in the United Kingdom is helped by sprinkler irrigation that can be predictably timed to coincide with early larval stages, which are knocked from the plant by the water. Irrigation can also be predictably avoided at critical times when it favors pest oviposition, e.g., by bollworms on cotton (Slosser, 1980).

A more subtle beneficial effect of improved water supply is by conferring host plant resistance, for example, to field beans, *Vicia fabae,* attacked by the black bean aphid, *Aphis fabae* (Cammell and Way, 1983). Table 3 shows that insecticide was unnecessary on the irrigated plants because they tolerated the particular aphid population without crop loss. In contrast, a similar aphid population severely damaged the untreated, unirrigated crop, as shown by a 38 percent yield increase from insecticidal control.

Fig. 1 (McEwan and Johnston, 1984) demonstrates the importance of understanding the interactions between irrigation and other inputs, namely, fertilizer and pesticides. Without added nitrogen fertilizer irrigation increased crop

Table 3. Effect of *Aphis fabae* control on unirrigated and irrigated spring-sown field beans at Silwood Park, United Kingdom.

	Peak Aphid Numbers per Plant in Untreated Crops	Yield (t/ha)		Percent Yield Change Caused by Insecticide Treatment
		Untreated	Treated	
Unirrigated	436	1.46	1.95	+38 (P = 0.05)
Irrigated	376	3.58	3.46	− 3 (P = 0.05)

SOURCES: Cammell and Way, 1983, and unpublished.

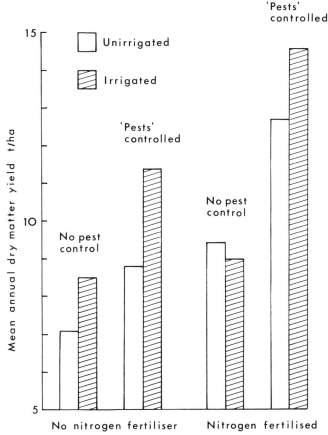

Fig. 1. Results of four-year trials on interacting effects of nitrogen fertilization, irrigation, and pest-disease control on yields of ryegrass/clover. McEwan and Johnston, 1984.

yield similarly on untreated and pesticide-treated crops. With nitrogen fertilizer, however, irrigation did not increase crop yield because fertilizer treatment, as already mentioned, helped pests cause damage that offset the beneficial effect of irrigation. This is evident from the combined fertilizer and pesticide treatments, where, with pests controlled, irrigation increased yield.

Pest Control

In the drive for increased yields, cultural, biological, and physical controls and host-plant resistance have often be-

come less effective or less practicable and have been replaced by chemical pesticides. There is no doubt that the high yields of crops in many developed countries could not possibly have been attained without the use of such cheap and effective chemicals. Nevertheless, Table 2 indicates that, despite the use of pesticides, high-yielding systems have not realized their potential because pests may still notably constrain yields. This limitation is partly associated with many insect species becoming dramatically resistant to insecticides that formerly controlled them, as shown in Fig. 2. Furthermore, there are many examples from the 1950s onward (Ripper, 1956) of pesticides being responsibile for "resurgences" of pests against which they were used and for development of new pests by upsetting biological controls. Such problems, together with other environmental hazards from pesticides, lead to the conclusion that present-day overdependence on chemical pesticides is unsatisfactory.

CASE HISTORIES

The following brief case histories exemplify problems caused by pests and illustrate how these problems change as crop production is intensified.

Wheat in Northwestern Europe

Mean annual wheat yields have greatly increased in northwestern Europe in the last forty years, e.g., in the United Kingdom, from less than 2.5 t/ha to more than 7 t/ha in 1984. The increase shows no sign of leveling off, and the objective is clearly for average yields of more than 10 t/ha, as already regularly attained by some farmers. Table 4 indicates what this means for control of aphids as pests. Yield data from the Netherlands have been used to develop a simulation model which shows the effect of a particular population of aphids as yield potential is increased. The aphids extract nutrients otherwise destined for grain production, and their honeydew falling on the leaves can critically decrease photosynthetic efficiency, a collective effect that cannot be compensated for by plants expected to fulfill an increasing yield potential. Thus the "acceptable" peak aphid density is decreased to an average of about two aphids per shoot for a yield objective of 11 t/ha. Fig. 3 also shows how the economic injury level—the level which justifies the cost of prior chemical control measures—decreases with any increase in anticipated yield. This means that if a yield of about 10 to 11 t/ha is expected, an aphicide must be ap-

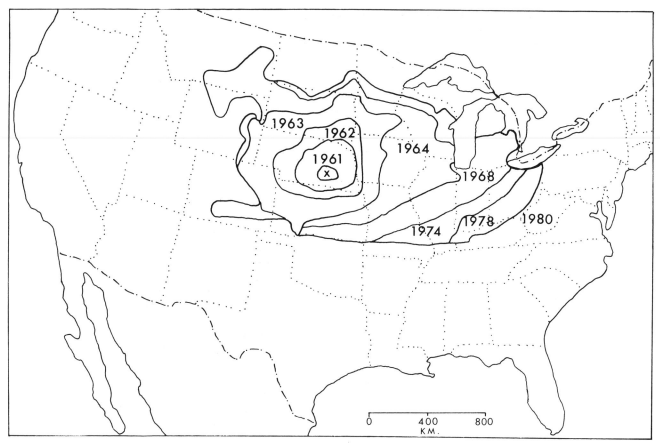

Fig. 2. Spread of the cyclodiene-resistant western corn rootworm, *Diabrotica virgifera,* from the original mutant. U.S. Department of Agriculture, 1978.

Table 4. Simulated effect of a mean of twenty-five cereal aphids per tiller at peak density on yield of winter wheat.

Yield Potential (t/ha)	Percent Yield Loss	Yield Reduction (t/ha)	Approximate "Acceptable" Peak Aphid Density
6.6	12	0.8	8
8.4	13	1.1	4
11.0	17	1.9	2

SOURCE: After Rabbinge et al., 1983.

plied before the aphid population reaches two per shoot if economic loss is to be avoided. Such a level is impossible to estimate in the field in view of sampling errors, so the inevitable outcome is routine aphicide application. Routine applications, as indicated later, have serious implications for the continued efficacy of current chemical control practices.

The multiplication rate of aphids is related to the amount of nitrogen fertilizer (Fig. 3b). Consequently, high-yielding nitrogen-dependent crops not only can tolerate fewer aphids but also favor rapid aphid multiplication, with the result that the ability of a particular number of aphid colonists to reach a damaging level is also increased.

In the above example the constraints imposed by aphids on increasing crop yield are largely limited to particular fields and depend on level of fertilizer applications, choice of wheat cultivar, and date of sowing. There may also be regional effects, particularly on the spread of aphid-borne pathogens by a larger overall population of aphids. Large-scale regional effects might be particularly important where aphids can colonize and build up on successive crops, for example, during seasonal northward migration in the United States.

Rice in Southeast Asia

The Green Revolution for rice involves a package of new high-yielding, early-maturing cultivars, fertilizers, pesticides, and improved irrigation. The combination of early-maturing rice cultivars and improved irrigation has often permitted an almost continuous and often widely over-lapping succession of two or three crops a year. These have provided a source of food for continued pest multiplication (Fig. 4), unlike situations where dependence on seasonal rainfall dislocated the pest's life cycle during the host-scarce dry season. Some rice insects have also become notably more serious under Green Revolution regimes, the most notorious being the brown plant hopper, which was previously almost unknown as a pest (Kisimoto, 1977; Kiritani, 1979). This pest exemplifies a vast regional problem with migrants

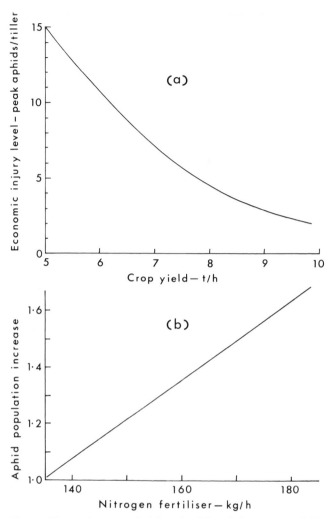

Fig. 3. Change in economic injury level in relation to crop yield (a), and aphid population increase in relation to nitrogen fertilizer (b). Rabbinge et al., 1983; Vereijken, 1979.

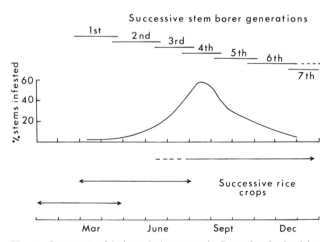

Fig. 4. Sequence of irrigated rice crops in Bengal colonized by rice stem borers showing buildup of severely damaging levels on the third crop. Momin, personal communication.

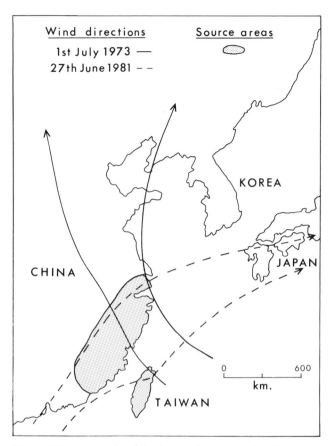

Fig. 5. Migratory paths of the brown plant hopper leading to annual outbreaks on rice in regions where it cannot overwinter. Rosenberg and Magor, 1984.

from outbreak areas that may cause infestations on rice as far as 1,000 km away (Fig. 5).

Rice pest problems in general and the brown plant hopper in particular exemplify a paradoxical situation that could perhaps be capitalized upon to reduce pest incidence rather than increase it in a continuous cropping regime. On the one hand, continuous cropping under irrigation allows pests such as the brown plant hopper to become outbreak pests because it allows the pest to more nearly fulfill its annual reproduction potential. On the other hand, continuity of rice cropping favors development of a more stable equilibrium between pests and their natural enemies because the pest–natural enemy equilibrium is not dislocated by an off season (Way, 1979). Consequently, biological control of pests can be favored on all-year cropped tropical rice, as is evident for the brown plant hopper, provided the natural enemies are not harmed by insecticide misuse (Kenmore et al., 1984). In general it seems that intensification of production has pushed the population of brown plant hoppers from a harmless status to a critical level where insecticidal destruction of natural enemies can tip the balance and cause damaging outbreaks.

This example demonstrates that a more sophisticated, integrated approach to pest management is needed. Such an approach would include host-plant resistance, which has already proved to be a crucially important component of pest management for higher-yield rice production in Asia, but it also depends on resolution of the dilemma over the need to favor biological controls rather than pest-dislocating cultural practices. A key question, therefore, is whether and in what conditions the cropping program should aim to enhance natural-enemy action or whether synchronous planting and similar practices inimical to natural enemies should be favored in order to upset the pests' life cycle.

Cotton in the Sudan Gezira and Elsewhere

The Gezira and other irrigation schemes in the Sudanese "desert" are the basis for the country's economy. Before the mid-1960s there was a clear break in the host-plant sequence which helped dislocate the life cycle of the bollworm, *Heliothis armigera*. Furthermore, a fodder crop, lubia, acted as a diversionary host, attracting the bollworm away from cotton so that it did little damage and required no control measures (Fig. 6). In general the crop production and protection system was highly successful. Intensification of cropping from the mid-1960s involved growing groundnuts in the break period and sowing cotton earlier, as well as virtually eliminating lubia. The bollworm then multiplied on the groundnuts and migrated to cotton in severely damaging numbers. Insecticides used against the bollworm created serious late-season problems with the whitefly, *Bemesia tabaci,* partly because they destroyed the insect's natural enemies. Moreover, the lack of cattle fodder—after cropping with lubia was discontinued—has been partly made up by irrigating fallow land to maintain weed growth and by prolonging the irrigation of cotton. Both these practices have exacerbated the whitefly problem, the former by creating a source of the pest and the latter by contamination of lint in the opening bolls by whitefly honeydew. This attempt to increase productivity has, therefore, proved disastrous to the cotton crop and to the Sudanese economy (Eveleens, 1983). It is a salutary example of the vital need to forestall such problems through studies aimed at forecasting the probable effects of proposed agricultural changes.

Serious problems with cotton have arisen elsewhere in the world, for example, in parts of Mexico and Australia, where intensification of crop production led to massive use of insecticides to which bollworms, *Heliothis* spp., became resistant, and cotton production ceased completely. Compa-

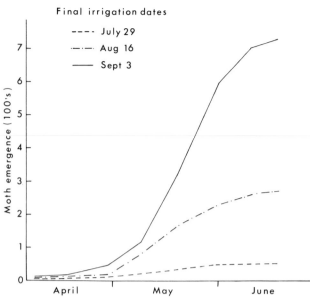

Fig. 7. Effect of final irrigation dates on numbers of pink bollworms emerging the following spring. Watson et al., 1975.

rable problems were averted in parts of Texas only by a combination of integrated pest-management practices, no doubt at the expense of some intrinsic yield potential (Adkisson and Gaines, 1960; Adkisson et al., 1966). At present an uneasy situation exists in the southwestern United States, where intensification of cotton production, beginning in the 1950s, based on a long growing season, is responsible for serious attacks by the pink bollworm, *Pectinophora gossypiella*. Here, extended cropping permits the pink bollworm to overwinter in numbers that can severely damage the crop in the following year. Considerable decreases in damage and in insecticide use, albeit at some loss of potential yield, could be accomplished by regionally coordinated early irrigation cutoff before the great majority of pink bollworms reach the overwintering stage (Fig. 7) (Watson et al., 1975; Bariola et al., 1981). The dilemma whereby extended irrigation increases intrinsic yield but incurs increased damage from pests has been resolved for one pest in Egypt, where an irrigation cutoff date for clover is legally enforced. This creates a host plant "break" for the cotton leafworm, *Spodoptera littoralis,* which would otherwise migrate to cotton in much larger numbers (Khalifa et al., 1979).

PEST CONSTRAINTS IN TROPICAL AGRICULTURE

The most crucial world need is to improve food supply in those tropical countries where crop yields per hectare have mostly remained low and sometimes have even decreased, in sharp contrast to yields of equivalent crops in temperate countries. High-yielding temperate farming systems depend on high inputs, including pesticides. As already indicated, reliance on pesticides, in part to compensate for lessened host-plant resistance and in part to replace traditional controls, is an increasingly important cornerstone of many high-yielding cropping systems in temperate regions. Cru-

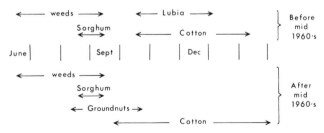

Fig. 6. Effect of cropping changes on pest incidence of the bollworm, *Heliothis armigera,* in the Sudan Gezira. *H. armigera* became a pest after farmers began replacing lubia with groundnuts. The limits indicate the approximate periods when each host plant is colonized by *H. armigera*. Updated from Way, 1974.

cial to such a strategy is the dependable climate of many temperate regions that permits a reliably high yield every year, guaranteeing the farmer's ability to repay with interest the cost of the large inputs needed each year to produce the crop.

Vast "dry" tropical areas in Africa and elsewhere have unreliable or insufficient rainfall to ensure dependable crop yields that in turn would justify costly high-yielding crop production and protection technologies. If water supply can be improved, how will this affect pest incidence and management? As already indicated for rice pests, tropical temperatures, with irrigation during dry periods, provides a climate and food supply that can be ideal for insect multiplication throughout the year. Many examples indicate that insects present a potentially much greater hazard in the tropics than in temperate regions, initially because tropical temperatures favor continuous pest multiplication and secondly because this situation will create more continuous and intensive selection pressure for pest populations to develop resistance to insecticides.

The evidence provided by Cramer (1967) indicates that losses from pests in tropical countries are already greater than those in temperate countries. Yet these losses occur in agricultural systems that are mostly low technology, without the large inputs of fertilizers or high-yielding crop cultivars that would enhance pest damage. Consequently, attempts to copy temperate-country high-yield technology in many tropical environments would undoubtedly exacerbate pest losses. The fundamental differences between tropical and temperate conditions are therefore due to other factors besides less effective developing-country technologies, economics, and organization, as is sometimes assumed. This is evident from the insect-induced catastrophe experienced in cotton production in the Ord valley of Australia, which is an example of complete failure in a tropical region of a developed country.

PEST MANAGEMENT IN THE FUTURE— DISCUSSION AND CONCLUSIONS

Developed-country temperate agriculture has been outstandingly successful. Yield increases have depended on an extraordinary array of chemical pesticides that fit well into high-technology crop-production strategies. The implications of such strategies are shown in the diagram in Fig. 8. Accelerating technology involves a combination of practices that increases the potential yield of the crop. There is a great increase in basic production costs, and also increased instability, particularly in terms of sensitivity to pests and other damaging organisms. This means that less and less risk of pest damage can be taken by the farmer and that there is increasing emphasis on risk-averse routine use of pesticides. In Fig. 8 the extent to which yield can fall below the potential level (a) and remain economic to the farmer is indicated by (b). The widening gap between (a) and (c) indicates increasing likelihood of pest damage and consequently increasing dependence on pesticides needed to attain or exceed the economically acceptable yield presented by (b).

In some developed countries in temperate environments,

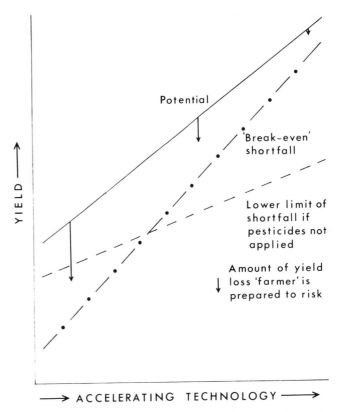

Fig. 8. Diagram indicating the decrease in "robustness" of annual cropping systems with accelerating technology that crucially affects crop-protection practices.

notably European Economic Community countries in northern Europe, technological inputs have reached the level on many farms where (a) and (b) in Fig. 8 are dangerously close. Any deterioration in efficiency, including failings in the pesticide-dominated regime, could cause catastrophes in such high-yielding systems. Even in Europe yields could be much increased on currently lower-yielding farms. This means that high-technology crop-protection systems could become more extensive. The associated extension of pesticide regimes is more likely to trigger pest-control failures than if high-technology farms remain buffered by a mix of less intensive regimes.

High-technology temperate agriculture therefore faces problems which have provided the incentive for the "integrated pest management" or "integrated crop protection" approach as a rational alternative to overdependence on pesticides. However, the evidence that present-day integrated approaches may involve inconvenience to the farmer and also some reduction in potential profit has, with some striking exceptions, made them unacceptable. It may be that pressures from environmentalists will stimulate legislation for more safe, integrated crop-protection strategies before pest-control failures force farmers to adopt them more widely.

In much of the tropics agriculture depends on low technology, and most small farmers, whose families may represent more than 75 percent of the population, use virtually no artificial inputs. Their crop-production strategy is indicated by the bottom end of the graph in Fig. 8. This indicates that, even without pesticides, an "economic" yield is obtained, though the crop is necessarily low-yielding. Yields *must* be increased from the currently low or deteriorating levels in many tropical countries. The question is how this can be done without following temperate-country technology, which most peasant farmers cannot afford and which, moreover, is likely to make pest problems worse than in temperate conditions? This is one of the greatest challenges facing us at the present time.

It is suggested (Way and Norton, 1984) that many farmers in the tropics should follow a different developmental path for crop production and protection than that adopted in most temperate systems; the emphasis should be placed on avoiding, rather than curing, pest infestations, using integrated cultural and biological controls together with appropriate (perhaps partial) host-plant resistance, and with pesticides as the final curative resort if other methods begin to fail. It must be emphasized that chemical controls remain essential and will be increasingly needed in the tropics if many crop yields are to be improved.

It should probably be accepted as a generalization that overall yields, particularly of many basic tropical crops, cannot in practice attain the levels of equivalent crops in temperate environments, but there is still ample opportunity

for doubling or trebling present crop yields, e.g., for tropical rice (Fig. 9). If doubling was accomplished in India, Bangladesh, and other countries with low rice yields, the world could be flooded with unwanted rice. There is, therefore, a considerable future for crop-production and protection strategies that are less intensive than those adopted in most temperate countries. The challenge is thus to identify and develop appropriate farming strategies that are between "relatively safe" low-yielding subsistence systems and "unsafe" high-yield capital-intensive systems. Research and development would involve relatively sophisticated approaches in which pest management, for example, is not to be envisaged as a fire-brigade operation to overcome pest problems created by other agricultural changes. Rather, it should be part of a systems approach in which interactions among all relevant components of the crop-production system, including pest problems, are analyzed and an optimum strategy adopted in the context of local socioeconomic conditions. This would almost inevitably demand restraint by agriculturalists and plant breeders, who have an understandable instinct to maximize rather than optimize yields.

Unfortunately, relatively little funding is being put into the imaginative "systems" research and development work that is needed in the tropics. Instead, such work still tends to mimic the piecemeal single-component approach that has characterized temperate agriculture. The failure to recognize what is needed must be rectified by ensuring that any new tropical agricultural development program, for example, a program using improved water supplies, should contain a large element of innovative and radical research and development work on crop protection. New management strategies should be developed in chosen object-lesson farms or areas through close collaboration among scientists, extension workers, and particularly farmers, many of whom have by trial and error developed cropping practices that contain important cultural components of pest avoidance that need to be capitalized upon (Way, 1974).

REFERENCES

Adkisson, P. L., and J. C. Gaines. 1960. Pink bollworm control as related to the total cotton insect control program of central Texas. Texas Agricultural Experiment Station Miscellaneous Publication 444. College Station, Texas.

Adkisson, P. L., D. R. Rummel, W. T. Sterling, and W. L. Owen. 1966. Diapause boll weevil control: a comparison of two methods. Texas Agricultural Experiment Station Bulletin 1054. College Station, Texas.

Bariola, L. A., T. J. Henneberry, and D. Kittuck. 1981. Chemical termination and irrigation cut-off to reduce overwintering populations of pink bollworms. *Journal of Economic Entomology* 74:106–109.

Bos, W. S. 1978. Root-knot nematodes in the Nigerian Savanna Zones with special reference to root-knot problems of irrigated crops in the Kano River Project at Kadawa. Pp. 38–46. *In* Proceedings of the 2nd research planning conference on root knot nematodes, *Meloidogyne* spp. Ibadan, Nigeria: International Institute of Tropical Agriculture.

Cammell, M. E., and M. J. Way. 1983. Aphid pests. Pp. 315–46. *In* P. D. Hebblethwaite (ed.) The Faba bean. London: Butterworth's.

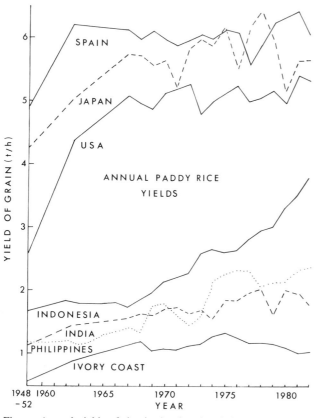

Fig. 9. Annual yields of rice in developed and developing countries. FAO yearbooks.

Cramer, H. H. 1967. Plant protection and world food production. Leverkusen: Farbenfabriken Bayer AG.

Eveleens, K. G. 1983. Cotton-insect control in the Sudan Gezira: analysis of a crisis. *Crop Protection* 2:273–87.

Food and Agriculture Organization. 1975. Pest control problems (pre-harvest) causing major losses in world food supplies. AGP, Pest/PH75/B31. Rome: Food and Agriculture Organization.

Kenmore, P. E., F. O. Carino, C. A. Perez, V. A. Dyck, and A. P. Gutierrez. 1984. Population regulation of the rice brown planthopper (*Nilaparvata lugens* Stal) within rice fields in the Philippines. *Journal of Plant Protection in the Tropics* 1:19–37.

Khalifa, A., R. R. Iss-Hak, and M. E. Foda. 1979. Effect of irrigation before and after the 10 May on the population fluctuations of the Egyptian cotton leafworm soil stages in clover fields. *Zeitschrift fur Angewandte Zoologie* 66:349–58.

Kiritani, K. 1979. Pest management in rice. *Annual Review of Entomology* 24:279–312.

Kisimoto, K. 1977. Bionomics, forecasting of outbreaks and injury caused by the rice brown planthopper. Taipei, Taiwan: Food and Fertilizer Technology Center for the Asian and Pacific Region.

McEwan, J., and A. E. Johnstone. 1984. Factors affecting the production and composition of mixed grass/clover swards containing modern high-yielding clovers. Pp. 41–55. *In* Proceedings of the 18th colloquium of the International Potash Institute, Gardone-Riviera, Italy.

Pimental, D. 1982. Perspectives of integrated pest management. *Crop Protection* 1:5–26.

Rabbinge, R., C. Sinke, and W. P. Mantel. 1983. Yield loss due to cereal aphids and powdery mildew in winter wheat. *Mededelingen van de Faculteit Landbouwhogeschool van de Rijksuniversiteit te Gent* 48:1159–67.

Ripper, W. E. 1956. Effect of pesticides on balance of arthropod populations. *Annual Review of Entomology* 1:403–38.

Rose, D. J. W. 1978. The epidemiology of maize streak disease. *Annual Review of Entomology* 23:259–82.

Rosenberg, L. J., and J. I. Magor. 1984. Flight duration of the brown planthopper. *International Rice Research Newsletter* 9(2):30.

Steadman, J. R., C. R. Maier, H. F. Schwartz, and E. D. Kerr. 1975. Pollution of surface irrigation waters by plant pathogenic organisms. *Water Resources Bulletin, American Water Resources Association* 11:796–805.

Slosser, J. E. 1980. Irrigation timing for bollworm management in cotton. *Journal of Economic Entomology* 73:346–49.

Tobar-Jiménez, A., and F. Palacios-Mejía. 1976. El agua como vehículo de disperión de nematodes fitoparasitos. *Revista Ibérica de Parasitología* 35:223–59.

U.S. Department of Agriculture. 1978. Farmers' use of pesticides in 1976. Agricultural Economics Report 418. Reprinted in Metcalf, R. L. 1982. Insecticides in pest management. Pp. 217–77. *In* R. L. Metcalf and W. H. Luckmann (ed.) Insect pest management. New York: John Wiley & Sons.

Vereijken, P. H. 1979. Feeding and multiplication of three cereal aphid species and their effect on yield of winter wheat. Centrum voor Landbouwpublikaties en Landbouwdocumentatie, Wageningen.

Watson, T. F., L. Moore, and G. W. Ware. 1975. Practical pest management. San Francisco: Freeman.

Way, M. J. 1974. Applied ecological research needs in relation to population dynamics and control of insect pests. Pp. 283–97. *In* Proceedings of the FAO conference on ecology in relation to plant pest control. Rome: Food and Agriculture Organization.

———. 1977. Pest and disease status in mixed stands vs. monocultures: The relevance of ecosystem stability. Pp. 127–38. *In* J. M. Cherrett and G. R. Sagar (eds.) Origins of pest, parasite, disease and weed problems. Oxford: Blackwell.

———. 1979. Significance of diversity in agroecosystems. Pp. 9–11. *In* Proceedings of the plenary session, symposium IX, international congress of plant protection. Washington, D.C.

Way, M. J., and G. A. Norton. 1984. Integrated crop protection. Pp. 212–18. *In* L. Hawksworth (ed.) Advancing agricultural production in Africa. Slough, U.K.: Commonwealth Agricultural Bureau.

38. RANGE-CROPPING INTERACTIONS— A DELICATE BALANCE

Gerald F. Gifford, Range, Wildlife, and Forestry, University of Nevada, Reno, Nevada

ABSTRACT

The interaction between rangeland and cropland in arid and semiarid environments is characterized as dynamic, regulated primarily by climatic irregularities, availability of irrigation water, and management in general. Population-induced land-use changes may result in water problems, erosion, and eventual desertification. Weather modification, water harvesting, snow harvesting, grazing management, contour furrows, fire, water spreading, and other techniques are discussed, as well as the various aspects associated with improved water-use efficiency of range and crop plants. The future is viewed in terms of improved education programs on an international level, easing of world economic problems and widespread poverty, and improved understanding within the policy-forming process. Increased awareness through increased research funding is a necessity.

INTRODUCTION

The delicate interaction between cropland and rangeland is indeed dynamic. The very fact that the Water and Water Policy Conference was concerned about that interface is an indicator that perhaps all is not well, that perhaps an international society is willing now to examine long-range implications of managing this important part of our global landscape.

The delicate balance between rangeland and cropland is perhaps most pronounced at the arid and semiarid ends of the climatic spectrum. Most of this chapter concentrates on this end of the scale; hence it is appropriate to characterize the world's arid and semiarid lands. Many examples of past descriptions are available; the following is taken from Box (n.d.):

> Between one-third and one-half of the earth's surface experiences some kind of drought during any given year. The exact amount of the earth considered as arid or semiarid will vary, depending upon the particular scholar's definition of aridity. Meigs (1953), using climatological indices, calculated that approximately one-third of the earth's surface is arid or semiarid. If biological criteria are applied (Perry 1967), then a much greater area of the earth can be considered arid. These lands vary from true desert (McGuinnis et al., 1968) to monsoonal tropics. . . .
>
> The people who occupy arid lands are different from those in the more humid regions of the world. Their environment is harsh, with particular constraints on what can and cannot be done. This leads to the development of a particular kind of individual and of particular kinds of institutions to help him survive. Neither the physical settings, the people, nor the institutions of arid lands are comparable to those of the more humid

areas where the decisions for the management of arid lands are usually made. . . .

> Climatic restrictions in arid regions impose severe biological constraints which directly affect man's economy. Production of vegetation is low and highly variable. Modifications that have developed to allow plants to survive the rigorous climate conditions are usually associated with low production of biomass. Such characteristics as dormancy, curling and dropping of the leaves, etc., may allow plants to withstand the severe conditions of deserts but make plant materials inaccessible as forage for grazing animals. . . .
>
> Arid ecosystems are delicately balanced, and, for the most part, succession is extremely slow. Once an ecosystem has been disturbed or altered it seldom heals itself within the lifetime of a man. Artificial revegetation of damaged ecosystems is also difficult because of the rigorous climatic and biological constraints of the system. . . .
>
> The isolation of people in arid areas tends to make them self-sufficient. They are strongly individualistic and tend to act on their own initiative rather than collectively. The traditional land use over many of the arid areas is nomadic pastoralism. . . . Even in developed countries the most efficient use of arid lands is usually a sophisticated nomadism, relying on motor transport other than driving of livestock. . . .
>
> Social and economic institutions that serve the arid regions of the world are usually weak. The combination of low population and little political organization usually tends to leave the arid regions under-represented in the political process. Therefore, such publicly supported institutions as schools, transportation systems, welfare systems, etc., do not tend to be as strong as they are in the more humid areas.
>
> Financial institutions—banks, lending agencies, credit unions, etc.—are usually not geared to the particular conditions of the arid regions. Long-term credit with payback schedules to fit the feast-and-famine productivity of arid regions usually is not available. Research efforts to obtain data necessary for development of the arid regions are scattered and poorly funded. Not only are the arid regions of the world in poor condition but both the forces of nature and the political and economic structure of the world seem to be operating against them.

WATER PROBLEMS, EROSION, DESERTIFICATION

As alluded to above, climatic variability is often the key in any mix of range and cropping enterprises. Extremes, the floods and droughts, are most impressive. Severity of extreme events is often characterized not by the amount that precipitation (or temperature) was below or above normal but by the impact of the event on crop yields, range forage, water yields, erosion, or animal behavior.

Population pressures or economic trends initiate land-use changes and, depending on scale, may change weather and climate (Chakrauarti, 1984). For example, removal of vegetation may change the albedo and dust loading of the atmosphere. Higher albedos result when vegetation is removed, and, therefore, more solar radiation is reflected and lost to space. Studies by Charney et al. (1975) and Otterman (1974) strongly suggest that lowered soil temperatures owing to increased albedos result in reduced precipitation and eventually drought or desertification.

Desertification is now perceived as an intensifying worldwide threat. More than 20 percent (850 million) of the world's population live in the 35 percent of the earth's land surface that consists of the arid, semiarid, and subhumid zones at risk of desertification. Three-fourths of this area is already at least moderately desertified (United Nations, 1984). Each year 21 million ha of agricultural land deteriorates through desertification to a point at which it is no longer economically productive. The principal cause of desertification is human overexploitation of drylands through overcultivation, overgrazing, poor irrigation practices, and deforestation. When drought strikes the overtaxed livelihood systems, desertification results (United Nations, 1984).

Erosion is a major problem at the rangeland-cropland interface. Soil erosion lowers soil productivity through loss of storage capacity for plant-available water, loss of plant nutrients, degradation of soil structure, and decreased uniformity of soil conditions within a field. The ability of soil to tolerate the impact of erosion is called the soil-loss-tolerance value (T). The relation of T values to actual rates of erosion and soil formation is highly important in establishing what constitutes excessive erosion from the long-term, society point of view. From 1967 to 1975, 24.4 million ha of cropland in the United States were converted to pasture, range, or forest (U.S. Department of Agriculture, 1980). At least some of these changes in land use were caused by accelerated soil erosion which made the land submarginal for intensive cropping in the view of the users. Land eroded so badly that it is not usable as cropland is also usually poor pasture, range, or forest land (Council for Agricultural Science and Technology, 1982). On the other hand, 16.4 million ha of rangeland was plowed and converted to cropland during the past five years (Halmans, 1985). The general lack of world interest in long-term stability and productivity of arid and semiarid lands as related to both wind and water erosion is appalling. Using the United States as an example, we are surrounded by intelligent but often unseeing individuals whose philosophy of an unlimited ability to produce ignores the relations between people and environmental balance. Improper land use results in gross alterations in the water cycle, with increased surface runoff, resulting in less soil water for forage or crops, less groundwater recharge, and accelerated erosion. A recent news article cites the Ethiopian example as follows:

> Ethiopia in the year 1900 was 40 percent forest. It is 4 percent forest today. It has had a steady decline in agricultural production since 1967—it has declined 1 percent a year.
>
> Three things contributed to all this. Africa had the fastest population growth of any continent in history. It has the fastest

soil erosion. And it had near national neglect of agriculture by the governments.

More seriously, there is not anything in sight in agriculture or family planning to arrest these trends.

WEATHER MODIFICATION—PRECIPITATION ENHANCEMENT AT THE RANGELAND-CROPLAND INTERFACE

Neyman (1977) reviewed the historical background of weather-modification technology. He commented:

> As indicated at the outset, the reliability of the emerging cloud seeding technology is a very controversial matter. . . . On the one hand, there are those who argue that techniques of modifying weather have been demonstrated successfully for so many years that the time has now come for a major push into the application stage. On the other hand, significantly altering certain important meteorological parameters (such as precipitation) has not been scientifically determined, and intensive well-designed experimentation is still very much needed to evaluate properly the potential usefulness of modification technology.

Neyman (1977) indicated that cloud seeding does affect precipitation and that it does so over areas far in excess of the intended targets, occasionally up to hundreds of kilometers. Effects may be either large increases or large decreases in precipitation. The several hypothetical mechanisms advanced to explain and predict these effects vary in their empirical support and persuasiveness.

With scientific and technological advancement, increased public acceptance, and a diminishing number of alternatives for new water supplies, there is an expanding demand to develop the full potential from weather modification. The increasing acceptability of this technology can be partly attributed to the water users and particularly utility companies in the western United States. They have pioneered support for weather modification by the long-term use of winter orographic cloud seeding to increase inflow to reservoirs. The fact that rational business people are willing to continue annual expenditures over many years has convinced some of the public that the programs are continued because an acceptable return is obtained from the investment. An important related fact is the apparent lack of undesirable environmental effects attributable to the long-term program.

Foehner (1977) cited the following conclusion, which appeared in the working document of the Western U.S. Water Plan entitled *Augmentation Potential through Weather Modification* in February, 1975. It is still appropriate:

> The advantages of using weather modification as a means of water supply augmentation are: (1) a source of high-quality water that does not deplete water supplies in other areas, (2) no known major ecological disadvantages, (3) increased water at high elevations permitting maximum hydropower generation, and (4) water supply enhancement at a relatively low initial investment and low annual operating cost. Taking into consideration availability, quantity, quality, and cost of the augmentation alternatives, weather modification is recommended as a promising source of new water supply.

The 10 to 15 percent potential increase (Foehner, 1977; Sherretz et al., 1983) in annual runoff from cloud seeding may not be overly promising on a global scale unless water can be transported to or stored on or near otherwise rain-fed arid and semiarid landscapes. Otherwise, the only benefit may be increased recharge to regional or localized water tables, while detrimental impacts may include increased surface erosion.

SURFACE RUNOFF MODIFICATIONS— ENHANCING SCARCE WATER SUPPLIES

Water Harvesting

Water harvesting (the process of collecting natural precipitation from prepared watersheds for beneficial use) can be a source of off-site water for a variety of purposes in arid and semiarid regions when common sources, such as streams, springs, or wells, fail (Cooley et al., 1975). Often the necessary water can be obtained without large expenditures of energy.

Water-harvesting methods are site-specific, requiring knowledge about the soil (especially characteristics of water holding, runoff, and erodability); the topography (slope and direction of natural runoff); the precipitation characteristics (amount, reliability, etc.); and the climate (wind, sunlight, temperature, etc.). Because of intermittent rainfall, storage must be an integral part of any rainwater-harvesting system. In some instances water may actually be "stored" in a suitable soil profile.

Water-harvesting techniques include land alterations, chemical and physical soil treatments, and soil covers. Land alterations may include digging ditches or constructing rock walls along hillside contours, clearing rocks and vegetation, or compacting the soil surface. Existing natural or man-made catchments like large rock outcrops, highways, airports, and parking lots can also be utilized (Burdass, 1975). Chemical and physical soil treatments and soil covers include sodium salts, silicons, latexes, fuel oils, asphalt wax, plastic films covered with gravel, rubber sheeting, corrugated sheet metal, and concrete. Water collected from the catchment is generally stored in excavated pits or ponds, bags, or tanks.

Use of water harvesting at the rangeland-cropland interface is not without limitations. Since water harvesting depends on natural rainfall, it is no more reliable than the weather. Without adequate storage facilities the system will fail in drought years. In locations with an average annual rainfall of less than 50 to 80 cm, water harvesting will probably never be economically feasible.

Poorly designed and managed water-harvesting systems can cause soil erosion, soil instability, and local flooding. All catchments require a certain amount of maintenance to keep them performing properly.

A water-harvesting system must withstand weathering and some foot traffic. Some may require fences. Contamination of the water must be constantly considered. Discolored or contaminated water will require treatment before it can be used for human consumption.

Snow Harvesting

In some situations the opportunity exists for harvesting snow. In snow country, when cold winter winds sweep open country, a third or more of the blowing snow is subject to evaporation by sublimation at subfreezing temperatures (Schmidt, 1972; Tabler, 1973). As an example of the existing potential, Hibbert (1979) indicated some assumptions that are necessary to illustrate the potential for snow management on sagebrush lands: (1) average winter precipitation is 20 cm or more in the form of snow, (2) roughly one-third of the snow evaporates under normal conditions, and (3) about one-half of the snow subject to evaporation can be trapped by snow fences. If these conditions prevail, about 3.3 cm more water would be present in the form of large drifts scattered over the landscape. Some of this water is subject to evaporation before it melts, leaving perhaps 2.5 cm in water to enter the soil or runoff. Rauzi (1968) and Reis and Power (1981) reported that grass stubble in Wyoming and North Dakota effectively holds snow on rangeland. Rauzi also noted that heavily grazed native rangelands were often almost devoid of snow cover during the winter, whereas moderately and lightly grazed rangelands had several inches of snow.

Better utilization of available water is extremely important at the interface of cropland and rangeland management, and snow harvesting may offer new opportunities.

Grazing Management

There exists today a relatively extensive literature on grazing impacts within specific plant communities. Though many knowledge gaps persist, it is readily apparent that grazing may influence community succession. A major conclusion from the review monograph by Ellison (1960) is that successional trends in plant communities are roughly proportional to grazing intensity: they are pronounced under severe grazing and in some instances difficult to distinguish at light or moderate levels. This conclusion is still valid.

Changes in plant composition are not nearly as important as changes in watershed protective cover and trampling disturbance. Review papers (Gifford, 1980; Meeuwig and Packer, 1976; Blackburn et al., 1982) indicate that overgrazing for extended periods may result in vegetation and soil changes that will lead to (1) reduced protective cover and thus increased raindrop impact; (2) lowering of soil organic matter, below ground biomass, and soil aggregates; (3) a possible increase in surface vesicular crusts; (4) decrease in infiltration rates with resultant increased runoff; and (5) possible increased erosion. It is well documented that grazing reduces standing crop (and therefore cover) (Lodge, 1954, and others). Grazing pressure also has an impact on mulch or litter cover, the greatest impact once again occurring under heavy grazing (Johnston, 1962, and others).

It is readily apparent that grazing within the rangeland-cropland interface may have a marked impact on the environment. This impact is most pronounced under heavy stocking rates or in conjunction with desertification processes.

Contour Furrows

Contour furrows in the United States are generally constructed 150 cm apart, 20 to 30 cm deep, and 50 to 76 cm wide and are dammed at intervals of 1.2 to 6.2 m. When furrows are newly constructed, their capacity exceeds 5 cm of precipitation. Because of the storage capacity of the furrows, little runoff or sediment would be expected to leave a treated site.

Several mechanical treatments were studied in the western United States, and Branson et al. (1966) found that contour furrowing was very effective in increasing yields of perennial grasses. They also found that storage capacity of furrows decreased rapidly during the first five years to less than 2.5 cm of precipitation and thereafter tended to stabilize at about 1.2 cm after nine or more years. Findings are similar elsewhere.

In short, contour furrows can have a marked impact on water relations on semiarid landscapes. Depending on the situation, contour furrows can be utilized on either rangeland or cropland.

Fire

Incorrect use of fire exerts pronounced effects on basic hydrologic processes, leading to increased sensitivity of the landscape to eroding forces and to reduced land stability (Rowe et al., 1954; Wright et al., 1976). This is manifested primarily as increased overland flow and greater peak and total discharge. These provide the transport force for sediment removal from the landscape.

Erosion responses to burning are a function of degree of elimination of protective cover, steepness of slopes, degree of soil nonwettability, climatic characteristics, and rapidity of vegetation recovery (Roundy et al., 1978, and others).

Sedimentation and mass erosion appear to be the most serious threats to land deterioration and water resources following fire (especially wildfire). Fire causes rapid mineralization and mobilization of nutrient elements that are manifested in increased levels of nutrients in overland flow and in soil solution. These nutrient relations are most important where rainfall accommodates greater quantities of vegetation than that commonly found on arid and semiarid landscapes.

Water Spreading

Water spreading involves diversion of water from arroyos or gullies onto the surrounding landscape through use of a system of dikes. The wet floodplains or valley floors can be used to grow crops or forage. Design criteria for water-spreading practices (Monson and Quesenberry, 1940, and others) indicate that spreading areas should be of such size that most sediment will settle in the upper 20 percent and that they must be large enough to accommodate exceptionally large flows. Slope of the spreading area should not exceed 2 to 5 percent. Floodwater spreader construction should be restricted to sites whose soils are deep enough to store at least 20 cm of water, and, to ensure forage increases, sites should receive at least one flooding a year.

Other Techniques

The rangeland-cropland interface breeds innovation in utilization of water. Other techniques not mentioned above include microcatchment farming (Shanan et al., 1970), where plant survival is enhanced if a rainwater-catchment basin is built around the planting. Conveyance losses are minimized with microcatchments; they provide runoff water from light storms when others will not, they are relatively cheap, and they can be used on almost any slope.

Another technique is desert-strip (or contour-catchment) farming. This technique employs a series of terraces that shed water onto a neighboring strip of productive soil.

These techniques are important, since runoff used to grow forage can relieve grazing pressures on nearby rangelands, extend the grazing season, and provide erosion control. Rainfall must generally exceed 80 mm per year, and soils must be at least 1.5 to 2 m deep to store the water.

IMPROVED WATER-USE EFFICIENCY

Breeding for drought tolerance will become increasingly important at the range-cropping interface in future years. To date breeding research has been directed primarily toward finding a better-adapted, more productive, or more palatable species, but it has not adequately addressed water-use efficiencies. The potentials of genetic engineering seem to open the door for development of more productive, water-use-efficient, and palatable species for use in both arid and semiarid range and cropland settings. Continued emphasis is needed in terms of enhancing photosynthetic efficiency (Cramer, 1983), nitrogen fixation potential (Burgess, 1983), plant-regulator use (Stutte, 1983), and pest-control strategies (Battenfield and Haynes, 1983), all of which interact with plant-water efficiencies. And certainly improved water management in general will help. Where applicable, conservation of moisture through improved irrigation systems, development of low-water-use and salt-tolerant plants, reduction of energy requirements for water transfer, control of vegetation in semiarid regions, improvement in the quality or reuse of wastewater, proper timing of fertilizer and pesticide applications, and protection of groundwater and surface-water supplies from mining and contamination all offer opportunities for progress (Schwab, 1983).

THE FUTURE

Education

Any solution to a better understanding of the range-cropping interface must involve education. As mentioned earlier, urban dwellers in more favorable environments often determine policy for arid and semiarid environments. The link between the land and food and an approved standard of living is often missing.

We must be actively involved in teaching modern but appropriate agriculture throughout the world. For the developing world education is the single most important assistance that we can provide. A high priority must be given to the development of suitable academic programs within the countries themselves. Qualified teachers must be recruited and field facilities developed to supplement the classroom. Extension programs, formal education, and research efforts should be developed together so that they support one another. Where training of foreign nationals is provided through a university in the United States, it is important that the university have a program appropriate for the candidate. Advanced-degree research should be accomplished in a student's home country if at all possible. Educational efforts must be directed at herders, farmers, administrators, and technicians alike, and high attrition rates must be anticipated.

In the United States the pervasive apathy about the range-cropping interface, especially in semiarid environments, must change. Many of our national agricultural policies reflect ignorance of the purest form. Increased research support is desperately needed to resolve management dilemmas that result from an eastern or urban perspective.

Other Aspects

As noted by the United Nations (1984), world economic problems and widespread poverty are continuing to force people into misuse of their natural resources. Resulting deterioration makes economic and structural reforms more difficult to achieve. Important long-term issues, such as climatic changes, soil degradation, and desertification, which have profound economic implications, are often impossible to deal with, given the existing structure of international economic negotiation. Such long-term issues are often inconspicuous, are not felt immediately, are difficult to quantify, and are not reducible to the standard cost-benefit equations, methods, and objectives that guide countries, negotiators, and decision makers in how they think and what they do.

At the rangeland-cropland interface the focus must be the maintenance of sustainable production. Mismanagement can only result in decreased yields and fertility levels, salinization, erosion, and desertification. The cost of mismanagement is not carried by the exploiting enterprise and its immediate region alone, but is, unfortunately, spread widely and over several generations. Side effects include deterioration of income, national wealth, or conditions of life.

In summary, despite world population problems, the world as a whole is producing enough food to sustain the present level of population. The immediate problem is one of inequality in food distribution, which leaves millions undernourished. Ramifications of this have been alluded to on a world scale, and the future of continued high production in developed countries (our crutch) is questioned by many. Certainly the rangeland-cropland interface is a dynamic zone, regulated primarily by climatic irregularities, availability of irrigation water, and management in general. Understanding at the policy level is often minimal, leaving a huge gap between what should be happening and what actually happens. It is imperative to keep working on causes of the many problems rather than simply treating the symptoms.

REFERENCES

Battenfield, S. L., and D. L. Haynes. 1983. Plant pest control strategies. Pp. 57–70. *In* Yao-chi Lu (ed.) Emerging technologies in agricultural production. USDA, Cooperating States Research Service, unnumbered publication.

Blackbum, W. H., et al. 1982. Impacts of grazing on watersheds. Texas Agricultural Experiment Station Publication MP 1496.

Box, T. W. N.d. The arid lands revisited 100 years after John Wesley Powell. 57th annual faculty honor lecture, Utah State University, Logan.

Branson, F. A., et al. 1962. Effects of contour furrowing, grazing intensities, and soils on infiltration rates, soil moisture, and vegetation near Fort Peck, Montana, *Journal of Range Management* 15:151–58.

Burdass, W. J. 1975. Water harvesting for livestock in western Australia. Pp. 8–26. *In* Proceedings of water harvesting symposium, USDA, Agricultural Research Service, W-22.

Burgess, B. K. 1983. Nitrogen fixation: research imperatives. Pp. 27–42. *In* Yao-chi Lu (ed.) Emerging technologies in agricultural production. USDA Cooperating States Research Service, unnumbered publication.

Chakravarti, A. K. 1984. Weather, climate, and the land. *Journal of Soil and Water Conservation* 39:350–53.

Charncy, J., et al. 1975. Drought In the Sahara: a biogeophysical feedback mechanism. *Science* 187:430–35.

Cooley, K. R., A. R. Dedrick, and G. W. Frasier. 1975. Water harvesting: state of the art. Pp. 1–20. *In* Proceedings of the symposium on watershed management, American Society of Civil Engineers, August 11–13, Logan, Utah.

Council for Agricultural Science and Technology. 1982. Soil erosion: its agricultural, environmental, and socioeconomic implications. Report 92.

Cramer, W. A. 1983. Enhancement of photosynthetic efficiency. Pp. 13–25. *In* Yao-chi Lu (ed.) Emerging technologies in agricultural production. U.S. Department of Agriculture, Cooperating States Research Service, unnumbered publication.

Ellison, L. 1960. Influence of grazing on plant succession on rangelands. *Botanical Review* 26:1–78.

Foehner, U. H. 1977. Weather modification—a major resource tool. 45:1–17. *In* Proceedings of the western snow conference.

Gifford, G. F. 1980. Watershed responses to grazing management. Pp. 147–59. *In* Proceedings of the interior West watershed management symposium April 8–10, Spokane, Wash.

Hibbert A. R. 1979. Vegetation management for water yield improvement in the Colorado River basin. National Technical Information Service, U.S. Department of Commerce, Report PB 300379/AS.

Johnson, A. 1962. Effects of grazing intensity and cover on the water-intake rate of fescue grassland. *Journal of Range Management* 15:79–82.

Lodge, R. W. 1954. Effects of grazing on the soils and forage of mixed prairie in southwestern Saskatchewan. *Journal of Range Management* 7:166–70.

McGinnis, W. G., G. J. Goldman, and P. Paylore. 1968. Deserts of the world. Tucson: University of Arizona Press.

Meeuwig, R. O., and P. E. Packer. 1976. Erosion and runoff on forest and rangelands. 105(1): 6. *In* Proceedings of the fifth workshop of the US-Australia Rangelands Panel.

Meigs, P. 1953. World distribution of arid and semi-arid homoclimates. 1:203–10. *In* Review of Research on Arid Zone Hydrology. Paris: UNESCO, Arid Zone Programme.

Monson, D. W., and J. R. Quesenberry. 1940. Range improvement through conservation of floodwaters. Montana Agricultural Experiment Station Bulletin 38.

Neyman, J. 1977. A statistician's view of weather modification technology (a review). 74:471C–472. *In* Proceedings of the National Academy of Science.

Otterman, J. 1974. Baring high-albedo soils by overgrazing: a hypothesized desertification mechanism. *Science* 186:531–33.

Perry, R. A. 1967. The need for rangelands research in Australia. 2:1–14. *In* Proceedings of the Ecological Society of Australia.

Rauzi, F. 1968. Pitting and interseeding shortgrass rangeland. *Wyoming Agricultural Experiment Station Research Journal* 17.

Ries, R. E., and J. F. Power. 1981. Increased soil water storage and herbage production from snow catch in North Dakota. *Journal of Range Management* 34:485–88.

Roundy, B. A., et al. 1978. Influence of prescribed burning on infiltration and sediment production in the piñon-juniper woodland, Nevada. *Journal of Range Management* 31:250–53.

Rowe, P. R., C. M. Countryman, and H. C. Storey. 1954. Hydrologic analysis used to determine effects of fire on peak discharge and erosion rates in southern California watersheds. California Forest and Range Experiment Stations, U.S. Forest Service, unnumbered publication.

Schmidt, R. A., Jr. 1972. Sublimation of wind-transported snow— a model. U.S. Forest Service Research paper RM-90.

Schwab, G. L. 1983. Water management. Pp. 123–36. *In* Yao-chi Lu (ed.) Emerging technologies in agricultural production. U.S. Department of Agriculture, Cooperating States Research Services unnumbered publication.

Shanan, L., et al. 1970. Runoff farming in the desert. 3. Microcatchments for improvement of desert range. *Agronomy Journal* 62:445–49.

Sherretz, L. A., et al. 1983. A comparison of the potential of cloud seeding to enhance mountain snowpack in Colorado during dry, normal and wet winters. Denver: Colorado Department of Natural Resources, Weather Modification Program.

Stutte, C. A. 1983. Plant regulators in agricultural production. Pp. 4A–55. *In* Yao-chi Lu (ed.) Emerging technologies in agricultural production. U.S. Department of Agriculture, Cooperating States Research Service, unnumbered publication.

Tabler, R. D. 1973. Evaporation losses of windblown snow, and the potential for recovery. 41:75–79. *In* Proceedings of the western snow conference.

United Nations. 1984. The State of the environment. Nairobi, Kenya: United Nations Environment Programme.

U.S. Department of Agriculture. 1980. Soil and water resources conservation act appraisal. Review draft, pts. 1–3.

Wright, H. A., et al. 1976. Effect of prescribed burning on sediment, water yield, and water quality from dozed juniper lands in central Texas. *Journal of Range Management* 29:294–98.

PART VII. ENERGY AND WATER INTERRELATIONSHIPS

39. GLOBAL ENERGY PERSPECTIVES, 1985

F. S. Patton, Martin Marietta Energy Systems, Inc., Oak Ridge, Tennessee

ABSTRACT

An ascendant and growing international trade characterized by the laissez-faire economic practices advocated by Adam Smith has greatly increased the availability of all forms of energy, forestalling, or at least delaying, the globally disruptive consequences of a crisis in energy supply. The capitalist industrial democracies, which constitute about 16 percent of the global population, consume about half of the global energy demand and earn nearly two-thirds of global income, have achieved important progress in energy conservation over the past decade. Further, their populations, except for migration from the less developed nations of the Third World, appear to be stabilizing. However, the Third World nations which have traditionally exported raw materials and energy supplies to the capitalist countries—and with which there is massive economic interdependence—continue to experience large increases in population growth with concurrent increasing energy requirements. Also, a trend toward transference of labor-intensive manufacturing to Third World countries adds to their energy demands.

At present, production capability for oil, natural gas, and coal is significantly in excess of overall global demand. It currently appears that the period of respite, before growing energy needs of Third World countries and communist nations overtake capabilities, will last at least through the 1980s.

THE GLOBAL ECONOMY

In 1969, U Thant, the Secretary-General of the United Nations, stated that "the members of the United Nations had 'perhaps' ten years left in which to subordinate their ancient quarrels and launch a global partnership to curb the arms race, to improve the human environment, to defuse the population explosion, and to supply the required momentum to development efforts." He added, "If such a global partnership is not forged within the next decade, then I very much fear that the problems I have mentioned will have reached such staggering proportions that they will be beyond our capacity to control" (Club of Rome, 1977). Subsequently a view emerged of an austere global future in which an increasing imbalance between growing energy demands and the needs of an expanding global population could lead to disaster (Club of Rome, 1977; Workshop on Alternative Energy Strategies, 1977; Council on Environmental Quality and the U.S. Department of State, 1980; International Institute for Applied Systems Analysis, 1981; World Energy Conference, 1978; Ehrlich et al., 1977; Brandt, 1980). The growing disparities between rich and poor countries and the increasing visibility of the negative consequences of pollutants and environmental damage gave additional weight to these pessimistic perceptions.

By 1985 no large-scale benevolent global partnership as called for by U Thant and others had come to pass. Instead,

a far different mechanism—an ascendant and growing international trade increasingly characterized by the laissez-faire economic practices advocated by Adam Smith—has greatly increased the availability of all forms of energy—at least for those having the financial resources to afford them. This global economy, which encompasses traffic in every conceivable item of commerce, including the manufacture in many different countries of the component parts of a final product, now overshadows the economies of individual nation-states to such an extent that their domestic markets and manufactures are not viable as self-contained arenas. In this dominant international economy, political, social, economic, and energy concerns are interrelated. Authorities charged with decision making—even on a parochial basis—cannot prudently plan without maintaining a conversancy with these sectors on a global scale.

The progressive lowering of trade barriers starting with the Kennedy round of talks in the 1960s, together with continuing advances in telecommunications, computers, and transportation, which greatly facilitate business—allowing hundreds of millions of dollars in transactions to occur between distant countries in the course of a day—are contributing heavily to growth. The United States, the world's wealthiest major nation, with only 5 percent of the global population but having about one-fourth of gross world product and consuming about one-fourth of the global supply of raw materials and energy (U.S. Department of Commerce, 1985; Sivard, 1983) has a leading role in this new era.

THE THREE WORLDS

Today there are more than 155 countries in the world. It has become common to group these countries along the lines of similarity in political and economic characteristics into three "worlds," as follows:

1. The First World: the capitalist-industrial democracies—the United States, Canada, Australia, the countries of Western Europe, and Japan. They import much of their raw materials and energy from the large group of countries making up the Third World. The First World at present has about 16 percent of the earth's people but consumes about half the global energy demand and has almost two-thirds of the global income (OPEC, 1981, 1984; Population Reference Bureau, 1983).

2. The Second World: the socialist-communist countries—the USSR, the Eastern European bloc, and the People's Republic of China and its allies. Within their own political and economic spheres these groups of countries are largely self-sufficient in raw materials and energy. These countries have centrally planned economies. In aggregate they have about one-third of the global population, consume

about one-third of the global energy demand, and have about 20 percent of global income.

3. The Third World: The more than 100 largely non-industrialized countries that have traditionally produced raw materials and energy, most of which has been sold to the First World. About 5 to 10 percent of their trade is with the communist-socialist Second World, and about two-thirds is with the capitalist-industrial democracies of the First World. Most of the Third World is poor and has been experiencing large population increases. The Third World currently has about half the global population, consumes slightly more than 15 percent of global energy demand, and has about 15 percent of global income.

Geographical and Resource Circumstances

Fig. 1 is a map of the globe in which liberties have been taken with the longitudinal positions of countries while their latitudes have been held true. The purpose of this arrangement is to bring into focus certain geographical features. It can be observed that the land masses of the First World, the Second World, and the Third World are roughly equivalent. Much of the land of the First World—including nearly the whole of the United States—is in the central sector of the North Temperate Zone. Most of the People's Republic of China also lies in the North Temperate Zone, while the mass of the Soviet Union is considerably farther north. The Third World is centered around the equator with relatively little land in the temperate zones. Most of the earth's temperate zone land mass is in the Northern Hemisphere; little lies in the Southern Hemisphere.

The importance of these geographic circumstances is that the First World countries and China have the advantage of a healthy and invigorating climate as well as a food advantage. About two-thirds of the caloric value of the foods consumed by the people of the world are derived from cereal grains. Most of the world's cereal grain is produced in the temperate zones. An abundance of these grains also stimulates the production of meat animals. A disadvantage of the Third World tropical areas is that food spoils quickly and food-destroying insects and rodents proliferate.

The population of the Soviet Union is only about 15 percent greater than that of the United States, but its land mass

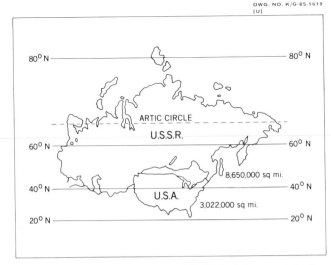

Fig. 2. Geographical comparison of the United States and the Soviet Union.

is about 2.5 times larger. It is not surprising, therefore, that the energy and raw-material resources of the Soviet Union are greater than those of the United States (Fig. 2). The People's Republic of China is almost exactly the same size as the United States and has a similar climate. However, the energy and mineral resources of both the Soviet Union and China have been exploited to a far lesser extent than have those of the capitalist democracies. With regard to oil and gas, probably less than 20 percent of Soviet reserves have been expended. There is uncertainty regarding China, but by Chinese account little of their oil and gas reserves has been extracted. In the United States, in contrast, over half of the oil and gas resources that constituted the original national endowment—and that have foreseeable prospects of economic recovery—has been extracted and consumed. More than 80 percent of known global coal resources are in three countries: the United States, the Soviet Union, and the People's Republic of China.

A most important element of international trade which has grown steadily since World War II has been the shipment of oil and raw materials northward from the developing tropical and semitropical nations of the Third World to temperate-zone countries, including Japan, the United States, and Western Europe. As payment quality manufactured goods and cereal grains have been shipped south.

The Soviet Union and the People's Republic of China have had only small roles in this international trade. These centrally planned economies, situated on large land masses, are essentially self-sufficient in energy supplies and raw materials. Indeed, on a small scale they are in competition with the Third World in the sale of oil and minerals to the capitalist-industrial democracies. Further, they too must import cereal grains from the capitalist democracies. Their principal manufactured exports have been armaments. Thus the only substantial export market the Third World has had for its oil and raw materials has been the capitalist democ-

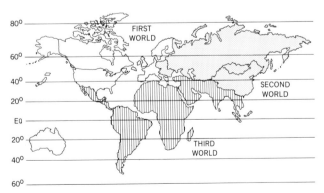

Fig. 1. The three worlds.

racies. This economic dependency on the capitalist bloc is a significant contributor to the limitation of communist influence in the Third World.

This north-south trade is now undergoing a partial structural alteration. To make any manufactured product, energy, raw materials, and labor are required. A decade ago, when energy was cheap, the higher cost of labor in the northern industrial democracies—associated with a high living standard—was offset by technology and liberal use of cheap energy. But energy has now increased substantially in price, while a large population increase in the Third World has produced an increasing pool of inexpensive labor. Thus in a free-trading global economy it is advantageous to shift labor-intensive manufacturing to Third World areas, in effect substituting inexpensive labor for expensive labor and expensive energy. This trend contributes to the already rapid urban growth occurring in the Third World. It is projected that by the year 2000, for example, Mexico City may have 30 million inhabitants, and Seoul, Korea, may have 15 million. Also, the People's Republic of China may have fifty cities each with a population of over one million.

POPULATION

Fig. 3 indicates the world population growth. In 1950 the population of the earth was approximately 2.5 billion. It is noteworthy that at the time the world was expected to reach a population of 4 billion by the year 2000. The 4 billion mark was actually achieved in 1975. The current projection for the earth's population is more than 6 billion by the year 2000 and approaching 8 billion by 2020. The earth's consumption of energy over the 1950–75 span was correspondingly underestimated, global consumption tripling in this period. This population increase is largely taking place in the Third World regions of Africa, Asia, and Latin America, which have an overall population rate increase about five times that of the aggregate of the First World regions of the United States, Western Europe, and Japan.

These population forecasts and figures (Population Reference Bureau, 1983) indicate that the earth's present 750 million capitalists will have increased to only about 825 million by the year 2020 while the inhabitants of the Third World nations will have approximately doubled from today's 2.5 billion to near 5 billion. At that time—under these demographic calculations—the First World would no longer comprise 16 percent of the earth's inhabitants—consuming half the global energy demand and earning two-thirds of the global income—but would be decreasing by 10 percent. The Third World nations would no longer have half the earth's inhabitants—consuming 15 to 20 percent of global energy demand and existing on about 15 pecent of global income—but would hold an expanding two-thirds of the total global population.

ENERGY ASSESSMENT

In 1983 total global production of commercial energy was between 270 and 280 quads (OPEC, 1984)—far below the projections made a decade earlier. These reduced requirements were most significantly due to energy-conservation

DWG. NO. K/G-85-1620 (U)

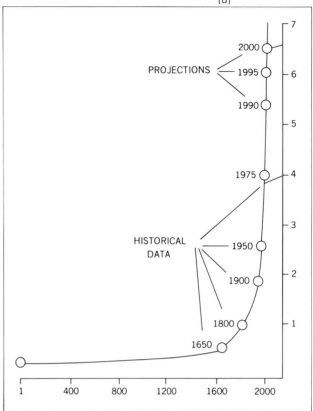

Fig. 3. World population growth.

measures adopted in the capitalist democracies. First World energy consumption in the period 1973–83 declined by about 5 percent, while overall energy consumption in both the Second World and the Third World increased by 40 to 50 percent. During this period oil consumption in the First World dropped by more than 15 percent. Global oil production is now 54 million barrels per day as compared with more than 55 million barrels per day in 1973, and much below the peak of approximately 63 million barrels per day in 1979 (API, 1984). During this same period oil consumption increased about one-third in both the communist and the Third World countries, but their consumption is still well under that of the capitalist bloc.

In the United States energy conservation has exceeded all expectations. In the decade 1973–83 oil consumption dropped from 16.5 million barrels per day to 14.5 million barrels per day, and natural-gas consumption declined from 22.5 trillion cubic feet (630 billion m³) per year to 17 trillion cubic feet (476 billion m³) per year. Coal consumption has remained nearly constant over the last five years. During this same period the average efficiency of automobiles in the United States increased by one-fourth. The potential of many conservation efforts under way is not yet fully realized.

Currently the world's commercial energy budget may be approximated as follows: oil, 42 percent; coal, 29 percent;

natural gas, 20 percent; hydropower, 6 percent; nuclear power, less than 3 percent. More than one-fourth of this energy is converted to electricity to produce in excess of 8,000 billion kWh per year. Nearly 10 percent of this electrical output is nuclear, generated by about 300 commercial reactors. The number of reactors in operation will probably be in excess of 500 before the end of the century. Almost one-fourth of global electrical production is from hydropower. Hydropower has significant promise, for only one-fifth of the global potential has been exploited (Deudney, 1981). Large-scale hydropower projects are under construction in South America and are planned in the People's Republic of China.

Oil—and the price of oil—holds a key position in the global economy. While today oil provides 42 percent of global energy, it can be argued that a far larger fraction of everything vital to mankind depends on this oil and on natural gas—transportation, synthetic fibers, synthetic rubber, plastics, medicines, pesticides, and food production.

The Organization of Petroleum Exporting Countries (OPEC) has the capability to produce about 33 million barrels of oil per day with little or no capital investment. Currently (1985) OPEC production is about 17 million barrels per day. United States production is approximately 10 million barrels per day of crude and natural-gas liquids. Thus OPEC has idle about 1 1/2 times the capability of the United States to produce. With this tremendous OPEC production capability "overhang" in a free-trading international economy, the difference associated with capital-investment needs is conclusive in competitiveness. Alternative energy technologies requiring large capital investment, such as production of synthetic gasoline from coal, have no chance for widespread application under these conditions.

Today the United States has nearly 600,000 oil wells and about 200,000 gas wells producing 8.5 million barrels of crude oil per day, 1.5 million barrels of natural-gas liquids, and 17 trillion cubic feet (476 billion m^3) of natural gas. About 70,000 new wells must be drilled each year to sustain this level of production. In contrast, Saudi Arabia has the potential to produce about 12 million barrels of crude per day from only 750 wells. Currently Saudi Arabia is producing only 5 million barrels per day to sustain price levels.

A consensus order-of-magnitude approximation of the original total global endowment of conventional oil that could be recovered by reasonable means is 2,000 billion barrels. About 1,200 billion barrels have been found, and about 800 to 1,000 billion barrels are thought to remain which have not yet been found. Of the 1,200 billion barrels that have been found, nearly 500 billion barrels have been extracted and consumed. In general, the most accessible oil deposits were located and exploited first.

PROSPECTUS

The capitalist-industrial democracies have been granted a respite from energy-supply concerns that should continue through the 1980s and possibly to the end of the century as a result of the effectiveness of cost-driven energy-conservation measures, the trend toward transference of labor-intensive manufacturing to Third World locations, and the stabilization of population. A principal cause for the slight increases in population in the First World is migration from the Third World. The energy demands of the Third World nations, while currently small in comparison with those of the First World, will continue to increase. The needs of expanding populations with desires for better living conditions and manufacturing growth argue for such a future. At some point these energy needs, coupled with the increasing energy demands of the Second World will have depleted the excesses of production capability beyond market demands that now exist for oil, gas, and coal. At that time will Adam Smith's "unseen hand" which guides the international economy be able, through advanced energy technologies, to supply the needs of the earth's teeming billions?

REFERENCES

API [American Petroleum Institute]. 1984. Basic petroleum data book. 4:2.

Brandt, Willy. 1980. North-south: a program for survival. Cambridge, Mass.: MIT Press.

Club of Rome. 1977. Summaries of four major reports to the Club of Rome: limits to growth; mankind at the turning point; reshaping the international order; goals for mankind. Paris.

Council on Environmental Quality and U.S. Department of State. 1980. The global 2000 report to the president of the U.S. entering the 21 century. New York: Pergamon Press.

Deudney, D. 1981. Rivers of energy: the hydropower potential. Washington, D.C.: World Watch Institute.

Ehrlich, P. H., A. H. Ehrlich, and J. P. Holdren. 1977. Rich nations, poor nations, and international conflict. Pp. 885–945. In Ecoscience. San Francisco: Freeman.

International Institute for Applied Systems Analysis. 1981. Energy in a finite world—A global systems analysis. Cambridge, Mass.: Ballinger.

OPEC [Organization of the Petroleum Exporting Countries]. 1981. Facts and figures: a comparative statistical analysis. Vienna, Austria.

———. 1984. OPEC Review 8(4): 381–91.

Population Reference Bureau. 1983. World population data sheet. Washington, D.C.

Sivard, R. L. 1983. World military and social expenditures. Leesburg, Va.: World Priorities.

U.S. Department of Commerce. 1985. Business conditions digest. Washington, D.C.

Workshop on alternative energy strategies. 1977. Energy supply to the year 2000. Global and National Studies. Cambridge, Mass.: MIT Press.

World Energy Conference. 1978. World energy resources 1985–2000. New York: IPC Science and Technology Press.

40. ENERGY FOR WORLD AGRICULTURE: WATER IMPLICATIONS

LeVern W. Faidley, Research and Technology Development Division, Food and Agriculture Organization of the United Nations, Rome, Italy

ABSTRACT

Agricultural production consumes only a small part of the world's total commercial energy—about 5 percent in 1982. However, this energy, which is used for the production and application of agricultural inputs, such as farm machinery, mineral fertilizers, chemical pesticides, and pump irrigation, is vital to provide the growing population with food, feed, and fiber. In 1982 in the developing countries mineral fertilizers accounted for more than 68.2 percent of the commercial energy used for agricultural production. They were followed by farm machinery, accounting for 25.5 percent; pump irrigation, 4.1 percent; and chemical pesticides, 2.2 percent.

Between 1972 and 1982 the use of commercial energy for agricultural production increased at an annual rate of 8.6 percent in developing countries, while the growth rate in the developed countries was 2.2 percent. As a result the developing countries' share of commercial energy used in agricultural production increased from 16.6 percent in 1972 to 26.7 percent in 1982, while their share of total commercial energy increased from 14.2 to 20.4 percent.

In 1982 pump irrigation consumed 5.1 million tons of oil-equivalent, developing countries accounting for 62 percent. Between 1972 and 1982 the growth rate for irrigation energy in the developing countries was 3.6 percent. This rate was lower than those for most other inputs, and the share of irrigation in agricultural commercial energy decreased from 6.6 percent in 1972 to 4.1 percent in 1982. While pump irrigation is heavily dependent on commercial energy, foreign-exchange problems, and high petroleum prices in relation to the value of developing countries' exports, have focused attention on the need to utilize, where appropriate, alternative sources of energy.

INTRODUCTION

Agriculture has the vital task of providing the growing world population with food, feed, and fiber. In addition, some of its products and many of its residues provide fuel for cooking and other uses, particularly in the less developed countries. Rapid increases in agricultural production, particularly in developing countries, are therefore required, if the demand for food and other agricultural products is to be met.

Although many developing countries still have some reserves of potentially productive land, most of them will be able to meet the food demands of their growing populations only by raising yields on both existing and new land. It has been estimated in the 1981 Food and Agriculture Organization study *Agriculture: Toward 2000* that up to the year 2000 the expansion of arable land in the developing countries can be expected to account for only about 28 percent of the required increase in agricultural production; the remaining 72 percent must come from increases in cropping intensity and yield on land already under cultivation. More intensive use of commercial energy inputs, particularly mineral fertilizer, farm machinery, pump irrigation, and chemical pesticides, will be required, as well as the appropriate application of renewable sources of rural energy.

This chapter presents an overview of commercial energy use for agricultural production, giving particular attention to the role of water in the form of pump irrigation. Estimates of agricultural energy consumption and trends in energy use in the major regions of the world for the period 1972–82 are also presented. In addition, the potential role of renewable energy in irrigation is discussed.

COMMERCIAL ENERGY FOR AGRICULTURAL PRODUCTION

Agricultural production is responsible for a small part of total commercial energy use. In 1982 the commercial energy used for agricultural production was 6.6 percent of the total consumption of commercial energy in the developing countries and 4.6 percent in the developed countries. Although total consumption is small, its crucial importance is illustrated by the increasing amount of energy devoted to agricultural production during the period of rapidly increasing energy prices which occurred after 1972. As shown in Table 1, the proportion of total energy used in agricultural production increased from an estimated 4.2 percent in 1972 to 5.0 percent in 1982. Only in Oceania and the Near East did the proportion of commercial energy used for agricultural production decline.

Total energy for agriculture production grew at a rate of 3.6 percent a year between 1972 and 1982, with a growth rate of 8.6 percent a year in developing countries and 2.2 percent in developed countries. This compares with a growth rate in total commercial energy of 5.5 percent in developing countries and 1 percent in developed countries during the same period.

Estimates of commercial energy used in the manufacture and operation of farm machinery and pump irrigation and the production and application of mineral fertilizers and chemical pesticides are shown in Table 2, while the share of agricultural energy devoted to each of these inputs in the various regions of the world is shown in Table 3.

The total energy consumption for agricultural production was estimated at 202 million tons of oil-equivalent in 1972, increasing to 287 million tons in 1982, over 50 percent of this increase occurring in the developing countries. As a result the developing countries' share of commercial energy used for agricultural production increased from 16.6 percent in 1972 to 26.7 percent in 1982. Although there were

Table 1. Total commercial energy and commercial energy used in agriculture.

Region	Total Commercial Energy 1972	Total Commercial Energy 1982 (× 1,000 tons oil-equivalent)	Commercial Energy Used in Agriculture 1972	Commercial Energy Used in Agriculture 1982	1972 (%)	1982 (%)
North America	1,763,212	1,668,188	67,973	66,161	3.9	4.0
Western Europe	954,024	1,004,146	51,654	67,912	5.4	6.8
Oceania	53,456	82,312	3,479	3,582	6.5	4.4
Other developed countries	295,573	354,249	6,104	16,204	2.1	4.6
Total developed market economies	3,066,265	3,108,895	129,211	153,859	4.2	4.9
Eastern Europe, USSR	1,080,113	1,474,460	39,574	56,510	3.7	3.8
Total developed countries	4,146,378	4,583,355	168,786	210,369	4.1	4.6
Africa	35,342	51,212	1,783	2,774	5.0	5.4
Latin America	187,326	297,730	7,158	11,203	3.8	3.8
Far East	135,069	146,930	8,789	20,738	6.5	14.1
Near East	53,931	231,675	3,989	9,946	7.4	4.3
Other developing countries	1,000	2,843	38	57	3.8	2.0
Total developing market economies	412,668	730,390	21,757	44,718	5.3	6.1
Asian centrally planned economies	276,278	444,425	11,743	31,844	4.3	7.2
Total developing countries	688,946	1,174,815	33,500	76,561	4.9	6.5
Total	4,835,324	5,758,170	202,285	286,931	4.2	5.0

SOURCES: United Nations Statistical Office, *Yearbook of World Energy Statistics 1982;* Food and Agriculture Organization estimates.

Table 2. Use of commercial energy for inputs to agricultural production.

Region	Farm Machinery 1972	Farm Machinery 1982	Pump Irrigation 1972	Pump Irrigation 1982	Mineral Fertilizer 1972	Mineral Fertilizer 1982 (× 1,000 tons oil-equivalent)	Chemical Pesticides 1972	Chemical Pesticides 1982	Commercial Energy in Agriculture 1972	Commercial Energy in Agriculture 1982	Share of Each Region 1972 (%)	Share of Each Region 1982 (%)
North America	48,853	44,212	747	943	17,102	19,630	1,271	1,377	67,973	66,161	33.6	23.1
Western Europe	33,937	45,123	335	404	16,535	21,485	847	900	51,654	67,912	25.5	23.7
Oceania	2,567	2,585	31	36	866	945	16	16	3,479	3,582	1.7	1.2
Other developed countries	3,630	13,336	84	86	2,372	2,764	18	18	6,104	16,204	3.0	5.6
Total developed market economies	88,988	105,256	1,197	1,469	36,875	44,824	2,152	2,311	129,211	153,859	63.8	53.6
Eastern Europe, USSR	18,854	25,396	302	461	19,571	29,753	847	900	39,574	56,510	19.6	19.7
Total developed countries	107,842	130,653	1,499	1,929	56,446	74,576	2,999	3,211	168,786	210,369	83.4	73.3
Africa	827	1,138	88	117	842	1,366	27	152	1,783	2,774	0.9	1.0
Latin America	3,306	4,515	119	157	3,611	6,300	123	231	7,158	11,203	3.5	3.9
Far East	1,533	4,552	627	1,236	6,596	14,809	33	142	8,789	20,738	4.3	7.2
Near East	1,382	4,269	527	676	2,049	4,888	32	113	3,989	9,946	2.0	3.5
Other developing countries	19	24	0	0	19	29	1	5	38	57	0.0	0.0
Total developing market economies	7,066	14,497	1,361	2,187	13,115	27,391	215	643	21,757	44,718	10.8	15.6
Asian centrally planned economies	2,052	5,004	839	958	8,323	25,246	530	635	11,743	31,844	5.8	11.1
Total developing countries	9,118	19,501	2,200	3,145	21,438	52,637	744	1,278	33,500	76,561	16.6	26.7
Total	116,960	150,154	3,699	5,075	77,884	127,213	3,743	4,489	202,285	286,931	100.0	100.0

SOURCE: Food and Agriculture Organization estimates.

Table 3. Commercial energy used in agricultural production and share of input in each region.

Region	Commercial Energy in Agriculture		Farm Machinery		Pump Irrigation		Mineral Fertilizer		Chemical Pesticides	
	1972	1982	1972	1982	1972	1982	1972	1982	1972	1982
	(× 1,000 tons)		(%)	(%)	(%)	(%)	(%)	(%)	(%)	(%)
North America	67,973	66,161	71.9	66.8	1.1	1.4	25.2	29.7	1.9	2.1
Western Europe	51,654	67,912	65.7	66.4	0.6	0.6	32.0	31.6	1.6	1.3
Oceania	3,479	3,582	73.8	72.2	0.9	1.0	24.9	26.4	0.5	0.4
Other developed countries	6,104	16,204	59.5	82.3	1.4	0.5	38.9	17.1	0.3	0.1
Total developed market companies	129,211	153,859	68.9	68.4	0.9	1.0	28.5	29.1	1.7	1.5
Eastern Europe, USSR	39,574	56,510	47.6	44.9	0.8	0.8	49.5	52.7	2.1	1.6
Total developed countries	168,786	210,369	63.9	62.1	0.9	0.9	33.4	35.5	1.8	1.5
Africa	1,783	2,774	46.4	41.0	4.9	4.2	47.2	49.2	1.5	5.5
Latin America	7,158	11,203	46.2	40.3	1.7	1.4	50.4	56.2	1.7	2.1
Far East	8,789	20,738	17.4	21.9	7.1	6.9	75.0	71.4	0.4	0.7
Near East	3,989	9,946	34.6	42.9	13.2	6.8	51.4	49.1	0.8	1.1
Other developing countries	38	57	49.6	41.6	0.1	0.1	48.9	50.0	1.4	8.3
Total developing market economies	21,757	44,718	32.5	32.4	6.3	4.9	60.3	61.3	1.0	1.4
Asian centrally planned economies	11,743	31,844	17.5	15.7	7.1	3.0	70.9	79.3	4.5	2.0
Total developing countries	33,500	76,561	27.2	25.5	6.6	4.1	64.0	68.8	2.2	1.7
Total	202,285	286,931	57.8	52.3	1.8	1.8	38.5	44.3	1.9	1.6

SOURCE: Table 2.

increases in each of the developing regions, the main increases were in the Asian centrally planned economies, where the annual growth rate in agricultural energy was 10.5 percent between 1972 and 1982, followed by the Near East with an annual growth rate of 9.6 percent and the Far East with an annual growth rate of 9 percent. In the developing regions of Africa and Latin America the growth rate in agricultural energy was about 4.5 percent a year.

While the use of agricultural energy has increased substantially in the developing countries, it is still low considering that in 1982 the developing countries had 54 percent of the world's arable land and land under permanent crops and produced 48 percent of the world's cereals and 62 percent of the world's roots and tubers.

As shown in Table 3, the manufacture and operation of farm machinery accounted for more than 50 percent of total commercial energy used in agricultural production in both 1972 and 1982. However, the growth rate of energy for farm machinery during this period was 2.5 percent a year, in comparison with 5 percent a year for mineral fertilizers. As a result the proportion of agricultural energy used for fertilizers increased, from 38.5 percent in 1972 to 44.3 percent in 1982, while the proportion used for farm machinery decreased from 57.8 percent in 1972 to 52.3 percent in 1982. The growth rate for pump irrigation was about 3.2 percent a year, and it maintained its share of agricultural energy at 1.8 percent. For pesticides the growth rate was 1.8 percent, and its share decreased from 1.9 percent in 1972 to 1.6 percent in 1982.

In the developing countries mineral fertilizer is by far the most important user of agricultural commercial energy,

and, as the result of a 9.4 percent average annual growth rate, the proportion of agricultural energy used for fertilizer increased from 64 percent in 1972 to 68.8 percent in 1982. During this same period the annual growth rate for the other inputs was 7.9 percent for farm machinery, 5.6 percent for pesticides, and 3.6 percent for pump irrigation. The low growth rate in pump irrigation, in comparison with the other inputs, caused its share of agricultural energy to decrease in the developing countries from an estimated 6.6 percent in 1972 to 4.1 percent in 1982. The largest change occurred in the Near East, where the proportion of agricultural energy devoted to irrigation dropped from 13.2 percent in 1972 to 6.8 percent in 1982, and in the Asian centrally planned economies, where it decreased from 7.1 percent to 3 percent.

The lack of foreign exchange and the relatively high interest rates on foreign capital have encouraged countries to concentrate more of their agricultural investment on inputs such as fertilizers that offer fast returns than on inputs such as irrigation equipment that require several years for the cost to be recovered. In addition, as foreign exchange has become limited and petroleum prices have risen, the import of petroleum fuels has been curtailed in developing countries.

In periods of energy shortage agriculture in isolated rural areas is often the first to be affected, since it is usually at the end of the distribution network and may be subject to erratic deliveries, even when overall energy supplies are adequate. Fuel shortages in Somalia, for example, are estimated to have resulted in a 40 to 60 percent yield reduction of irrigated crops in some areas during 1984, when irrigation could not be carried out during the crucial flowering period because of a lack of diesel fuel for pump operation.

The recent emphasis on mineral fertilizers seems justified by the economic conditions in the developing countries. However, in areas with low and erratic rainfall an assured water supply is often a prerequisite for the effective utilization of other inputs. Therefore, care must be taken that the financing of irrigation, which is needed to develop the base for increasing agricultural production, is not unduly restricted.

COMMERCIAL ENERGY FOR IRRIGATION

Controlled irrigation is mainly of two types: large-scale gravity-flow irrigation, in which dams or water-diversion structures and channels are built to bring water to the fields and pump irrigation, in which water is pumped from either ground or surface sources. Agricultural production is often only a secondary use of water from large dams, the primary use being generation of electrical power, and the energy used in the construction of dams is therefore excluded from the estimates made here. Also, since the development and maintenance of irrigation canals are usually performed with agricultural machines, the energy for these purposes has been included under farm machinery. The irrigation equipment discussed here is limited to pumps, engines, pipes, and material such as equipment for sprinkler and drip irrigation.

In 1972 the irrigation equipment in use in the world amounted to about 2.3 million tons, 1.2 million tons (52 percent) of which are in developing countries. In 1982 the total irrigation equipment was estimated to have increased to 3 million tons, 1.6 million tons (53 percent) of which are in developing countries. The annual production of irrigation equipment supplied to agriculture was about 265,000 tons in 1972 and increased to about 360,000 tons in 1982. It is assumed that the average energy required to produce this equipment was 2 kg oil-equivalent per kilogram of equipment.

In addition to the energy needed for the manufacture of irrigation equipment, energy, usually in the form of petroleum fuel, is required for its operation. The fuel required per hectare of land irrigated varies with the depth of the water being pumped, the type of irrigation system, and the water requirements of the crops. It is estimated that fuel requirements vary from 160 kg/ha in the developed countries to 200 kg/ha in developing countries of Africa and the Near East. Estimates of the commercial energy for pump irrigation based on these assumptions are shown in Table 4.

In 1982 pump irrigation consumed 5.1 million tons of oil-equivalent, developing countries accounting for 62 percent. However, while developing countries increased their share of all inputs between 1972 and 1982, the increase for irrigation was only 2.5 percent (from 59.5 percent to 62 percent) in comparison with a 13 percent increase (from 28 percent to 41 percent) for fertilizer, an 8 percent increase (from

Table 4. Commercial energy for pump irrigation equipment manufacture and operation.

Region	Area Irrigated by Pumps		Energy for Manufacture[a]		Energy for Operation		Total Irrigation Energy		Share of Each Region	
	1972	1982	1972	1982	1972	1982	1972	1982	1972	1982
	(× 1,000 ha)				(× 1,000 tons)				(%)	(%)
North America[b]	3,862	4,875	133	168	614	775	747	943	20.2	18.6
Western Europe[b]	1,741	2,103	58	70	277	334	335	404	9.0	8.0
Oceania[b]	161	187	5	6	26	30	31	36	0.8	0.7
Other developed countries[b]	449	456	13	13	71	73	84	86	2.3	1.7
Total developed market economies	6,213	7,622	209	257	988	1,212	1,197	1,469	32.4	28.9
Eastern Europe, USSR[b]	1,520	2,316	61	93	242	368	302	461	8.2	9.1
Total developed countries	7,733	9,938	270	350	1,229	1,580	1,499	1,929	40.5	38.0
Africa[c]	389	523	10	14	77	104	88	117	2.4	2.3
Latin America[d]	553	732	20	26	99	131	119	157	3.2	3.1
Far East[c]	2,815	5,547	68	134	559	1,102	627	1,236	17.0	24.4
Near East[d]	2,562	3,288	69	88	458	588	527	676	14.2	13.3
Other developing countries[d]	0	0	0	0	0	0	0	0	0.0	0.0
Total developing market economies	6,319	10,090	167	262	1,194	1,925	1,361	2,187	36.8	43.1
Asian centrally planned economies[e]	4,164	4,756	94	108	745	851	839	958	22.7	18.9
Total developing countries	10,484	14,846	261	370	1,939	2,776	2,200	3,145	59.5	62.0
Total	18,217	24,784	531	719	3,168	4,356	3,699	5,075	100.0	100.0

SOURCE: Food and Agriculture Organization estimates.

[a] Energy requirements for manufacture assumed to be 2 kg of oil-equivalent per kilogram of equipment with 10 years' average life of pump and equipment.

[b] Weight of equipment assumed to be 140 kg/ha irrigated, and fuel requirement, 160 kg/ha.

[c] Weight of equipment assumed to be 100 kg/ha irrigated, and fuel requirement, 200 kg/ha.

[d] Weight of equipment assumed to be 140 kg/ha irrigated, and fuel requirement, 180 kg/ha.

[e] Weight of equipment assumed to be 100 kg/ha irrigated, and fuel requirement, 180 kg/ha.

20 percent to 28 percent) for pesticides, and a 5 percent increase (from 8 percent to 13 percent) for farm machinery.

The main increase in the area under pumped irrigation was in the Far East, where pumps were estimated to have been used on 2.7 million ha (21 percent) of the 13 million ha of the additional land brought under irrigation between 1972 and 1982. This area accounted for more than 62 percent of the estimated 4.4 million ha of additional land brought under pump irrigation in the developing countries during this period, with the result that the Far East accounted for 24.4 percent of the total irrigation energy in 1982, in comparison with 17 percent in 1972.

Irrigated areas need to be expanded in the developing countries. However, because of the increasing investment and operating costs of the present pump-irrigation systems, these systems must be used as effectively as possible, and alternative sources of energy must be examined. More efficient use of irrigation water is feasible in many areas and could result in savings in energy consumption. The interdependence of land-development methods, irrigation practices, and systems of cultivation and crop production is seldom fully appreciated. Both increased efficiency in use of irrigation water and higher cropping intensities can be achieved by (1) improving water-distribution channels and providing appropriate drainage, (2) improving field layouts, (3) grading and leveling the land before irrigation, and (4) using better implements and methods of water application. Improved maintenance and operation of mechanical equipment can also improve the efficiency of the energy used for irrigation. However, fragmented landholdings and the difficulty of organizing the group action required to implement new projects often impede irrigation improvement. The lack of an adequate infrastructure to support and maintain mechanical equipment may also limit its efficient use.

ALTERNATIVE ENERGY FOR IRRIGATION

In many developing countries the high capital cost and long lead time required by large irrigation schemes have slowed their development and increased the emphasis given to small-scale systems. Many farms in developing countries are less than 2 ha in size, and the water table in some areas is within a few meters of the ground surface. While the quantity of water needed to irrigate a given area depends on soil type, land topography, climate, method of water distribution, and crop water requirements, the peak pumping capacity needed for 1 ha is typically in the range of 2 to 6 $L \cdot s^{-1}$. For water within a few meters of the ground surface this may require as little as 100 to 300 W of energy input per hectare. It is for these small areas requiring low power inputs that alternative energy sources seem to have the greatest potential.

People have irrigated small areas near water sources for centuries and continue to do so in many developing countries. The work efficiency of humans is relatively low, however, only about 75 W on a sustained basis, particulary in developing countries with high temperature and humidity.

Therefore, while improved hand pumps and water-lifting devices could reduce somewhat the drudgery and increase the irrigated area, other forms of power are needed to substantially expand irrigated areas.

The use of draft animals for irrigation is widespread in both Asia and the Near East, where a pair of bullocks operating a Persian wheel or other water-lifting device can irrigate 1 to 1.5 ha. The efficiency of present methods of lifting water with draft animals is often low and could benefit from improved water-lifting devices and drive mechanisms, better harnesses, and improved animal nutrition and management. The additional area irrigated through such improvements is limited, however, since the need for draft-animal power for other agricultural operations increases as the irrigated area becomes larger.

Solar-energy resources are generally good in developing countries, and the utilization of photovoltaic solar cells appears to be one of the most promising alternative energy technologies for water pumping. Several types of photovoltaic pumping systems are commercially manufactured and have been operating on a limited basis in developing countries for several years. While technical feasibility has been proved, photovoltaic systems are currently too expensive for pumping irrigation water in most developing countries. A reduction in the price of solar cells and improved system designs seem possible, however, and could make photovoltaic systems economically viable for small-scale irrigation in the future.

Wind power is another alternative. Wind speeds are generally low in the tropics, where most of the developing countries are situated. However, water-pumping windmills have been used to supply water for livestock and human consumption in some developing countries for many years, and most commercially available windmills are reliable and safe and seldom require repair if properly maintained. Since topographical features can augment wind speed and doubling the wind speed increases the power output eight times, windmills may be an appropriate source of power for irrigation water pumping, though at present they appear economically viable only at selected locations in developing countries.

The power of flowing water may also be used to pump water for irrigation where irrigated areas are near rivers and streams having an average water velocity of 0.75 $m \cdot s^{-1}$ or more. In addition, opportunities exist in selected locations to substitute petroleum fuels in internal-combustion engines with alternatives such as biogas, producer gas, alcohol, and vegetable oil which can be derived from agricultural products or their residues.

To meet future food needs, irrigated areas in the developing countries must be further expanded. This will require the appropriate application of both conventional and renewable sources of energy. The main concern must be to ensure the energy needs of agriculture from whatever energy sources are available and can be effectively utilized at a particular location.

41. CALIFORNIA AGRICULTURAL WATER MOVEMENT AND ITS ENERGY IMPLICATIONS

L. Joe Glass, Department of Agricultural Engineering, California Polytechnic State University, San Luis Obispo, California

ABSTRACT

California climate and topography provide for a unique agriculture in the state. Water development and transportation are necessary to grow crops through the summer months in the Central Valley. As a result energy is both generated and consumed. A system of canals and rivers is used to transport the water from northern California to the Central Valley by the U.S. Bureau of Reclamation as part of the Central Valley Project and by the California Department of Water Resources as part of the State Water Project. Some local irrigation districts have their own water supplies and hydroelectric power.

Energy use and its implication for agriculture are projected to the year 2000.

CALIFORNIA CLIMATE AND TOPOGRAPHY

California is a land of plenty. The state has plenty of people, plenty of water, plenty of food, and plenty of problems related to its people, water, and food. Problems arise in the midst of these plenties primarily because of mislocation relative to each other. This mislocation is largely due to the climatic and topographic features of the state.

The topographic features of mountains and valleys in conjunction with a Mediterranean-type climate are very significant to the state. Much of the precipitation, occurring mainly from October to May, falls as snow in the Sierra Nevada. This snow melts in the spring, and much of the resulting water flow is caught in reservoirs built to provide irrigation water for summer crops, flood control, hydroelectric power, and recreation. The absence of rainfall during the summer and early fall allows proper timing of water application by irrigation to many diverse agricultural crops. This climate allows the opportunity to maximize yields and quality of the produce grown which would otherwise be dramatically affected by untimely rainfall during the growing season.

Because of the arrangement of the mountains in the state, there are several valleys of agricultural significance. The major valley is the Central Valley (Fig. 1). It is surrounded by mountains, the high Sierra Nevada on the east and the Coastal Range on the west. Two of the rivers flowing into this valley are considered the major rivers. The Sacramento River is the major south-flowing river in the northern portion of the valley, and the San Joaquin River is the major north-flowing river in the southern portion. The rivers join and flow into the San Francisco Bay, which in turn outlets through the Golden Gate into the Pacific Ocean. Several other rivers flow into this major valley, but these two are used to identify each of the subvalleys within the Central Valley.

The mean annual precipitation varies throughout the state. The net effect is that three-fourths of the precipitation falls in the northern fourth of the state. However, the land and the most suitable climate for the maximum production of the diverse crops are mainly in the lower three-fourths of the state. The net effect is that water must be transported and energy consumed to maximize the potential food and fiber production.

DEVELOPMENT OF WATER RESOURCES AND HYDROELECTRIC POWER

Surface Water

The California Department of Water Resources (1983, 7) states that water resources planning and development in California have a long and often complex history that dates back to the late eighteenth century. The Franciscan fathers began water development by damming small streams and diverting water through canals to their missions. Later the gold rush of the mid-1800s brought a need to provide water from the high mountain streams for washing the gold-bearing deposits. This was provided primarily by private individuals and companies. As the state grew from the influx of gold seekers, people began to farm. Needing water for their crops, the farmers formed groups and cooperatives to construct canals for water diversion from rivers to their farms.

In 1887 the state passed the Wright Irrigation District Act, which provided the legal means for forming local irrigation districts with the authority to acquire water by development and to buy out private irrigation enterprises. By 1930 more than a hundred irrigation districts were operating in the state.

By this time the legislature had directed the state engineer to make a comprehensive statewide survey of the water resources. The state submitted its first water plan to the legislature in 1931. The primary focus of this plan was to develop water resources for agriculture in the Central Valley. According to Gill et al. (1971, 6), the plan was authorized by the 1933 legislature, and state bonds to finance the plan were approved by the voters, but because of the Great Depression there were not enough bond purchasers. The state then turned to the federal government for help.

U.S. Bureau of Reclamation. In 1937, Congress authorized the U.S. Bureau of Reclamation to proceed with the

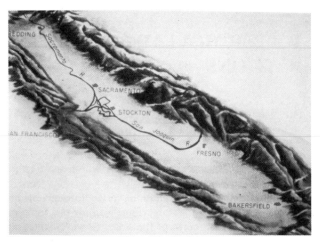

Fig. 1. Relief map of the Central Valley of California.

Fig. 3. Overview map of the state water project in California.

Fig. 2. Overview map of the Central Valley project in California.

plan, which became known as the Central Valley Project. The major works of the project are shown in Fig. 2. They include (1) Shasta Dam and Keswick Dam, on the Sacramento River near Redding; (2) a diversion dam downstream and the two associated canals, the Tehama-Colusa and Corning, at Red Bluff; (3) the Trinity Dam and associated works to transport water from the Trinity River to the Sacramento River; (4) Folsom Dam and associated work on the American River near Sacramento; (5) Friant Dam, on the San Joaquin River, near Fresno, which includes the Madera Canal and the Friant-Kern Canal, taking water from storage behind the Friant Dam; and (6) the San Luis Unit (a cooperative venture between the bureau and the state Department of Water Resources), consisting of San Luis Dam, the Dos Amigos Pumping Plant, and the San Luis Canal. A power transmission system which included power plants at several of the dams was also a part of the project.

State Department of Water Resources. In 1947, at the request of the state legislature, the Division of Water Re-

sources began a three-phase investigation of the state's water resources. The final phase was published in 1957. The Division of Water Resources had been renamed the Department of Water Resources (DWR), and the plan became the State Water Project. In the election of November, 1960 California voters approved $1.75 billion for general obligation bonds to begin the State Water Project (Fig. 3). The major works of the project include (1) the Oroville Dam and Power Plant, (2) the Thermalito Afterbay and Power Plant, and (3) the main line of the California Aqueduct System, which includes nine pumping plants, the San Luis Dam and Power Plant, the Castaic Dam, the Silverwood Dam, and the Terminus Dam. Other, smaller works are also included.

State Irrigation Districts. Only a few districts have developed water resources and generate hydroelectric power. Each district is subject to the state only within the guidelines established in its formation and operation, which were laid down through the Wright Irrigation District Act, passed by the state legislature in 1887.

Table 1 shows the reservoir capacities and the capacities for generation of hydroelectric power of each of the federal and state districts that provide agricultural water.

Groundwater

Groundwater comprises approximately 35 percent of all the water used for agriculture in the state. Its availability varies throughout the agricultural areas requiring irrigation. According to California Water Plan Bulletin 160-83 (1983, 85), the statewide overdraft of groundwater is estimated at 2.2 dkm³ a year. Overdraft is expected to be a continual problem in some areas because the demand for water exceeds the supply of accessible water outside the local area.

TRANSPORTATION OF AGRICULTURAL WATER

With the availability and development of water resources principally in the northern quarter and the major agricultural areas in the lower three-fourths of the state, transportation of water is necessary. Rivers are used to transport water from the Sacramento Valley south to the San Joaquin

Table 1. Reservoir and hydroelectric power generation capacities for federal, state, and districts providing agricultural water.

Location	Reservoir capacity (dam^3)	Generation capacity (kW)
Shasta (F)	5,615,000	422,300
Trinity (F)	3,020,000	105,600
Whiskeytown (F)	297,500	141,400
Spring Creek (F)	—	150,000
Keswick (F)	—	75,000
Folsom (F)	1,246,000	186,500
Friant (F)	642,000	—
San Luis (F, S)	2,517,500	424,000
Oroville (S)	4,364,000	714,600
Thermalito (S)	101,000	194,700
Devil Canyon (S)	—	126,000
Castaic (S)	400,000	1,470,000
McClure (D)	1,264,000	80,100
New Don Pedro (D)	2,504,000	157,000

(F) = federal, (S) = state, (D) = district.

Table 2. Canal capacities and lengths for federal and state agencies delivering agricultural water in the Central Valley.

Name	Capacity (m^3/s)	Length (km)
Corning (F)	14	54
Tehama-Colusa (F)	65	316
Folsom South (F)[a]	99	111
Contra Costa (F)	10	77
Delta-Mendota (F)	130	182
San Luis (F)[b]	371	164
Coalinga (F)	31	19
Madera (F)	28	58
Friant-Kern (F)	113	245
California Aqueduct (S)	286	620

[a] Canal length not yet completed.
[b] Portion of the California aqueduct.

Valley. Because the land in the San Joaquin drains to the north, canals are used to transport water south throughout this valley.

U.S. Bureau of Reclamation

The U.S. Bureau of Reclamation has constructed approximately 800 km of canals to deliver irrigation water to irrigation districts, which in turn deliver the water to individual farmers. The capacities and lengths of each canal are given in Table 2. Several pumping plants are used in the total canal system. Their energy requirements and pumping capacities are given in Table 3.

State Department of Water Resources

The one major canal of the DWR is the California Aqueduct (Fig. 3). Its capacity and length are given in Table 2. Nearly half of the water transported by this system is used for municipal and industrial purposes in southern California.

The aqueduct system includes seven pumping plants along its main channel in the San Joaquin Valley. Each

Table 3. Plant capacities, lifts, and energy requirements for pumping agricultural water along federal and state canals in the Central Valley.

Location	Pump capacity (m^3/s)	Lift (m)	Output Energy Load (kW)
Tracy (F)	130	60	100,700
O'Neill (F)	119	15	26,900
Banks (S)	292	76	272,900
San Luis (F, S)	311	88	376,000
Dos Amigos (F, S)	374	38	180,000
Buena Vista (S)	159	64	111,700
Wheeler Ridge (S)	139	73	110,500
Wind Gap (S)	134	160	246,420
Edmonston (S)[a]	125	600	838,200

[a] Minimal agricultural water.

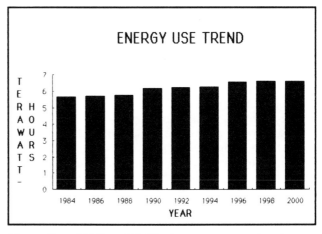

Fig. 4. Central Valley of California energy use trend to the year 2000.

pumping plant's energy use and its pumping capacity are given in Table 3. The agricultural development of the western side of the southern portion of the San Joaquin Valley is dependent on the water from this aqueduct. Limited amounts of the water transported by this canal are used for agriculture after the water has been lifted over the Tehachapi Mountains and out of the San Joaquin Valley.

ENERGY USE AND PROJECTIONS TO THE YEAR 2000

Energy use and projections are limited to the agricultural sector in the Central Valley. Of the total agricultural energy in the state, 80 percent is used in pumping water for crop production, according to the California Energy Commission (1984, 56). For the Central Valley alone it is probably closer to 85 percent and is affected by the availability of surface water. Fig. 4 shows the trend of estimated energy use for pumping and moving agricultural water to the year 2000.

The California Energy Commission developed the projected energy use by considering (1) the eleven major crops grown in the area, (2) the amount of water needed per hectare for each crop, (3) the percentage of irrigation water

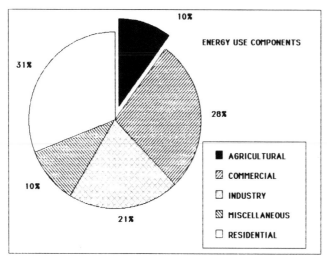

Fig. 5. Percent of energy used by component in California in 1981.

Table 4. Water costs in the southern San Joaquin Valley.

Location	Water Charge ($/dam^3)
Entrance to Kern County	$13
Past Buena Vista Pumping Plant	20
Past Wheeler Ridge Pumping Plant	29
Past Wind Gap Pumping Plant	48

supplied from surface and groundwater sources (and the amount of energy needed to pump water from each source), (4) the amount of land irrigated by surface and pressure-required methods and the energy requirements of each, and (5) the future crop acreages by crop type.

To suggest the significance that agriculture has on energy use, which is primarily water movement, Fig. 5 shows the percentage of energy use for each component of the total energy used in the state. As can be noted in the figure, agricultural energy use is small considering that it is the largest single enterprise in the state.

The percentage of energy use by agriculture varies depending on water conditions. When limited precipitation occurs during the winter months, the availability of surface water decreases, and groundwater pumping is increased. The amount of the increase depends on the reservoir storage carryover from previous years. The drought conditions in 1976–77 increased groundwater pumping by about 20 percent. The percent of energy use increased slightly because of the lower groundwater levels.

Because energy is a nonrenewable resource, its costs will continue to climb and further stimulate conservation and more efficient energy use in all sectors, including agriculture. However, because of the uniqueness of the climate in the Central Valley for growing a wide variety of crops, many of which have a high cash value, a continued use of water transportation and energy is anticipated. This will occur as long as the crops grown can produce a margin of profit. Other factors, such as drainage and maintenance of a certain level of water quality, may have a more significant effect on agriculture in the Central Valley than will energy costs and water availability.

Energy costs to agriculture depend on whether federal or state water is being used. The State Water Project charges the water user in relation to his location from the water source and its associated costs. The farther the user is from the source, the more costs will be incurred. There are three basic components of the cost to the water user: the capital component or payback for the construction, the operation and maintenance charge, and the energy costs in water transportation to the user's turnout. The first two costs are related to the user's annual water entitlement, which was contracted before the construction of the system. The third component is a variable charge depending on the power cost to the DWR.

Until 1983 the DWR contracted with the Pacific Gas & Electric Company (PG&E) for a fixed energy charge beginning with the start-up of the system. When the contract was completed, rather than being forced to negotiate short-term energy contracts through PG&E because of the rapidly increasing energy costs, the DWR became a bulk power supplier and user in exactly the same manner as a public or private utility company. Now the DWR negotiates with many other suppliers, buying and selling electricity in the same manner as the utility companies. The energy cost to the water user of the State Water Project may vary dramatically from year to year depending on the ability of the DWR to generate or purchase least-cost electrical energy. The present cost for energy charge is approximately 30.3 mills/kWh. This translates into the water costs shown in Table 4 for the southern San Joaquin Valley as related to the number of times that the water is lifted through a pumping plant on the California Aqueduct.

These water charges include the charges that the individual water and irrigation districts assess the water user to offset their costs in transporting the water from the California Aqueduct to the individual farm. On some farms where additional pumping lifts are required by the district, the costs may be as much as $100/dam^3. These costs dramatically affect the choice of crops grown. The crops are generally tree crops—fruits and nuts, grapes, and vegetables. For these high water costs the market prices for the crops must be good, or the farmer cannot continue to grow them. The land will revert back to predevelopment barrenness. Only areas where lower-cost water is available will continue to be agriculturally productive.

REFERENCES

California Department of Water Resources. 1983. The California water plan: projected use and available water supplies to 2010. Bulletin 160–83.

California Energy Commission. 1984. California energy demand: 1984–2004. Vol. I: Summary staff report.

Gill, G. S., E. C. Gray, and D. Seckler. 1971. The California water plan and its critics: a brief review. Pp. 3–27. In D. Seckler (ed.) California water. Berkeley: University of California Press.

42. RECENT EXPERIENCE IN THE APPLICATION OF SMALL HYDROPOWER AS A PRINCIPAL ENERGY SOURCE IN RURAL AREAS OF DEVELOPING COUNTRIES

Jack J. Fritz, National Research Council, Washington, D.C.

INTRODUCTION

The dependence of economic development on low-cost energy supplies was established with the oil-price shocks of 1973 and 1979. Many economies came to a halt as an increased fraction of their foreign exchange had to be allocated for imported fuels. Unfortunately, half of the world's energy is consumed in the form of wood collected at great cost to the environment and individual productivity. Electricity available in more prosperous communities through either grid extension or small diesel generator sets, is expensive in capital costs (extending the grid) and operating costs (diesel fuel). Both of these approaches are well represented in the foreign assistance programs of the World Bank and the U.S. Agency for International Development (AID). A possibility barely under consideration is small or mini-hydropower, particularly in those countries blessed with adequate water resources and favorable topogrphy.

Traditionally, large irrigation and hydropower schemes have been developed simultaneously. Examples include the dams at Aswan, in Egypt, and Tarbela, in Pakistan. In both of these projects water for irrigation remains the first priority and water for hydropower second, indicating that food production is of the highest importance to both Egypt and Pakistan. On occasion problems arise if water needs for irrigation do not coincide with the requirement for firm power, leading to the use of thermal power plants that consume imported fuels.

However, such large projects benefit from economies of scale, low and essentially constant operating costs, and nondependence on fossil fuels. At the time these projects were constructed, the above attributes were the key factors in making them competitive with large-scale petroleum-fired power plants using low-cost and readily available fuels. In recent years, however, high construction costs, environmental concerns, and long delays in planning and construction have reduced the attractiveness of such large-scale projects.

Small hydropower facilities situated near load centers either on irrigation canals primarily in control structures or on mountain streams can provide and regulate scarce water resources and power to the more isolated communities. This approach is appropriate for areas far from the grid or at some distance from traditional transportation systems capable of providing diesel fuel. Although clearly not a substitute for large-scale systems such as Tarbela or Aswan, small hydropower facilities can be considered as complements, especially for those areas that the government is seeking to develop.

In rural areas recent technical advances in water-turbine design, construction, and efficiency, combined with increasing petroleum fuel costs, have enhanced the competitive position of smaller hydroelectric projects in relation to diesel-powered generators of similar size. When compared to large-scale projects, small hydroprojects can be planned and built in less time and are less likely to create extensive environmental problems. These plants are reliable and, within the limits of the water resources available, can be tailored to the needs of the end-use market. Although the unit cost per installed kilowatt of generating capacity is higher for small-scale projects, the benefits are easier to identify. These characteristics make small hydropower projects particularly attractive for developing countries in which near-term installation of dispersed energy systems is essential for economic and social development.

THE TECHNOLOGY: SOME COMMENTS

Potential Energy in Falling Water

On a global basis the usable potential energy in falling water as it makes its way to the seas is considerable. Annual precipitation over the earth's surface is between 4 and 5×10^{14} m^3, one-fourth of which falls on land. Of this, approximately 3.5 to 4×10^{13} m^3 returns to the oceans in the form of direct runoff. Much of its potential has already been tapped with large-scale water and hydro projects. About 23 percent of electrical generation capacity, or approximately 375,000 MW on a worldwide basis is provided through hydropower. In the developing countries only about 10 percent of available hydropower resources have been developed. Because of the availability of large rivers, hydropower development along small watercourses has been principally a function of local demand, distance to the nearest grid, and availability of diesel fuel. The economic realities of the 1980s have made the development of mini-hydropower once again attractive.

The power potential of each cubic meter of water falling through a distance of 1 m·s^{-1} is 9.8 kW, or 13 HP, assuming negligible efficiency losses. Ideally this same flow over a period of one year could produce approximately 85,000 kWh or 306,000 MJ of energy.

Determining Power and Energy Production

The two important determinants of power and energy are the vertical distance through which water falls, or "head," and the quantity of water passing through the turbine per unit time, or "flow." Mini-hydropower installations, in particular turbines, are specified in terms of "head" in meters, "flow" in cubic meters per second, power capacity in kilowatts or megawatts, and annual energy production in kilowatt-hours. Clearly a turbine generator will not operate at peak capacity throughout the day or year. The portion of power produced as a fraction of power capacity is called the "load factor." The load factor is always less than one because there is little probability that power will be drawn to a maximum capacity by energy uses simultaneously. In fact, the annual energy production of mini-hydro installations may only be 15 to 20 percent of its total potential.

Expanding upon the above, if our cubic meter per second of flow were to drop through 20 m of head, as might be typical for a high or medium head site, then our capacity would reach 194 kW, which is sufficient to service a community of about 1,100 consumers, assuming a load factor of 20 percent. Therefore, each additional meter will ideally increase capacity some 9.8 kW.

The well-known relationship defining power as a function of head and flow is:

$$P = 9.81 \; Qhe$$

where P = power output, kW
Q = flow, $m \cdot s^{-1}$
h = net head, m
e = system efficiency

For rough estimates of potential at a specific site, and assuming a system efficiency of 82 percent, the above equation simply reduces to:

$$P = 8 \; Qh$$

Description of a Mini-Hydropower Installation

The hydraulic components of a mini-hydropower installation consist of an intake structure, a penstock, guide vanes or distributor, generator, turbine, and draft tube, as shown in Fig. 1. The intake is designed to withdraw flow from the forebay, or canal, as efficiently as possible with minimal energy losses. Trash racks are commonly provided to prevent ingestion of debris into the turbine. Intakes usually require some type of shape transition to match the passageway to the turbine and also incorporate a gate or some other means of stopping the flow in an emergency or for turbine maintenance. Some types of turbines are set in an open flume; others are attached to a closed-conduit penstock. An effort should always be made to provide uniformity of the flow, which affects the efficiency of the turbine. For low-head installations the diameter of a closed penstock must be quite large to accommodate the large discharges necessary for a given power output. Determination of penstock size is a compromise between head loss and cost. The selection of

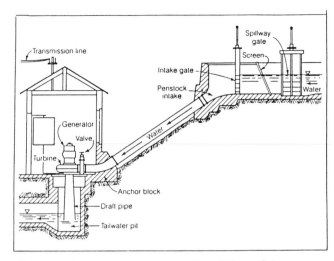

Fig. 1. Typical mini-hydro scheme. (From Fritz, 1983).

Fig. 2. Medium-head mini-hydro plant in Ecuador.

Fig. 3. Low-head plant on irrigation canal in California's Imperial Valley.

the actual penstock configuration depends on the location of the powerhouse with respect to the dam or headworks.

For some types of reaction turbines the water is introduced to the turbine through casings or flumes which vary widely in design. The particular type of casing is dependent on the turbine size and head. For small heads and power output open flumes are commonly employed. Steel spiral casings are used for higher heads, and the casing is designed so that the tangential velocity is essentially constant at consecutive sections around the circumference. This requirement necessitates a changing cross-sectional area of the casing.

Discharge control for some reaction turbines is provided by adjustable guide vanes or wicket gates around the outer edge of the turbine runner. The vanes are tied together with linkages, and their position is regulated by a governor. Flow velocity at the entrance and exit is a function of the position of the guide vane, and, therefore, the efficiency of the turbine also changes. Wicket gates can also be used to shut off the flow to the turbine in emergencies. For turbines without wicket gates various types of shutoff valves are installed upstream of the turbines. The water exits by way of the draft tube. Fig. 2 shows a typical medium head mini-hydropower

plant in a hilly region of Ecuador. Fig. 3 shows a low-head plant on an irrigation canal in the Imperial Valley of California.

RELATIVE ECONOMICS

Fig. 4 summarizes the results of an analysis performed by the Intermediate Technology Development Group comparing a micro-hydro system of 40 kW to a diesel generator of the same capacity installed in Nepal. The figure illustrates the unit-cost electricity characteristics of both systems. The total annual operating cost is basically constant for the hydro system, irrespective of the percentage of capacity utilized because recovery of the capital investment is the major component of the cost. The total annual cost for the unused diesel system (no electricity production), i.e., the cost of recovering the capital, is lower than that for the hydro system because of the lower unit cost per kilowatt installed for the diesel. As electricity is produced, the annual cost of the diesel unit increases in a linear fashion, reflecting the cost of the fuel consumed. Annual costs for the two systems intersect at about 32,000 kWh, or about 10 percent of capacity utilization. This is noteworthy since in many developing countries initial demand for electricity may be

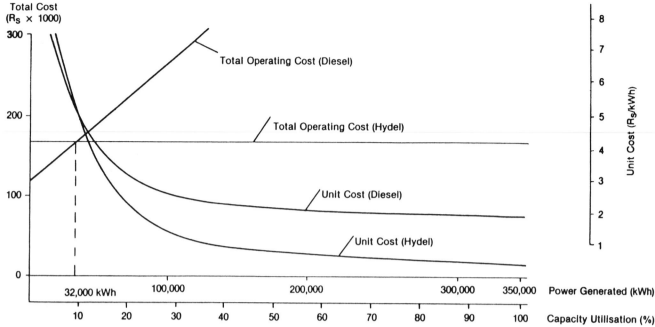

Fig. 4. Annual total cost and unit cost against power generated and capacity utilization for 40 kW diesel and hydroelectric installations. (From Holland et al., 1980).

high during specific periods (such as for lighting at night) and very low during the remainder of the day (minimal services), creating a high peak demand but low capacity factor. As is suggested by the data in the figure, under such circumstances the diesel system remains economically attractive. This is an example of site-specific conditions (in this instance market demand) which could reverse the validity of general statements suggesting that hydropower is more attractive than diesel. Analysis of typical demand patterns in villages in India suggest that capacity factors of about 30 percent might be achieved. Under those conditions hydro systems appear more attractive than diesel units as demonstrated.

Hydro systems have the obvious disadvantage of being restricted to specific sites, which may be distant from the end user of the energy product. Electricity distribution must then be added to the cost of production, thereby reducing the cost advantage of hydro versus fossil fuel–fired systems. The data in the figure nevertheless suggest that under favorable conditions, i.e., proximity of source and end user, sufficient capacity factor, and high prices for petroleum fuels, small or mini-hydropower systems are viable alternatives to diesel systems.

HYDROPOWER PROFILES OF SELECTED DEVELOPING COUNTRIES

In a number of developing countries significant progress is being made in the implementation of small to mini-hydropower systems. Many countries are developing unique approaches suited to their cultures, energy demands, and natural resources. Comparison of these efforts yields valuable information regarding the opportunities and limitations surrounding this technology.

Peru

Hydropower is one of the most promising options for decentralized electricity production in the villages and secondary towns of Peru. A large number of potential sites are near inhabited areas in mountain regions, primarily on the western slopes of the Andes. Mini-hydropower development in Peru is coordinated by the Ministry of Energy and Mines through ElectroPeru, the national electricity utility. Plans call for the construction of fifty small hydropower projects by 1990 at a cost of $12 million. Since 1980 foreign-assistance programs in this area have been initiated primarily with the United States and Germany.

Peru's census data for 1972 suggest that there are more than 3,000 rural villages with a total population of over 4 million. About a hundred of these villages are settlements with populations of between 6,000 and 10,000. Ninety-five percent are without electricity. Of the remaining 5 percent, 1 percent have hydropower stations and 4 percent utilize diesel or gasoline generators. The total installed capacity of these communities by the year 2000 with a large mini-hydropower program could be 120 MW.

As previously mentioned, electricity requirements in rural areas are generally characterized by low capacity factors, in the range of 15 to 20 percent. This is also true for Peru. Agricultural demand derives largely from irrigation water pumping, a highly seasonal activity, while domestic demand is linked primarily to lighting, particularly in the initial stages of electrification. Assuming an annual capacity factor of 20 percent, the total electricity consumed based on a 120 MW installed power will be about 210 GWh by the year 2000, or 0.75×10^{15} J.

Peruvian officials expect the installation cost of mini-hydropower systems to average $500 (1978) per installed kilowatt, assuming an abundance of local volunteer labor to complete the necessary civil works. Site-specific capital costs, however, can be expected to vary considerably, depending on the head and the size of the installation. The low cost of $500/kW is based on actual experience in installing a micro-hydro (4 kVA) Michell-Banki turbine at a pilot plant in a rural community. To further reduce cost, local manufacture of equipment will be encouraged and coordinated through such groups as the Institute of Industrial Technology Investigation and Technical Normalization, whose job will be to develop plant designs and equipment-manufacturing techniques.

Indonesia

Hydropower development in Indonesia dates back to the early twentieth century. Units installed by Dutch engineers before 1940 and ranging in size from 35 kW to 3 MW, are still in operation. By the mid-1940s hydropower accounted for more than 80 percent of total electricity generation. Since that time, however, this fraction has steadily declined despite continual increases in capacity. By 1968 the annual hydropower energy output climbed to 941 GWh generated from an installed capacity of 283 MW. In 1976 capacity has risen to 532 MW. Today's 552 MW represents only 20 percent of the total electricity-generating potential utilized by the public utility, the National Power Agency. Most of this capacity is in Java, where it is used primarily in conjunction with irrigation and water-supply projects. Currently exploited hydroelectric capacity is estimated as only 1.5 percent of Indonesia's total hydropower potential.

Most opportunities for small to mini-hydropower appear to be in remote areas of Sumatra, Kalimantan, Sulawesi, and Irian Jaya—areas not served by a central grid. This potential is essentially unexploited and has been only cursorily explored through general geographic and rainfall data obtained for recent studies (Fritz, 1984). In terms of precipitation and the ratio of mountains to lowlands, Kalimantan and Sulawesi are the most attractive for hydropower development. North Sumatra and parts of Java also appear attractive, but Irian Jaya may be the most economical for development, though the use of small-scale hydropower there is limited by a very small population.

From recent analyses it is estimated that approximately 9 million people in rural Sumatra, Kalimantan, and Sulawesi could be served by small-scale hydropower in the next fifteen years. With a per capita capacity of 50 W, 450 MW could be installed requiring about 3,000 units. Although there is currently no large-scale utilization of small hydropower in Indonesia, there appears to be a widespread recognition of its potential to achieve the government's policy goal of developing rural energy sources especially in the transmigration areas.

People's Republic of China

With more than 5,000 rivers, each with drainage areas of more than 100 km², as well as about 2,000 lakes and 80,000 reservoirs, the People's Republic of China has abundant water resources. The exploitable hydroelectric potential has been estimated at 370 GW with an existing installed capacity of only 70 GW. China's program in small and mini-hydropower can be traced to 1949, when only about fifty small plants with individual capacities of less than 6 MW had been installed for a total capacity of 7.1 GW. A 1979 survey reported the average-sized plant to be 61 kW, operating with a plant factor of 20 percent.

The major push for the construction of small hydropower plants in China occurred during the 1950s in conjunction with rural small-scale industrialization programs. By the end of 1960s installed capacity had reached some 520 MW. By 1966, however, many plants were retired when electrical distribution systems were extended. During the 1970s widespread construction of small plants was resumed with installed capacity growing from 500 MW in 1969 to 3,000 MW in 1975.

Early plants were built with local financing, material, and labor. Equipment was manufactured in village shops, wood, for example, being used for turbine runners. Dams were built of earth and stone, and penstocks were constructed of cement, wood, and occasionally bamboo. The readily available labor and the large number of rural industries made it possible to build low-cost plants, but they required frequent repair and maintenance. As they began to be interconnected into regional grids, alleviating typical control and outage problems, irrigation, flood-control, and water-supply benefits from these projects began to accrue.

China's leaders are currently seeking to expand rural electrification by consolidating planning and construction. The new policy limits the local, self-help approach in favor of greater collaboration and system standardization. These steps appear to follow a pattern of rural electrification similar to that which developed in the United States in the early twentieth century.

INSTITUTIONAL CHALLENGES

One of the major impediments to widespread use of mini-hydropower systems is lack of expertise in organization and management of planning, construction, and operation. Such efforts could be organized in various ways with the costs shared among users.

An approach suggested by the Intermediate Technology Development Group, of Great Britain, is to identify industrial and agricultural users of electricity first. Thus both capital and operational costs can be economically justified through the increased productivity of certain enterprises. These systems can be built with extra capacity to serve the community as well. Local residents pay only a marginal rate for the additional capacity needed to serve them.

The use of microcomputers for analysis, design, and operation is becoming standard practice in the developed countries. This approach coupled with geographical information systems and the new software environments can easily be brought to the developing countries for local application. Several firms are also developing feasibility-study approaches using microcomputer-based methods (World Bank, 1984; Broadus, 1981; Crawford, 1981).

Today various international donor organizations such as AID, the World Bank, the United Nations Development

Program, the Inter-American Development Bank, and the Asian Development Bank have begun to consider mini-hydropower as a serious option. Planning and execution are slow processes, owing in part to lack of information on the appropriate application of this technology in rural and agricultural energy schemes. Today, however, as many countries seek solutions for their rural energy problems, small hydropower is emerging as one of them.

REFERENCES

Broadus, C. R. 1981. Hydropower computerized reconnaissance packages version 2.0. April. Washington, D.C.: U.S. Department of Energy.

Crawford, N. H., and Thurin, S. M. 1981. Hydrologic estimates for small hydroelectric projects. September. Washington, D.C.: National Rural Electric Cooperative Association.

Fritz, J. F. 1984. Mini-hydropower potential at selected sites in Kalimantan: a preliminary analysis for field evaluation. September. Setauket, N.Y.: Energy/Development International.

———. 1983. The potential of small scale hydro in developing countries. December. New York: Civil Engineering, American Society of Civil Engineers.

Holland, R. E. A., R. J. Armstrong-Evans, and K. Marshall. 1980. Community load determination, survey and system planning: Small hydroelectric plants. Washington, D.C.: National Rural Electric Cooperative Association.

World Bank. 1984. A methodology for regional assessment of small scale hydropower. May. Washington, D.C.

43. ENERGY IN IRRIGATION IN DEVELOPING COUNTRIES

Ernest T. Smerdon, Department of Civil Engineering and Lyndon Baines Johnson School of Public Affairs, University of Texas at Austin, Austin, Texas, and Edward A. Hiler, Department of Agricultural Engineering, Texas A & M Univeristy, College Station, Texas

ABSTRACT

Information is provided on the worldwide scope of irrigation, and an overview of the energy use in irrigation is given. Energy use is divided into several categories: the energy (direct and indirect) which must be expended to provide the water supply from either surface or groundwater sources, the energy required to provide the on-farm irrigation system, and, finally, the energy to operate the system. A procedure for estimating the potential energy savings from irrigation improvements is also provided.

Curves are given to show the total annual energy inputs for various types of irrigation systems, including surface, sprinkler, and trickle irrigation and a new system called low-energy precision application system (LEPA). A method of calculating the potential energy savings from improved practices is developed.

Alternate renewable energy technologies for irrigation in less developed countries (LDCs) are summarized from the standpoint of costs, dependability and risk factors, state of the technology and its suitability for LDC conditions, the supply of raw materials, and competing uses. Finally, although irrigation is energy-intensive, it is essential for high crop productivity in many developing countries. This fact must be recognized by government policymakers as a national energy policy is formulated.

INTRODUCTION

This chapter is taken from a study for the U.S. Agency for International Development (AID) that resulted in a comprehensive report (Smerdon and Hiler, 1980). In 1981 parts of that work were summarized in two papers (Smerdon and Hiler, 1981a, b). For more details on the background investigations supporting the work, the reader is directed to the 1980 AID report. This chapter updates that work and introduces new irrigation approaches designed to save energy.

WORLD IRRIGATION

The world contains approximately 13,401 million ha of land surface with crops occupying about 1,439 million ha, or about 11 percent of the land area (Framji and Mahajan, 1969). About 40 percent of the cropped land is in humid regions, about 40 percent in subhumid regions, roughly 15 percent in semiarid regions, and 5 percent in arid regions. The irrigated lands of the world exceed 210 million ha (FAO, 1983). This amounts to approximately 15 percent of the world's cropland. In addition there are more than 500 million ha of potentially irrigable land in the world if water can be provided to it. Of the world's irrigated land, more than 150 million ha are in the developing countries. The people in many of these countries are heavily dependent on irrigation for their food.

The annual energy required for irrigation in all developing countries, excluding that energy required to provide the water supply, has been projected to be 161.6×10^{15} J by 1986 (FAO, 1976). This is a 55 percent increase in the irrigation energy from that used in 1973 and is equivalent to 27 million barrels of oil per year (1 barrel = 0.159 m^3). Most of the energy used in irrigation is for pumping.

On a global basis only 15 percent of the cropland is irrigated, but it produces 30 percent of the world's food. It also provides food security against droughts such as those that have occurred in recent years in parts of Africa. The importance of irrigation in food production is clearly evident.

ENERGY USE IN IRRIGATION

Energy in irrigation includes that required for constructing the water-supply source, providing the conveyance works, installing the field irrigation systems on the farms, and operating and maintaining the system. Both the direct and the indirect energy uses must be considered. The indirect energy requirement includes the energy for manufacturing the materials in dams, canals, pumps, pipe, and equipment as well as the energy for constructing the works and building the farm irrigation systems. The direct energy uses, which are recurring energy expenditures, are those for pumping and operating the farm irrigation systems (Smerdon and Hiler, 1980).

Energy for the Water Supply

When surface water can be used, dams usually must be built and canals constructed to deliver the water to the fields. From analyses of the cost of constructing typical irrigation-supply reservoirs and associated canal sytems and the total energy required for this type of construction, it is possible to determine the total energy that must be committed to providing a surface-water supply for irrigation (Smerdon and Hiler, 1980). Expressed as the annual energy required per hectare of land to be supplied with irrigation water from surface sources, the energy requirement for developing the surface water supply is 748 MJ·ha^{-1} per year. (Energy is herein expressed in joules [J] or megajoules [MJ]. Conversions of other units are as follows: 1 MJ = 10^6 J = 239 kcal [kilocalorie] = 0.278 kWh = 948 Btu's = 1.7×10^{-4} barrels oil-equivalent = 3.4×10^{-5} kg coal-equivalent. Conversions to oil or coal are approximate and depend on the source of the oil or coal.)

When groundwater is to be used, wells must be drilled and pumping units installed. Considering the energy required to drill wells, manufacture, and install pumps and pump motors, a corresponding energy requirement to provide irrigation water from groundwater sources is determined. The figure for groundwater sources, again expressed as energy required annually per hectare served, is 1,727 MJ·ha^{-1} per year (Smerdon and Hiler, 1980).

These figures are for representative conditions for irrigation in the world. They consider the expected life of the various components in the irrigation water-supply works, and the energy requirements are, therefore, recurring annual energy needs. Therefore, for typical water-supply systems it takes an energy investment of 748 MJ·ha^{-1} per year and 1,727 MJ·ha^{-1} per year to provide the water supply from surface water and groundwater sources, respectively (these values are equivalent to 0.13 and 0.29 barrels of oil per hectare per year).

Energy to Provide Field Irrigation

Farm irrigation systems include surface irrigation of various types, sprinkler systems, and sometimes trickle systems. To determine the energy required to provide a surface irrigation system requires a determination of the energy required to construct ditches, level fields, manufacture and install the necessary equipment, and provide other inputs. For a sprinkler or trickle irrigation system the energy to manufacture all the components and install them must also be determined. These calculations have been made for nine common types of irrigation systems (Batty and Keller, 1980). The results for four typical field irrigation systems are as follows: surface irrigation, 466 MJ·ha^{-1} per year; surface irrigation with and irrigation runoff recovery system (IRRS), 1,219 MJ·ha^{-1} per year; hand-moved sprinkler, 808 MJ·ha^{-1} per year; side-roll sprinkler, 1,155 MJ·ha^{-1} per year; and trickle, 4,215 MJ·ha^{-1} per year.

Energy to Operate Irrigation Systems

The primary energy requirement to operate irrigation systems is that for pumping water. When the water supply is groundwater, pumping is always required, and the energy increases in proportion to the depth of the supply. Also, when pressurized systems such as sprinklers or tricklers are used, additional pumping energy is required. This pumping energy is in addition to that required to provide the water supply and construct the field irrigation system discussed in the preceding sections.

It is not possible to have an irrigation system without some water losses. These losses occur in seepage and leakage, evaporation, and percolation in the fields below the crop root zone and beyond reach of the crop. The greater the amount of water lost, depicted by a lower irrigation efficiency, the greater the wasted energy. Therefore, properly operated systems designed to have high irrigation efficiency save energy as well as water.

Similarly, efficient pumping systems save both money and energy. Irrigation pumps theoretically may have pump efficiencies of greater than 70 percent, but field tests of irrigation pumps in the United States show typical pump efficiencies to be between 50 and 55 percent and are often lower (Coble and LePori, 1974). Irrigation pump efficiencies in developing countries are unlikely to be higher than those in the United States and probably do not exceed 50 percent. This efficiency could be increased with properly designed and operated pumps kept in good repair. The efficiency of converting the fuel energy to mechanical energy is about 25 percent for diesel engines and electric systems (when the efficiency of power generation (33 percent), electricity transmission (85 percent), and electric motors (88 percent) are considered). This gives a typical combined efficiency

Table 1. Annual energy required for irrigation.

Irrigation System Type (% Efficiency)	Instal- lation Energy	Surface Water Supply			Ground Water—50-m Lift			Ground Water—100-m Lift		
		Energy for Supply	Pumping Energy	Total Energy	Energy for Supply[a]	Pumping Energy	Total Energy	Energy for Supply	Pumping Energy	Total Energy
Surface (50)	0.47	0.75	4.7[b]	5.9	1.29	83.3	85.0	1.72	161.8	164.0
Surface (70)	0.47	0.75	3.4[b]	4.6	1.29	59.5	61.2	1.72	115.6	117.8
Surface (85)[c]	1.22	0.75	4.6[b]	6.6	1.29	50.8	53.3	1.72	97.0	99.9
Sprinkler (75)[d]	0.81	0.75	55.5	57.1	1.29	107.9	110.0	1.72	160.1	162.6
Trickle (90)[e]	4.22	0.75	30.6	35.6	1.29	74.3	79.8	1.72	117.8	123.7
LEPA (90)[f]	1.20	0.75	14.3	16.2	1.29	58.0	60.5	1.72	101.6	104.5

SOURCE: Data in this table (except for the low-energy precision application [LEPA] system) are adapted from research in Utah (Batty and Keller, 1980). Energy figures are in gigajoules per hectare per year (1 gigajoule = 10^3 MJ = 10^9). Systems are designed to meet a peak water-use rate of 8.4 mm per day and provide 1 m net irrigation. Pump efficiency is assumed to be 50 percent and pump power unit is assumed to have a net efficiency (thermal energy to mechanical energy) of 25 percent.

[a]Energy to provide supply (drill and equip the well) for a well with a 50-m pumping lift was estimated to be 75 percent as much as for a deeper well with 100-m pumping lift.

[b]Some pumping energy is assumed even for surface irrigation with open ditch to account for friction head loss in pipe and a slight elevating of the water to the level of the ditches. In systems in which canal water is supplied at sufficient elevation to permit gravity flow, pumping energy is 0 except for the modest amount of energy required for the system with an irrigation runoff recovery system (IRRS).

[c]This is a gated pipe surface system with a pumped IRRS. These data can also be used for a surge system.

[d]A hand-moved sprinkler system.

[e]Designed for orchard crops.

[f]Low-energy precision application system (LEPA). It has an operating pressure of 140 kPa at command platform.

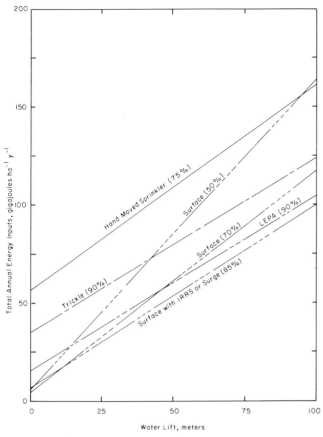

Fig. 1. Total annual energy requirement to provide 1 m net irrigation for different irrigation systems with irrigation efficiencies as indicated in parentheses. Pump efficiency is assumed to be 50 percent and net power unit efficiency (thermal energy to mechanical energy) to be 25 percent.

(pump and motor) of 12.5 percent for pumping units in converting fule (thermal) energy to lifted water for irrigation (mechanical energy) (Smerdon and Hiler, 1981a).

Using the data on total energy to provide the water supply, install the farm irrigation system, and operate the system permits curves to be drawn relating the total annual energy required per hectare to irrigate with water provided with different pumping lifts for various kinds of irrigation systems. Pumping lifts for systems supplied with surface water would be small and in some cases zero. Table 1 and Fig. 1 illustrate the results for typical irrigation systems designed to provide 1 m of net irrigation annually and satisfy a peak water use rate of 8.4 mm per day (Smerdon and Hiler, 1981a). The six irrigation systems illustrated, with assumed irrigation efficiencies in parentheses, are hand-moved sprinkler (75 percent), surface (50 percent), surface (70 percent), surface with IRRS (85 percent), trickle (90 percent), and LEPA (see below, 90 percent). Pump efficiency is 50 percent, and pump-engine efficiency is 25 percent.

The low-energy precision application irrigation system (LEPA) was introduced in 1981 by Texas A&M University (Lyle and Bordovsky, 1981). Basically it is a continuously

moving sprinkler system (side roll or center pivot) modified to distribute water at low pressure from drop tubes instead of high-pressure sprinklers. The water drops into small basins created by miniature furrow dams established with a special machine in the cultivation process. The pressure required is about 140 kPa for a 57 L·s^{-1} system. The installation energy is estimated to be 1.2 MJ, similar to that for a side-roll sprinkler system (Batty and Keller, 1980). The energy savings in experimental work with LEPA irrigation system was reported to have ranged from 43 to 86 percent compared to conventional sprinkler systems (U.S. Department of Energy, 1982). By comparison, the figures from Table 1 give a total energy savings of 36 to 72 percent compared to sprinkler systems supplied from groundwater with 100 m lift and surface water, respectively.

Surge irrigation is a recently developed surface irrigation method with considerable potential for saving both water and energy (Walker et al., 1982). It is well suited to conditions in developed countries such as the United States, where fields tend to be large with long irrigation runs. Its applicability is judged to be somewhat less in developing countries, where many farms are very small. Nonetheless, an estimate of the energy requirement for surge irrigation is presented. Surge irrigation uses gated pipes and requires extra valves to control the on-off pulsing of flow to the furrows. However, the installation energy and pumping energy would be similar or perhaps slightly less than the gated-pipe surface system with irrigation return system used in Batty's calculations (Batty et al., 1975). The expected irrigation efficiency of 85 percent for the two systems is also similar. Therefore, the same energy-use data for the surface irrigation with irrigation runoff recovery system is appropriate for the surge irrigation (see Table 1 and Fig. 1).

It is evident from Fig. 1 that the total annual energy required increases markedly with increased water lifts. This illustrates the importance of pumping lifts, including the operating pressure of pressurized systems, in irrigation energy considerations. Also, in a comparison of the surface systems, the curves dramatically show the importance of providing well-designed systems with high irrigation efficiency.

POTENTIAL ENERGY SAVINGS IN IRRIGATION

A general equation can be developed showing the energy savings of improvements in individual components of an irrigation system (Smerdon and Hiler, 1980). This equation for potential energy savings (PES) from improvements in the irrigation system, is

$$PES = \left\{ 1 - \left(\frac{D_a}{D_b}\right)\left(\frac{H_a}{H_b}\right)\left(\frac{E_b}{E_a}\right)_1\left(\frac{E_b}{E_a}\right)_2 \cdots \left(\frac{E_b}{E_a}\right)_n \right\} 100\%$$

where D is the depth of net irrigation required by the crop; H is the total head (pumping lift) required of the irrigation pump; E represents the efficiency of the various components of the irrigation system (including the pump efficiency, the efficiency of the watercourse in conveying water, and the efficiency of the irrigation application system on the farm); the subscript b indicates conditions before improvements;

the subscript a indicates the conditions afterward; and the subscript numbers outside the parentheses denote the individual components in which the efficiency is improved and any number of components, n, may be included.

As an example, assume the following: the net irrigation application is reduced from 800 to 700 mm, giving D_a/D_b = 0.875; the total head is reduced from 50 to 30 m, giving H_a/H_b = 0.60; the efficiency of the pump is increased from 0.55 to 0.67, giving $(E_b/E_a)_1$ = 0.821; the watercourse conveyance efficiency is increased from 0.50 to 0.70, giving $(E_b/E_a)_2$ = 0.714; and the efficiency of water application in the fields is increased from 0.65 to 0.80, giving $(E_b/E_a)_3$ = 0.812.

The combined effect results in the following potential energy savings:

$$PES = \{1 - (0.875)(0.60)(0.821)(0.714)(0.812)\}\,100\%$$
$$= (1 - 0.25)\,100\% = 75\%$$

Therefore, in this hypothetical case 75 percent of the energy originally used can be saved by this combination of improvements in the irrigation practices. Stated another way, only one-fourth as much energy would be required to provide irrigation as before. Although it would seldom, if ever, be possible to make all these improvements in a single system, the equation can be used to assess the magnitude of the energy savings resulting from each improvement, individually or collectively.

How might these savings occur in developing countries? It is possible through the use of improved crop varieties to reduce the water required by crops, D. The total head, H, required may be reduced by providing low-pressure irrigation systems where high-pressure systems existed before. Irrigation pumps in the field often have low efficiencies and can be repaired or replaced to markedly improve their efficiency. Watercourses can be renovated and the water-delivery efficiency thereby improved. And, finally, fields can be leveled and better on-farm irrigation practices can be installed to decrease the water losses that result from poor on-farm irrigation practices. Some of these improvements are usually feasible in developing countries, resulting in energy savings.

POTENTIAL RENEWABLE ENERGY SOURCES FOR IRRIGATION

Developing countries derive more than half their total energy from wood and agricultural or animal wastes (World Bank, 1980). The predominant power sources for irrigation have been oil and gas used in internal-combustion engines and electricity. Hydroelectric energy is important where sites suitable for hydropower are available. In the long term local applications of biomass, solar, wind, and other forms of renewable energy may hold promise of more abundant energy, but the economic costs should not be underestimated. A brief assessment of the advantages and shortcomings of each technology is presented here.

At the outset it must be emphasized that as of this time, none of these alternatives is economically competitive with energy from fossil fuels (oil, gas, coal), nuclear power, or hydroelectric power, where it is available. This is particularly true for an operation such as the irrigation of agricultural crops in which the amount of energy required for pumping can be very great, as shown in Fig. 1.

Much of the developing world has ample solar energy and a considerable potential for biomass resources (Stout, 1979). These resources are best suited to helping meet the widespread need for small, decentralized sources of energy in places where, because of lack of conventional energy supplies, renewable sources could prove to be economical earlier than in the industrialized countries (World Bank, 1980). However, it must be stressed that the economics of renewable energy resources for pumping irrigation water in developing countries are dependent on many yet unproved factors.

It is difficult to generalize about the economic feasibility of alternate fuels. The economics of biomass fuels are site-specific and depend heavily on feedstock cost and availability, end use, transport distances of feedstock, and a host of other factors (OTA, 1980). Solar- and wind-power costs are also very site-specific, depending on abundance of solar or wind resources. Given that solar, wind, and biomass resources are available in abundance, rankings are made regarding energy production costs based on currently available technology (Smerdon and Hiler, 1980). These rankings, which consider the likelihood that a technology will be suited to developing countries, are (1) wind (40 to 240 kW range), (2) biomass (all technologies), and (3) direct solar energy. Within biomass the ranking is as follows: (1) direct combustion, (2) gasification, (3) methane production, (4) plant oils, and (5) ethanol production.

Pyrolysis is not technologically developed to the extent that a meaningful ranking can be made. Direct solar conversion with current technology is much more expensive (five to ten times) than any of the other conversion technologies, though research and development breakthroughs could change this. It should be reiterated, however, that in general none of these technologies compete well with present conventional energy sources (fossil fuels, nuclear power, and hydropower). An exception might be wind energy at ideal sites with consistent winds of greater than 19 km per hour.

For irrigation purposes the source of power must be dependable because the entire crop can be lost if water is not applied at critical growth stages. Usually both solar- and wind-power depend on intermittent sources of energy, and some energy-storage mechanism is needed if these are to be the sole sources of power for irrigation.

Research and development efforts are continuing for all the alternate energy technologies. Wind conversion and direct combustion technologies are the most advanced at this time, followed by methane production, gasification, ethanol production, and solar-power technology. Plant-oil extraction is a simple process, but not as much research and development effort has been made in this area using simple screw presses. This technology could rapidly move ahead of the others with appropriate research and development emphasis, but much remains to be accomplished before the technology can be generally applied.

Very few of the alternate energy technologies score well

in terms of suitability for developing country conditions. Direct combustion, gasification, methane production, and windmills would rank highest on a "suitability" list, with plant-oil extraction having great promise, but all still have many problems to be solved. The "solar pond" technology coupled with photovoltaic cells and wind turbine generators is fairly complex and likely to remain very expensive. Ethanol production comes next on the list, pyrolysis being least suitable with the current technology.

Solar- and wind-energy sources, where abundantly available, have a distinct advantage over biomass energy sources in that they have no competing uses, such as for food and fiber. If a surplus exists or more biomass can be grown over and above the needs for human and animal diets, they may be considered for fuels. But if biomass is used for fuel, its impact on food prices and availability must be very carefully considered (OTA, 1980).

Many forms of biomass are not edible by humans and are undesirable as animal feed or fiber. Also, some waste biomass products, such as municipal solid wastes and food-processing wastes, require an expenditure to dispose of them, and conversion of such wastes to useful fuels should be explored. However, in developing countries such wastes are to a large extent already recycled, burned for fuel, or otherwise consumed. Moreover, many by-products or residues are put to alternate uses, such as being returned to the soil for plant nutrients and erosion control. If biomass is to be used for fuel, its value as a fuel must compete with alternate uses, particularly food—a critical issue in any food-deficient nation.

The probability is not high that in the next fifteen years there will be significant changes in the source of energy supplies that support irrigation in the developing nations. There will be expansion of the experimental irrigation pumping systems using solar energy and other renewable energy sources. There are more than sixty small photovoltaic pumping systems over the world (Halcrow, 1979). The water output of these solar pumps will likely continue to be small, on the order of 100 m^3 per day or less, and of local importance but not of sufficient magnitude to have any significant worldwide impact. It is questionable that solar pumping technology will have advanced within the next ten years to make the systems economically justified under free-market conditions except in rare circumstances.

Supplies of biomass energy sources in developing countries will continue in short supply in arid and semiarid nations. This factor, coupled with the food-fuel conflict, will restrict use of biomass fuels for irrigation on a widespread basis even though the technology will have advanced to make it practical in many settings. Wind energy will be utilized to a greater extent in locations where adequate wind resources are available.

Although there will be many advances in irrigation in the next fifteen years, the most likely actions to reduce energy use in irrigation during this term will be reducing irrigation water losses and improving the efficiency of the irrigation systems.

In the period from fifteen to forty years hence there will likely be several practical solar-powered pumping systems.

Two of the systems judged to be the most probable are solar ponds, which could power relatively large irrigation pumps, and small solar photovoltaic systems. It is not farfetched to think that the cost of solar photovoltaic arrays may have decreased in price to between $150 and $250 (1980 U.S. dollars) per peak kilowatt by 1995 or soon thereafter (Halcrow, 1979). This is still quite expensive as an irrigation power source in developing countries. The photovoltaic collector arrays should be more durable and dependable by that time and have better-adapted motors. In our judgment the biomass energy uses will still not be overly promising owing to the competition for biomass materials and the continuation of the food-fuel conflict.

In looking at energy in irrigation in developing countries, three issues are of primary importance. First, there must be a clear understanding of the magnitude of the total energy requirements in irrigation as well as the critical nature of the timing of these energy demands. Second, the level of technological sophistication required for on-farm irrigation powered by alternate energy sources must be carefully assessed so that systems do not fail because the technology, and all of its potential problems, were not understood. Finally, the total economic costs must be carefully considered to ensure that systems are not proposed that are well beyond the reasonable economic reach of farmers in developing countries.

CONCLUSIONS

This report provides data on the general magnitude of energy requirements for various types of irrigation systems supplied from surface-water or groundwater sources. The surface irrigation systems require the least energy to operate and are also the least expensive to construct. Therefore, in developing countries, when soil and topographic conditions permit and when the system is well designed and managed, surface irrigation is the best choice from both energy and monetary-cost considerations. Above all, the water losses in irrigation should be reduced as much as possible so that the energy invested in providing the supply and pumping the water is not wasted. Although alternate renewable energy sources may serve irrigation in developing countries, many technological and economic problems remain to be solved before widespread use of alternate energy sources can be expected.

The energy demands for irrigation, or other agricultural needs, in a developing country cannot be viewed in isolation from the other energy requirements of the nation. In arid nations or in nations with long dry seasons irrigation is quite likey an essential input for increasing food production. This very circumstance exists in much of the developing world (Hargreaves, 1977). Government policymakers must realistically assess the energy which their nation's agriculture (including irrigation) will require to meet the food-production goals. Ensuring energy for agriculture may be a most critical policy decision. For irrigation, logical steps to achieve the goals should be identified and followed. The first and most important is to improve farm irrigation systems to minimize waste of water and energy.

ACKNOWLEDGMENT

The authors wish to acknowledge the U.S. Agency for International Development, Project No. 930-0091, under which the work reported herein was conducted.

REFERENCES

Batty, J. C., and J. Keller. 1980. Energy requirements for irrigation. Pp. 35–44. *In* David Pimentel (ed.) Handbook of energy utilization in agriculture. Boca Raton, Fla.: CRC press.

Batty, J. C., S. N. Hamad, and J. Keller. 1975. Energy inputs to irrigation. *Journal of the Irrigation and Drainage Division, American Society of Civil Engineers* 101:293–307.

Coble, C. G., and W. A. LePori. 1974. Energy consumption, conservation, and projected needs for Texas agriculture. Report S/D-12. College Station: Texas Agricultural Experiment Station.

FAO [Food and Agriculture Organization]. 1976. Energy and agriculture. Pp. 81–111. *In* The state of food and agriculture, 1976. FAO Agriculture Series, no. 4. Rome.

———. 1983. 1982 FAO production yearbook. Vol. 36. Rome.

Framji, K. K., and I. K. Nahajan. 1969. Irrigation and drainage in the world. International Commission on Irrigation and Drainage.

Gilley, J. R., and R. J. Supalla. 1983. Economic analysis of energy saving practices in irrigation. *Transactions of the American Society of Agricultural Engineers* 26:1784–92.

Halcrow, W. 1979. Testing and demonstration of small-scale solar-powered pumping systems: State-of-the-art report. UNDP Project GLO/78/004. Washington, D.C.: World Bank.

Hargreaves, G. 1977. World water for agriculture. Logan: Utah State University.

Lyle, W. M., and J. P. Bordovsky. 1981. Low energy precision application (LEPA) irrigation system. *Transactions of the American Society of Agricultural Engineers* 24:1241–45.

OTA [Office of Technology Assessment]. 1980. Energy from biological processes. Vol. 2. Technical and environmental analyses. OTA-E-128. Washington, D.C.: Government Printing Office.

Smerdon, E. T., and E. A. Hiler. 1980. Energy in irrigation in developing countries: Report to Agency for International Development. Project 930-0091. Washington, D.C.: National Technical Information Service.

———. 1981a. Energy use in irrigation. Pp. 1837–95. *In* Proceedings of the 3rd international conference on energy use management. Oxford: Pergamon Press.

———. 1981b. Energy in irrigation in developing countries. *In* Energy in agriculture. London: Elsevier.

Stout, B. A. 1979. Energy for world agriculture. Rome: Food and Agricultural Organization.

U.S. Department of Energy. 1982. Conserving energy through new irrigation technologies. Technical briefing report by Battelle Northwest. PNL-4339. Washington, D.C.: Office of Industrial Programs, U.S. Department of Energy.

Walker, W. R., A. A. Bishop, and A. S. Humphreys. 1982. Energy and water conservation with surge flow. American Society of Agricultural Engineers Paper 82-2101.

World Bank. 1980. Energy in the developing countries. Washington, D.C.

44. ENERGY REQUIREMENTS AND MANAGEMENT FOR PUMPING IRRIGATION WATER

James R. Gilley and Raymond J. Supalla, University of Nebraska, Lincoln, Nebraska

ABSTRACT

The energy used for pumping and distributing irrigation water has an impact on a significant portion of the irrigated land in the United States. In those areas where irrigation is required for continuous agricultural production, the energy use for irrigation may approach 75 percent of the total energy demnands of crop production. The relatively large energy demands of irrigation systems supplied with water which must be pumped (groundwater) and the rapid expansion of pressurized irrigation systems have provided impetus to the development of improved energy management of current irrigation systems as well as increased energy considerations in the design of new systems.

Potential enegy-conserving practices include reductions in the volume of water pumped, reductions in total dynamic head, and improvements in the efficiencies of the pump, drive, and power units. Many potential areas of improvement are not realistically available to existing systems, and not all the practices are economically viable in all situations. However, depending on the initial energy efficiency of irrigation systems, several procedures are economically attractive and are being undertaken at the present time.

INTRODUCTION

With modern irrigation equipment and current irrigation management technology, it is possible to apply water precisely and at the correct time. Yet the incorporation of this technology often requires a significant expenditure of energy for its effective use. Because of intensive energy requirements the profitability of pumped irrigation is highly sensitive to energy prices. Thus, efficient energy utilization is an important consideration in the management of irrigated agriculture.

Many of the energy-saving practices available to irrigators require capital investments to improve the operation of the sytem. Thus the decision to incorporate these practices must consider not only the energy savings from a particular change or adjustments but also the economic feasibility of such alternatives. The primary purpose of this chapter is to evaluate alternative energy-saving practices, given a range of irrigation-system characteristics. More specifically, the objectives are to (1) estimate the energy requirements for irrigation pumping plants, (2) estimate the potential energy savings from selected management, and (3) analyze the economic feasibility of selected practices.

ENERGY REQUIREMENTS FOR PUMPING PLANTS

Whenever irrigation water is pumped, energy is consumed. The amount of energy used depends on the efficiency with which water is pumped, distributed, and used on the farm. The energy required can be calculated as follows:

$$PE_d = (C_1 \, H \, D_n \, A) / (E_i \, E_p \, E_o \, E_e)$$

where PE_d is the pumping plant input energy requirement, in megajoules; H is the total dynamic head on the pump, in meters ($H = L + 0.102 \, P$); L is the pumping lift plus the column and distribution pipe and other friction losses, in meters; P is the system pressure in Kilo Pascals; D_n is the net amount of irrigation water applied, in millimeters; A is the effective irrigated area, in hectares; E_i is the irrigation efficiency, or the fraction of the pumped water that is stored in the crop root zone, expressed as a decimal ($E_i = D_n/D_g$); D_g is the gross amount of irrigation water pumped, in millimeters; E_p is the pump efficiency, decimal; E_o is the efficiency of the gearhead and drive shaft, etc., if present, decimal; E_e is the efficiency of the power unit (engine or motor), decimal; and C_1 is a conversion factor to account for the units, 0.0979. The amount of fuel required to drive the irrigation pumping plant can be found by dividing equation (1) by the energy content of the particular fuel used (column 2 of Table 1) and is given in column 5 of Table 1.

To provide a means of comparing the results of field tests of pumping plants (pump and power unit), Schleusener and Sulek (1959) proposed a performance criteria for each of the fuel types. Measurements of the parameters E_o and E_e in equation (1) were combined with an assumed pump efficiency ($E_p = 0.75$) to calculate the fuel requirements of an average pumping plant. These results are given as the performance criteria in Table 1 (K_f). Thus the fuel requirements of any irrigation pumping plant can be found by

$$FR = C_1 \, H \, D_n \, A/(E_i \, K_f \, R)$$

where Fr is the actual fuel used, in fuel units (liters, kilowatt-hours, cubic meters); K_f is the Nebraska performance criteria given in Table 1, in megajoules per unit of fuel; and R is the performance rating of the pumping plant, expressed as a decimal.

The performance rating is further defined as

$$R = FR_c/FR_a$$

where FR_c is the amount of fuel used by a pumping plant meeting the criteria; and FR_a is the actual fuel used by the pumping plant. The performance rating, R, is an indicator

Table 1. Energy content, power-unit output, and performance criteria of irrigation pumping plants.

Fuel Type	Representative Energy Content	Power Unit Brake Energy Output per Unit of Fuel[a]	Performance Criteria[b] (K_f)	Fuel Used per 1,000-m³ Volume and 100-m Lift
Diesel	39.02 MJ·L⁻¹	11.81 MJ·L⁻¹	8.86 MJ·L⁻¹	111 L
Propane	26.34 MJ·L⁻¹	6.51 MJ·L⁻¹	4.88 MJ·L⁻¹	210 L
Natural gas	34.46 MJ/m³	7.79 MJ/m³	5.84 MJ/m³	168 m³
Gasoline	34.56 MJ·L⁻¹	8.16 MJ·L⁻¹	6.12 MJ·L⁻¹	160 L
Electricity	3.60 MJ·kWh⁻¹	3.26 MJ·kWh⁻¹	2.45 MJ·kWh⁻¹	400 kWh

[a]Nebraska performance criteria, water energy per unit of fuel, modified from Gilley and Watts (1977).

[b]Fuel requirements of a pumping plant with a performance rating of 1 (pump efficiency of 0.75).

of the efficiency of a pumping plant; that is, if R = 1, the plant has a fuel consumption equal to that of a pumping plant meeting the Nebraska criteria. If the value of R is less than unity, the pumping plant is using more fuel than the criteria.

ALTERNATIVE ENERGY MANAGEMENT PRACTICES

The fuel requirement of irrigation pumping plants is calculated by equation (2) and is dependent on: (1) volume of water pumped ($D_n A/E_i$); (2) total dynamic head (H = L + 0.102 P); and (3) pumping-plant performance (R), which includes pump, drive, and power-unit efficiencies (E_p, E_o, and E_e). Reductions in fuel requirements for pumping water can be achieved by improving the performance of the pumping plant, reducing the volume of water pumped, and/or reducing the total dynamic head. A thorough discussion of these improvements has been presented by Gilley (1983) and is summarized here.

In addition to the topics described herein, three other possible cost- and energy-saving areas related to irrigation are off-peak irrigation scheduling to reduce peak electrical demands, reduction of nitrogen losses through reduction of deep-percolation losses, and reduced tillage practices.

Improved Pumping-Plant Performance

While some energy is required to operate or propel the irrigation system, most irrigation energy demands are for the pumping plant. Thus an efficiently designed and operating pumping unit is necessary to minimize this energy requirement. The specific fuel requirements for a pumping plant with a performance level that can reasonably be obtained by pumps, engines, or motors and drives that have average or above-average efficiency are given in Table 1.

Many of the pumping plants in the field have fuel efficiencies far below those given in Table 1. The primary causes of poor fuel performance are reduced pump, driver, or power-unit efficiency, including pumps mismatched for either flow rate or total head; improper maintenance of pump and power unit; improper sizing of power unit; and excessive wear of pump and engine.

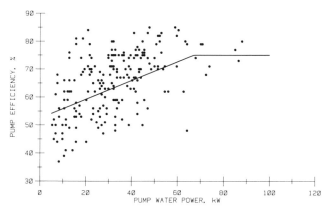

Fig. 1. Irrigation pump field efficiencies (data from Lundstrom et al., 1980; Schroeder and Fischbach, 1983).

Several field tests on irrigation pumping plants have been conducted over the last few years and are summarized in Fig. 1. The data were collected with the use of a torquemeter, which permits distinguishing between the pump- and power-unit efficiencies. A good design and installation yields a pump efficiency approaching 75 percent. The field data given in Fig. 1 indicate that improvement is needed and achievable.

Criteria similar to those given in Table 1 were used by Schleusener and Sulek (1959) as a basis for appraising the field performance of 209 pumping plants. The average performance rating of the pumping plants was 0.75. Lundstrom et al. (1980) found average performance ratings of pumping plants of 0.87 in North Dakota. Schroeder and Fischbach (1983) summarized the results of field tests taken from 1980 to 1982 and found an average rating of 0.77.

Reduced Pumping Volume

A reduction in volume of water pumped (A D_n/E_i) will yield a corresponding reduction in fuel used to pump irrigation water, even if no other changes are made to the pumping plant or irrigation system. Reductions in total water pumped (gross irrigation depth) can be achieved through improvements in irrigation efficiency (E_{i1}/E_{i2}) or reductions in net irrigation applications (D_{n2}/D_{n1}). Separation of the benefits of these two components is extremely difficult in the field and for discussion purposes will be combined.

The net irrigation requirements of a particular crop are relatively independent of the type of irrigation system. However, the amount of water that must be pumped (gross irrigation, D_n/E_i) is dependent on the type of irrigation system (Batty et al., 1975) and the particular irrigation water management practices used by the operator. The efficiency of a particular type of irrigation system may change during the growing season. Thus it is difficult to specify completely the irrigation efficiency values to be used in the preceding equations.

There are instances in which selection of an improper irrigation system coupled with inadequate irrigation water management has created reduced irrigation efficiencies. In these instances significant improvements in irrigation efficiencies can result in reduced energy consumption. A shift in method of irrigation from one of relatively low efficiency to one of higher efficiency will, of course, depend on the economics of the given situation. As energy costs increase, such systems may become more attractive in selected applications.

Irrigation scheduling procedures calculating both the amount and time of the net irrigation have been used to reduce the quantity of water pumped without yield reductions in several locations (Stegman and Ness, 1974; Heermann et al., 1976). These studies have indicated that water-balance methods of irrigation scheduling could save between 15 and 35 percent of the water normally pumped in semiarid to subhumid climates. More complex irrigation scheduling methods incorporating plant sensors, remote sensing, and other procedures may further reduce the average annual irrigation requirement when compared with other, simpler scheduling procedures. Although the total area under some form of irrigation service is relatively small compared with the total area being irrigated, the concept of improved water management has been shown to be beneficial and is rapidly increasing in importance.

Additional savings of water and energy are possible if the irrigations are limited in such a way that the crop will suffer some moisture stress during part or all of the growing season. Stegman et al. (1981) suggested that it is usually possible to select an efficient scheduling process to produce the maximum yield for the attainable level of water use. However, only a relatively few irrigation management regimes are of primary interest because net profit is frequently maximized near the maximum yield level.

Reduced Pumping Head

Reductions in total pumping head can be achieved by (1) reduced-pressure sprinkler systems, (2) replacement of sprinkler systems with surface systems, (3) substitution of surface water for groundwater, (4) pipeline modifications to reduce friction losses, and (5) design changes in irrigation wells to reduce head losses. Many of these methods will not be feasible in all situations. In particular, the replacement of sprinkler systems with surface sytems may not be possible because of costs or topography. In fact, there is a growing trend to replace surface systems with sprinkler systems because of improved efficiency and reduced labor requirements. Efficient well designs and pipeline distribution systems to reduce head loss should be used in all irrigation systems, and yet modification of these components in existing systems is extremely difficult, and replacement is costly. In established systems these two energy-saving practices are limited to replacement wells and pipelines.

Reducing the pressure of sprinkler systems is another method which can be adopted to save energy. Conversion of conventional high-pressure sprinkler systems to reduced-pressure systems may require redesigning at a considerable expense, and management practices such as set times or irrigation depths will also have to be changed. In all cases the energy savings resulting from reduced pressure must be greater than the cost of additional equipment and the extra labor required for more frequent moves of the systems.

Reducing the pressure of center-pivot systems will also save energy. However, there may be management problems caused by increased runoff and soil erosion caused by the higher application rates from reduced-pressure systems. Gilley (1984) presented a general guide for allowable irrigation amounts on different soils and various reduced-pressure systems. This guide indicates that because of small allowable irrigation amounts, some low-pressure devices may not be practical for some soil and slope conditions, especially on fine-textured soils. If, however, the soil surface can be increased by artificial means or if the spray systems are modified by booms to provide wider spray patterns, spray nozzles can still be used. Microbasins (Lyle and Bordovsky, 1979) provide the artificial surface storage needed to store the water that is applied at rates exceeding the soil intake rate.

The costs of converting a center pivot to a reduced-pressure system must be evaluated. In some instances costly changes in the pump and power unit may be necessary, and these costs must be included in the economic analysis of reduced-pressure systems. The energy requirements of the end-gun booster pump, while small, should also be added when reduced pressure is considered.

Combined Effects of Irrigation Management

The energy savings from various combinations of reductions in volume of water pumped, reductions in total head, and improvements in pump performance are shown in Fig. 2. Depending on the initial conditions of the various components of equation (1), the application of these energy-reducing practices can result in significant energy savings. Annual energy savings of between 15 and 50 percent for surface irrigation systems and savings of between 10 and 45 percent for sprinkler irrigation systems are possible, depending on the initial conditions and the energy-reduction procedures used (Gilley and Watts, 1977).

ECONOMIC EVALUATION OF IRRIGATION MANGEMENT PRACTICES

Many of the energy-saving practices require capital investments to improve the operation of the irrigation system

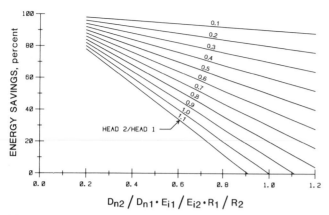

Fig. 2. Energy savings from combined improvements in irrigation management practices.

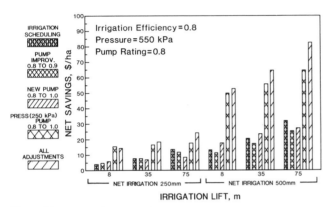

Fig. 3. Net economic benefits from various energy-saving practices for center-pivot sprinkler systems.

the financial savings depended on the energy savings, the price of the particular fuel used, and the costs associated with the various modifications.

In general, however, it was found that irrigators wishing to conserve energy should first reduce the pressure requirements (accompanied by a pump adjustment), then incorporate irrigation scheduling, and only as a final action attempt to reduce water application through improvements in irrigation efficiency (Fig. 3). It should be pointed out, however, that the irrigation efficiency did not change with reduced pressure. This analysis also indicated that it paid to make all the available adjustments only when lifts or irrigation water requirements were high.

Surface Irrigation Systems

Gilley and Supalla (1983) also analyzed the economic feasibility of these energy conservation options (except for low pressure) for surface irrigation systems. As with sprinkler systems, the specific results depended on initial conditions and prices, but in general it was found that improvements in pump performance were nearly always economically attractive. Second on a scale of financially attractive adjustments were improvements from irrigation scheduling. Improving irrigation efficiency was much less attractive in all situations and did not become profitable until lifts were relatively large, and then the gains were small, especially if the pump performance had already been improved.

or pumping plant. Thus it is not sufficient to consider only the energy savings resulting from particular modifications or adjustments; the economic feasibility of each modification must also be considered. An economic analysis of alternative irrigation management practices for both surface and center-pivot sprinkler irrigation systems was developed by Gilley and Supalla (1983). While the data used in their analysis centered around conditions found in the Great Plains states, the procedures they developed can be used to determine the economic feasibility of various energy-saving practices in other locations.

Sprinkler Irrigation Systems

Gilley and Supalla (1983) analyzed the major energy-conservation practices available to center-pivot irrigators, including (1) improved irrigation efficiency, (2) reduced pumping volume through improved water management (irrigation scheduling), (3) reduced-pressure systems, and (4) improved pump performance or replacement. The energy savings resulting from incorporation of these practices depended on the conditions under which the existing irrigation system was operating and the magnitude of the improvements which could be made to the system. Likewise,

REFERENCES

Batty, J. C., S. N. Hamad, and J. Keller. 1975. Energy inputs to irrigation. *Journal of Irrigation and Drainage Division, American Society of Civil Engineers* 101 (IR4):293–307.

Gilley, J. R. 1983. Energy utilization and management in irrigation. Pp. 31–59. *In* Daniel Hillel (ed.) Advances in irrigation. New York: Academic Press.

———. 1984. Suitability of reduced pressure center-pivots. *Journal of Irrigation and Drainage Engineering, American Society of Civil Engineers* 110 (1):22–34.

Gilley, J. R., and R. J. Supalla. 1983. Economic analysis of energy saving practices in irrigation. *Transactions of the American Society of Agricultural Engineers* 26 (6):1784–91.

Gilley, J. R., and D. G. Watts. 1977. Possible energy savings in irrigation. *Journal of Irrigation and Drainage Division, American Society of Civil Engineers* 103 (1R4):445–57.

Heermann, D. F., Haise, H. R., and R. H. Mickelson. 1976. Scheduling center-pivot sprinkler irrigation systems for corn production in eastern Colorado. *Transactions of the American Society of Agricultural Engineers* 19 (2):284–87, 293.

Lundstrom, D. R., W. E. Burbank, and R. C,. Bartholomay. 1980. Operating efficiency of recently installed irrigation pumping plants. American Society of Agricultural Engineers paper 80-2552.

Lyle, W. M., and J. P. Bordovsky. 1979. Traveling low energy precision irrigator. Pp. 121–31. *In* Proceedings of the American Society of Civil Engineers, Irrigation and Drainage Division, speciality conference, 1979.

Schleusener, P. E., and J. J. Sulek. 1959. Criteria for appraising the performance of irrigation pumping plants. *Agricultural Engineering* 40 (9):550–51.

Schroeder, M. A., and P. E. Fischbach. 1983. Improving the efficiency of irrigation pumping plants. American Society of Agricultural Engineers paper 83-5009.

Stegman, E. C., and L. D. Ness. 1974. Evaluation of alternative scheduling schemes for center pivot sprinkler systems. North Dakota Agricultural Experiment Station research report 48.

Stegman, E. C., R. J. Hanks, J. T. Musick, and D. G. Watts. 1981. Irrigation water management-adequate or limited water. Pp. 154–65. *In* Proceedings of the American Society of Agricultural Engineers, 2nd national irrigation symposium.

45. WIND-ENERGY SYSTEMS FOR PUMPING WATER

R. Nolan Clark, U.S. Department of Agriculture, Conservation and Production Research Laboratory, Bushland, Texas

ABSTRACT

For centuries Asians have used windmills to lift water for growing crops, while Europeans have used windmills to pump drainage water for land reclamation. Americans have used wind power primarily for year-round water supply for livestock and domestic needs. The type of windmill used depended on the pumping application and the design of the pump. Screw and paddle-wheel pumps used in drainage pumping required large mills with rotating shafts, while deep-well pumps required smaller mills with reciprocating shafts.

Wind-powered pumping systems with reciprocating pumps are used with the American multibladed design because it offers a high starting torque and the self-regulation in high winds needed by the piston pump. Even though several improvements have been made in the windmill, the pump is almost identical to ones used a century ago. Rotary- or scoop-paddle pumps are used in pumping irrigation or drainage water where lifts are less than 1.5 m.

Both electrical and mechanical wind-powered pumping systems that operate in conjunction with the electric utility or diesel engine and as stand-alone systems have been developed. The electrical systems, both utility-interconnected and stand-alone, are better than the mechanical systems because they will allow more flexibility in optimizing the windmill output.

INTRODUCTION

The origin of the windmill is unknown, but Cretans and Asians were the first to use a fixed-sail type to pump water and grind grain. Most of these early units were small, less than 5 m in diameter, with sails, reeds, or boards for rotors. Europeans began using wind power about the thirteenth century and by the 1700s had developed the post and tower mills. The Dutch are famous for their use of windmills to reclaim land for agricultural production. Dutch windmills were mostly made of wood, and the sails were made of canvas stretched over a wooden frame (Fig. 1). Rotor diameters were approximately 25 m, and water was lifted 1 to 1.5 m.

Windmill development in the United States began with duplications of the European designs, but these machines did not provide the flexibility needed to withstand the fickle weather of the Midwest and provide for deep-well pumping. The first American-designed machines used self-regulating paddle-shaped blades that pivoted or feathered as the wind speed increased. Major changes in wind rotors occurred during the early 1900s with the development of metal fans and enclosed gears. These drag-type windmills have proved to be a reliable and low-cost means of pumping water, primarily from wells. These multibladed units have a fan diameter of between 2 and 6 m and can lift water in excess of 100 m.

The water-flow requirements for different agricultural uses vary from 0.13 L·s^{-1} for range cattle to more than 1.0 L·s^{-1} for irrigation. Domestic uses normally require less than 0.30 L·s^{-1} for a household of fewer than five members. Because of similar flow rates and pump designs, domestic pumping and livestock pumping are usually treated together. Wind-powered pumps for domestic and livestock water have primarily been the piston type, whereas the screw pump or paddle-wheel pump has been used for wind-powered irrigation and drainage. The type of pump used has dictated the design of the windmill rotor and power transfer shaft, creating a unique water-pumping system. The Dutch windmill and the American multibladed windmill are good examples of a total pumping system designed for particular applications.

RECIPROCATING PUMPS

The piston pump is the most common type of reciprocating pump used with windmills. This pump consists of a plunger with an internal valve moving up and down in a fixed cylinder. The diameter of the cylinder and the length of the plunger stroke are the major factors that determine the volume of water pumped. Cylinder sizes range from 47 to 100 mm and are usually one size smaller than the drop pipe to allow easy access of the plunger through the pipe into the cylinder. A check valve at the bottom of the cylinder holds water in the pipe so that water is pumped on each stroke (New Mexico Energy Institute, 1978). This column of water creates a large starting torque requirement for the windmill.

The piston pump is normally used to lift water from wells, with pumping lifts from a few meters to more than 100 m. Typical flow rates using a 47-mm cylinder and a 30-m lift would be 0.25 L·s^{-1} in wind speeds above 5 m·s^{-1}. The pump is used primarily with the multibladed windmill, which produces a large torque at low rotational speeds. At high wind speeds the damping effect of the pump rod working up and down in a column of water somewhat retards overspeeding of the windmill rotor.

Windmills like the one shown in Fig. 2 have been used since the 1930s to provide water for livestock and domestic uses. Some type of storage reservoir is used to provide water during times of low winds and maintenance. These units are manufactured primarily in Argentina, Australia, South Africa, and the United States—many with almost identical designs and constructed entirely of metal. Through the years these units have proved to be a reliable and economical means of providing water, especially where electricity is not readily available.

Researchers and manufacturers have attempted to increase the efficiency of these multibladed water pumpers by adding counterweights, springs, and cams to reduce the

Fig. 1. Seventeenth-century Dutch water-pumping windmill used for land drainage.

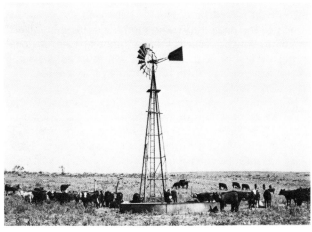

Fig. 2. Multibladed windmill used to pump water from deep wells for livestock and domestic uses.

starting torque. The purpose of counterweights and springs is to offset the static load on the windmill from the weight of the pump rods and the standing water in the discharge pipe (McKenzie, 1984). These efforts have reduced the wind speed required for starting, but the extra costs have not proved beneficial. The automatic stroke control has more promise than any other recent modification. This device helps adjust the pump load to better match the windmill output. Additional work is needed before this device is ready for widespread use.

Wind-powered pumping systems using the all-metal, multibladed windmill and piston pump have not been adapted worldwide because many areas cannot afford the high cost of an all-metal, imported machine. Several groups have been working on developing low-cost, locally constructed water-pumping windmills. They include Consultancy Services Wind Energy Developing Countries (CWD), of the Netherlands; the Intermediate Technology Development Group (ITDG), of Great Britain; and Volunteers in Technical Assistance (VITA), of the United States. CWD has been successful in developing a low-cost machine that

Fig. 3. Windmill designed by CWD, Netherlands, for manufacture and installation in developing countries.

Fig. 4. Multibladed windmill used to pump water in Peru. Water is lifted 2 m by this 100-mm-diameter pump.

will produce 0.75 to 2 L·s⁻¹ against a lift of 1 to 5 m (Fig. 3). Much of this new effort has been directed toward the countries of southern Asia and Africa, where many pumping lifts are less than 10 m (Veldhuizen, 1981).

Local groups in many countries have developed low-cost, locally made windmills similar to the one shown in Fig. 4. Metal and wood are the predominant materials for the windmill, and almost all of the pumps are made of brass or similar metal. Countries with few construction materials and individuals with few manufacturing skills have built units constructed of wood and canvas. Pumps are usually of the rotary rather than the piston type.

ROTARY PUMPS

The screw, paddle, gear, and vane pumps are examples of rotary pumps, but only the screw and paddle-scoop pumps are primarily used with windmills. Many old Dutch windmills use the screw pump to lift the water from one canal to another. Oftentimes several screw pumps are used in series to lift the water from a polder to a reservoir at a higher level. Each pump will normally lift water about 1.5 to 1.75 m at a rate of 1000 L·s⁻¹ in a moderate wind. The screw and the

paddle scoop are not used much today because they require large wind turbines that are more costly than large engines or electric motors. However, they have proved to be an effective means of providing drainage pumping where there is some flexibility in pumping times.

Some developing countries are constructing wind-driven rotary pumps using flaps made from old automobile tires. The rubber flaps are rotated and act as scoop paddles, allowing small windmills to be used (Nelson and Caldera, 1984).

CENTRIFUGAL- OR AXIAL-FLOW PUMPS

Centrifugal- or axial-flow pumps were developed to operate with electric motors and internal-combustion engines that operate at a constant speed. When these pumps are operated at a constant speed, they have a much improved efficiency over reciprocating or rotary pumps and allow users to pump large volumes of water from a variety of pumping lifts. These pumps are used almost exclusively for irrigation and municipal pumping in countries around the world where either electricity or petroleum products are available for fuel. Two operating characteristics that are important when these pumps are considered for use with wind energy are the low starting torque and the requirement for constant speed. Modern windmills with slimline rotors produce little torque in low winds and can easily stall when they are overloaded.

The USDA–Agricultural Research Service, Bushland, Texas, has been examining the feasibility of using modern, high-speed wind rotors to power centrifugal-type irrigation pumps. These systems include pumps that incorporate conventional power sources with wind power and are called "wind-assist" and "stand-alone" wind-powered pumps. Boht electrical and mechanical systems using horizontal-axis and vertical-axis units have been examined. In each instance at least 20 L·s⁻¹ were pumped to irrigate crops, with pumping lifts varying from 5 to 105 m.

Electrical Wind-Assist Systems

A wind turbine operating in a wind-assist mode will supply power to the loads, the excess being passed through the meters into the utility system. If additional power is needed, it is supplied by the utility. The main advantages of the wind-assist pumping concept is that it allows for constant-speed operation of the pump, and water can be pumped regardless of the wind speed. A disadvantage is that it requires a connection to the electric utility with associated demand charges.

Electricity-generating wind machines usually have either an induction generator or a synchronous inverter which interfaces with the electric utility. In 1984 more than 90 percent of the electrical wind machines sold were of the induction-generator type (Fig. 5). Because the induction generator uses the utility line for its excitation, the generator operates at a constant speed, thus maintaining the wind rotor at near-constant rotational speeds. The main components of the system are wind rotor, gearbox, generator, controller, and brake. With this generating sytem any electric pump can be operated without modification.

Data from machines operated by the USDA-ARS indicate that the wind generator must have a rated capacity as

Fig. 5. Modern electrical-generating wind machine used to provide electrical power for centrifugal irrigation pumps.

large as that of the pump motor to provide a significant enough amount of energy to make the system feasible, unless the system is used for more than seasonal irrigation pumping. Machines normally operate 5,500 hours a year, or 64 percent of the time, in regions where the average wind speed is 6 m·s^{-1} (Clark and Vosper, 1985). Electricity-generating units with induction generators average 20 to 25 percent of their rated capacity.

Mechanical Wind-Assist Systems

Two mechanical wind-assist pumping systems have been developed and tested by USDA-ARS, Bushland. In each system a vertical-axis wind turbine was mechanically coupled to a combination gear drive, which in turn was used to power a deep-well line-shaft turbine pump. The first experiment used an electric motor in combination with the wind turbine, and the second experiment used a diesel engine. An overrunning clutch was used to synchronize the speed of the two power units and prevented the engine from transferring power to the wind turbine. The wind turbine reduced the load on the engine rather than replacing it, reducing the energy consumption.

The energy provided by each component was measured independently and was compared to the energy required to pump the water. The engine load remained constant until the wind speed exceeded 6 m·s^{-1} and then the load was reduced as the wind speed increased, reaching a minimum of 9 percent at a wind speed of 16 m·s^{-1} (Clark, 1984). Actual fuel consumption was reduced by 50 percent at wind speeds above 12 m·s^{-1}, but predictions of seasonal savings were less than 15 percent. A mechanical wind-assist system must be operated more than 2,000 hours a year to be feasible.

Electrical Stand-Alone Systems

The operation of an electrical wind machine that is independent of the electric utility has the advantage of not having to be situated at the water source. Many times the location of the water source is not the best windmill site; therefore, the overall performance can be enhanced by placing the windmill on a nearby hill. A method developed by USDA-ARS, Bushland, used variable-voltage, variable-frequency electric power directly from a three-phase permanent magnet or self-excited alternator. The wind turbine used with a permanent magnet alternator operates at variable speed and usually has some rotor-blade pitch control to prevent overspeeding.

The output from the permanent magnet alternator varies with the rotational speed of the wind rotor. Power varied from 0.5 to 7 kW, with a frequency of 30 to 65 Hz and a voltage of 81 to 210 V. The voltage to frequency ratio (V/f) was 3 to 3.2, slightly less than the 3.8 calculated from the motor nameplates. While operating a centrifugal pump, the pump motor varied in speed from 800 to 1,940 r/min, and water-flow rate varied from 8 to 20 L·s^{-1} (Vosper and Clark, 1984). System efficiency, including motor and pump losses, varied from 44 to 54 percent, almost the same as when operated off the utility power. Keeping the voltage-frequency ratio constant is the key to making this system perform satisfactorily. Also, the system will work with a conventional three-phase electric motor and pump.

Mechanical Stand-Alone System

A small vertical-axis wind turbine was mechanically coupled to a progressive-cavity pump to determine the operating characteristics of a stand-alone, mechanical irrigation system. Power was transferred from the rotating shaft through a gearbox to the pump, and a clutch was used to unload the wind turbine for starting. The system worked satisfactorily in moderate and high winds but easily stalled in winds of less than 9 m·s^{-1} (Clark, 1983). The progressive-cavity pump did not have the operating characteristics needed to interact with the wind turbine efficiently and provide self-regulation.

REFERENCES

Clark, R. N. 1983. Irrigation pumping with wind energy only. *Agricultural Engineering* 64 (12):15–18.
———. 1984. Co-generation using wind and diesel for irrigation pumping. American Society of Agricultural Engineers paper 84-2603.

Clark, R. N., and F. C. Vosper. 1985. Electrical wind-assist water pumping. *Journal of Solar Energy Engineering, Transactions of the American Society of Mechanical Engineers* 107 (1):97–101.

McKenzie, D. W. 1984. Improved and new water pumping windmills. American Society of Agricultural Engineers paper 84-1625.

Nelson, V., and E. M. Caldera. 1984. Wind energy potential and wind projects in Latin America. *In* Proceedings of the European wind energy conference and exhibition, Hamburg, Germany.

New Mexico Energy Institute. 1978. Selecting water pumping windmills. Report NMEI 11-0-6m. Las Cruces, N.Mex.

Veldhuizen, L. R. van. 1982. Windmills for small-scale irrigation. ILRI Reprint 32. International Institute for Land Reclamation and Improvement, Wageningen, Netherlands.

Vosper, F. C., and R. N. Clark. 1984. Water pumping with autonomous wind-generated electricity. American Society of Agricultural Engineers paper 84-2602.

46. CURRENT DEVELOPMENTS IN PHOTOVOLTAIC IRRIGATION IN THE DEVELOPING WORLD

Richard McGowan and George Burrill, Associates in Rural Development, Inc., Burlington, Vermont

ABSTRACT

Recent technical developments and significant reductions in equipment costs have expanded the potential for the use of solar photovoltaic (PV) water pumping for irrigation in the developing world. The last seven years have seen an ever-widening awareness of the inherent advantages of PV pumps and their consequent increased use. This article discusses those advantages and the liabilities of the use of PV for irrigation, typical system configurations and component options, and capacity limitations of commercially available equipment. The problems encountered in the first-generation PV pumps are discussed, as well as the solutions to those problems, which have resulted in the decreased cost and increased efficiency and reliability of the current generation of systems. A life-cycle cost analysis comparing representative diesel, wind, and PV irrigation systems is given. Finally, policy issues which could have a significant effect on the rate of widespread acceptance of the developing technology are discussed.

WHY CONSIDER SOLAR PHOTOVOLTAIC FOR IRRIGATION?

Traditionally, irrigation systems at remote sites in the Third World have been powered by human beings, animals, wind, or diesel engines. Although diesel, wind, and photovoltaic (PV) systems have much higher capital costs than human- and animal-driven pumps, the latter are very labor-intensive and are unable to meet irrigation demands beyond those of very small fields. With the advent of relatively low-cost PV modules, irrigation engineers and farmers are beginning to look at PV as an alternative to diesel for low- to medium-capacity irrigation needs. Renewable energy-driven pumps are normally characterized by high initial capital costs and low long-term recurrent operation and maintenance costs. Typical costs per unit of water delivered are discussed in detail in a later section.

The use of PV in small-scale low-head stand-alone irrigation systems has several distinct advantages over the common diesel alternative. The most important of these is the very long lifetime of PV modules, in which there are no moving parts. Anyone familiar with diesel engines in the field can appreciate the great advantage of having no moving parts, which neccessitate frequent overhauls and constant attention.

PV systems are modular, allowing farmers to increase the water output from a system by simply increasing the number of modules in the array, subject to well-yield constraints and the operating parameters of the pump set. This modularity allows for more precise matching of the needs of the farmer in the low end of the range of power-supply equipment (die-

sel costs per installed kilowatt increase markedly in the ½ to 3-HP range for which PV irrigation is currently considered economical). PV systems require very little operator interaction, and users frequently mention their appreciation of the silent operation. The skilled labor necessary for the successful long-term operation and maintenance of diesel engines is not required. Unlike diesels, PV pumps are not inherently dependent on the vagaries of rural transportation networks for a continuous supply of fuel and spare parts, the cost of which in the long term can go nowhere but up.

The primary disadvantage of the use of small-scale PV irrigation systems is their comparatively high initial capital cost, as well as the expenditure (as with diesels) of precious foreign exchange. This has resulted in the impression that the initial costs of PV will make the delivered cost of water acceptably high over the long term. Farmers and government decision makers are often not truly aware of the magnitude of the long-term recurrent costs associated with the use of diesel pumps.

The reliability of PV systems is no longer the concern it once was. An estimated 1,000 solar pumps are operating in the Third World. On the basis of this experience manufacturers have developed high-quality systems and components which are much more energy-efficient and reliable than the first-generation equipment, which did little to establish consumer confidence in PV. PV systems have developed to the point that their outage rate is less than that of most electric utilities. This has led to their use as power supplies for critical loads such as remote-site telecommunications for which power outages cannot be tolerated.

Extensions of the electrical grid are sometimes suggested as a possible alternative to diesel or PV for irrigation. A number of studies in India have indicated that the extremely low load factors frequently encountered in many rural electrification schemes make the cost per kilowatt-hour generated much more expensive than initially planned for (Bhatia, 1984). Stand-alone systems, whether PV, diesel, or wind (where sufficient wind and solar radiation occur) merit closer examination under such circumstances.

Appropriate Applications of PV in Irrigation

Irrigation water needs for crops are based on several factors: the type of crop, the method of water application, and soil and climatic conditions, such as the evapotranspiration rate. The cost of the energy input required is a function of the volumetric demand, the total pumping head (including any head losses in the distribution system), and the application schedule. The schedule is important in PV systems because of storage considerations, which are discussed below.

PV pumping is most cost-competitive where levels of solar radiation are high and water requirements and pumping head are low. Pumping low flows from shallow sources such as springs, pools (natural or man-made), ditches, cisterns, and low-head wells are appropriate applications of PV. Such sites would normally use surface-mounted centrifugal pumps, which are relatively inexpensive and easily serviced. Suction pumps are limited to sites with suction heads of less than 6.1 m at sea level and decreasing with altitude. Centrifugal suction pumps are the most likely candidates for PV irrigation pumping because of their high capacity at low head compared with other common types of PV pumps.

The unexploited potential for PV pumping on small plots in the Third World is immense. For example, many of the small farms in Nigeria are intensively farmed plots of 2 to 5 ha. PV pumps can be used for pumping from river valleys into small irrigation canals, a lift of 2 to 5 m. Commercially available systems could pump as much as 1,000 m^3 per day under good solar-radiation conditions, enough to satisfy a wide variety of crop demands.

Matching Irrigation Demand and Solar Energy Supply

Large variations in water demand as a function of time are an inescapable fact of irrigation practice. In addition, a large percentage (as much as 50 percent) of the water pumped is lost because of inefficient distribution networks and application methods. With the use of PV, wasting water through inefficient irrigation practices means more than simply adding fuel to the tank and turning on the engine for a few more hours. Flood irrigation is not appropriate for use with PV owing to its low application efficiency. Sprinklers, while more efficient in their use of water, require considerable pressure head to operate properly. Trickle irrigation also requires some pressure head for proper water distribution, but much less so than sprinklers, and the use of PV is appropriate, given the high efficiency of trickle techniques. Similarly, channel and furrow distribution is moderately efficient with low-head losses, and it too can be used with PV.

While PV systems normally deliver maximum output concurrent with peak irrigation demands for most crops (when solar radiation peaks in the summer), PV cannot supply water on demand as diesels can by simply running for longer periods. PV systems supply a limited amount of water, directly proportional to the level of solar radiation and array and pump size. To smooth demand peaks, provision must be made for storage so that energy (electrical or hydraulic) can be accumulated during off-peak periods (between irrigations) to satisfy peak loads.

Commercially Available Systems

Most currently available commercial pump sets designed for use with PV are in the fractional to 3-HP range. Most use high-efficiency (about 76 to 85 percent) DC permanent magnet motors, although some use DC-to-AC inverters with AC motors. Since farms in less developed countries are fre-

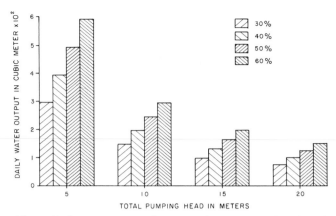

Fig. 1. Daily water output of a 3-HP solar pump as a function of pumping head and pump efficiency ranging between 30 and 60 percent.

quently between 0.5 and 3 ha, with water requirements of between 20 and 80 m^{-3} ha per day, PV irrigation systems must be capable of delivering between 10 and 240 m^3 per day. The graph in Fig. 1 shows the range of capacity of a 3-HP pump set at various heads and pump and motor efficiencies. It is apparent that PV pumps are capable of delivering water for small farms over the head range given in the graph without necessarily requiring large-capacity storage. While larger-capacity systems can certainly be had, the costs per unit of capacity are appreciably greater because of the smaller number of units manufactured.

PV pumping systems normally consist of the following components: PV modules and the balance of system (BOS), which includes array support structures, controls of power conditioning units (PCUs), pump/motor set, wiring, and frequently some form of energy storage, either electrical storage (batteries) or hydraulic storage (water tanks). The simplest systems consist of PV modules mounted on the array support structure and connected directly to the pump motor. Its low-cost configuration does not necessarily result in the least cost of water delivered.

Since water must be delivered to crops on a given schedule, PV irrigation systems frequently include some form of storage, either batteries or water tanks or both. Because of the unavoidable maintenance problems (deep discharging and electrolyte boiling) and considerable cost of batteries, the large energy requirements in irrigation suggest the use of water storage tanks. Batteries (or PCUs) are used with pumps which require high surge currents to start.

Modules are blocks of about 33 to 40 individual cells mounted together and encapsulated to isolate them from harsh operating environments. Several types of PV cells are in wide use. There are some differences in the performance characeristics as well as in the cost of the cell types, but at the present time the prices per delivered watt for the common power-generating cells are nearly identical. Extensive accelerated testing has been performed on all commercial cells, and under most conditions of use modules are likely to have lifetimes of up to twenty years, with less than 10 percent degradation in performance over that period.

This does not necessarily apply to the BOS components (batteries, for example, have an inherently limited lifetime and must be replaced well before twenty years).

Modules are mounted on the array support structure at a fixed angle chosen to maximize the array output during the critical months where the ratio of electrical demand to available solar radiation intensity is highest. The modules are wired in series and parallel to match the electrical demand of the pump motor.

Many types of pumps are used in PV systems, each with its advantages and disadvantages. Irrigation systems normally use centrifugal pumps because of their efficiency, reliability, and ease of maintenance. Surface-mounted centrifugals are used for high capacity at low head, and vertical turbine centrifugals are used for deeper wells, because they are relatively inexpensive and easily serviced. Other common pumps used with PV systems are submersibles and positive displacement pumps (rotary and jack). Positive displacement pumps are not recommended for PV irrigation because of their high starting torques, their lower efficiency than centrifugals, and sand problems likely to be encountered. The PV subsmersibles currently available are nominal 1-HP units, and their capacity is restricted at present (5-HP units will soon be commercially available).

Controls, batteries, and PCUs can be used to increase the output of the system as an alternative to using a larger array. All these devices exact a price in terms of both power use and system cost. Battery losses reduce system efficiency by up to 25 percent; PCUs, 5 to 10 percent; and regulators, less than 5 percent. Inverters used with AC normally have about 10 percent losses. The ideal system is that which uses the optimum combination of components to give the lowest cost per unit of water supplied over the lifetime of the system.

Controls can increase system efficiency and safety of operation. Charge controllers or regulators are used to prevent overdischarge of batteries and to prevent motor damage resulting from low-voltage operation. Some PCUs force the array to operate at its maximum power point (significantly increasing system efficiency), as well as to supply starting surge to stiff pumps. Batteries can smooth out the delivery of power to the pump (increasing its operating efficiency) as well as provide backup power when water is required during periods of low radiation.

EVOLUTION OF PV IRRIGATION PUMPING

PV irrigation systems are being used in many areas around the world, including Africa; Asia; Central, South, and North America; and the Pacific Islands. Systems range in size from an experimental 25-kWp (peak kilowatt) unit using a 25-HP pump to irrigate grain fields in Nebraska in 1978 to 320-Wp arrays with ½-HP systems pumping water for small vegetable plots in Botswana and Zimbabwe.

Problems Encountered in Early Systems

Many of the first-generation PV pumps did not perform as well as expected owing to immature technology. Systems were designed without much knowledge of the solar resource of the intended site. Since solar radiation is now being monitored in many countries where solar applications are most likely to be cost-effective, designers of future systems will not be similarly hampered. The best sites for solar pumps have not only high radiation levels but also more uniform seasonal variations, and thus little extrapolation from existing data is necessary. For irrigation systems annual data are not such a crucial requirement as is the solar-radiation level during the irrigating season(s). The PV system is then sized (Halcrow and IT Power, 1984) so that irrigation demands can be met under worst-case conditions, during the period when the ratio of hydraulic-energy demand to solar-energy supply is highest. Well data on yields and depths are critical. If the water level in a well drops 10 m during the dry season when irrigation is required, a low-head pump designed with wet-season data will perform dismally. To compensate, designers can overdesign a system, but this will greatly affect the initial cost of the system.

Another major design problem was the impedance mismatching of the power supply and the BOS. PV operation is characterized by a current-voltage (IV) curve. Maximum system output occurs when the system operates at the maximum power point (MPP) on the IV curve. This happens when the impedance of the array and the load are properly matched. The early French Pompes Guinard in Africa were particularly plagued by impedance mismatching, and their output was well below expectation. As awareness of the seriousness of this problem spread throughout the industry, pump manufacturers began designing their DC pumps with PV-array characteristics in mind, greatly increasing overall performance.

Operation and maintenance problems also included battery degradation, owing either to underestimation of battery requirements and consequent deep discharging and rapid deterioration or to failure of the charge controller and subsequent boiling away of the electrolyte. Early versions of some power-conditioning units had quality-control problems. Some systems have experienced varying degrees of performance degradation because of vandalizing of modules, and goats have shorted more than one circuit by their penchant for inadequately protected wire insulation. Typical pump-maintenance problems such as seal and impeller degradation and brush replacement occur in PV pumps with the same frequency as in standard pumps. On the whole, compared with diesel installations, PVs have much less downtime because of equipment failure or operator error. This is due primarily to the exceptional reliability of the power modules.

Decreasing Cost and Increasing Efficiency

The PV module is by far the most expensive component of a pumping system. Significant cost reductions have occurred over the eight years that PVs have been used for water pumping. Modules that cost $20 per peak Watt (Wp) in 1978 are now selling for $7 per peak Watt. The cost of modules is still dropping, albeit more slowly than was earlier expected. Single-crystal cell efficiencies in the laboratory are now approaching 20 percent, and commercial *module* efficiency is currently 12 percent. Semicrystalline module efficiency is 10 percent. The amorphous (ASi) modules that are just becoming available for small-scale power generation have module efficiencies of about 5 to 6 percent and bulk costs of $15 to $18 per Wp. The first-generation commercial PV systems experienced some significant problems with module degradation; these problems have been solved by virtually all the major manufacturers. Ten-year warranties that specify less than 10 percent maximum output degradation are now standard.

Considerable effort has been made by several pump and motor manufacturers (e.g., Jacuzzi, MacDonald, Franklin Electric, Grundfos, Honeywell, KSB, and AEG Telefunken) to develop higher-efficiency pump sets for use with PV. Some of their efforts have met with considerable success. Pump sets now on the market are considerably more efficient and reliable than typical pumps that were reviewed in Halcrow and IT Power (1983). Effort has been directed toward the development of brushless submersible DC pumps, which would eliminate maintenance costs associated with pulling a down-hole pump every 6,000 hours (or oftener) to replace brushes. Thus far, product development has not met manufacturers' expectations. This has led some manufacturers to turn to synchronous AC motors with DC-to-AC inverters for submersibles, which have thus far achieved an enviable reputation for reliability and simplicity of installation.

NEW COMPONENTS AND APPROACHES FOR COST REDUCTION

More power can be obtained from the same size array by several different strategies. PV systems work best when operating at their maximum power point (MPP). Several PCUs force the array to operate at the MPP, thereby considerably increasing the array output. Their cost varies considerably (from $200 to $3,500). The more expensive PCUs follow the MPP very precisely, while the less expensive ones merely approximate it by forcing the array to operate at a preset constant voltage. Manufacturers claim annual output increases of up to 15 percent. These increases must be balanced against the incremental cost of the devices, as well as compared to the cost of simply adding more modules to increase the array output.

Another way to increase power production is to physically move the array so that it is always oriented perpendicular to incoming solar radiation. Very large PV arrays use computer-driven continous tracking devices, which are quite complex and expensive. For small, remote systems, manual seasonal adjustment of arrays has met with little success because users fail to adhere to the adjustment schedule, leaving the array at a less than optimal tilt angle, with the result that annual array output actually drops.

A third and more promising approach is a passive, gravity-driven Freon tracker which tracks the sun continuously throughout the day and then returns to its eastward-facing position in anticipation of the morning sun. These single-axis trackers are mechanically very simple and have been used on a small scale for several years of trouble-free operation, increasing array output as much as 40 percent. They are particularly useful for irrigation since the greatest additional output occurs during the summer.

Concentrators multiply the amount of solar energy falling on individual cells, thereby increasing electrical output. The cost of the concentrator can sometimes offset the cost of additional modules to generate the same amount of power. The simplest concentrators are mirrored surfaces mounted alongside standard modules, which effectively double the level of incident radiation. Alternatively, Fresnel lenses integrally mounted in a module above the cells also concentrate solar radiation. The popularity of this type of module is evident in its increasing sales, which, though currently a small fraction of the sales of standard flat nonconcentrating modules, are steadily increasing.

For all of these devices the critical issue is whether or not the increase in system performance has greater value than the consequent increased cost and complexity. In remote Third World applications system longevity has been inversely proportional to complexity. In comparing the economics of different system options, some financial value must be assigned to simplicity of operation and consequent reliability. Every additional component represents an additional opportunity for failure.

FINANCIAL-COST ANALYSIS

Life-cycle-cost (LCC) analysis, which calculates the present worth of all costs, capital, operation and maintenance, and replacement parts over the lifetime of the system, is used to compare the various alternatives. A cost/benefit ratio is also calculated, though a benefit value per unit of water pumped must be assumed, and this can be highly site- and crop-specific.

For the small-scale systems discussed here, the module cost is normally between 85 and 90 percent of the entire system cost. While it is likely that the cost of modules will continue to decline (though not as rapidly as has been forecast from 1977 to 1985), it is improbable that BOS costs will drop comparably. While there will be certain economies of scale as the number of units manufactured increases, BOS costs are spread over array structures, pumps, motors, and controls. The technology for manufacturing these devices is now relatively mature, and it is unlikely that costs of these components will drop significantly. Since the cost of the BOS is a small fraction of the overall system cost, moderate decreases in BOS costs will have little effect on system LCC.

The most obvious cost consideration for any irrigation scheme is that its annualized cost should not be greater than the incremental benefits that the farmer can reasonably expect from each growing season as a result of the investment in irrigation equipment. Since these benefits are highly site- and crop-specific, and since the value of water is independent of the equipment used to supply it, only the relative costs of supplying a given amount of water at several different pumping heads are calculated here. In Table 1 the breakdown of costs is given for three systems: diesel, windmill, and PV. A graph of the effective water cost is shown in Fig. 2. A detailed breakdown of all costs and assumptions is available from the authors.

The costs considered in this analysis do not include the costs of well drilling or development, the water distribution

Table 1. Cost analysis of three irrigation pumping systems.

	Photovoltaic Pump				Windmill				Diesel			
Total pumping head (meters)	5	10	15	20	5	10	15	20	5	10	15	20
Amortization period (years)	20	20	20	20	20	20	20	20	20	20	20	20
Pump/motor lifetime (years)	7	7	7	7	2	2	2	2	4	4	4	4
Discount rate (percent)	10	10	10	10	10	10	10	10	10	10	10	10
Costs:												
Initial capital cost	$24,200	$24,200	$24,200	$24,200	$12,500	$12,500	$12,500	$12,500	$4,349	$4,349	$4,349	$4,349
Shipping	1,200	1,200	1,200	1,200	2,500	2,500	2,500	2,500	0	0	0	0
Installation	700	700	700	700	1,000	1,000	1,000	1,000	500	500	500	500
Total initial cost	$26,100	$26,100	$26,100	$26,100	$16,000	$16,000	$16,000	$16,000	$4,849	$4,849	$4,849	$4,849
Annual O&M costs	$100	$100	$100	$100	$400	$400	$400	$400	$2,365	$2,365	$2,365	$2,365
NPV of replacement-parts costs	$2,368	$2,368	$2,368	$2,368	$2,216	$2,216	$2,216	$2,216	$10,631	$10,631	$10,631	$10,631
Life-cycle cost	$29,320	$29,320	$29,320	$29,320	$21,621	$21,621	$21,621	$21,621	$35,615	$35,615	$35,615	$35,615
Benefits:												
Water pumped per year (m^3)	179,945	89,790	59,860	44,895	108,004	53,984	35,989	27,010	161,220	80,592	53,728	40,304
Value of output @ $0.05/m^3	$8,997	$4,490	$2,993	$2,245	$5,400	$2,699	$1,799	$1,351	$8,061	$4,030	$2,686	$2,015
NPV of benefit stream	$76,599	$38,222	$25,481	$19,111	$45,975	$22,980	$15,320	$11,498	$68,628	$34,306	$22,871	$17,157
Effective water cost ($/m^3)	0.02	0.04	0.06	0.08	0.02	0.05	0.07	0.09	0.03	0.05	0.08	0.10
Benefit/cost ratio	2.61	1.30	0.87	0.65	2.13	1.06	0.71	0.53	1.93	0.96	0.64	0.48

Assumptions: Equipment costs inflate at 5 percent per year. No storage costs are included. Diesel fuel cost inflation is zero. All initial capital costs are current. Diesel shipping is included in the capital cost.

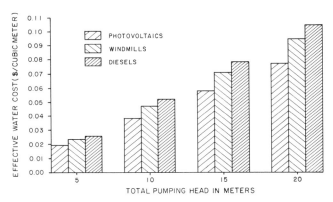

Fig. 2. Cost of water from photovoltaic, wind, and diesel powered pumps as a function of pumping head.

system, or storage tanks. System components that are common to all the systems are omitted. It was assumed that village drinking-water supply over the entire year would be supplied by the irrigation pump, and the benefits include this. All the example systems supply approximately the same amount of water at the indicated head. The costs of this example comparison are actual costs for systems in the Yemen Arab Republic (McGowan and Cassam, 1985). It should be borne in mind that Yemen has some of the highest solar-radiation levels in the world. The windmill is a Kenyan Kijito (with an assumed average wind speed of 3.5 m·s^{-1}), and the PV is a vertical turbine centrifugal with a DC motor. The diesel is standard equipment. Assumptions of fuel consumption and maintenance schedules are standard. From the table and graph it is clear that PV is competitive with diesel for the conditions of low head and flow and high solar radiation assumed in this example. Varying

the assumptions certainly has some effect on the relative ranking, but the point is that the cost of the systems examined is quite similar under the current costs. As the cost of diesel fuel rises (as it surely will in the long term) and the cost of PV continues to drop, the comparison can only become more favorable to PV and windmills.

Economic-Cost Considerations

Economic analyses attempt to place a "true" value on various cost components, which is not necessarily what these costs would be in the marketplace. They attempt to quantify such real costs to the national economy as the cost of government subsidies (hidden or otherwise), anomalies in the marketplace, imbalances in exchange rates, and scarcity in the availability of foreign exchange. In Yemen, for instance, retail diesel price is about $0.27 per liter. Given current world prices for crude oil of about $29 per barrel and allowing $0.12 per liter for refining and transportation costs, the price of diesel should be $0.30 per liter. Thus there is a subsidy of approximately 10 percent of the real cost. In many areas this subsidy is much greater. This would not matter to consumers but should be taken into account by government planners who are concerned about the scarcity of foreign exchange, much of which is caused by importation of fossil fuel. Similarly, dependence on fuel supplies from politically volatile areas, centralized electrical grids of varying reliability, and uncertain future costs of fuel must be considered when planners are making policy choices that will affect the long-term economic and social goals of a country.

Policy Issues

To address the cost issue, several countries are initiating local manufacturing of some or all of the components for PV systems. Charge controllers are being manufactured in

Botswana. PV irrigation systems, including everything from PV modules to batteries to controllers to small DC-driven jack pumps are being manufactured and used in India with the help of extensive government subsidies.

Since the principal obstacle to the widespread use of PV for small-scale irrigation is the initial capital cost (not the LCC), it will be necessary to overcome the lack of awareness of most farmers, governments, and financing institutions of the long-term benefits of this promising technology. Many people are simply unaware of its existence or view it as a totally experimental technology that is many years away from commercial availability. If LDCs wish to take advantage of the savings in the recurrent costs of energy for water pumping and reduce their ever-increasing export of precious foreign exchange, some method of financing the purchase of PV pumps must be developed.

In rare instances (in the Yemen Arab Republic, for example) there is sufficient rural liquidity and willingness to try new technologies that a public-awareness program would probably be sufficient to disseminate the technology. In most countries, however, individual farmers are unlikely to have sufficient assets or be willing to invest such large amounts of cash on unfamiliar equipment such as PV pumps. Thus in most situations it would be necessary for governments, PV manufacturers, or perhaps agricultural cooperatives to provide financing, given present PV costs. Having limited access to or experience with long-term capital financing, Third World farmers would expect very short payback periods and implicitly high discount rates. Convincing potential consumers of the reasonableness of balancing high initial costs with reduction of long-term recurrent costs would require a carefully planned public-awareness program, perhaps through existing government agricultural extension programs. A positive government perspective, evidenced by allowing PVs to quality for favorable import tariff rates, would have a considerable effect on the rate of dissemination of the technology.

RECOMMENDATIONS FOR PV APPLICATIONS IN IRRIGATION

Field research programs in small-scale PV irrigation are under way in several countries, and one major study, funded by the World Bank, covering first-generation PV pumps has already been published (Halcrow and IT Power, 1983). Comparisons of the economic and technical performance of diesel, wind, and PV systems are going on in Africa, southeast Asia, India, and Central America (McGowan and Ashworth, 1984). Engineers, economists, and water-resource specialists should take advantage of the results of these tests to make decisions about allocations of financial resources for the development of small-scale low-head remote-site irrigated agriculture. Photovoltaics have an important role to play in this development, which can be implemented by government policy decisions that carefully weigh the advantages and liabilities connected with the range of available pumping technologies and that take into account the true costs associated with the widespread use of each.

REFERENCES

McGowan, R., and J. Ashworth. 1984. Comparative testing for water-pumping systems installed in Botswana. Botswana Renewable Energy Technology Project, U.S. Agency for International Development. July. Burlington, Vt.

McGowan, R., and M. Cassam. 1985. Yemen rural energy assessment: final report. U.S. Agency for International Development, Sana'a YAR. January. Burlington, Vt.

Bhatia, Ramesh. Energy alternatives for irrigation pumping: an economic analysis for northern India. World Employment Program working paper. December. Geneva: International Labor Office.

Halcrow, Sir William, and Partners and IT Power, Ltd. 1983 Small-scale solar-powered pumping systems: the technology, its economics and advancement. June. London: World Bank, United Nations Development Program.

———. 1984. Handbook on Solar Water Pumping. February. Washington, D.C.: World Bank, United Nations Development Program.

PART VIII. TECHNOLOGY

47. WORLDWIDE VIEW OF IRRIGATION TECHNOLOGY DEVELOPMENT

Jack Keller, Department of Agricultural and Irrigation Engineering, Utah State University, Logan, Utah

ABSTRACT

Considerations related to irrigation development in both the industrial and the Third World countries are discussed. The need for more clearly defining and dealing with the objective for developing irrigation projects (i.e., for commercial production, for sociopolitical, and/or for geopolitical reasons) is stressed. An outline of the various irrigation application system options is given, along with a discussion of the advantages of modern irrigation technologies and the planning options for selecting appropriate technologies. The framework related to managing traditional large-scale irrigation systems serving small farmers, which requires managing the government's main system, the farm community's middle system, and the farmer's individual application system, is presented. And finally, some thoughts on using modern irrigation technologies to solve some of the management and start-up problems associated with traditional irrigation systems are presented.

INTRODUCTION

Irrigation has been considered mainly as a means to bridge annual drought periods and to water desert lands. Since variability in weather and climate is becoming an increasingly important factor influencing national and regional food situations, it is recognized that extending the area with an assured water supply has become particularly urgent. Through modern technology, irrigaton can stabilize and increase agricultural production and employment opportunities for the rural poor so they can partake of the increased production. But irrigation can do more; it permits optimum utilization of fertilizers, the introduction of highly responsive seeds, and advanced tillage techniques and practices. The lack of an assured water supply has been one of the main bottlenecks in the successful introduction of high-yielding varieties. Irrigation thus has become an input of agricultural production—where natural conditions are unfavorable, the most important one. Investment in irrigation work must, therefore, be regarded as basic to agricultural development and, consequently, to long-term goals for social and economic development.

DEVELOPMENT TRENDS

From a worldwide perspective, irrigation development is progressing along numerous paths throughout industrial and Third World countries. Irrigation development is, in a sense, like an organic process, continually evolving from whatever state it is on along a path of events consistent with the whole environment. The socioeconomic aspects of a system or project's environment are as important as the physical aspects, yet they are less well understood. In fact, it is the in-

sensitive transfer of irrigation technologies from one farm to another, or, more important, from one region or country to another, without adequate consideration of the socioeconomic aspects that has led to a great many disappointments. Obviously, careful consideration must also be given to the physical and biological site conditions in arriving at good irrigation designs and management practices, but this is not sufficient in itself.

Industrial Countries

The thrust of irrigation development in the industrial countries is concentrated mostly on techniques that will systemize management decisions, reduce labor inputs, and provide more precise and timely water applications. The socioeconomic factors driving the evolutionary process are the need (desire) to reduce labor, management, and resource input expenses while at the same time increasing agricultural output.

The new irrigation application machines and new techniques and control systems that are evolving for managing, conveying, and applying water achieve these goals. They provide automation, which reduces both management and labor input needs while delivering precise and timely applications of water. The consumption of resources is reduced by designing to minimize energy input and providing uniform and optimally scheduled irrigations to minimize water and fertilizer losses. Furthermore, with optimum applications of water, crop production per unit of land area as well as per unit of water is significantly improved.

Third World Countries

The thrust of irrigation development activities in the Third World countries is concentrated mostly on increasing the irrigation potential by investments in new infrastructure, and more recently, on improving the utilization of the existing and new potentials created. For the most part, in the public sector the system or project design standards and concepts are too similar to what has been utilized (often with disappointing results) in the past. However, some significant changes in both the design standards and the variations in the conveyance and application technologies are being tried. Furthermore, some limited attention is being given to designing public systems to make them more manageable. On the other hand, where crop returns are high, Third World private developers often are relatively quick in developing groundwater resources and in selecting and adopting new irrigation technologies that appear promising.

The real problem with underutilization of the irrigation

potential created by public systems has now been broadly recognized and is the subject of much study. Where farm units are fragmented and small, the outlets on public canal systems are typically sized to serve rather large groups of farmers. The farmers are expected to organize and participate in maintaining and managing the delivery of water from the public outlet to the individual landholdings. Ten to fifteen years ago this farmer participation aspect was essentially ignored. When the shortcoming was discovered and revealed, the true multidisciplinary nature of irrigation development was broadly accepted. More and more attention is now being given to farmer participation, but this in itself is not sufficient to overcome underutilization.

The most recent blind spot to be revealed in the management of canal irrigation systems is that of "main system management" to ensure reliable and timely deliveries of water to the public outlets. This, coupled with an emphasis on organized, as well as individual, farmer participation in system operation and management, holds the promise of significantly improving the utilization of public projects wherever the microeconomic and microenvironmental conditions are favorable. These are some preliminary signs that attention is now being directed to designing new systems and modernizing existing ones to facilitate better main system management. However, this trend is still in an embryonic stage.

Svendsen (1985) points out that there is increasing concern with the high cost of new projects based on reservoirs and traditional surface irrigation system development. He also notes that the benefits derived from the high-cost systems have been disappointing in too many cases, and goes on to say that in view of this there is increasing interest in small-scale and community-operated systems. This interest is based on the realization that such systems are less management intensive (from the government's point of view), quick yielding, and less costly to construct or improve. It also reflects the recognition that there is a wealth of positive experience with such systems in Asia and Latin America.

DEVELOPMENT OBJECTIVES

An initial look at the subject of irrigation development makes it apparent that many irrigation projects are developed and designed in the absence of a clear concept of the objective. I can see three somewhat different objectives for developing an irrigation project. These are: for commercial production, for sociopolitical, and/or for geopolitical reasons. A commercial production objective refers to a project where the principal purpose is to produce food and fiber for markets. A social benefit objective refers to a project that is directed principally at improving the well-being of a large number of farmers with small landholdings. By geopolitical I refer to projects that are initiated for security or purely political reasons rather than for either of the above purposes.

Obviously, most projects contain elements of all three objectives. However, it appears useful to delineate the main thrust of the objective at the outset so that it can be optimized, rather than to make all projects appear to be commercially oriented using standard benefit/cost analysis techniques. Clearly, for commercial projects a relatively high discount rate is appropriate. However, for sociopolitical projects, directed essentially to providing social benefits to peasant farmers and landless laborers, a much lower discount rate may be in order. On the other hand, a geopolitical project that is developed for security reasons is an undertaking similar to a military operation, in which the economic benefit/cost analysis is inappropriate.

The above does not imply that a project with a principal objective of social benefits should not be productive and, in a sense, economically feasible. However, at the beginning of the project the principal interests might be institution building and improving the well-being of the local population, with the commercial economic benefits being delayed until these have taken place. Thus, the project might be designed to optimize the social benefits at the outset in such a manner that the project's productivity supports the building of needed institutions. For such projects, a maximum amount of community self-help and involvement is essential. An alternative to using reduced discount rates might be to allocate a portion of the project cost to a subjective evaluation of social benefits. This could be done in a manner similar to that used in allocating environmental benefits within projects in developed nations.

Shifting to the social or geopolitical objectives should not be used as an excuse for careless planning without rigorous technical and economic analyses or a lack of attention to broader social, environmental, and economic consequences. If there are social or political values, these ought to be accounted for by surrogate values in the decision process and the best commercial project built under these circumstances. The principal argument here is that all projects should not be designed, implemented, and managed as though they are commercially viable. When this is done, the management task becomes practically impossible. Thus, ultimate project performance is apt to be considerably worse than what might have been achieved had more realistic appraisal techniques been utilized.

NATURE OF IRRIGATION SYSTEMS

The anatomy of an irrigation scheme may consist of gigantic dams to impound and store water, large pumping plants and extensive canal or pipe systems to distribute water to the fields, and elaborate mechanized irrigation systems to apply the water to the land, or it may be merely a farm pond and a clay jar. But irrigation requires an irrigator and the development necessary to supply water to the field and service the irrigation system. Thus, a functioning irrigation system is first a mental image, which consists of the irrigator, his tools (requiring capital), and labor. An endless number of trade-offs can be made between management, labor, capital, and energy inputs, and, through man's inventive genius, numerous irrigation techniques have evolved.

In contrast to traditional irrigation systems, there are completely automatic systems, where the irrigator's job becomes deciding when to punch the "start" and "stop" buttons (scheduling the irrigations), keeping energy supplied to the pump and drive systems, and servicing the machinery and equipment. A professional service can be employed to make the scheduling decisions, or the farmer can rely entirely on moisture-sensing instruments to turn the system on and off. By mechanizing the system, the mental images and certain management skills of the inventor, engineer, and technicians who designed and installed it are transferred to the farmer through the irrigation hardware. Obviously, an irrigator with a mechanical system can handle a larger area, perhaps as much as 1,000 times more, than an irrigator with a traditional system. But when the army of people involved in the manufacture, sales, service, and energy supply network for the mechanized system is included, the numerical contrast is much less dramatic.

Major advantages of modern systems over traditional systems include greater ease of management, reduced labor costs, less drudgery, less skill required to operate efficiently, and more precise water application. Furthermore, mechanized systems can be made to operate effectively in sandy and hilly lands that are impractical to irrigate by traditional methods. Thus, through innovative irrigation tools, we are able to expand our capacity to produce food and, if the rest of the farming is done using traditional methods, to increase and stabilize rural employment opportunities. For example, center-pivot sprinklers that can provide daily irrigations have reduced the need for the soil to hold water and have made the sand hills of the U.S. Midwest into a major maize-producing region, and trickle irrigation, which can be used on almost any terrain, has made the 50 to 60 percent mountain slopes in San Diego County, California, into prime avocado-growing areas.

The modern irrigation applications have their disadvantages, especially in Third World countries. They require energy for pumping and special support systems to provide repair parts and mechanical services, as well as fuel and off-farm maintenance facilities. While the farmers who utilize may not need much specific training to manage and operate them, the technicians providing the support services do need special training. Furthermore, the fuel, repair, and maintenance required to operate modern systems cost money; thus, the farmers must be involved in a cash economy or be continuously provided with fuel and mechanical services at public expense.

In contrast to modern systems, traditional systems can be constructed, or at least maintained, within the indigenous capacity of Third World communities. Commercialization is not needed, for once public resource transfers have been made to construct the system it can be maintained with little or no outside input.

One point worth noting is that about one-third of the world's irrigation must depend on water pumped from wells, rivers, tanks, and canals. Where an engine- or motor-driven pump is employed the system has the disadvantages of modern irrigation, even if traditional techniques are used to distribute and apply the water to the fields. Thus, where pumpsets are employed it becomes a relatively minor step to utilize modern water distribution and application techniques, especially for upland crops.

USE OF MODERN IRRIGATION TECHNOLOGIES

The higher the relative value of irrigation water in terms of net added crop value per unit of water, or the higher the water supply development costs or pumping lift, the greater the cost incentive to utilize modern irrigation systems. This is especially important in view of the rising awareness of the difficulties in developing irrigation projects and achieving cost-effective operation using traditional systems. Some advantages of using these new systems are: the speed of development, which produces quicker returns; the relatively simple training needs for "controlled" irrigation, because the systems have what is often called "built-in management"; and the elegant simplicity of both the systems themselves and the new infrastructure needed.

By utilizing modern irrigation techniques, the efficiency of water deliveries to the crop root zone can often be doubled. For example, a recent diagnostic analysis of traditional irrigation systems utilizing surface irrigation and unlined tertiary and field channels in Egypt (EWUMP, 1984) and Pakistan (Clyma et al., 1981) indicates that typical overall "on-farm" irrigation efficiencies are in the neighborhood of 20 to 50 percent. These low overall efficiencies result from the combined series of efficiencies, ranging from 55 to 85 percent in the tertiary canals (watercourses serving groups of farms) and 80 to 90 percent in the field channels between the tertiary canals and farm fields, along with field application efficiencies from 30 to 80 percent, depending on the degree of under- or overirrigation, land preparation, and soil conditions. With modern irrigation using piped distribution systems, the tertiary conveyance losses are nil, and potential on-farm efficiencies range from 70 to 90 percent.

In addition to the improved overall efficiency, with the management built into modern irrigation systems giving rise to more timely and accurately controlled applications, the yield per unit of water received by the crop can be improved considerably (perhaps by 50 percent). For example, in the traditional systems of northwest India and Pakistan, rotational deliveries are often scheduled at two-week (or longer) intervals, which is not frequent enough for optimum production of most crops. On the other hand, a modern system such as a center pivot could be conveniently scheduled to apply irrigations daily, or as frequently as needed for optimum production. These two factors of improved scheduling efficiency and application uniformity combine to give a total increase in productivity of perhaps 300 percent from a given investment in water supply capacity.

Typically, water resource development costs range from $1,000 to $10,000 per hectare for more recently constructed and/or planned irrigation projects employing traditional surface irrigation. The added cost of replacing a traditional system with a mechanical application system for upland crops ranges from $500 to $1,500 per hectare (Keller et al., 1984; Keller, 1985). Therefore, irrigation projects utilizing modern irrigation technologies having a 2:1 efficiency advantage over traditional upland surface irrigation systems may be considerably less expensive per unit of land irrigated. For example, assume a water resource development cost of $3,000 per hectare for a traditional system. If center-pivot systems costing $1,000 per hectare were utilized to irrigate twice as much area with the same water supply, the total development cost would be reduced to $2,500 per hectare. Furthermore, with twice as much land irrigated, agricultural production as well as employment would also be doubled.

Planning Options

It is this phenomenal increase in realized production potential, along with rapid full utilization of irrigation water resource investments and the possibility of even lowering investment costs per unit of irrigated land, that makes modern irrigation technologies attractive despite the relatively high equipment cost and complexity. A principal dilemma in the strategy for improving the performance of irrigated agriculture by utilizing modern technologies in developing countries is the apparent incompatability of those technologies with the management skills and lack of commercialization associated with the small farm sizes and the diversification of agriculture so important to the small landholders. Our challenge is: How can we creatively take advantage of the economies and benefits of modern (and perhaps large-scale) irrigation delivery and application systems while preserving the vitality and human-initiative advantages of small-scale, traditional irrigation farming enterprises?

A partial list of modern irrigation technologies includes hose basin, gated pipe surge flow furrow, and precision-leveled border or basin irrigation systems; hose-fed, hand-move lateral, periodic-mechanical-move lateral, and continuous-moving center-pivot sprinkle irrigation systems; and point-and-line source trickle irrigation systems.

Theoretically, most of these systems (except the mechanical-move and center-pivot sprinkler systems) are divisible and can be designed for practically any size or shape of field. But since all the systems utilize piped- or lined-channel distribution networks, their economic practicality and effectiveness are considerably reduced where large-scale water supplies serve many individual small landholdings. On the other hand, pipe- and hose-fed surface, sprinkle, and trickle systems are particularly attractive where both the water supply and the field to be served are small-scale—for example, 1 to 10 $L \cdot s^{-1}$ water supplies serving 0.2- to 2-ha farm units.

Some interesting planning and design options for using modern irrigation technologies in Third World developing countries were summarized by Keller (1985) as follows:

1. *Large-scale modern irrigation with large-scale farms.* Fields of 20 to 50 ha or more must be developed where both large-scale modern irrigaton (such as center-pivot and surge flow) and large-scale farming are to be utilized. Thus, unpopulated areas such as the deserts of the Middle East must be selected for development, or existing small holdings must be consolidated into large cooperative units. Furthermore, state or cooperative management structures are needed to carry out large-scale operations. But such enterprises typically fail because of the "state farm mentality" or the shortcomings of the "law of the commons," unless there is strong (and often expatriate) management along with sufficient incentives. Furthermore, the people (farmers) usually resist consolidation to the point of its being politically untenable unless the land is already owned by the state.

2. *Random small-scale modern irrigation with small-scale farming.* Small-scale modern irrigation systems such as hose-fed sprinkle and trickle can be designed to fit random existing boundaries associated with small landholdings. This allows farm boundaries and most farm practices to remain traditional. However, such systems require very complex pipe networks to distribute the water to each plot and are very costly and complicated to operate and maintain except where the water supplies are also very small, as in the case of shallow tubewells, dug wells, and small springs.

3. *Consolidated small-scale modern irrigation with small-scale farming.* Unpopulated lands can be settled or random small holdings can be consolidated and distributed to give farmers small rectangular plots complete with modern irrigation systems such as hand-move lateral sprinkler and trickle. This has been done in order to maintain the fully independent nature of the on-farm irrigation systems on small holdings (as in Option 2 above) while at the same time reducing irrigation development costs and management difficulties by simplifying the pipe network required to deliver water. Rightfully, farmers often resist consolidating, for they feel they get "cheated" by losing good land and/or diversity (which gives them a degree of insurance over complete catastrophe) to gain relatively uniform (and usually smaller) rectangular plots of land. Even with such land realignment, serving individual small rectangular plots is quite expensive, and recent experience in Morocco and Jordan with the overall productivity and manageability of such schemes has been somewhat disappointing. Furthermore, the operation and maintenance of the distribution system (and even the on-farm components) often remain the responsibility of the irrigation department.

4. *Large-scale modern irrigation with random small-scale farming.* One cost-effective way to achieve this would be to install large center-pivot sprinklers (40 to 80 ha) on all land falling under an irrigation scheme and to provide timely irrigation as a service to the farmers, rather than only to supply a source of irrigation water for them to apply. Such a development scheme might be referred to as "controlled rain." But there are questions concerning the practicality of such a scheme:

- How can this be practical? The various crops and fields don't all need water on the same schedule.
- What about farm fields lying outside of the circular irrigated areas?
- How can farmers diversify or raise rice?
- Who would operate and maintain the systems?
- Haven't large public wells been a failure? So, why won't the same types of problems occur with a center-pivot scheme?

Option Selection

To take full advantage of large-scale modern systems such as center-pivots, either Option 1 or Option 4 is most appropriate from the engineering point of view. But can either be made to work? With small-scale modern systems (such as trickle, hand-move sprinklers, and piped surface systems) all options may be feasible, but Option 3 is undoubtedly the most practical for large-scale water supplies, and Options 2 and 3 are most suitable for small-scale supplies.

For the most part, the recent extensive irrigation development projects in Saudi Arabia have been accomplished using center pivots and Option 1. Most of the systems have been installed in arid areas that have not been farmed previously; therefore, land consolidation has not been necessary. Furthermore, since labor is scarce in such regions, there is incentive to utilize mechanized large-scale farming practices.

Essentially all of the almost 6 million ha of center-pivot-irrigated land throughout the world is irrigated and farmed under Option 1. In most of the more developed countries where center pivots are used, the individual farms are relatively large (50 ha or more) and are either privately or state owned and farmed. As far as I know, Option 4, using center pivots with random small-scale traditional farming, has not been tried. I have heard, however, that some surplus pivot systems from Libya are being given to Nicaragua for possible use, as in Option 4.

One note of caution, which was alluded to earlier, is in order where modern irrigation technologies, which require fuel and other purchased inputs to maintain the systems, are being contemplated. That is that the implementation of such projects must be contingent on the development of a market (or commercial) economy with adequate profitability, so that farmers can purchase the needed inputs plus reliable physical and technical services for maintaining the systems and supplying the needed inputs.

TRADITIONAL SYSTEMS

In large traditional canal irrigation systems with many small (up to 2 ha) farm units, it is very expensive and complex to have a bureaucracy and water delivery network that can deal effectively with each farmer. Thus, farmers are induced to organize into groups so that they can deal collectively with the main system management, and the main system management, in turn, needs to deal with only relatively few collective groups.

Traditional systems servicing small landholdings are easiest to operate and seem to work best for paddy rice irrigation. This is because in large flooded paddy areas a considerable amount of paddy-to-paddy distribution of water is practical, and the need for small distribution channels serving individual landholdings is reduced. Furthermore, where standing water is maintained, the need for precise land leveling is eliminated.

One of the principal concerns of farmers is the reliability of the water supply (Chambers, 1982). Without a reliable system, farmers view irrigation more or less the same as natural rainfall and act accordingly. They are reluctant to level their land for traditional irrigation or add the other high-cost inputs that are necessary to obtain the benefits needed to justify irrigation development. So, too often the water that is delivered has limited value to the farmers, and they spend little effort in utilizing it efficiently. Such systems increase neither production nor employment opportunities to any significant degree. Moreover, equitable water allocations are achieved only within well-managed systems. With inadequate management, "head end" farmers take a disproportionate share of water, leaving scarce and unpredictable supplies for "tail enders."

Conjunctive use of surface water and groundwater plays a very important role in irrigation development. In many situations the surface water lost to seepage and deep percolation recharges the groundwater stored in shallow aquifers. Individual farmers and/or groups of farmers can construct wells and pump water when they need it, provided the necessary fuel is available. Thus, the aquifer serves as both an auxiliary water conveyance and a storage system. The stored groundwater provides the farmers with a standby irrigation water supply that is independent of the vagaries of surface water deliveries. Furthermore, the groundwater affords an important means for providing more equitable distribution of project benefits between head enders and tail enders.

Management

There are three potential management levels in traditional irrigation systems: the main system, the "middle system," and the farmer system. Typically, in the United States the farm systems are so large they encompass what might be called the "middle system." That is, water is delivered directly from the main system to the individual farmer's holding. In fact, the main system typically delivers water to several outlets serving a given farmer's contiguous holdings. Thus, the main system actually forms part of the on-farm irrigation infrastructure, and there is only one management interface—that between the farmer and the main system. Furthermore, there are relatively few farm systems; thus, the main system needs to communicate with only a few users.

On projects involving main systems in developing countries, where the farm sizes are small, there is a need for management of middle system. This is because the bureaucracy operating the main system can hardly be expected to communicate and deal with all the farmers. The best solution to this problem is for the farmers themselves to organize into groups so that the main system managers can communicate with groups of farmers. This gives the farmers access to local management and allows the main-system managers to deal with relatively few large-system subsets.

Growing attention is being given to "main-system management" (MSM), which combines computer-assisted management techniques and improved water control structures and mechanisms. There has been a recognition of the fact that MSM and what we have called "on-farm water management" depend critically on each other. The need to accelerate the development and testing of MSM tools and to understand better the nature of the crucial interplay between farmers and system managers is also recognized.

Farmer management of the middle system is also important from the standpoint of maintenance. For example, if the bureaucracy operating the main system endeavors to deal directly with each farmer, it also overtly assumes the responsibility of maintaining the entire canal network down to each farm holding. Thus, an inordinate operation and maintenance burden is placed on the bureaucracy. Without costly subsidies, the bureaucracy usually fails in this area, and the middle system becomes a no-man's zone with deteriorated, inefficient tertiary watercourses. Unfortunately, it is also difficult to organize farmers, and it is costly for them to work together to operate and maintain this middle system.

In addition to the direct costs of operation and maintenance are the costs associated with organizing and with the rigid rotational water schedules often imposed to achieve equity. Much of the irrigation research, training, and rehabilitation activity is directed at dealing with the complexities and almost universal poor performance in terms of equitable water distribution, maintenance, and efficiency of the middle system (Barker et al., 1984).

For farmers to increase their water use efficiency at the field level in traditional irrigation systems, they must increase the labor, capital, and management inputs. Thus, it costs them more to use water efficiently than to misuse it. This extra cost is not necessarily offset by additional benefits from higher crop yields unless the water is in short but reliable, supply. Increasing the price of water actually allows the farmers less leeway for providing the additional on-farm cost of using it well.

An Example Alternative

Except for a fully automated mechanical system, irrigation is essentially a "happening." A traditional system does not irrigate—it is merely a network of channels feeding prepared fields. Human enterprise does the irrigating. Furthermore, the control and allocation of the water to the fields also requires continuous and direct human action. In other words, irrigation involves people and their tools. People provide the labor and management. Capital and energy must exist to obtain hardware and energy to operate. In addition, for successful irrigated agricultural production other physical inputs such as seed, fertilizer, and pesticides are required. These, in turn, take additional management, labor, capital, and energy.

The delivery of all of the above must come together in a more or less optimum mix in order to achieve high production. The modern technology development (Option 4) utilizing center pivots to provide controlled rain to otherwise undisturbed communities of small farms might be one means of greatly enhancing the probability of accomplishing this objective. Farmers would continue to cultivate their existing fields with ensured favorable moisture conditions and could concentrate their efforts on optimizing production and income. They would be relieved of organizing and competing for their individual irrigation supply and the very difficult task of effectively using it. Irrigation bureaucracies could concentrate on the proven and cost-effective industrial-type process of operating center-pivot projects to deliver controlled rain to communities of farmers. Operation and maintenance of the center pivots could be handled by the irrigation authorities, farmer groups, or private operation companies.

Option 4 presents intriguing possibilities not only for doubling or even tripling productivity per unit of water developed but also for increasing employment opportunities, especially for the landless and very small landholders. By combining modern irrigation with traditional farming methods, labor requirements will increase along with production. Furthermore, higher-value, more labor-intensive crops can be grown with limited but more precisely applied irrigation. Thus, modern irrigation applied in Third World developing countries not only may provide an important means for improving food production but also increases the employment opportunities for the rural poor so they can partake of the increased production.

Obviously, irrigation developments utilizing center pivots to provide controlled rain will eliminate many management and operation difficulties. These include difficulties related to the following: the interface between the main and middle systems, collective farmer operation of the middle system, communication between farmers and the irrigation supply, efficient conveyance of water from the main system to the field, efficient water allocation in the fields, and equitable (uniform) distribution to all plots. With a center-pivot project, the irrigation bureaucracy's responsibility would be to supply controlled rain uniformly and efficiently over the entire irrigation command area. Controlled rain would be scheduled to meet average crop water requirements, and the individual farmers could concentrate their efforts on optimizing production. This should be quite workable, since crop water requirements are similar for broad ranges of crops.

Admittedly, some flexibility would be lost in terms of controlling irrigation in individual fields and the selection of crop mixes and planting dates, but there will still be more than 20 percent of the gross area lying outside the irrigated circles. This should leave ample area for a diversity of other farming and irrigation practices and uses, such as rain-fed farming, irrigation of alternate crops (such as trees) from small wells, farmsteads and housing, etc. We believe farmers will consider themselves fortunate to be within the controlled-rain areas and gladly submit to farming under "ideal" rainfall conditions even with the implied restrictions—that is, providing the controlled rain is reliable and predictable.

CONCLUSIONS

We began by noting that the vast majority of irrigation systems fall short of expectations as a result of poor system management. With only about half of the targeted basic irrigation development now in place, there is ample scope for rehabilitating old systems and constructing new systems to make them more manageable. First, however, the public planning objectives of each system, be it for commercial production, sociopolitical, and/or geopolitical reasons, must be more clearly defined and system analysis and design pursued accordingly.

The objective of the farmers who are the beneficiaries of public irrigation systems is to maximize their net benefits from irrigation by maximizing the productivity per unit of land, which is usually their scarce resource. For an individual farmer, water may not be his scarce resource unless it is rationed, allocated, and distributed equitably. Therefore, he is not usually concerned about water use efficiency or fair and equitable distribution of water to other farmers, although these are the typical operational objectives for public irrigation systems. This dichotomy between the operational objectives and the private beneficiaries of public irrigation systems is the root of many problems in managing them.

Contrary to conventional wisdom, modern high-technology irrigation techniques not only are feasible but may be preferable methods of irrigation in a variety of circumstances in Third World countries for both recently commercialized agriculture and traditional agriculture. There exists the promise of increased employment opportunities, lower per-unit-area irrigation development costs, lower organizational costs to be borne by small-scale cultivators, a curtailed bureaucratic system, increased flexibility for farmers to respond to market prices, and even decreased competition between cultivators for limited water supplies. Quite possibly center-pivot irrigation systems, with their elegant and cost-effective simplicity, or other modern irrigation techniques may be found at the forefront of the charge to develop irrigated agriculture around the globe.

REFERENCES

Barker, R., E. W. Coward, G. Levine, and L. E. Small. 1984. Irrigation development in Asia: past trends and future directions. Cornell Studies in Irrigation Ithaca, N.Y.: Cornell University.

Chambers, R. 1982. Canal irrigation in India: some areas for action, analysis and research. Pp. 44–69. *In* General Asian Overview/USAID Water Management Synthesis Project Report no. 7. Logan, Utah: Utah State University.

Clyma, W., W. D. Kemper, and M. M. Ashraf. 1981. Reducing farm delivery losses in Pakistan. *Transactions of the ASAE* 24 (2):367–74.

EWUMP (Egyptian Water Use and Management Project). 1984. Improving Egypt's irrigation system in the old lands. Final Report. Cairo, Egypt.

Keller, J., B. Smith, A. LeBaron, P. Aitken, R. Meyer, M. Walters, and J. Wolf. 1984. Irrigation development options and investment strategies for the 1980s—USAID/Peru. Water Management Synthesis Project Report no. 14. Logan, Utah: Utah State University.

Keller, J. 1985. Taking advantage of modern irrigation in developing countries. *Agribusiness Worldwide,* March–April.

Svendsen, M. 1985. Current issues in irrigation management in Asia. Asia Bureau ADO conference, April 21–26, Los Baños, Philippines.

48. IRRIGATION TECHNOLOGY *

Dale F. Heermann, U.S. Department of Agriculture-Agricultural Research Service, and Agricultural Engineering Research Center, Colorado State University, Fort Collins, Colorado

ABSTRACT

Irrigation technology has a major impact on water resource use since irrigation is the major user of water. Current irrigation technology practices, trends in technology adoption, and research directions are discussed. Sprinkler and trickle systems can achieve higher efficiencies than surface systems, primarily because the irrigator can more easily control the delivery of water to the crop. The actual irrigation efficiency is affected as much by scheduling and management as by the delivery system. The public perceives that if irrigation efficiencies were increased we would have substantial additional available water. This is a misconception, since most of the water lost to surface runoff and deep percolation is available and often appropriated by downstream users. The major benefit of developing and improving irrigation technology is to increase production, improve net returns, decrease water quality degradation, and to a limited extent make more water available for other uses.

IRRIGATION TECHNOLOGY

Irrigation technology has been practiced around the world for several thousand years, including in the American Southwest since long before it became the United States. Many of the irrigation projects and systems currently operated in the United States began in the mid-1800s. The irrigated area in the United States in 1984 was about 25 million ha (1984 Irrigation Survey, 1985), 15 percent of which was added in the last decade. The mid-70s saw a more rapid growth in irrigated area than have the 80s. The southwestern United States and the Central Plains showed a slight increase in irrigated area for 1984. Small decreases occurred in the Southern Plains, with larger decreases in the southeastern United States, attributed primarily to Florida.

Early projects were irrigated almost exclusively by gravity methods. Today, approximately 36 percent of the irrigated area is sprinkler irrigated (1984 Irrigation Survey, 1985) and of this two-thirds is irrigated by center-pivot systems. The largest concentration of center pivots is in the Central Plains, followed by the Southern Plains and Pacific Northwest. Trickle irrigation, a newer technology, irrigates approximately 2.7 percent of the area in the Southwest and 4.9 percent in the Southeast. The major development of trickle irrigation systems has occurred in the last five to 10 years. Generally, trickle irrigation is best adapted to and most successfully used to produce high cash-value crops where water is expensive.

*Contribution from USDA-Agricultural Research Service in cooperation with Colorado State University.

TRENDS OF IRRIGATION DEVELOPMENT

The first irrigation developed in the western United States was adjacent to rivers and streams. Many individual irrigators and/or cooperatives developed small-scale canal systems which diverted water and delivered it to the irrigators' head gates. The water, transported in farm ditches to individual fields, was then diverted to furrows through "cuts" in the ditch bank. The major tool for irrigation farmers was the shovel.

The U.S. Bureau of Reclamation (USBR), established in 1902, brought about an expansion of the irrigated area by designing and constructing dams and canals to store and distribute water to areas for a more seasonally stable water supply. Most projects were irrigated by surface gravity methods and developments were concentrated in the arid and semiarid West along the major rivers. Many small private irrigation companies still provide water for crop production; some of them receive supplemental water from USBR projects.

The major improvements in the on-farm irrigation system in the 1940s and 1950s included replacement of the "cut" in the ditch bank with siphon tubes, use of ditch linings to prevent seepage losses, and burying pipeline with risers at the head of a field.

Gated pipe systems, introduced in the 1950s are currently used by many irrigators, particularly where water is pumped from groundwater sources directly into closed conduits. Gated pipe can be moved from field to field to facilitate operations, thus reducing equipment costs, or can be installed as solid sets to reduce labor costs. Gated pipe improves the control of the irrigation water and increases the irrigation efficiency. Application efficiencies are highly variable but are estimated to be an average of 50 percent for surface irrigation systems.

Groundwater development in the Central and Southern plains and in the southwestern United States, which also used gated pipe systems, was the next major area for development.

Center-pivot sprinkler systems became popular because automation provided the ease of irrigating large areas (53 to 200 ha under one pivot) with minimal labor input. Center-pivot development began in the mid-1960s, with rapid expansion into the 1970s not only in the Southern and Central plains but also in the Southeast on sandy, droughty soils. During the same period, large-scale private projects were also developed in the Pacific Northwest with water pumped from the Snake and Columbia rivers. Current economic conditions, increased pumping costs, and declining water tables are forcing some areas to revert to either dryland or limited irrigation. This is particularly true in the High Plains, where the groundwater tables in the Ogallala aquifer have dropped significantly.

EMERGING AND NEW TECHNOLOGY

Rapid increases in energy costs and the continual competition for limited water resources have been the impetus for continuing research to develop new irrigation systems and improved technology.

Surface Irrigation

Level basin irrigation has recently gained greater acceptance and adoption because of new technologies for constructing and operating level basins. The cost and difficulty of constructing and maintaining such basins were prohibitive prior to the use of laser leveling technology. Coupled with laser leveling was the development of reliable automation. Haise et al. (1981) designed and Dedrick and Erie (1978) demonstrated the use of jack-gates to automate the diversion of large streams. The acceptance of this technology has been concentrated in the southwestern United States, where large stream flows are available. It reduces labor and water costs. These systems can attain irrigation efficiencies of 90 percent when properly operated. Both close-growing and row crops are irrigated in level basins, with row crops generally grown on beds.

In the absence of large irrigation streams, surface irrigation automation requires smaller level basins. Adaptation of available farm machinery makes this impractical, and sloping, larger fields are more desirable. Laser leveling becomes less important and the use of the automation devices for large flows is not easily transferable. Many more water control points are required for these irrigation systems, thereby increasing the cost for automation.

A gated pipe sytem can be automated either by installing, at risers or in the lateral, pneumatic valves, which can be remotely controlled by radio or wire, or by using portable controllers to regulate the distribution of water. Commercially available valves can control flow into individual sections of gated pipe to irrigate a number of furrows. Farmer acceptance of this technology seems to be limited. The cost and the lack of a complete or turnkey irrigation system are probably deterring factors to adoption. Haise et al. (1981) developed valves to control the flow for each furrow, but they have not become commercially available and are expensive per unit area. Much of the system cost is in design requirements that need technical expertise; thus, profits of hardware sales are diminished. Sprinkler systems, on the other hand, are easier to design and install, with more profit potential for system components.

Kemper et al. (1981), Kincaid and Kemper (1982), and Goel et al. (1982) have developed and tested cablegation for automation of furrow irrigation systems. Cablegation is a unique system which provides for a cable-controlled plug to continually move inside a graded perforated supply pipe and thereby change the set of furrows receiving water. A water brake controls the cable and plug speed. A bypass system also has been added to improve the uniformity of water application and the simplicity of controlling the rate of plug movement without an external power source to control the time of irrigation. A number of systems have been installed in several of the western states.

Surge irrigation on graded surface irrigation systems (Stringham and Keller, 1979) has also attracted considerable interest by many irrigators. The general approach is to introduce a maximum nonerosive stream into a furrow for a short period of time (i.e., until water advances a quarter of the length of furrow) and then to divert it into an adjacent set of furrows. The stream is alternated between furrow sets until it reaches the end of the field, at which time the stream is divided. Irrigation continues at one-half the stream flow until all furrows in the combined sets are adequately irrigated. Advantages include greater uniformity of application and reduced runoff. These advantages are accomplished by decreasing the time required for the stream to advance to the end of the irrigated furrow and minimizing the infiltration at the upper end of the field, thus increasing the uniformity of irrigation. The smaller discharge rate or cutback stream for the latter part of the irrigation period reduces the volume of surface runoff. Cutback irrigation has been recognized as beneficial but has been labor intensive and expensive to implement.

Industry has responded to the development of surge technology by supplying a number of surge controllers and valves which allow the irrigator to select the cycle time and frequency for alternating the stream flow. In the Texas High Plains, where falling groundwater tables are limiting the available water, the number of surge irrigation systems currently in use exceeds 1,000. Research scientists still have the challenge of developing the recommended frequency and cycle times best suited for surge irrigation on different soil types and topography. There is a wide variability as to the current recommendations and practices.

Stewart et al. (1981) have developed and tested an irrigation system referred to as an LID system (limited irrigation–dryland). The system minimizes the cost for pumping water and maximizes the use of natural precipitation. It is particularly adapted to low-intake soils with high water-holding capacities and where irrigation water supplies are insufficient to meet the irrigation requirement. It is a furrow irrigation system where the inflow stream does not reach the end of the furrow. The upper portion of the field has the soil profile filled, while the lower end of the field is left nonirrigated. The system uses small furrow dams to prevent surface runoff. Sufficient rainfall must be available for some dryland production for the LID system to be effective.

Sprinkler Systems

Center-pivot systems have sprinkler heads mounted on a pipeline which is suspended on towers, rotates about a pivot, and supplies water very uniformly over the field, with very little labor required. As energy costs increased, many center pivots were converted from high-pressure (600 kPa) to low-pressure (300 kPa) impact sprinklers, or even lower pressure, using spray nozzles (150 kPa) to reduce pumping costs. Conversion to low pressure results in higher application rates with reduced sprinkler pattern radii and thus increases the possibility of runoff. Minimum tillage and other cultural practices such as furrow diking increase infiltration rates or provide surface storage to reduce or eliminate surface runoff. Researchers have demonstrated that an effective way to prevent surface runoff under center-pivot systems is to install furrow checks or pits to capture surface water. Several equipment manufacturers have equipment commercially available for that purpose.

Lateral-move irrigation systems have sprinkler heads mounted on an elevated pipeline, with more uniform and lower application rates along the lateral than are typical near the outer end of a center-pivot system. These systems can irrigate square or rectangular fields. The major problem with lateral systems is that the inlet continually moves and requires a pump to be mounted on the system pumping from an open ditch. The other alternative is to drag a flexible hose connected to a riser from a buried pipeline.

LEPA

The low-energy precision applicator (LEPA) irrigation system reduces the energy requirements and simultaneously obtains very high irrigation uniformities (Lyle and Bordovsky, 1981). The system is similar to a lateral-move sprinkler system except that the water is discharged into drop tubes, which effectively operate as a traveling surface or trickle system. The water is discharged just above the soil surface into furrows that have small earth dams to store the water while it infiltrates. These systems have been demonstrated to offer a very effective way of reducing energy costs and providing high irrigation efficiencies (95%). By applying the water very near the soil surface, spray or drift losses are nearly eliminated. Evaporation loss is limited to that from the wetted soil surface.

Trickle

Trickle irrigation is one of the newest technologies used by irrigators. The major areas of application are the Southwest and Florida in the Southeast. Trickle systems are economically feasible with high cash-value crops such as fruits and vegetables. Hawaii has installed trickle systems for at least half of its sugarcane and pineapple production. Sugar production is generally increased by approximately 10 percent when compared to surface irrigation. This increase is attributed to better timing of water application where water supplies are limited. The current economics for trickle irrigation has not favored adoption of this technology for many row crops which have low cash value. Trickle systems can be operated to obtain irrigation efficiencies of 90 percent.

Subsurface

The term *subsurface irrigation* is used herein for reversible drainage systems. Buried trickle systems with low-discharge emitters are classified as trickle irrigation. The primary development of subsurface irrigation is in the southeastern United States. The systems require high water tables, which may be effectively controlled for crop production. In the corn belt, drainage problems are more prevalent than the need for irrigation. The nonuniform seasonal distribution of rainfall makes irrigation profitable in many years, primarily on the soils with low water-holding capac-

ity. Water is pumped back into the drain lines and refills the soil profile with water for crop production. Sandy and/or shallow soils are the most affected by short periods of deficit precipitation. The timing of interrupting drainage and starting to pump water back into the system is a key to successful management of subsurface irrigation and crop production. Drain lines must be spaced close enough to raise and lower the water table over the entire field.

IRRIGATION WATER MANAGEMENT

The key to improve water use efficiency is not only in the design of the irrigation system but also in the management and operation. Many still have the misconception that irrigation efficiency depends only on the irrigation system design. Each type of irrigation system has different labor and management requirements. However, the degree of water control obtained with an irrigation system is dependent on the quality of management and on irrigation scheduling. The best-designed trickle system can be operated less efficiently than many surface irrigation systems.

Irrigation Scheduling Approaches

There are a number of techniques and tools available for irrigation scheduling. One technique calculates a water budget with meteorological data to maintain the current water status for individual fields and forecast future irrigation dates and amounts. Jensen (1969) pioneered much of the work in adapting these techniques to computers. Many researchers have developed various computer programs for the many different styles of computers and calculators now available for implementing this technology. Updating the water budget with feedback requires other tools and devices which can monitor the status of soil water or plant-available water—that is, tensiometers, gypsum blocks, neutron probes, plant sensors, and thermal infrared sensors. An irrigation schedule should forecast the time and amount of water that should be applied. If water is available on demand and can be controlled by a sensor a schedule is not required. Where the water supply comes from direct diversion or storage reservoirs, it must be ordered in advance and cannot be turned on instantaneously as a sensor reaches a set point. Even with groundwater systems the supply may not be large enough to supply all fields based on field-sensed demand. Scheduling also needs to be accomplished to avoid conflicts with cultural practices.

Irrigation-Scheduling Delivery Systems

There are a number of ways that water budgets and irrigation scheduling technology can be used by an irrigator. Nebraska has implemented an AG-NET central computer network with a data base that includes irrigation scheduling programs that can be operated from terminals throughout the state. Weather stations are installed at a number of locations and automatically or manually input current data into the central data base for access by an individual irrigator.

Many private consulting firms provide water budget computer programs and technical assistance to recommend irrigation scheduling dates and amounts to individual farmers. Most consultants use trained technicians who make frequent visits to the farm for monitoring the actual soil water conditions. Some water districts employ the services of trained technical people to provide irrigation scheduling service to their irrigators. The state extension service and Soil Conservation Service provide training and technical assistance to farmers for improving their water management.

Readily available home computers provide a tool which can be used by the irrigator to maintain his own water budget. Climatic data for calculating reference ET are being published in newspapers, made available on dial-up telephone, and broadcast on radio and television. Field sensors are also readily available for use by individual irrigators to monitor the current soil water status.

Scheduling for Peak Electrical Load Control

Heermann et al. (1984) developed a system that integrated an irrigation scheduling program with a program for controlling peak electrical demands. This system includes a radio telemetry system and a microcomputer for monitoring the irrigation systems, controlling the pumping plants, providing irrigation scheduling, and implementing peak electrical load control programs. The system has been used successfully for three seasons and has been accepted by both the suppliers and the irrigators. Several commercial companies are currently manufacturing and marketing the radio telemetry—computer equipment which provides for the adoption of this technology. The systems include weather stations, which automatically collect real-time climatic data for use in irrigation scheduling programs and provide recommendations of future irrigations based on current water budgets. The automatic feedback of rainfall and irrigations will simplify the implementation of irrigation scheduling technology. The combination of improved management for increased production and reducing electrical demand costs provides the economic incentive to adopt this technology.

Frost Protection and Bud Delay

Irrigation systems can be used for purposes other than to provide water for crop production. Many producers of vegetables and fruits use sprinkler irrigation systems to provide frost protection. Alfaro et al. (1973) demonstrated the use of sprinkler systems to delay bud development. The principle in using irrigation for bud delay is to keep the fruit cooler during extended warming spells in late winter, which will cause many fruit trees to flower before the frost danger is past.

CHEMIGATION

Surface, sprinkler, and trickle systems are used for timely application of fertilizers. Center-pivot systems are also used to apply insecticides and herbicides. The practice is becoming widely accepted, but the big concern now is to ensure the safe handling of chemicals and to prevent pollution. Preventing back flow and contamination of groundwater sources is one area of concern. Many states are preparing legislation governing the use of irrigation equipment for chemical application.

FUTURE DEVELOPMENTS

Current research concerns new approaches, subsystems, and components to improve irrigation efficiencies in sprinkler, surface, and trickle irrigation systems. Surface irrigation has the potential of requiring the least amount of energy, often a major operating cost for irrigation. The spatial and temporal variability of infiltration has a major effect on the irrigation efficiency with surface systems. Basic studies of infiltration theory and field studies of tillage and cropping practices are essential to develop and design more efficient surface systems. Real-time feedback from surface irrigation systems to control the distribution of water is also being investigated. Such systems include the use of field sensors to monitor the advance of the stream, as well as water measurement devices for determining the flow rates. These signals can then be input to microcomputers to solve mathematical models for controlling and changing of sets for irrigations on a real-time basis.

A number of studies concern basic principles and optimum operating criteria for implementing surge irrigation, such as determining the proper stream sizes, cycle frequencies, and cycle durations. Commercial companies are developing the necessary control valves and irrigation controllers which could implement the optimum operating criteria for surge systems.

Limited research has addressed techniques for optimizing water allocation (Pleban et al., 1983). These programs are particularly important where the water supply is not available on demand for satisfying all irrigation requirements. Field testing of models for real-time optimization of water allocation is needed.

Models may become significantly more important as water supplies become limited. Improved yield response functions for limited water conditions at various growth stages are needed. Simulation models can then be used to develop strategies for planning the best methods for using limited water supplies and maximizing the use of natural precipitation.

The next generation of computers and artificial intelligence and expert systems will provide new tools which will certainly have an impact on new irrigation system controls and management strategies.

REFERENCES

Alfaro, J. R., R. E. Griffin, J. Keller, G. R. Hanson, J. Anderson, G. L. Ashcroft, and E. A. Richardson. 1973. Preventive freeze protection by preseason sprinkling to delay bud development. ASAE Paper no. 73-2531. St. Joseph, Mich.: American Society of Agriculture Engineers.

Dedrick, A. R., and L. J. Erie. 1978. Automation of on-farm irrigation turnouts utilizing jack-gates. *Transactions of the ASAE* 21(1):92–96.

Goel, M. C., W. D. Kemper, R. Worstell, and J. Bondurant. 1982. Cablegation: Ill. Field assessment of performance. *Transactions of the ASAE* 25(5):1304–1309.

Haise, H. R., E. G. Kruse, M. L. Payne, and H. R. Duke. 1981. Automation of surface irrigation: 15 years of USDA research and development at Fort Collins, Colorado. USDA-SEA-AR Production Research Report no. 179.

Heermann, D. F., G. W. Buchleiter, and H. R. Duke. 1984. Integrated water-energy management system for center pivot irrigation: implementation. *Transactions of the ASAE* 27(5): 1424–29.

Jensen, M. E. 1969. Scheduling irrigations using computers. *Journal of Soil and Water Conservation* 24(8): 193–95.

Kemper, W. D., W. H. Heinemann, D. C. Kincaid, and R. V. Worstell. 1981. Cablegation: I. Cable controlled plugs in perforated supply pipes for automatic furrow irrigation. *Transactions of the ASAE* 24(6): 1526–32.

Kincaid, D. C., and W. D. Kemper. 1982. Cablegation: II. Simulation and design of the moving-plug, gated pipe irrigation system. *Transactions of the ASAE* 25(2): 388–95.

Lyle, W. M., and J. P. Bordovsky. 1981. Low energy precision application irrigation system. *Transactions of the ASAE* 24(5): 1201–45. 1984 Irrigation Survey. 1985. *Irrigation Journal* 35(1).

Pleban, S., J. W. Labadie, and D. F. Heermann. 1983. Optimal short term irrigation schedules. *Transactions of the ASAE* 26(1): 141–47.

Stewart, B. A., D. A. Dusek, and J. T. Musick. 1981. A management system for the conjunctive use of rainfall and limited irrigation of graded furrows. *Soil Science Society of America Journal* 45: 413–19.

Stringham, G. E., and J. Keller. 1979. Surge flow for automatic irrigation. Pp. 132–42. *In* Proceedings of the 1979 irrigation and drainage specialty conference. Albuquerque, N.Mex. American Society of Civil Engineers.

49. DRAINAGE

Richard Wayne Skaggs, Department of Biological and Agricultural Engineering, North Carolina State University, Raleigh, North Carolina

ABSTRACT

All soils require drainage for agricultural production; many need improved or artificial drainage. Agricultural drainage systems have traditionally been installed for three reasons: (1) to provide trafficable conditions so that seedbed preparation, planting, harvesting, and other operations can be conducted in a timely manner; (2) to protect crops from excessive soil water conditions; and (3) for salinity control. While these objectives are still of primary importance, drainage should be considered only one component of the water management system. Thus the design and evaluation of a drainage system should consider its effects on drought stress and the amount of irrigation water required, as well as the primary drainage objectives. In some cases combination drainage-subirrigation or water table control systems can be used to satisfy both drainage and irrigation needs. Off-site impacts should also be considered as a constraint in the design of drainage sytems. Where possible, both agricultural production objectives and water quality and quantity requirements of the receiving waters should be considered in the design. Water management simulation models and new methods for predicting crop response to excessive and deficient soil water conditions promise to be effective tools for analyzing and designing drainage and associated water management systems in the future.

Drainage of water from the soil profile is an important hydrologic component in most agricultural soils. Natural drainage processes include groundwater flow to streams or other surface outlets; vertical seepage to underlying aquifers; or lateral flow (interflow), which may reappear at the surface at some other point in the landscape. In many soils, the natural drainage processes are sufficient for the growth and production of agricultural crops. In other soils, artificial drainage is needed for efficient agricultural production.

Soils may have poor natural drainage because they have low surface elevations, are far removed from a drainage outlet, or receive seepage from upslope areas, or because they are in depressional areas. Water drains slowly from soils with tight subsurface layers, regardless of where they are in the landscape; so soils may have poor natural drainage due to restricted permeability or hydraulic conductivity of the profile. Climate is another important factor affecting the need for artificial drainage. Natural drainage at a rate that may be sufficient for agriculture in a section of Nebraska, where annual rainfall is 600 mm, may be inadequate in Louisiana, where the annual rainfall is 1400 mm. Nowhere is this factor more evident than in irrigated arid and semiarid areas. Lands that have been farmed for centuries under dryland cultures often develop high water tables and become waterlogged after irrigation is established. By contrast, natural drainage may be adequate in other arid-region soils and the severalfold increase in the amount of irrigation water applied to the surface will not result in poorly drained conditions. Seepage from unlined irrigation canals or from man-made reservoirs may also result in poorly drained soils in areas where they did not previously exist.

In summary, all soils require drainage for efficient agricultural production; many need improved or artificial drainage. In most cases improved drainage practices can be used to satisfy agricultural requirements. Drainage requirements and methods used to design systems to satisfy those requirements are discussed in the following section. A case study is presented to describe the design and operation of a drainage system in a humid region. The chapter concludes with a discussion of the need to consider off-site impacts of drainage and related water management practices.

DRAINAGE REQUIREMENTS

There are basically three reasons for the installation of agricultural drainage systems: (1) for trafficability, so that seedbed preparation, planting, harvesting, and other field operations can be conducted in a timely manner; (2) for protection of the crop from excessive soil water conditions; and (3) for salinity control.

Trafficability

The effect of good drainage on timeliness of farming operations was discussed in detail by Reeve and Fausey (1974). Soils with inadequate drainage may experience frequent yield losses because essential farming operations cannot be conducted in a timely fashion. The result may range from complete crop failure, if planting is delayed too long, to reduced yields, if tillage, spraying, harvesting, or other operations are not performed on time.

Protection from Excessive Soil Water Conditions

It is well recognized that the major effects of excessive soil water on crop production are caused by reduction in exchange of air between the atmosphere and the soil root zone. Wet soil conditions may result in a deficiency of O_2 required for root respiration, an increase in CO_2, and the formation of toxic compounds in the soil and plants. Under field conditions, soil-water-plant systems vary continuously. Evaluating the effect of water content and aeration status on plant growth requires integration of these conditions over time during the entire growing season. One of the parameters that give a certain integration of these factors in soils requiring artificial drainage is the water table depth (Wesseling, 1974). Although the depth of water table has no direct influence on crop growth, it is an indicator of the pre-

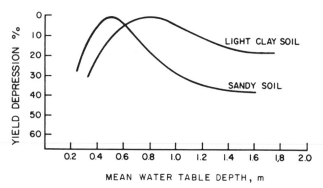

Fig. 1. Yield depression as a function of mean water table depth during the growing season for two soils. After Wesseling, 1974.

vailing soil water status, water supply aeration, and thermal conditions of the soil.

Numerous laboratory and field experiments have been conducted to determine the effect of water table depth on crop yields. Probably the main reason yield has been related to water table depth is that water table depth is easier to measure than other variables such as the distribution of oxygen in the profile. Most experiments have been directed at relating yields to constant water table depths (Williamson and Kriz, 1970). An example of the effect of water table depth on yield is given in Fig. 1. The results were obtained from Wesseling (1974) and are based on original research conducted in the Netherlands by W. C. Visser. Both relationships show reduction in yield at shallow water table depths because of excessive soil water conditions, an optimum range, and a decrease in yield at deeper water table depths because of deficient soil water conditions. Clearly, the relative position of curves such as those given in Fig. 1 would depend on climate, soil properties, the crop, and cultural and water management practices. Williamson and Kriz (1970) found that optimum water table depths were greater when irrigation water was applied at the surface.

While cause-and-effect relationships for crop yields are easier to identify for constant water table depths, such steady-state conditions rarely occur in nature. The effects of fluctuating water tables and intermittent flooding on crop yields depend on the frequency and duration of high water tables as well as the crop sensitivity. Approximate methods have been developed to quantify the effect of excessive soil water conditions caused by fluctuating water tables for corn (Hardjoamidjojo et al., 1982) and grain sorghum (Ravelo et al., 1982). The method employs the SEW_{30} concept originally defined by Sieben (Wesseling, 1974) and the stress-day index method, defined by Hiler (1969) in a water management simulation model (Skaggs, 1978) to estimate the effects of drainage design parameters, soil properties, weather data, and crop parameters on yields. Results of the model will be demonstrated in a later section of this paper.

Salinity Control

It seems somehow unjust that the dry lands of arid and semi-arid regions, when irrigated, often require artificial drainage. Luthin (1957) documented drainage problems that have

beset irrigators since the earliest recorded times in history. Accumulation of salts in the surface soil layers caused the once fertile Tigris and Euphrates river valleys of ancient Mesopotamia to return to desert. A present-day example is the annual loss of thousands of acres per year in the San Joaquin Valley of California because of salt accumulation and waterlogging.

Practically all irrigation water contains some salt. Evaporation and consumptive use of water by plants concentrate the salts in the residual soil water, resulting in a solution that is usually more saline than the irrigation water. Repeated irrigations continually increases the salinity of the soil water, even if the irrigation water is of relatively good quality. In order to prevent the buildup of soil water salinity to a point that it harms plant roots and reduces productivity, irrigation water in excess of the amount needed for evapotranspiration is applied to leach the concentrated soil solution from the root zone. If drainage is adequate, the excess irrigation water will carry the concentrated salt solution out of the root zone. If it is not removed, the water table will rise in response to the excess irrigation water, the salinity will continue to increase in the root zone, and crop yields will be reduced as a result of high salinity as well as high water tables.

Artificial drainage systems are often needed to remove the excess irrigation water from the soil profile. Because the salinity below the water table is usually several times that of the irrigation water, drainage systems are normally designed to hold the water table well below the root depth. Drains are typically placed 2 to 3 m deep in irrigated lands, as compared with 0.75 to 1.5 m deep in humid areas.

DRAINAGE DESIGN

Drainage materials and installation methods have been tremendously improved in the last twenty years. Corrugated plastic tubing, the drain tube plow, laser grade control for both surface and subsurface drainage machines, and synthetic envelope materials represent some of the advances that have occurred. Both subsurface and surface drainage systems can be installed quickly and efficiently using modern technology. The challenge, from the engineering and scientific perspective, is to tailor the design and operation of drainage and associated water management systems to soil, crop, and climatological parameters and to specific site conditions.

Both surface and subsurface drainage systems are used to meet drainage requirements of poorly drained sites. A schematic of a drainage system is shown in Fig. 2. Subsurface drainage is provided by drain tubes or parallel ditches spaced at some distance, L, apart. Most poorly drained soils have a restrictive layer at some depth, shown here as a distance, d, below the drain tubes. When rainfall occurs, water infiltrates at the surface, raising the water content of the soil profile. Depending on the initial soil water content and the amount of infiltration, some of the water may percolate through the profile, raising the water table and increasing the subsurface drainage rate. If the rainfall rate is greater than the infiltration rate, water begins to collect on the surface. If good surface drainage is provided so that the surface

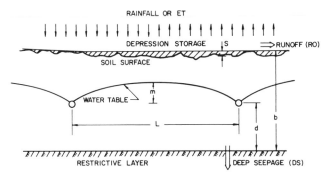

Fig. 2. Schematic of a drainage system. The subsurface drainage intensity depends on the depth and spacing of the drain tubes, while the quality of surface drainage is inversely proportional to the depth of depression storage.

is smooth and on grade, most of the surface water will be available for runoff. However, if surface drainage is poor, a substantial amount of water must be stored in depressions before runoff can begin. After rainfall ceases, infiltration continues until the water stored in surface depressions is infiltrated into the soil. Thus, poor surface drainage effectively lengthens the infiltration event for some storms, permitting more water to infiltrate and producing a larger rise in the water table than would occur if depression storage did not exist. Once excess water enters the soil profile, it may be removed by evapotranspiration from the surface and through the plants; by natural drainage processes via deep and lateral seepage; and through man-made systems consisting of drainage tubes, ditches, or wells.

Numerous drainage theories, based on both steady-state and transient analyses, have been developed (van Schilfgaarde, 1974) to relate drain spacing and depth to soil properties and site conditions. In general, transient methods have been preferred in humid areas, where the drainage criterion is often to lower the water table at a specified rate. Steady-state methods are also used in humid areas (Luthin, 1957), as well as in arid areas, where the drainage criterion is related to the volume of water to be removed. While there are many steady-state and transient methods available to treat a wide range of boundary and site conditions, practically all are based on criteria that are only indirectly related to the actual objectives of a drainage system. Simulation models developed in the last ten years provide a more direct link between design parameters and objectives of the drainage system. Simulation of the performance of a drainage system over several years of climatological record can be used to determine if a given design will satisfy trafficability and crop protection requirements. Several models have been developed (Lagace, 1973; Belmans et al., 1983). The water management simulation model, DRAINMOD, developed at North Carolina State University (Skaggs, 1978, 1980), will be used herein to demonstrate the approach and to examine further the interactions and effectiveness of surface and subsurface drainage.

The reader is referred to the references for details of the DRAINMOD model. Inputs to the model include soil properties, crop parameters, drainage system parameters, and

climatological data. The model is based on a water balance in the soil profile, which is computed on an hourly basis by using approximate methods to calculate infiltration, drainage, subirrigation, and evapotranspiration (as limited by both atmospheric and soil water conditions). The quality of surface drainage depends on the depth of depression storage, which may vary from about 1 mm for land-formed fields that have been smoothed to greater than 30 mm for fields with numerous potholes and depressions (Gayle and Skaggs, 1978). Thus the effect of improving surface drainage can be simulated by varying the average depth of depression storage.

Approximate methods based on the stress-day index concept (Hiler, 1969) were incorporated in the model (Skaggs and Tabrizi, 1983) to predict the effect of excessive and deficient soil water conditions on corn yields. The effect of trafficability is estimated from experimental data relating yield reduction to planting date delay.

As an example of the use of simulation models for the analysis of drainage systems, results for an eastern North Carolina soil, Rains sandy loam, will be presented. This soil has a nearly level surface, a hydraulic conductivity of about 1 m/day, and a profile depth of 1.4 m. It requires artificial drainage for trafficability and protection from excessive soil water during wet periods. Details of the soil properties and other input data are given elsewhere (Skaggs and Tabrizi, 1983). Simulations were conducted for several drain spacings with both good and poor surface drainage, using weather data from Wilson, North Carolina.

Average predicted relative yields for the twenty-six-year simulation period are plotted in Fig. 3 as a function of drain spacing. Relationships for both good (depression storage, S = 2.5 mm) and poor (S = 25 mm) surface drainage are presented. A maximum average relative yield (YR) of 0.78 was predicted for a drain spacing of L = 20 m for good surface drainage and for L = 17 m for poor surface drainage.

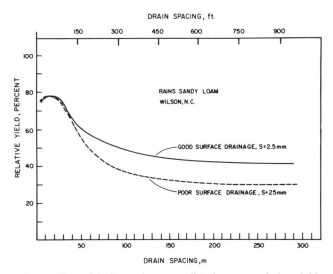

Fig. 3. Effect of drain spacing on predicted average relative yields for a Rains sandy loam soil at Wilson, North Carolina. Predictions for both good and poor surface drainage are plotted.

Because of deficient soil water conditions, which caused drought stresses during several years, higher average yields were not obtained. Yields increased with better drainage (decreasing drain spacing) until the maximum was obtained. Further decreases in drain spacing caused the average YR values to drop slightly, showing a tendency toward overdrainage when drains are placed too close together.

These results clearly show that yield response to surface drainage is dependent on subsurface drainage intensity. For good subsurface drainage (e.g., drain spacings of less than about 30 m), surface drainage has little effect on predicted yields. However, surface drainage is very important when subsurface drainage is poor. For example, the predicted relative yield on the Rains soil for a 100 m drain spacing is YR = 0.48 for good surface drainage versus YR = 0.37 for poor surface drainage. Economic analyses using present costs and prices were conducted to determine the drainage treatment that would produce the maximum net profit. Results showed that the maximum profit for this soil would be obtained for a 24-m drain spacing with unimproved subsurface drainage.

Annual relative yields predicted for years 1950 through 1975 are plotted in Fig. 4 for the Rains sandy loam with drain spacings of 24 and 100 m. Average predicted relative yields were 0.76 and 0.47 for the 24-m and 100-m spacings, respectively. However, differences in the predicted yields between the two spacings varied widely from year to year. In wet years, the closer drain spacing gave much higher yields. For example, in 1961, YR = 0.90 for L = 24 m, as opposed to YR = 0.23 for L = 100 m. For that year the closer spacing allowed planting on time (by April 15), and the only decrease in yield was due to a short period, early in the growing season, when the water table was high. However, planting for the 100-m spacing was delayed until the last of May. High water table conditions after planting and dry conditions later on during the delayed growing season caused additional yield reductions. The cumulative effect resulted in a relative yield of 0.23 for the 100-m spacing.

During years when yields were limited by deficient soil water conditions, very little yield difference between the 24 m and 100 m drain spacings occurred. Examples are 1952 and 1964. In a few years (e.g., 1956 and 1970), predicted yields for the 100-m spacing were higher than for the 24-m spacing. This was caused by a sequence of weather events that allowed planting to be completed on time for the closer spacing but delayed planting for twenty to thirty days for the wider spacing. Subsequently, deficient soil water conditions occurred at a time when the early-planted corn was most susceptible to drought. The later-planted corn fared better because rainfall occurred before its period of maximum susceptibility.

Results given in Fig. 3 and 4 show that average yields are significantly increased by improved drainage. However, the benefits of drainage are widely variable from year to year. Improved drainage increases not only average yields but also the reliability of production.

SUBIRRIGATION

The same drainage system that removes excess water during wet periods can also be used in some soils for irrigation during periods of deficient soil water. Subirrigation involves raising the water table and maintaining it at a position that will supply water to the growing crop. A sketch of both a drainage system and a combination drainage-subirrigation system is given in Fig. 5. Drains outlet to a ditch, as shown on the right side of the drawing, or to a head control tank. For conventional drainage the water level in the outlet is maintained at or below the depth of the drain tube. During subirrigation the water level in the outlet is raised to force water back through the drains and raise the water table, as shown in the bottom part of Fig. 5. Subirrigation has been practiced in scattered locations for many years (Clinton, 1967; Renfro, 1955) and has advantages over other alternatives in certain conditions. However, until recently the method has not been widely used because of the lack of established design criteria and information characterizing the operation of systems in the field. Research in recent years has provided answers to many of these questions, and subirrigation is now being promoted by the drainage industry and by public agencies. As a result its use is currently increasing rapidly.

In order for the subirrigation systems to be practical, cer-

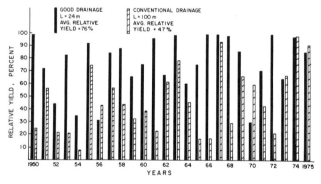

Fig. 4. Yearly predicted relative corn yields for the optimum drain spacing of 24 m and the conventional open ditch spacing of 100 m for a Rains sandy loam soil.

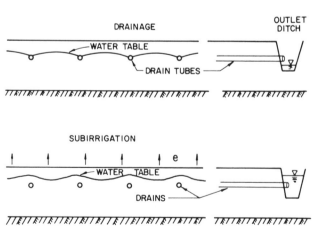

Fig. 5. Schematic of a system used for both conventional drainage (top) and subirrigation (bottom).

tain natural conditions must exist: an impermeable layer or a permanent water table at a rather shallow depth (within 6 to 8 m of the surface), to prevent excessive seepage losses; relatively flat land; a moderate to high soil hydraulic conductivity, so that a reasonable spacing of ditches or drain tubes will provide subirrigation and drainage; and a readily available source of water. These topographical and soil conditions exist in several million acres of land in the humid regions of the United States. Where suitable conditions exist, combined subirrigation-drainage systems offer a number of advantages and can play a significant role in water management strategies. Probably the most outstanding advantage is the cost; both drainage and subirrigation can be provided in one system, often with a considerable cost reduction in comparison to separate systems. In addition, energy requirements for pumping irrigation water may be considerably lower than for conventional irrigation systems (Massey et al., 1983). While salt buildup at the soil surface poses no problem in humid regions, subirrigation is not feasible in arid and semiarid areas because of this problem.

The most critical aspect of design and management of subirrigation-drainage system is the interaction between the irrigation and drainage functions. It is nearly impossible to determine, a priori, what the most critical sequence of weather events might be for a given management strategy. The most effective way of analyzing the performance of such systems is to use simulation methods, such as those discussed in the previous section. The DRAINMOD model is now being used by the Soil Conservation Service and others for design and analysis of subirrigation systems.

Research continues to develop better methods for managing or controlling these dual-purpose systems. Smith et al. (1982) used both field experiments and simulation methods to show that controlling subirrigation applications based on field water levels rather than outlet conditions reduced both water and energy requirements. Fouss (1983) modified the DRAINMOD model to analyze various control strategies for a subirrigation system.

OFF-SITE EFFECTS

The preceding sections have discussed drainage and water table management in terms of agricultural requirements. Traditionally, the efforts of engineers, technicians, farmers, and contractors have been aimed at one goal: to design and install systems that will satisfy agricultural drainage requirements at the least cost. However, recognition in recent years of agriculture's role in non-point source pollution of surface waters places additional constraints on the design and operation of drainage and related water management systems. This is particularly true where farms are located in environmentally sensitive areas, or where downstream users of water have stringent water quality of quantity requirements. In most cases there are several design and operational alternatives that can be used to satisfy agricultural drainage needs. Some of those alternatives have different effects on the rate and quality of water leaving the fields than do others. The challenge is to identify those alternatives that will satisfy agricultural requirements while minimizing detrimental effects on the receiving waters.

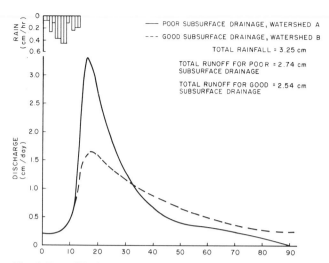

Fig. 6. Runoff hydrographs for 3.25 cm rainfall event on Feb. 28, 1983. The peak runoff rate for watershed A, with poor subsurface drainage, was more than twice that from the adjacent watershed B, which had good subsurface drainage.

Although research is by no means complete on this subject, considerable work has been done to determine water quality and hydrologic effects of drainage and associated water management practices. In general, systems that depend primarily on surface drainage tend to have higher rates of runoff with more sediment, phosphorus, and pesticides than do systems with good subsurface drainage. However, good subsurface drainage increases the outflow of nitrates with the drainage water. Associated water management practices such as controlled drainage and subirrigation will also have an effect on both the rate and the quality of drainage water leaving a field.

An example of the effect of subsurface drainage on peak outflow rates is given in Fig. 6. The runoff hydrographs were measured on adjacent flat (less than 0.05 percent slope) 32.5-ha eastern North Carolina watersheds with identical soils and crops. Watershed A has parallel ditches spaced 100 m apart, which provide good surface drainage but relatively poor subsurface drainage. Watershed B has the same surface drainage system but has drain tubes at 33 m intervals between the ditches, which provide good subsurface drainage. The results show that, while total drainage from the 3.25 cm storm was about the same for both watersheds, the peak outflow rate from the fields with good subsurface drainage was less than half that from the fields with poor subsurface drainage. Good subsurface drainage removes excess water from the profile slowly over a longer period of time. It lowers the water table and provides more storage for infiltrating rainfall than systems that depend primarily on surface drainage. Thus, in areas where high surface runoff rates cause flooding and related problems, subsurface drainage would tend to reduce the peaks. These effects may be very important in lands close to estuarine nursery areas, where high runoff rates are perceived to cause unnatural salinity fluctuations and a consequent reduction in productivity of finfish and shellfish.

Table 1. Effect of subsurface drainage on concentration of nitrogen and phosphorus in outflow from adjacent 35 ha watersheds.

Watershed[a]	Concentration (mg · L^{-1})			
	NO$_3$ – N	TKN	Total P	Ortho P
A (poor subsurface drainage)	1.3	1.9	0.16	0.04
B (good subsurface drainage)	3.8	1.6	0.08	0.01

[a]Both watersheds have good surface drainage.

The effect of subsurface drainage on water quality parameters is shown in Table 1 for watersheds A and B, discussed above. The values given are mean concentrations of nitrogen and phosphorus measured continuously over a one-year period. These results show that good subsurface drainage increases nitrate outflow but reduces the loss of phosphorus to drainage waters. Improvement of surface drainage has the opposite effect. Thus, if P concentrations in receiving waters are critically high, better subsurface drainage would improve the situation. Likewise, improved surface drainage or the use of drainage outlet controls to increase surface runoff would reduce nitrate outflow.

These examples emphasize the fact that various drainage and associated water management practices have different effects on the rate and quality of runoff water. By careful design and operation of water management systems, it may be possible to satisfy agricultural requirements while minimizing off-site detrimental effects. To achieve this goal requires understanding of the factors controlling the off-site conditions and requirements as well as of agricultural drainage needs.

REFERENCES

Belmans, C., J. G. Wesseling, and R. A. Feddes. 1983. Simulation model of the water balance in a cropped soil: SWATRE. *Journal of Hydrology* 63:271–86.

Clinton, F. M. 1967. Invisible irrigation on Egin Bench. *Reclamation Era* 34:182–84.

Fouss, J. L. 1983. Simulated controlled operation of subsurface drainage-irrigation systems. ASAE Paper no. 83-2567. St. Joseph, Mich.: American Society of Agricultural Engineers.

Gayle, G. A., and R. W. Skaggs. 1978. Surface storage on bedded cultivated lands. *Transactions of the ASAE* 21(1):102–104, 109.

Hardjoamidjojo, S., R. W. Skaggs, and G. O. Schwab. 1982. Predicting corn yield response to excessive soil water conditions. *Transactions of the ASAE* 25(4):922–27, 934.

Hiler, E. A. 1969. Quantitative evaluation of crop-drainage requirements. *Transactions of the ASAE* 12(3):499–505.

Lagace, R. 1973. Modèle de comportement des nappes en sol agricole. *Genie Rural-Laval* 5(4):26–35.

Luthin, J. N. 1957. Drainage of irrigated lands. Pp. 344–71. *In* J. N. Luthin (ed.) Drainage of agricultural lands. Madison, Wis.: American Society of Agronomy.

Massey, F. C., R. W. Skaggs, and R. E. Sneed. 1983. Energy and water requirements for subirrigation versus sprinkler irrigation. *Transactions of the ASAE* 26(1):126–33.

Ravelo, C. J., D. L. Reddell, E. A. Hiler, and R. W. Skaggs. 1982. Incorporating crop needs into drainage system design. *Transactions of the ASAE* 25(3):623–629, 637.

Reeve, R. C., and N. Fausey. 1974. Drainage and timeliness of farming operations. Ch. 4. *In* J. van Schilfgaarde (ed.) Drainage for agriculture. Madison, Wis.: American Society of Agronomy.

Renfro, George, Jr. 1955. Applying water under the surface of the ground. Pp. 173–78. *In* Yearbook of agriculture. U.S. Department of Agriculture.

Skaggs, R. W. 1978. A water management model for shallow water table soils. Water Resources Research Institute of the University of North Carolina, Technical Report no. 134. Raleigh: North Carolina State University.

Skaggs, R. W. 1980. A water management model for artificially drained soils. Technical Bulletin no. 267. Raleigh: North Carolina Agricultural Research Service, North Carolina State University.

Skaggs, R. W., and A. Nassehzadeh-Tabrizi. 1983. Optimum drainage for corn production. Technical Bulletin no. 274. Raleigh: North Carolina Agricultural Research Service, North Carolina State University.

Smith, M. C., R. W. Skaggs, and J. E. Parsons. 1982. Subirrigation system control for water use efficiency. ASAE Paper no. 82-2520. St. Joseph, Mich.: American Society of Agricultural Engineers.

van Schilfgaarde, J. 1974. Nonsteady flow to drains. Pp. 245–70. *In* J. van Schilfgaarde (ed.) Drainage for agriculture. Madison, Wis.: American Society of Agronomy.

Wesseling, J. 1974. Crop growth and wet soils. Ch. 2. *In* J. van Schilfgaarde, (ed.) Drainage for agriculture. Madison, Wis.: American Society for Agronomy.

Williamson, R. E., and G. J. Kriz. 1970. Response of agricultural crops to flooding, depth of water table and soil composition. *Transactions of the ASAE* 13(1):216–20.

50. IRRIGATION TECHNOLOGY FOR FOOD PRODUCTION: EXPECTATIONS AND REALITIES IN SOUTH AND SOUTHEAST ASIA

Sadiqul I. Bhuiyan, International Rice Research Institute, Manila, Philippines

ABSTRACT

The remarkable achievement in food production increase in South and Southeast Asia during the past two decades has been possible because of substantial irrigation development, which allowed a wider adoption of high-yielding production technology. Rapid irrigation development, however, has not been without problems. Most irrigation systems suffer from low performance efficiency, with the actual irrigated area much smaller than the designed area, as well as such problems as water distribution inequity, waterlogging, and loss of land productivity. The result is that the benefits obtained from these systems are much less than expected.

Poor management is often cited as the reason for unsatisfactory performance of irrigation systems. Whereas management deficiencies are a major contributing factor, the sources of many inadequacies, which ultimately limit performance capacity, are often introduced into the systems when they are designed and constructed. The nature of and underlying reasons for these limiting factors are identified and analyzed. Further, selected technological or development options concerning the use of irrigation technology are discussed. Finally, recommendations are made for action toward the removal of the major constraints to achieving better performance of the existing irrigation facilities and developing future irrigation systems on a more sound basis.

IRRIGATION AND FOOD PRODUCTION

Agriculture in South and Southeast Asian countries is still highly dependent on rainfall, and therefore food production is largely at the mercy of the vagaries of nature. High risk and low production are the norm in most rainfed agricultural systems. These countries support a population of nearly 1.5 billion, about 80 percent of which is dependent on agriculture for living (Population Reference Bureau, 1984). The population is expected to double in the next thirty years, and therefore, increased food production is needed to meet the expanding demand.

Early efforts to increase food production were mainly in the form of opening new lands for rainfed agriculture. But as new arable lands became scarcer, crop intensification became a more appropriate strategy and the potential role of irrigation was better recognized. In the humid and semihumid areas of the two regions, for example in southern India, Sri Lanka, the Philippines, and Indonesia, most early irrigation development was for supplemental watering of rice fields in the wet seasons. But with the advent in the mid-1960s of the new agricultural technology, popularly called the Green Revolution, which made available early-maturing, input-responsive wheat and rice varieties, a dramatic shift toward year-round irrigation systems took place in order to utilize the production potential of the new technology.

The total irrigated area of the countries of South and Southeast Asia rose from 41.5 million ha in 1960 to 65.8 million ha in 1980, a 58 percent increase over the period. National growth figures are given in Table 1. India had the largest share of the development of new irrigation facilities, about 13.3 million ha, during the period.

Several studies aimed at meeting the long-term food production growth requirements in these countries indicated the need for making much greater investments in the years to come than in the past. In a report to the Trilateral Commission, Colombo et al. (1978) recommended that rice production in thirteen countries of South and Southeast Asia should be doubled in fifteen years, from 1978 to 1993, by increasing irrigated area at an annual rate of 6.7 percent and at an estimated capital cost of $52.6 billion (1975 prices), or $3.5 billion per year. In a more comprehensive study of eight countries (Bangladesh, Burma, India, Indonesia, Nepal, Pakistan, Philippines, and Sri Lanka), Oram et al. (1979) projected growth in gross irrigated area at 2.3 percent and estimated total capital requirements from 1975 to 1990 at $52 billion, or $3.5 billion per year (1975 prices).

At what rate development of new irrigation facilities will actually take place over the next ten years or so depends on many factors and can only be speculated about now, but what seems certain is that the importance of the use of irrigation water for crop production will continue to increase in order to keep pace with the increasing demands for food grains in these countries.

PERFORMANCE RECORDS OF IRRIGATION TECHNOLOGY

In general terms, the adoption of irrigation technology has yielded substantial food production benefits. For example, during the past twenty years, rice yields in Asia have increased at an average rate of more than 3 percent per year. About 30 percent of the total rice production increase during the 1965–1980 period in the main rice-producing countries of Asia has been attributed to the effect of irrigation alone, as opposed to other factors such as fertilizer and modern variety (Herdt and Capule, 1983). Barker and Herdt (1979) estimated that about 50 percent of total rice production in the mid-1970s in the countries of South and Southeast Asia was contributed by the irrigated areas, which constituted about 32 percent of total rice area. Their

Table 1. Growth in irrigated area in South and Southeast Asia, 1960–1980.

Country	Arable Land	Irrigated Area		Av. Annual Increase (1960–1980)
		1960	1980	
		000 HA		
South Asia				
Bangladesh	8,915	316	1,620	62.1
India	164,500	23,393	36,665	632.0
Nepal	2,305	n.a.	230	—
Pakistan	19,835	10.234	14,300	193.6
Sri Lanka	1,023	255	525	12.9
Total	196,578	34,198	53,340	900.6
Southeast Asia				
Burma	9,558	549	999	21.4
Indonesia	14,168	4,100	5,418	62.8
Malaysia	3,150	214	370	7.4
Philippines	5,250	808	1,300	23.4
Thailand	15,773	1,636	2,650	48.3
Vietnam, Kampuchea (Cambodia), and Laos	7,404	—	1,700	—
Total	55,303	7,307	12,437	163.3

SOURCE: Barker et al., 1984.

projected figures for the mid-1990s are 57 percent of total rice production from the approximately 40 percent of total rice area that will have irrigation facilities. A similar study by the Food and Agriculture (FAO, 1979) estimated that in the year 2000 about 70 percent of all rice production in ninety developing countries of the world would come from irrigated lands.

The above figures, however, are not indicative of the level of efficiency at which the irrigation systems are generally operating. In recent years, concern about the performance of existing irrigation systems has been growing. Objective assessments of their performance are limited, but, encouragingly, a growing body of information based on field investigations conducted in the various countries is becoming available. It is now a well-accepted fact that by and large the performance of the irrigation systems falls much short of what is desirable and can be reasonably expected. The area benefitting from the developed water resource potential is generally much below the level for which the systems were planned and designed—the gap is perhaps widening with time. Water distribution inequity problems, created by system deficiencies of various kinds are widespread, allowing excessive use of irrigation water by the advantageously located farmers at the head end of the distributory canal at the expense of those at the tail end. Unreliability of water supply from the system, in terms of both quantity and timing, is a common problem, which discourages farmers from using optimum levels of production inputs and prevents them from reaping the expected benefits from the system. Deficiencies in system planning and design and system management have contributed to the aggravated environmental problems of waterlogging and have resulted in reduced productivity of the affected lands in many irrigation systems.

The above description, summarized from various studies of performance of large as well as small irrigation systems in Bangladesh, India, Pakistan, the Philippines, and Thailand, reflects the nature of the problems that afflict most irrigation systems today. In most cases, the problems are serious. Take, for example, the waterlogging and land degradation aspect. In India, the productivity of millions of hectares of land is known to be affected by irrigation-induced waterlogging and associated salinity. High seepage loss, overirrigation, and the use of vast areas for growing crops that require a great deal of water, with attendant high percolation losses, resulted in a steady rise of the water table in the command areas of many Indian irrigation systems (Swaminathan, 1980). More than half of the Indus Basin Canal system in Pakistan, some 8 million ha, is waterlogged and about 40 percent of it has salinity problems (WDR, 1982, 62). About 17 percent of all irrigated areas covered by the public sector systems in the Philippines are reported to suffer from inadequate drainage facilities (NWRC, 1979). Most rice irrigation systems face significant waterlogging problems in 10–15 percent of their service area within several years of their operation.

If we accept the proposition that use of irrigation technology is an essential means to meet the food production needs of the population, the primary concern should then be to identify and assess the factors responsible for the present undesirable conditions and determine what should be done to help existing as well as future irrigation systems overcome these problems.

WHY IRRIGATION SYSTEMS ARE FAILING TO FULFILL PROMISES

It is important to recognize that irrigation development is a process in which both water users and managers steadily upgrade their understanding and strategies and proceed toward an optimum level of effectiveness and efficiency within the given economic and socioinstitutional milieu. In this context, the analysis of Levine (1981) is relevant. Taking a historical perspective, Levine reasons that irrigation systems in Southeast Asia go through three definable development stages. The first stage is when the system operates primarily as a "hydrologic-hydraulic" entity, with emphasis on water capture, conveyance, and equity in allocation; management capability is scarce at that stage. In the second stage the system becomes "agriculture based" when management capability improves and land becomes the scarcest production factor. At the third, or "farmer-oriented" stage, the system efficiency becomes a priority management objective and water becomes the scarcest production factor. Levine has also suggested that irrigation system performance should be evaluated in relation to its position in the development continuum.

Ideally, well-planned and well-managed systems should progress from one stage to the next harmoniously and within a relatively short period of time. Systems with prolonged discord and ineffectiveness suffer irrecoverable economic loss. Unfortunately, most irrigation systems are developed without conscious planning to facilitate this transformation process. Weaver (1984) suggests that the failure of irrigation system planners and managers to understand and plan for irrigation development as a dynamic process may be the number-one problem with that development today. I believe this shortcoming is certainly at the core of many of the irrigation system performance problems that we see today. These problems are discussed below on more specific terms.

Three phases are involved in the development and functioning of an irrigation system: planning and design, implementation, and operation and maintenance. Each of these phases is critically important in determining how successfully the system will perform when it is operated. In each of the phases there are a number of problems that I believe contribute significantly to the inefficient performance of irrigation systems. The assessment below concerns mostly irrigation systems that are created and managed by the public sector agencies.

Planning and Design

In many cases, the seeds of a variety of system performance problems are sown during the planning and design phase. Despite its most critical role, the irrigation planning and design process is still more of an art than a science. Currethers (1978) has criticized the irrigation system planning process for its lack of scientific focus as well as political economy and its preoccupation with certain issues that are not of central importance to irrigation's success. The unreliability and consequent futility of the analytical procedures commonly used in ex ante benefit-cost assessments to determine the economic feasibility of irrigation projects are a growing concern (Pant, 1984; Sundar, 1984). Clearly, a major problem is that the analytical tool used in estimating benefits and costs is amenable to easy manipulation to serve specific biases or interests of the user.

The chronic unavailability of good field data for new project areas and the short time usually allowed for completing feasibility studies provide opportunities for such manipulations. Planners and designers are required to make assumptions to fill up data gaps, and even their best efforts may be far from the actual field situation. Use of overoptimistic assumptions is often made in technical matters such as life of reservoir, life of equipment, water conveyance efficiency, and the like. Systems are assumed to be operated and maintained with overoptimistic estimates of resources. In matters related to farmers' water use behavior, preference, and motivation, hypothetical notions of the planner-designer rather than field realities seem to have often dominated in the past. In many cases, the only perceivable reason for the use of specific assumptions or design standards is found in the fact that they were used before in another project.

Related to the aforementioned problems is the fact that the lessons of operating experience of existing irrigation systems are hardly given a chance to influence the planning and design of new irrigation systems. The planning and design task is traditionally considered by the engineers within the agency as a more prestigious job than other jobs such as system operation and maintenance, and it is often performed in isolation from other activities of irrigation development or management. Ex post evaluations of existing projects are rarely conducted to assess the validity of the design standards and assumptions used and to upgrade them. Thus, planning and design mistakes tend to be repeated.

A "hardware bias" usually dominates the planning and design process. As a result, only the visible physical infrastructure, such as dams, reservoirs, canals, gates, etc., becomes the major focus of the development effort, leaving the software components with low priority. Thus, the manpower development needs of the agency for proper operation and maintenance of the system and farmers' organizational development needs for effective and equitable use of the water are always underestimated. Waterlogging and associated problems, which normally do not appear on a large scale until after a few years of the system's operation, are, in many cases, not given due consideration. In some cases, the initial provision of adequate drainage facilities becomes a victim of final economy measures imposed because of financial limitations.

Ecological considerations are most often given least attention in the planning-design phase, just when they are most critically important. Inadequate understanding of the relationship between the natural ecosystem and the sustainable productivity of land, which is exacerbated by the hardware bias as well as the quick-fix attitude of many a planner-designer, has been responsible for the development of various unintended ecological problems that have degraded the productive environment of lands. A classic example of such inadequacy is found in the spillway-regulator project in Kuttanad, Kerala, India, which was intended to prevent flood damage and to increase land productivity by controlling salt-water intrusion into the area but has actually produced the opposite results, affecting the livelihood of thousands of farmers and fishermen and endangering the health of the local population because of increased incidence of mosquito-borne diseases (Cerescope Report, 1984,

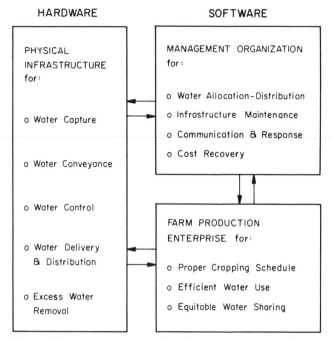

HARDWARE   SOFTWARE

PHYSICAL
INFRASTRUCTURE
for:

o Water Capture

o Water Conveyance

o Water Control

o Water Delivery
  & Distribution

o Excess Water
  Removal

MANAGEMENT ORGANIZATION
for:

o Water Allocation-Distribution
o Infrastructure Maintenance
o Communication & Response
o Cost Recovery

FARM PRODUCTION
ENTERPRISE for:

o Proper Cropping Schedule
o Efficient Water Use
o Equitable Water Sharing

Fig. 1. The main component of an irrigation system model and their major functions in relation to system performance.

11–12). Somewhat similar results were obtained, for perhaps similar reasons, in parts of the gigantic Coastal Embankment Project in Bangladesh.

The performance of future irrigation systems depends a great deal on how the planning and design process is made more effective today. A better understanding of the various elements that make up an irrigation system, their respective roles, and their complementarities is desired of those involved in the planning process (Fig. 1). In-depth studies of the specific weak links in the currently used planning process are essential to developing principles and procedures that could effectively guide future planning.

Project Implementation

The project implementation phase, during which the physical infrastructure development activities dominate, is primarily the domain of engineers, technicians, and contractors. This is perhaps the least studied area in irrigation but is of critical importance to the success or failure of the system when it is operated. Many things can, and indeed do, go wrong at this stage, to the detriment of the system's performance capacity.

Mislocation of tertiary-level structures, such as turnouts or offtakes, with respect to their position as well as elevation relative to the water supply level in the canal, is a commonly found inadequacy that originates mostly during the implementation stage. Problems of misalignment of main farm ditches and their defective, often negative, slopes are created by faulty construction. These defects inhibit the expected delivery of water to the farms, create frustrations among the affected farmers, and encourage them to have recourse to illegal diversion of water by cutting canal banks,

installing pipes, or other means. Such practices promote a laissez-faire state with respect to system water management and allow uncontrolled use of water by those who have access to canal water. Consequently, the "stronger" and the more favorably located farmers get more water from the system at the expense of the "weaker" and the more distant farmers (NIA-IRRI, 1984, 53). This is one major reason for the so-called head end–tail end problem of water distribution in irrigation systems.

Good data on the problems that usually originate at the project implementation stage and their relationship to system performance capacity are limited. Barker et al. (1984, 51) reported on a study in the Philippines that found that about 40 percent of the terminal structures in the large Upper Pampanga River Integrated Irrigation System were inappropriately located, resulting in unauthorized cuts in the canals to serve areas missed by the official structures. In a much smaller and more recently constructed system, also in the Philippines, a joint investigation by representatives of the farmers and the system manager identified numerous problems with the tertiary-level structures, including inadequacies in the capacity of the drainage structures. But the extent of the problems was not fully realized until it was determined that more than 10 percent of the designated service area could never get canal water through gravity flow because of design and/or construction faults and that five out of six large concrete Parshall flumes constructed in situ were not useful at all because of faulty construction. Another example of similar problems is found in the work of Corey (1982), who reported that in the Mahaweli Project in Sri Lanka, more than 50 percent of the structures were nonfunctional, because of either inappropriate location or damage. These are certainly not unique cases of nonfunctionality of tertiary-level infrastructure.

Faulty irrigation infrastructures cannot perform their functions properly. Thus, the existence of some inadequacies in the infrastructure implies a correspondingly reduced performance capacity of the system. Further, it often remains unrecognized that infrastructural inadequacies generate social problems among farmers with respect to water distribution and sharing, which also inhibit the system's performance capacity.

Infrastructural inadequacies can have a variety of causes, but most of them are related to shortcomings in either design or construction or both. It is generally believed that design-related shortcomings are due mainly to unavailability of necessary good-quality field data, especially data related to hydrology and land topography. The difficulty of accurate field data collection, which is compounded by the existence of small landholdings in most of the countries of South and Southeast Asia is well recognized. But we must also admit that behind the data gap there is a lack of proper appreciation of the need for good-quality field data for the development of successful irrigation systems. Construction-related inadequacies, on the other hand, generally reflect a lack of adequate supervision by the concerned personnel at various stages of the work. Contributing to this problem is the unfortunate tendency to give less importance to the supervision needs of tertiary- and field-level construction works compared with those at the water source or at the primary level.

Delay in the implementation of the irrigation projects is responsible for not only cost overruns but also a degrading influence on the quality of the irrigation and drainage infrastructure affected by the delay. Nonlined irrigation and drainage canals constructed at the beginning of a project suffer from degradation because of delays, and often they are not restored to the original specifications when the system is to start functioning. Use of shortcuts and incomplete facilities and, in general, low-quality works tend to become more acceptable under conditions of delayed schedule and cost overruns.

Delays in implementation are a common feature in irrigation development. Each of the nine irrigation projects in South and Southeast Asia completed by 1980 with assistance from the Asian Development Bank had suffered an average time delay of 72 percent over the scheduled implementation period and an average nominal cost overrun of 66 percent. The complicated process used to administer projects and the generally weak management capacity of the local agencies are cited as two important reasons for the delayed implementation (Seki, 1982). Sundar (1984) attributed delays in India to an excess of projects under construction and inadequate funding.

Operation and Maintenance (O&M)

This aspect of irrigation management has received some research attention during the last several years, specifically in the assessments of the increase in system performance potential through adoption of improved methods of system operation. Such research has been conducted in India (Rao, 1984) and the Philippines (Miranda, 1984), and also, on a more limited scale, in Bangladesh (Khan, 1984), Sri Lanka, and Thailand (Thongtawee, 1984). Although most of these field studies were conducted in diverse biophysical and socioeconomic backgrounds and different methodologies were involved, they indicate that there is scope for significant improvement in system performance through implementation of improved operation procedures. However, from these studies no information is available on the extent of system operation problems that are created or induced by deficiencies at the planning-and-design and implementation stages of irrigation development.

In the planning and design of irrigation systems, O&M is often taken for granted. Irrigation system management is a highly complex task that demands understanding and application of principles of not only engineering but also the agronomic, economic, and socio-institutional realms. However, the management functions are often most inadequately defined for the system managers. I believe the essential functions for which the management team should acquire adequate capacity in order to successfully operate and maintain irrigation systems are the following:

1. Ability to plan and execute a water allocation and distribution schedule during each crop season to best utilize the available water resource, keeping in mind the following

goals: reliability of supply, minimum wastage, and equity among users. In short, this requirement could be termed "water allocation-distribution capacity."

2. Ability to assess field water conditions and use that information in taking appropriate measures toward achievement of the goals stated in item 1 above and for improvement of future performance—"feedback and response capacity."

3. Ability to develop and maintain reliable communication mechanisms with the water users for the exchange of relevant information—"communication capacity."

4. Ability to organize and sustain active involvement of farmers at mutually agreed levels in both decision making and execution of decisions—"organizational capacity."

5. Ability to maintain and improve, where possible, the given irrigation facilities to enable their continued use to the best advantage of the farming community—"maintenance capacity."

6. Ability to foresee and observe land productivity problems, such as waterlogging or salinity development, and take appropriate measures to prevent or minimize such developments—"productivity protection capacity."

7. Ability to successfully realize water service fees from the water users as per the prevailing laws—"cost recovery capacity."

The above requirements should apply to the management of all irrigation systems regardless of their type, scale, or management organization. However, there may be variations in the importance attached to any of these requirements. For example, the productivity protection function may be extremely important in some systems but not in others. Likewise, the cost recovery function differs substantially from country to country depending on local laws.

In general, the required capacities for successful system operation and maintenance are all in short supply. The most compelling reasons for the shortcomings include the following:

Financial constraint. Insufficient finance and staffing for the O&M activities, as recognized earlier by Bottrall (1978), are serious common problems. The allocation by the government of resources for irrigation system O&M is in continued decline in most countries, leading to deterioration of the performance capacity of the systems. For example, a recent study by the Work Bank in Bangladesh concluded that the underutilization and deterioration of operating irrigation schemes were a direct result of inadequate funding for O&M (GOB-WB, 1979, 21). Sundar (1984) criticizes the Indian irrigation administration for providing an inadequate budget for O&M and allowing system deterioration, which, he argues, reflect a lack of concern for system output. Barker et al. (1984, p. 64) warn of serious productivity consequences if careful budgetary planning to help future infrastructure maintenance and rehabilitation of irrigation systems of South and Southeast Asian countries is not pursued.

Many irrigation agencies appear to be tuned more to building new projects than to operating and maintaining well those that are in place. Ironically, it sometimes seems easier for the agencies to muster financial resources for new projects than for improving or even sustaining the level of O&M that is most sensible. This situation must be improved if expected returns are to be gained from irrigation systems.

Inadequate staff training. Despite the high complexity of the tasks they are expected to perform, few irrigation managers are adequately trained for them. Irrigation managers are mostly civil engineers who have had little opportunity through their college or university curricula to learn about the concepts and issues relevant to system management. On-the-job training opportunities for them are also limited. A similar situation exists with respect to the support staff responsible for various field O&M activities. It is reported that in India more than 80 percent of the irrigation system O&M staff have had no training related to their jobs whatsoever (Wade, 1982).

The potential benefits from the introduction of irrigation mangement related subjects, such as management science, canal operation principles, agronomy, etc., into the civil engineering curricula of Indian colleges and universities have been emphasized by various authors in recent years. Wade (1982) reasons that perhaps the single most important reason why Indian irrigation systems are performing poorly is the neglect of the relevant education and training of the professional irrigation staff. I believe this argument applies equally well for most other countries of South and Southeast Asia.

Lack of accountability and incentives. The problem of accountability is at two levels. At the institutional level, it is often the case that the agency that builds and operates the irrigation systems is not directly responsible for the use of the water at the farm level. Usually, the responsibility for distribution of water after it leaves the main system network lies with the extension staff of the agriculture department, which, in most cases, not only is a department separate from the irrigation agency but also may be under a different ministry in the government. In this situation, coordination of the activities of the two departments is often difficult, and there is the inherent problem of institutionalizing accountability for irrigation system performance at the departmental level. Within the irrigation agency, there is prevalent a lack of enforced accountability with respect to the O&M functions of the systems by the various cadres of the staff. In some cases, the job descriptions are well defined, but these are considered mostly for record purposes. There is often a serious lack of supervision of the work of various field staff by the supervising officers, who have to spend too much time on routine administrative duties imposed on them. Sundar (1984) summarizes this lack of accountability for Indian irrigation systems with the statement: "Since performance is never measured, who cares?" India must not be considered unique in this situation.

A related problem is the lack of incentives. Incentives for staff for to perform well are sometimes inadequate, and promotions are based more on length of service than on performance in assigned roles. Since the irrigation manager is not required to be concerned with the farm-level distribution and use of the water, extraordinary personal initiative is needed for the manager to be concerned with the ultimate purpose of the development of the system.

Inadequate farmer participation. The critical role the farmers must play in the successful O&M of an irrigation system has been underestimated in the past. It has traditionally been assumed that farmers should get organized to support the system's water allocation and distribution plans, maintain the on-farm irrigation and drainage facilities, and, in some situations, also help to collect the irrigation service fees. It has also been implicitly assumed that in their own ultimate interest the farmers will be supportive of these activities. Some inputs from the agency are all that has been considered necessary to develop and sustain organized farmer groups for these purposes. This approach has acheived very limited success. Farmers often view the demands of the agency as unreasonable because they think they are asked to do only the manual or "dirty" work. Compounding this problem is the lack of good communication and, often, of proper understanding between the agency staff and the farmers. Clearly, there is an urgent need to devise means to ensure the participation of farmers in the various O&M functions if better use of water is to be achieved.

Recent studies in the Philippines have shown that in small irrigation systems that are agency developed but community owned and managed, the participatory approach to irrigation development, in which both the irrigation agency personnel and the intended beneficiaries are jointly involved in decision making from the planning stage to system O&M, is much more likely to succeed in the long run than the conventional approach in promoting and maintaining farmers' participation (Bagadion and Korten, 1980). This approach is being used now for communal irrigation development in the Philippines. The concept merits serious consideration and testing for its possible applicability, perhaps with appropriate modification, to similar small-scale irrigation development in other countries.

SELECTED ISSUES CONFRONTING DEVELOPMENT STRATEGY OR CHOICE OF TECHNOLOGY

Several important issues are faced by the policy and decision makers in choosing a strategy or a component technology in relation to irrigation development from among the options available to them. Three important issues are discussed here, with a view to developing an extended understanding of the various facets involved in them.

New Expansion versus Upgrading of Existing Irrigation Systems

Upgrading existing irrigation systems is sometimes mentioned as a more desirable alternative to developing additional areas with new irrigation facilities for the countries of South and Southeast Asia. Basically, the argument is for qualitative improvement in lieu of the popular quantitative development approach.

Implicit in recommending the upgrading option is the assumption that we know well how improvements of existing irrigation systems should be made to achieve higher levels of crop production. In reality, however, our knowledge base relative to irrigation system upgrading and its relationship to crop production increase is more limited than that relative to food production increase through development of new irrigation systems. Most upgrading efforts in the past have been to "rehabilitate" deteriorated physical facilities of irrigation systems to the original design standards. It is logical to think that the improved facilities will deteriorate again, perhaps as quickly as or even quicker than in the past, unless better arrangements have been made for their maintenance. Also, these rehabilitations per se may not yield significant crop production benefits unless the deteriorated facilities were the primary reason for the earlier low production or poor system performance. There is evidence that some of the recent rehabilitation or upgrading of on-farm infrastructure of irrigation systems has produced no positive effects on either system performance or crop production, for reasons similar to those stated above. In two such cases, one in India (Ali, 1984) and the other in the Philippines, major water problems were in the management of the main system and as such, farm-level improvements did not make any significant difference with respect to farmers' water availability or crop production.

Cumulative evidence from a number of pilot studies in several countries, as mentioned earlier, suggests that significant benefits could be realized by improving the water allocation-distribution procedure in the main system. The emphasis in such improvement or upgrading efforts should be on establishing reliability and predictability of the water supply, equity in its access to farmers at various locations within the system area, and reduced water wastage. The specific interventions needed to achieve these goals beyond the pilot level and their economic viability under given conditions have not been established, however, and these matters therefore deserve serious research. Clearly, any successful effort along this line will require farmer cooperation and participation. To what extent substantive investment for physical infrastructure improvement is needed for such efforts depends on site conditions, but in most situations attempts to apply improved water allocation-distribution procedures are likely to show numerous weaknesses in the main system itself.

Upgrading the management capacity of the irrigation bureaucracy is often likely to be a necessary, though not always a sufficient, condition for upgrading the irrigation system's performance and the productivity of water. In most situations, an upgrading scheme along this line is likely to require two important elements: (1) adequate resources, both manpower and financial, to enable proper O&M of the system, and (2) proper training of the different cadres of the staff. The training activity should aim at enhancing the staff's capacity to perform the various O&M functions described earlier.

There is no doubt that as self-sufficiency in food grain production is achieved and maintained in a country and as new irrigation developments become more expensive, the option of upgrading existing irrigation facilities will gain greater importance. For most of the countries of South and Southeast Asia, where water for irrigation is becoming a scarcer and more limiting commodity for additional food production, there is a need to conduct immediate in-depth studies to assess the feasibility and practicality of upgrading the productive capacities of existing irrigation systems, taking into full account all relevant technical, economic, and socioinstitutional factors.

Large versus Small Irrigation Projects

By and large, researchers and critics of the maladies associated with irrigation development tend to favor small irrigation systems, for various reasons.* Large systems can be justifiably criticized for their many weaknesses, including the following:

1. There is overemphasis on economy of scale and overoptimistic projection of benefits in planning. Also, as Levine (1977) points out, there is neglect of "diseconomies" associated with more stringent requirements for data, for accurate projections, and for specialized skills. Large systems generally require long gestation periods.

2. The planning, implementation, and management of large systems require coordinated action of several concerned agencies or institutions, a match that is very difficult to achieve in developing countries (Madeley, 1983).

3. There are major weaknesses in sustaining the productive capacity of reservoirs, this due to difficulty in designing and/or implementing viable measures to protect the reservoirs from silting.†

4. Large systems are prone to waterlogging and consequent land productivity problems.

Small systems are generally less affected by most of the problems listed above. But problems of inefficiency in system performance and inequity in water distribution as well as unreliability in water supply are also common in small systems. Such examples abound in most of the countries using small systems with deep tubewells, tanks, and diversion dams. On the other hand, there are examples of relatively large irrigation systems that are performing at reasonably high levels of efficiency. In Malaysia, relatively large systems, those with a service area of 10,000 ha or more, are found to perform much better and more productively than the scattered small-scale systems (Lim, 1984).

Large systems are unjustifiably criticized sometimes for their dependence on sophisticated technology and foreign know-how and capital. Certainly, the level of sophistication in modern irrigation technology is very much within the capacity of the Asian developing countries to properly absorb and utilize, if there is institutional commitment to it. Further, whereas full utilization of indigenous know-how is a desirable goal, we must not advocate closing doors to suitable foreign know-how unless it is entirely irrelevant. Local adaptation and adoption of foreign technology has proved

---

*A universal definition of "large" or "small" irrigation systems is not applicable. In the context of this discussion, large systems would be those that serve greatly extended areas, perhaps 50,000 ha or more. An "intermediate" or "medium" category may be used for systems serving 10,000 to 50,000 ha.

†For example, the effective life of the Tarbela Reservoir of the Indus Basin Project in Pakistan is apprehended to be half the life expectancy originally calculated (Borlaug, 1982). Unchecked deforestation in the watershed of the Mahaweli River irrigation project in Sri Lanka, which is partly complete, is now gravely threatening its reservoir's potential capacity (Madeley, 1983).

successful in many instances in the developing countries. Ultraconservative planning based only on readily available local resources will not be sufficient to solve our food production problems. New resources, especially in the manpower sector, will have to be generated through forward-looking but realistic planning.

The development of large irrigation systems should be avoided in favor of smaller systems when there is a reasonable alternative choice. But is there always a choice? A number of factors complicate the decision-making process in this regard. First, a policy to develop only small systems can slow down the irrigation development pace, which may be critical for a country, and it may turn out to be more expensive in the long run. Also, often a large river basin may not be amenable to development into a number of small basins. Furthermore, economy of scale will remain an important factor in planning and project selection. Second, large irrigation systems with reservoirs are mostly multipurpose projects in which electric power generation is a major component. Power is in short supply in most of the countries and hydroelectric power is still the most favored means of developing the energy. Third, it is not evident that system management problems can be eliminated or reduced and system performance significantly improved by only scaling down the size of the systems.

In view of the above, it is likely that large irrigation system development will remain a strategy attractive to policymakers and planners. Perhaps the right question, then, is not whether systems should be large or small but what the right size should be. The size should be determined based on not only a realistic, rather than hypothetical, analysis of expected benefits and costs of the alternative projects but also taking into full account the planning, designing, implementation, and management capacities that can be realistically acquired and maintained within the agencies concerned. Many large systems today suffer from various problems for not considering properly the limitations with respect to these capacities. Ecological and environmental considerations, which have often been neglected in the past, must also be at the forefront when medium or large projects are considered. Proposals for developing large but unsound systems are likely to be logically discarded if these precautions are taken properly. Since our understanding of the ecological and environmental dynamics of water development is very limited, research efforts along this line should be greatly strengthened.

Management Organization: Centralized Bureaucracy versus Farmer-Shared Model

In the past, irrigation systems have been viewed mostly as merely technological solutions to the food production problem. The importance of the role of farmer participation is only beginning to be fully appreciated, and our understanding of the nature of a truly effective agency-farmer interface is still limited.

In general, agency-managed irrigation systems have attempted to develop a management organization pattern in which the agency takes control of the main system, usually up to the secondary or tertiary canal. In effect, all system operation related decisions are made by the agency and the maintenance responsibility is divided between the agency and the farmer groups, the latter being responsible for the maintenance of the farm-level irrigation and drainage facilities. But, as discussed earlier, field application of this model has faced serious setbacks, since farmer participation in most agency-managed irrigation systems has been highly inadequate and has in fact contributed to their unsatisfactory performance. Farmers generally are considered unable to contribute to main system management decision making and are blamed for nonparticipation in the execution of system operation and maintenance plans worked out by the agency. It is only fair to say that in many cases the nonparticipation is due to failure of the agency to fulfill its share of the responsibility, creating lack of confidence in the farmers about the agency and disinterest in its programs.

It is logical to assume that irrigation system performance would be improved if farmers could be made active partners with the agency not only in the maintenance of their farm-level facilities but also in the decision-making process for water allocation-distribution in their respective portions of the main system, its upkeep, and the implementation of these decisions. This shared-management model should elicit local leadership, the lack of which has been a problem in earlier efforts to organize farmers, and should utilize local wisdom in the rational planning and execution of the key activities within the system. Further, this process should enlist farmer commitment to the needed jobs from the conceptual stage. If this model is agreed on in principle, the organizational structure and specific functions of the two parties involved could be developed considering the prevailing sociocultural background as well as local resources. It is conceivable that some agencies may consider such a model an infringement on their authority. But it is expected that a successful sharing of responsibility will strengthen the agency's true authority and also bolster its image with the farmers. There will have to be a perceptive and attitudinal change within a traditional irrigation agency to implement a model along this line.

How can farmers be effectively organized in a given sociocultural background to help achieve and sustain the irrigation system goals? What should be the most effective and mutually acceptable delineation of the limits of responsibility between the agency and the farmer groups? In what way must the agencies change to implement a shared-management model? We need research-based answers to these and other relevant questions. Past research along this line has been most limited. A number of pioneering attempts by the National Irrigation Administration in the Philippines to organize farmers to share the management responsibility in large irrigation systems are currently under way. A most interesting feature of these efforts is that farmer organizations also are sharing the responsibility of irrigation service fee collection from the beneficiaries, and the agency is trying out a number of incentive formulas to allow a percentage of the collection to be shared by the farmer organization if it can fulfill a given time target for collection. Also, the agency contracts out canal maintenance work to the organizations, generating mutual financial as well as other benefits (Bagadion, 1984).

CONCLUSION AND RECOMMENDATIONS

Our increasing dependence on irrigated agricultural production systems to provide adequate food and food security for the expanding population makes it imperative that existing irrigation systems be more efficient and productivity of irrigated lands be maintained. The problems of inefficiency and land degradation faced today in most irrigation systems are indeed, very serious. If these are allowed to remain unsolved, not only will the economic losses associated with the foregone production and related effects continue, but in addition the severity of the problems will become more acute with time. Consequently, the much-needed food production momentum gained over the years will suffer serious setbacks. Further, without thoughtful studies and practical reforms to make improvements in planning, implementing, and managing irrigation facilities, there is little hope that future investments in irrigation will be more rewarding. With a population in South and Southeast Asia that is expected to double in the next thirty years, bold measures are essential if the problems of irrigation systems and retarded food production are to be avoided.

Consonant with the discussions in this chapter, the following recommendations are made for appropriate action by the national and international agencies concerned with increasing the benefits from irrigation development.

1. There is a great need to examine critically the planning-design process currently used for irrigation development and to develop principles and procedures that will allow it to be free from the current weaknesses. The planning-design process has to be made adequately sensitive as well as responsive to the potential problems of waterlogging and land degradation and to other environmental-ecological concerns. The planning and design functions must be broadened to integrate into them such critical aspects as planning for field implementation of physical infrastructure, development of institutional infrastructure for effective and sustained management, and as evaluation of system performance.

The above will require in-depth studies conducted by multidisciplinary teams, and strong support from the irrigation agencies concerned will be essential to bring about the desired changes in the planning-design process. The international lending institutions should play a vital role in financing the needed studies on and actions toward those changes.

2. Research on increasing benefits obtained from existing irrigation systems should be strengthened greatly. Such research should set forth one or more of the following component goals: (a) improving the water allocation-distribution procedures in the main irrigation system to increase equity in farmers' access to water and to enhance efficiency of their water use; (b) upgrading the field operation and maintenance capacity of the irrigation agency; and (c) improving farmer cooperation in efficient and equitable use of water and, for this purpose, organizing farmer participation in planning and implementing relevant functions of system management. The scope of the benefits achievable from the pursuit of each of these goals in given irrigation systems and their complementarities should be assessed in depth.

In relation to the above main goals, comprehensive assessment should be made of the possible need for policy and institutional reforms to establish much-needed resource mobilization for effective and sustained O&M of irrigation systems on one hand and, on the other, enhanced accountability as well as an incentive mechanism within the agencies responsible for making irrigation technology work.

3. There is a clear indication that waterlogging and related land degradation are a serious problem in many irrigation system areas. In many others, they are an impending problem of great magnitude. New irrigation development may turn out to be a self-defeating pursuit if these problems are not resolved satisfactorily. However, our knowledge of these problems is sketchy and highly inadequate. Major research efforts should be made immediately in appropriate locations to quantify the extent of the problem, study the process of land degradation, and explore viable solutions. Special emphasis should be placed on identifying the genesis of the problem and determining how other existing or future irrigation systems could prevent its occurrence or minimize its adverse effects.

4. A vast amounts of information and experience relative to irrigation planning, design, and operation and maintenance is available in the various countries, and if properly assembled and systematized it could create a priceless storehouse of knowledge useful for various important purposes in future irrigation development and management. What is needed is more than merely a databank; it should be a central facility that can deliver analyzed information relative to specific problems experienced in the irrigation sector in the different countries. Such a facility would serve as a mechanism to promote feedback of past experience to present planning and allow coverage of not only the different irrigation systems within a country but also those of other countries. Also, it would help to avoid repetition of past mistakes in planning-design as well as in management decisions. International initiative is recommended for this purpose.

5. In the long run, the irrigation development and management quality of a country will be determined by the amount of well-trained manpower that is available in the country. The shortage of trained manpower is already perceived as a major limitation to achieving higher levels of irrigation system performance in most countries at the present time. Close attention to this problem should be given by concerned educational institutions.

The importance of water in the national economy is most often not reflected in the education that technical graduates receive in the college or university. Engineering curricula should be modified to educate civil and agricultural engineering students on the major problems of the irrigation sector and on principles and procedures that can help to solve them. Well-supported institutions should be developed within, or in close association with, the irrigation agencies of each country to impart relevant on-the-job training to the different cadres of the staff to enhance their technical capacity as well as their motivation for good work. Special attention is needed in the area of development of pertinent textbooks and training materials, which are in short supply, for this purpose.

REFERENCES

Ali, S. H. 1984. Planning and implementation of measures to ensure productivity and equity under irrigation systems. Pp. 211–40. *In* N. Pant (ed.) Productivity and equity in irrigation systems. New Delhi: Ashish Publishing House.

Bagadion, B. U., and F. F. Korten, 1980. Developing viable irrigators' associations: Lessons from small scale irrigation development in the Philippines. *Agricultural Administration* 7(4): 273–87.

Bagadion, B. U. 1984. Personal communication.

Barker, R., E. W. Coward, Jr., G. Levine, and L. E. Small. 1984. Irrigation development in Asia: past trends and future directions. Cornell Studies in Irrigation. Ithaca, N.Y.: Cornell University.

Barker, R., and R. W. Herdt. 1979. Rainfed lowland rice as a research priority—an economist's view. Pp. 1–50. *In* Rainfed lowland rice: selected papers from the 1978 international rice research conference. Los Baños, Philippines: International Rice Research Institute.

Borlaug, N. 1982. Planning to avert chaos. *Mazingira* 6(3): 80–81.

Bottrall, A. 1978. Evaluating the organization and management of irrigated agriculture. Pp. 235–53. *In* Proceedings of the Commonwealth workshop on irrigation management. Hyderabad, India: Commonwealth Secretariat.

Cerescope Report. 1984. An engineer's dream transformed into an ecological nightmare. *Ceres* 17(6): 11–12.

Colombo, U., D. G. Johnson, and T. Shishido. 1978. Reducing malnutrition in developing countries: increasing rice production in South and Southeast Asia. Triangle Papers, no. 16. New York: Trilateral Commission.

Corey, A. T. 1982. Unpublished report at workshop on water management in Sri Lanka. Colombo, Sri Lanka: Agrarian Research and Training Institute.

Currethers, I. 1978. Contentious issues in planning irrigation schemes. Pp. 301–308. *In* C. Widstrand (ed.) The social and ecological effects of water development in developing countries. New York: Pergamon Press.

Food and Agriculture Organization (FAO). 1979. Agriculture toward 2000. 20th session. Rome.

The Global 2000 Report to the President. 1983. New York: Penguin Books.

Government of Bangladesh and the Work Bank (GOB-WB). 1979. Review of the Bangladesh Water Development Board. Report no. 2327-BD.

Herdt, R. W., and C. Capule. 1983. Adoption, spread, and production impact of modern rice varieties in Asia. Los Baños, Philippines: International Rice Research Institute.

Khan, H. R. 1984. Irrigation management research in Bangladesh. Workshop on research priorities for irrigation management in Asia. Digana Village, Sri Lanka: International Irrigation Management Institute.

Levine, G. 1977. Management components in irrigation system design and operation. *Agricultural Administration* 4(1): 37–48.

———. 1981. Perspectives on integrating findings from research on irrigation systems in Southeast Asia. Workshop on investment decisions to further develop and make use of Southeast Asia's irrigation resources. Bangkok, Thailand: Agricultural Development Council.

Lim, C. C. 1984. Irrigation management research in Malaysia. Workshop on research priorities for irrigation management in Asia. Digana Village, Sri Lanka: International Irrigation Management Institute.

Madeley, J. 1983. Big dam schemes—value for money or nonsustainable development? *Mazingira* 7(4): 16–25.

Miranda, S. M. 1984. Status report on irrigation management research in the Philippines. Workshop on research priorities for irrigation management in Asia. Digana Village, Sri Lanka: International Irrigation Management Institute.

National Irrigation Administration and International Rice Research Institute (NIA-IRRI). 1984. On-farm facilities study, a final report. Manila.

National Water Resources Council (NWRC). 1979. Irrigation inventory, 1977. Report no. 17-B.

Oram, P., J. Zapata, G. Alibarubo, and S. Roy. 1979. Investment and input requirements for accelerating food production in low-income countries by 1990. Research Report no. 10. Washington, D.C.: International Food Policy Research Institute.

Population Reference Bureau (PRB). 1984. World population data sheet. Washington, D.C.

Rao, P. S. 1984. Status report on research on irrigation management in India. Workshop on research priorities for irrigation management in Asia. Digana Village, Sri Lanka: International Irrigation Management Institute.

Seki, A. 1982. Irrigation projects: typical problem areas in planning and execution. Thursday seminar paper. Los Baños, Philippines: International Rice Research Institute.

Sundar, A. 1984. Modern techniques for management of irrigation systems: what can they do in the absence of commitment to manage? *Wamana* 4(3): 1, 20–22.

Swaminathan, M. S. 1980. Past, present and future trends in tropical agriculture. *In* Perspective in world agriculture. London: Commonwealth Agriculture Bureau.

Thongtawee, N. 1984. Irrigation management research in Thailand. Workshop on research priorities for irrigation management in Asia. Digana Village, Sri Lanka: International Irrigation Management Institute.

Wade, R. 1982. The World Bank and India's irrigation reform. *Journal of Development Studies* 18(2): 171–84.

Weaver, T. F. 1984. Problem areas and researchable issues in irrigation. Workshop on research priorities for irrigation management in Asia. Digana Village, Sri Lanka: International Irrigation Management Institute.

World Development Report 1982 (WDR). 1982. New York: Oxford University Press.

51. SOIL PROPERTIES AND WATER REGIME MANAGEMENT AS AFFECTED BY OPTIMIZED TILLAGE ENERGY AND PRACTICES UNDER SEMIARID CONDITIONS

Dan Wolf, Department of Agricultural Engineering, Technion-Israel Institute of Technology, Haifa, Israel, and Amos Hadas, Department of Soil Physics, Institute of Soil and Water, Agricultural Research Organization, Bet Dagan, Israel

ABSTRACT

About one-third of the world's cultivated area is in semiarid lands, most of it in developing countries. A large portion of the semiarid soils is susceptible under wet conditions to compaction by tractors and other farm machinery. The soil compaction causes a reduction in rain and irrigation water infiltration and storage, difficulties in nutrient uptake and root development, and yield decrease. Tillage of the dry precompacted soil, using implements and methods adapted from temperate lands, requires high tractor energy, forms large soil clods, and dictates the need for many operations to achieve a reasonable soil aggregation. Overdusting by the mechanical activities may cause crusting, pollution, and soil erosion.

Intensive field research and agrotechnological system analysis brought about a successful, widely applied controlled traffic, and precision optimum tillage methods. The separation between permanent compacted lanes and the plant-growing zones, as well as the gradual development of machinery, implements, and other subsystems to suit the semiarid soil constraints, resulted in improved soil structure, better water regime, reduced tillage energy, and improved plant response.

Still, there is a need to investigate potential technologies, such as the wide tractive frame or the nontractive lateral operating systems, for even better productivity, efficiency, economy, and soil and plant reaction.

INTRODUCTION

The need for greater crop yields to provide food, fibers, and plant materials for industries is growing. These goals can be met only by increasing production rates in prime, currently producing agricultural areas and introducing new lands into modern agricultural production.

Increased production from currently cultivated land requires intensification of current agronomic practices, namely increased inputs in energy, water, labor, chemicals, and mechanization, which in turn create pollution, soil compaction, and salinization hazards. Introduction of new lands means developing new marginal soil and water resources in developed countries and modernizing agronomic practices in developing countries.

Modern practices and proper utilization of resources in agricultural enterprises have been developed mostly in temperate zones by trial and error and thus cannot be directly applied to the new locations or environments under consideration, especially when these are located in the semiarid and tropical zones of the world. Therefore, it is imperative that wise decisions, pertinent to utilization of such resouces as water, soil, labor, energy, and machines for developing new areas or for modernizing cultivated areas, be made, based on sound, proven database knowledge obtained through systems analysis of agricultural practices, with special attention to optimizing input-output relationships.

This systems analysis concept for agriculture calls for the understanding that, for increased production and yields, the farmers have to work the soil and to apply water and chemicals into man-controlled ecological habitats optimized for the crop's needs throughout the growing and yielding season.

Among the means to achieve this the farmer may consider tillage operations and irrigation systems, through which soil water storage and hydraulic properties may be changed while pests and weeds are controlled.

Soil tillage as a soil properties–controlling practice imposes a drastic change in soil structure orientation at first; but these newly affected physical properties consequently change with consecutive tillage operations (e.g., deep, aggressive primary tillage for root bed and shallow secondary tillage passes for seedbed preparation), wetting and drying, swelling and shrinkage cycles, or heavy traffic across the fields. The seasonal trend is toward the initial soil properties (that is, those prior to tillage) or even the worsening of these as a result of traffic-caused compaction.

Tillage and compaction diminish the physical properties of the soil, thus affecting the crop. In order to optimize production, one must study the crop-environment relationships as a systems analysis case in which the parameters and variables are changing with time and operations and the crops yield responses to these changes. Such an approach was partially presented by Hadas et al. (1980, 1983). In their works the main problem was whether the soil-crop water regime could be optimized through proper manipulation of soil properties by various combinations of tillage operations (e.g., fragmenting, inverting, rotavating, reorienting soil crumbs, or reshaping the soil surface).

This chapter discusses some aspects of an agrotechnological systems analysis while pointing out the benefits and hazards involved in modernizing practices. The ideas and data presented are based on the authors' experience, gained under Israeli semiarid climatic conditions on clod-forming soils.

SOIL TILLAGE IN SEMIARID LANDS

As described by Wolf and Luth (1979), about one-third of the world's 1.4 billion cultivated ha is in semiarid lands (Fig. 1). The agroclimatic term *semiarid* refers to

- Inadequate or nonuniform rain distribution interspersed with long dry seasons.
- High temperatures, intensive solar radiation, and little frost to affect soil structure.
- Lack of water for softening the soils by pretillage irrigation.

Most of the semiarid lands are in the central and southern sections of the world, while the temperate areas are in the northern part. At least half of the semiarid lands, both irrigated and nonirrigated have potentially clod-forming soils: a total of 250 million ha (Fig. 2). Large hard clods may be exposed during primary tillage, and seedbed preparation becomes time consuming and expensive.

The texture of these soils is similar to temperate soils, but the mechanical characteristics are different (Wolf, 1970).

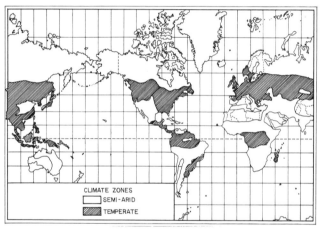

Fig. 1. Temperate and semiarid agricultural areas in the world. Wolf and Luth, 1979.

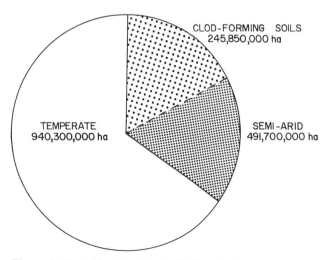

Fig. 2. Cultivated land by climate. Wolf and Luth, 1979.

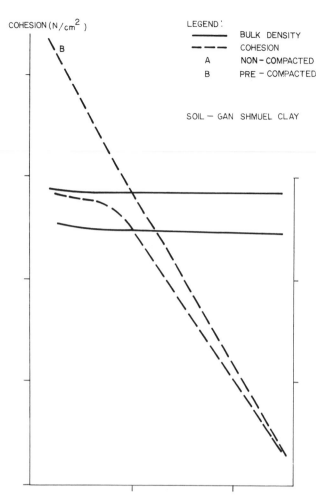

Fig. 3. Bulk density and cohesion as affected by decreasing moisture content and pre-compaction. Wolf and Hadas, 1983.

Most of the semiarid soils have very little or even no soil structure stabilizing organic material and thus susceptible to compaction by traffic. Wet soils may be compacted during the previous cropping season by tilling, planting, cultivating, spraying, and harvesting activities. A survey analysis (Wolf et al., 1984) shows that the number of passes and operations involved in cropping dryland and irrigated cotton is fifteen to twenty-five, most of these being done on wet soils. After intensive drying during the growing season, by climate, planting, and sun radiation, the soil forms large, hard blocks or clods, bounded by cracks. The strength of the soil mass is high and nonuniform because of the presence of the low cohesion boundaries and cracks.

Wolf and Hadas (1983) described the effect of interaction between external, machine-made compaction and the natural drying process on low organic colloid content semiarid soils. The residual effect of soil compaction when moisture content decreases was analyzed after field and laboratory studies and is illustrated in Fig. 3.

Soil samples were compacted, at lower plastic limit moisture content, to two levels of bulk density. Then, a slow, low temperature drying process was used to decrease the moisture content down to the hygroscopic level. Through the process, samples were taken out, and bulk density and cohesion (from shear tests) were measured.

The effect of drying on bulk density was equivalent for both compacted and noncompacted soil samples; it increased slightly, primarily as a result of the montmorilonite clay shrinkage. On the other hand, there was a distinct precompaction effect on soil strength. As long as moisture content is high, cohesion of noncompacted soil increases at a lower rate than that of the compacted samples, but their values were close together. However, once moisture content reaches 40 percent of the lower plastic limit, the difference increases fast. At the hygroscopic m.c. level, cohesion of the precompacted soil is 55 percent higher than that of the noncompacted soil.

By comparing aggregate strength from fields and neighboring natural, never-tilled soils, this phenomenon was verified (Fig. 4).

Tillage should produce a soil tilth that provides crops with adequate air and water and produces low mechnical resistance to crop roots (Slipher, 1932). In the subhumid, subtropical, semiarid regions of the world tillage is the most important practice to improve the soil's physical condition and hence, crop establishment and development. Under these climatic conditions, a common practice is to till the soil toward the end of the dry season. Seedbed preparation for winter crops or primary tillage for the next summer's crops is done frequently under conditions of dryness perhaps as low as the hygroscopic moisture content. This is done so that farmers can get the maximum benefit from the limited rainfall period. The practice prevails because, although water would soften the clods, the moisture range for optimum tilling is narrow, and excess water may wash the soil away or puddle, and it is technically difficult to till wet soil since it provides no traction.

Tillage may be performed by heavy machinery at depths up to 45 cm or by draft animals to depths of 10 to 20 cm.

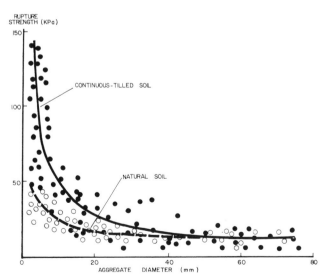

Fig. 4. Effect of aggregate size on rupture strength. Wolf and Hadas, 1983.

The dry compacted soils, when tilled, produce large clods because of the anisotropy and heterogeneity of their structural framework. High energy is required for primary tillage of the clod-forming soils. Many secondary tillage passes are required to pulverize the hard clods. The result is often a poor seedbed composed of fine dust and large aggregates. The excess of dust may cause erosion and pollution problems and form a crust or compacted layers when wetted.

Since a large portion of clod-forming soils is in the less-developed countries, relatively little research on tillage has been done in these areas.

TILLAGE ENERGY AND ITS EFFICIENCY

Draft requirements for implements in semiarid lands are very high compared with tillage in temperate soils, as shown in Table 1 (Wolf and Luth, 1979). Representative data of energy required for tilling in cotton growing areas in semiarid zones were presented by Wolf et al. (1977, 1984) and then compared to energy consumed in tilling temperate soils, as analyzed from the ASAE data (1983).

It can be seen in Fig. 5 that for most operations and implements, the specific energy required for semiarid soils is higher, because of the tough conditions, than that for the temperate soils. As a result, powerful tractors—tough and heavy implements—are required, although their productivity in the semiarid land is rather low. Low efficiency in cutting, breaking, and pulverizing the hard soil clods is the main energy consumer in tilling clod-forming soils.

Pressing the soil mass causes shear stresses in a large soil volume around the implement. The conventional failure pattern, as affected by the implement characteristics under temperate soil conditions, is entirely different in the semiarid soils. The soil clods cleave along low-cohesion surfaces rather than the designated primary and secondary shear planes.

Wolf (1970) found experimentally that primary tillage, done by moldboard plows of different sizes and characteristics or by subsoiling, did not increase pulverization of soil relative to its pretillage natural condition. No significant differences in mean-weight diameter between the various treatments could be identified, as shown in Fig. 6.

The primary tillage operation only separates the naturally interlocked clods and rearranges them in a new order. It does not pulverize the soil by shearing the clods into smaller aggregates. But the new arrangement means increases pore space elevates the soil surface.

Considering the nonpulverizing effect of primary tillage in clod-forming soils, the input energy efficiency of a simple implement can be demonstrated numerically. Data are based on results of field experiments in relatively moderate soils.

For example, subsoiling to a depth of 0.4 m requires an average draft of 12 kN/standard for a 0.8-m lateral spacing. Energy input is then 15 kNm per square meter of field area.

As there is no pulverizing effect on soil, the only useful work from the agricultural point of view is invested in increasing the pore space. For a soil bulk density of 1,500 kg/m^3, the weight of a soil block with a surface area of 1 m^2 and a volume of 0.4 m^3 is 600 kg. If the soil surface is ele-

Table 1. Tillage implement draft in clod-forming soils.

Operation		Mean Depth (mm)	Mean Velocity[a] (m/s)	Mean Draft Clod-Forming Soil	Mean Draft Temperate Soils
Disking	—preprimary tillage		0.7–1.5	6.0–16.0 kN/m	
Subsoiling	—1.0-m lateral spacing	400–500	0.6	22.0–24.0 kN/standard	4.0–14.0 kN/standard
Subsoiling	—0.5-m lateral spacing	350–400	0.7–0.9	11.0–12.0 kN/standard	4.0–14.0 kN/standard
				22.0–24.0 kN/m	8.0–28.0 kN/m[b]
Deep plowing	—following subsoiling	400	0.9–1.2	90–120 kPa	
Deep plowing	—down to compacted layers	300–500	0.5–1.2	100–200 kPa	
Shallow plowing	—above compacted layers	200–300	0.7–1.2	70–100 kPa	30–80 kPa
Disking			0.5	15.0–22.0 kN/m	3.6–5.8 kN/m[b]
Floating			0.5–0.9	15.0–24.0 kN/m	4.3–11.5 kN/m[c]
Packing			0.8–2.5	7.0–17.0 kN/m	0.300–2.2 kN/m
Chisel plowing	—300-mm lateral spacing, primary tillage	300	0.5	220 kN/m	
Chisel plowing	—300-mm lateral spacing, secondary tillage	250–300	0.5–0.7	12.0–22.0 kN/m	2.0–9.5 kN/m

SOURCE: Wolf and Luth, 1979.

[a] Assumed top velocity, primary tillage, 2.0 m/s; secondary tillage, 3.0 m/s.

[b] At higher velocities.

[c] Land plane.

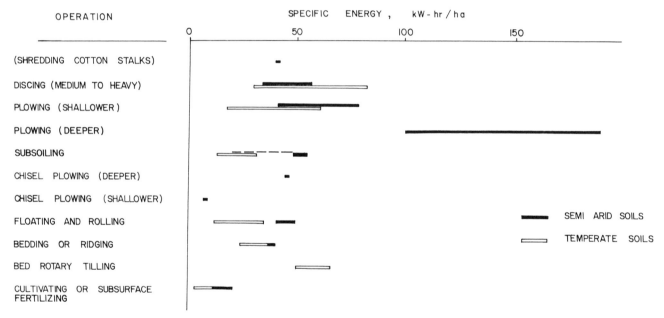

Fig. 5. Specific energy requirements for various tillage operations. Wolf and Hadas, 1983.

vated on the average by 0.1 m after subsoiling (a 25 percent increase in pore space), the center of gravity of the soil block is lifted by 0.05 m. The net energy required to do the work is 0.3 kNm for each square meter of field area.

Defining implement energy efficiency as

$$\frac{\text{net energy required for useful work}}{\text{energy invested in implement}}$$

it will in our case be as low as 0.3/15 = 0.02.

The other 98 percent of the energy required by the implement is wasted on moving the soil clods, bulldozing, friction, and nonutilized cutting and shearing stresses. Hadas et al. (1978) analyzed field research results, performed in typical clod-farming soils, and correlated total energy of tillage operations and combinations with the resulting aggregate distribution (Table 2).

The energy consumed for all operations is very high compared with the representative levels of energy used to till temperate soils or when one considers the quality of the soil pulverization.

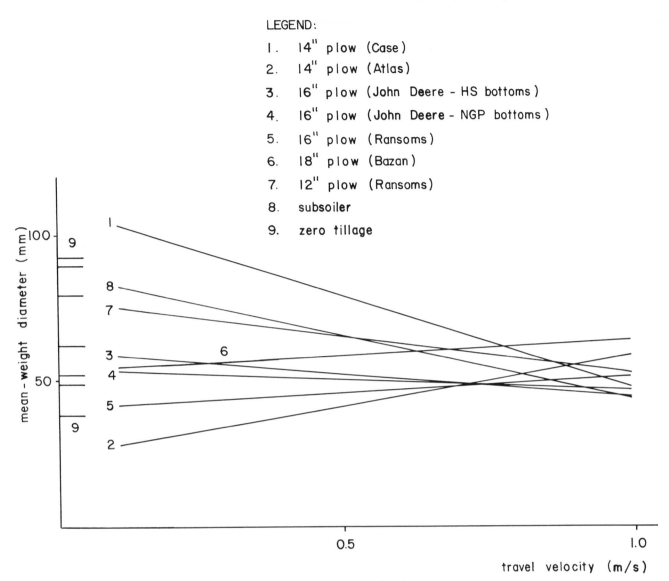

LEGEND:

1. 14" plow (Case)
2. 14" plow (Atlas)
3. 16" plow (John Deere - HS bottoms)
4. 16" plow (John Deere - NGP bottoms)
5. 16" plow (Ransoms)
6. 18" plow (Bazan)
7. 12" plow (Ransoms)
8. subsoiler
9. zero tillage

Fig. 6. Effect of primary tillage operations on mean-weight diameter of clod-forming soils.

To evaluate the efficiency involved in these tillage operations, the minimum net energy required for breaking soil clods and aggregates was measured by using the drop-shatter test (Hadas and Wolf, 1983). The results of the efficiency analysis are presented in Tables 3 and 4. The soil discussed in Table 3 is a poor-structured, loessial clay loam. The second soil is clay. The energy efficiency was calculated by comparing the net minimum energy from laboratory tests to the actual field tillage energy for the same degree of soil pulverization. Its quality is measured in three ways, as shown in Tables 3 and 4.

It can be seen that in dry, precompacted soils containing little organic matter, the reorientation of clods and aggregates is determined by abrasive action rather than shearing impact. Thus, the use of tillage implements in clod-forming soils is less energy efficient than in moist soils, especially in dry soils with a distinct structure.

TILLAGE—SOIL COMPACTION—PHYSICAL PROPERTIES IN MOIST SOILS

After winter rains or irrigation, tilling the moist soil of the spring seedbed provides weed control, but the weight of the tractor or other equipment will compact the moist soil. When the soil's bulk density changes, its degree of saturation, water characteristics, capillary and hydraulic conductivities, and air content change as well (Fig. 7). The effect of compaction and tillage cycles is demonstrated in Fig. 8.

Prior to tillage the soil's density was 1.3 g/cm^3 and its gravimetric water content was 16 percent (A); after tillage, part of the soil volume was increased to 1.2 g/cm^3 (B), whereas the soil under the tractor's wheels reached a density of 1.55 g/cm^3 (C). The chart shows that the free porosity to conduct or retain water diminishes in the compacted soil (A to C) and increases when the soil is tilled. If the field is then

Table 2. Aggregate size distribution as affected by sequence of tillage operations.

Tillage Treatment	Aggregate Size (mm)				Total Energy (kg mm²)
	<10	10–25	25–75	>75	
	%				
Deep plow (dry soil)	55.9			44.1	4,660
Subsoiler (dry soil)	27			73.0	2,100
Deep plow (wet soil)	59.7	19.9	9.2	11.2	4,326
Subsoiler, deep plow (dry soil)	7.2	14.7	78.1		2,100 / 4,660 / 6,760
Subsoiler, deep plow, disking (dry soil)	25.4	8.3	66.6		2,100 / 4,600 / 1,000 / 7,760
Subsoiler, deep plow, disking, heavy roller, leveling box (dry soil)	39.3	13.5	47.6 (20.9)	(26.7)	2,100 / 4,666 / 1,000 / 600 / 1,200 / 9,560
Deep plowing, heavy roller, leveling box, heavy roller (dry soil)	37.5	8.1	54.4 (25.9)	(28.5)	4,660 / 600 / 1,200 / 600 / 7,060

SOURCE: Hadas et al., 1978.

Table 3. Median aggregate diameter, specific energy to reduce aggregate size, energy input, and energy efficiency in breaking up the soil, as affected by different implements and tillage sequences at Nir Am-Gevim.

Tillage Treatment of Sequence	Initial Dry Bulk Density (g · cm⁻³)	Median Aggregate Diameter (mm)	Specific Surface Area (m² · kg⁻¹)	Soil Volume Affected by Implements (m³)	Specific Energy		Energy Input (kN · m⁻³)	Energy Efficiency (η)		
					Median Aggregate Diameter Reduction (J · kg⁻¹)	Specific Surface Area Increase (J · kg⁻¹)		Median Aggregate Diameter Reduction	Specific Surface Area Increase	Soil Surface Elevation
Natural clods	1.45	253	0.09	—	—	—	—	—	—	—
Chisel plow	1.45	97	0.13	0.26	24.3	11.4	21.0	0.44	0.21	0.05
Deep moldboard plow	1.45	76	0.14	0.40	34.4	16.8	46.6	0.31	0.21	0.03
Deep chisel plow + deep moldboard plow	1.45	61	0.14	0.40	45.2	23.1	67.6	0.39	0.20	—
Deep chisel plow + deep moldboard plow + disc	1.45 / 1.20	52 / 44	0.15 / 0.16	0.47 / 0.20	54.2 / 20.9	28.5 / 36.1	77.6 / 10.0	0.39 / 0.50	0.21 / 0.87	—
Deep moldboard plow + heavy roller + land plane + heavy roller	1.45 / 1.20	71 / 26	0.14 / 0.20	0.47 / 0.05	37.5 / 69.3	18.6 / 71.1	70.6 / 24.0	0.30 / 0.17	0.15 / 0.18	—
Deep chisel plow + deep moldboard plow + disc + heavy roller + hardplane	1.45 / 1.20	50 / 21	0.15 / 0.22	0.47 / 0.05	57.4 / 62.2	30.5 / 92.1	95.6 / 18.0	0.34 / 0.21	0.18 / 0.31	—
Deep chisel plow	1.45	50	0.15	0.47	57.0	—	96.2	0.34	—	—

SOURCE: Hadas and Wolf, 1983.

Table 4. Median aggregate diameter, specific energy to reduce aggregate size, energy input, and energy efficiency in breaking up the soil, as affected by different implements and tillage sequences at Gan Shemuel.

Tillage Treatment of Sequence	Initial Dry Bulk Density ($g \cdot cm^{-3}$)	Median Aggregate Diameter (mm)	Specific Surface Area ($m^2 \cdot kg^{-1}$)	Soil Volume Affected by Implements (m^3)	Specific Energy Median Aggregate Diameter Reduction ($J \cdot kg^{-1}$)	Specific Energy Specific Surface Area Increase ($J \cdot kg^{-1}$)	Energy Input ($kN \cdot m^{-3}$)	Energy Efficiency (η) Median Aggregate Diameter Reduction	Energy Efficiency (η) Specific Surface Area Increase	Soil Surface Elevation
Natural clods	1.45	324	0.21	—	—	—	—	—	—	—
Deep chisel plow	1.45	24	0.30	0.28	13.5	12.6	20.6	0.27	0.08	0.02
Deep moldboard plow	1.45	39	0.26	0.38	9.2	7.0	44.2	0.16	0.25	0.02
Shallow plow	1.38	28	0.29	0.22	12.0	10.4	18.8	0.19	0.17	0.02
Deep chisel plow with 4 lister attachments	1.45	24	0.30	0.18	13.3	12.6	16.6	0.20	0.19	0.02
Deep chisel plow with 5 lister attachments	1.45	24	0.30	0.18	13.3	12.6	13.1	0.26	0.25	0.01

SOURCE: Hadas and Wolf, 1983.

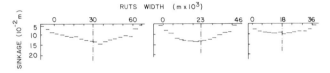

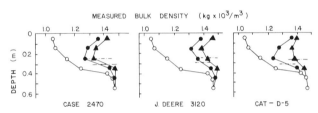

Fig. 7. Typical rut cross sections after the first pass and mean measured bulk density distributions—initital (o), after the first pass (●), and after the third pass (▼)—of the three different tractors used. Broken lines represent depth from center of ruts to the untilled soil layer. Wolf and Hadas, 1984.

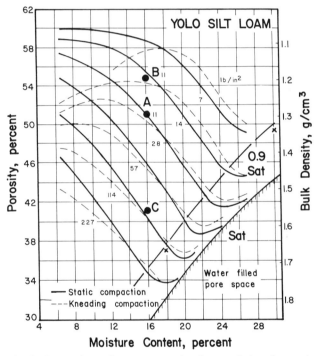

Fig. 8. Comparison of pressure-porosity characteristics of an agricultural soil subject to both kneading and static compaction. Chancellor, 1976.

irrigated or gets water from precipitation, then, for the soil's initial bulk density, the soil's water content can increase to approximately 31 percent, almost twice its initial content, before saturation is attained. In the compacted layer (C) only a 10 percent increase in water content can be achieved.

The higher the density of the soil, the less water can be stored in it. Furthermore, the higher its density, the narrower its pore system becomes, and as a consequence the soil water potential becomes more negative and the capillary and hydraulic conductivities decrease very rapidly (e.g., a reduction of 10 or 25 percent in a pore's radius will cause a change in its hydraulic conductivity by 27 to 36 and 58 to 70 percent, respectively). This means that the crop must waste more energy to get the small amount of water from a compacted soil.

Under field conditions the farmer can witness the water runoff from compacted lanes to noncompacted zones or to drainage systems. The reduction in infiltration is due mostly to reduced soil conductivity.

Tillage operation can alleviate to some extent the compaction effects by opening cracks in the soil mass or fragmenting it into small, rearranged clods with a great volume of large voids, into which water infiltrates very easily and at higher rates when compared with the initial infiltrability rates of the soil.

The effects of tillage on infiltration are presented in Fig. 9. Plowing, which leaves larger clods, improves infiltration,

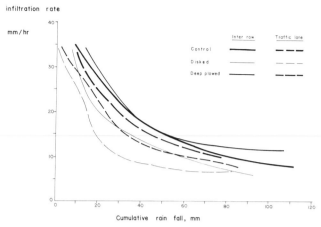

Fig. 9. The effect of cumulative rainfall on infiltration rate. Rawitz et al., 1980.

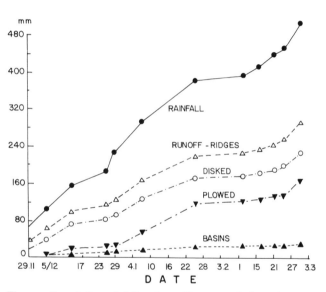

Fig. 10. Cumulative rainfall and runoff amounts during rainy season. Rawitz et al., 1980.

whereas recompacting the soil by traffic on plowed fields reduces the infiltration to rates below those attained on nontilled trafficked fields (control/traffic lane). Disking is an operation that causes heavy pulverization of the soil, and thus once the soil is wetted a crust is formed and the infiltration decreases even further than that of the nontilled control soil. In order to increase soil infiltrability and thus decrease water losses, the soil relief is modified by forming water-retaining basins on the soil surface, which reduce or even prevent runoff on fields or lanes in the field, the infiltrability of which is low, as shown in Fig. 10. Increased soil infiltrability by tillage is only part of controlling the soil water storage. According to Hadas and Hillel (1972) and Hadas et al. (1980), deep tillage operations performed prior to the precipitation season can increase soil water storage by increasing infiltration and reducing runoff and evaporation from the soil, resulting in increased amounts of stored, potentially available water for the crop before planting. There is a certain amount of precipitation or irrigation water below which soil storage is unaffected or even practically reduced by tillage operations, whereas above that certain amount, deep tillage operations conserve up to 15 percent more water in a given soil profile depth, as shown in Table 5. These results are found in other regions, as reported by Unger and Stewart (1983). If the soil is compacted so as to impede root development, this extra stored water as well as the nutrients will not be available to the crop (Trouse, 1971), and consequently the yield may be impaired. On the other hand, with very loose topsoil, even though more water is stored in the soil underneath under rainfed conditions, crop like cotton may yield less than it would have if less water had been stored in nontilled soil. This is due to over-transpiration followed by total collapse and boll shedding, whereas with a crop like sorghum no shedding occurs and the yield corresponds to the added water storage capacity (Tables 6 and 7).

The complexity of this system can now be appreciated. In order to control crop yields the whole system should be monitored and analyzed in order to achieve the very complicated experimental setup needed. The amount of data to be collected and interrelated, such as data on continuous collec-

Table 5. Amount of rainwater (mm of water head) stored in the soil (0–1.50-m profiles) before sowing.

Rainfall (mm)	Primary Tillage Operation			
	Deep Plowing	Shallow Plowing	Chisel Subsoiler	No Tillage
110	67	69	74	73
237				
(+250 mm irrigation in February)	221	189	193	181
247	210	201	208	203
609	523	504	485	470
450	426	403	375	365
No. of winter weeds per m²	66	70	227	241

SOURCE: Hadas et al., 1980.
[a]Midwinter determination.

Table 6. Response of cotton plants to primary tillage operations (Lakhish).

Tillage Treatment	1 Year		2 Years									
	Stand (pl · ha⁻¹ × 10⁴)	Lint Yield (kg · ha⁻¹)	Stand (pl · ha⁻¹ × 10⁴)	Leaf Dry Matter Production[a] (kg · ha⁻¹) at Day				Bolls Dry Matter Production (kg · ha⁻¹) at Day				Lint Yield (kg · ha⁻¹)
				54	61	68	102	54	68	102	132	
No autumn tillage	10.3	603.0	12.5	268 (0.42)	620 (0.64)	884 (0.83)	1,036 (0.98)	16	78	2,306	2,810	774
Shallow plowing	10.9	622.2										
Deep plowing	10.6	622.2	10.9	285 (0.41)	493 (0.59)	726 (0.80)	820 (0.79)	15	60	157	2,495	766
Deep plowing × 2	—	—	9.03	249 (0.34)	381 (0.41)	694 (0.62)	886 (0.69)	10	43	1,579	2,200	558

SOURCE: Hadas et al., 1980.
[a]Numbers in parentheses are the Leaf Area Index.

Table 7. Response of sorghum plants to primary tillage operations (Revadim).

Primary Tillage Treatment	Field Plot								
	1				2			3	
	Germination[a] (pl · ha⁻¹ × 10⁴)	Final Stand[a] (pl · ha⁻¹ × 10⁴)	Panicles (no · ha)10⁴	Yields (kg · ha⁻¹)	Final Stand (pl × ha⁻¹ × 10⁴)	Panicles (no · ha)10⁴	Yield (kg · ha⁻¹)	Yield (kg · ha⁻¹)	Total Yield (kg · ha⁻¹)
Shallow plowing	8.98	9.05	8.94	4,079 a	8.28	8.21	4,190 a	2,303 b	10,572
Deep plowing	9.51	9.45	8.51	4,185 a	7.89	8.10	4,120 a	2,463 b	10,768
Sub-soiling	8.06	8.95	7.70	3,895 ba	7.85	8.26	4,190 a	2,710 a	10,768
No tillage	8.84	—	—	3,164 c	8.28	7.84	2,720 b	2,200 c	8,084
Rainfall	483 mm, well distributed				608 mm			451 mm, mostly at the beginning of winter	

SOURCE: Hadas et al, 1980.
[a]10–12 × 10⁴ seedlings ha⁻¹ were planted.
Value classes (a, b, c) differ significantly at $P = 0.05$.

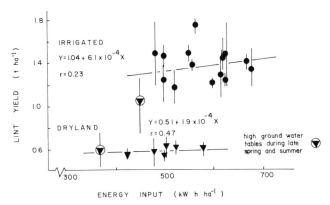

Fig. 11. Lint yield as a function of energy input by tillage for irrigated and dry-land cotton, respectively. Wolf et al., 1984.

tion of soil water regime, root activity, and plant phenology, is enormous. Some of these complexes were brought up by Hadas et al. (1980, 1983) and Hadas and Wolf (1984). A simple analysis carried out by Hadas et al. (1983) to assess the ability to detect the effects of water application, soil water storage, and tillage energy inputs on yield of rainfed and irrigated cotton showed that there was a statistically significant correlation between these inputs and the yields (Figs. 11 and 12). These could explain only a rather small fraction of the total yield variations, a higher fraction (0.5) for water application and a lower share for tillage. Better correlations were attained for irrigated cotton (Hadas et al., 1983, 1985) by combining the effects of residual soil compaction on crop stands and variations in soil water storage throughout the cotton-growing season.

Soil compaction effects on rooting capabilities, or dimin-

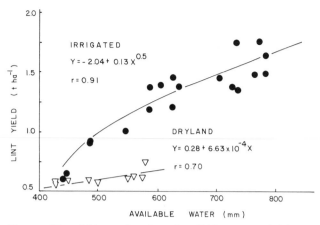

Fig. 12. Lint yield as a function of available water (rainfall and irrigation) (in mm) for dry-land and irrigated cotton, respectively. Wolf et al., 1984.

ished and more variable crop stands, are carried from one season to the next (Voorhees, 1983; Hadas et al., 1983, 1985; Hadas and Wolf, 1984; Wolf and Hadas, 1984). An impaired stand is caused by a coarser seedbed produced on compacted soil (Hadas et al., 1985; Wolf and Hadas, 1984; Rawitz et al., 1980). This fact is demonstrated for different crops; for example, in Fig. 13 the stand of cotton plants depends on the mean aggregate diameter, which is larger under trafficked and compacted spots in the field. Furthermore, not only does the stand diminish but the variability around the mean increases (bars on the data dots). The effect of the stand and the stand's variability on cotton yield is also shown in Fig. 13.

For a mean stand of 6.3 plants per meter of row length, the greater the stand's variation becomes, the lower the yield will be. For a mean stand of 7.2 plants per meter of row length, the same pattern is obtained, but the slope is almost doubled and the intercept is greater. These data show the effect of stand density and its variation on the yield of irrigated cotton, but the mean crop stand and the variability around the mean can be attributed to soil compaction or bad farming—negligent sowing or planting. Similar results are presented for sorghum (Fig. 14) and groundnuts (Fig. 15).

POTENTIAL PRACTICES AND TECHNOLOGIES

There is a cycle of compacting the semiarid soils by tractors and machinery, as a result worsening the soil structure,

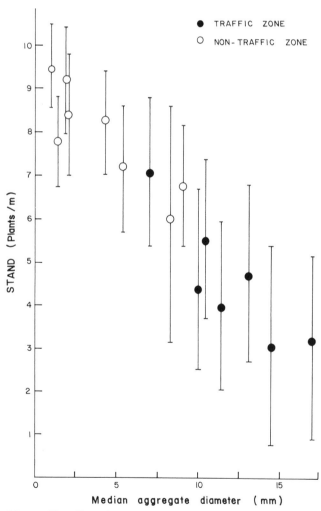

Fig. 13. The effect of aggregate size on cotton stand. Gupta et al., 1985.

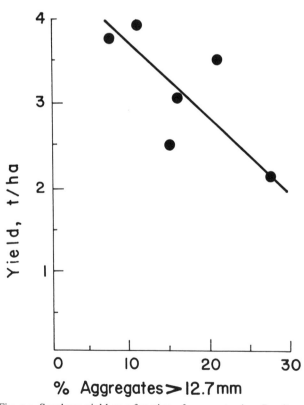

Fig. 14. Sorghum yield as a function of aggregate size. Rawitz et al., 1980.

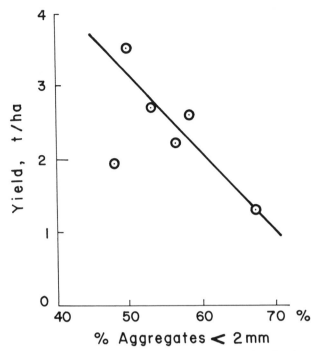

Fig. 15. Groundnut yield as a function of aggregate size. Rawitz et al., 1980.

wasting water and other resources, affecting plant growth and production, and then, to overcome the tough soil conditions, investing more tillage energy. This is done by using more powerful and heavier tractors and machinery systems, which increase soil compaction when wet. Done without caution, this process may be accelerated and could endanger food production.

New approaches to research, development, and application of practices and technologies have to be taken in order to improve soil structure, conserve resources, and optimize growth conditions. Quality soil tillage systems have to be introduced.

The development potential of temperate lands and the adaptation of such systems to these lands, based on the authors' research experience in semiarid conditions, is discussed in this section.

Taylor and Gill (1984) report on one system:

Controlled traffic research was begun three decades ago to increase crop yields by eliminating compaction from the cropping area. While yield increases have been obtained, reduced production costs may be of more benefit. Timeliness of operations, especially harvesting and spraying, made possible by firm, permanent traffic lanes has to be fully evaluated but appears very beneficial.

Wolf and Hadas (1983) define the goals of applying controlled traffic to semiarid soils:

• Restrict wheel traffic to pre-selected permanent minimum areas. Separate between the compacted surfaces and the plant growing zones.
• Soil strength of the growing zones will gradually decrease as

compaction will be kept away. The potential benefits are: lower bulk density, lower impedance, higher water intake and storage, better aeration and drainage, lower resistance to tillage, formation of smaller aggregates and a potential for reduced number of tillage operations. Better growing conditions and saving in tillage energy may be expected.

Gradually, following intensive research, controlled traffic systems based on the conventional tractor wheel tread came into use in Israeli agriculture, first in the cotton field, then in cotton-wheat double cropping, and finally in almost all irrigated field crops. All kinds of soils, with a common denominator of being in the semiarid areas, came under this controlled traffic systems approach.

Within five years of the introduction of this approach, about half of the country's major irrigated field crop areas had incorporated the concept. Growing techniques and machinery were modified to suit the permanent traffic lane spacing. The preferred fall primary tillage was done in single-pass operations, subsoiling-bedding first and then subsoiling-rotavating-bedding.

For treating the cotton residue a new technology was applied successfully. Following a few years of R&D by the Technion the uprooter-shredder-mulcher (USM) combine was introduced to farmers. Many of them are in use in Israel, and export to other semiarid lands in the world is increasing.

After picking the cotton, the USM uproots the stalks and chops them into small pieces. Then the farmer has these options of handling the chopped material:

a. Let it fall on the ground behind the combine, in a concentrated windrow.
b. Mount a powered centrifugal mechanism and spread the chopped matter evenly over the surface.
c. Mount a blower system and convey the material to a trailer pulled by the combine.
d. Let the material fall into a subsurface mulching system, attached to a subsoiler standard that is mounted on the combine's rear frame. Mulching depth can be adjusted between 0 and 0.5 m.

Options a and b require an inverting tillage operation for a reasonable incorporation unless a surface mulching is desired to fight soil erosion. Option c can be used if there is a need for the material somewhere else (for animal feed or burning for farm energy) and if continuous clearing of the organic material from the field can be justified, considering the soil requirements.

Subsurface mulching of the chopped material solves four major problems:

• It inverts the residue to control insects and answer the legal requirement.
• It returns the organic matter to improve soil condition.
• If placed in traffic lanes, the accumulated elastic material may reduce soil compaction.
• In soils where water infiltration is poor, especially in traffic lanes, this process may increase porosity, build up subsurface reservoirs, and decrease water runoff.

The USM may replace the primary tillage operations by adding sweeps to the mulching subsoiler and shattering

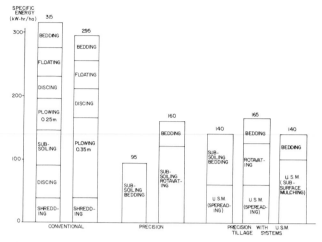

Fig. 16. Specific energy required for conventional and precision tillage systems. Wolf and Hadas, 1983.

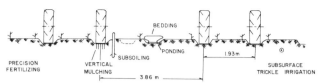

Fig. 17. Controlled traffic and precision tillage. Wolf and Hadas, 1983.

the whole bed. The result is a lower energy investment, a single fall run, and a combined residue treatment and tillage operation.

Energy savings by replacing conventional tillage systems with controlled traffic and precision tillage are presented in Figure 16.

To improve the controlled traffic and the precision tillage systems, research projects are being carried out in two more directions:

- *Subsurface trickle irrigation.* This serves to place water accurately where needed. It will save labor, cost, and water. Preliminary investigations show a high potential.
- *Precision fertilizing.* Unlike conventional systems, where fertilizers are spread and inverted, an accurate quantifying mixing and placing can be beneficial for the crop, prevent pollution, and save on costs.

The combined concept of controlled traffic, precision tillage, residue mulching, subsurface trickle irrigation, ponding, and precision fertilizing is presented in Fig. 17.

Recently developed technologies in the area of controlled traffic and energy conservation are under research now. They are the wide tractive frames and the lateral-travel nontractive frames.

The United States and Israel have a joint research project (BARD) on the feasibility of using the wide tractive frames. The wide tractors (6 and 10 m) were built on both sides of the ocean and are being used now in an intensive study with the goals of decreasing the noncompacted field area, developing tillage systems for improving the noncompacted soil condition for better production, and optimizing it with energy input. Taylor and Gill (1984) survey similar projects in the Netherlands and in the United Kingdom.

Another approach, with a similar objective, was investigated by Le Pori et al. (1983), who described the Alternative Machinery Propulsion System (AMPS), which is a modernized cable-towing system. Another joint BARD project is dedicated to investigating the feasibility of the system. Hood (1985) is developing and investigating the lateral-travel frames for fruit and vegetable production.

Crossley and Kilgour (1983) reported on a winch-based small tractor for developing countries. The power unit is cheap and its productivity and efficiency are high.

An intensive research effort is still required to prove the feasibility of these new approaches and to optimize them for wide-scale use. The potential is high and improving soil condition, especially in the semiarid lands, is a must. Such systems may increase yields, save resources, and improve the worsening soil condition.

REFERENCES

ASAE Data. 1983. Agricultural machinery management data. ASAE D.230.3. ASAE Yearbook 1983. St. Joseph, Mich.: American Society of Agricultural Engineers.

Chancellor, W. J. 1976. Compaction of the soil by agricultural equipment. Division of Agricultural Sciences, University of California, Davis. Bulletin no. 1881.

Crossley, C. P., and J. Kilgour. 1983. The development and testing of a winch based small tractor for developing countries. *Journal of Agricultural Engineering Research* 28:149–61.

Gupta, S. C., A. Hadas, W. B. Voorhees, D. Wolf, W. E. Larson, and E. C. Schneider. 1985. Development of guides for estimating the ease of compaction of world soils. BARD Research Project no. US-337-80. Final Report.

Hadas, A. 1975. Drying of layered soil columns under nonisothermal conditions. *Soil Science* 119.

Hadas, A., and D. Hillel. 1972. Isothermal drying of structurally layered soil columns. *Soil Science* 113:65–73.

Hadas, A., and D. Wolf. 1983. Energy efficiency in tilling dry clod-forming soils. *Soil and Tillage Research* 3:47–59.

Hadas, A., and D. Wolf. 1984. Soil aggregates and clod strength dependence on clod size, cultivation and stress load rates. *Soil Science Society of America Journal* 48:1157–64.

Hadas, A., D. Wolf, and I. Meirson. 1978. Tillage implements–soil structure relationships and their effect on crop stands. *Soil Science Society of America Journal* 42:632–37.

Hadas, A., D. Wolf, and E. Rawitz. 1983. Zoning soil compaction and cotton stand under controlled traffic operations. Paper no. 83-1042. ASAE meeting, June 26–29.

Hadas, A., D. Wolf, and E. Rawitz. 1985. Residual compaction effect on cotton stand and yields. *Transactions of the ASAE* (in press).

Hadas, A., D. Wolf, and A. Stibbe. 1980. Tillage practices and crop response analysis of agro ecosystems. *Agro Ecosystems* 6:235–48.

Hood, C. E. 1985. Personal communication. Department of Agricultural Engineering, Clemson University, Clemson, S.C.

LePori, W. A., A. Mizrach, C. R. Harrison, M. D. Evans, and D. B. Carney. 1983. Functional evaluation of field machinery operation using a cable towing system. ASAE Paper no. 83-1545. St. Joseph, Mich.: American Society of Agricultural Engineers.

Rawitz, E., W. B. Hoogmoed, and J. Monin. 1980. Development

of criteria and methods for improving the efficiency of soil management and tillage operations with special reference to arid and semi-arid regions. Report no. 2. Faculty of Agriculture, Rehovot, Israel.

Slipher, J. A. 1932. The mechanical manipulation of the soil as it affects structure. *Agricultural Engineering* 13:7–10.

Taylor, J. H., and W. R. Gill. 1984. Soil compaction: State-of-the-art report. *Journal of Terramechanics* 21 (2):195–213.

Trouse, A. C. 1971. Soil conditions as they affect plant establishment, root development and yield. Pp. 225–91, 306–13. *In* K. K. Barnes et al. (ed.) Compaction of agricultural soils. St. Joseph, Mich.: American Society of Agricultural Engineers.

Unger, P. W., and B. A. Stewart. 1983. Soil management for efficient water use, an overview. Pp. 419–60. *In* H. M. Taylor et al. (ed.) Limitations to efficient water use in crop production. Madison, Wis.: American Society of Agronomy.

Voorhees, W. B. 1983. Relative effectiveness of tillage and natural forces in alleviating wheel induced soil compaction. *Soil Science Society of America Journal* 47:129–33.

Wolf, D. 1970. Effect of moldboard plow characteristics on energy consumption-soil reaction interaction in the plowing of clod-forming soils. Unpublished D.Sc. dissertation (Hebrew).

Wolf, D., and A. Hadas. 1983. Conventional vs. controlled traffic and precision tillage systems for cotton. ASAE Paper no. 83-1040. St. Joseph, Mich.: American Society of Agricultural Engineers.

Wolf, D., and A. Hadas. 1984. Soil compaction effects on cotton emergence. *Transactions of the ASAE* 27(3):655–59.

Wolf, D., A. Hadas, and I. Meirson. 1977. Tillage systems for cotton under semi-arid conditions. ASAE Paper no. 77-1018. St. Joseph, Mich.: American Society of Agricultural Engineers.

Wolf, D., A. Hadas, and A. Newman. 1984. Analysis of mechanized cotton cultivation practices under dryland and irrigated conditions. *Soil and Tillage Research* 4:55–66.

Wolf, D., and H. T. Luth. 1979. Tillage equipment for clod-farming soils. *Transactions of the ASAE* 22(5):1029–1032.

52. WATER ON THE THIRD PLANET*

J. R. Philip, Commonwealth Scientific and Industrial Research Organization, Division of Environmental Mechanics, Canberra, Australia

ABSTRACT

The unique physicochemical properties of water and our unique planetary environment make possible the Earth's great diversity of phenomena involving water. This chapter looks at the history of the growth of man's understanding of the behavior of water on the Earth; the broad characteristics of the distribution and turnover of the Earth's water; and the global and the local, smaller-scale physical processes of the hydrologic cycle.

INTRODUCTION

I feel that the best contribution I can make to this conference is to offer a perspective on the Earth's water from the viewpoint of natural science; and I am grateful that the organizers agree. I expect that many of you decision makers may feel a little impatient at being called on to listen to a scientific talk rather than to hear news of some grand scheme or model or new technological fix. I respectfully suggest, however, that the more you understand the context in which you make your decisions, the wiser those decisions are likely to be. The special role of water on this special planet, and our understanding of where the water is and how it behaves, are important elements in the background to your decisions.

Let's imagine a traveler from outer space who encounters the solar system and inspects our own star, the Sun, and the nine planets that orbit it. Long before he discovers the most special thing about the third planet, Earth, namely that it supports life, he will realize, just from what he can detect from space, that Earth is unique among the planets of the solar system.

Seen from space, Earth looks like a white, blue, green, and brown swirling paisley pattern. The colors and the pattern are a vivid expression of the existence of water on Earth. As the planetary sciences have developed, it has become more and more clear that Earth is unique with respect to water—that Earth is the water planet of the Solar System. Among the nine planets it is only on Earth that liquid water exists, and here it is plentiful indeed. H_2O is by far the most abundant liquid molecule on Earth.

Not only is the Earth unique in relation to water, but water, in its turn, is quite unique in its physicochemical properties. It is this conjunction of two brands of uniqueness

*This contribution has drawn on material first presented in my chapter, "Water on the Earth," in *Water, Planets, Plants and People*, ed. A. K. McIntyre (Australian Academy of Science, 1977). I am grateful to the Australian Academy of Science for granting me permission to use Figures 3–7 and Tables 1–6 of that work.

that leads to the beautiful diversity of terrestrial processes involving water and to the subtlety and the complexity of the interactions between them.

I shall begin by considering briefly the history of the growth of man's awareness and understanding of the behavior of water on the Earth, and I'll go on to look at the geography of water. Then I'll say a word about the large-scale physical processes undergone by the Earth's water and, finally, a little about the smaller-scale physical processes of the hydrologic cycle.

HISTORICAL BACKGROUND

Early Hydraulic Civilizations

The early historical record is fragmentary indeed. Many early societies depended on the management of water for their survival, but there seems to be no evidence of curiosity about whence the water came or whither it went. By the third millennium B.C. the Sumerians had an elaborate code of irrigation practice, but the water supply was safeguarded by propitiation of the water god, Enki, not through the pursuit of hydrology.

Other hydraulic, but incurious, civilizations go back as far as Sumer—those of the Nile and of the Indus valley. That of China was similar, but came rather later: the earliest record dates from about 2300 B.C. The hydraulic dynasties of Egypt had gone on for nearly three millennia before Greeks such as Herodotus started to ask questions about the Nile.

Hydrology in Classical Greece

Like so many elements in our intellectual life, hydrology had its beginnings in classical Greece. The conscious search for rational descriptions and explanations of the behavior of the water on Earth began about 600 B.C. Judged by its outcome, the hydrologic thinking of the Greeks was not especially successful. One or two of them came close to a correct qualitative account of the hydrologic cycle, notably Anaxagoras (500–428 B.C.) and Theophrastus (371–288 B.C.). The influential pronouncements, however, were those of Plato (428–348 B.C.), who was hopelessly wrong, and of Aristotle (384–322 B.C.), who was mostly, but not wholly, wrong. Plato asserted that all springs, rivers, and seas were connected by underground channels to Tartarus, a vast, bottomless pit of water, and that some kind of hydraulic perpetual motion circulated water from Tartarus into the rivers and back again via the underground channels. Aristotle, on the other hand, declared that the water in rivers originated in the main through the subterranean condensation of air into water, but also partly from rainfall and percolation.

Leonardo da Vinci

There was little progress until the Renaissance and Leonardo da Vinci (1452–1519). Leonardo needs no introduction, but it may not be known to all that, of the 7,000 sheets of notes and sketches that Leonardo left, more are devoted to hydrology and hydraulics than to any other single topic. Leonardo was fascinated by the movement of water. His sketches are beautiful evidence of the loving care with which he observed water in motion. It is doubtful if Leonardo's interest in hydrology led him to a correct understanding of the hydrologic cycle. Leonardo's unequivocally important contribution was not to hydrology but to hydraulics. It was through his hydraulics that Leonardo provided an impetus to quantitative hydrology.

Leonardo was the first to understand the principle of continuity that, in a channel carrying a constant discharge, the mean flow velocity varies inversely with the flow cross section. Before Leonardo it was thought that the flow in a channel or pipe was simply proportional to the flow cross section (that is, the mean flow velocity was assumed to be a universal constant), with disastrous consequences for any quantitative effort to study water flows and water balances.

The Beginnings of Scientific Hydrology

Leonardo had been innocent of Latin and of the conventional learning of his day. We pass on now to another outsider, Bernard Palissy (1510–1589), who began life as a poor apprentice in the Dordogne. Palissy put forward an accurate description and explanation of the hydrologic cycle. He was a keen and precise observer of nature, and he convincingly demolished the prevalent notions ascribed to Plato and Aristotle.

If qualitative scientific hydrology began with Palissy, quantitative scientific hydrology began with another Frenchman, Pierre Perrault (1608–1680). Perrault's great achievement was to make some actual measurements and do some sums. The last-ditch stand of the Plato-Aristotle school rested mainly on the assertion that the quantities of rain and snow that fell were far too small to maintain the flow of rivers. Perrault disposed of that argument. He measured precipitation over three years and estimated both the river flow at a point on the Seine and the catchment area above it. He thus computed that the precipitation on the catchment amounted to six times the river discharge. A third Frenchman, Edmé Mariotte (1620–1684), working on two catchments and making more careful measurements, repeated and fully confirmed Perrault's work.

Perrault and Mariotte thus pioneered quantitative treatment of the rainfall-runoff sector of the hydrologic cycle. It was left to Edmund Halley (1656–1742) to close the atmosphere-ocean arc of the cycle. Edmund Halley, F.R.S., was the discoverer of the comet and the man who encouraged Newton to write down and publish the *Principia*. In 1687, a year after Mariotte's work was published, the first of Halley's papers on evaporation appeared.

By then, the one surviving argument for Plato's Tartarus was the age-old observation that, as the author of Ecclesiastes put it 3,000 years ago, "All the rivers run into the sea; yet the sea is not full." Surely, the argument went, evaporation from the sea is not enough to balance the river flows: subterranean channels must pipe the excess to Tartarus and thence back to the rivers. Halley put this to the test by measuring the evaporation rate under conditions he judged appropriate to the Mediterranean; he then compared the evaporation with his estimate of the total river discharge into the Mediterranean. He concluded that the inflow from the rivers amounted to only about one-third of the evaporation loss.

I must abandon the narrative at this point, the very beginnings of quantitative scientific hydrology. The related fields of meterology and oceanography follow similar evolutionary patterns, but we cannot pursue them here.

Table 1. Distribution of land and ocean.

	Area (10^6 km^2)		Percentage	
	Ocean	Land	Ocean	Land
Northern Hemisphere	154.8	100.3	60.7	39.3
Southern Hemisphere	206.5	48.7	80.9	19.1
Total	361.3	149.0	70.8	29.2
Planet	510.3		100.0	

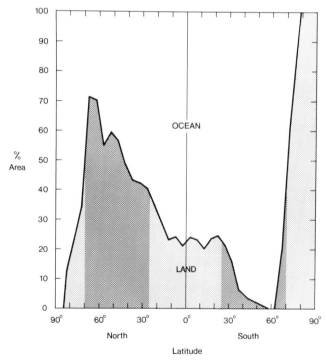

Fig. 1. Variation with the Earth's latitude of the percentage distribution of land and ocean. The heavily shaded areas signify land in the latitudinal zones from 25° to 70°. Note the great contrast between the hemispheres.

Table 2. Distribution of water on the earth.

	Volume as Liquid Water (10^6 km^3)	Percentage of Total Water	Average Depth (m)	Based on Area of
Ocean	1338	97.3	3700	Ocean
Ice caps and glaciers	29	2.1	80	Ocean
Groundwater	8.4	0.61	56	Land
Lakes and rivers	0.23	0.17		
Atmosphere	0.013	0.00094	0.025	Planet
Biological water	0.0006	0.000005	0.004	Land
Total	1376	100	2700	Planet

Table 3. Distribution of groundwater.

	Volume 10^6 km^3	Percentage of Total Water on the Earth	Average Depth Based on Land Area (m)
Unsaturated zone	0.15	0.011	1
Groundwater above 1 km	4.20	0.305	28
Groundwater below 1 km	4.05	0.294	27
Total	8.40	0.610	27

THE GEOGRAPHY OF WATER

Distribution of Ocean and Land

You will see from Table 1 that the oceans occupy 70.8 percent of the Earth's surface and that only 29.2 percent is land. Note especially that the distribution is far from even; there is more than twice as much land in the Northern Hemisphere as in the Southern. Fig. 1 shows the latitudinal distribution of land in more detail. Note, in particular, the 45° broad zones from 25° latitude to 70° latitude—that is, roughly the temperate zones. In the Northern Hemisphere there is actually more land than water in this zone, with 51.5 percent of the surface being land and only 48.5 percent ocean. In the Southern Hemisphere the ratio is only 8.6 percent to 91.4 percent. The relative abundance of land is 11.3 times greater in the northern zone than in the southern. This very strong asymmetry has significant effects on the global circulations of the atmosphere and of the oceans. Note, in particular, that the paucity of land between 35°S and 65°S makes for the uninterrupted west wind drift, which has no analogue in the northern oceans.

Inventory of Water on the Earth

Table 2 is an inventory of the Earth's water. Of all the water on Earth, 97.3 percent is in the oceans and is, of course, saline. The mean ocean depth is 3.7 km. Most of the rest is frozen and in the ice caps and glaciers. If the ice were to melt, the oceans would rise almost 80 m. We shall break down the categories "groundwater" and "lakes and rivers" a little later. Note the infinitesimal fractions of the total

water in the all-important categories of "atmosphere" and "biological water." The latter represents the water in all plants and animals. Tables 3 and 4 give more details of the distribution of the Earth's water.

The Global Water Balance

Table 5 gives the components of the mean annual global water balance. The runoff from the land to the ocean (315 mm) is the excess of the precipitation on the land (800 mm) over the evaporation from it (485 mm). This is balanced by the excess of evaporation from the ocean (1400 mm) over the precipitation on it (1270 mm).

Air moving over the ocean picks up 46.9×10^3 km^3 of water per annum and air moving over the land loses the same quantity. The net effect is that the horizontal advection of water vapor from ocean to land just balances the runoff from land to ocean. Fig. 2 illustrates these processes. Note that 315 mm runoff from the land exactly balances 130 mm advection of vapor from the ocean. The figures are different

Table 4. Distribution of surface water on land.

	Volume (10^6 km^3)	Percentage of Total Water on the Earth
Rivers	0.0017	0.00012
Freshwater lakes	0.125	0.0091
Saline lakes	0.105	0.0076
Total	0.23	0.017

Table 5. Annual global water balance.

	Precipitation		Evaporation		Runoff	
	10^3 km^3	mm	10^3 km^3	mm	10^3 km^3	mm
Ocean	458.9	1270	505.8	1400	−46.9	−130
Land	119.2	800	72.3	485	46.9	315
Planet	578.1	1133	578.1	1133	0	0

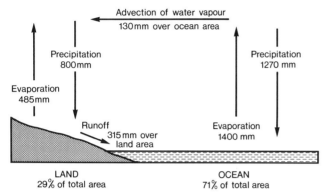

Fig. 2. Global water balance. Note that 315 mm over the land area is equal in volume to 130 mm over the ocean area. (i.e., runoff = advection of water vapor from ocean to land).

because the areas are different. It will be seen that, overall, the ratio of runoff to precipitation comes out at about 0.39.

Turnover Rates

It is useful to fill out our picture of the hydrologic cycle on the Earth by looking at the turnover rate of water involved in its various parts. A naive way of doing this is to evaluate the mean residence time of the various categories of water. We calculate the mean residence time simply by dividing the volume of water involved by the rate of turnover. Table 6 shows the result. The entries are based on the data of the previous tables or are consistent with those data. Note the very great spread of residence times—from 2,600 years for the ocean and 1,100 years for the ice caps and glaciers to 8.2 days for the atmosphere and 3.4 days for biological water. At any one time there is only enough water in the atmosphere to supply 8.2 days' worth of the world's rain. The world's organisms would be desiccated in 3.4 days if they continued to lose water at their average rate and couldn't take up any more. It is these very rapid turnovers that tend to concern us most directly. The slow turnover water is mostly saline, most of what isn't is frozen, and the remainder tends to be inaccessible.

Although these mean residence times are useful in giving us a more immediate feeling for the character of the various parts of the hydrologic cycle and for how they interact, I must reiterate that mean residence times represent only a first naive single-number index of what goes on. The distribution of residence times is what we really require. Take the figure of 2,600 years for the ocean, for example. It is the molecules that have just arrived in the ocean by rainfall or

runoff that are most likely to be at the surface and to be candidates for evaporation, and there is a strong tendency for new arrivals to be the first departures. Equally, the chance that molecules of the deep ocean—below 3 km—will surface must be very small indeed.

Continental Water Balances

Fig. 3 compares the water balances of the continents. The vertical scale is in mm of water per annum and the horizontal one is surface area in 10^6 km^2. The vertical ordinate thus expresses precipitation, evaporation, and runoff as annual water depths, but the rectangular areas for each continent represent these quantities as annual volumes. The most obvious point of the comparison, other than the miserable plight of Australia, is that South America is so much wetter than anywhere else. The Amazon is way out on its own as a very big river. Its discharge is 11 times that of the second river, the Mississippi, and more than 18 times the total discharge of *all* Australian rivers.

THE GLOBAL CIRCULATIONS

So much for the geography of water, for the straightforward questions of bookkeeping. We turn now to the physical processes that lie behind the bookkeeping.

We have seen that the global hydrologic cycle is a gigantic distillation scheme. The whole Earth forms a vast heat engine and the distillation process is simply one element of this engine. In essence, the total engine converts solar energy into the fluid motions of the atmosphere, the ocean, and the rivers and lakes. It is water, of course, that is the working fluid, the fluid whose motions and phase changes bring about the energy transformations. As Leonardo da Vinci expressed it, "Water is the driving force of all nature."

The effectiveness of this engine depends on the tightness

Table 6. Mean residence time of the Earth's waters.

	Volume (10^6 km^3)	Rate of Turnover (10^6 km^3 · year^{-1})	Mean Residence Time	
Ocean	1338	0.5058	2,600	years
Ice caps and glaciers	29	0.00255	1,100	years
Groundwater	8.25	0.0119	700	years
Lakes	0.23	0.00173	13	years
Soil water	0.03	0.0706	155	days
Rivers	0.0017	0.0469	13	days
Atmosphere	0.013	0.5781	8.2	days
Biological water	0.0006	0.0651	3.4	days

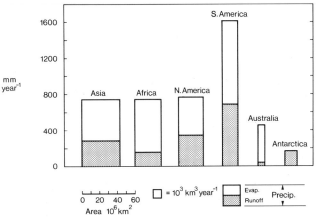

Fig. 3. Water balance of the six continents. The total rectangles represent precipitation, the unshaded rectangles evaporation, the shaded rectangles, runoff. The vertical scale represents annual water depth and the horizontal scale represents area, so that annual volumes are proportional to the area of the relevant rectangle.

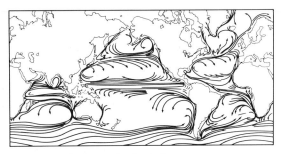

Fig. 4. Mean surface oceanic circulation.

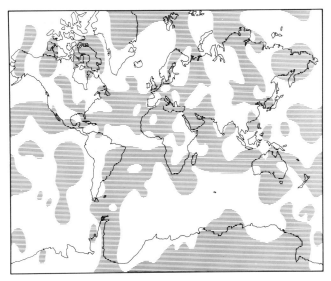

Fig. 5. Global distribution of the annual net pickup and net deposition of water by the atmosphere. Shaded areas: regions of net pickup. Unshaded areas: regions of net deposition. Note that annual net pickup and deposition are both typically about 200 mm.

of the linkage between the energy cycle and the cycle of the working fluid, water. This depends primarily on the unique properties of water, which I stressed at the beginning of this chapter. In some degree, it depends also on the uniqueness of the Earth, which I also emphasized. As you know, the latent heat of evaporation of water is greater than that of any other substance. This, and, to a lesser extent, the fact that the heat capacity of water is so great (greater, in fact, than that of any solid or liquid other than liquid ammonia), ensures the highest possible correlation between water transport and energy transport. The tight linkage between water and energy also depends on the fact that the temperatures on Earth are such that H_2O is always present in at least one phase besides vapor, and that the saturated vapor density is great enough to ensure rates of evaporation and condensation, and of advection of vapor in the atmosphere, that involve fluxes of latent heat of a magnitude comparable to that of the fluxes of total energy. (On Mars, on the other hand, surface temperatures are about 90°K less than on Earth, and saturated vapor densities are only about 1/6,000th those on Earth. In consequence, even if water were abundant, latent heat fluxes would be a trivial fraction of total energy fluxes on Mars, and, as a result, the linkage between the energy balance and the water balance would be, at best, extremely weak.)

The great ocean circulations are profoundly influenced by the atmosphere; and yet, to a large extent, the atmosphere in turn owes its nature to, and derives its energy from, the ocean. Everything depends on everything else, and a simple acount seems almost impossible. Fig. 4 shows a map of the mean surface oceanic circulation. This is a deceptively simple representation of the global pattern of oceanic movements. But we must leave it at that.

The story for the atmosphere is almost as frighteningly complicated as that for the ocean. The global circulation of the atmosphere is governed by the Coriolis force, by friction, by the irregularities of input of energy at the bottom of

the atmosphere, and by other processes that we shall not discuss here.

For our immediate purpose, it suffices to examine the hydrologic end product of the global circulation. Fig. 5 presents a first estimate of the global distribution of the annual net pickup and net deposition of water by the atmosphere. This map is derived from calculations of the global transport of water vapor by the atmospheric circulation. The shaded areas are regions of net pickup, where the atmosphere gains water; the white areas are regions of net deposition, where the atmosphere loses water.

SMALLER-SCALE PROCESSES

Finally, a very brief word on some of the smaller-scale processes of the hydrologic cycle.

Most of the water involved in the land phase of the hydrologic cycle is located in unsaturated soil between the time of its arrival as rain at the soil surface and that of its return to the atmosphere. A small fraction of precipitation does not enter the soil, but moves overland directly into streams or lakes; a second small fraction percolates downward through the unsaturated zone and joins the groundwater. In dry lands such as Australia, about 93 percent of the precipitation enters the soil; of this, 92 percent returns directly to the atmosphere, only about 1 percent reaching the groundwater.

The processes of water movement in unsaturated soil thus play a central part in the scientific study of the land sector of the hydrologic cycle and in the related problems of irrigated and dryland agriculture, of plant ecology, and of the biology of soil flora and fauna. They are, in addition, of great significance in connection with the transport through the soil of materials in solution, such as natural salts, fertilizers, and urban and industrial wastes and pollutants. Phenomena of great interest and importance include infiltration, drainage and retention of water in the soil strata, extraction of soil water by plant roots and its subsequent transpiration, and evaporation of water from the soil.

The character of these everyday, but all-important, processes depends on yet another aspect of the physical uniqueness of water, namely the fact that its surface tension is so great. This means that the soil can hold appreciable quantities of water against gravity. This is a great advantage to plant life and, moreover, makes possible the whole range of moisture conditions at the surface. In the absence of the surface tension of water, the land surface would be either desert or swamp.

Some of these hydrologic processes, of course, do not involve the soil alone. It will be noted, for example, that the soil, the plant, and the atmosphere form a thermodynamic continuum for water transport, so that the proper study of natural evaporation from the Earth's surface involves not only soil physics, but also micrometeorology and, in the case of vegetated surfaces, plant physiology.

Two or three decades ago the level of understanding of many of these processes was at little better than the folklore level. Today folklore has been supplanted by a coherent body of quantitative science, which we might call microhydrology.

I conclude by urging both decision makers and scientists to ensure that we make maximum use of what we know about water in our world. Planners, systems analysts, and the like sometimes mistake their beautiful models for reality; and it is all to easy for decision makers to accept their seemingly rational models gratefully as surrogates for the perplexing, intractable, real-world situation. But neither scientist nor decision maker can ignore what really happens, and we both must insist that our models be to the full what we know about the real processes of the real world.

53. WATER CONSERVATION TECHNOLOGY IN RAINFED AND DRYLAND AGRICULTURE*

B. A. Stewart, U.S. Department of Agriculture, Agricultural Research Service, Conservation and Production Research Laboratory, Bushland, Texas, and Earl Burnett, U.S. Department of Agriculture, Agricultural Research Service, Grassland, Soil and Water Research Laboratory, Temple, Texas

SUMMARY

Interest in dryland and rainfed farming systems has increased in recent years because of escalating costs of developing new irrigation projects and the high costs associated with irrigated agriculture in general. Rainfed and dryland are often used synonymously, but they are considered vastly different by many workers. They both exclude irrigation, but beyond that, they can differ significantly. Dryland agricultural systems emphasize water conservation, sustainable crop yields, limited inputs for soil fertility, and wind and water erosion constraints. Rainfed systems, although they include dryland systems, can also include systems which emphasize disposal of excess water, maximum crop yields, and high inputs of fertilizer. This chapter deals primarily with dryland agriculture. There are three components of a successful dryland management system: (1) retaining the precipitation on the land, (2) reducing evaporation, and (3) utilizing crops that have drought tolerance and that fit the rainfall patterns. Although these components have been known for centuries, new technologies are developing that increase crop production in water-short areas. Some of these technologies are presented and the principles on which they are based are discussed.

INTRODUCTION

In recent years, there has been a growing awareness of the importance of rainfed and dryland agriculture. This growing awareness has resulted largely from the rapidly increasing costs for developing new irrigation projects as well as the high costs associated with irrigated agriculture in general. There is no area that has been more affected than the Southern High Plains of the United States, where increasing energy costs and low commodity prices have resulted in some irrigated lands being returned to nonirrigated conditions. Nonirrigated agriculture is also being emphasized more in the developing nations because nonirrigated areas must product the vast majority of food grains upon which an expanding population is dependent for subsistence.

At the outset, it is important that we understand what is meant by rainfed and dryland agriculture. Clearly, they both exclude irrigation. Beyond that, the definitions become less evident because the terms rainfed agriculture and dryland agriculture are often used synonymously, but they are considered vastly different by many workers. We view them as different and offer the following definitions for farming areas in the United States.

*Contribution from USDA, Agricultural Research Service, Bushland, Texas.

- *Dryland Agriculture*—where dry farming is practiced, including farming systems without irrigation, in regions of limited rainfall, usually < 750 mm per year.
- *Rainfed Agriculture*—where crops are produced without irrigation in subhumid and humid regions, usually > 750 mm per year.

The annual rainfall values are not absolute because seasonal rainfall distribution and temperature affect crop water requirements and thus the kinds of soil and water management practices. A region with annual rainfall of 700 mm with good monthly distribution is a cool climate might utilize rainfed agriculture–type management systems, whereas in a hot climate a region with poorly distributed rainfall of 1,000 mm per year might appropriately require dry farming techniques.

Table 1 highlights the important differences between dryland and rainfed agriculture. This paper deals primarily with dryland agriculture in the Southern Great Plains of the United States, but some of the principles and practices discussed also apply to other areas and to rainfed agriculture.

DRYLAND AGRICULTURE SYSTEMS

The key to successful dryland farming in semiarid regions is using systems and practices that can take advantage of the favorable years. Dryland farming has been and will continue to be a high-risk undertaking. There is clearly a need to become more aware of the historical weather data and to begin thinking in terms of probabilities as an alternative to averages. An understanding of the probabilities will provide a foundation for making management decisions.

There are three components of a successful dryland management system in a semiarid region. These are (1) retaining the precipitation on the land, (2) reducing evaporation, and (3) utilizing crops that have drought tolerance and that fit best with the rainfall patterns. Although we have known these components for centuries, progress in adapting them to specific areas and situations has been slow. However, there are technologies emerging that show real promise, and these technologies, or the principles on which they are based, can be applied to other regions and countries.

Retaining Precipitation on Land

The most important component for dryland farming is conservation of rainfall, which must start by preventing runoff. Conservation of rainfall is very important in the Southern High Plains because water is both the beginning and the end

Table 1. Major differences between dryland agriculture and rainfed agriculture.

Dryland	Rainfed
Emphasis on:	Emphasis on:
Water conservation	Disposal of excess water during certain periods
Sustainable crop yields	Maximum crop yields
Limited inputs for soil fertility	High levels of fertilizer inputs
Wind and water erosion constraints	Water erosion constraints

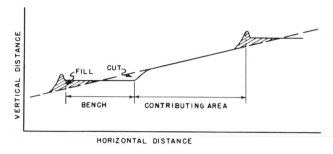

CONSERVATION BENCHING

Fig. 1. Schematic drawing of a conservation bench terrace at Bushland, Texas.

Fig. 2. A field at Bushland, Texas, immediately following a major rainfall event. Part of the field had furrow dams installed to prevent runoff.

of agriculture. Plants cannot grow without it, of course, and soil erosion, particularly by wind, cannot be controlled successfully without vegetation.

Runoff from cropland in the Southern High Plains is highly variable because of varying amounts of average rainfall, specific rainfall events for a given year, topography, soil type, and soil surface conditions. Runoff from cropland on Pullman clay loam (a fine, mixed, thermic, Torrertic Paleustoll) at Bushland, Texas, where the average rainfall is 460 mm, has averaged about 40 mm annually (Jones et al., 1985). However, runoff occurred in only about one-half of the twenty-six years studied, so the amount was very significant in some years. Long-term studies at Riesel, Texas, in a subhumid area on Houston Black clay (a fine, montmorillonitic, thermic, Udic Pellustert), show that about 125 mm of runoff occurs annually. The average annual rainfall at Riesel is 800 mm. In subhumid regions, such as at Riesel, practices to allow runoff without excessive soil erosion are required because rainfall rate frequently exceeds soil infiltration capacity. However, in the lower-rainfall areas typified by the data from Bushland, it would be desirable to entirely eliminate runoff from cropland. Furrow diking, conservation bench terraces, and land leveling have proven very effective. These practices not only result in additional water for crop production but provide an effective means for controlling water erosion. Fig. 1 shows a schematic drawing of a conservation bench terrace and Figure 2 shows a field with furrow dams immediately following a major rainfall event. Jones et al. (1985) describe these systems in more detail and summarize the results. Richardson (1973) compared storm runoff from watersheds with a graded-furrow system, designed to convey all runoff originating in the furrow to a waterway, to that from watersheds with a conventional terrace system. Runoff was significantly lower from the graded-furrow watersheds, and soil erosion was within acceptable limits. The reduced runoff was probably due to more uniform distribution of excess water by the graded furrows. On the terraced watershed, excess water accumulated in the terrace channels. As stated previously, it is not possible to eliminate runoff in such regions because of the excess rainfall at certain times. Water for crop growth does become limiting in most years, and runoff should be minimized when possible. Recent evaluation of hydrologic data suggests that furrow dams might be feasible on long, uniform slopes in this subhumid region (Krishna and Arkin, 1985).

Reducing Evaporation

Evaporation from the soil surface during periods when a crop is not growing results in a major loss of water in water-deficient areas. This is illustrated in Table 2, which summarizes long-term data at Bushland, Texas. The amount of precipitation during the rotation lost as evaporation during the nongrowing season ranges from 36 percent for the continuous wheat (*Triticum aestivum*) system to 61 percent for the wheat-fallow system. In the wheat-fallow system, where the fallow period is 15 to 16 months, only about 15 percent of the precipitation that occurs during the fallow period is stored in the soil for use later by the growing crop. Even under the continuous wheat system, where the fallow period is only three to four months, the fallow efficiency is less than 20 percent. However, in spite of the very low efficiency of water storage during fallow periods, fallow is practiced widely because of the importance of sustaining crop yields under dry farming conditions. Again, referring to the data in Table 2, soil water storage during a four-month fallow is only 37 mm, compared with about 80 mm for an eleven-month fallow and almost 100 mm for a fifteen-month fallow. This additional stored water is highly important in reducing the risk of a crop failure.

Much more efficient use of the limited water resources

Table 2. Water balance for various cropping systems at Bushland, Texas.

CONTINUOUS WHEAT (ONE CROP ANNUALLY)[a]			
	Wheat	Fallow	Total
	mm		
Precipitation	256	202	458
Evapotranspiration	293		293
Soil water change	−37	37	
Evaporation (and runoff)		165	165

TWO CROPS IN THREE YEARS[b]					
	Wheat	Fallow	Sorghum	Fallow	Total
	mm				
Precipitation	256	462	241	416	1375
Evapotranspiration	329		286		615
Runoff	13	25	27	43	108
Soil water change	−86	86	−72	72	
Evaporation		351		301	652

ONE CROP IN TWO YEARS[c]			
	Wheat	Fallow	Total
	mm		
Precipitation	256	660	916
Evapotranspiration	354		354
Soil water change	−98	98	
Evaporation (and runoff)		562	562

SOURCE: O. R. Jones, personal communication; Johnson and Davis, 1972.
[a] Fallow period between crops is three to four months. Runoff was not measured but would be minimal under annual cropping.
[b] Fallow periods between crops are about eleven months.
[c] Fallow period between crops is fifteen to sixteen months. Runoff was not measured but was a minor portion of the total.

could be achieved if the high evaporation losses discussed above could be reduced. The most effective practice for reducing evaporation is a mulch. The use of mulches to conserve water and to reduce soil erosion is an age-old practice. Many materials, such as stones, gravel, plastic, film, asphalt emulsions, paper, and plant residues, have been used as mulches. Porous mulches may reduce raindrop impact, thereby increasing water infiltration. They may also reduce soil water evaporation by cooling the soil by insulating it, reflecting solar energy, and decreasing wind speed near the soil surface (Willis, 1982). Artificial mulches are seldom used in the United States because application is so labor-intensive. There is some use of plastic mulches for high-value crops where application can be automated. However, crop residues are the only practical source of mulching material for most situations in the United States, and this is particularly true for the dryland areas of the Southern High Plains.

In the semiarid Great Plains, water storage efficiency has been low even with mulch because of the limited amounts of residue produced under dryland farming (Unger, 1983; Wiese et al., 1967). Unger (1978) studied the effect of increasing rates of wheat straw mulch on water storage efficiency during an eleven-month fallow period and subsequent grain sorghum (*Sorghum bicolor* [L.] Moench) yields

Table 3. Straw mulch effects on water storage efficiency and grain sorghum yield.

Mulch Rate (t/ha)	Water Storage Efficiency[a] (%)	Grain Yield (kg/ha)
0	22.6 c[b]	1780 c[b]
1	31.1 b	2410 b
2	31.4 b	2600 b
4	36.5 b	2980 b
8	43.7 a	3680 a
12	46.2 a	3990 a

SOURCE: Unger, 1978.
[a] Water storage determined to a 1.8-m depth. Precipitation averaged 318 mm.
[b] Column values followed by the same letter are not significantly different at the 5% level (Duncan multiple range test).

on Pullman clay loam in the Southern High Plains (Table 3). Water storage efficiency values increased sharply with increasing mulch levels, which shows the high potential for increasing soil water storage when sufficient amounts of residue are available. Greb (1983) also reported very significant soil water gains at four Great Plains locations at the end of the fallow period with increasing rates of straw mulch (Table 4). Storage efficiency is usually lower in the

Table 4. Net soil water gain at the end of fallow as influenced by straw mulch rates at four Great Plains locations.

Location	Number of Years Reported	Mulch Rate (t/ha)			
		0	2.2	4.4	6.6
		Soil Water Gain (cm)			
Bushland, Tex.	3	7.1	9.9	9.9	10.7
Akron, Colo.	6	13.4	15.0	16.5	18.5
North Platte, Neb.	7	16.5	19.3	21.6	23.4
Sidney, Mont.	4	5.3	6.9	9.4	10.2
Average		10.7	12.7	14.5	15.7
Gain by mulching			2.0	3.8	5.0

SOURCE: Greb, 1983.

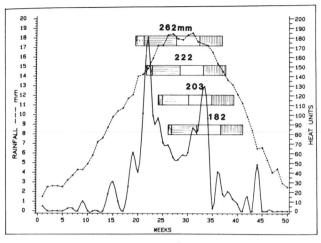

Fig. 3. Weekly precipitation and heat unit (zero C base) values for Bushland, Texas, that are exceeded in 50 percent of the years (0 weeks begin on January 1). The four boxes represent grain sorghum seeded at four different times, and the values above the boxes are the amounts of rainfall exceeded in 50 percent of the years during the cropping season.

southern part of the region because of the higher evaporative demand. Adams (1966) showed that straw mulches decreased soil water evaporation, storm runoff, and erosion and increased crop yield on Houston Black clay in the subhumid part of the Great Plains. Similar results have been reported under humid conditions in many parts of the world (Jacks et al., 1955).

Matching Cropping Systems with Rainfall Patterns

In the final analysis, dryland cropping depends on matching a cropping system with the climate so that there is a good probability of producing a harvestable crop. Increased emphasis is being placed on probability levels as compared with average values of rainfall data. Average values, particularly in low-rainfall regions, can be very misleading because a few very high, but rare, rainfall events can raise the average substantially. Probability levels can be set at any desired level and are a good way of assessing risks. Dancette and Hall (1979) have developed methods for improving management of water resources, using principles for soil and plant sciences. They have prepared maps for the Sudanian and Sahelian zones of Africa showing maximum cycle lengths for millet that will result in crop water needs being satisfied to at least the 80 percent level, and for eighty years out of a hundred. The information needed for such estimates is rainfall, evaporative demands, crop coefficients of water use, rooting depths, water retention characteristics of the soil, and availability of water in the soil.

A rather simple approach to matching a cropping pattern with the climate is shown for grain sorghum at Bushland, Texas, in Fig. 3. The solid line represents the weekly rainfall amounts that are exceeded in 50 percent of the years, and the dashed line represents the number of weekly heat units (degrees C above 0) exceeded in 50 percent of the years. The rectangular boxes represent a crop of grain sorghum planted at four different times, and the numbers above the boxes are the 50 percent probability amounts of rainfall that occur during the periods. The four divisions within each period represent the emergence, vegetation, reproduction, and grain-filling stages of crop production. Although the same cultivar is pictured for each of the planting dates, the length of growing season decreases from 121 days

for the earliest planting to 104 days for the latest because of higher temperatures at the later planting dates.

Grain sorghum is traditionally seeded in the area on about June 15 (represented by the third box from the top of Figure 3). The rainfall pattern readily shows the advantage of this seeding date because the rainfall preceding this time results in good soil water conditions for seeding. Also, the crop has a relatively short vegetative growth period, there is a high probability of rainfall's occurring during the reproduction growth period, and temperatures decrease during the grain-filling period. The disadvantage of this time of planting, however, is that there is substantially less precipitation during the growing season than for an earlier seeding date. For example, seeding on May 10 (top box in Fig. 3) results in a growing season with substantially more rainfall. However, the vegetative growth period is lengthened and the reproduction portion of the crop season is now shifted to the hottest and driest portion of the growing season. Nevertheless, an early seeding date may still be the most desirable, particularly if the soil profile is fully recharged so that a later seeding would not conserve much of the rainfall that normally occurs during late May and early June. Early seeding may be combined with increased row spacing and decreased plant population to maintain lower evapotranspiration rates so that the soil water reserves will not be excessively depleted before the reproductive phase of the growth cycle is reached (Bond et al., 1964). Under different conditions, particularly in the subhumid parts of the Southern High Plains, grain sorghum yields can be increased by narrow row spacing. Adams et al. (1976, 1978) found that grain sorghum in 50-cm rows established a more complete canopy earlier than sorghum with conventional (100-cm) row spacing. The improved plant canopy intercepted 12 percent more radiant energy and resulted in grain

Table 5. Effect of row spacing on grain sorghum yields on Houston
Black clay soil at Temple, Texas, 1972–74.

Year	Row Spacing (cm)	
	50	100
	Grain Yield (kg/ha)	
1972	3890 (25%)[a]	3115
1973	3850 (20%)[a]	3200
1974	5050 (18%)[a]	4275

SOURCE: Adams et al., 1976.

[a] Parentheses show percentage increase in grain yield over grain
sorghum with 100-cm conventional row spacing.

yield increases averaging 20 percent (Table 5). The earlier
and more complete ground cover also reduced runoff and
erosion.

The above discussion is simply an example of how cropping systems and climatic databases can be matched. Insofar as feasible, a crop should be growing during the periods
of high rainfall probability. This allows for more of the
water resource to be used for evapotranspiration, which will
increase water use efficiency. Crop growth models such as
the grain sorghum model of Arkin et al. (1980) can be used
to estimate crop yields under various climatic conditions.
Such models will be extremely useful in developing cropping systems for specific areas as these models are validated
and improved by the use of field data sets.

CONCLUSION

Crop production under rainfed conditions, and particularly so when rainfall is so limited that dry farming methods
must be practiced, requires a three-pronged attack—rainfall
retention, evaporation reduction, and cropping systems that
take advantage of the rainfall and temperature patterns.
Rainfall retention can be enhanced either by increasing infiltration rate or by containing the water long enough for it
to infiltrate. The use of furrow dams is one technology that
has proven very effective. Evaporation can be reduced by
mulches, or by plant spacings that result in a more complete
and earlier canopy. Cropping systems should match the specific crop with the climate insofar as feasible so that there is
a good probability of producing a harvestable crop. As a
general guideline, a crop should be growing during the periods of the year that have a high probability of rainfall. This
allows more of the rainfall to be used for transpiration and
less for evaporation. Another important technological development is increasing the drought tolerance of crops
through improved germ plasm.

REFERENCES

Adams, J. E. 1966. Influence of mulches on runoff, erosion, and soil moisture depletion. Soil Science Society of America Proceedings 30:110–14.

Adams, J. E., G. F. Arkin, and E. Burnett. 1976. Narrow rows increase dryland grain sorghum yields. Texas Agricultural Experiment Station MP-1248. College Station, Texas.

Adams, J. E., C. W. Richardson, and E. Burnett. 1978. Influence of row spacing of grain sorghum on ground cover, runoff, and erosion. Soil Science Society of America Journal 42:959–62.

Arkin, G. F., S. J. Maas, and C. W. Richardson. 1980. Forecasting sorghum yields using synthetic weather data and updating techniques. Transactions of the ASAE 23(3):676–80.

Bond, J. J., T. S. Army, and O. R. Lehman. 1964. Row spacing, plant populations and moisture supply as factors in dryland grain sorghum production. Agronomy Journal 56:3–6.

Dancette, C., and A. E. Hall. 1979. Agroclimatology applied to water management in the Sudanian and Sahelian zones of Africa. Pp. 98–118. In A. E. Hall et al. (eds.) Agriculture in semiarid environments. Ecological Studies, vol. 34. Berlin–Heidelberg–New York: Springer-Verlag.

Greb, B. W. 1983. Water conservation: Central Great Plains. Pp. 57–72. In H. E. Dregne and W. O. Willis (eds.) Dryland agriculture. Agronomy 23. Madison, Wis.: American Society of Agronomy.

Jacks, G. V., W. D. Brind, and R. Smith. 1955. Mulching. Commonwealth Bureau of Soil Science (England) Technical Communication no. 49.

Johnson, W. C., and R. G. Davis. 1972. Stubble-mulch farming of winter wheat: A history of 28 years' experience at USDA Southwestern Great Plains Research Center, Bushland, Texas. USDA Agricultural Research Service Conservation Research Report no. 16.

Jones, O. R., P. W. Unger, and D. W. Fryrear. 1985. Technology effects on soil and water conservation in the Southern High Plains. Journal of Soil and Water Conservation (in press).

Krishna, J. H., and G. F. Arkin. 1985. Furrow diking in Central Texas: a hydrologic assessment. Texas Agricultural Experiment Station Progress Report-4264. College Station, Texas.

Richardson, C. W. 1973. Runoff, erosion, and tillage efficiency on graded-furrow and terraced watersheds. Journal of Soil and Water Conservation 28:162–64.

Unger, P. W. 1978. Straw-mulch rate effect on soil water storage and sorghum yield. Soil Science Society of America Journal 42:485–91.

Unger, P. W. 1983. Water conservation: Southern Great Plains. Pp. 35–55. In H. E. Dregne and W. O. Willis (eds.) Dryland agriculture. Agronomy monograph series 23. Madison, Wis.: American Society of Agronomy.

Wiese, A. F., E. Burnett, and J. E. Box, Jr. 1967. Chemical fallow in dryland cropping sequences. Agronomy Journal 59:175–77.

Willis, W. O. 1982. Soil water management practices for wheat production in semiarid climates of the United States. In J. Burgos (ed.) Proceedings of the United States–Argentina bilateral workshop on drought. Mar del Plata, Argentina: Institut Nacional di Tech. Agropec., Buenos Aires.

54. ACTION EXPERIMENTS IN IRRIGATION DEVELOPMENT: IDENTIFYING POLICY AND PROGRAM IMPLICATIONS

E. Walter Coward, Jr., Department of Rural Sociology, Cornell University, Ithaca, New York

ABSTRACT

This paper discusses three action experiments in irrigation development, currently under way in Indonesia, Sri Lanka, and the Philippines. Each of these experiments is concerned with increasing farmer involvement in project decisions and activities in both the pre- and the postconstruction periods. It is suggested that such action experiments are an effective means for discovering and testing country-specific means for reorienting the mix of state and locality rights and responsibilities in irrigation development. To implement such action experiments, one needs to begin with a broad definition of irrigation development, an irrigation agency that is tolerant of testing alternatives, a knowledge-generating partner institution, and a supportive project donor. The action projects reviewed suggest (1) that irrigation development is a process requiring a set of implementing institutions rather than a single agency, (2) that it benefits from greater involvement in pre- as well as postconstruction activities, and (3) that the use of a catalyst role is an effective means of improving interaction between the irrigation agency and water users.

INTRODUCTION: A TIME OF TESTING

During the past several decades the state has become increasingly involved in irrigation development—both creating new commands and rehabilitating and "modernizing" existing commands. In many countries, the result is an irrigation structure heavily dependent upon continuing state actions and less connected to local responsibilities and inputs. While this situation has resulted in a number of undesirable consequences for irrigation system performance, it is the present fiscal crisis of many governments, in both industrial nations and the so-called Third World, that is accelerating interest in reexamining irrigation investment policies. As irrigation departments are required to function in resource-limited rather than resource-rich contexts, there is an increased interest in formulating investment strategies that represent a different mix of State/local rights and responsibilities—limiting the state role while inducing a larger local role.

While there is growing interest in such a reorientation, the means for planning and implementing such strategies is not well understood at present. However, there are several experiments under way in Asia that are suggestive. This paper briefly discusses three such experiments and derives lessons and implications from them. Perhaps the most important conclusion reached is that these new strategies can only be done in the context of such agency-locality experiments. This requires agencies to practice what D. Korten (1980) has called a "learning process" of program development.

THE HIGH PERFORMANCE SEDERHANA IRRIGATION SYSTEMS IN INDONESIA

Indonesia has a rich legacy of small-scale irrigation systems locally built and managed by indigenous water users' groups—the best known of these being the *subaks* of Bali. Beginning in 1974, the U.S. government initiated a program to assist Indonesia in rapidly developing a number of small-scale irrigation works as one means to overcome the then pressing shortfall in rice production. This program was known as the Sederhana Program (*sederhana* in Indonesian meaning "simple"). While the intent of the planners was that the majority of these sederhana projects would be new small-scale facilities, in reality a majority of the projects were overlaid on local systems—planned to improve those systems in some way and/or to expand their service areas.

In the early years of the program the approach used was very much an agency-dominated one. All the initial activities of planning, designing, and construction were implemented by government agencies or private contractors. Farmers became involved with the activities only at a very late stage—usually after construction was completed—when they were formed into water users' groups and assigned responsibility to operate and maintain parts of the irrigation layout.

There were a number of negative consequences associated with this construction-first approach. Often the most obvious problem was that the users did not assume responsibility for the facilities, and maintenance problems rapidly appeared. At other times there were glaring problems with the physical infrastructure—components that did not operate, layouts that were misaligned, etc. In fact, it can be said that many of the sederhana projects suffered the "Rao effect"—facilities were built in these existing systems that were "unproductive, irrelevant, and extravagant" (Rao, 1984,3).

The High Performance Sederhana Irrigation Systems (HPSIS) experiment was designed to try to improve these two programmatic problems that were seen as linked to one another—the problem of poor system design and construction and the lack of effective farmer involvement in the postconstruction projects. The experiment was built on ideas and propositions that had then been under development in the Philippines for several years. There, an approach for providing government assistance to similar small-scale, local irrigation systems was evolving. One of its basic premises was the following (F. Korten, 1982, 11):

> Involving the local water users' association in the preconstruction and construction activities is an important means of developing more functional physical systems and developing the skills and structures of the associations. It is important also for insuring that farmers are willing to contribute towards maintenance of the investments.

Effective farmer involvement in these preconstruction and construction activities requires a number of conditions; paramount among them is that farmers have some organized means of participating with the agencies and contractors involved in these activities. To assist farmers in ordering their experiences, opinions, and demands during these initial project steps, a new staff role was created: the community organizer. The community organizers, usually young college graduates, were hired by the government and assigned to work in irrigation systems that were to be assisted by the sederhana program. A nongovernmental organization, the Institute for Economic and Social Research, Education and Information, was contracted to assist the government in selecting candidates, providing training, and monitoring progress in the field. This institute, while not having prior experience with irrigation activities, was skilled in working with community organizers in other social settings such as urban neighborhoods.

The community organizers, though hired by the government, are not meant to be government representatives in the local area. Their role is a more difficult one—attempting to act as a liaison between the agencies and contractors and the local groups. Following the principle of involving farmers in various preconstruction decisions and activities, quoted above, the work of the community organizers begins with organizing farmers at the smallest units in the command area, ultimately proceeding to the total system level. The initial activities are concerned with organizing farmers to interact effectively with the agency staff and contractors to identify irrigation problems at the local level, review agency suggestions for improvements in view of local knowledge and experiences, and monitor the construction activities.

Morfit and Poffenberger (1984, 28–29) reached the following conclusion based on their analysis of the community organizer approach in one small-scale system:

> The data presented in this article show the extent to which community organizers, working through local institutions, were able to establish a more effective channel of communication between government agencies controlling both funds and technical expertise for irrigation development and farmers responsible for managing and maintaining completed systems. This improved communication resulted in identification of several problems in the original design. Because of the willingness of the Ministry of Public Works engineers and the private contractor to listen to the views of farmers and incorporate many of their recommendations, approximately 11 hectares were irrigated which otherwise would not have received water. This effectively constitutes a 7 percent increase in the area actually irrigated by the project. Although sufficient data is not available to do a thorough cost-benefit analysis, this research indicates that the benefit of the changes in terms of increased rice production surpassed the cost of the pilot project (i.e., the use of the community organizers in one year).

THE GAL OYA PROJECT IN SRI LANKA

This experiment is being implemented in the context of a project to rehabilitate a large reservoir-based system in the dry zone of Sri Lanka—the Gal Oya project. With support from the U.S. government, this project was planned to reinstate the physical facilities in the Left Bank service area of the system—improvement of the main and distributary canals and construction of various control structures (gates, turnouts, regulators). Since field channel improvements were to be the responsibility of farmers themselves, the project also called for creating irrigator groups in the project area. In fact, the original plan very much equated farmer participation with "free labor to reshape and improve all field channels, as funding was budgeted only for primary and secondary level rehabilitation work" (Uphoff, 1985a, 3).

To assist the Irrigation Department in the task of creating the irrigator groups, the project included a social science group, the Agrarian Research and Training Institute (ARTI, located in Colombo), with collaboration from Cornell University. The overall strategy identified by the ARTI/Cornell team for implementing the farmer organizations component of the project involved four key ideas:

- A blueprint approach to the organizations was unlikely to be successful—rather, something like a "learning approach" would be used, identifying some likely actions, implementing them, learning from the outcome, and making changes as necessary.
- The farmer organizing efforts needed to proceed parallel with the physical rehabilitation rather than come after it. In this way the incipient farmer groups would have significant functions from the start.
- Building on knowledge of the Philippines activities discussed above and similar programs using group organizers in Nepal, it was decided that some form of "catalysts" would be used to work with the irrigator groups.
- It was assumed that the success of the work with the irrigator groups would be partly dependent upon the irrigation agency's modifying some of its programs and policies—what came to be referred to as bureaucratic reorientation (Korten and Uphoff, 1981).

A key component of the organizing effort was the recruitment, training, and fielding of a catalyst staff—here called institutional organizers (IOs). To fill this role, university graduates were recruited by ARTI (with the hope that eventually this role would be made a permanent staff position in the Irrigation Department). The IOs were assigned as teams to the hydraulically defined area of a distributary canal, with individual IOs assuming responsibility for one or more field channels.

The organizing work began with emphasis on informal organization at the level of the field channels and attention to various self-help activities that these groups could implement on their own—primarily ditch cleaning and other maintenance activities and water distribution within the field channels. The latter activity was especially successful in the early months that the IOs were fielded, when the system experienced a severe water shortage.

A major concern of the organizing effort is to increase the participation of the water users in the planning and implementation of the rehabilitation effort. This has occurred in several ways. First, the self-help activities of the farmers at the level of the field channels and, to some extent, the distributary canals have helped change the image of the farmers held by the Irrigation Department and made the latter more willing to discuss with farmers both plans for improvements and ongoing water distribution matters.

Second, the Irrigation Department has instituted changes in the design process so that the initial survey of field conditions in a given area is done in collaboration with farmers of that area. The initial technique used was a rehabilitation design meeting involving irrigation staff and farmers. The IOs played a critical role in helping farmers prepare for these meetings so that their priority concerns were effectively communicated to the agency engineers. As Widanapathirana and Perera (1984, 414) indicate, this initial procedure has been modified:

> The design meetings were subsequently substituted by a walk-along-the-canal, where the engineer, assisted by a technical assistant, walked along the canal together with the specific farmer group, observing actual conditions in situ and discussing possible solutions. At the end of the meeting, an agreement was entered into between the farmer representative and the engineer under which the farmer group was to carry out rehabilitation earthwork, and the Irrigation Department to undertake construction of structures. In addition to specific hydraulic problems, farmer groups have also pointed out where places for wallowing pits for buffaloes, bathing spots, etc., were required, so that provision for such structures could be made in the design plan. Some field channels, which hitherto did not exist, were designed purely on the suggestions made by farmer groups.

> Farmer consultation for design work did not end with the planning stage. The experiment had not anticipated using farmer consultation for the design work beyond the field channels. However, the activities of some of the farmer organizations, in respect of design work above the channel, have been useful.

In this way the local knowledge and experience of farmers over the past thirty years can be incorporated into decisions about canal realignments, the need for particular structures, and other matters, and increase the likelihood of farmer commitment to operating and maintaining the improvements that are provided.

Third, there has been a significant increase in the routine interaction between the irrigation agency and farmer representatives through periodic meetings called by the farmer groups, and through the regularized participation of farmer representatives in the formal meetings of the District Agricultural Committee, composed of district-level department heads and local members of parliament.

THE PALSIGUAN IRRIGATION PROJECT IN THE PHILIPPINES

The third example, the Palsiguan project in the Ilocos region of the Philippines, is different from the others in that the project began with one conceptualization of its activities and then, when considerable problems were encountered, the approach was radically reoriented.

Above, we have referred to the innovative program that the Philippines has developed for assisting the small-scale, communal systems that cover about half the irrigated land in the country. The Palsiguan project is very interesting because most of the area to be covered by the project (about 8,000 ha) is already irrigated by approximately 170 local irrigation groups—called *zanjeras*. However, because this project was originally conceptualized as building a large government system, rather than assisting a number of existing communal systems in improving their facilities, the innovative approach to irrigation development being tested in one unit of the irrigation agency was not being implemented in the project.

Fortunately, the project began with an initial 1,000-ha pilot area to carry out its development activities. As work proceeded on this pilot effort, the zanjeras in the affected area began coming forth with their various objections—some indicating they did not wish to be included in the project at all, others indicating their dissatisfaction with the manner in which things were being done. Visaya (1982, 6) succinctly summarizes what went wrong:

> The design of the pilot project was based on maximum engineering efficiency, without considering the existing communal irrigation systems and irrigation organizations in the area. [The] Majority, if not all, designed canals are new ones, crisscrossing the canals of the existing zanjera systems. The proposed rotational areas, consequently, disregarded existing area boundaries of the irrigation associations.

In brief, project planning in the pilot area proceeded as though the 1,000 ha was an open field devoid of existing irrigation structures or institutions. With this image in mind, the engineers developed their notion of an optimal canal reticulation, including the concept of 50-ha rotation areas being used in other modern national systems in the Philippines. Moreover, they attempted to recreate a pattern of local irrigation leadership that would fit this new canal alignment—a three-tiered pattern with leaders at the rotation area, a zone area, and, finally, a federation for the entire 1,000-ha pilot. Little of this new organization coincided with the existing pattern of zanjera leadership in the area. Finally, again following national policies, the project planned to charge farmers regular irrigation fees for the "irrigation services" that were to be provided.

As a result of the many problems encountered in the pilot area, the project staff began to call on researchers familiar with the zanjera organizations. The outcome of some rapid appraisal work by these researchers and a series of discussions with project-level staff and top-level National Irrigation Association (NIA) administrators was a decision to radically reconceptualize the project, not as a national irrigation scheme but as a communal irrigation project. The orientation of this "zanjera strategy" is again best described by Visaya (1982, 13–14):

> to rehabilitate existing zanjera communal irrigation systems and construct facilities for new areas, through the maximum participation of the farmers in planning and implementation of the

project, and improve the farmers' capability to effectively operate and maintain *their irrigation systems* [emphasis in the original].

To implement this approach, several broad policies were immediately established. First was the decision to reorient the planning of canal layouts to make maximum use of existing canals and retain the integrity of the established zanjera boundaries. A second broad policy that has finally evolved is to deal with financial matters in this project in the same way that finances are dealt with in other communal projects. Farmers will be responsible for the O&M (operation and maintenance) activities of the system through their existing zanjera organizations and through the creation of zanjera federations combining all the zanjeras to be served in each of five zones to comprise the total project area. In addition, farmers will repay a portion of the capital costs of construction through small annual payments over a fifty-year period.

A third broad policy has been to establish procedures for greater farmer involvement in the project planning and implementation. A cadre of institutional workers has been established for the specific purpose of improving liaison between the existing zanjera groups and the agency staff. A major procedure for involving the zanjeras in planning and design activities is the so-called walk-through. This refers to a procedure whereby the agency staff and zanjera leaders go together to the field location to see where planned canals and structures are to be placed and to agree on or suggest other modifications. The following quote from Angeles et al. (1984, 57) illustrates how this works:

> In Paor-Patoc, which is one of the zanjeras in the Neuva Era area, the confirmation of structures along the Nueva Era main canal (NE-MC) was conducted on September 1 and 5, respectively. A team composed of an agri-institutional worker, a technical staff member, a member of the field survey section, and the zanjera officials was present during the confirmation.
>
> On September 1, 1983, structures along the stations 0+00 to 0+700 on NE-MC were/surveyed identified by the party starting from the upstream and going downstream. The extent of the canals to be lined was also shown and identified. At station 0+00 the technical staff . . . explained to the zanjera officials that a closed conduit will be constructed up to station 0+203.50. The technical staff also explained what a closed conduit is and its importance. This manner of conducting the walk-through was carried all through the different stations. In every station where a structure is to be located, the zanjera officials were asked whether they had any proposal for the relocation of any structures. Neither relocation was suggested nor any negative attitude shown by the farmers.

Farmers do not always concur, of course, and there has been disagreement about the location of one of the lateral canals in this section. What is impressive about the resolution of this problem is the considerable interaction that occurred between the agency and the zanjeras regarding possible alternative locations (see Angeles et al., 1984, 61–65). Farmers unhappy with a section of the original layout explored other possibilities and identified an alternative acceptable to the agency.

ORGANIZING FOR ACTION EXPERIMENTS

As noted above, there is a growing interest in achieving a new mix of state-locality rights and responsibilities for irrigation development. Achieving this reorientation is not likely to be done through a blueprint approach that specifies the procedures for accomplishing this new mix in any particular case. Rather, there is need for a more experimental mode of action directed toward identifying what is possible and effective in particular sociotechnical settings. Action experiments are one means to identify and test alternatives.

1. *An enlarged definition of irrigation development.* While this new definition of irrigation development does not have to be precise to begin with, it does need to recognize that irrigation development is more than designing and constructing civil works, and that agencies and groups other than the irrigation agency have an important role to play in irrigation development.

2. *A tolerant irrigation agency.* While the agency may not begin with a full commitment, it does need to be willing to have approaches tested that are different from business as usual and to allow time for these new approaches to mature. In each of the cases discussed above, the irrigation agency has been willing to allow a new institutional actor to come into the irrigation domain—for example, the Institute for Social and Economic Research, Education and Information, in Indonesia. The agencies have also been willing to modify their own procedures to accommodate farmer involvement in preconstruction activities—the rehabilitation design meetings and walk-along-the-canal activities in Sri Lanka and the walk-through exercises in the Philippines. This agency tolerance is important for getting the process initiated and for sustaining it because increased farmer involvement in irrigation development depends, in part, on changes in the administrative policies and procedures of the agency (Alfonos, 1981).

3. *A knowledge-generating organization.* Action experiments are unlikely to succeed unless the irrigation agency is willing to join with an institutional partner that has a knowledge-generating mandate. Often, this will be a research group of some type—such as the ARTI in Sri Lanka or the Central Luzon State University in the Palsiguan project. The research group performs the important role of keeping track of what is going on—not just in terms of broad evaluation indicators such as number of groups formed or number of rehabilitation design meetings held but in terms of processes occurring such as the decisions made in walk-throughs or actions taken by farmers in response to agency procedures. Moreover, in the context of action experiments, the information gathered by the research group is not merely stored away until the time of final evaluation but is fed back to the project team (which includes staff of the research group) for immediate consideration and project modification, as required. A knowledge-generating group that is an independent partner with the irrigation agency provides a means by which bad news about the program can be communicated to the agency and questions about the fundamental assumptions and procedures of the agency examined.

The reality of bureaucratic behavior will severely inhibit these things from happening if the irrigation agency works alone on the experimental effort.

4. *A supportive donor.* Since so many of the irrigation projects under way around the world are donor supported, it is important to note the important role that donor objectives, expectations, and procedures can have on action experiments. To begin with, there is the point that some donor agencies, or some representatives of those agencies, will be uncomfortable with the risk associated with an experimental approach—an approach that seems to imply we are not sure about how to do something, in contrast to the usual assertiveness about procedures and outcomes explicit in most project documents. Since, as noted above, the experimental approach will depend upon actions by several agencies (some of which may be unfamiliar to the donor) rather than the single irrigation department, there may also be a reluctance on the donor's part to enter into these more complex, interorganizational projects. Action experiments also imply a phasing of activities in which the initial coverage of the project activities may be quite limited and expand only after an extended trial and learning period—again, a strategy that might be in conflict with a donor's needs to move funds rapidly and demonstrate widespread effects. All of this suggests that if a donor is involved in the action experiment, that donor needs to understand the various implications identified above and have a means by which to make those implications acceptable within the ideology and procedures of the agency.

EMERGING LESSONS

The several action experiments in irrigation development under way in Asia suggest some lessons that might be useful to consider in planning irrigation development elsewhere.

A first lesson that emerges is that innovative irrigation development projects are being implemented by networks of people and organizations rather than by a single department such as irrigation or agriculture. D. Korten (1982, 1) has characterized such a network as a "working group," which he describes as

a mechanism for legitimizing and supporting an informal coalition committed to the change objectives and composed of: (1) key people within the action agency concerned about how well the agency serves the needs of its intended beneficiaries, (2) a number of talented individuals external to the agency who are unfettered by the usual bureaucratic constraints, and (3) a donor which provides an independent source of flexible financial resources and assistance in forming and helping the members of the coalition work together.

The areas of expertise that can complement the skills of the irrigation department will include the following: agriculture, public management, and research—both technical and social science.

A second lesson that emerges is recognition of the direct utility of farmer involvement in the preconstruction planning and design activities. It is during this phase of the project that the location-specific information and experiences of farmers can be tapped and incorporated into pre-construction decisions. The result can be layouts and structures more suitable to the local situation—that is, better engineering decisions—as well as greater farmer commitment to the O&M activities required by these new artifacts. It also is the case that phasing the farmer organization effort to follow construction means that a very important opportunity to use preconstruction activities as a locus for group formation and strengthening is lost. The conventional procedure of attempting to organize irrigator groups after construction is completed needs to be reversed.

A third lesson emerging is the utility of a catalystlike worker to act as the important interface between the irrigation agency and the farmer groups. This is a specialized role that requires preparation and freedom from other responsibilities. Thus, it is unlikely to be suitably performed by staff such as the field workers of the irrigation agency or the local agricultural extension agents. It has been somewhat surprising that the catalyst strategy has worked so effectively in the three very different national settings represented by the action experiments discussed above.

Uphoff (1985b, 2) has suggested that development of the catalyst approach is "a promising social science analogue to the biological technology of 'high-yielding varieties' (HYV's)." Like the HYVs, the catalyst approach, with appropriate modifications, may be a suitable strategy for a number of irrigation development situations.

Finally, we can note simply that the action experiments we have discussed also suggest that there are real possibilities for rearranging the mix of state and local responsibilities and rights in irrigation, When effectively involved, irrigator groups can provide critical inputs for the state's planning and design activities. As organized groups more effectively participate in irrigation activities, their talents and resources can substitute for, or complement, the resources that the irrigation agency has been expected to devote to irrigation. New mixes are possible—but they require changes and modifications both in what farmers are doing and in what agencies are doing. Action experiments have helped to identify what is possible and what needs to be changed to achieve those possibilities.

REFERENCES

Alfonso, F. B. 1981. Assisting farmer controlled development of communal irrigation systems. Pp. 44–52. *In* D. C. Korten and F. B. Alfonso (eds.) Bureaucracy and the poor: closing the gap. Manila: McGraw-Hill International.

Angeles, H. L., et al. 1984. Process documentation research on the development of the Palsiguan River multi-purpose project. Second Annual Report. Muños, Philippines: Central Luzon State University.

Korten, D. C. 1982. The working group as a mechanism for managing bureaucratic reorientation: experience from the Philippines. NASPAA Working Paper. Washington, D.C.

Korten, D. C. 1982. The working group as a mechanism for managing bureaucratic reorientation: experience from the Philippines. NASPAA Working Paper. Washington, D.C.

Korten, D. C., and N. Uphoff. 1981. Bureaucratic reorientation and participatory rural development. NASPAA Working Paper. Washington, D.C.

Korten, F. F. 1982. Building national capacity to develop water users' associations. World Bank Staff Working Paper no. 528. Washington, D.C.

Morfit, M., and M. Poffenberger. 1984. Community participation and irrigation development: a case study from Indonesia. Paper presented to USAID, Asia Bureau Committee on Community Management, Bangkok, Thailand.

Rao, P. K. 1984. Comments on cost recovery and irrigation water pricing. ODI Irrigation Management Network Paper 10f. London.

Uphoff, N. 1985a. Experience with people's participation in water management: Gal Oya, Sri Lanka. In J. C. Garcia-Zamor (ed.) Public participation in development planning and management: cases from Africa and Asia. Boulder, Colo.: Westview Press.

———. 1985b. Activating community capacity for water management: Experience from Gal Oya, Sri Lanka. In D. C. Korten (ed.) Community management: Asia experience and perspectives. West Hartford, Conn.: Kumarian Press (in press).

Visaya, B. P. 1982. The Palsiguan River multi-purpose project and the zanjeras. Paper presented at conference on organization as strategic resource in irrigation development, Makati, Metro Manila, Philippines, November 15–19.

Widanapathirana, A. S., and I. R. Perera. 1984. Farmer participation in the design, construction, operation and maintenance of a major rehabilitation project: evidence from an exploratory approach in Sri Lanka. Paper presented at African regional symposium on small holder irrigation, Harare, Zimbabwe.

PART IX. PANEL DISCUSSION—MAKING INSTITUTIONS WORK

55. EVOLUTION AND DEVELOPMENT OF IRRIGATED AGRICULTURE IN THE SUDAN

Hussein Idris, United Nations Development Programme, New York, New York

ABSTRACT

The experience of the Sudan in developing the second largest irrigation system in Africa during the century is presented. A brief account in the evolution of patterns of water use for agriculture since ancient times is given. To reconcile conflicting interests of Egypt and the Sudan in the utilization of the Nile waters international agreements were signed in 1929 and 1959. Tripartite partnership between a foreign private sector, the Sudan government, and the Sudanese tenants laid the early foundation for irrigation development in the Zeidab and the Gezira schemes. Since 1950 public parastatal bodies, rather than the foreign private sector, have been used in the tripartite arrangements. The roles of public sector departments of irrigation and agricultural research and the managerial bodies were crucial, as were those of the tenants and their associations, with whom the public sector officials worked. Successes of the schemes followed years of high cotton prices. The impact of the energy crisis of the early 1970s in the economy of the country led to a sharp decline of all schemes from a lack of appropriate investment resources. The cooperation of the government and the parastatals with the World Bank in planning and implementing rehabilitation measures has started a remarkable recovery. The Sudan experience could be of interest to African nations and other developing countries.

INTRODUCTION

The Sudan is considered in this chapter as an example of a semiarid Sahelian African country. It has developed, since the beginning of this century, the largest irrigation system in Africa south of the Sahara. It ranks second to Egypt in the whole continent. Table 1 shows irrigated areas of leading African countries in irrigation as estimated by the Food and Agriculture Organization (FAO). Sudan's experience is very relevant to the problems of drought in the rest of Africa.

BACKGROUND

The distribution of rainfall in the Sudan and the Nile River and its tributaries has influenced the extent of irrigation use. Average annual rainfall decreases gradually from a maximum of 1,200–1,450 mm in southwest Equatoria Province in the southern Sudan to almost zero rainfall along the northern borders of the country. Rainfed farming dominates in the lateritic high-rainfall areas of the southern Sudan and the black cracking clays (vertisols) of the central Sudan fed by rains amounting to 400–1,000 mm. The White and Blue Niles and their tributaries divide the Sudan, from south and east, forming the main Nile at Khartoum. The Nile flows north of Khartoum across the great North African desert, through Egypt, and its remaining few drops drain into the Mediterranean.

THE PERIOD PRIOR TO 1914

Until World War I there were four means of irrigation from the Nile, its tributaries, other seasonal rivers, and underground sources: (1) natural flooding; (2) basin irrigation; (3) lift irrigation by various means—*shaduf* (manually operated lever and bucket), *saqia* (ox-driven waterwheel), and engine-driven pump (internal combustion and later electric motor); and (4) flush irrigation from river spate.

Natural Flooding

This is the oldest method, the least costly, but it is directly influenced by fluctuations in the level of the river from year to year. Area covered by the main Nile north of Khartoum ranges from 25,000 to 60,000 ha.

Basin Irrigation

This is practiced mainly along the main Nile north of Khartoum. Basins are depressions beyond the outer banks of the Nile and are flooded with water drawn through man-made feeder canals from the river at higher levels. The basin is flooded for a period sufficient to build up the proper moisture content of the soil. Excess water is led back by a drain canal to the river. The effective cultivable areas fluctuate considerably from year to year. The largest basin (Kerma in the Northern Province) covers an area of 30,000 ha, but several basins range from 200 to 3,000 ha in area.

Lift Irrigation

Shaduf. The Shaduf consists essentially of two wooden posts supporting a crossbar, on which a long wooden lever pivots. The shaduf is worked by manpower at lifts of up to 3 m and an output of 24–30 m per day, which would support 0.20–0.30 ha of vegetables. The shaduf supported a few thousand hectares on the main Nile during the flood season and was also used to a lesser extent to lift water from low drift wells in Kassala and Kordofan provinces.

Saqia (Persian waterwheel). The saqia, like the shaduf, is made of local material. The saqia lifts water from 3 to 8 m. The area which a saqia can irrigate varies considerably with the lift and ranges from 1.0 to 2.0 ha. About 10,000 saqias, predominantly in the main Nile, were registered in 1943. Both shadufs and saqias have been gradually superseded by pumps during the last decades.

The saqia is driven by animal power, which demands about half the irrigated area to be put under fodder crop for the animals' consumption. Both the shaduf and the saqia could provide only subsistence income for a small number of people.

Table 1. Irrigated areas of leading African countries by country and region (1982).

Country	Area (10^6 ha)
Egypt	2.47
Sudan	1.90
South Africa	1.03
Madagascar	0.48
Morocco	0.53
Algeria	0.35
Libya	0.23
Senegal	0.18
Tunisia	0.18

SOURCE: 1983 Food and Agriculture Organization Production Yearbook, vol. 37.

The evolved partnership arrangements between the parties supplying the various inputs in the operation of the saqia have greatly influenced relations between partners on large-scale irrigation schemes developed after World War I. The inputs involved include: landownership, provision and maintenance of the saqia, ownership of bulls and supply of fodder, provision of seed and implements, and labor. Animal power, labor, and land are the most important inputs. The cost of seeds and taxes are shared according to the magnitude of the inputs. The crop produce is shared according to the relative importance of the inputs. Labor and animal power are highly valued inputs, and land becomes equally important where it is scarce. In general, labor takes roughly a half share, and those who supply land, irrigation water, and the means whereby it is raised take the other half share of the total crop.

Pump Schemes. The engine-driven pumps were introduced in the beginning of the century; about thirteen pumps were in operation in 1904. The total artificially irrigated area along the Nile was about 40,000–50,000 ha. The pump schemes were under government or private ownership. They enabled the irrigation of larger areas distant from the river and helped to mitigate the uncertainties inherent in flood and basin cultivation.

However, several factors hindered rapid expansion of pump irrigation. These were mainly the restriction of pumping during the low flood period (January 1 to July 16), which is an important measure to ensure availability of adequate water for Egypt, which lies downstream. The second factor was the doubts about the economics of pump irrigation. Pumps were imported and incurred sundry costs, which included transportation; installation; operation using wood fuel and, later, oil; employment of foreign engineers and managers; land clearing; leveling, and canalization. Working capital requirements were high during the development stage, involving untried cropping patterns and various other risks.

The period before World War I and immediately after witnessed important trial ventures on the use of pump irrigation that paved the road for the establishment of the large-scale schemes.

Lessons of Zeidab Scheme. The Zeidab Scheme was the first venture by the government to attract foreign capital and enterprise to work in association with the local cultivators and develop pump irrigation agriculture in the Northern Province.

The Zeidab agreement was for 4,000 ha. The Sudan Experimental Plantation Syndicate Ltd. was registered in England in 1904. During the course of implementing the schemes, several changes and adjustments were made and many lessons were learned.

The company operated the first two seasons with direct paid labor. By the 1908–1909 season it had developed the idea of land and water tenancies on the grounds that these would give a more certain return than the doubtful, and, to that time disappointing yields by its own farming. Restriction of perennial pumping to only 1,600 ha of the estate reduced returns on investment. Flood pumping irrigated the rest of the estate. This restricted the cropping pattern in these areas to quick-maturing crops, like sorghum, which was not profitable when cultivated by direct labor. In view of the low value of cereals the government urged production of cotton. Cotton, if it was to be picked before the cold spell, had to be planted before July, while flood pumping began in mid-July. The switch from Egyptian (long staple and long maturing) to American (medium staple and early maturing) cotton varieties solved that problem. Wheat required irrigation until April, while pumping stopped at the end of February. Neither cotton nor wheat could give a reasonable return on the heavy capitalization.

These difficulties, together with others relating to landownership, contributed to the company's decision to continue as a landlord and manager, instead of as a farmer. The estate was divided into tenancies of 12.6 ha each, and in return for an inclusive rent (land, tax, and water) tenants could cultivate the land and were provided with water according to the needs of the crops. A rotation was enforced of cotton-wheat-fallow or legumes (usually fodder legume) on each 12.6-ha holding.

The company provided foreign management staff to superintend the rotations and to advise on crop husbandry, the tenant being required to follow the technical advice offered. Plowing, ridging, threshing, and ginning were also done for the tenant against the inclusive rent.

By 1914, Zeidab had demonstrated the technical, economic, and social feasibility of pump irrigated agriculture, revealing both the positive and the negative sides.

THE PERIOD AFTER 1918

Identification of sources of revenue, particularly exports, had preoccupied the attention of the Sudanese government in the beginning of the century. Following the example of Egypt, development of irrigated agriculture and cotton as a promising export crop was seriously considered. An early survey showed that soils of good quality and suitable slope were abundant. As for water, even at that time the whole of the natural flow of the river was used by Egypt from early in the year (January–March) until the rise of the flood in July, and it was clear that either the crops to be grown in the Gezira must require no irrigation from the beginning of March onward, or storage must be provided. Cotton was then and is now grown in Egypt from March to November.

Fortunately, in the Sudan cotton was found to grow best from July or August to March. The idea of building a dam on the Blue Nile near Sennar, to store water for irrigation during the shortage period, was conceived in 1908. Preparations for building the dam were interrupted by World War I. Building of the dam and canalization of the Gezira area, between the Blue and White Niles, were commenced in 1918 and completed by 1925.

To investigate the feasibility of growing cotton and other crops under irrigation in the Gezira environment, the government established two experimental pump schemes on the Blue Nile at Tayiba in 1911 and at Barakat in 1914. Cotton and several other crops (sorghum, wheat, sesame, legumes, etc.) were found suitable for the area. Cotton grew best when sown in the beginning of summer rains from mid-July to mid-August. This was the time when the Blue Nile was in flood and pumping of water was not restricted. The long staple Egyptian type (*Gossypium barbadense*) of cotton would be irrigated from August until February or March. Two other pump schemes at Hag Abdalla (1921) and Wad el Nan (1923) have also contributed to the training of the supervising staff and cultivators and provided additional data on agronomy and water requirements.

The lessons from Zeidab and the experimental pump schemes; the role played by the Department of Irrigation in surveys, identification, and supervision of building of the Sennar Dam and canalization; and the efforts of the Agricultural Research Division together with the pioneer farmers or tenants laid the foundation for expansion of systematic irrigation by gravity in the Gezira and other areas. Significant interplay of these rural institutions and others had also started.

Gezira Scheme

Some of the main forces behind the Gezira Scheme's development are:

1. The establishment of systematic gravity irrigation, which made possible irrigation on a large scale at low cost. The signing of the Nile Water Agreement in 1929 between Egypt and the Sudan cleared the way for development. The agreement allocated to the Sudan sufficient water to warrant high levels of capital investment. Sudan's share of the Nile waters was fixed at 1.47 billion m^3 during the restricted period, from January to mid-July. The Sennar dam had a gross capacity of 0.93 billion m^3.

2. The choice of cotton as the main crop, which was in high demand as an export commodity. The Agricultural Research Division of the Department of Agriculture conducted the necessary research for the production and protection of cotton in the Gezira. Excellent agricultural research in crop agronomy, plant breeding for resistance to disease and entomology made possible continued growing of cotton in the Gezira over the years.

3. The organization and administration of the scheme based on the tripartite partnership between the government; the two allied concession companies, the Sudan Plantations Syndicate Ltd. and the Kassala Cotton Company Ltd.; and the tenant cultivators. Their respective functions could be summarized as follows:

a. *Government:* provided land, rented compulsorily from its owners at about 23.8 piastres (100 piastres = £1,000) per hectare per annum, and allotted to tenants, without rent or land tax. Provided the water, by means of the Sennar Dam and the canalization down to the minor canal. Provided auxiliary services such as public health, security, telephones, etc. Provided support in agricultural research.

b. *Concession companies:* managed agricultural activities in the scheme through resident inspectors, who supervised the tenants' watering, cotton husbandry, picking and bringing in cotton, and cleanup of dead cotton plants at the end of each season. The companies kept individual accounts for each cultivator and undertook ginning, transport, and marketing of cotton. The companies also operated a light railway system for cotton transport to their ginneries and a fleet of cable plows for ridging the cotton areas on the tenant's behalf.

c. *Tenants:* were responsible for agricultural work on their holdings, including excavation and upkeep of the water courses and water channels. Supplies such as seed, and work done on their behalf, such as plowing, were debited to them. Cash advances were made to them at suitable periods to meet their expenditures in sowing, weeding, picking, etc. The size of the standard tenancy was 12.6 ha; one-third was put under cotton, another third under legume and sorghum, and the remaining third was left fallow. The whole of the food and fodder crops were retained by the tenant. From the gross proceeds obtained from the sale of cotton were deducted the costs of ginning, transport, and marketing, and the balance was divided, 40 percent to the tenants, to each according to the yield from his holding, and roughly 40 percent to the government and 20 percent to the concession companies.

The period from 1925 to 1931 witnessed rapid expansion of the scheme from 33,613 ha cotton area (101,610 ha gross) in 1925–1926 to 80,506 ha cotton area (244,149 ha gross) in 1930–1931. Further expansion until 1958 (cotton area 135,915 ha, gross area about 544,000 ha) was shown, and a plateau was reached because of the utilization of the major portion of the stored water in the dam.

Because of the drastic reduction in yield in 1930–1931 and 1932–1933, attributed mainly to leaf-curl and bacterial blight, the rotation was changed from three course to four course. The standard tenancy was increased from 12.6 ha to 16.8 ha. Rigorous cleanup and pulling of cotton stalks and burning were strictly observed.

The company concessions (the Sudan Plantation Syndicate) ended, and management of the Gezira Scheme was nationalized and undertaken by an independent corporation, the Sudan Gezira Board. The board manages production, markets the crop, and promotes social development and the scheme population.

Since 1950 few changes have occurred and the Gezira Board is directly responsible to the Minister of Agriculture. The tripartite structure includes the government, the tenants, and the board. The government provides the land and irrigation. The tenants undertake production of crops. The board is the overall coordinator and manager. It provides financing of inputs and services and markets the crop.

Until 1979 the Gezira followed the crop production relation system of sharing the net proceeds of the cotton crop, as follows: 36 percent to the government, 49 percent to tenants, 2 percent to local government councils within the irrigated area, 3 percent to the Social Development Department, and 10 percent to the Sudan Gezira Board.

The net proceeds from the cotton are derived by deducting the Joint Account Charges from the gross proceeds. The Joint Account Charges include cost of seed sown, fertilizers, spraying, transportation of cotton to ginneries and to Port Sudan, picking advances, cost of jute sacks, ginning, storage, insurance, etc. The tenants have full control on the production and returns of other crops, which included groundnuts, wheat, sorghum, and fodder legumes.

The production relations were revised in 1979 in favor of the land and water charge on all crops.

The Sudan Gezira Board is composed of a chairman/managing director and representatives of ministries of Agriculture, Irrigation, Finance, and Planning, Agricultural Research Corporation, commissioner of the Blue Nile Province, and the tenants union.

A new Nile Water Agreement was signed in 1959, which increased the Sudan's share of the Nile waters to 18.5 billion m³, providing the possibility of a considerable expansion of irrigated agriculture. Since that time the scheme has doubled in size through the addition of the Managil Extension and now covers more than 840,000 ha. The cotton area is about 200,000 ha. The tenant farmers exceed 75,000 ha. The Gezira Scheme is the world's largest irrigation scheme under single management. The building of the reserves dam in the late 1950s and early 1960s and the availability of more Nile waters enabled implementation of a progressive plan of intensification and diversification of cropping in the Gezira Scheme. The older part of the scheme followed a wide, double four-course rotation (fallow-fallow-cotton-fallow-sorghum-fallow or legume-fallow-cotton) including 50 percent of the land under fallow. The Managil Extension adopted from the start of a three-course rotation of cotton—one half sorghum/one half legume—fallow, resulting in only 30 percent of land under fallow. As from the early 1960s wheat, groundnuts, and vegetables were gradually introduced in the rotation. At present the old Gezira follows the following four-course rotation: cotton-wheat-groundnuts-fallow/sorghum/vegetables. The Managil Extension follows an intensified three-course rotation: cotton-wheat-groundnuts/sorghum/vegetables.

New Wadi Halfa Scheme (Khashim El Girba Scheme)

Expansion in the development of systematic gravity-irrigated projects continued by the establishment of the Kashim El Girba Dam on the Atbara River in 1964 and the launching of Kashim El Girba Scheme, later called the New Wadi Halfa Scheme. The dam had a storage capacity of 1.3 million m³, which is enough to irrigate a total cropped area of about 210,000 ha. The scheme was settled with displaced farmers from the Wadi Halfa region whose lands were submerged as a result of the building of the Aswan High Dam in Egypt. Some members of the local seminomadic tribes were also settled in the scheme.

As from the 1964–1965 season medium staple cotton, wheat, and groundnuts were grown in a three-course rotation. The scheme experienced numerous difficulties in later years: structural problems attributed to progressive silting of the reservoir behind the dam and socioanthropological constraints related to adaptation problems of the settlers.

The Rahad Corporation

The World Bank assisted in the building of the Roseires Dam, establishment of the Managil Extension, and financing of the development of the Rahad Corporation. The Rahad Scheme is located east of the Blue Nile, 160 km southeast of Khartoum. It draws water from the seasonal Rahad stream and by pumps from the Blue Nile. The scheme started production in 1977–1978.

A pilot project at Tambul at the northern tip of the Rahad begun in 1969 conducted innovative trials, including new methods of irrigation such as long furrows using syphon tubes and requisite thorough leveling of land, mechanized sowing of cotton and groundnuts, and mechanical picking of cotton.

Institutional organization and development is of special interest as it is intended to be an improvement over the Gezira model. The project is managed by a parastatal body, called the Rahad Corporation, which is managed by the Rahad Corporation Council. The council is composed of a chairman, who is the managing director, and nine other members, who are representatives of government ministries and units such as irrigation, agriculture, and Gezira Board, the Agricultural Research Corporation, the provincial commissioners, the Cotton Marketing Corporation, and the tenants' union. The council is directly responsible to the minister of agriculture. This structure is similar to that of the Gezira Scheme.

The project covers an area of 126,000 ha, divided into 1,300 tenancies of 9.14 ha each growing mainly cotton and groundnuts, with a small number of tenancies of 2.1 ha each under fruits and vegetables, and some 100 tenancies of about 5.0 ha each for livestock and dairy production. The tenants are also given land to build a home on an allotted village site. The tenancy has indefinite tenure and would be terminated only in death or default by the tenant. The corporation purchases and distributes on credit most inputs required by tenants especially fertilizers, pesticides and spraying services. It purchases and collects tenants' crops and delivers to Port Sudan the produce to be exported. Storage and marketing are undertaken by the Cotton Marketing Corporation and the Oil Seeds Marketing Corporation. Fruits, vegetables, and livestocks are marketed directly by the tenant himself.

Following initial settlement and a grace period of three years, an annual land and water charge was levied. Public health and environmental measures were built into the project.

The Ministry of Irrigation has the responsibility of constructing, operating, and maintaining the irrigation and drainage system. Field inspectors on the corporation's staff are responsible for the agricultural managment of the scheme. Responsibilities include interunit coordination, scheduling water indent with irrigation engineers, supervision of irrigation in the field, monitoring timely delivery of inputs and services to the tenants, and advising the tenants on agricultural practices.

Although the Rahad was conceived on the Gezira pattern, it differed in the following areas: production relationship; settlement of tenants; cropping pattern, practices, and intensity; size of tenancy; level of mechanization; approach to horticulture and animal production; irrigation layout and use of long furrows; social development and services approach; and tenants' participation.

The Rahad Scheme has started fairly well but has been facing several difficulties. Some of the constraints are common to all the agricultural sector and are of national proportions. Specific problems related to the scheme include shortage of trained personnel to cope with the requirements of mechanized agriculture, new irrigation methods, and highly intensive cropping.

Expansion in the Private Pump Schemes

An important development in irrigated agriculture, parallel to that which has occurred in irrigation by gravity, has taken place in the private pump schemes along the Nile and its tributaries. Since 1925 two categories of schemes have developed; the private cotton estates, mainly on the Blue Nile and the White Nile, and noncotton schemes of the Northern Province.

The pump schemes of the Northern Province. Until before World War II in 1937 there were 77 private pump schemes, but in view of increased prices of food crops during World War II, the number of schemes increased to 147 by 1943. The schemes were operated purely by the private sector, which included local notables, merchants, retired government officials, and cooperatives. Some owners farmed the land themselves, but mainly owners provided water to tenants on a crop-sharing basis.

Other factors which influenced expansion were the introduction in the 1930s of diesel engines, which gradually replaced the steam engine; the Nile Water Agreement of 1959; and the demand for vegetables, fruits, and fodder to meet increasing human and animal population needs. By 1963 the number of schemes reached 1,014, covering an area of about 96,000 ha. The government had established eight pump schemes covering an area of more than 10,000 ha.

The private cotton estates. The first private cotton estate was established in 1929 at Aba Island on the White Nile. Estate development was stimulated by raising of the White Nile level after completion of the Jebel Anlia Dam in 1937 and by high cotton prices in 1951 and 1952. During the decade of the fifties the area under cotton increased eightfold, but because of an exceptionally poor yield caused by pests on the 1957–1958 crop and the fall in cotton prices in the 1958–1959 season, further development was checked. For this reason the Nile Water Agreement of 1959 did not result in more expansion.

In 1963 there were 741 cotton pump schemes growing 97,440 ha of cotton, predominantly of the long staple type. Eighty-six percent of these schemes and 93 percent of the cotton area were in the Blue Nile Province. Licensing of pump schemes was governed by the Nile Pumps Control Ordinance of 1939. The Nile Pumps Control Board was vested with issuing or withholding of licenses. Most of the land was leased from the government.

The relationship between tenants and licensee on pump schemes in the Blue Nile Province on which cotton was grown by tenants on a profit-sharing basis was controlled by the Nile Pumps Control (Blue Nile Province Tenancies) Regulations of 1947.

Estates were financed by owners, who were a few rich merchants or, in partnership with financiers, mainly commercial banks; the Agricultural Bank of Sudan, a government corporation, was established in 1959, and since 1960 it has formed the major source of credit to these schemes.

The setting up of the Sudan Cotton Growers Association in 1956 has been an important factor in safeguarding the interests of private cotton growers.

In view of low cotton prices and feuds between tenants and the estate owners during the second half of 1960s, the government nationalized most of the private cotton estates and put them under the Agrarian Reform Corporation. Since then these estates, in common with several major irrigated schemes in the country, have faced several difficulties. These problems are discussed in the following paragraphs.

General Performance of Irrigated Agriculture in the Sudan

The Gezira Scheme, which embodied in its design and planning the lessons learned from the saqia (Persian waterwheel) and the Zeidab Scheme and influenced greatly, as a model, succeeding irrigation projects like New Halfa and the Rahad, is taken in this study as an example of the successes and failures of irrigation development in the Sudan. The results of interaction among various institutions belonging to the government and the private sector will be reviewed.

The Gezira Scheme and the cotton crop in particular have dominated the economy of the Sudan for most of the present century. Revenue from the export of cotton accounts for more than 50 percent of all exports. Other exports include groundnuts, seasame, gum arabic, and livestock.

Cotton productivity over the years has been marred with periodic fluctuations of yields. Early setbacks in productivity in seasons 1930–1931 and 1932–1933 were attributed to diseases of leaf-curl and bacterial blight. The government agricultural research institutions at the Gezira Research Station succeeded in selecting and breeding disease-resistant strains of Egyptian cotton, which ensured the continuation of cotton growing in the Gezira.

The scheme's performance in twenty-two years, during the period 1958–1959 to 1979–1980, was as follows:

Average area under cotton	208,733 ha
Average production of seed cotton	292,524 t
Average yield	1.40 t/ha
Highest yield recorded 1968–1969	1.95 t/ha
Lowest yield recorded 1963–1964	0.77 t/ha

Serious depressions in yield during this period were attributed mainly to pests such as bollworms and whiteflies.

The sharp and consistent decline of cotton yields in 1978–1979, 1979–1980, and 1980–1981, which recorded yields of 0.95, 0.82 and 0.75 t/ha, respectively, is a new phenomenon. Besides the Gezira Scheme, all the other five parastatals which produce cotton experienced similar declines, and overall cotton production in the country dropped to 306,000 t of seed cotton in 1980–1981, compared with 659,000 tons in 1974–1975.

The main reason for the decline of cotton production and productivity were:

1. *Shortage of essential inputs.* This resulted from (a) deficiencies in water supply due to silted irrigation canals, which were neglected and not maintained because of a lack of spare parts and machinery; (b) disruption of field water management because of total breakdown of the telephone system and, consequently, inefficacy of the water indenting mechanism; and (c) shortages in fertilizer and pesticide supplies because of insufficient financial resources and malfunctioning of the Sudan railways and the Gezira light railway.

2. *Low and declining producer prices and incentives.* This resulted from (a) overevaluation of the exchange rate; (b) export duties on cotton; (c) the revenue-sharing formula between the government, the parastatal, and the tenant, which acted as a disincentive to the more productive tenant; (d) delays of payments to tenants, sometimes for as long as two years, diminishing the link between effort and reward; and (e) the bias created in the minds of tenants against cotton, because input costs of other crops (groundnuts, wheat, and sorghum) that were privately marketed were recovered from cotton revenues.

3. *Poor performance of parastatals.* This resulted from (a) brain drain losses of senior and skilled personnel, who migrated to the neighboring oil-producing countries for more remunerative jobs, and (b) inadequate management supported by weak information and accounting systems.

The general deterioration of the Sudan economy as a result of the energy crisis and the spending of more than 60 percent of the export revenue for oil had an overriding effect. The declining productivity of the main export crop, together with the burden of external debt and its service commitments, created a critical balance-of-payments situation in late 1978.

The Rehabilitation Measures

In the same year the government, in cooperation with the IMF and the World Bank, embarked on a Financial Stabilization Program (FSP) and an Export Action Program (EAP), a medium-term economic recovery program, designed to achieve stabilization and structural change through emphasis on rehabilitation, export growth, and import restraint, was initiated.

The EAP envisioned (a) provision of external assistance to satisfy the immediate import requirements of the major irrigation schemes, (b) a series of rehabilitation projects in the 1980s covering all major irrigation schemes, and (c) policy and institutional reforms to remove major constraints inhibiting higher cotton production and productivity.

The government and the World Bank commenced jointly in 1980 three key studies in the areas of (a) cotton pricing and marketing, (b) production relationships and the recovery, and (c) government supervision and support of parastatals. The government was prompt in implementing recommendations of the studies, which included abolition of the export tax on cotton, improvements in the exchange rate applicable to cotton exports, application of export parity principles for determining the domestic cotton price, replacement of the Joint Account System by the Individual Account System for each crop, announcement of producer prices prior to harvest, and prompt payment for cotton supplied by tenants.

These measures, in addition to the provision of $70 million worth of equipment and spare parts, resulted in a marked revival within two years of cotton production:

	1980–1981	1981–1982	1982–1983
Production (10^3 t)	306	461	573
Yield (t/ha)	0.75	1.26	1.42

The rehabilitation program scored a remarkable success. Appropriate investments restored capabilities of the scheme, and the new appropriate policies and measures created a favorable environment of incentives to the tenants.

As a consequence of these initial successes IDA rehabilitation projects for the Gezira Scheme, the New Halfa Scheme, and a project each for the White and Blue Nile pump schemes are now being implemented. Additional projects involving cotton processing and marketing, as well as research, extension, and training, have been prepared.

EXPERIENCES TO SHARE WITH OTHER DEVELOPING COUNTRIES

Lessons learned from the experiences of the Sudan in the development of irrigated agriculture could benefit developing countries in Africa and other regions. Both successes and failures are relevant.

REFERENCES

Allan, W. N., and R. J. Smith. 1948. Irrigation in the Sudan. Pp. 593–632. *In* J. D. Tothill (ed.) Agriculture in the Sudan. Oxford University Press.

Idris, H. 1975. Agricultural research capabilities and scope in the Sudan. Khartoum: National Council for Research.

Idris, H. 1984. Accelerating food production in Africa. *In* Proceedings of 1984 world food production conference. Honolulu International Minerals and Chemical Corporation.

Moir, T. R. G. 1954. Some aspects of agricultural development in the Sudan. Memoirs of Field Division, no. 5. Khartoum: Ministry of Agriculture, Sudan Government.

Osman, S., and H. E. El Haq. 1974. Irrigation practices and development in the Sudan. Pp. 96–110. *In* Sudan notes and records, vol. 55. Khartoum: Philosophical Society of the Sudan.

Shaw, D. J. 1965. The development and contribution of irrigated agriculture in the Sudan. Pp. 174–224. *In* Agricultural development in the Sudan. Papers for the thirteenth annual conference. Khartoum: Philosophical Society of the Sudan and Sudan Agricultural Society. Sudan Ministry of Agriculture and Irrigation. 1984. Yearbook of agriculture statistics—1984. Khartoum.

56. MAKING INSTITUTIONS WORK—DEVELOPMENT PROGRAM

C. Subramananiam, "River View," Kotturpuram, Madras, India

SUMMARY

The challenges of managing both supply and demand for water are assuming urgency worldwide. Developing countries are making sizable investments in water development, but the projects are yielding poor returns because of poor management, user indifference, and institutional bottlenecks. A major international effort is now necessary to alert all concerned to the dangers of continued haphazard use of water, and to provide technical and financial assistance for bringing about more sensible use of water for all purposes. Sensitive political questions need to be faced before nations will engage in cooperative action. A participative approach that involves users, technologists, and officials for evaluating current trends and for evolving programs of action in each country holds promise of achieving sustained results. Local community involvement is crucial to success. Public sector institutions have a crucial role to play in many aspects of water supply, conservation, and use, and they need to be encouraged to take up a sustained improvement program. At the international level, findings of the present conference need follow-up for identifying country-specific programs of assistance, as well as for evolving a framework for mobilizing resources and monitoring and evaluating results.

"If you wish to establish your reputation among your people", sang the sage by way of advice to his ruler in the Tamil epic "Purananuru" 2,000 years ago, "store great quantities of water in the valleys of your Kingdom. Those who fail to store water will fail to store their glory." The reasoning was simple. Those who give food give life. And food is but the union of land and water. This argument has not lost its validity even today. Successive World Development Reports convey this very message. Only the phraseology has changed.

Perceptions relating to water among the common people are not uniform around the globe. The nomadic tribes in deserts, the inhabitants in arid zones, the residents of foothills with heavy precipitation and fishermen on seacoasts each have their own way of looking at and utilizing this resource. India mirrors this great variety, and 20 percent of the world's irrigated area is in India (Kanwar, 1973, 226).

Historically in India, the initial attitude toward water was one of reverence (with rivers being named after goddesses). In the course of time, however, a number of irrigation cum flood control systems were established. A network of man-made tanks (of which more than 500,000 have survived to this day), percolation ponds, irrigation canals, and drainage channels was constructed. While the rulers took the initiative for the initial investigation for and construction of these works, responsibility for maintenance was generally assumed by the community. There are parallels in Tamil Nadu to the kind of initiative that the inhabitants of the Negev Desert had shown in harvesting rainwater runoff in rough terrain thousands of years ago. The gazetteers compiled by the British record this astonishing achievement (Satya, *Shrava*, 1951, p. 5). Also, the "Grand Anicut" built across the river Kaveri by Karikala Chola nearly 2,000 years ago, continues to serve its purpose even today. The engineering aspects of this solid work of masonry, laid in brick and stone on a sand bed which has stood the test of time, constitute an unheralded wonder of the world.

Population growth, attainment of political independence, and burgeoning economic ambitions have occurred in recent decades in India, as in many other developing countries, providing a new thrust for augmenting irrigation and drinking water supplies. Of the 23 million ha increase in irrigated area that materialized in Asia between 1966 and 1982, 14 million ha was in India alone (Asian Development Bank, 1984, p. 41). As irrigation needs grow, water requirements for domestic, industrial, transportation, and animal uses are also on the increase. Challenges in managing water supply and demand are assuming urgency worldwide. In assessing the nature and dimensions of the problem in the decades to come, we need to take critical stock of our experience in the past and devise policies and institutions that will facilitate a balanced and scientific exploitation of this valuable resource between different regions, uses, and generations.

LESSONS FROM EXPERIENCE

The major lessons that can be drawn from recent experience in water utilization are given below

Indiscriminate Use

In many localities there is a tendency toward indiscriminate water use (National Academy of Sciences, 1974, 2). Paddy tracts in the southeast coast of India provide examples of overindulgent and often indiscriminate use of water for crop cultivation. Local farmers tend to use water at much greater intensity per crop year hectare than agronomists consider necessary or even advisable. This phenomenon is particularly prevalent in areas where water flows from field to field without being regulated through properly designed watercourses. This contributes to waterlogging and erosion of soil and its nutrients and results in loss of productivity. Yet the wasteful practices continue. Any attempt at diverting water to more needy areas is strongly resisted. Vohra estimates that India has already lost at least 6 million ha to waterlogging and salinity and that large additional areas are being affected year after year even in the commands of comparatively new projects (Vohra, 1980, 6). Similar developments have been recorded in Pakistan, Egypt, the United States, and the Soviet Union. Lester Brown cites United Nations data to show that one-tenth of the world's total irrigated area is already waterlogged (Brown, 1981, 25). The obstacle to more rational use appears to be a very localized perspective and lack of awareness among farmers and local leaders of the long-term implications of continued indiscriminate use.

Inefficient Use

A tendency for inefficient use of water, even in areas where it is in short supply, is apparent. The reasons are many and include ignorance of (or lack of access to) water-saving technologies, unenlightened public policy, and unsuitable institutional factors. In the densely crowded agrarian economies of Asia, for instance, land holdings tend to be small and scattered. There are crisscross ridges everywhere, and scientific water distribution arrangements are the exception rather than the rule. Water flow in such an environment erodes rather than enriches the soil. Property laws are often such that over the years the already small holdings are further subdivided into minuscule proportions where the individual farmer acting on his own can hardly be expected to practice any scientific agriculture. Writing on irrigation management in Taiwan, Y. T. Wang of that country's Joint Commission on Rural Reconstruction refers to the chaotic conditions that prevailed in that country before a land consolidation program was initiated (Wang, 1973, 218–19). But the kind of drive for consolidation that Taiwan went through has not occurred in most other countries of Asia.

Lack of Participation

There has been a widespread breakdown of community spirit and farmer participation in arranging even routine maintenance of irrigation works. Irrigation development, on which the state has sunk vast resources under successive Five Year Plans in India, has failed to activate old practices or to set up more formal institutions like those in Taiwan (Stavis, 1974, 105–108) or in Korea (Wade, 1983, 32–33).

Public Policy

Public policy has not responded quickly or substantially to these emerging threats and at times has even accentuated the pressures. In many developing countries there is no effective incentive for good use or disincentive for inefficient use of water by various users. Rich urban dwellers misuse scarce potable water to water their gardens; giant industries pollute major watercourses and render them unfit for use downstream, and affluent farmers resort to overexploitation of groundwater.

Research and Development

Even in terms of research and development priorities in agriculture, it appears that the main effort has been to maximize crop yields per unit of land rather than per unit of land *and* water. There is, no doubt, ongoing research to evolve drought-resistant seed varieties, but concern for the long-term scarcity aspects of water does not appear to have been as explicitly built into research and development programs as the concern for scarcity of land as such.

Fragmented Action

Even where there has been some appreciation of the emerging problems and the need for public intervention, the policies and programs have tended to be isolated and fragmented. Experiences in Asia and the Far East indicate that in most cases centralized or unified water administration did not exist and that the various functions were performed without adequate and effective coordination (ECAFE, 1968). In order to get over this well-identified problem of multiplicity of regulatory and promotional agencies and to ensure a more coordinated approach in the planning and operation of irrigation systems, the concept of an integrated Command

Area Development has been tested in India in some of the new irrigation projects. However, even here the experience has not been very pleasant (Ali, 1982).

TASKS AHEAD

The major tasks facing planners and managers alike as a consequence of the above experience are listed below.

1. Objectives of water policy need to be stated in clear and concrete terms on the national as well as global level, along with a firm commitment to achieve these goals.

2. Prevailing water use policies and practices at various levels and for various purposes must be critically assessed, and guidelines for better water use as part of the overall development strategy must be developed.

3. A technological base must be established in each country to facilitate continual improvements in water management and use.

4. An effective package of incentives and disincentives for water use efficiency by all users must be enforced.

5. A coordinated and participative approach in various aspects of water management must be adopted.

6. Resources must be mobilized to ensure that the needed programs are backed by adequate financial, technological, and physical inputs.

INSTITUTIONAL FRAMEWORK—MICRO AND MACRO, PUBLIC AND PRIVATE

Merely highlighting the dangers inherent in the present pattern of water use around the world would be a useful role for this conference. However, it should reach beyond such a limited objective and indicate how the challenges are to be met. It can provide a useful forum for exploring at least in broad outline the main features of an institutional framework that would be needed to initiate and pursue a sustained program of improvement. Any such framework needs to be highly flexible to respond adequately to differing physical, socioeconomic as well as political environments. Any attempt to impose a rigid framework from above, whatever its theoretical refinement, would find little acceptance and might prove counterproductive.

At the same time bold initiatives are necessary for breaking down political obstacles or other barricades to a rational utilization of at least the major rivers within and between countries. The India-Nepal and the India-Bangladesh river systems provide ready examples from the Indian subcontinent. Similar examples could be cited from the other continents. Existing arrangements are not merely suboptimal in terms of flood control, power generation, and irrigation but positively harmful to the long-term ecological balance. Yet the barriers to cooperative action have so far proved formidable. The question that we might ask ourselves at a gathering like this is: Can we break these barriers by pressing into service eminent individuals of outstanding public reputation and with no bias for or against the interest of any particular country? Their efforts, coupled with the backing of international science and finance, can prod leadership in these countries to work for their mutual benefit. Success in one or two cases initially might prove infectious for the more recalcitrant ones in course of time. Let the first steps in this direction be initiated at this conference.

Much of the action for improved water management will be internal to the countries, more particularly at subnational and local levels. A question that needs to be considered in this context is the role of private and public agencies, respectively. It is possible to argue that governments with so many demands on their time and resources, and with an uninspiring record of achievement in this field in the past, are ill equipped to take on a major role in any new ambitious endeavor to rectify this situation. Voluntary agencies, universities, business corporations, and financial institutions, it may be argued, could instead be encouraged to develop their own networks to interact with users of water directly, which would involve minimum interface with governmental authorities.

I am, however, of the view that in the context of the developing countries, any programs that bypass the authorities can have but marginal impact. It is a fact of life in these countries that governments are involved in virtually every aspect of economic significance to its people. Water, as a vital national resource, is already subject to varying control by governments in these countries. Regulating its use involves sensitive social engineering. No long-term improvement in its use pattern can be brought about unless the governments themselves are convinced of the need for action and are ready to take the proper action. Autonomous institutions, research agencies, and donor institutions nevertheless have a critical role in bringing relevant facts to the attention of the highest decision-making bodies, in highlighting the long-term implications of a policy of continued drift, and in outlining the broad areas of potential assistance by them.

One way to provide additional momentum initially would be to stimulate popular debate on these issues within these countries under the auspices of reputed local institutions and thereby build up public opinion in favor of change.

Another supportive action would be to provide training facilities to both officials and community leaders so that technical capabilities as well as public awareness grow simultaneously.

The assessment of requirements of a program of action in each country and identification of their relative priorities should emerge through a consultative process. however, materials already available do provide some clues in identifying an initial set of water management problems of fairly general relevance. Perhaps this conference could devote some attention to pinpointing critical problem areas that prima facie lend themselves to international assistance.

Here we might distinguish between programs (such as provision of field channels, drainage courses, evaporation and seepage less devices) that are badly needed and can be put into effect on the basis of available know-how on the one hand, and activities that may have to await further refinements in technology and equipment on the other. For the developing countries, the first category itself poses a massive challenge. The international community would be doing a disservice if it were to give the impression that it is going to come up with some miraculous breakthroughs in water-control methodologies or water-sharing agreements which

the countries can then painlessly adopt and from which it can reap rich rewards.

This is not to deny the importance of continued research and development in various facets of water conservation. Adaptive research for localized needs, regular field trials, and systematic diffusion of findings deserve high priority. International assistance could be particularly valuable in the following areas:

- remote-sensing techniques in surveying and mapping different sources of water, particularly groundwater, and in monitoring changing river flows and crop status.
- better techniques of harvesting and storing water to minimize soil erosion and evaporation loss.
- increased irrigation efficiency by reducing loss in conveyance and application.
- evolving cropping systems and cultural practices to take full advantage of available water (e.g., use of saline water) and improving drought resistance.
- recycling of water for the same use (e.g., industrial) and for different uses (e.g., fishing and irrigation).
- formulation of water codes and strengthening the machinery for enforcement.

Assuming that we broadly agree on the need and urgency for international action in this vital area of concern for humanity as a whole, let me say a few words as to how we might approach the question of follow-up action. Possibilities and modalities of acting in concert with ongoing initiatives under the auspices of the United Nations, the World Bank, and other such bodies need to be evaluated, even if it is ultimately decided that we should pursue our main concerns independently. At the minimum we should draw lessons from previous efforts and learn what pitfalls to avoid. A core group could perhaps be identified and entrusted with this task. A budget and a time schedule would also have to be agreed upon.

Assuming that the efforts of this group evoke favorable response and that necessary funding can be ensured, an important step further would be to arrange national-level consultations with political leaders, officials, scientists, and relevant community organizations. The purpose would be to crystallize perspectives and priorities of water management problems relevant to each country in the short run and in the long run. As part of these consultations, willingness to participate in possible areas of international cooperative action, taking note of ongoing national programs, will also need to be delineated.

Nations need to be encouraged and assisted in critically reviewing the prevalent water management practices, identifying specific areas and potential for improvement, and assessing requirements of technology, skill, and finance. This can be followed by a selection of specific programs of international cooperation that would best serve the needs of each country.

Simultaneously, efforts to attract pledges of support—money, manpower, and machines—will need to be pursued with all potential donors. The follow-up institutional arrangements can be given further shape for the purpose of mobilizing international resources on the one hand, and marrying them to national needs on the other, on a continuing basis. Procedures will also have to be built up for ensuring proper use of the aid that is provided and for evaluating results periodically. Ideally, on the basis of mobilized political will and donor support, an institutional network can be thought of at the operating level that minimizes political control in the management of programs. Indeed, the needs of ecosystems rather than the vicissitudes of political boundaries, should become the touchstone for providing assistance. Perhaps the arrangements that have been worked out in the field of crop research, through a partnership of donor agencies and centers of technological excellence, provides one tested model for promoting international collaboration.

In the formulation of programs for international support, it would be necessary to take note of ongoing work and results already achieved in various national and international forums. The temptation to launch comprehensive programs on all aspects, ignoring work already done elsewhere, should be strongly resisted from the outset.

An early kind of program activity that recommends itself is to identify specific demonstration projects drawing upon results achieved at one place for application in other areas. A data bank, a reference service, and a specialists pool are also potential areas of assistance internationally. Recasting legislations and codes relating to water supply and use, methodologies for their more effective application, techniques for successful interdepartmental and interagency cooperation in planning and implementation, and stimulating community awareness and involvement are other possible areas for international support.

We live in an age where techniques for mutual destruction are getting refined and perfected faster than techniques for mutual advancement. Governments seem to be caught in a mad race where there is greater urgency to allocate scarce resources for armaments than for development. Affluence is becoming synonymous with indulgence, even as poverty extends its vise-like grip on millions. Our nonrenewable assets are getting depleted, and our environment is being ravaged remorselessly in the meantime. We can no longer look upon these ominous trends with indifference or a sense of helplessness. There is still room to act, but the time to act is now, before the impending damage proves irreversible.

Enlightened public opinion has to assert itself in every possible way and at every conceivable forum to reverse the trends. Water is in the forefront among the resources that now calls for cooperative and rational management. Let us proceed further with this mission as part of the same endeavor that brought us together at this conference, with optimism tempered by realism, but undeterred by cynicism.

REFERENCES

Ali, H. 1982. Report of the Commission for Irrigation Utilisation. Government of Andhra Pradesh, Hyderabad, India.

Asian Development Bank. 1984. Agriculture in Asia. Manila.

Brown, L. R. 1981. Building a sustainable society. New York–London: W. W. Norton & Company.

Economic Commission for Asia and the Far East (ECAFE). 1968. Water legislation in Asia and the Far East. New York: United Nations.

Kanwar, J. S. 1973. Water management and crop planning in India. *In* Regional workshop on irrigation water management. Manila: Asian Development Bank.

National Academy of Sciences. 1974. More Water for arid lands. Washington, D.C.

Satya, Shrava. 1951. Irrigation in India. Simla: Department of Archaeology.

Stavis, B. 1974. Rural local governance and agricultural development in Taiwan. Ithaca, New York: Cornell University.

Vohra, B. B. 1980. A policy for land water. Sardar Patel Memorial Lectures, Bhavan's Journal. Bombay.

Wade, R. 1983. World Bank is urged to stop, look and listen. In World water. Liverpook, England.

Wang, Y. T. 1973. Development impact and management of irrigation in Taiwan. *In* Regional workshop on irrigation water management. Manila: Asian Development Bank.

57. THE OPTIMUM ROLE OF THE PRIVATE SECTOR IN THE AGRICULTURAL DEVELOPMENT OF LDCs: AN INVESTIGATION OF THE ENTREPRENEURIAL AND DEVELOPMENTAL DYNAMICS OF SMALL PRODUCERS ORGANIZED AROUND A CORPORATE CORE

Ruth Karen, Business International Corporation, New York, New York and Orville L. Freeman

POLICY RECOMMENDATIONS

The successful agribusiness enterprises in developing countries investigated in this study have four major actors:

1. The small farmer-producer who wants to move from subsistence agriculture into an active role in the market economy and is ready to transcend traditional constraints to create socioeconomic conditions that offer greater opportunities for him and his family.

2. The company—foreign, domestic, or joint venture—which envisions the opportunity, takes the risk, and transfers the required technology in all facets of the undertaking.

3. The government of the country in which the enterprise is located (referred to as the "host government"), which promulgates the laws and regulations that directly affect the enterprise and provides and/or supports a range of institutions with which the enterprise necessarily interacts.

4. The industrial country in which the parent company is based, which interacts both with the host government and with the operating enterprise in a number of ways. In this study that industrial country is described as the "donor country," and usually refers either to the United States or to the United Kingdom.

The policy recommendations outlined below address each of the actors separately and have evolved directly from the case histories. However, it is important to recognize that the success of an agribusiness enterprise in a developing country, with success measured in both bottom-line and developmental terms, stands in measurable ration to the degree with which the four actors pursue a coherent policy.

THE SMALL FARMER-PRODUCER

For small farmers in the developing world, the traditional goal has been survival. Generally speaking, they have had neither the resources nor recourse to the ingredients required to move beyond that goal. As a result, rural areas in the developing countries have become increasingly impoverished, and farm children, for whom there was no more family land to cultivate, have moved to the cities. There, most of them have become the denizens of socially and politically incendiary slums.

The systematic approach to agricultural development investigated in this study, in which small farmers are organized around a corporate core, regards the farmer as a vital ingredient of the enterprise, as each of the case histories bears out.

A farmer in the Dominican Republic, participating in the melon-growing venture of a core company (Agro Inversiones), spells out in his own telling terms what the system means in his life:

> I got my own land, under the Dominican Republic's agrarian reform, in 1971. I don't own it, but I have the right to work it for my lifetime, and my son has the same right when I die. It can be taken from me, or from him, only if I sell it, or if I let it lie idle. I don't intend to do either.
>
> Here is my pay-off: From 1972 to 1978, my income was DP10 per tarea [6 tareas = 1 acre]. From 1978 to 1980, it was DP40 per tarea. In 1981, it was DP90 per tarea. Now, since I have moved mostly into melons, and grow two crops a year for Agro Inversiones, my income is DP160 per tarea. I, my wife, and my two eldest sons do most of the work on the farm. For a few weeks during the harvest season, we hire about 15 people to help.
>
> What do I do with the extra income? I spend it on my family, on clothes, on fixing up the house, and mainly on education. Two of my children are in high school, and both intend to go on to university. I want both my boys and my girls to have that opportunity.

THE COMPANY

The assumption here is that the paramount company goal consists of maximizing profit potential, minimizing risk, and achieving a satisfactory return on investment. The research shows that while some trade-offs come into play in all three elements of the company goal, organizing small farmers around a corporate core achieves a satisfactory bottom line more quickly than any alternative form of production organization. For example, the case history of an agribusiness enterprise (pig raising) in Thailand reports an ROI (return on investment) with three dimensions:

> The first dimension is a financial ROI that begins the very first year of operation. Tactically, the company considers the first five years of each project the developmental phase, after which the training and direct supervisory functions of the company are attenuated.
>
> The second dimension of the company's ROI comes into play at that stage when the company encourages the farmers to manage their own affairs via a Board of Directors made up of se-

lected farmers, with the company assuming an advisory role, compensated by a management contract.

The third dimension, operative throughout both processes, is the company providing inputs such as feed and breeding stock, at a reasonable profit, and doing the processing and marketing—at a reasonable profit.

In the long term, the company sees the college-educated children of these prosperous farmers managing their own family farms, with minimal outside services in either technology or management, but becoming increasingly larger customers for the company's products, and sources of supply for the company's processing and marketing activity.

A U.S.-based company operating in the Dominican Republic, without the integrated structure of the Thai company cited above, also reports a satisfactory ROI the first year, and full recovery of invested capital within three years. It should be noted, however, that both cases involve crops with short production periods and, in the case of the Dominican Republic, the special advantage of duty-free access to the U.S. market. For tree crops and other crops with a longer cultivation/production cycle, the calculations for a satisfactory ROI would necessarily involve a different time frame.

For enterprises such as the Dominican Republic undertaking (melons and vegetables for the U.S. winter market), the policy implications, both financial and operational, are clear:

1. Hands-on commitment and involvement at the managerial level, the technical level, and the field supervision level are essential for success. Given these three ingredients, a relatively modest scale of operations can produce a net profit on sales during the first year, and a respectable return on investment, including full recovery of capital, within 2–3 years.

2. This applies even when there is on-site competition for the farmers' output.

3. For export-oriented products, it is vital to have a well-defined market plus a market organization, in the case of a bigger company; or a well-structured relationship with food brokers and wholesalers for a smaller company.

4. Transportation is a major cost consideration, and available options have to be analyzed carefully.

5. Financing, even if available locally at subsidized rates, may not be the most desirable form of credit. Given the snarls and obstacles of bureaucratic delays, it may be more cost-effective for a company to finance farmers directly.

6. From a sociopolitical point of view, in any operation designed for the long term it is advisable for a company, particularly a foreign company, *not* to own land. If land holdings are needed for pilot projects or a nuclear estate, the land should be leased. From a sociopolitical perspective, as well as a productive one, the most desirable arrangement is to work with producer farmers who own their own land and work it largely with their own family members.

In the Philippines, a company with integrated operations in a wide range of food products reports an ROI on its seed-corn enterprise that spills over strategically into other aspects of company operations:

Working directly with small farmers represents a range of business opportunities that strengthen vertical integration of company products and/or provide a synergetic horizontal extension of product lines for the domestic market as well as for export.

A carefully structured outreach program that involves technical support in a number of ways, and includes social activities and contributions to community concerns, formulated on the basis of an ongoing dialogue with relevant community groups, has direct bottom-line results. It helps to create markets for company products; it serves as an innovative aspect of advertising; it alleviates, or even eliminates, law and order problems for company activities; and it creates a relationship with producers that represents potential for additional profitable activities.

While companies, in their feasibility studies for agribusiness ventures in developing countries, have corporate-specific strategies to determine the suitability of soil, climate, water, transportation and appropriate financing mechanisms, generally useful policy implications emerge from the case histories in the areas of marketing, relationships with farmer-producers, management, and macroeconomic aspects of the enterprise.

In *marketing,* vertical integration works best. Thus, in the Philippines, the San Miguel Corporation, with an internally integrated market for its seed-corn enterprise, reports a four-pronged result:

1. A stable quality supply for its feed operations and its downstream animal products.

2. A stronger market for its other product lines, with resulting better profitability.

3. An increased market share of seed corn (the company's market share in 1983 was 24 percent, targets are 33 percent for 1984, 44 percent for 1985, and 50 percent-plus thereafter).

4. A return on investment of 20 percent on funds employed, which includes amortization of research and development activities.

In Turkey, Pinar, a milk-processing operation based in Izmir on the Aegean coast, developed a range of consumer products with which it successfully penetrated the domestic market nationwide, as well as developing an export market, primarily in the Middle East.

In the Sudan, Haggar Ltd. notes that the payback for its tobacco operations is immediate because it is vertically integrated in the production of blended cigarettes, which the company manufactures and sells. In contrast, the payback for the company's coffee and tea operations not only takes longer because of the nature of the crop but also requires volume and/or processing facilities for added value. The company points out that the highest payoff is obtained when coffee and tea operations are extended to include packaging and retailing.

In *company relationships with farmer-producers,* farmer loyalty is vital. The secret of success in this relationship is stated succinctly by an executive of Adams International's operation in Thailand: "You have to deal with the farmer not only as a producer, but as a person."

The multi-facetedness of this process is spelled out by the manager of a major milk processing facility in Turkey, who couches his recommendations in corporate-specific terms, which, nevertheless, are applicable to all agribusiness undertakings in developing countries.

> Our company is aware of the fact that its own success depends not only on the increased population of milch cows it can induce and the higher yield and quality of milk it can help farmers produce. It knows that in Turkey, for small farmers, an economically viable and developmentally desirable farm requires an appropriate mix of livestock and crops, with a balance of food and cash crops. It knows, as well, that achieving this mix and this balance calls for sociopolitical and cultural skills as well as economic organization and technical expertise.
>
> Current plans call for a broad diversified production base that would provide a market, and act as a technology transfer agent for such integrated development.
>
> What should probably be added to the company's plans is a systematic effort to broaden its existing base to include among its shareholders as many farmer cooperatives and individual small farmers as is feasible, given economic realities.

As an operational matter, establishing a satisfactory ongoing relationship with its producers requires that the company offer not only a fair purchasing contract, but an appropriate mix of four additional contributions to the farmer's welfare. These are:

a. Competent, dependable extension services that are responsive to the farmer's needs not only in the product he furnishes the company but in other activities important to the farmer's economic base. This means giving the farmer whatever help the extension agent can in the cultivation of crops or the raising of livestock that does not represent direct income of immediate sourcing for the company. It is vital, in this context, for the company to encourage a balanced use of land by the farmer, i.e., a division between food crops and cash crops that adequately meets the direct needs both of the company and of the farmer and his family.

Typically, with small farmers in developing countries this balance is tantamount to having no more than one-third to one-half of the farmer's land devoted to the market crop, with the remainder allocated to food crops for family consumption or for sale to the local market. An important fringe benefit of this arrangement is that the company-farmer relationship does not result in economic dependencies with explosive sociopolitical overtones.

b. Improving and enhancing, as far as corporate resources permit, the social environment of the farmer and his family. This includes, but is not limited to, sports, health, education, and access to appropriate consumer goods.

c. Acting as a catalyst between the farmer and existing government institutions designed to serve the farmer. In most developing countries, competent bridge-building is required between small farmers and their needs and the bureaucracies intended to serve these needs.

d. Assisting farmers, in locally appropriate ways, in structuring and strengthening their own organizations, and organizations involving their families and communities. Hindustani Lever Ltd. (a subsidiary of Unilever), operating in the district of Etah, state of Uttar Pradesh, one of the least developed regions of India, has formulated "Ten Commandments for Rural Development," which, with relevant modifications and alterations, are applicable in any LDC (less developed country):

1. Establish credibility through honesty and integrity. These qualities have to be not only internal but externally visible as well. They are best conveyed by committed supervisors who are honest, apolitical, and corruption-proof, and can earn the respect both of elected officials from the village level up and of appointed civil servants from the district magistrate down.

2. Ensure that plans are generated at the grassroots by the farmers themselves. There is an initial hesitation by the farmers to make such plans, but the resistance can be broken down by supervisors who know their business and their communities, and by management trainees who actually live in the villages. Both the supervisors and the management trainees have to establish the kind of relationship with the farmer in which they can say "no" as well as "yes" and still retain the respect and trust of the villagers.

3. Set up an effective organizational structure for follow-through. Frequently, government and voluntary agencies have marvelous ideas and brilliant concepts but no one who is competent or interested enough to follow through.

4. Provide or organize financial support. The need is for on-site banking institutions that operate effectively at the village level.

5. Build a viable communications system, both physical and people-to-people. This includes roads that are accessible throughout the year, and every form of transportation.

6. Upgrade agricultural practices. This involves everything from water management to crop rotation, from seed improvement to livestock care.

7. Introduce animal husbandry, not as a replacement for existing cultivation of food or cash crops, but as a viable secondary occupation for the farm family.

8. Promote appropriate alternative energy resources, such as biomass, fueled by cow dung.

9. Aid village industries, particularly those relevant to women.

10. Help to build health and educational infrastructure.

In *management*. For the top management of the enterprise, at least initially, the company, wherever based, must reach for the best: not the best it can spare, but the best it can muster. This applies to both executive and technical staffing. It is important to recognize that "the best," in this context, has to be defined in a way that exceeds narrow, or even broad-gauged, expertise. At the executive side, the top manager must not only know his product and his market but be sensitive to people in their social and cultural context. On the technical side, crop knowledge and people knowledge are pragmatically intertwined and equally important. The history of agribusiness companies in developing countries is replete with problems and outright failures created by executives with unquestionable technical and managerial expertise who failed to relate effectively to the people in the undertaking's host country environment.

When the company is a foreign concern, it is also available to work as assiduously as feasible toward the goal of replacing foreign managment with local management. Systematic and thoughtful recruiting and training programs designed to achieve this goal are a major ingredient in the success of the enterprise over the long term.

For all companies, whether foreign or domestic, "people contact" works best when it is closest to the peer level. For example, one company discovered that for its hands-on extension services to farmer-producers, a team of local graduates from agricultural institutions did not work out. What did work was a system of recruiting extension agents from the farm families themselves and giving these best and brightest farmers the technical and administrative training they needed to become effective and respected extension agents.

At a more senior level of peer relationship, companies have found that local research and development is conducted most effectively when host-country technical and professional people—and indeed more adventurous and experiment-minded farmers—are involved in the process as soon as feasible.

In the *macroeconomic area,* a successful agribusiness enterprise produces visible economic and social results that penetrate the community both horizontally and vertically in measurable developmental terms. This enhances the image of the private sector in general and, where applicable, multinational corporations in particular; and validates both in their role as important engines of growth. In most developing countries, such image enhancement is important. In some, it is crucial.

Another macroeconomic consideration is the fact that successful agribusiness enterprises involving small farmers in the developing countries substantially raise the purchasing power of these small farmers and their families. There are today approximately 1 billion small farmers in the developing world. If, by way of the simplest of calculations, the income of these farmers were raised by only U.S.$100 per year, the stimulative effect on the global economy would be staggering, with multiplier effects not only for agricultural output but for manufactured goods and services as well, both in the developing countries and in the industrialized world.

THE HOST COUNTRY

Almost without exception, political leaders in the host countries today recognize the importance of agricultural development. Indeed, agriculture is, and always has been, the key to economic development. No country in human history, with the exception of a few merchant or military city-states, has ever prospered and built a sound economy without a solid agricultural base.

The problem is that while the recognition of this is prevalent, most host countries are at least baffled, and more often overwhelmed, by the magnitude, the complexity, and the political problems involved in carrying forward an effective, sustained program of agricultural development. There is no doubt that sound agricultural policies are difficult to develop and carry out. The time span required to put into place an appropriate land/people balance; to make available credit and necessary inputs to the grower; and to construct stor-

age, processing, and marketing capacity is longer than the usual time span of a political officeholder. In addition, carrying out a sound, meaningful agricultural policy calls for changes which, by their very nature, shake up traditional social and management patterns, with the result that changes are fiercely resisted. This is true in industrialized as well as in developing countries, as even current EEC and U.S. policies demonstrate.

The problems host countries need to address most urgently fall into ten categories:

1. *Food policies that have an urban bias.* Food policies with a persistent urban bias may have short-term political payoff, but are clearly counterproductive in the long haul. They slight agricultural producers, undercut production, and motivate mass population movements from country to city, creating in the process the socially explosive slums that bedevil almost every host country.

The clearest manifestation of this urban bias is price policy, with governments using a range of price-setting mechanisms to keep producer prices low, sometimes even below cost. An illustrative example, with counterparts in every host country, is the support price of cotton in Turkey. That price was set at T£70 (in 1983) when the market price was T£150.

2. *Agricultural taxation.* In most host countries, the bias against farmer-producers' manifest in pricing policies is equally prevalent in taxation policies. Agricultural output is taxed at too high a rate, a policy that extends even to such measures, cleary counterproductive from a macroeconomic viewpoint, as levying substantial taxes on agricultural exports and on imports required for optimum output in the agribusiness sector.

3. *Exchange rates and exchange rate controls.* In many host countries, exchange rates that overvalue the local currency are maintained, often for image concerns that have no realistic economic base. These currency value distortions are particularly harmful to farmers producing for export.

A recent example of a reasonably policy in this area, leading to productive results, was a policy implemented by the Dominican Republic, which introduced a multi-tier exchange rate, with the most realistic rate available to exporters of nontraditional products, specifically including agricultural products.

4. *Restrictions on internal food movement.* Some host countries actually have laws and/or regulations that restrict domestic movement of food crops, mainly for political reasons. In many, indeed in most of the host countries, internal food movement is effectively restricted, and to a considerable extent prevented, by inadequate infrastructure and transportation, as well as by inadequate and quite often nonexistent storage facilities.

5. *Credit availability.* While most host countries make an effort to provide agricultural credit, with widely varying degrees of resource allocation and administrative competence, none of the host countries in the study has yet managed to get anywhere near enough credit to the small farmers, who constitute the backbone of the agricultural sector. Indeed, the case histories indicate that with rare exceptions it is only when private sector companies, foreign or domes-

tic, supply supervised credit themselves or act as catalysts and/or mediators between farmer-producers and host country financial institutions that small farmers actually get the financial assistance which, in theory, has been designed for them.

6. *Redistribution of land.* Evidence around the world has demonstrated that the family farm, with a land holding adequate to apply modern technology effectively, is the most productive size. The incentive that results when the producer benefits directly from his efforts cannot be duplicated by large holdings whether they are privately held, communal, cooperative, or state owned. Results from the factory-sized organization of state farms and large collectives in the Soviet Union are dramatic demonstrations of how not to organize agriculture. A system whereby the producer on the soil benefits directly from his efforts is the single most important element in increasing productivity. In most places in the world, this means producer ownership, and it requires egalitarian land policies, adequately supported by the government. Adequate support, in this context, can be defined as a network of physical and social infrastructures that make possible economically rewarding farm production and provide enough social services to induce farm families to resist the lure of the cities.

A demonstrative example of successful agrarian reform and its results is the effort made by the Dominican Republic in the Azua valley. The reform, allocating land to family farmers, was complemented by a web of infrastructure services, including irrigation, electrification, farm-to-market roads, effective credit institutions, health and education facilities, and help with housing. The result was a 300 percent increase in per capita income in less than a decade.

7. *Expropriation or nationalization of food industries.* A number of host countries have pursued such policies, with results that range from paralysis to disaster. Every case history in this study showed that competitive government enterprises required 2 to 5 times the resources that companies employed, and took at least twice, and in some instances 3 and 4 times as long, to achieve comparable results.

8. *Political patronage and bureaucratic ineptness.* Where government is involved in providing or supporting services to small farmers, it is desirable to make farmer productivity, not political patronage, the yardstick. In the Philippines, for example, where the KKK (Kilusang Kabuhayan at Kaunlaran or National Livelihood Program) is generally assessed as being both imaginative and sound in the design of its programs, the implementation of these programs is hampered by the fact that too much of the KKK's money still goes to feudal leaders in the countryside and their political allies, instead of being channeled to the small producing farmer. If small farmers were supported more effectively, desirable economic and political results could be achieved. Farmer income and community standing would increase, and the political leadership, now very hierarchical in the rural areas, would have to listen more attentively to its constituents.

An illustration of obstructive bureaucratic ineptness occurs in India, where the effectiveness of a comprehensive set of services the government offers its rural population is marred by bureaucratic corruption and by paperwork too incomprehensible and too cumbersome for villagers to understand and deal with. At present, the paperwork required for villagers to obtain any government service is daunting to a point where the overwhelming majority of the rural population simply has no way of obtaining the service to which it is entitled.

9. *Private sector involvement.* If host governments want to attract and support private sector activity in agriculture, domestic or foreign, the host country government will have to make clear its commitment to agriculture, and its determination to implement policies it has proclaimed, and to honor promises it has made. This includes, but is not limited to, access to foreign currency; admittance of necessary expatriates; prompt approval of necessary imports; and, as noted above, the development of needed infrastructure. Perhaps most important, it requires a commitment not only in the political and governmental institutions at the top but also in provinces and localities. Concurrently, the political leadership at all levels must lead the way in building public understanding and support of this commitment to the country's agricultural base.

10. *Relations with multinational corporations.* Most governments' relations with multinational corporations in the agribusiness sector, whose technology, organization, processing, and marketing expertise can make a major impact, have several special aspects of complexity. A blueprint for mutual understanding and successful collaboration is limned below.

a. *Profitability and responsibility.* Both multinational corporations (MNCs) and developing countries must recognize the dual, fundamental facts that (1) private companies are (and by their structure must be) motivated to make a profit on their operations and investments, and that (2) host governments are (and naturally must be) concerned about the development of their countries. Each side should clearly recognize the legitimate interests of the other. The essential point is that governments must allow MNCs to make and remit a reasonable profit, while MNCs must acknowledge and fulfill the full range of their economic and social development responsibilities to the host countries. Further, it should be recognized by both sides that contributions to the progress of a developing country can be made in many forms, both economic and noneconomic (e.g., training and educating people), and that all forms of contribution applicable to each investment should be given full recognition.

b. *Information and reporting procedures.* Access to certain kinds of information is often a key point of contention between MNCs and developing countries. On the one hand, governments often feel that MNCs are "secretive" and do not fully reveal their activities and practices. On the other, companies are sensitive about proprietary information getting into the wrong hands—for example, commercial competitors or social adversaries. If developing countries wish MNCs to reveal sensitive information to tax and other government regulatory authorities, they must be able to guard against the misuse of that information.

c. *Technology.* Technology in the broadest sense—including material, managerial, marketing, organizational and other skills, as well as advanced technical information such as secret know-how—is at the heart of the problem differentiating developed from developing countries. Developed countries should, in the overall context of seeking to assist and aid countries working hard to improve themselves, address this problem and seek to facilitate the transfer of technology. However, MNCs that are private properties cannot and should not be expected to give away skills and knowledge that may have taken years (if not decades), as well as great expense, to develop. Nor is it reasonable that a country should expect to get something for nothing. Reasonable payments for technological contributions by MNCs to developing countries should be expected. If the technology is continuously updated by injections of fresh advances, these too should be compensated. However, payments should cease after a number of years in which new injections do not occur.

d. *Employment and labor.* Countries should clearly outline and communicate their manpower objectives and expectations to MNCs, and MNCs should do their best to fulfill those objectives. Where appropriate, free union activity should be permitted, but MNCs should not be picked out as targets for demands not made of local companies. MNCs should pay prevailing rates as a minimum; on the other hand, if they do more than the minimum, either in terms of direct pay or of other benefits and fringes (e.g., housing, schooling, lunch programs), the effect of such costs on the MNC's local operations should be taken into account by the host government.

e. *Consumer protection.* Minimum international health and safety standards should be worked out, and a standardized international labeling system introduced. Any prohibitions or restrictions in process or product imposed by home countries should be revealed to host countries.

f. *Competition and market structure.* Countries and MNCs should work out export and purchasing policies at the time investments are made, and they should clearly establish the length of time that such policies (and any restrictions on them) are to be in effect.

g. *Transfer pricing.* Transfer pricing is a difficult and extremely complex area of international business. At the outset, two things should be honestly recognized: first, by the host country, that the subject cannot be dealt with by simplistic slogans or formulas, and second, by the MNC, that there have in fact been cases of serious abuse in pricing policies.

A reasonable transfer price for a product imported into a developing country for further use in an MNC operation in that country will cover the full costs (including R&D and engineering costs) involved in making and shipping that product, plus a fair profit on the *imported product.* The transfer price should not include any "hidden" forms of return to the MNC, such as special services rendered by parent company specialists that are not reimbursed (or not permitted to be reimbursed) by the government or central bank of the host country subsidiary. Companies are sometimes tempted to take out returns for their investments via the transfer price when they are not permitted to charge what they consider reasonable royalties, service fees, trademark fees, and the like. It is the interrelationship of all these factors—affecting both local subsidiary and parent company profits—that makes transfer pricing such a complex area. The only reasonable way to approach this problem is through openness and honesty on both sides: through recognition that constructive economic activity is entitled to profit for its efforts, but that, at the same time, considerations of simple humanity and relative ability to pay must temper specific expectations of return.

h. *The economic role of women.* Both host countries and MNCs must address attentively, constructively, and immediately the economic role of women, particularly in agriculture. Women do 78 percent of the farmwork in developing countries, including production, processing, and marketing. Though results and needs vary from region to region and from culture to culture, some elements of the effects of technology transfer on women are constant. Technology—and especially the operation of large machinery—is traditionally seen as work for men. In agriculture, this leaves women both with a greater workload in manual tasks (some of which they will pass on to children) and also with a loss of prestige or pride of place in the community.

At the same time, women throughout the developing world are interested in domestic technology and in crop processing and storage technology that will lighten their workload. Host countries and MNCs need to include women in the planning stages of development strategy, particularly in the agricultural sector, thereby enhancing family solidarity and offering greater possibilities for the long-term success of the family farm.

MNCs must remember that dealing with farmer-producers involves women as well as men and, in one way or another, the entire farm family.

An Evolutionary Process

A description of the evolution of host government thinking vis-à-vis agribusiness, with clear policy implications, is offered by a senior private sector executive in Thailand who earlier served in the public sector at the cabinet level. He said:

> Initially, the Thai government pursued what was essentially a welfare policy vis-à-vis the farmer. It treated the farmer as a backward child, poor and uneducated, and provided him with handouts in the form of free seed, subsidized fertilizer and support prices. But it offered neither the full package of know-how and services nor the motivation to make him self-supporting.
>
> In addition, the government's attitude toward the private sector in agriculture was that the private sector would exploit the farmer and was therefore not to be trusted. This attitude is beginning to change as the government realizes that it cannot create meaningful rural development alone. At this stage, the government is thinking in terms of cooperation from the private sector in rural development, and has long-term intentions of encouraging private sector activity in agribusiness, with the government gradually pulling out.
>
> A conceptual difference remains between the government and the private sector of what rural development is and means. The government is still inclined to think of rural development as helping poor farmers in subsistence areas, while the private sec-

tor thinks of rural development as creating and supporting motivated farmers to cultivate products that meet market criteria.

Conceptually, what is needed on the government side is the recognition that any country, in order to industrialize successfully, must have a strong agricultural base. Sound development is not possible by leapfrogging the agricultural component. A sound agricultural base raises farmer income which, in turn, increases demand for consumer industries; and that, in turn, creates the need and market for heavy industry. All industrialized countries, and all successful developing countries, have followed this pattern.

In this process, governments must remember that the private sector company is not a development agency, but it is an agent—a very dynamic agent—in the development process.

THE DONOR COUNTRY

Donor countries—if they are prepared to formulate the appropriate long-term policies, commit the indicated financial resources, and follow through with the required implementation at both the diplomatic and the administrative levels—can play a major, positive role. They can exercise an important influence in guiding host countries toward formulating appropriate policies and implementing sound practices, thereby laying the foundation for sustainable economic and social development.

They can also furnish practical support and concrete incentives to private sector risk-takers, domestic and foreign, who are prepared to put on the line their expertise, technology, and shareholders' money, to launch agricultural ventures that can make a meaningful contribution to the goal of meaningful development.

At the *policy level*, donor countries must impress the governments of host countries with the imperative of making a clear commitment to the importance of the agricultural sector, its growth and expansion. This commitment must include specific undertakings to set product price levels that will stimulate the acceptance of new and, in many cases, untried technology and cultivation methods by small growers.

As a political issue (clearly not an easy one to confront), this means that host governments must be persuaded to formulate and support an adequate agricultural policy rather than a cheap food policy. There is no doubt that this will require wisdom, insight, and political courage from host country leaders, who will need the staunchest possible support from donor nations.

This support must be expressed and delivered not only in donor country capitals but, on an articulate and consistent basis, in the host countries. Donor country diplomatic posts, starting at the ambassadorial level, need to understand that providing this support is a high-priority item on their overall diplomatic mandate.

At the *implementation level*, ambassadors and the directors of donor country aid programs should be directed to make contact at the highest level with the government of the host country in which they serve, beginning with the chief of state and including all appropriate ministers as well as other relevant government institutions. The thrust of this effort should not be to exercise pressure in the usual sense, but to convey unmistakably the support of the donor government for an active agricultural policy directed at the small farmer and implemented by the private sector.

For the United States specifically, it would be important to strengthen the staff of the Agency for International Development (AID) director in the host country by assigning, at the highest possible level, a representative of the Bureau for Private Enterprise, with competence for and insight into private sector approaches and operations.

To host countries prepared to follow the policies described above, donor countries should offer the maximum assistance feasible in constructing the infrastructure networks, both physical and social, that will provide optimum conditions for agricultural growth through the instrument of small farmer-producers acting in a private sector context.

To the *private sector*—local or multinational—donor countries can provide a number of practical services that will help reduce the considerable and inevitable risk inherent in all agricultural enterprises: risks exacerbated in developing countries.

Specifically, donor countries can: (1) finance or participate in the financing of feasibility studies; (2) provide appropriate insurance or reinsurance; (3) supply financing for small farmer-producers in the form of supervised credit. This financing can be channeled through existing host government financial institutions where these are competent and capable of reaching the small farmer. Where this is not the case, supervised credit can be channeled through the private sector company, local or multinational, that works directly with small farmer-producers and whose own interest in the farmers' economic performance dovetails with that of the institution or organization that supplies the financing; (4) offer the services of development experts with a sound grasp of economic realities and hands-on experience in working with institutions, communities, and families in developing countries. Such experts could help companies—especially, of course, foreign companies—to address some of the sensitive cultural, social, and sociopolitical issues that inevitably arise when traditional practices and methods are altered to achieve maximum production. These development experts could, where indicated, help build farmer organizations that would facilitate company negotiations and, where advisable, work with intermediate institutions to achieve a harmonious integration of the goals of the private sector company, the small farmer-producer, and the host country.

These experts could be furnished by donor countries either to the company or to the host country on a reimbursable basis.

ON-SITE SUGGESTIONS

Case histories in this study yielded policy recommendations from on-site sources that concretize the general recommendations outlined and provide some specific additions.

From Thailand

In the past, US policy has channeled AID funds only to governments and to the military. The new emphasis on the private sector, and direct bilateral contact between the private sector of the US and Thailand, with government encouragement and support, is likely to bring a positive dynamic to the entire aid process. The allocation of USAID resources to bringing together the private sector of the donor country with the appropriate partner in the recipient country will undoubtedly have more immediate and direct results than channeling funds to government organizations and institutions, where demonstrable development results may or may not be achieved.

From the Sudan

Three positive action-points seem plausible:

(1). To find, or create, mechanisms that will channel funds as expeditiously and inexpensively as possible to "bush planters" for the production of cash crops to supplement their food crops and raise their living standard.

(2). To devise ways in which a portion of counterpart funds (which will amount to the equivalent of $100 million in 1984) can be channeled to the private sector.

(3). Using whatever policy-making leverage the U.S. government has to persuade the government of Sudan that encouraging private investment in agribusiness would be an effective method to make use of Sudan's comparative advantage of arable land to raise the living standards of its people and to contribute meaningfully to adjusting the presently lopsided balance of payments.

From Turkey

First, the donor country can exercise its persuasive powers to move the Turkish government toward a policy of letting the private sector do what it does efficiently and effectively while concentrating public sector attention on infrastructure undertakings, economic and social, that are beyond the private sector's competence or resources.

Donor countries should provide scholarships for junior and middle management, not only in the public sector, but in the private sector as well.

Some USAID funds could be allocated specifically for the importation of high-yield cattle and of frozen semen from the U.S.

From the Philippines

Donor country funds should be channeled, at least in part, through the private sector in the agribusiness area. Such funds could be earmarked, for example, for appropriate research and development as well as a range of other private sector activities in agribusiness designed to make small farmers optimally productive and increase their earning capabilities and purchasing capacity. An example of how such donor country funds could be used in innovative ways is the creation of a pilot project in which the private sector would support a group of farmers organized as a cooperative or association by guaranteeing financing, providing technology, and monitoring the farmers' activities for a profit and loss orientation.

For the United States specifically, a final policy recommendation manifests an additional dimension relating to the vital role of the United States as leader of the free world. That dimension was limned in a recent editorial of *Financier: The Journal of Private Sector Policy:*

At a time when the world has grown bitter and skeptical about U.S. leadership, agriculture could be the way for this country to reclaim the moral high ground it occupied not so many years ago, when it devoted its vast unharmed industrial power to rebuilding the world after World War II. In those helping, confident years, the U.S. exemplified leadership, in a moral as well as a material way.

It has the stuff to do it again—to meet a great and growing material need, to feed the starving, to kindle hope, to regain confidence.

58. MAKING INSTITUTIONS WORK—A SCIENTIST'S VIEWPOINT

Norman E. Borlaug, Distinguished Professor of International Agriculture, Texas A&M University, College Station, Texas

Those of us who have been involved in attempting to assist food deficit nations to increase food production are especially aware of the constraints imposed on crop yields and production by moisture shortages during certain critical phases of plant development. The constraints of water on potential food production are greatest in semiarid and tropical regions where temperatures are favorable for crop development throughout the year.

Only within the last two decades has much attention been given to breeding new crop varieties specifically for greater drought tolerance. However, it is my belief that for many decades much of the benefit derived from agronomic research and its application, which has collectively resulted in higher grain yields (e.g. fallow, stubble mulch, minimum tillage, weed control, and correction of soil infertility, combined with use of improved crop varieties), is primarily the result of better utilization of soil moisture.

Unfortunately, it is only in time of widespread famine resulting from crop failures triggered by drought, such as exist in many African countries at present, that the world's attention is focused on the vital importance of water for the well-being of mankind. Moreover, it is only in time of crisis that most of us reflect on the importance of all of the interacting factors that affect crop production and the availability of food.

It is at such times that urban people in the affluent developed nations, who know very little about the agriculture of their own country, ask questions about why agriculture remains so primitive and unproductive in the developing nations despite more than three decades of foreign technical assistance programs designed to correct its deficiencies.

The neglect of the agricultural sector in development programs in virtually all developing nations, worsened by cheap food policies that favor the urban consumer minority, has contributed to perpetuating a stagnant, low yielding traditional agricultural production system. Exploding population growth and resultant food demand have outpaced the ability of traditional agriculture to produce the required food. Moreover, inadequate economic support for agricultural education, research, and extension programs in developing nations has made it impossible to develop improved production technologies capable of coping with the increased demand for food. Finally, the inadequately financed young research and extension programs are further handicapped in virtually every developing country by a bloated bureaucracy that further limits their efficiency.

SOME FACTORS THAT INFLUENCE THE EFFECTIVENESS OF FOREIGN TECHNICAL ASSISTANCE PROGRAMS

I have spent the past four decades attempting to assist farmers, scientists, and political leaders of many food-deficit countries of Latin America, Asia, and Africa in increasing their food production. It has been both a frustrating and gratifying experience. In some cases the results have been spectacular, while in others they have been only modest.

I would like to share with you some of my experiences relating to foreign agricultural technical assistance programs. At the outset let me emphasize that there is no fast-fix technological solution that can assure the rapid transformation of a stagnant, traditional, low yielding agrarian agricultural system into one that is highly productive and modern. Essential ingredients for such a transformation are: (1) the development of a corps of well-trained and highly motivated scientists, (2) a well-executed multidiscipline research program to develop a reliable and appropriate package of improved technology capable of increasing yields by 50 to 100 percent when properly applied, (3) widespread demonstration on farms of the potential benefits of the new technology, and (4) the "marriage" of the new technology to economic policies that will stimulate its widespread adoption by farmers.

This is a slow process, especially when an attempt is made to transform a traditional agriculture system in a country where there are few trained scientists. Experience in a number of developing countries indicates it takes 20 to 25 years to identify, train and provide adequate research experience for a sufficiently large number of young scientists and technicians so that a national research institute can be organized and staffed effectively with the capability of carrying out an effective research, extension, and production program. While the team is being trained, foreign technical assistance personnel can be very useful, if properly educated and trained, in helping national programs to organize and execute research, extension, and production programs.

Experience has shown that no matter how excellent and spectacular the research is in each scientific discipline, its application in isolation will have little or no positive effect on crop production. Consequently, I have been forced to become an integrator across scientific disciplines in order to develop a reliable package of production technologies capable of dramatically increasing yields when it is properly applied. Moreover, new production technologies must be tested on hundreds of farms over a range of soil and climatic conditions in order to establish both their potential to increase yield and, in the process, establish the level of risk likely to be encountered in the use of new technologies under farm conditions. Finally, I have found that once a package of improved production technologies has been developed, verified for reliability and widely demonstrated, it must be "married" to a governmental economic policy that will encourage and permit its adoption by the majority of small farmers to increase food production.

I would like to comment briefly about why I believe so many of the world's foreign agricultural technical assistance programs are ineffective.

In the first place, the turnover among scientific personnel is too frequent. It takes from six to eight years for an expatriate scientist to become thoroughly familiar with the order of importance of various constraints that limit yield and production in a host country and to develop the research information, improved varieties and agronomic practices capable of overcoming these obstacles. Moreover, scientists must develop, evaluate, and establish the reliability of the technological package of improved practices on many farms and, while doing this, gain the confidence of the scientists of the host country and of its farmers, policy makers, and political leaders. All this is required to convince leaders of the need for a sound, stimulatory economic agricultural policy that will encourage widespread, timely adoption of new technology by farmers and, in the process, increase food production. Unfortunately, expatriate scientists in most foreign assistance programs remain only two to three years at a given post before being shifted back to their home country or to another developing country. With this handicap it is not surprising that they are relatively ineffective.

Another factor that reduces the effectiveness of technological assistance programs is that most expatriate scientists want to confine their research to their own discipline. It is more comfortable to stand and work in the shadow of the tree of your own speciality without acknowledging that the forest is made up of many trees of different sizes and usually of several species. What is also needed to manage the forest properly are a few venturesome scientists who are both comfortable and willing to integrate across the shadows (disciplines) cast by all the trees in the forest and thereby assemble a package of improved production practices capable of increasing and sustaining the production of the "forest" as a whole. Finally, many foreign assistance programs are organized so that the expatriate scientist operates strictly as a consultant, which limits his effectiveness, in contrast to where the expatriate scientist actively participates as a "hands-on" collaborator.

THE CURRENT AFRICAN FOOD PROBLEM

Let us now examine the cause of the present food crisis in African countries and possible means of mitigating the misery it has brought. In recent months the international news media have focused the world's attention on the human tragedy that is widespread in many of the drought-stricken countries of Africa, especially Ethiopia and the Sudan. To most citizens of the affluent nations who have never personally experienced hunger, the tragic scenes of starving people and their dying animals staggering aimlessly across desolate, drought-stricken landscapes in search of food and water are deplorable and incomprehensible.

When one speaks of the world food shortage, however, one must recognize that in reality, there are three intertwined aspects of this problem. The first is the need to produce sufficient food to meet the needs of the present world population of 4.8 billion, while at the same time assuring the potential for expanding production to provide the additional food required for the 84 million people being added to the population annually. The second predicament is in trying to assure equity of distribution of food; this is complicated by poverty resulting from lack of purchasing power at two different levels in food deficit nations. At the governmental level, a shortage of foreign exchange often limits the amount of food imports that can be made by a food-deficit nation, even when there are ample stocks available in exporting nations. Even after adequate food has been imported into food-deficit countries there remains the problem of equity of distribution at the consumer level. Many low-income families lack purchasing power because of unemployment or underemployment and are unable to buy adequate food. The paradox of the current world food situation is that while famine is widespread in Africa, huge surpluses in the United States and Canada have depressed agricultural prices and are driving many farmers into bankruptcy.

The third factor that must be considered in order to assure a stable world food supply is the year-to-year variation in production resulting from unfavorable weather (e.g., droughts, untimely frosts), and losses caused by disease and insect pests. Consequently, an adequate world reserve of grain must be carried in stock as insurance against a poor harvest. If this reserve increases too much, as is currently the case, it depresses grain prices to a level which is a disincentive to production. The middle course must be steered to meet the needs of both consumers and producers.

The seriousness of the current famine in Africa mandates that a two-pronged approach be used to attain a stable solution to the problem. In the short term, emergency food aid must be provided to alleviate the suffering of those left destitute by drought. In the longer term, means must be found to increase the productivity of African agriculture.

Many public and private organizations have recently given generously to provide emergency food for the hungry and suffering in Africa, especially in Ethiopia and the Sudan. It is essential that this aid be continued until the drought is broken. Unfortunately, the effects of food shortages, undernutrition and malnutrition are not restricted to these two countries, but are widespread in more than 20 countries.

Regrettably, most donors, both private and governmental, believe that once the drought is broken agricultural production will promptly recover and again provide an abundance of food. This will not happen. Over the past 15 years the rate of increase in food production has been falling behind the rate of increasing demand for food, caused by explosive population growth. Many fail to understand the limitations on yield and production imposed by traditional agricultural methods. Moreover, they do not comprehend that the present disasters, in a large part, are the result of long-term neglect by political leaders of the agricultural sector in economic development programs.

Since about 80 to 85 percent of the total population in most African countries are subsistence farmers, the only practical way to improve their income and standard of living is to improve production and sale of agricultural products. Moreover, increased food production will also reduce the threat of recurring famine.

A striking similarity can be seen between the food deficit, famine, drought and stagnant agricultural production conditions now present in Africa, and those which existed in India, Pakistan, and the People's Republic of China from 1960 to 1966.

During the food crisis of India and Pakistan from 1962 to 1966, high yielding, semi-dwarf, rust-resistant wheat varieties, together with a package of improved agronomic production practices, were introduced from Mexico. The package of improved management production practices was tested on hundreds of farms in India and Pakistan over a period of three years with modifications made as needed to fit local soil and climatic conditions. The revised package of improved practices was then married to an economic policy that provided fertilizer, seed of the improved semi-dwarf varieties, and credit to purchase them. Also, an announcement was made by the government before planting that the farmer would receive a price for his wheat at harvest equivalent to the international market price. With these provisions in place, a national wheat production campaign was launched in both countries, based on the importation of 60,000 tons of seed from Mexico in 1965 and 1966 (and two years later in rice) that increased wheat production spectacularly. The dramatic jump in production by 1968, dubbed the "Green Revolution," had its genesis in the first foreign agricultural technical assistance program, known as the Cooperative Mexican Government—Rockefeller Foundation Agricultural Program, which was launched in 1943.

What is needed now to alleviate food shortages is a "Green Revolution" in sorghum and maize production in African countries where these cereals are important basic foods. The time is right. Considerable potentially valuable scientific data and a number of improved crop varieties are now available to fuel such a revolution. During the past fifteen years the international centers for agricultural research—the International Maize and Wheat Improvement Center (CIMMYT), in Mexico, and the International Crops Research Institute for the Semi-Arid Tropics (ICRISAT), in India—have developed improved varieties of maize and sorghum, respectively, as well as considerable information on improved agronomic production technology. These materials and data have the potential for greatly increasing yield and production in several African countries. However, we must remember that it will take many years to transform the traditional low yielding African agricultural production systems into higher yielding systems throughout the large and diverse African continent. The transformation must happen as soon as possible, beginning first in those countries where data and varieties developed by CIMMYT and ICRISAT, in collaboration with national African programs, best fit.

I would be remiss if I failed to emphasize that most African countries are handicapped by a shortage of trained agricultural scientists. Consequently, training of large numbers of scientists must be an integral part of the program effort.

Today there are some political leaders, and also a few naive scientists, that are advocating that developing nations of Africa and Asia should use an approach to rural development and industrialization similar to that which was used by the United States to slowly transform its economy from a traditional agricultural society to an industrial society underpinned by a highly productive agricultural sector. To me this is absurd; the situations are entirely different. The developing nations of Asia and Africa are currently densely populated, employing primitive, unproductive agricultural methods, while when the United States was going through its slow transformation from a traditional agrarian society to an industrial society, it was not burdened by heavy population pressure. In fact, it was blessed with a vast frontier of largely uninhabited fertile land which provided 160 years to make the transition. The African and Asian nations must make this transformation in a few decades.

One of the most pertinent questions of our time is how the food-deficit nations of the developing world, especially those generally burdened by the double curse of overpopulation and a fragmented, stagnant, traditional, agricultural production system can industrialize fast enough to move some of the population from the land into better opportunities in industry and commerce, while at the same time increasing food production, and slowing population growth to manageable levels. In many instances with agricultural development in the United States there was a gestation period of more than 80 years from the time research was initiated until the technology was applied on a large commercial area to impact production. It is obvious that shortcuts must be found if the agricultural production of the developing world (where yields are currently very low) is to be dramatically increased in the next two decades to offset rapid population growth and avert disaster.

FOREIGN TECHNICAL AGRICULTURAL ASSISTANCE PROGRAMS

For the past 41 years I have been privileged to participate in technical assistance programs designed to help increase food production in more than 30 developing nations. As a result of this experience I have seen some dramatic changes in yield and production of a few crops, especially wheat, in a number of countries. I take this opportunity to sketch how some of these changes were achieved and what factors had to be manipulated in order to increase yield and production.

The success story of the Cooperative Mexican Agricultural Program is now well known. This program was undertaken jointly by the Mexican Ministry of Agriculture and the Rockefeller Foundation in 1943 and represented the first attempt by either a philanthropic organization or foreign government to assist a developing nation in improving its agriculture.

The original directives in establishing the Cooperative Mexican Program were to: (1) develop a research program to produce technology capable of increasing the yield and production of basic food crops such as corn, wheat, and beans (later other crops were added), (2) develop a modest network of agricultural experiment stations on which to conduct the research, although at the outset it was agreed that much of the research should be done on farmers' fields, (3) to train a corps of young Mexican agricultural scientists in all of the disciplines that influence crop production: genetics and plant breeding, soil fertility and agronomy, irrigation, weed control, plant pathology and entomology (agricultural economics and cereal technology were added later), (4) to formulate a package of improved agronomic production practices, based upon the research results, and transfer them to farmers' fields to increase production as soon as possible, and (5) to "work ourselves out of the job" as soon as possible by transferring the responsibilities for continuation of the program to young Mexican scientists as soon as sufficient numbers had been trained and acquired sufficient experience to effectively carry out the program.

Many challenges were met and overcome in the intervening year, but the ultimate success of the program is unquestioned. In 1945 Mexican wheat yields were low and stagnant at 750 kilograms per hectare. Production was merely 365,000 metric tons, only 40 percent of consumption. By the early 1950s the impact of research and its application on yield and production was becoming evident. This resulted from the development of a package of improved technology (improved high yielding, early maturing, broadly adapted, rust-resistant varieties grown employing improved agronomic practices) and its rapid and widespread transfer to farmers' fields under the incentive of stimulatory economic government policy. Compared with the 1945 base period by 1956 yields had increased 83 percent, to a level of 1,370 kilograms per hectare, whereas production had risen from 365,000 to 1.25 million tons and Mexico had achieved self-sufficiency in wheat production. Both wheat yields and production have continued to increase dramatically in Mexico. The 1984 national average yield reached 4,300 kilograms per hectare and production increased to 4.5 million tons. At the present time the better farmers harvest 6.5 to 7.0 tons per hectare in favorable years compared to 2.0 tons in 1945. The improvement in yield from 1945 to 1984 is shown in Fig. 1.

The important point to be emphasized from this experience is that the dramatic yield and production increases were the result of the development and widespread use of an appropriate technology package. The package not only provided early maturing, high-yielding, broadly adapted varieties that were disease and lodging resistant (dwarf), but they were also more efficient in the utilization of both fertilizer and moisture and generally responded more favorably to better husbandry. Government economic policies provided incentives which encouraged rapid, enthusiastic adoption of the technology by farmers.

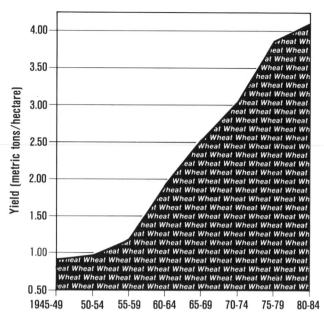

Fig. 1. Mexican wheat yields from 1945 to 1984 (averaged over five-year periods).

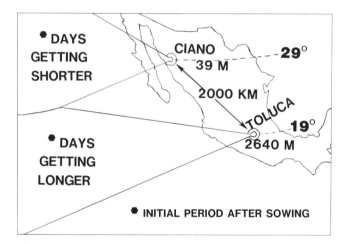

Fig. 2. Locations, elevations, and latitudes where Mexican wheats were grown for the "shuttle breeding" program.

The unique broad adaptation of the new Mexican varieties resulted from the then-unorthodox "shuttle breeding" method that was used in their development (Fig. 2). The shuttle breeding technique involved growing and selecting two segregated populations each year under two environments that differed widely in climate, latitude, soil, and diseases. Only the best individual plants were selected in each generation from each segregated population at each of the two locations (Ciano and Toluca). Seed from the selected plants was shuttled for re-growing and reselection during the next segregating generation at the alternate site. Only those segregates (plants) with good yield potential, plump grain, broad disease resistance and good adaptation to both locations were continued in the breeding program to eventually become commercial varieties. The broad adaptation of the new varieties simplified the seed multiplication and distribution problem in Mexico, a mountainous country where the crop is grown under a wide range of planting times, latitudes, elevations, and soil types. Many years later the importance of this unique breadth of adaptation permitted the Mexican varieties (after adequate testing) to be successfully grown commercially in many other spring wheat regions of Asia, Africa, Europe, South America, North America, and Australia.

Most important, the Cooperative Mexican program developed and left in place a well-trained cadre of national scientists to continue the task.

By the late 1950s, it was evident that the food situation in Asia was becoming more and more critical. Anticipating a forthcoming crisis in the 1960s, Dr. J. G. Harrar, then director (later president) of Agricultural Sciences of the Rockefeller Foundation, and Dr. F. F. Hill, vice-president of the Ford Foundation, took the initiative to establish, in collaboration with the Philippine government, the first truly International Agricultural Research Institute, namely, the International Rice Research Institute (I.R.R.I.). IRRI began to function in 1962. Today there are 13 international institutes in the system, including CIMMYT. The Mexican wheat research program was used as a model for establishing the international rice research program.

THE ROCKEFELLER FOUNDATION AGRICULTURAL PROGRAM COMPLETES ITS MISSION IN MEXICO

By 1960 the Rockefeller Foundation had completed its mission in Mexico with the following results: (1) more than 700 scientists and technicians had been trained, (2) the research program was well organized and functioning smoothly, (3) the technology that was being generated by research was being transferred to farms, (4) Mexico was self-sufficient in cereal grain production, and (5) a graduate school had been established to provide advanced degree training in agricultural sciences. The Rockefeller Foundation's scientists had indeed "worked themselves out of their jobs."

To achieve these objectives the Rockefeller Foundation had invested $6.1 million ($23 million in 1965 dollars) from 1943 to 1960 in the Cooperative Mexican Government—Rockefeller Foundation Agricultural Program. Without doubt the enormous benefits derived were far greater than were anticipated when the program was initiated. Even more amazing were the immense unanticipated, indirect economic and social benefits that were derived during the 1965 to 1970 period as the seeds and technology of the Mexican wheat revolution spread to India, Pakistan, Turkey, and many other countries.

The research program and the team of young Mexican scientists trained in the Cooperative Mexican Government–Rockefeller Foundation project were then transferred to Mexico's newly formed National Institute of Agricultural Research (INIA). Most of the Rockefeller Foundation staff either had been transferred to other programs or had re-

turned to their home country. Several, including myself, remained in Mexico temporarily to assist in the transfer of responsibility and to serve as consultants to the new organization. Visits made to several South American countries in the late 1950's confirmed that Mexican wheats also were performing well under many conditions throughout Latin America.

During 1960, under the joint sponsorship of the Rockefeller Foundation and the Food and Agriculture Organization of the United Nations (FAO), I visited all the nations of North Africa, the Near East, and the Middle East to observe wheat production problems and to try to determine whether the Mexican wheat research experience and genetic materials might be of some value for increasing production in these countries.

It became apparent that in many countries I visited, with the possible exceptions of India and Egypt, there was an extreme shortage of trained scientists. Moreover, the few scientists that were available were generally ineffective because of poor research orientation and inadequate financial and organizational support. In India and Egypt, however, where there were a considerable number of well-trained scientists, most were working on theoretical problems only remotely related to solving their countries' wheat production problems. Nonetheless, almost everywhere I visited, and especially in India and Pakistan, I thought I saw opportunities to effectively utilize the Mexican wheat varieties and research experiences to increase production. At the end of the trip, I recommended that FAO and the Rockefeller Foundation jointly sponsor a scholarship program to train young North African and Near and Middle Eastern scientists in Mexico under my supervision. As part of the proposal, I also suggested that we organize a Near and Middle East–Mexican Wheat Yield Nursery to be grown in all of the Near and Middle East and North African countries, as well as in Mexico. The nursery was to include the principal commercial varieties from each country in the region, as well as the best commercial Mexican varieties and the most promising Mexican experimental lines. It was to be prepared in Mexico as a training exercise under my supervision. The proposal was accepted and the first group of trainees came to Mexico in the fall of 1960.

Little did I imagine then that the establishment of this ("hands-on" or intern) training project would have a tremendous impact on wheat production in a number of Near and Middle East countries within the next seven years.

The young trainees arrived in Mexico in time to be infected by the euphoria of the high-yielding Mexican semidwarf wheats, which were then in the final stages of evaluation on farms. When they returned to their countries, they took with them many small samples of experimental lines of the Mexican wheats.

Three years later, I was invited by the Government of India, whose scientists had not participated in the training program in Mexico, to visit their wheat research program. By then, the euphoria connected with the Mexican wheat varieties had spread to many countries. Dr. M. S. Swaminathan, then a young Indian wheat scientist and now the director of IRRI, had obtained seed of five of the early dwarf Mexican wheat lines through an international wheat disease nursery, and was fascinated by their appearance. He asked me whether I thought they had any potential value for increasing Indian wheat production. I refused to make a judgment on the basis of the performance of these five inferior, obsolete lines. I told him that I would withhold a decision until I had visited Pakistan and Egypt en route back to Mexico to see how the Mexican semi-dwarf wheats were performing there, since I knew that trainees from these two countries who had been in Mexico had taken back with them many advanced experimental lines.

I was invited by the director of research, the senior wheat scientists and the minister of Agriculture of Pakistan to review their wheat breeding nursery at Lyallpur (now Faisalabad). Trailing along in the background were the two young Pakistani scientists who had been in Mexico in the training program. I was disappointed to see the performance of the Mexican dwarf wheats in the demonstration plots. They were inferior to the Pakistani wheats under best conditions. However, I could see that the wheats had not been properly fertilized or irrigated, although the senior wheat scientists assured me that the methods that had been used in growing the demonstrations were optimum for conditions in Pakistan. I stayed at the guest house on the research station that night and was scheduled to leave the next morning at ten o'clock. At daylight I was awakened by the two young wheat scientists who had been trained in Mexico, who said they had

something to show me. We walked to a remote corner of the research station and there I saw four superb plots of Mexican semi-dwarf wheats, growing as beautifully as in their native home in the Yaqui Valley, halfway around the world. When I asked why they had not used the same agronomic practices to grow the Mexican dwarfs in the main demonstration plots we had seen the day before, I was informed that they were prevented from doing so by the senior scientists. It was then I learned that when one reaches the grade of senior scientist in a government organization in a densely populated developing country, one prefers the condition of "status quo" (the known), rather than risk "change" (the unknown). The visit to Egypt revealed the same state of affairs. After returning to Mexico, I wrote a report to the Government of India informing them that the Mexican semi-dwarfs could indeed play an important role in increasing wheat production in both India and Pakistan. Within a few weeks, many additional small experimental samples of Mexican wheats were sent to both Pakistan and India and the race was soon on between scientists in the two countries to find out whether Mexican wheat varieties could contribute to increasing food production in their respective countries.

I will briefly describe the happenings in the Indian program. The average production of wheat over the 1959 to 1966 period was 10.95 million metric tons. The high-yielding dwarf Mexican wheats, together with improved agronomic practices which permit them to express their high genetic yield potential, were introduced into India on a

Table 1. The impact of improved technology on Indian wheat yield, production, and land use before and after the wheat revolution.

Year (Harvest)	Area Harvested 1,000 ha	Yield M.T./ha	Production 1,000 M.T.	Gross Value of Increased Production (Million $)[b]	Adults Provided with Carbohydrate Needs by Increased Wheat (Millions of Persons)[c] over 1961–66 Period	Area Required to Produce Crop at 1961–66 Yield 1,000 ha	Area Saved by Yield Increased Over 1961–66 Base 1,000 ha
1961–66[a]	13,191	0.830	10,950	—	—	—	—
1967	12,838	0.887	11,393	88	3	13,726	888
1968	14,998	1.103	16,540	1,118	41	19,928	4,928
1969	15,958	1.169	18,652	1,540	56	22,472	6,513
1970	16,626	1.209	20,093	1,828	67	24,208	7,582
1971	18,241	1.307	23,833	2,576	94	28,714	10,472
1972	19,154	1.382	26,471	3,092	113	31,893	12,738
1973	19,461	1.271	24,735	2,758	101	29,801	10,339
1974	18,583	1.172	21,778	2,166	79	26,238	7,655
1975	18,111	1.338	24,235	2,630	96	29,198	11,087
1976	20,458	1.410	28,846	3,580	131	34,754	14,295
1977	20,966	1.387	29,080	3,626	133	35,036	14,069
1978	20,946	1.480	31,000	4,010	147	37,349	16,402
1979	22,560	1.574	35,510	4,912	180	42,783	20,222
1980	21,962	1.437	31,560	4,122	151	38,024	16,061
1981	22,104	1.649	36,500	5,110	186	43,976	21,872
1982	22,308	1.696	37,833	5,370	196	45,582	23,274
1983	23,567	1.816	42,790	6,368	232	51,554	27,987
1984 Sept. 1 Est.	24,395	1.851	45,144	6,833	250	54,390	29,995

SOURCE: Ministry of Agriculture of India.

[a] Average for the six year period 1961–66.

[b] Wheat value calculated at US $200/metric ton, similar to landed value of imported wheat in India, 1970–80 period.

[c] Calculation based on providing 375 g wheat/day or 65 percent of carbohydrate portion of a 2,350 kcal/day diet.

commercial scale in the 1965–66 crop season. Since then, both yield and production have increased spectacularly, as shown in Table 1. Indian wheat production reached a peak of 45.1 million metric tons in 1984, more than quadruple the production of the 1959 to 1966 period, and yields increased more than 123 percent in the same period. The increase in gross value of product in 1984 due to increased wheat production over the base period was $6.8 billion dollars, most of which found its way into the pockets of several million small farmers. The additional production in 1984 over the 1959–66 base period was sufficient to provide 65 percent of the calories for 250 million people. Had the 1959–66 yield/hectare prevailed, it would have required 54.5 million hectares to have produced the 184 harvest instead of the 24.4 million hectares that actually were involved, thus resulting in a saving of 29.4 million hectares for other uses. Perhaps even more important is that the increase in wheat production, combined with a corresponding increase in rice production resulting from the introduction of high yielding rice varieties in 1968, made India self-sufficient in cereal production for the first time in 1977. Moreover, during the wheat and rice harvest of 1978 and the wheat harvest of 1979, a grain reserve stock of 22 million metric tons was accumulated. The monsoon failed in the summer of 1979, resulting in what was reputed to have been the worst drought in 90 years. Despite the drought, resulting in a drop in rice production of 12 million tons, India fed its people from the reserve grain stock and emerged having a reserve of about 7 million tons of grain in storage when the wheat harvest of 1980 commenced.

The dramatic increase in production of wheat and rice in India in this past 15 years is the result of the interaction of the use of high-yielding dwarf varieties, the use of more fertilizer (Fig. 3), improved cultural practices, and wise government economic policies that stimulated production.

The changes in wheat and rice production technology,

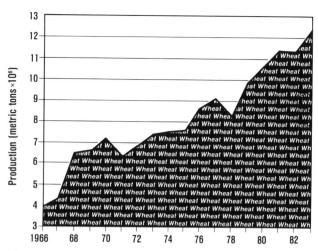

Fig. 4. Wheat production in Pakistan from 1966 to 1983.

combined with the use of more fertilizer, have also ushered in the widespread use of double and sometimes triple cropping on the same land which have further contributed to food production.

Pakistan has also made spectacular progress in increasing wheat and rice yields, employing the dwarf Mexican wheats and dwarf IRRI rice varieties. Since 1966, wheat production has increased from about 4 million metric tons to a high of 12.5 million metric tons in 1983, an increase of more than threefold (Fig. 4). Yields have more than doubled in the same period. In fact, up until 1969 when political instability set in, Pakistan was making faster progress than India. It became self-sufficient in wheat production for the first time in 1968, and then retrogressed to become a modest importer as progress in production slowed because of political instability, and per capita production fell because of rapid population growth. In recent years its wheat research and production program is back on track producing enough wheat for domestic needs. Although its rice production is only about one-fourth that of its wheat production, it has been a rice exporter for the last 12 years.

Turkey has more than doubled its wheat production in the last 10 years and has again become a modest exporter. Bangladesh, although still a small producer of wheat, has made spectacular progress in increasing production in the last five years.

The People's Republic of China has made fantastic progress in increasing cereal production during the past decade. It has long been the number-one nation in rice production and ranks second only to the United States in maize production. In 1984, China harvested 87.7 million tons of wheat and thereby displaced the Soviet Union, which harvested 76 million tons as the number-one wheat producer in the world (Fig. 5) Most of the wheats grown in China are winter varieties. However, the dwarf Mexican spring wheats have been used commercially in the south, along the eastern coast where winters are less severe, and in the northeastern provinces, especially in Kirin, where they are sown in the spring.

The CIMMYT (Mexican) dwarf wheats or their derivatives selected in national programs in developing countries

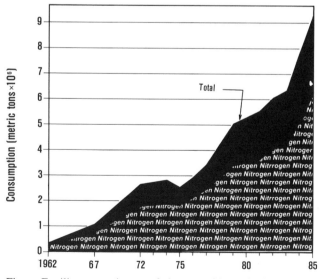

Fig. 3. Fertilizer usage in tons of nitrogen with emphasis on nitrogen fertilizers, 1962 to 1985.

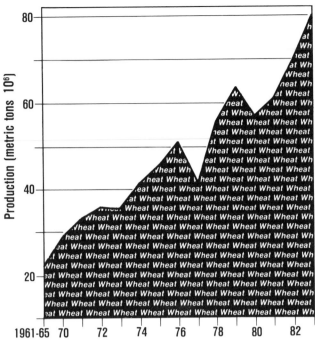

Fig. 5. Wheat production in China from 1961 to 1983.

are now grown on about 45 million hectares in the developing nations. They are also grown on large commercial areas in such developed nations as the United States, Canada, Australia, New Zealand, Spain, Portugal, South Africa, Israel, and Argentina.

The spectacular increase in wheat production and rice production that has been achieved in many developing countries during the last two decades should bring hope to food-deficit African nations. To convert the hope to reality will require drastic changes in governmental attitudes and policies. If the governments of the food-deficit African nations are to become serious about increasing food production they must have the political will to: (1) abandon the policies of cheap food for the benefit of urban consumers (minority), a policy that has been maintained at the expense of the large, poor, subsistence food-producing rural majority, (2) invest more capital in rural development, (3) provide greater investments in rural education, (4) provide greater support for the training of agricultural scientists, and (5) provide increased and more continuous economic support for dynamic programs in agricultural research, extension and production.

There currently exists in several African food-deficit nations, several improved varieties of sorghum and maize that are superior to local varieties. Moreover, there is considerable information on improved agronomic and plant protection practices that, when applied properly, will permit the improved varieties to manifest their clear superiority over the traditional varieties and practices. The improved varieties and agronomic practices for sorghum and maize have been developed jointly by national programs, ICRISAT and CIMMYT, respectively. At present, most of this research

lies unused or underutilized. What is needed now is the political and scientific will to launch and support aggressive extension and production programs in both sorghum and maize in areas where these improved varieties and agronomic practices are appropriate. A revolution in sorghum and maize production in a few areas, where the research materials indicate this is possible, must be made to happen. Success in one area will catalyze enthusiasm and provoke changes in other areas as soon as the research data justify such an undertaking.

A LOOK AHEAD AT FOOD PROBLEMS FOR THE NEXT DOUBLING OF WORLD POPULATION:

I would be remiss if I did not express my concern about the human population explosion.

As I look ahead at the magnitude and complexities of the world food needs for the next half-century I am apprehensive. In 1975, when world population reached 4 billion, the world produced an all-time record harvest of 3.3 billion metric tons of all kinds of food, for example, grains, pulses and grain legumes, tubers, oil seeds, sugar, vegetables, fruits, nuts, eggs, milk, cheese, meat, and fish. It took from the beginning of agriculture and animal husbandry (some 12,000 to 14,000 years ago) until 1975 to gradually increase production to those record levels. If human population growth continues at the 2 percent levels of 1975 it will double to 8 billion in about 40 years or by the year A.D. 2015; consequently, food production must be doubled and more equitably distributed in the same period. There is evidence that worldwide population growth is beginning to slow somewhat, especially in the developed countries, but it continues to grow at a frightening rate in most of the developing countries. But even if we assume that this reduced rate will prevail, and that the time to double to 8 billion will increase by 50, 60, or even 80 years to A.D. 2025, 2035, or 2055, respectively (which I feel is optimistic)—the necessary food production increases are staggering. In essence these projections mean that within the next 40 to 80 years, depending on how population growth changes, world food production must again be increased at least as much as was achieved during the 12,000- to 14,000-year period from the beginning of agriculture up to 1975 just to maintain per capita production at the inadequate 1975 level. Moreover, most of this increase in production in the future must come from increases in yield from land already under cultivation, since in most of the densely populated countries there is little additional land suitable for agriculture that can be brought under cultivation without huge investments in irrigation, which are both extremely costly and slow to bring on line.

Lest we forget, the world population growth rate expressed as annual percentage of natural increase is deceiving. Although the percentage of annual increase has fallen from 2.0% to 1.8% in the last five years, the annual increment in human numbers continues to increase frighteningly because of the larger population base. We need to remember that it took perhaps 1 to 2 million years for the human population to grow to 1 billion, which it reached in about 1850. It required only 80 years to reach a population of 2 billion

(1930), and the 3 billion figure was reached in 1975; and it now appears that the addition of the 5th billion will be completed in 12 years or, by 1987.

I am cautiously hopeful that food production can be doubled within the next doubling period of world population (40–60 years) provided that world governments have the political will and give high enough priority and continuing support to the agricultural sector in their development programs. It cannot be achieved with the miserly and discontinuous support that has been given to agriculture and forestry by governments over the past 50 years. Today the horror of the famine and human misery in Ethiopia and Sudan shown on television screens around the world shocks the general public and political leaders, but tomorrow it will be forgotten by most viewers.

To double food production will require a change in focus in development programs and an upgrading of the effort in agriculture and forestry, especially in the food-deficit developing nations, where crop yields are still low. We must train more and better agricultural scientists, expand our scientific knowledge and improve and apply better technology if we are to make our finite land and water resources more productive. If our foreign technical assistance programs designed to assist developing Third World food deficit nations are to be effective, their administrative procedures must be streamlined. Bureaucracy and paperwork must be drastically reduced while field-orientated, action-type production programs are greatly expanded. To become more effective scientists must have longer assignments at a given post. This must be done promptly and in an orderly manner if we are to meet the growing needs for food. We must educate the public to realize that producing more food and fiber and protecting the environment can, at best, be only a holding operation while the population monster is being tamed. More-

over, we must recognize that in the transition period, unless we succeed in increasing the production of basic necessities and more equitably distributing the benefits to meet growing human needs, the world will become more and more chaotic and social and political systems will collapse. In recent years the "human rights" issue has generated much interest and debate around the world. It is a utopian issue and a noble goal to work toward. Nevertheless, in the real world, the attainment of human rights in the fullest sense cannot be achieved as long as hundreds of millions of poverty-stricken people lack the basic necessities for life. The right to dissent does not mean much to a person with an empty stomach, a shirtless back, a roofless dwelling, the frustrations and fear of unemployment and poverty, the lack of education and opportunity, and the pain, misery, and loneliness of sickness without medical care. It is my belief that all who are born into the world have the moral right to the basic ingredients for a decent, human life. However, to speak glibly and sanctimoniously about the morality of the "right to life" while ignoring the morality of the "quality of human life" only adds confusion to this fundamental, complex issue.

Those of us who work on the food production front, I believe, have the moral obligation to warn the political, religious, and educational leaders of the world of the magnitude and seriousness of the arable land, food, and population problems that loom ahead. If we fail to do so in a forthright, unemotional manner we will be negligent of our duty and inadvertently contribute to the pending chaos of incalculable millions of deaths by starvation. A solution to this complex problem is imperative. The imminence of the disaster is before us. It is closer than most people realize, or are prepared to admit. The problem will not vanish automatically and to continue to ignore it will make its solution ultimately more difficult.

59. MAKING INSTITUTIONS WORK—A CANADIAN VIEWPOINT

A. H. Macpherson, Environment Canada, Ottawa, Ontario, Canada

INTRODUCTION

Every country, every society, has its own recipes for success: its own memory of what worked and what did not in similar circumstances in the past. Canada is certainly that way. Although we are of diverse ethnic origins and we live in an equally diverse country, we have developed a distinct and recognizable institutional culture, our own ways of doing things together.

I need go no further than to outline how we feel our institutions differ, however subtly, from those of our closest neighbor, the United States, with whom we share many bonds and ideals.

Fundamentally, I think we see ourselves as more prosaic, and you may find evidence for that in the contrast between the primordial American ethic "life, liberty, and the pursuit of happiness" and ours, "peace, order, and good government." Also, we like to say that we have undergone no civil war in Canada. In fact, we did have a brief, lopsided one, a century ago this year. But is is generally true that Canada is built on compromise between interests: regional, linguistic, religious, cultural, and economic, rather than on contests in which one side won and one lost.

In fact, our approach to problem solving has been unusually nonadversarial. An example is to be found in the comparison of the environmental assessment and review process in the two countries. In Canada, federally, the relevant policy is specified in various forms of cabinet decision: there has been no law passed to enshrine it as there has been in the United States. There being no legal basis for the environmental assessment and review process federally in Canada, there is therefore no recourse to the courts, no appeal except at the political level. We could, I am sure, find a number of parallel examples, contrasting the American tradition of problem solving through the courts, and the preference of Canadians for using their legislatures.

Institutions can take a variety of forms. They can be built of people and physical facilities, and we can think of many examples, such as universities and hospitals. They can also be entirely abstract, as is the institution of property. All, however, are social expressions of a collective perspective, directed at the achievement of specific objectives. Perhaps institutions can best be visualized as forming a continuum: at one extreme they are concerned with specific social benefits, such as equitable delivery of educational or medical services; and, at the other, they may take the form of a broad complex of norms, internalized in our behavior as an expression of our culture.

In a fast-changing world, institutions in the broad sense require continuous redefinition, and institutions in the narrow sense must adapt or lose their places to more relevant ones. And this is a fast-changing world, whether we look at our monetary system, energy, agricultural resources, or trade.

With this introduction, I would like to survey relevant institutional arrangements in Canada, then discuss the environment and its economic dimensions, of which water management for agriculture is one, and finally note some current initiatives in the international institutional field.

Canada is a federation with ten provinces. It is a fundamental fact that the four founding provinces were, in 1867, at the time of confederation, separate colonial territories evolving toward separate states. Their union was negotiated, not imposed, and they ceded to the new federal level of government only those powers they felt impelled to. As new provinces were added, they acquired essentially the same rights as the founding provinces.

Natural resources, generically, fell to the jurisdiction of the provinces, though with exceptions. Fisheries, for example, were seen as a federal interest, although the administration of inland fisheries was later generally ceded to the provincial jurisdiction. Agriculture was seen as a shared responsibility, trade being regarded as federal.

There is one departure from this clear division between federal and provincial levels of government. This lies in the status of the northern territories, the Yukon and the Northwest Territories. These are federally administered; the territorial councils, though in practice regional governments (albeit with restricted powers), are legally only advisory councils to a federal minister. The resources of the northern territories are mostly administered by the federal government.

Many institutional arrangements have been established to facilitate economic development and promote social harmony in this diverse and complex state. We have, from the beginning, made considerable use of state enterprise—the Crown Corporation—particularly in the transport sector. And there are several examples of committees made up of provincial and federal representatives on equal footing, to harmonize activities for which the jurisdiction is shared.

One of these is the Canadian Council of Resource and Environment Ministers (CCREM), a ministerial level body, with representatives from all ten provincial governments and the federal government. Established approximately twenty-five years ago, CCREM operates as a national forum for discussion and exchange of views on environmental and renewable resource issues among the federal, provincial, and territorial governments (the latter officially present as observers but in reality playing an active role in deliberations). Its purpose is to stimulate and develop compatible policies and cooperative programs between the two levels of government.

CCREM, with its decisions based on consensus, is a key actor in Canadian interjurisdictional environmental affairs. However, although CCREM has played a role in a wide variety of resource issues, it has not inhibited the development of separate institutional arrangements directed at particular problems.

Of these separate arrangements, the most useful, and ubiquitous in Canada, is the "shared-cost agreement," of which Environment Canada has more than 250 currently active, under which such disparate activities as native wildlife harvest surveys, flood zone mapping, and hazardous waste management planning are conducted.

Constitutionally, we have allocated the administration of our inland waters to the provincial governments, although the federal government holds certain responsibilities, for example, for navigation. There are obviously a number of problems with this approach, and I will touch also on the international dimensions in a few minutes.

A public inquiry is now under way into the federal responsibility for water. It has completed hearings nationwide, and some 300 interested parties have made presentations. The inquiry will report during the summer, but it has already provided a useful review of our record in water management.

Canada has, of course, encountered numerous interjurisdictional water problems. The Saskatchewan River system, for example, runs generally west to east through the three prairie provinces, arising in Alberta on the slopes of the Rocky Mountains, flowing through arid parts of Alberta and Saskatchewan, and emptying into Hudson Bay through Lake Winnipeg and the Nelson River, in Manitoba. The Prairie Provinces Water Board was created in 1948 to determine the best use of the eastern-flowing streams' waters on the basis of cooperative planning between the federal government, on the one hand, and the three provincial administrations. Since 1969, when the Prairie Provinces Water Apportionment Agreement was signed by the four parties, the equitable apportionment of all eastward flowing waters has been agreed to, and water planning and other management studies have been undertaken to clarify specific concerns.

In this case, the sharing of a major and vital water resource is first a matter of sharing consumptive use, particularly in irrigation, and second one of sharing assimilative capacity. For another large western Canadian water resource, that of the Mackenzie River, the question is one of managing flows for the collective benefit of people in several jurisdictions.

The Mackenzie River system includes large rivers draining parts of British Columbia, Yukon, Alberta, Saskatchewan, and the Northwest Territories. The closing of a hydroelectric dam on one of these, the Peace River in British Columbia, in the late 1960s, had serious downstream effects.

In 1971, the six governments concerned began to exchange information formally on the water resources of the basin. Currently, work is under way on a whole series of bilateral agreements, and an "umbrella" agreement, to allow for better coordination in the future.

The current federal water inquiry has revealed a deep public concern not only for the quality of our surface waters, but also over the adequacy of our planning and policy framework for managing this vital resource. The recommendations of the inquiry are thus likely to be directed particularly toward improved institutional arrangements.

The Canadian experience necessarily includes a considerable history of bilateral relations of an institutional nature concerned with the waters that are shared with the United States at the Canadian border. The Boundary Waters Treaty of 1909 established the principle that neither nation shall pollute the other's boundary waters to the extent of causing "injury to health or property," and it gave each one "equal and similar" rights to use of the border waters.

The Boundary Waters Treaty also provided for the establishment of the Canada/U.S. International Joint Commission (IJC) with the mission of resolving common water problems through cooperation, rather than adversarial proceedings.

The IJC (made up of six members, three from each country) acts as a single body seeking common solutions in the joint interest of both parties and the prevention of disputes between the parties, in accordance with rules and principles as laid down and agreed on in the 1909 treaty. Without going into detail, it can be said that Canada's experience with the operation of the IJC has been very positive, with many expanding political problems being brought to resolution by means of a practical and pragmatic approach. One fairly recent and to date very successful outgrowth of this process was the signing in 1972 of the Great Lakes Water Quality Agreement, which launched a major international pollution control program.

There are several international initiatives of which to take note. First, however, we might examine how each category of environmental problems has its specific institutional dimension. For example, though soil degradation may perhaps be seen as a consequence of international market forces, it is nonetheless a problem essentially amenable to local resolution. On the other hand, a problem of acid rain originating through the long-range transport of atmospheric pollutants is one that demands regional, national, and even international institutional remedies. And in between are such problems as toxic chemical pollution and eutrophication of surface waters, normally amenable to point source or regional waste management control, or regional drainage and sewage treatment works.

Although water management institutions tend to be regional and national, and only rarely international, the indirect environmental effects of trade agreements and other international arrangements lead us inescapably into the international arena to seek harmonious policies that will provide a degree of market security conducive to the application of good environmental practices.

Many countries, including Canada, have subscribed to the

World Conservation Strategy, which seeks to establish new norms of sustainable development, and, more recently, such initiatives have received unprecedented encouragement.

For example, the 1984 London Economic Summit resulted in a statement indicating that the leaders of the Summit Nations recognized the international dimension of environmental problems and the role of environmental factors in economic development. A follow-up report was presented to the heads of state and government attending the May, 1985, Bonn summit, and the conference's closing communiqué contained a number of statements on environmental policy, emphasizing the need for strengthened international cooperation and new approaches to solving environmental problems. Included among these was the pledge to "harness both the mechanisms of governmental vigilance and the disciplines of the market to solve environmental problems." It was also agreed that the "polluter pays" principle should be developed and applied more widely and that science and technology must contribute to reconciling environmental and economic growth.

Concern has recently arisen in Canada over soil degradation. In addition to the growing problem of salinization, resulting largely from the practice of summer fallowing, there has been a rapid loss of carbon from certain soils, amounting to as much as 50 percent in fifty years of cultivation.

As humanity presses more and more heavily on the world's arid and marginally productive areas, so the danger of irretrievable desertification becomes of increasing concern. We put at risk not only what people need now, to support themselves, but also their futures—whether these will involve current land-use practices, or options yet unknown.

Increasingly, then, if we are to manage our resources on a sustainable basis, land managers must manage for sustained biological productivity the one certain value in a maze of uncertainties. As lands become more intensively and more extensively managed, so must land managers recognize an increasing responsibility, as stewards of the productivity of the planet.

Here the issue of agricultural productivity becomes one with that of environmental protection. Several speakers have already pointed to the quality of water, whether from precipitation, surface or ground, as a constraint, and increasingly so, to agriculture. The degradation of soil and water resources and the diminution of genetic diversity are issues which fall as much in the "environment" dossier as in that for agriculture.

It should be acknowledged that this point was implied in the recent summit communiqué, which commits the summit nations to work with developing countries toward avoiding environmental damage. No doubt it will be aired further, in the course of the investigations of the World Commission on Environment and Development, which recently held its first hearings in Indonesia and is scheduled to visit Canada in spring, 1986.

As already mentioned, the link between agriculture and water is one of those which relates the environment most closely to economic development. Agriculture is a production-oriented industry the inputs and outputs of which we can for the most part subject to economic analysis. Water, on the other hand, is an essential agricultural input that has rarely been considered in the same economic sense. Water is usually unpriced or, at best, drastically underpriced. Often, when pricing does exist, it is based on the cost of supply, not on any pricing policy derived from water's replacement cost. Also, many competing uses exist for a finite water resource.

In the absence of an economic value for water, allocative decisions may be subject to distortion and resources may not be developed in a sustainable manner. A current example may be found in the prairie provinces (Alberta, Saskatchewan, and Manitoba) of western Canada. Agriculture is an economic mainstay of the region, which accounts for most of Canada's cereal production. The southern portion of this region experienced a higher rate of economic growth than in any other part of Canada during the 1970s and early 1980s. A recent report showed that water use in the Saskatchewan basin had doubled over a twenty-five-year period. It is expected that such rates of growth could well recur.

A serious constraint on future growth in this region, however, is that economic activity in a number of river basins has absorbed essentially all the available water supply. It is a familiar story of a semiarid climate, variability of river flows and precipitation, and periodic recurrence of severe drought conditions already introducing rigid natural constraints. A growing concern is that the climate could become even drier in future if the forecasts of a greenhouse effect come true. While proven institutional mechanisms, such as the Prairie Provinces Water Board, exist for dealing with apportionment and control, the problem for the future is such that new combinations of environmental practices and sustainable development limits will probably have to be pursued.

A more realistic approach to valuing water may not, of course, lead to increases in the agricultural uses of water. Indeed, and if I may speculate, the future for agriculture of the kind now practiced on the Canadian prairies is far from assured. It will, however, contribute to a more efficient management of that portion of the water resource devoted to irrigation and should also contribute to the overall wealth of society by ensuring that water is put to its most productive uses. If this type of decision making is to take place, the foundation for it must become established within institutions, by means of economic, constitutional or legislative initiatives.

The use and management of water resources thus exemplify a vital relationship between the environment and the economy. How we manage our water resources will depend on our economic opportunities and our future economic options, just as our economic future will depend on the sustained productivity of the biosphere.

Canada's great geographic expanse and small population formerly led us to see our country as limitless. However, we have come to realize that all our land resources have limits, if sustainable development is our goal. The need for concern becomes apparent when we consider that 40 percent of our country's GNP and 25 percent of its jobs are directly related to the land resource—the extraction, harvesting and processing of raw materials.

Though success will require a common societal understanding of the importance of sustaining our environment, governments must lead in the development of new institutional mechanisms. In Canada, the federal government has developed a policy on land use, and each provincial government in Canada has either developed or is in the process of developing comprehensive land-use policies. Recently, a committee of the Canadian Senate undertook a study of one aspect of our land resource—the problem of agricultural soil degradation—and made a number of knowledgeable recommendations which are now under study. Soil degradation is of concern primarily in western Canada, which accounts for 55 percent of Canada's agricultural receipts and provides the basis for our grain export industry. Additional investigative undertakings, and responses, will likely take place as Canadians gain a fuller appreciation of emerging problems and of the need for innovative solutions. It seems clear already that we will have to stop making allocative decisions in isolation, permitting the treatment as a free good of the vital environmental resources upon which all depend for survival. "The tragedy of the commons," applied to such dilemmas by Garret Hardin, has been alluded to already in this conference by Robert Chambers.

To summarize, let me restate the view that to be effective, specific institutions have to spring from their own, individual societal roots. They must incorporate appropriate representation from the stakeholders. Their scope will be appropriate to the problems they address, whether local, regional, national, or international. They must reflect societal values. Increasingly, they will be called upon for acceptable decisions, in the context of other environmental objectives and future options.

60. MAKING INSTITUTIONS WORK—STATE AGRICULTURAL RESEARCH VIEWPOINT

Neville P. Clarke, Texas Agricultural Experiment Station, Texas A&M University, College Station, Texas

PRINCIPAL ROLE OF THE STATE AGRICULTURAL EXPERIMENT STATIONS

The state agricultural experiment stations in the United States represent a unique partnership between state and federal government to conduct research of both national and regional application. The state agricultural experiment stations are part of a broader institutional arrangement of so-called land-grant institutions, which have, in addition to their research mission, academic and outreach or extension components of the total activity. Taken together, the research, education, and extension missions of the land-grant institutions form a major component of the infrastructure which has allowed a highly productive agriculture to emerge in the United States. The state agricultural experiment stations, in most cases, have a dominant funding from the individual states, but a substantial support from the federal government. The federal component of support provides for a coordinated and jointly planned program of research which addresses not only local but also regional and national research needs in agriculture. One of the principal characteristics of the state agricultural experiment stations is a close coupling to agricultural commodity groups and other clientele in the individual state. The mission of the individual state agricultural experiment stations as well as the state agricultural experiment stations in the aggregate is broad and multifaceted. In its most simple context, the missions of the state agricultural experiment stations must include at least three dimensions: (1) the dimension that deals with the impact on agriculture of geographic diversity within the state and the nation, (2) the various food and fiber commodities and natural resource issues that must be dealt with in agriculture, and (3) the increasingly large array of scientific disciplines that must work together to solve the complex problems facing agriculture today. The state agricultural experiment stations view the broad programs that address these three dimensions of their mission as the "base program" which in itself must be dynamic and sustained to meet the continuing needs of agriculture across the country. Related to this are a series of new research initiatives which emerge from time to time, initiatives based either on research opportunities or on new problems that must be solved in production agriculture. The combination of base program and new initiatives forms the overall program of research in the state agricultural experiment stations.

WORLD AGRICULTURE RELATIONSHIPS—A SHRINKING GLOBE

As has been well described in other parts of this symposium, in almost all dimensions, agriculture has become international in its scope and applications. The issues related to international trade and competition call to mind the similar capabilities and the common needs for technology as well as needs for interdependent understanding of the operations of the agricultural institutions of the various countries and the way in which they meet together in world trade. We share many common pest and disease problems that can be most effectively attacked by complementarity of coordinated research activities. Many of the geographic barriers to the transmission of various pests and diseases no longer exist in today's world with modern transportation operating as it does. These factors present to the agricultural research institutions of the various countries of the world a variety of existing and new opportunities for collaboration in research. Making institutions work to achieve the kind of collaboration that will make the most effective use of the total agricultural research resources is an effort that deserves considerable new attention.

STATE AGRICULTURAL EXPERIMENT STATIONS—THE ENABLING MECHANISM FOR RESEARCH IN INTERNATIONAL AGRICULTURE

Without appearing to be immodest, it would be reasonable to say that the capability for the United States to participate in international agricultural research is due in major proportion to the existing state agricultural experiment station infrastructure, coupled with the remainder of the land-grant institutions in each of the fifty states. Taken together with the capabilities of the Agricultural Research Service at the federal level, this offers a major opportunity for incremental efforts in the areas of international agriculture. One of the most important factors related to the success of international programs of research conducted by the state agricultural experiment stations is the linkage within the land-grant systems to the complementary academic and extension programs that exist in this structure.

THE TWO-WAY STREET IN RESEARCH

The state agricultural experiment stations have as their primary reason for being the conduct of research that supports the agricultural enterprises and agribusiness within each of the individual states. However, as previously stated, there are many opportunities for complementary research in the international arena, research which provides a synergistic engagement with other developed countries, as well as research in the developing countries. There are many geographical similarities between a state like Texas and many parts of the world. There are many common livestock and crop species that share similar problems in both the developed and developing countries of the world and many areas of related science that can be engaged in complementary activity. It is important to the long-term health of international research in the state agricultural experiment stations for the effort to be mutually complementary in terms of application of results. This is because, as previously stated, the agricultural experiment stations have as their first mission providing service to the state in which they exist. It is not at all difficult, in my view, to develop broad and very meaningful programs of agricultural research that represent a two-way street; areas of research in which the presence of teams of people from an individual state agricultural experiment station in another country represents a positive investment in the parent state's agriculture. Selecting complementary research objectives that are mutually supportive is one of the key concepts in making the state agricultural research institutions work in the international arena.

DEVELOPING VERSUS DEVELOPED COUNTRIES—RESEARCH IMPLICATIONS

Often, agricultural research in the public's eye is viewed as essentially research done by the developed countries in the developing countries. Obviously, this forms a major part of the total activity and provides an opportunity to work on problems with common physiographic, pest and disease, or other geographic relationships. The research between developed and developing countries provides for our future research linkages, often involves the training of scientists in the developing countries as a complementary part of the total activity, and works toward the building of institutions in the developing countries with which more effective research linkages and collaborative activities can be established in the future. Not as well amplified in the public's eye but perhaps just as important are the opportunities for collaboration between the agricultural research institutions of the developed countries. Here there is the opportunity for shared science, for an immediate synergism and for a more effective and efficient use of total research resources. The relationships tend to be institution-to-institution in this kind of international collaboration rather than depending upon governments to stimulate international research and development in the developing countries.

OUTREACH VERSUS RESEARCH

In the developing countries, the outreach activities from the developed countries may often be initially of more importance or at least of equal importance to the research activities. While both of these activities represent highly visible and highly important linkages to the developing countries from the developed countries with regard to agri-

culture, it is important in making institutions work to maintain a clear definition of the difference between the two objectives. Precise expectations of accomplishments need to be clearly stated in the relationship between agricultural research institutions in developed and developing countries with regard to research. As indicated above, there is often a key element of scientists' education and training associated with the effort and an institution-building component that enables research in the future where opportunity might not exist at the moment. There are many complementary relationships associated with work on agriculture in the developing countries, but a clear definition of the specific objectives is a key component to maintaining a long-term viable relationship.

EXAMPLES OF INTERNATIONAL OPPORTUNITIES

The opportunities to work together in international agriculture are multiple and might be illustrated by several classes of examples.

1. International collaboration on a broadly used single commodity, sorghum. The sorghum research program of the Texas Agricultural Experiment Station has a broad geographic diversity corresponding to the diversity of our state's agricultural climate and cropping systems. Because of this, we have established very important worldwide linkages with research on sorghum in both the developed and developing countries. Wild germ plasm, work on common diseases, sharing of overall production techniques, research in pathology and entomology have brought a rich and rewarding collaboration between scientists and between countries across the world.

2. Water, the major theme of this conference, is a common problem to almost all countries. It is a global agricultural issue. There are many examples of common linkages on a natural resource issue such as water. Perhaps one of the most effective ones at work today is the relationship between the United States and Israel and the binational agricultural research and development fund program (BARD). Water is a principal area of common concern between Texas scientists and Israeli scientists, and the BARD mechanism has provided a major enabling collaboration and communication on this common resource issue.

3. A third linkage, in addition to specific commodities and natural resources, would be geographical proximity. In the case of our Texas Agricultural Experiment Station, this is exemplified in our collaborative programs of research with Mexico. We work very closely with Mexico on plant and animal pests and disease as well as on common production problems and natural resource activities. A winter cotton nursery, located in southern Mexico, amplifies the effectiveness of our plant breeding program for that commodity by a factor or two through growouts that occur in the winter in that part of Mexico. Major collaboration in animal disease and in plant disease areas is also under way in that country. Through sharing of common resources and working together on common problems, the effectiveness of the research of our two countries is amplified and U.S. scien-

tists working in Mexico become aware of and know how to deal with a variety of exotic diseases and other pest problems that do not exist in the United States.

MAKING INSTITUTIONS WORK

As has been stressed several times in preceding comments, the state agricultural experiment stations are a mission oriented, problem solving set of research institutions whose first allegiance is to the state of origin, whose second allegiance is to the regional and national problems of agricultural production in the United States and whose other activities need to be complementary to these principal missions. Recognizing the fundamental motivations for the state agricultural experiment stations does not detract in any way from a very active and substantive involvement in international agricultural research. The most important and most relevant management principle that must be recognized to make the state agricultural experiment stations work in the international arena is to identify and deal with common institutional objectives and common production and research problems.

One of the key issues to be overcome in making the state agricultural institutions work in the international arena is to develop explicit understandings with regard to the commitment of time of key scientists in the state agricultural experiment stations. The individuals who have the capability of making the greatest contribution in international agricultural research are the ones who are most badly needed at home. In our state, a model which is working well recognizes that key individuals will have a difficult time being available for long-term overseas assignments but that such individuals can make meaningful shorter-term commitments to overseas activities and bridge the gap between with key graduate students and individuals more committed to full-time international activities.

There are a number of new and innovative methods for linkage that are emerging today that allow for better coupling of the state agricultural experiment stations to the other elements of international agriculture. I have already mentioned the BARD mechanism for linking agricultural scientists in Israel and the United States on problems of mutual interest. This mechanism is funded by the interest earnings from a pool of money jointly provided by the governments of Israel and the United States. The CGIAR International Laboratories represent areas of excellence in international agriculture scattered throughout the world. The U.S. Agency for International Development is making a substantial effort at developing linkages between the areas of excellence in science in the United States and these various international laboratories to have a two-way scientific exchange and collaboration. Through this mechanism, more can be learned from the international laboratories for use in the United States, and certainly scientists in the United States can effectively collaborate with world-class scientists in the CGIAR laboratories. More and more, we see emerging institution-to-institution relationships in international agricultural research, particularly in the developed countries. These institutional relationships also grow stronger each year by virtue of the training that the international scientists have had in the developed countries and the remaining linkages to the parent academic institution when they return home to take major leadership roles in their countries. More and more, as scientists in agriculture become experienced in the international arena, there is a scientist-to-scientist communication and from that, a collaboration that is effective in mutually complementary ways.

CONCLUSIONS

In conclusion, the state agricultural experiment stations constitute a major resource to enable an effective communication and collaboration in international agricultural research and development. There are many complementary international research capabilities that can be exploited between scholars and institutions with common motives and objectives. There is a growing mutual commitment to a series of common problems that must be solved through agricultural research and development among the scientists of the world. There are emerging a series of innovative approaches that will allow for a more effective communication and collaboration between institutions and scientists capable of addressing key questions in agricultural research around the world. It is incumbent upon all institutions to take advantage of the major opportunities that exist to enhance this communication toward the common goal of providing more affordable, wholesome, and healthy food and fiber for the increasing population of the world.

PART X. PANEL DISCUSSION—THE PRIVATE SECTOR

61. THE TREND OF U.S. POLICY IN DEVELOPMENT WITH LARGE-SCALE AGRIBUSINESS AROUND THE WORLD

Edgar C. Harrell, U.S. Agency for International Development, Washington, D.C.

I want to talk about the relationship between the delivery of services through the private sector and development.

Four years ago Peter McPherson, the administrator of AID (Agency for International Development) set up a new bureau in AID to study how bilateral donors such as the U.S. government's AID can work with and through the private sector to achieve developmental goals, particularly in agriculture. What was different about the bureau's mandate was that McPherson wanted us to try and work directly with private companies and institutions. This is different from the more familiar, traditional AID government-to-government programs. We chose to work primarily with the private companies and institutions in the developing countries rather than directly with the U.S. companies. We decided to start with the market and marketable opportunities rather than with a particular problem area or technology and let those opportunities be identified by the people who knew the market, that is, the companies and institutions in the developing world or the U.S. companies that had experience there. There are a few advantages to this approach: One is that the people who develop the ideas are closer to the market. Second, most of the business opportunities are fairly well developed by the time they come to AID, and so we are able to react much more quickly. Third, there would be full sharing of risk. Traditionally, AID is in the risk business, and that is precisely where a bilateral or multilateral donor should be. We decided that we also would take risks, but that we would share those risks equally with private companies and with institutions. That is, if we lost, they lost, and if they gained, we gained as well. So there would be equal sharing of both the losses and the gains. And finally we financed basically small projects to test ideas and experiment with new approaches that if demonstrated to be successful and viable, could be replicated by the rest of the agency or by multilateral donors or by LDC (less developed country) governments themselves.

We really started with two programs, and all the focus was on agribusiness. We did set up an investment window, and over the course of the four years that I was deputy assistant administrator of the bureau, we invested about $40 million. The average size of a project was about $1.5 million. We leveraged about $160 million in private agribusiness investment. All the investments with the exception of one were in agribusiness in the developing world. The average term of our lending was about 12 percent, eight years repayment. To some people this may sound onerous. The enterpreneurs that we worked with in the developing countries basically had no access to institutional credit. It is not the price that is important; it is the fact that they now had access to credit and someone willing to work with them. Moreover, we were conscious of the costs of our funds (U.S. Treasury borrowing rate) and the cash flow potential of projects we invested in.

The second area we worked on was policy, particularly in trying to strengthen and deepen capital markets to mobilize and allocate savings for private investment. One of the biggest problems today in the developing world is the crowding out of the private sector from the capital markets by governments. About 60 to 70 percent of the capital available in developing countries in many parts of the world, and I speak specifically of Africa and Latin America, is taken by the government sector, leaving very little for the private sector to continue their businesses.

What we discovered from this experience was first of all, that the developing countries' governments liked the program. There is a change of philosophy going on in the developing world. Partly because we worked in agribusiness, we discovered that many governments are not satisfied with their own managed extension programs, that they are very costly. The private sector can and does provide the extension program, and this is a subject in a book that Ruth Karen and Simon Williams are publishing with some case studies. The private sector has a self-interest to continue the program and to make it service-oriented and cost-effective.

The second thing we found was that many governments are interested today in privatizing some state-owned enterprises, and not only in agriculture. They have found that they cannot run them efficiently. Their investments are not market driven, and they are a drain on the capital and operating expense budgets.

Third, new markets could be developed which are good for the countries. The governments liked the idea of market-driven opportunities which lead to foreign exchange, higher value added to farmers, and allocation of savings directly to productive investment and not consumption. They liked the idea of better use of agricultural land. One of the interesting cases that will come out of the Simon Williams/Ruth Karen book is the Mumias project in Kenya, which was basically a nuclear estate sugar project in an area that was not producing sugar. After four or five years the company provided technical service to about 20,000 to 25,000 farm facilities outside the nuclear estate that provided sugarcane for production by the factory. The company found that they also had to provide extension services for other crops such as maize and sorghum because the farmers had to have food or cash during the period when they were waiting for their cane to grow and be harvested. A whole new relationship developed between the company and small farmers that was not necessarily contractual; it was in the self-interest of both parties. The company provided services not only in terms of productive inputs and technology and markets for sugarcane but also for other crops that could be given and marketed by the farmers.

The second thing we found was that the general wisdom that "if there was a good opportunity, the private sector would find it," was not necessarily correct. We discovered that private institutions, particularly the financial institutions, were missing some good opportunities. The first projects we financed were as agribusiness investment funds in Kenya and in Thailand. In both cases this was the first medium-term, fixed interest rate financing available for small, rural, private agribusiness firms. We shared the financing 50/50 with the banks, but they assumed the risks of on-lending. And what these banks found out was that not only did they generate new customers in terms of deposits and other new banking services but they also had the opportunity to be in the forefront of new investment opportunities. In the case of Thailand the bank involved is becoming a leader in private financing of aquaculture and animal husbandry projects.

The other thing that was interesting was in the case of Kenya the cost of jobs created through sub-lending to small rural agribusiness processing firms was about $2,000 per job. This is quite a good figure in terms of relative experience and job creating by investment.

Another area that we entered was retail leasing. We financed a project in Pakistan to develop new farm implements for small farmers. What became interesting in this project is that the company not only will begin production of the small farm implements, but they may set up a retail leasing operation where instead of selling implements to the farmers they will lease and service them. So again you have a direct relationship between the production and, in terms of a farm implement or an input to farming, service to the farmer in using it, and also a way of financing that will be very cost-effective for the farmer. We also financed a retail leasing facility with a financial intermediary in Pakistan.

We also found that the programs could be quite complementary to the government programs. The one that I want to mention particularly was our participation on the financing of the first private meatpacking project, or slaughter project, in Thailand. All others are currently owned by the central government or municipal governments. The interesting part of the project to us was that the meat processing plant would provide the extension to small farmers for raising pigs and cattle on their farm where manure could be recycled and improve the fertility of the land. But this also became very complementary to the government program in eliminating hoof and mouth disease because the government wanted most of the production from the meat processing plant to be exported. So the government found this is a very complementary program to the traditional kind of extension in terms of vaccines, etc. for agriculture.

The third interesting area we found was, and this is really the very important part of the study by Ruth Karen and Simon Williams, was the social and development equity aspects of it. Again, in the case of Thailand one of the cases in the book they are publishing is an agribusiness firm called Charoen Pokphand. That company decided that there was a market for pork, and they went out to help small farmers raise piglets for slaughter. They provided all the infrastructure: they bought the land, they resettled the farmers, they provided the health services, and so forth, to go along with these villages they helped to establish. They found that after seven years profits had been sufficient that they could give the farmers the houses, the land, and the infrastructure that had been developed. Moreover the value added to the farmers in terms of incomes was about three to five times from growing pigs than it was for growing traditional rice or cassava. So there was a situation again where working through the private sector the governments won in terms of income, in terms of rural employment, in terms of new markets; the private company won in terms of developing relations with farmers, plus profit, and the farmers won in terms of social services as well as income, and in this case, additional assets that they would own.

From this experience we also found two major opportunities emerging that we as part of the agency are going to spend more time on. One is technology development. We found that we were receiving opportunities that we'd like to finance: they had good management, good development impact, and good marketing, but the technology wasn't fully developed. The agency has a long history in financing research through the Science and Technology Bureau. We found that there were opportunities to work with private companies to develop new technologies that would only take a year or two to develop. In the case of Costa Rica, we had a company come to us for assistance in expanding a plan to use coffee waste as animal feed. They did not have a very good process because it could not take out the impurities that were not good for animals such as caffeine lignins and tannins. The first thing we did, and this is technology transfer where Americans are excellent, we contacted some engineering firms who helped the Costa Rican firms to refine their process so that they could take out the impurities and raise the proportion that coffee waste would substitute for sorghum and maize.

In addition, one of the by-products of taking the coffee bean from the kernel is a mucous which is high in pectin. Pectin is a very good enzyme. There has never been a process developed to commercialize pectin from the mucous of coffee waste. Here is a case where, with a limited amount of money, $50,000 each, or a total of $100,000, we would jointly work with that company and an American engineering firm to develop that process.

So we feel that there is a real opportunity for AID to share the risks with private companies in developing technology for developing countries markets. This is where America is so strong in terms of our research institutes and our private sector. Many development institutions work on technology transfer but technology development in developing countries with private companies is a new opportunity.

The second area which I have already mentioned is that we are very pleased with this linking of markets to production. That is an area where we have now financed three or four projects. We believe we are developing enough background data and experience that we can replicate these. We feel that the linkage brings in the production technology. The private company brings in help on the crop selection; there's a big market potential in developing countries if they could access it and produce it, for example, exotic fruits, vegetables, and plants. There is also diversification of U.S. agriculture melon production, etc., in the developing world, particularly in the Caribbean.

Third, you have the processing done on-farm for value added. I gave the coffee example plus the social infrastructure and equity example in Thailand that comes along in this mutual relationship between private processing companies who will stick with it for their own self-interest and farmers.

Four points summarize this experience over the last four years. First, nothing is inconsistent between development and working with private companies and institutions. Private companies are not development agencies—I think we agree on that—but they can be excellent vehicles for achieving developmental objectives. It is a situation where all win. The government wins, the farmer wins, and business wins, if it is done properly.

Second, there is growing dissatisfaction not only in the private sector but in the governments themselves trying to do the whole job. It is too costly and ineffective.

Third, there is a new self-confidence. I'm always surprised, having worked in developing countries all my pro-fessional life, at the number of new entrepreneurs that are cropping up everywhere. I can think of Thailand where I first went in 1956 and look today at their strong private entrepreneurial risk-taking private sector as compared with what it was ten or fifteen years ago.

Fourth, there is awareness of technological advances worldwide. There are going to be tremendous opportunities to work with private companies and institutions in developing countries and help them to adopt and use the biotechnology and bio-genetic engineering know-how and the basic technology that has been developed in this country. I think there are tremendous opportunities for everyone, and this also applies to the water sector, which is an important part of this conference.

In terms of policy within the agency, I think these efforts at working with the private sector will continue, will be a complement to the traditional government-to-government programs, and I think that basically we will be in the four areas where advances will be made. One, we will be working with private intermediary financial institutions to provide new types of financing or services to private companies, and that means AID will probably be spending more of its money directly to private intermediary financial institutions to provide credit to small farmers or small businesses. Two, farmer outreach programs through private companies. Three, new technology development. And four, continuation of work with the governments on improving the macro and sectoral policies to provide the incentives for the private sector to do the kinds of things that are important for development.

62. THE PRIVATE SECTOR AS A FORCE IN AGRICULTURAL DEVELOPMENT

Tracy S. Park, Tenneco, Inc., Houston, Texas

Corporate endeavor in less-developed areas of the world helps maximize the social welfare of the people. Without a healthy society, there are no stable markets and no prospects for sound business growth. Corporations should be able to relate their long-range goals to those of the countries in which they work. They should identify with major economic and social goals of their host country.

As a major U.S. firm concerned with these considerations and one which is engaged in both domestic and international business, Tenneco is a diversified company whose divisions and subsidiaries span eleven major industries. It provides products and services in four basic areas: energy, manufacturing, natural resources, and insurance. Tenneco has grown to be a major worldwide organization with annual revenues of $15 billion and assets of $18 billion. It is ranked as the sixteenth largest U.S. company in sales, and employs about 100,000 people worldwide.

Of immediate interest to this conference, Tenneco's subsidiary, Tenneco West, Inc., owns and manages over 1 million acres (400,000 ha) of land in the United States devoted to grazing and intensive crop production. It leases a considerable amount of its land to independent farmers and ranchers, makes information available to them to encourage optimum utilization, and handles and markets the crops grown on these lands on behalf of the independent farmers. Simply stated, Tenneco has for years in the American Southwest been implementing the corporate core and satellite farming management techniques which have been proven so successful in certain developing countries, as recently documented by joint USAID/Business International studies. Ruth Karen has given this conference a detailed report on the results of their research in this area.

Commencing about six years ago, Tenneco demonstrated its commitment to international agriculture by starting the first of its several international agribusiness ventures in one of the most remote and environmentally harshest regions of the world. It, and two additional examples in other international regions, will be briefly reviewed.

THE SUDAN

Tenneco pioneered the transfer of modern agricultural technology to a remote area in northern Sudan by building and operating an irrigated farm. This project offered all the challenges a company would want: saline and sodic soil; searing ambient temperatures; fine, blowing dust; no infrastructure; and an unskilled labor force. This farm evolved from discussions in 1976 between the president of the Sudan and the chief executive officer of Tenneco. Simply stated, Tenneco decided to establish a model farm in the Northern Province which would demonstrate modern methods of crop production and provide insights on how it could best act as a catalyst to develop the area.

The Northern Province is one of the most arid regions of the world. Nonetheless, it has great potential as a producer of agricultural commodities. With more than 81,000 ha acres of rich alluvial soil watered by the Nile River and a relatively small population, it is capable of producing surplus food. However, the area remains underdeveloped, and its people continue to subsist on traditional methods of crop production.

Based on its experience, Tenneco concluded that the near-term future of the Northern Region lies not in developing large corporate or government farms, but in improving the productivity of the area's existing small farms. Most of these farms are located on the fertile land nearest the river and are producing far below their potential.

The main reason for the Northern Region's low productivity is the continued use of traditional cultivation techniques. Farmers do virtually all their work by hand or with animals, following a routine that has remained basically the same for centuries. As a result, a single farmer can handle no more than about 1 ha of field crops, which is barely sufficient to pay back his costs and feed his family, much less provide surplus cash. The key to increasing productivity on these local farms is mechanization. If farmers can achieve economies of scale and then produce and market surpluses, the land is rich enough that they will be able not only to support the cost of mechanization but to substantially boost their incomes.

Successful mechanization in the Northern Province will first require that farmers modify their irrigation practices. They still use the small basin practice of flood irrigation, a practice which involves diversion of water from one small plot (often no more than 10 to 20 m square in size) to another. This small basin practice is a major impediment to any mechanized farming operation insofar as it seriously handicaps the capabilities of farm machinery to till, plant, cultivate, and harvest crops. However, border strip or long furrow irrigation on land that has been leveled eliminates these problems. Furthermore, such improved systems of irrigation represent only a modification of the farmers' present understanding and capabilities.

Tenneco has found that the cheapest and most effective means of land leveling, particularly well suited to the Sudan, is that which employs laser-controlled equipment. In effect, the laser automates the entire process, thus reducing the number of skilled personnel needed to do the work and ensuring a precise grade. Unlike conventional leveling, laser leveling does not require a survey crew since the laser itself is used to map the surface of the field and determine the cuts and fills necessary to create the desired slope. The laser unit can then be programmed to that slope, and it will continually check and correct the grade as the earth-moving machine moves across the field. Once complete, leveling allows water to flow evenly through furrows or between border strips for distances up to several hundred meters. The result is reduced water consumption and evaporation, better drainage, higher crop yields, and less labor.

Land leveling opens the way for fully mechanized crop production. With long furrow or long border irrigation, farmers are relieved of their most time-consuming task, that of constructing borders around dozens of small plots and then diverting water from one plot to the next. Without the cross-borders, machinery can operate easily, and it can then take over the tasks of land preparation, seeding, spreading fertilizer, harvesting and threshing. This allows each farmer to devote his attention to maintaining the primary irrigation canals or to spend more time at outside work, such as cultivating fruit and vegetable gardens. Once machinery is fully incorporated into a local farm operation, one farmer working full time during the growing season can handle up to 24 hectares, in stark contrast to the one or two hectares he farms with traditional methods.

Besides allowing farmers to extend their acreage, leveling and mechanization have other important benefits. First, with heavy tillage and uniform application of seed and fertilizer, yields increase significantly. In addition, machinery enables the farmers to maintain a strict timetable. That is, they can plant and harvest on time and do so fast enough to allow for two crop rotations per year on a single piece of land. This not only increases yields through timely planting, but transforms the neglected summer season into an important part of the crop cycle. The concept has been very well accepted and Tenneco hopes to continue the program.

After five years of direct farming and assisting numerous other private farmers and agricultural cooperatives in northern Sudan, Tenneco now plans to produce certified seed for distribution to farmers in the area and around the country.

PUERTO RICO

Another example of overseas corporate involvement in agriculture is Tenneco's Vieques Island spice farm project in Puerto Rico. The U.S. Defense Department has considerable activity on Vieques, many of whose inhabitants are jobless. To improve the situation, the Defense Department asked each of its top ten contractors to assist in economic rehabilitation of the island. As one of the top ten, Tenneco and one of its large subsidiaries, Newport News Shipbuilding, have responded by embarking on a joint venture project with a successful New York City spice and herb growing company to build a spice and herb farm on Vieques Island in Puerto Rico.

Working with the U.S. Navy and Vieques Island community development officials, an aerial survey was made of the island to select good potential sites for the farm. Soil samples were taken and an excellent farm site was selected. Field growing trials are already under way. Positive findings are expected from the business and marketing study now being completed.

The project as designed will grow such spices as basil, oregano, tarragon, rosemary, sage, thyme, nasturtium, bay laurel, chives, and parsley for the fresh and dry markets. It is envisioned that there will be a core farm of one hundred to several hundred hectares of spices with a similar area of various spices that will be grown by the surrounding small farmers and packaged and marketed by a joint venture company.

The most limiting factor on the small island is fresh water. The farm will be designed to include some of the latest techniques of water management. A catchment basin will trap rain in ponds to recharge the aquifer and also to serve as a source of water for the drip system. The use of a drip system will allow us to provide irrigation scheduling with only enough water applied to meet the evapotranspiration of the growing plants. To supplement the irrigation system, small wells will be drilled to produce the fresh water from an underlying aquifer. The total discharge rate of the wells will not exceed the recharge rate. This will ensure that saltwater intrusion will not become a problem.

We are optimistic that this project will enable Tenneco and Newport News Shipbuilding to fulfill their objective and make a significant contribution to the island's economic development.

TUNISIA

As a third example, Tenneco instigated the establishment of a joint venture date processing company to process and export common variety invert dates from Tunisia to North America.

As the largest single processor of dates produced in the U.S., Tenneco's date division pioneered the development of several techniques to utilize dates as ingredients in processed foods. Examples include date paste, date sugar, and chopped dates which are widely used in pastries, confectioneries, and granola-type cereals. To ensure a stable supply of ingredient dates to the industrial users, Tenneco was interested in locating additional sources of quality dates to meet this growing market demand.

Historically, Tunisia's common variety dates have proved difficult to market both domestically and abroad. Development of the country has brought a gradual shift in the preferences of Tunisian consumers, away from the common date to the sweeter and softer-textured dessert date, called Deglet Noor.

An attractive feature allowing for increased exports of the common dates is that their processing season falls after the Deglet Noor season. Local processors can thus extend their processing season. This not only generates extra returns for the plant and equipment, but it also keeps labor employed for a longer part of the year.

To meet the high standards of the U.S. Department of Agriculture, a number of cultural and processing techniques need to be implemented within the Tunisian date industry. Tenneco is willing to help the date growers improve their quality in return for the opportunity to market these dates in North America. Therefore, it is possible to bring together the Tunisian date growers association, a Tunisian investment bank, and Tenneco into a mutually beneficial investment opportunity.

In addition to the three projects just outlined, Tenneco has completed or currently is engaged in agricultural feasibility studies in:

Australia	Gabon	Pakistan
Cameroon	Kenya	Saudi Arabia
Colombia	Mexico	Turkey
Costa Rica	Morocco	
Ivory Coast	Nigeria	

In summary, I believe we all realize that many agribusiness companies, large and small, know how to mobilize, relate to, and energize small farmers, in both developed and developing countries. Believe me, private business can do it. There are numerous regional and global financial and technical assistance institutions who would like to see small farmers and corporations working together with complementary goals.

Just as companies can motivate small farmers around a "corporate core," I believe the companies likewise can be motivated to accept the challenges and risks of investing in projects overseas reflecting their areas of expertise. It seems to me that one of the most dramatic actions that this great university could take in follow-up to this fine conference is almost self-evident. Find ways of encouraging and motivating the U.S. agribusiness private sector to seek out management and investment opportunities. An individual company must find its niche, and it is most certainly out there waiting to be filled.

63. PRIVATE SECTOR DEVELOPMENT OF COCOA IN LESS DEVELOPED COUNTRIES

B. K. Matlick, Agribusiness Department, Hershey Foods Corporation, Hershey, Pennsylvania

Ten years ago Hershey thought that cocoa beans grew on the docks of New York or Philadelphia; we knew absolutely nothing about the production of cocoa. Sure, we knew from the maps where it was produced and had nice pictures, but we knew nothing about it. We fortunately had a chairman who was very concerned. The violent fluctuation of the price of cocoa beans was very upsetting to our company— we constantly had to be changing the size of our product in the marketplace—so we sat down in a long-term strategic planning session to see what could be done. Hershey Foods Corporation was determined to try to do something about the long-term supply of cocoa beans. We knew it was a tree crop and we knew that it was growing in underdeveloped countries in the tropics, but we really didn't know very much more.

My associate Glenn Trout and myself were given the challenge. We were professionals in agriculture. Hershey makes milk chocolate, and my training was in dairy manufacturing. I was purchaser of all the milk for the Hershey Foods Corporation, and I was working with dairy farmers. Glenn called one day and said, "Do you want a new challenge?" and I said, "Sure, why not?" We first went around the world meeting with ministers of agriculture and large agribusiness companies to try to convince them to produce more cocoa. They responded by saying, "If we thought cocoa production was such a good crop, why didn't we grow it ourselves." We decided to grow cocoa on a demonstrational and experimental basis to gain experience and knowledge about the production of cocoa.

Our particular expertise at Hershey is in manufacturing, sales, and marketing of chocolate, so this was something really new to us. There was one thing we thought we could do and that was to understand the technology of cocoa production, but we felt that we had to get hands-on experience. For various reasons we selected a site in the little country of Belize, which is just south of the Yucatan Peninsula, bordered by Guatemala to the west and Honduras to the south. We purchased about 800 ha there and set up the task of growing cocoa. We have an agribusiness technical staff of three professional agriculturalists. One thing we consciously did was staff the farm with local people. All we did was visit the farm regularly, giving the technical requirements and letting them do the job.

The technology was basically from the Tropical Agricultural Research Station, CATIE, in Turrialba, Costa Rica. We also visited Ecuador, Ghana, Nigeria, Malaysia, New Guinea, the Philippines, and other major cocoa-growing areas. We picked up what we thought was the best technology and applied it. We had some problems, of course, because we were growing a crop we did not understand. We were growing cocoa in a country that was not a major producer and we were using people who were not familiar with cocoa; so, we had three strikes against us and in all probability we should have failed. However, we didn't. We now have more than 240 ha of cocoa. We have a very extensive laboratory where we are doing research on fermentation, irrigation, drought stress, field spacing, fertilizer, and the various field problems of cocoa.

This was started in 1978, and up to 1982 we kept it quiet. We really didn't say anything because we knew we didn't have anything to talk about. We really didn't know if we were going to succeed or fold up our tents and go home, but it became apparent about this time that we did have something, so we did start talking. Originally, our plan was that once we developed the technology we were going to go back to those large agribusiness companies who were growing tropical crops. At that time all these companies weren't interested; they had all the problems they could handle.

Cocoa, being a tree crop, requires about four to five years of development before you get a positive cash flow, and the financial officers of these companies did not like that sort of investment. So, we turned again to the question of how we were going to transfer this technology. We kept knocking on doors. If you think it is tough being a government employee trying to get to know somebody in private industry, you should be on this side trying to get to know how the government works. I have not figured it out yet; it is very, very complicated. We spent three or four years just trying to figure out who in our government or who at World Bank were the decision makers, how to get in to see them, and how they operated. It was very much of a maze to me because our industry is very small and simplified. We were at the point, however, where we had something to transfer and the opportunity to transfer was, quite frankly, to the foreign governments and through USAID. They were looking for an agricultural crop they could recommend to LDC that would generate foreign exchange. They needed a crop in which marketing was no problem. Cocoa is a crop that is traded every day in international trading, so it has a market and it is a nonperishable product. The farmer can sell cocoa when he wants or needs to.

We are currently providing technical assistance for USAID-sponsored projects in Belize and Honduras and are in the talking stages in Panama, Jamaica, and Grenada. We started out with a very large objective, and we are still a long way from achieving that objective, but we now see light at the end of the tunnel. We have developed a research farm in Belize. We have a technical staff and regularly invite the extension people to come to the farm and visit. We also have held seminars. Last fall we held a seminar in which technicians from Haiti, Honduras, Costa Rica, the Dominican Republic, and Belize attended.

We have what we think is a small way of returning to the developing and cocoa-producing countries a small bit of our success. We hope that the technology transfer that we have will allow us to make a contribution to the world cocoa producers. The current world average yield of cocoa production, especially the Caribbean and Central American areas, is about 280 kg · ha^{-1}. Under the technology we have available they can easily increase that to 1,120 kg · ha^{-1}. The world price now is about in country price $0.34 per kilogram. This results in about U.S. $305 per hectare gross income.

I feel that a small farmer can handle 4 ha of cocoa, so it is a crop in which we feel he can make a living and improve his life-style. If he makes a profit, then his neighbors will look around and suddenly say, "That house is painted, the kids have new shoes, the older son is going to school; I would like to have that too. I would like to learn to grow cocoa." We feel that once they do that, it will ensure a long-term supply of cocoa at a reasonable price. It is a small venture on our part, but is it something to which we feel committed. We felt for years that anything we did would have no impact; therefore, we did nothing. Finally, however, we decided to do something.

The keys to our project are marketing and technology. We have a market and we also now, through our research farm in Belize, have the technology. With that combination and with land, labor, and the hard work of local farmers, we believe that cocoa can be a successful crop. Recently, we were approached by the local farmers about how they could get started in cocoa farming. After a couple of years of planning, we have a project in which local farmers are being financed by the local government to purchase about 10 ha of land; Hummingbird-Hershey Ltd. is providing the extension service, and the local government is making land available. The first land is now partly planted with cocoa. We feel that if these people show some degree of success then we can duplicate this project in other parts of the country so that it will eventually grow into a major export crop.

Belize has only about 150,000 people; therefore, we are not looking at a large amount of money to make an impact on this country. It is something that Hershey has set out to do. We spent a significant amount of money in developing the farm; we spent the last six years in developing the agricultural techniques, and now we are trying to transfer that technology. We feel that the technology we have developed will result in a profit for small farmers and that this will stimulate further development. We will then be more confident about the future of the basic raw materials we need to continue to make Hershey chocolate.

PART XI. PANEL DISCUSSION—THE ROLE OF VARIOUS GROUPS IN INTERNATIONAL AGRICULTURAL DEVELOPMENT

64. THE WORLD BANK AND IRRIGATION

Montague Yudelman, World Resources Institute, Washington, D.C.

INTRODUCTION

Irrigation development has been a major source of growth in agricultural output over the past thirty years. Between 1950 and 1980, the area under irrigation expanded from 95 million to 260 million ha. This expansion was most pronounced in Asia, where China and India, the world's two most populous countries (with a combined population of approximately 1.8 billion) now have around half of the world's irrigated acreage. The area with the smallest acreage under irrigation is Africa, where only 3 percent of total output comes from irrigated land. In general, the regions with the highest growth rates in agricultural output have been those with the most rapid expansion in area under irrigation while the converse is true about those with the slowest growth rates.

Irrigation will continue to play an important role in increasing food production—projections are that around 75 percent of the increase in food supplies in Asia in 1990 will have to come from irrigated land. Technically, irrigation is important for three reasons. First, it can eliminate or reduce plant stress during periods of water shortages, thus giving higher and more stable yields. Second, irrigation can supply water in seasons when it is not normally available so allowing more than one crop to be grown on the same land during a year. Finally, irrigation can support crop production in arid areas previously too dry to sustain any crop growth. Whatever the technical merits of irrigation, though, due consideration has to be given to the economies of water use—and the management of irrigation systems—a topic discussed at greater length below.

The World Bank is a very large investor in irrigation development. The Bank's investments in irrigation in Asia have contributed to the "yield" revolution that has done so much to allay short-term concerns about a Malthusian crisis in that region. Nonetheless, while irrigation has expanded, major problems in designing and implementing irrigation projects have arisen. In retrospect, it seems that the Bank has had unrealistic expectations. Fortunately, unrealistic expectations about costs, time required, area to be irrigated, and yields have been compensated by unexpectedly high prices for farm products. Irrigation costs per hectare are rising—with investment reaching $2,000 per hectare—and the terms of trade have now turned against agriculture. Consequently, greater realism is required in preparing projects, as well as in their management.

BANK LENDING FOR IRRIGATION

Between 1974 and 1984, the World Bank extended loans and credits for around $120 billion for a wide range of projects—transport, utilities, industry, mining, and education. The largest proportion of these loans, close to 30 percent, were for agricultural development, including more than $11 billion for irrigation projects. This represents nearly 10 percent of the Bank's portfolio and one-third of all lending for agricultural development. It also represents more than half of all the external aid (bilateral and multilateral) for irrigation development. Thus, the Bank is unquestionably a major actor in the development of irrigation among its member countries, especially those in Asia.

The Bank lends primarily for projects. Perhaps, though, one of its most notable successes in dealing with "water-related" issues was in its role as a supranational agency helping to resolve an international problem of riparian rights. I refer to the division of the waters of the Indus following the partition of the Asian subcontinent into India and Pakistan. The Bank, a multilateral agency with the confidence of the major parties involved in the dispute, was able to draw up an acceptable plan for allocating the waters of the Indus. Thereafter, it was able to mobilize resources to construct the reservoirs needed to implement the plan and help finance and supervise the construction of these reservoirs, including the Tarbela Dam—the world's largest earth-filled dam.

No doubt, the Bank will continue to play an important diplomatic role of this kind, a role open only to a multilateral agency that is seen to be objective, that has a large and capable technical staff, and that can help finance and implement any proposed solution. I do not think it is entirely fanciful to believe that a multilateral agency such as the World Bank will be in a position to help resolve some of the major international riparian issues that influence water use in the Middle East and the Ganges Plain. And the resolution of riparian issues in these regions will have an enormous impact on development in the years to come.

Most of the Bank's lending is for projects—a well-defined set of activities that can be implemented over a limited time period. Lending for irrigation projects is intended to support national efforts to intensify water use to increase agricultural output and reduce annual fluctuations in food production. Bank-financed projects cover a wide range of activities: from large dams to financing of hand pumps and shallow wells; from completely new irrigation systems for desert lands to the rehabilitation or extension of existing systems in monsoon climates; from large canal distribution systems to on-farm water management; from land leveling and land consolidation to the use of sprinkler and drip-irrigation systems; from planning new projects to operation and maintenance and training for ongoing or new systems; from large systems with more than a million hectares to groups of small irrigation subprojects with individual sizes of from 50 to 500 ha; from support of large state irrigation systems to providing rural credit for small farmers to acquire irrigation pumps.

Bank-supported projects to promote irrigation often include other components. Typical are rural roads, credit, extension, marketing, research, education and training, health, potable water, and electrification. In practice, actual irrigation system costs may be anywhere from 45 percent to 90 percent of total project costs. Nonirrigation components are included in projects only when they are necessary for the project benefits to be realized, can be independently justified, or are part of preparatory work for future projects. In the main, most of these components are deemed essential to improving the livelihood of small farmers and to generate rural employment opportunities, two important objectives in Bank-supported projects.

Usually, it is preferable that projects be planned so that they are technically and economically viable as entities—economic viability being linked to a reasonable economic rate of return. However, the Bank also finances "time slices" of very large projects that cannot be completed within normal project loan periods of five to seven years, and this raises an interesting issue regarding the "duration" of a project for purposes of evaluation. By way of illustration: a project with an irrigation area of 425,000 ha requires about fifteen years to complete; the first time slice of five years would bring about 105,000 ha under cultivation. The economic rate of return (ERR) for the first phase is estimated to be about 10 percent, and the overall rate of return for the final project is projected to be about 16 percent. Such a project meets the criterion of economic viability. In another project of about 630,000 ha in size, though, the ERR for the first time slice is estimated to be negligible because of the heavy initial investments. This raises some important concerns, and several tests must be met by such projects before the Bank agrees to finance a "time slice" of this kind. Is the overall ERR for the full project satisfactory? Can the Bank rely on the government's commitment to complete the project expeditiously and soundly, especially since the Bank will not give any advance guarantee that it will participate in the financing of later phases? Fortunately, Bank experience with financing "time slices" has been positive in the sense that governments have fulfilled their commitments to sustain their investments to complete projects.

RECORD OF IMPLEMENTATION

The Bank's experience with implementing irrigation projects has been mixed. The record shows substantial differences in the implementation of projects between what was expected and what actually happened. This is especially so in regard to cost overruns during construction and overestimation of the area to be irrigated.

A sample of twelve projects in Asia, Latin America, and Africa is analyzed in Table 1. This small sample includes new and rehabilitated projects; the data are from published reports. The most notable feature of the projects is that the actual costs of completing them was nearly twice the expected cost—$1,059 million compared with $816 mil-

lion—and this figure was close to a 26 percent shortfall in the acreage expected to be irrigated. As a consequence, the cost per hectare was $1,128 rather than $461. In only one project was the actual cost per hectare less than the planned cost, and this arose because the area irrigated by the project was more than two times that planned.

The World Bank itself has reviewed forty projects. This larger sample—in which the Bank invested an average of $22 million per project—revealed a similar pattern to that of the twelve projects in Table 1. Only 25 percent of these projects were completed on time, and the average cost overrun was 38 percent. This sample also included estimates of output that were produced from the projects, as well as estimates of the economic rates of return on the projects. About half of the projects led to a greater volume of output than was expected, but the most favorable effect on the economic rate of return for this group of projects came from a pronounced rise in commodity prices—average prices being 40 percent higher than expected. As a result, thirty-two out of the forty projects had economic rates of return greater than or equal to 10 percent—a rate of return analogous to the opportunity cost of capital and so considered to be "acceptable." Eight projects did not achieve acceptable results.

The projects in the two samples were planned and completed at a time when the terms of trade were relatively favorable for agriculture. Higher prices for output helped offset the delays, cost overruns and shortfall in areas irrigated. So why did problems arise in the implementation and operation of these projects?

LESSONS FROM EXPERIENCE

The evidence indicates that Bank-financed irrigation projects in developing countries seldom meet their expected performance levels in issues of cost, completion, coverage, and production targets. While many factors have contributed to the shortfalls in performance, three broad categories of problems appear to be pervasive: (1) inadequate project preparation, (2) poor management and organization, and (3) poor operation and maintenance.

Inadequate Project Preparation

Many issues have to be resolved before projects get under way. Delays occur while riparian rights are resolved or legislative issues are settled over sharing costs and benefits of irrigation. Then, too, there are delays stemming from the fact that most bureaucracies handling irrigation are in the public sector and have little flexibility in dealing with the additional demands for staff and budgets that arise from development projects. Once the project is approved, though, experience has indicated that inadequate project preparation has been a major cause of cost overruns, time overruns, poor water coverage and, frequently, failure to meet production targets.

Design failures in projects stem, in good measure, from a lack of adequate information and understanding of the project area—a direct result of inadequate project preparation. A very revealing—though by no means unusual—example of insufficient preparation can be illustrated from experience in Thailand. Most of Thailand's irrigation devel-

Table 1. Performance data for twelve World Bank irrigation projects.

Region/Type	Project Number	Area (10^3 ha)		Cost ($/ha)		Time Overrun (years)	Total Cost ($ millions)	
		Target	Actual	Target	Actual		Target	Actual
Asia								
New irrigation	1	100	34	1,270	6,205	8	127	211
projects	2	102	102	815	883	3	83.1	90.1
	3	77	65	812	1,968	9	62.5	127.9
	4	19.7	19.7	939	1,188	3	18.5	23.4
Subtotal		298.7	220.7	975*	2,050*	—	291.1	452.4
Rehabilitated	5	186	200	199	390	NA	37	77.9
irrigation projects	6	200	177.8	146	366	NA	29.1	65.1
	7	229	184	102	254	NA	23.4	46.8
Subtotal		615	561.8	146*	388*	—	89.5	189.8
Other areas								
New irrigation projects								
Latin America	8	203	202.6	468	1,293	11	95	262
Africa	9	126	126	786	3,175	NA	99	400
Africa	10	488	184	362	640	NA	176.5	117.7
Subtotal		817	512.6	454*	1,521*	—	370.5	779.7
Rehabilitated								
Latin America	11	10	7.88	780	1,923	1	7.8	15
Latin America	12	35	35	1,646	2,074	1	57.6	72.6
Subtotal		45	42.88	1,454*	2,046*	—	65.4	87.6
Total new projects		1,115.7	733.3	594*	1,680*	—	661.6	1,232.1
Total rehabilitated		660	604.68	235*	459	—	154.9	277.4
Total		1,775.7	1,337.98	461*	1,128*	—	816.5	1,509.5

* = weighted average.
NA = not available.
— = not applicable.

opment has been in the Central Valley, a very productive rice-growing region responsible for the bulk of Thailand's rice production for export. The Central Valley has soils that are high in clay—ideal for rice production. In contrast, northeast Thailand has soils that are very sandy, resulting in water losses through the soil from 3 to 20 times higher than those of the Central Valley soils. Some years ago, several irrigation schemes were developed in northeastern Thailand, primarily for rice production. The engineers who designed these projects, rather than taking soil surveys for the area, assumed that the soils were the same as those of the Central Valley and designed the projects accordingly. Because the designs failed to account for the high water losses of the northeast soils, less water is available than planned and the projects are not nearly as effective as was expected.

Another widespread illustration of poor preparation is the manner in which soil surveys are done. Frequently, surveyors look at the soil to a depth of only 1 m. Drainage barriers often occur within 5 to 10 m of the surface. When these barriers are not discovered, waterlogging and salinity problems occur within a short period of time. These problems have arisen in many projects in Latin America and Asia and have added enormously to the final costs of projects.

The preparation and design of projects must include concepts about how the water will be distributed at the farm level and what it will be used for. This requires a close working collaboration between engineers and agricultur-

alists so as to achieve timely deliveries of water to producers, consistent with a realistic production patterns. Experience indicates, though, that the agriculturalists are seldom heeded, so that designs include elaborate schemes for water use that are unrealistic; as a result, many irrigation systems are overdesigned and operate below their productive capacity. The resolution of this issue depends on the project leadership. Experience in some projects in Asia has been very positive. Project managers have undertaken deliberate efforts to foster a dialogue among staff with different disciplines. The results has been a much better appreciation of the issues linking conveyance and distribution of water to cropping patterns with subsequent improvements in design.

Experience also teaches that it is important that farmers in the project area participate in preparation and management. Failure to take account of their needs and desires can hurt the performance of a project. A case in point is in a project in Africa that was intended to increase rice production by rehabilitating and extending a relatively small irrigation scheme. Production of rice from the area was expected to increase dramatically. However, project planners incorrectly assumed that the prevailing socioeconomics of the area were favorable to the intensification of rice production. In fact, though, paddy farming was considered an undesirable occupation, having low social status and yielding a much smaller income than other on- and off-farm activities. Paddy farming was desirable only as a means to produce food for family consumption. As a result of this oversight, while the product was designed for rice monoculture, the project's farmers did not plant rice intensively. Other food crops were planted, and the benefits accruing to the irrigation investment were very low.

Irrigation projects that encompass the settlement or resettlement of farmers require special consideration in terms of project preparation. The previous example pointed out the need to design for an appropriate cropping scheme. Experience in land settlement projects in Latin America and Asia makes it clear that research should be undertaken to determine which cropping schemes are appropriate for the prevailing cultural practices and soil and water conditions present in the new lands. The success of the project should not be premised on cropping schemes alien to the farmers as unusual patterns of production—often planned by non-agriculturalists to generate high incomes for settlers—do not find wide acceptance. Research should also include careful study of the amount of land that should be made available to each farm family. If given enough land, irrigation schemes for small owner-operators can be very successful and efficient. If too little land is provided, however, the hope of increasing rural incomes and productivity may come to nothing but create rural poverty and despair.

The World Bank has recognized that some of the policies of the past have not produced the anticipated results. With respect to the tendency toward inadequate preparation for irrigation projects, the Bank has instituted a new requirement to correct this problem. Specifically, the Bank now requires that both hardware and software designs be well advanced at the time of the loan approval. Designs for large monolithic dams should be finalized, and design for other facilities should be completed for at least the first year of construction or implementation. Research on the agricultural aspects of the project should be well under way and the management and organization of the project formulated. This policy has helped to improve project preparation by increasing the probability that the most glaring errors will be caught before the project is undertaken.

Management and Organization

A number of issues that fall under the general rubric of management and organization have an important bearing on the effectiveness of irrigation projects. One is what kind of institutional framework is most conducive to high performance in the irrigation sector. In some countries, autonomous institutions or authorities organize and manage irrigation projects; in others, there is a national irrigation agency; while yet in others, governments have an overall ministry of agriculture that includes an irrigation department. In still other countries, success in project operation is dependent upon the coordination of several ministries. Some countries have a high degree of decentralization in project management that includes a great deal of control at local levels; in others, especially in centrally planned economies, there is very little local autonomy.

It is difficult to draw conclusions based on Bank experience about the form of organization that leads to the best performance of an irrigation system. Generally, projects operated under the umbrella of nationwide irrigation agencies have performed well compared with those operated under autonomous or specialized authorities. But there are so many exceptions that it is not possible to draw any general conclusions about which form of organization works best. Be that as it may, evidence shows that weak institutions—whether national, regional or autonomous—are one of the main causes of poor management of delivery-systems. Experience makes it clear that a key to improved institutional performance is linked to securing enough qualified personnel, especially for location on the site of the project—even if it is necessary to pay hardship allowances. Other improvements that have helped institutions be more effective include: making allowance for staff housing; ensuring that there is adequate financing for fieldwork; establishing clear project objectives, policies and lines of communication; understanding farmers' needs and goals and, in some instances, ensuring adequate administrative and legal authority to operate effectively.

The Bank's experience in many projects is that "poor management" is an important reason why many projects fail to meet expectations. Experience has shown that good managers can raise the productivity of poorly designed systems while poor managers can and do lower returns on well-designed and previously well-managed systems. Consequently, one of the recent priority areas in Bank actions is to encourage increased investment in training managers and other key project staff; and to discourage high turnover of project managers.

One of the important issues in organization and management of irrigation projects is farmer participation. There are very few major projects where farmers participate in management, although as a general rule, many projects rely on groups of farmers playing some role in handling water beyond the primary and secondary delivery points. When farmers operating in groups have participated in the management of systems, then the Bank's experience has been that they have assisted in ensuring more efficient and equitable use of water. Unfortunately, farmer groups or associations tend to be weak, poorly organized, and poorly financed. Insofar as the Bank is concerned, the promotion of farmer participation has been one of the most elusive aspects of project implementation. As yet, there is no ready solution to this issue, although increasing efforts are under way to work with farm groups and associations.

Operation, Maintenance, and Cost Recovery

Bank experience is that inadequate attention is paid to operation and maintenance (O&M). Yet, effective O&M is an essential requirement for the efficient working of irrigation systems. Leakages, seeping, clogging of canals, wastage, and destruction of distribution systems are all symptoms of poor maintenance, and many of these symptoms are prevalent in most Bank-funded projects and in most national systems. One estimate is that improved operation and maintenance alone would add the equivalent of 10 percent to the area that could be irrigated from existing systems—needless to say, improved O&M would raise the return on many of the large investments already made by governments and the Bank.

Despite the gains to be made—and losses to be prevented—low priority is given to operation and maintenance in national programs. A recent survey of thirty-one Bank-funded projects confirmed that the responsible authorities had made very little in the way of allowance for improving operations and postproject maintenance. The survey showed that maintenance efforts are viewed as having low priority and so budget allocations are meager and good staff prefer to be assigned to design and construction. This becomes a self-defeating system as the neglect of O&M makes the whole system less effective than it could be.

One consequence of the difficulty of convincing governments or irrigation authorities to pay more heed to operation and maintenance is that there is a tendency to favor more capital-intensive systems that require less maintenance. In some cases, this has involved a "technological" substitute for "better management." For example, on one Bank project, pumping equipment, which in traditional systems is attended by operators, was made so as to operate without attendants. This eliminated an important source of inefficiency and corruption. Modern pumping equipment *can* be made reliable by better quality control in manufacturing and by installing appropriate control and protective relays. Preventive maintenance and good repair services *can* minimize downtime. Indeed, experience has shown that while modern equipment is more costly, it is much more reliable than traditional systems. The economies of one revolve around the comparison of high initial capital costs and low recurrent costs with low capital costs and high recurrent costs. Recent experience has been positive. The lesson is that it is very difficult to modify administrative bureaucracies so as to have a level of operation and maintenance of traditional systems that can compete with effective modern systems.

The same principle applies to the introduction of polyethylene pipes as conveyances of water from the source to the farmgate. The use of pipes eliminates water losses through seepage and spillage and greatly reduces water distribution problems among farmers. Periodic maintenance of channels by farmer groups—a difficult task to organize in the best of circumstances—becomes unnecessary. The cost of an underground pipe distribution network is much higher than the construction of ditches. But experience has shown that the performance of the costlier solution is such that there are greater returns to the high-technology alternative than to the traditional system.

There are other examples of Bank-promoted design standards to overcome poor maintenance. A rigid concrete-lined watercourse reduces seepage losses and is easier to maintain than earthen conveyance systems; more important, concrete-lined systems make illegal diversions of water more difficult and easier to detect. Yet, wherever such concrete-lined minor systems have been constructed, the distribution of water has become more efficient and corrupt practices have been reduced.

The issue of cost recovery for financing operation and maintenance is a vexing one. The Bank has always maintained that farmers should be charged for their irrigation water for many reasons. Farmers are made aware that water is not a free commodity and thus, it is not used wastefully. Water charges also help reduce inequalities in income between those who have irrigation water and those who do not by capturing some of the benefits from irrigation. Water charges also provide funds for essential maintenance work on the irrigation systems. Unfortunately, few public agencies—and most systems are in the public sector—are disciplined about recovering costs, and the level of collections is low. Furthermore, in many instances, those funds that are collected are not earmarked for maintenance.

The worst aspect of poor cost recovery and system operation is that they increase the likelihood of poor performance in the future. As has been emphasized, most irrigation schemes depend on the water users to help maintain the physical structures by organizing to do some of the maintenance work on the system themselves and by paying fees on water charges to support the cost of maintenance. If the system does not provide reliable and timely water deliveries, it is difficult to motivate farmers to aid in the provision of the systems support. It becomes difficult to collect water charges, and the water users become unwilling to organize to do maintenance. Consequently, the physical structures are not properly maintained and the system deteriorates, becoming less and less able to provide adequate irrigation.

CONCLUSION

Irrigation has played and will continue to play an important role in the production of food in many developing countries. Developing countries have placed great hope in the development of irrigation in the past, and will continue to do so in the future. Given the limited financial resources and the needs for development, it becomes increasing important that each investment produces maximum benefit. In this regard, irrigation development has fallen short of its potential, even though it has yielded substantial returns. There is much room for improvement, though it is expected that future projects will come closer to realizing their potential. Irrigation projects are complex social as well as physical systems that are difficult to design, implement, manage, and operate. It will not be easy to improve the performance of irrigation projects in developing countries, but the reward will be well worth the effort.

65. THE ROLE OF BILATERAL AGENCIES IN WATER AND WATER POLICY IN WORLD FOOD SUPPLIES

N. C. Brady, U.S. Agency for International Development, Department of State, Washington, D.C.

INTRODUCTION

Water resources have been a major factor in enhancing the economic and social development of the United States. Many of you may be keenly aware of the role water conservation and use have played in the western part of this country, not only in relation to agriculture, but to energy and domestic and industrial development. Water has played a different but equally significant role in the more heavily populated and industrialized eastern United States where environmental quality and health issues tend to dominate.

With our own development experiences in mind, it was only natural that from the inception of the Point Four program, in 1949, water considerations have been a major part of the bilateral aid program of this country. Irrigation projects, for example, have dominated our aid water efforts, but significant attention has also been given to power generation, flood control, and health and sanitation issues.

In the 1950s and 1960s, our technical cooperation program placed primary emphasis on the development of numerous irrigation projects. In cooperation with other donors we helped accelerate the worldwide increase in land under irrigation from 94 million ha in 1950 to about 261 million ha today. Most of this increase, of course, occurred in the developing countries.

Initially, most of our resources were used to finance capital construction. We helped design and build large dams and major distribution canals. The emphasis was on engineering, the aspect which we thought required priority consideration. We paid less attention to the institutional, management, and on-farm distribution aspects, perhaps assuming that the developing countries, utilizing their own cultural mechanisms, would take care of these other problems.

CONSTRAINED IMPACT OF SOME NEW SCHEMES

The irrigation schemes which we and other donors helped construct have had a remarkable and positive impact on food production and power generation in the developing countries, especially those in Asia. But in general they have been much less successful than was originally anticipated. Today, far less land than was planned is irrigated by new projects, and power production is likewise below design levels. I am sure you have devoted much time at this conference to ascertain why performance has been far below expectations. I will not attempt to enumerate all the factors which have influenced this performance but instead will identify a few major lessons AID feels have been learned over the past thirty-five years in water conservation and use. These lessons have helped determine the nature of the current programs which the U.S. Agency for International Development is supporting. They have called to our attention the fact that several criteria must be met if effective and sustained water conservation and utilization systems are to be developed. This is true whether we are discussing water for agriculture, health and sanitation, flood control, or power generation.

I would like to focus on three major lessons we have learned and show how our current programs are responding to these lessons.

THREE MAJOR LESSONS

Scope of Development

First is the recognition that the development of a water project involves far more than the construction of a dam and power plant and of major distribution canals. All aspects of water use must be considered, especially the management of the system and all its parts. This lesson has had a major impact on the nature of water projects we support. We now leave to the World Bank and other donors most of the responsibility for supporting major capital construction projects. We focus our efforts, through some 120 irrigation projects, on such activities as:

1. Improving the performance of *existing* systems rather than creating new ones.

2. Strengthening existing water-related *institutions* in host countries.

3. Initiating and supporting training courses to educate technicians on improved management techniques. Thus far, such courses have been held in India, Pakistan, Nepal, Sri Lanka, Bangladesh, Bolivia, and Peru.

4. Holding two senior officials workshops, one in Colorado and one in India. The decision makers must recognize the wisdom of a total systems management approach.

5. Holding eight *diagnostic workshops:* three in Sri Lanka, three in India, and one each in Nepal and Bangladesh.

6. Making seven *irrigation sector surveys,* in India, Nepal, Bangladesh, Thailand, Sri Lanka, Peru, and Haiti.

7. Making a major irrigation strategy review in India.

8. Developing handbooks and operational guides with primary emphasis on water management.

9. Provision of design assistance, especially on the modification of existing systems to provide more efficient on-farm delivery of the water. Much of the technical assistance for these activities is provided through our Water Manage-

ment Synthesis II project, which has a global mandate as well as a special focus on Asia. The project involves several U.S. universities and cooperators oversees and there is great demand for the services being offered. The project is now increasing its attention to African irrigation development problems.

Irrigation System Components Other than Water

The second lesson we have learned is that irrigation systems often do not meet expectations if they focus only on water and its conservation and utilization. From experience in Asian agriculture, for example, we have learned that much of the success of new irrigation schemes has been due to the concomitant availability of high-yielding and pest-resistant varieties of wheat, rice, and maize along with the greatly expanded use of fertilizers and, in some cases, pesticides. Through our support for national agricultural research programs, international agricultural research centers, and U.S. universities we have helped develop these high-yielding technologies, which, in turn, have increased the effectiveness of the irrigation systems. We have also placed emphasis on the need for fertilizers to utilize more fully the yield potential of the new varieties. Without additional fertilizer inputs the miracle cereal seeds would have had little impact with or without irrigation. Likewise the seeds and fertilizer alone would have had only modest impact without irrigation water.

User Involvement

A third lesson suggests that water systems are most succesful if there is at least some involvement of the potential users of the system from the very beginning of project development. Likewise, the most successful systems involve these users and their institutions in basic decisions as to how the system is to be managed and financed. I am certain this point has received adequate attention at this meeting.

A number of AID projects focus on the involvement of users early in the process and more completely than in the past. We encourage greater farmer involvement by helping to establish and operate water users' organizations. We also help develop better communications between farmers and government officials. Specific farmer involvement activities include:

1. A joint workshop with FAO in 1984 on farmer participation in irrigation water management.

2. Assisting efforts to organize a water users' association in Sri Lanka.

3. Training Pakistani extension personnel to organize water users' associations.

4. Studies of macroeconomic public policies which influence a farmer's ability to profit from irrigation.

SPECIAL CONSTRAINTS IN AFRICA

Unfortunately, most of the conditions which have led to at least some degree of success in Asian water management projects are missing in much of Africa south of the Sahara. High-yielding food crop varieties adapted to African conditions are only now being developed. Fertilizer use is lower by far in Africa than in any other major food producing

area. Human and institutional developing is generally not as well advanced as in Asia. Furthermore, Africa has a much lower overall water availability per hectare in Asia or Latin America.

As a consequence of these facts, irrigation projects in Africa generally have been only marginally successful at best. New irrigation schemes often supply water to only a fraction of the land area for which the project was designed. In many of these cases the actual costs per irrigated hectare are astronomical.

AID has recognized these conditions in Africa and is taking steps to help change them. While our direct involvement in major irrigation schemes is not too great, we are trying to help Africa develop other technology packages. For example, we provide about $100 million annually to support agricultural research efforts in Africa. Most of this support is made available to national research centers. Some, however, is provided through five International Agricultural Research Centers (IARCs) and several U.S. universities that are involved in collaborative research support programs (CRSPs) on major food crops and farm animals. While progress has been slow, significant results have been achieved. For example:

1. A new drought-tolerant hybrid sorghum has been developed and released.

2. New high-yielding maize hybrids are in wide use in Kenya and Zimbabwe.

3. New pest-resistant cassava and cowpea varieties have been released.

4. A new biological system has been developed to control the cassava mealy bug.

5. Potential vaccines for East Coast Fever of cattle and for pleuropneumonia in goats have been developed.

Much of the collaboration with national research centers is through research networks coordinated by IARCs or U.S. universities. We are working with other donors to expand these research networks.

If Africa's food production is to be increased significantly, fertilizer availability and use must grow markedly on that continent. Worldwide, increased crop production has been closely correlated with fertilizer use as well as with increases in irrigated land area. There is no reason to believe that this situation will not prevail in Africa. Consequently, steps must be taken to help the Africans provide sufficient fertilizer for food crops. The experiences of Asia and Latin America which clearly demonstrate the symbiotic effects of fertilizers and water must be heeded in Africa.

Another aspect of water management which must receive priority attention, particularly in Africa, is water management on unirrigated drylands where most of the crop production occurs. Innovative soils and crop management systems must be developed to capture rainwater and keep it in the soil to support crop growth. Farming systems research using so-called alley cropping is showing considerable potential. Leguminous trees and shrubs are grown in rows along with food crops. When properly fertilized with phosphorus, the trees and scrubs can enhance resistance to runoff and erosion while simultaneously, through fallen leaves and other residues, providing a mulch to reduce evaporation losses from the soil surface. We are supporting research on alley cropping at two international agricultural research centers and at national centers in cooperation with a cropping systems research project involving a number of U.S. universities.

AID is also supporting a number of upland soil and water conservation projects. For example, we have helped initiate a dryland research network for cooperating countries in the Middle East. The goal is to help these countries increase the efficiency of water use through improved soil and crop management practices. In the semiarid tropics, we have partially supported the development of a simple land farming practice which helps capture precipitation on heavy clay soils. This practice has successfully doubled the number of crops which can be grown each year.

The agency is also supporting efforts to improve watershed management as a means of controlling soil erosion and enhancing water conservation. Included are extensive efforts to help reforest badly denuded areas, thereby reducing the silting of reservoirs and municipal supply systems.

HEALTH AND SANITATION

Even though I have concentrated my remarks on agriculture, it should be emphasized that some of the same principles we have discussed for irrigation projects also apply to health and sanitation projects. AID and other donors have provided hundreds of millions of dollars to help improve community water systems. As was the case with past efforts in agriculture, however, most of the attention has been given to the development and installation of pumps and associated equipment. All too little emphasis has been placed on other aspects of water utilization such as waste disposal and sanitation. As a consequence, most of these projects have not lived up to expectations. We are now trying to couple these capital inputs with concentrated educational programs to help the water users understand other aspects of sanitation which must be included in an overall health and sanitation program. I received a report only this week of a successful pilot project in Togo which has used this broader approach. Users are involved through the development of user institutions with some responsibility for the system's management.

CONCLUSION

I would like to close on a personal note.

Water resource considerations have always been an important part of my life. I was born in southern Colorado and spent my early years on an irrigated farm. My forefathers were among those who transformed desertlike western areas into productive agricultural land, and many of my family members still make their living on irrigated farms. Their experience proves that water deficiencies can be overcome.

As I broadened my knowledge of agriculture and extended it to international concerns, I noted that while the causes and effects of agricultural failure are usually similar, the real difference is often in how to solve the problem or get around the constraint.

This then is what AID and other bilateral donors often deal with—helping the developing countries find that correct solution. We are succeeding, and we are struggling for greater and faster success. Our vision is to help the people of the world to feed, clothe, and sustain themselves while, at the same time, cherishing and conserving our precious natural resources.

66. THE LAND-GRANT SYSTEM IN INTERNATIONAL AGRICULTURAL DEVELOPMENT

John Patrick Jordan and Edward M. Wilson, Cooperative State Research Service, U.S. Department of Agriculture,
Washington, D.C.

ABSTRACT

The most significant contributions the United States of America can make to the developing nations are to assist in the building of human capital and institutions which encourage research and education in food production, food processing, post harvest technology, human nutrition, and water.

The United States participation in international development not only is justifiable on humanitarian grounds, but is in the interest of our economic stability and national security.

The involvement of the land-grant universities/state agricultural experiment station system in technical assistance to developing countries comes as a natural extension of their mission.

One of the outstanding achievements of these institutions was the partnership with India from 1952 to 1972. This partnership resulted in nine Indian agricultural universities' developing strong programs of agricultural research, teaching, and extension using a land-grant concept adapted from the U.S. model.

Over the past three decades we have learned much about the processes of international development and world hunger. We now know the strengths of a collaborative approach, the need for long-term commitment, and the importance of emphasizing human capital and institution building. These are appropriate roles for our universities and will help developing countries build indigenous capacities for meeting their own needs on a long-term, self-sustaining basis.

With a world which is becoming more crowded, more polluted, less stable ecologically, and more vulnerable to disruption, it is imperative that we look at ways of building closer relationships among us to solve worldwide food problems. The issue of peace revolves to a large extent around the availability and distribution of food; therefore, the significance of our work should not be under-emphasized. We are engaged in issues of life and death, of war and peace.

INTRODUCTION—WHY BE INVOLVED?

The most significant contributions the United States of America can make to the developing nations are to assist in the building of human capital and institutions which encourage research and education in food production, food processing, post harvest technology, human nutrition, and water. It is important that development bring insight and the knowledge base so necessary for human beings to live life to its fullest, in harmony with the natural environment and at peace with each other.

The involvement of our nation and its land-grant universities in international agricultural development is a commitment propelled by the potential for global famine and the overwhelming need to relieve general and chronic poverty that keeps millions of people hungry even in time of plenty.

The *Global 2000 Report to the President* in 1977 concludes that if present trends continue, the world in the year 2000 will be more crowded, more polluted, less stable ecologically, and more vulnerable to disruption than the world we live in now. It projects that by the year 2000 we will have an additional 2.35 billion people to feed. This population growth alone will cause requirements for water to double in nearly half the world. Still-greater increases would be needed to improve standards of living.

Serious deterioration of agricultural soils will occur worldwide as a result of erosion, loss of organic matter, desertification, salinization, and alkalinization.

These projections would justify increased United States participation in international agricultural development on humanitarian grounds alone. In reality, however, our participation is also in the interest of economic stability and national security.

In the 1970s developing countries accounted for most of the growth in U.S. exports. The value of agricultural exports rose from $7.8 billion in 1970−71 to $43.8 billion in 1980−81. As farm prices rose through the 1970s, American farmers increased production and came to view the export market as their source of prosperity.

In 1981 and 1982, global recession hit the developing countries especially hard and this had an immediate impact on the U.S. export trade. Export of U.S. agricultural products to developing countries declined by 11 percent in value in 1982, and another 11 percent in 1983, a direct result of slowing of economic growth in those countries.

The inequity in per capita GNP and in access to food between developing countries and industrial countries is not consistent with global peace and stability. Unless there is change, the report of the Presidential Commission on World Hunger predicted the following in March, 1980: "The most potentially explosive force in the world today is the frustrated desire of poor people to attain a decent standard of living. The anger, despair, and often hatred that result represent real and persistent threats to international order." The involvement of the land-grant universities/state agricultural experiment station system in technical assistance to developing countries comes as a natural extension of their mission. These universities were created to bring knowledge and the capacity to change to those at the grassroots. They were chartered by Congress through the Morrill Act ". . . to teach such branches of learning as are related to agriculture and the mechanic arts . . . in order to promote the liberal and practical education of the industrial classes. . . ."

THE LAND-GRANT MODEL

Clearly the U.S. farmer is the backbone of our agricultural industry, but much of the credit for making this industry the most productive in the world must go to the agricultural programs of our land-grant universities. These universities, through their research and education programs, provided the knowledge for progress.

Before the establishment of the land-grant system, there was nothing uniquely American about higher education on this continent, even though we have had higher education institutions since the 1630s. The University of Georgia was the first state-chartered institution of higher learning and the University of Virginia was the first tax-supported collegiate institution in America. But when the doors of the University of Virginia opened under the leadership of President Thomas Jefferson in 1824, there was nothing special about the curricula nor the structure of the university that made it any different from all the other seminaries and colleges in the New World. They were based upon a good solid liberal arts curriculum, but exposure to science was principally through the fields of mathematics, natural history, and perhaps some introductory courses in chemistry and physics. No one had suggested that knowledge ought to be applied to the solution of real-world problems.

This did not become a viable idea until the latter portion of the 1840s, when Professor Jonathan Baldwin Turner of Illinois came up with the idea that we ought to have institutions dedicated to the agricultural and mechanic arts in which science would be applied to the solution of real-world problems. He published his first paper on this idea in 1850 and by 1857 Congressman Justin Smith Morrill of Vermont proposed legislation to authorize the establishment of such institutions. The act passed both houses of Congress and was sent to President Buchanan, who promptly vetoed it.

In spite of entering into the most devastating and divisive war in the history of the United States, the next Congress readdressed this issue, passed the Morrill Act, sometimes called the Land-Grant Act, and President Abraham Lincoln signed it into law in 1862. The idea provided a framework against which the first uniquely American contribution to higher education was established. We now had schools dedicated to applying knowledge to issues of agriculture and natural resources across the length and breadth of the nation.

The agriculture program of these institutions has three basic functions—teaching, research, and extension. All three are interrelated and mutually supporting. The system includes fifty-eight state and territorial experiment stations, seventeen historically black colleges and universities known as the 1890 institutions, plus sixty-two schools of forestry and twenty-eight schools of veterinary medicine. The system supports some 24,000 research projects using 12,500 scientists (7,500 full-time equivalent), 13,000 graduate and postdoctoral researchers and professionals, and 7,000 technical support personnel. The bulk of the involvement of the land-grant institutions in international development has been in agriculture and has used the state agricultural experiment stations, Cooperative Extension Service, and related teaching faculties in agriculture as a foundation of talent.

INTERNATIONAL PROGRAMS—THE BEGINNING

The involvement of U.S. agriculturally related colleges in technical assistance and in the training of foreign students spans more than a hundred years. In 1876, the Massachusetts State College of Agriculture, now the University of Massachusetts, assisted in developing the Sapporo Agricultural School in Japan, and in 1924 Cornell University began its Cornell-in-China program.

Early participation was on a small scale involving individual faculty members, and only a few of the largest universities which had the capabilities and the interest to take on international projects. The approach was given a boost by President Harry S. Truman, who, in his inaugural address on January 20, 1949, pledged to set forth a program by which the United States would help developing countries help themselves. President Truman's administration marked the beginning of official U.S. government cooperation in international agricultural development. The U.S. Department of Agriculture was given the responsibility of implementing many aspects of the international agricultural development program and in turn asked the land-grant institutions for help.

THE INDIA EXPERIENCE

One of the outstanding achievements of that period was the partnership with India, which wanted to build institutions that through study and practice would enhance the rural communities and increase food production. Six U.S. land-grant universities—Illinois, Kansas State, Missouri, Ohio State, Pennsylvania State, and Tennessee—were invited by the government of India to help. The program was initiated in 1952 with the financial support of the U.S. government. When the program ended in 1972, nine Indian agricultural universities had developed strong programs of agricultural research, teaching, and extension using a land-grant concept adapted from the U.S. model.

Over the twenty years of this linkage program, the six U.S. universities sent 217 staff members to India for tours of two to seven years and 124 for shorter periods, totaling more than 600 professional years of effort. More than a thousand Indians came to the United States for study.

The phenomenal progress made in India in the production of food and fiber can probably be attributed to this inter-university cooperation.

INTERNATIONAL AGRICULTURAL RESEARCH CENTERS

Another accomplishment in which the land-grant institutions were involved was the establishment of international agricultural research centers in the developing countries. In the 1960s, the Ford and Rockefeller Foundations sponsored a small number of international agricultural centers in developing countries many of which were staffed initially from the U.S. land-grant institutions. An excellent example of this involved Norman Borlaug, who left the University of Minnesota to work at the International Maize and Wheat Improvement Center in Mexico, where he won a Nobel Prize.

The inter-university cooperation between Cornell and the Philippines' College of Agriculture at Los Baños provided a strong base for development and led to the selection of Los Baños as the site for the world-famous International Rice Research Institute, which helped launch the Green Revolution in Asia.

Recognizing the need to expand the scope and to build new centers, The World Bank, the Food and Agriculture Organization of the United Nations (FAO), and the United Nations Development Program (UNDP) joined forces to sponsor and manage a new kind of international association.

As a result, the Consultative Group on International Agricultural Research (CGIAR) was organized in 1971. The objective of CGIAR is to bring together countries, public and private institutions, international and regional organizations, and representatives from developing countries in support of a network of international agricultural research centers and programs. Today there are twelve centers supported by some thirty donors.

TITLE XII

A significant landmark was achieved in 1975 when Congress enacted Title XII of the Foreign Assistance Act. Congress recognized the capabilities of the land-grant universities and through this legislation provides for an expanded long-term involvement of these universities in international agricultural development. It also provides for collaboration between the land-grant universities and the U.S. Agency for International Development (AID) in program selection and planning.

The task has been accomplished through diverse mechanisms including: strengthening grants, memoranda of understanding between AID and some universities for continuing long-term cooperation, the establishment of a joint professional career system to allow university faculty to work for AID and AID professionals to spend some time on university campuses, and a joint enterprise mode, which is a mechanism to improve AID's access to the resources of the smaller universities.

In the ten years following its enactment, the Title XII program has had significant impact on attitudes, communication, and understanding of the development processes. The land-grant universities have been called on to contribute in every part of the developing world. The Collaborative Research Support Program (CRSP) is an effective mechanism of operation which has evolved and needs to be highlighted in a discussion on the role of the state agricultural experiment station in international development.

The CRSPs are long-term research programs, supported by AID for collaboration of U.S. universities, AID, USDA, and other research institutions with institutions in developing countries. The CRSP may target any aspect of the food production chain, including nutrition, socioeconomic, or cultural factors. This arrangement brings together the resources necessary to successfully conduct a multidisciplinary, multifaceted, international research program. The overriding objectives of the CRSPs are to improve agriculture both in the developing countries and in the United States.

Foremost among the CRSPs are the sorghum-millet CRSP, the small ruminant CRSP, the bean-cowpea CRSP, and the pond dynamics–aquaculture CRSP. These programs are extensive and involve several of our universities and large numbers of scientists. In the case of the sorghum-millet CRSP there are some eighty-two scientists from eight U.S. land-grant universities collaborating with scientists in thirteen host countries.

A new cooperative program will soon be started. The purpose of this program is to assist the International Agricultural Research Centers (IARC) with research problems when the IARCs lack needed specialized facilities, such as highly technical, costly equipment, or specifically trained personnel. The USDA's Cooperative State Research Service, working with the land-grant universities, will assist in carrying out this program with AID.

THE BENEFITS TO THE UNITED STATES

Humanitarian, economic, and political reasons are those most often cited for the U.S. involvement in international agricultural development. The need to free the world from starvation and malnutrition, to find markets for U.S. agricultural products, and to foster social and political stability in the world are magnanimous reasons and need no further elaboration, but there are several benefits derived by individuals, institutions, the U.S. agricultural industry, and the United States in general which are often overlooked.

Personal Benefits

It is said that U.S. agricultural professional who has lived and worked in a developing country is never the same again. There is much truth in that statement because the professionals gain a clearer understanding of world problems related to their fields of study. They become more sensitive to the need for an ecological approach to problem solving and the importance of integrated systems of production and pest control. A sense of humility and an enhanced comprehension of gratitude is often an added bonus. The participants return to the United States with increased vigor and enthusiasm.

Land-Grant Universities—Windfall

In a time of declining national enrollment and fiscal exigency the international dimension provides an opportunity for the universities to augment their enrollment and provide added opportunities for the research and extension faculties.

The presence of foreign students on the campuses enhances the learning environment with its multicultural and multiethnic dimensions. The overseas experience can provide a new dimension for the faculty and enrich the curricula for all students.

Foreign Graduates

Following graduation, international students often return to prominent positions with their governments and over time become influential leaders. They often provide the avenue through which trade and programmatic advantages may accrue to the United States. This is particularly true in the area of farm inputs such as tools, machinery, seed, fertilizer, pesticides, and feed additives.

Enhanced U.S. Agricultural Productivity

Agriculture is a science, and science knows no national boundaries. The facts uncovered in one country usually have application in another. U.S. agriculture has benefited from both plant and animal germ plasm introduced from other countries, particularly with respect to disease and drought resistance. It is often forgotten that, for example, our soybean industry was founded on the introduction of germ plasm from China. This effort has been a two-way street, with the United States improving varieties and sending them back to the originating country. The United States has made substantial contributions to the international crop germ plasm resources including so-called minor crops such as the sunflower (*Helianthus annuus*) and blueberry (*Vaccinium spp*). Two excellent examples of foreign genetic resources benefiting U.S. agriculture are the potato (*Solanum tuberosum*) and tomato (*Lycopersicon esculentum*).

The modern potato varieties obtained much of their disease resistance from genes derived from wild germ plasm resources imported from developing countries. The late blight resistance genes came from the Mexican *Solanum demissum* and other wild species. These sources also have provided genes for immunity or resistance to frost; bacterial wilt; viruses A, X, and Y; races of golden and root knot nematodes; potato aphids; Colorado potato beetle; hopper burn; scab; leafroll; and other potato disorders.

The wild tomato species from South America, the original home for tomatoes, have provided most of the disease-resistant genes which have been incorporated within modern U.S. tomato varieties. Resistance to Fusarium and Verticillium disease pathogens obtained from these imported wild tomato species have saved the U.S. tomato growers millions of dollars each year. Additional promising tomato germ plasm resources include salt-tolerant and drought-tolerant species from the Galapagos Islands.

Moreover, modern history is resplendent with examples of developing countries' buying considerably more U.S. agricultural products because they have strengthened their own economy through U.S. agricultural aid, thus providing the capital with which to buy U.S. food commodities, machinery, fertilizer, seed, etc.

THE FUTURE

Since President Truman's commitment in 1949 to provide assistance to developing countries, we have learned much about the processes of international development and world hunger. Today we are sensitive to related social, political, economic, moral, and educational challenges. In the words of Clifton R. Wharton, Jr., chancellor, State University of New York, "It challenges us to set aside differences of ideology and institutions in pursuit of the common good of humankind."

Our land-grant universities having made significant contributions, often long-term support which is now possible through the Title XII legislation. The collaborative approach to research and training encouraged by Title XII will result in mutual benefit to the United States and developing countries. Speaking on the role of universities in international affairs at Michigan State University, Erven J. Long, director of the Office of Research and University Relations, AID, said, "I see the universities' potential role as of enormous significance; as having greater significance to the future of international relations of this country than any other institution, public or private—save only one! That one exception of still greater importance is our system of constitutional government with its supporting system of periodically recurring free elections."

The experiences in Asia and Latin America have demonstrated that the land-grant universities in cooperation with local institutions can make significant improvements in the agricultural sector of developing countries. The challenge is to adapt this experience in working effectively with the diverse developing African nations. Several of these nations are faced with severe agroecological problems, eroding natural resource bases, and declining per capita food production. In addition the cultural, social, economic, political, and communication systems are significantly different from that of the United States, Asia, and Latin America and differ markedly among African nations.

For U.S. agricultural professionals to work effectively in Africa they must have a working knowledge of the local language. Our universities should orient their social and political science curricula to global topics and expand their language training capability. Consideration should be given to including a foreign language requirement in our undergraduate agricultural curricula. In the area of economics, more research and training is needed in international trade, marketing, and monetary policy. Our graduates must be prepared to function in an increasingly interdependent world. They should be taught systems approaches to problem solving in agriculture and be prepared for the interaction between agriculture and the social processes, with all of the humanistic implications.

Development projects must be collaborative and long term. The donor countries should coordinate their efforts among themselves and with the developing countries. This would improve priority setting, reduce unnecessary duplication, and provide adequate resources to tackle pressing problems. An example of a multidonor collaboration model is the Cooperation for Development in Africa (CDA). Cooperation for Development in Africa is an informal association of donor countries consisting of Belgium, Canada, the Federal Republic of Germany, France, Italy, the United Kingdom, and the United States.

The idea for CDA originated in France, where it was noted that certain economic problems could not be solved by one donor country alone, but needed to be coordinated to prevent duplication and overlapping among donors. It was also noted that Africans themselves have formed Africa-wide institutions to foster development. These institutions include: the Organization of African Unity/Scientific, Technical and Research Commission (OAU/STRC), the African Development Bank (AFDB), the Association for the Advancement of Agricultural Sciences in Africa (AAASA), and the Southern Africa Develoment Coordination Conference (SADCC). The CDA donor countries found it useful to join African groups to work on sectors considered critical to development in Africa.

The CDA framework for developing agricultural research initiatives is very broad. It permits a broad scope of activities and is designed to accommodate a wide range of donor and recipient country funding and administrative styles and procedures. The CDA Ad Hoc Technical Committee on Agricultural Research serves in an advisory and consultation capacity to ensure that individual activities are initiated by CDA members in concert with African governments and regional entities. CDA-supported initiatives within any given ecological zone or country would aim to strengthen and complement current research activities. In consultation with African organizations, CDA donor-supported activities would be based on an analysis of the research programs as related to agricultural productivity.

It will be necessary for us to find new and creative ways to work together as the science of agriculture becomes more complex. With the great visibility given at this time in the United States to the new technologies broadly labeled "biotechnology," it is appropriate to initiate discussions on an international basis. The developing countries stand as an untapped source of germ plasm, a genetic pool which could be engineered to greatly improve agricultural productivity worldwide.

What do we mean by biotechnology? There are many definitions, but the Biotechnology Committee of the Division of Agriculture, National Association of State Universities and Land-Grant Colleges, defines biotechnology as the use of living organisms or their components in agricultural, food, and other industrial processes. These include technologies emerging through advances in molecular genetics, molecular biology, and closely associated disciplines, particularly as these research areas continue to elucidate the molecular details of growth and development. Biotechnological research uses recently developed research techniques such as cell and chloroplast culture, plant regeneration, somatic hybridization, embryo manipulation and transfer, and recombinant DNA approaches, including gene splicing, replication, and transfer. But much simpler technologies used in artificial insemination of livestock and in plant breeding are also included.

The availability of these technologies increases the worldwide need for an inventory of the entire biota on the planet. This is a massive undertaking which will only be achieved by international cooperation, but the land-grant institutions can be a major source of information contributing to such a global effort. Toward that end the land-grant universities of America and the USDA are jointly championing the establishment of a National Biological Impact Assessment Program which will be built upon decades of experience within the state agricultural experiment station system.

In addition to the new technologies, there are a number of innovative, emerging concepts. An example is the concept of coupling the Caribbean Basin Initiative with the research and extension programs in the land-grant system. The Puerto

Rico Agricultural Experiment Station and Cooperative Extension Service have proposed the establishment, at their station in Mayagüez, of a staging area and support program for any and all agricultural research and extension programs that might be targeted to assist the Spanish-speaking nations around the Caribbean. The emphasis is on nations at the west end of the Caribbean. The University of Puerto Rico would provide translators, individuals with background on specific agricultural commodities and technologies currently used in various areas of the Caribbean, knowledge of the individuals who are holding positions of authority in the Spanish-speaking Caribbean nations, and test plots on Puerto Rico that could be used for preliminary work since the island contains almost all of the varied environmental and soil conditions found in the western Caribbean.

The same concept has been developed by the Virgin Islands Experiment Station, emphasizing the eastern Caribbean nations that are principally English speaking. The Virgin Islands program is already in its initial stages. The idea in each case is for the land-grant system to use these Caribbean stations as conduits and facilitators through which agricultural research and extension techniques and developments can be applied in support of the Caribbean Basin Initiative. A similar approach is being discussed among those institutions involved in the Pacific Basin. Such efforts are a natural extension of CSRS's Tropical, Subtropical Agriculture program, which has had strong leadership from the universities of Florida and Hawaii.

Unequivocally we need to look at ways of building closer relationships among us to solve worldwide food problems. The key to maintaining world peace does not lie solely in aircraft, missiles, and troop units. The issue of peace revolves to a large extent around the availability and distribution of food. Therefore, the significance of our work should not be underemphasized. We are engaged in issues of life and death, of war and peace.

REFERENCES

Barney, G. O. 1977. The global 2000 report to the president. Vol. 1.

Johnson, W. F., and P. Upchurch. 1985. Guidelines for collaborative research support programs under Title XII.

Long, E. J. 1980. The university's role in international affairs—a personal perspective. Address delivered at Michigan State University.

Morgan, R. P. 1978. The role of U.S. universities in science and technology for development. St. Louis, Mo.: Washington University.

Ordfield, M. L. 1984. The value of conserving genetic resources. Washington, D.C.: U.S. Department of the Interior, National Park Service.

Read Hadley. 1974. Partners with India building agricultural universities. University of Illinois at Urbana-Champaign.

Scoville, O. J. 1979. World hunger and the land-grant universities. AUSUDIAP Publication no. 3.

Thomas, G. W. 1983. The international dimension: Unrealized potential. Address delivered at Oregon State University.

Wharton, C. R., Jr. 1982a. U.S. bilateral development assistance:

Three observations for the future. Commencement address, John Hopkins University, Baltimore, Md.

Wharton, C. R., Jr. 1982b. International development and institutional development and institutional-Building: is human capital the key to success? E. T. York Distinguished Lecture, Auburn University.

Wharton, C. R., Jr. 1983. BIFAD's sixth birthday: a personal exaugural. Administrator's International Development Leaders Forum. Washington, D.C.: U.S. Agency for International Development.

PART XII. RECOMMENDATIONS OF THE CONFERENCE

RECOMMENDATIONS OF THE CONFERENCE

Conference participants took part in the Nominal Group Technique (NGT) process to determine recommendations to resolve critical issues of water supply, water management, water and energy, technology, water salinity, and integrated ecosystems management. Conference participants were asked to respond to the question: "What are the most significant issues in (insert group name) that must be resolved over the next decade to help alleviate world hunger?" Their responses are grouped by subject category and listed in priority ranking.

WATER SUPPLY

1. Conduct research on atmospheric/oceanic interrelationships to obtain a better understanding of climatic patterns and their changes and weather modification, especially with regard to precipitation.

2. Apply soil/water conservation techniques in watersheds which enhance on-site water-use efficiency and downstream water quality and quantity.

3. Make provision for sustainable and prioritized use of surface and groundwater to meet the needs of people, crops, livestock, and industry, and to balance food and economic needs against environmental concerns.

4. Evaluate and quantify aquifers and regulate groundwater withdrawals for priority food crops and urban uses.

5. Develop flexible agriculture production systems which can withstand extended, recurrent droughts.

6. Conduct research to optimize the use of water and land resources in the production of crops, livestock, and wildlife.

WATER SALINITY

1. Develop drainage on existing and future irrigation projects.

2. Improve water-use efficiency.

3. Educate farmers concerning effects of soil salinity, recognition of its symptoms, and changes that can be made in cropping systems when salinity problems occur.

4. Prevent salinity problems through improved water management and distribution systems.

5. Improve water distribution systems and delivery systems to reduce excess irrigation application.

6. Grow crop species, develop new varieties, or use natural vegetation tolerant to salinity as conditions permit to utilize saline waters effectively.

WATER MANAGEMENT

1. Develop national policies for water and agriculture.

2. Improve water management of existing irrigation systems.

3. Increase incentives to farmers to manage water more effectively.

4. Provide training in irrigation management.

5. Use farm inputs and services more effectively in existing systems.

INTEGRATED ECOSYSTEMS

1. Preserve natural resources (water, plants, and soil) and encourage their optimal use in the context of existing agricultural, ecological, and social conditions.

2. Develop government policies to achieve equilibrium between population and support areas.

3. Create more understanding of the causes of failure of crop plants to yield their genetic potential given water availability and quality.

4. Consider all alternative sources of water, including ocean water.

5. Improve integrated ecosystems management within targeted communities through multidisciplinary research and extension using local institutions and personnel with priority on farmer inputs.

WATER AND ENERGY

1. Select or develop alternative energy sources with particular emphasis on small (½ to 3 hp) systems to replace or supplement conventional energy resources in agriculture to exploit site-specific energy resources.

2. Develop national policies to remove energy constraints to irrigation development and to provide incentives to farmers.

3. Involve local people in water and energy development.

4. Establish information exchange, vocational education, and demonstrations for local people to improve technical skills in cost-effective water and resource management.

5. Install transportation infrastructure for getting resources to and from markets on a timely basis.

TECHNOLOGY

1. Develop appropriate agrotechnology and management systems for higher and more stable yields in dryland and rainfed agriculture.

2. Improve existing irrigation systems to increase productivity and efficiency within existing social and cultural contexts.

3. Provide practical and relevant education and training to users of technology.

4. Develop appropriate incentives for adoption of water efficiency measures by farmers.

5. Integrate technologies—planting, tillage, harvesting, water management, pesticide control, crop selection, and climate. We must attack the problem with a system rather than one technology in order to be successful.

6. Develop technology to prevent and alleviate waterlogging and land productivity degradation within irrigated areas.

PART XIII. ATTENDEES AND COMMITTEE MEMBERS

INVITED PARTICIPANTS, SPEAKERS, RAPPORTEURS, AND DISCUSSANTS

I. P. Abrol
Everardo Aceves-Navarro
Perry L. Adkisson
Manzur Ahmad
José F. Alfaro
Gerald F. Arkin
Eduardo Armas
Alan R. Aston
Benjamin U. Bagadion
Tom Bahr
Yehia Barrada
Anson R. Bertrand
Sadiqul I. Bhuiyan
Wilbert H. Blackburn
Martin Ramirez Blanco
Ferrari Bono
Norman E. Borlaug
Thadis Box
John S. Boyer
Nyle C. Brady
Daniel W. Bromley
William L. Brown
J. Artie Browning
Pieter Buringh
George Burrill
Glenn W. Burton
Robert Chambers
J. Jesus Romero Chavez
Muhammad Sidiq Cheema
V. H. Choga
R. Nolan Clark
Stanley J. Clark
Neville P. Clarke
R. James Cook
E. Walter Coward
Michael E. Curtin
Ian Dalbogni
Iel DeGreeter

N. G. R. DeSilva
K. William Easter
Zein el-Abedine
LeVern W. Faidley
Carlos Fernandez
Richard A. Frederiksen
Raymond E. Frisbee
Jack J. Fritz
W. Fuller
Herbert H. Fullerton
G. Fred Gifford
James R. Gilley
L. Joe Glass
Lalit Godammunne
Martin H. González
John F. Griffiths
Neil S. Grigg
Charles T. Hallmark
Arthur G. Hansen
Arselan Harahap
Thorant W. Hardeware
Edgar C. Harrell
Dale F. Heermann
Amin Hidyat
Edward A. Hiler
Rafiqul Hogue
H. M. Horning
Garald H. Horst
John R. Hoyle
S. Shahid Husain
Hussein R. Idris
Samba Idrissa
Kurt J. Irgolic
Wesley P. James
Marvin E. Jensen
John P. Jordan
Wayne R. Jordan
A. M. H. Kango

Ruth Karen
Jack Keller
Michel Doo Kingué
Waewchak Kongtolprom
H. O. Kunkel
Roberto Revera Lanza
Robert J. Lascano
Roberto L. Lenton
Wayne A. LePori
Helmut L. Lieth
Arthur Maas
Andrew H. Macpherson
Khalil H. Mancy
Brian K. Matlick
Gerald Matlock
Dick McConnen
Richard McGowan
Marshall J. McFarland
Robert G. Merrifield
Shem Edwin Migot-Adholla
Chrysanthus Osoro Mogere
Louis J. Mostertman
Zheng Naibo
Syed Navaid Ali Nasri
John L. Nieber
Henry A. Nix
Juan Novara
Orlando Olcese
John O'Toole
M. G. Padhye
Tracy S. Park, Jr.
Finis S. Patton, Jr.
J. R. Philip
Thomas D. Potter
Bhuvanesh Kumar Pradhan
George E. Radosevich
W. Robert Rangeley
Ned Raun

Donald L. Reddell
Carlos Sarria Remy
James D. Rhoades
Kirk P. Rodgers
Stephen G. Sandford
D. Sanni
Joseph L. Schuster
Eduardo Seminario
Sach Sethaputra
Jael Silliman
R. Wayne Skaggs
Ernest T. Smerdon
K. Mitchell Snow
Soewasono
Lukono Sowa
B. A. Stewart
William A. Stout
Kenneth M. Strzepek
C. Subramananiam
Raymond J. Supalla
Robert Sweazy
Ananda Bahadur Thapa
Gerald W. Thomas
Nukool Thongthawee
H. W. Underhill
Frank E. Vandiver
Enrique Polacios Velez
Grant H. Vest, Jr.
Carlos Corrales Villalobos
T. Vivekananthan
Robert Wade
Michael J. Way
Lowell O. Weeks
Simon Williams
Dan Wolf
Robert A. Young
Montague Yudelman

CONFERENCE REGISTRANTS

John Abernathy
Johnathan Afolabi
William H. Aldred
Sonia Alianak
Ilan Amir
Arachchi Ariyaratne
Gary Arnold
Bill Babacz
Danita S. Bailey
Julian Baker
Punnee Barrera
George W. Bates
James B. Beard
Fred J. Benson
Arthur Benton
Roberto Berges
Reginald Berland
Shyamala Bhaskaran
Annette Bingham
Luther S. Bird
Wes Birdwell
James D. Brace
E. Cabell Brand
Jane P. Breen
Ron Brimhall
Charles R. Britton
Oscar Brauer-Herrera
Meryl Brossard, Jr.
Herman D. Brown
Kirk W. Brown
Mary S. Brown
T. J. Bulat
John Calhoun
Charlotte M. Cameron
Josephine Campbell
Patrick Carriere
C. Andrew Carson
Pedro Castillo
Michael Cate
William J. Clark
Tyrone Clauero
Wayne Clyma
B. Gregory Cobb
Clint Coleman
Marty Coleman
Edwin H. Cooper
Dean Corrigan
C. R. Creger
Kathryn Crenwelge
Rodney Crenwelge
Hafid Debarrh
Fred Davies
Douglas R. De Cluitt
Rodolfo de la Garza
Daniele De Wrachien
Frank Di Matteo
Joe B. Dixon

Pat Domenico
Randy Dominy
Peter B. Dreisbach
Nelson D. Durst
Ralph James Echols
Richard Egg
Milton C. Engelke
Vance Engleman
Cecilio Escareno
John P. Fackler
Donald E. Farris
Janine Finnell
Worth Fitzgerald
Gretcha Flinn
Daniel Forbes
Richard K. Ford
Ellen Friedman
Hamzal Gafar
Luis Galaz
Col. Gerald Galloway
Charles A. George
Charles Giammona
Earl Gilmore
Cindy Goldman
Mario Gonzalez-Lacayo, Sr.
James T. Goodwin
James H. Gramman
Gordon A. Grant
Alton M. Gray
Carl Gray
Ethan Grossman
Gary Hallbauer
P. G. Harms
Sharon Haughee
Robert W. Heard
James L. Heilman
Otto Helweg
Don R. Herring
Douglas C. Hicks
Gerald Higgins
Charlotte Hill
Henry C. Hill
Cliff Hoelscher
J. W. Holloway
Howard Hogg
Wendell Horne
Altaif Husain
Aly Indiaye
Marilyn Ivins
Michael Jeger
Sarah Johnson
Ralph Jones
Roger K. Jones
Alan Journet
John H. Judd
Waldon Kerns
James H. King

Robert Koenig
Raymond E. Kitchell
David Kittleson
D. Earl Kline
Ron Knutson
Rose Kress
Karen Kubera
Leon Kubera
Otto R. Kunze
Benson J. Lamp
Fritz H. Langer
Curtis F. Lard
Alvin Larke, Jr.
Harold F. Latortue
Dan Lattimore
J. Charles Lee
Wayne LePori
Phillip Limbacher
Gene Lindemann
Richard H. Loeppert
Cathleen Loving
William Lucez
Aaron Kim Ludeke
Terry McAdams
George G. McBee
Darrel McDonald
George Ray McEachern
Deborah Mahavier
Howard Malstrom
Fritz Marcelin
Gene Mata
M. A. Matthews
Fred D. Maurer
Fowden G. Maxwell
Kevin R. Mazziotta
C. E. Meier
Carl Menzies
Glynda Mercier
Pat Miles
Murray H. Milford
Creighton Miller
Jim F. Mills
Tom Mings
Lawrence G. Mix
Roger L. Monk
James A. Moore
Jaroy Moore
D. D. Moss
Saied Mostaghimi
Steve Murdock
H. Murray-Rust
J. Stephen Neck
John Neiber
Larry Ness
Ronald J. Newton
John P. Nichols
K. A. T. Nikapitiya

John Norris
Joe Novak
Blas Oddome
Yvonne Ottman
Dan Padberg
Rev. A. A. Palermo
Melville L. Palmer
Leonard Panella
Bob Pauline
Ed Peacock
Marcos Pena-Franjul
Daniel C. Pfannstiel
Allan L. Phillips
Leonard M. Pike
Karen Pilant
Rick Piltz
Mary Alice Pisani
Francisco A. Planco.S.
W. Arthur Porter
Sandra Postel
Maxwell Poswal
Bob Provart
David Pugh
Sylvia Brown Putnam
Nihal Rajapakse
Ann Reilly
Herbert Richardson
James Richardson
William B. Richardson
Ron Richter
Carlos Rivas
Lewis M. Roberts
Dan Robertson
Bill Roof
B. B. Ross
Paul Roth
Barry G. Rought
Robert H. Rucker
M. B. Russell
Rebecca Sanchez-Orosco
E. G. Sander
Mark L. Sandlin
Ruth C. Schaffer
Michael C. Schiefer
John P. Schneider, Jr.
Vernon E. Schneider
W. S. Schneider
Herb W. Schwertner
Mary C. Scott
D. H. Seastrunk
Nora Seton
Yacoub Shaer
Carl E. Shafer
Milo Shult
George Slater
Charles L. Smith
Charles R. Smith

Dudley Smith

Edward G. Smith

Gary C. Smith

Roberta Smith

Crispin A. Sorhaindo

Randal Stahl

Jim Stansel

Susan Steinberg

Charles Stockton

Dr. Arthur Stoeker

Glenn E. Stout

Kirk Strawn

Duwayne Suter

Wayne Sweatt

Donald A. Sweeney

G. B. Thompson

Terri Tongco

John Velehradsky

Victor Vinas

Jaime A. Vinas-Roman

Kevin C. Vining

Raymond Waldron

A. H. Fred Walker

Bill Walker

Bret Wallach

Flora C. Wang

Mamadou Watt

Dave Weaver

Milton W. Weller

Fred E. Westbrook

J. Westphal

Robert B. Wheaton

Greg White

Robert E. White

Raymond Whitley

Lambert H. Wilkes

Michael D. Woods

ORGANIZING COMMITTEE

Perry Adkisson
Kenneth L. Bader
Charles E. Ball
Harry Beachell
Osvaldo Bedini
Robert J. Berg
W. T. Berry, Jr.
Art Blair
Jorge Blanco
Norman E. Borlaug
Peter K. Bourne
Cabell Brand
Oscar Brauer
David Burns
Mayra Buvinic
Jose Cabeza
John Caple
Charles Cargill
Zerle Carpenter
Neville Clarke
Vincent R. Clephas

Jack Cross
Marian Czarnecki
Douglas R. DeCluitt
T. L. de Fayer
Heitor Guruglino De Souza
Murray Fasken
Eduardo Feller
Douglas G. Fleming
Davis L. Ford
Orville Freeman
Jack Fritts
Luis Garibay
Carlos Grassi
Herbert Grubb
Jon L. Hagler
Robert Hanson
Robert W. Heard
Fred Hutchinson
George D. Kennedy
Harry O. Kunkel
Roberto Lenton

Gilbert Levine
Phil Limbacher
Stephen McGaughey
M. H. Manning
William T. Mashler
Bruce Maunder
Fred Maurer
Augustin Miller
George Mitchell
J. Hiram Moore
Orlando Olcese
J. W. O'Meara
Herbert H. Ortega
Robert W. Page
Tracy S. Park, Jr.
Eber H. Peters
Arthur Porter
Michael Potashnik
Thomas D. Potter
Jay Pumphrey

Jack Rains
Sheran Riley
Lewis M. Roberts
J. D. Sartwelle, Sr.
Charles Scruggs
George William Sherk
Wayne A. Showers
Wayne Slovacek
Jim Spicola
J. Paul Sticht
M. S. Swaminathan
Peter Thatcher
Leland S. Turner
Frank E. Vandiver
Michael Vaughn
Denise Weiner
Robert Wheaton
Joseph H. Williams
F. Caddo Wright
Montague Yudelman

PROGRAM COMMITTEE

William A. Stout, Chairman

J. Artie Browning

Thomas C. Cartwright

Steven C. Chapra

Richard A. Frederiksen

Ronald C. Griffin

John F. Griffiths

Ed Hiler

John R. Hoyle

Wayne R. Jordan

Ronald D. Lacewell

Donald L. Reddell

Edward C. A. Runge

Fred E. Smiens

Cornelius H. van Bavel

Grant H. Vest, Jr.

Ralph A. Wurbs

LOCAL ARRANGEMENTS

John Abbott
Clark Adams
Perry L. Adkisson
David N. Appel
Steve Archer
Gerald F. Arkin
George Baker
George Bates
Tom Baxter
Don Bender
W. H. Blackburn
W. L. Born
Shirley Bovey
Mary Helen Bowers
Gary Briers
W. Brown
Marifran Bustion
O. D. Butler
Zerle Carpenter
David Byrne
Charles Cargill
James R. Cate
A. B. Childers
J. Christiansen
Harold Conway

Vi Cook
Jack Cross
Bill Dugas
J. S. Duggal
G. Eckols
Vance Edmondson
Kamal El-Zik
Rusty Etheredge
R. Feldman
Jim Ferguson
John Fluth
Joe Foster
Ray Frisbie
Albert Garcia
Fred Gardner
David Gay
C. Gilliand
J. Goodenough
Nancy Granovsky
Jon Gresham
Charles T. Hallmark
Arthur G. Hansen
Kelley Harris
Kurt Irgolic
Wesley P. James

Ricard W. Jensen
Eldred Keahy
B. Keegan
C. Kenerly
W. Klussman
J. Hari Krishna
W. F. Krueger
H. O. Kunkel
V. McDermott
P. Mendelson
Robert Merrifield
J. Mulkey
John Mullet
Garry Nall
J. Nichols
Daniel Padberg
R. Reed
John Richards
J. Richardson
R. Richter
Sharon Riley
Dave Ruesink
Ed Rykiel
Tep Sastri
M. Schroeder

John Schueller
Steve Searcy
Douglas Slack
Tom Sneed
John Sodolak
G. Sorensen
Jim Stack
W. Sterling
J. Benton Storey
J. Stribbling
John Stropp
Ken Strzepek
John Sweeten
Ruth Taber
George Teetes
J. Townsend
H. van Cleve
Bob Walker
Dale Webb
Cliff Whetton
Bob White
J. R. Wild
Larry Wilding
W. P. Worley
Y. H. Yang

EDITORIAL COMMITTEE